THE COLLECTED ESSAYS
JOURNALISM AND LETTERS

GEORGE ORWELL

Volume 1

An Age Like This

1920–1940

THE COLLECTED ESSAYS
JOURNALISM & LETTERS

GEORGE ORWELL

Volume 1 *An Age Like This*

1920–1940

EDITED BY

SONIA ORWELL

AND

IAN ANGUS

NONPAREIL BOOKS
DAVID R. GODINE
Publisher · Boston

This is a *Nonpareil Book*, first published in 2000 by

David R. Godine, *Publisher*
Post Office Box 450
Jaffrey, New Hampshire 03452
www.godine.com

This edition originally published by
Harcourt, Brace & World, Inc. in 1968

LIBRARY OF CONGRESS CATALOGING-IN-PUBLICATION DATA

Orwell, George, 1903–1950
The Collected essays, journalism, and letters of George Orwell /
edited by Sonia Orwell and Ian Angus.
p. cm.
Originally published: New York : Harcourt, Brace, and World, 1968.
Includes bibliographical references and indexes.
Contents: v. 1. An age like this, 1920–1940 —
v. 2. My country right or left, 1940–1943 —
v. 3. As I please, 1943–1946 —
v. 4. In front of your nose, 1946–1950.
ISBN 1–56792–133–7 (alk. paper : v. 1)
ISBN 1–56792–134–5 (alk. paper : v. 2)
ISBN 1–56792–135–3 (alk. paper : v. 3)
ISBN 1–56792–136–1 (alk. paper : v. 4)
1. Orwell, George, 1903–1950—Correspondence.
2. Authors, English—20th century—Correspondence.
3. Journalists, Great Britain—Correprsondence.
I. Orwell, Sonia. II. Angus, Ian. III. Title.
PR6029.R8 A6 2000
828'.91209–dc21 00–037540

SECOND PRINTING, 2019
Printed in Canada

MIX
Paper from
responsible sources
FSC® C004071

Contents

	Acknowledgements	xi
	Introduction	xv
	A Note on the Editing	xxi
1.	Why I Write	1

1920–1929

2.	Letter to Steven Runciman	11
3.	A Farthing Newspaper	12
4.	Letter to Max Plowman	15

1930

5.	Review of *Herman Melville* by Lewis Mumford	19
6.	Review of *Alexander Pope* by Edith Sitwell, etc	22
7.	Review of *Angel Pavement* by J. B. Priestley	25
8.	Letter to Max Plowman	27

1931

9.	Lettercard to Max Plowman	33
10.	Review of *The Two Carlyles* by Osbert Burdett	33
11.	The Spike	36
12.	A Hanging	44
13.	Letter to Dennis Collings	49
14.	Letter to Dennis Collings	51
15.	Hop-Picking	52
16.	Letter to T. S. Eliot	72
17.	Letter to T. S. Eliot	73

1932

18. Letter to Leonard Moore 77
19. Review of *The Spirit of Catholicism* by Karl Adam 79
20. Letter to Eleanor Jaques 81
21. Letter to Eleanor Jaques 83
22. Letter to Leonard Moore 84
23. Letter to Leonard Moore 84
24. Letter to Eleanor Jaques 85
25. Clink 86
26. Review of *Byron and the Need of Fatality* by Charles du Bos 95
27. Common Lodging Houses 97
28. Letter to Brenda Salkeld 100
29. Letter to Eleanor Jaques 101
30. Letter to Eleanor Jaques 102
31. Letter to Leonard Moore 104
32. Letter to Eleanor Jaques 105
33. Letter to Leonard Moore 106
34. Letter to Eleanor Jaques 107
35. Letter to Eleanor Jaques 108
36. Letter to Leonard Moore 109

1933

37. Introduction to the French edition of *Down and Out in Paris and London* 113
38. Letter to Leonard Moore 115
39. Letter to the Editor of *The Times* 115
40. Letter to Eleanor Jaques 117
41. Poem 118
42. Letter to Brenda Salkeld 119
43. Letter to Eleanor Jaques 119
44. Letter to Brenda Salkeld 120
45. Letter to Eleanor Jaques 122
46. Letter to Eleanor Jaques 122
47. Poem 123
48. Letter to Leonard Moore 125
49. Letter to Brenda Salkeld 125
50. Letter to Leonard Moore 129

1934

51. Letter to Leonard Moore 133
52. Letter to Leonard Moore 134
53. Poem: On a Ruined Farm near the His Master's Voice Gramophone Factory 134
54. Letter to Leonard Moore 135
55. Letter to Brenda Salkeld 136
56. Letter to Brenda Salkeld 137
57. Letter to Brenda Salkeld 139
58. Letter to Leonard Moore 141
59. My Epitaph by John Flory 141
60. Letter to Leonard Moore 142

1935

61. Letter to Leonard Moore 147
62. Letter to Brenda Salkeld 147
63. Review of *Caliban Shrieks* by Jack Hilton 148
64. Letter to Brenda Salkeld 150
65. Letter to Rayner Heppenstall 152
66. Letter to Rayner Heppenstall 153
67. Review of *Tropic of Cancer* by Henry Miller 154

1936

68. [On Kipling's Death] 159
69. Review of *The Lively Lady* by Kenneth Roberts, etc 160
70. Letter to Cyril Connolly 162
71. Letter to Sir Richard Rees, Bt. 163
72. Review of Penguin Books 165
73. Letter to Jack Common 168
74. *The Road to Wigan Pier* Diary 170
75. Letter to Jack Common 214
76. Letter to Jack Common 215
77. Letter to Sir Richard Rees, Bt. 217
78. Review of *Bastard Death* by Michael Fraenkel, etc 219
79. Letter to John Lehmann 221
80. Letter to Geoffrey Gorer 221
81. Letter to Anthony Powell 223

82. Letter to Denys King-Farlow 224
83. Review of *The Rock Pool* by Cyril Connolly, etc 225
84. Letter to Henry Miller 227
85. Review of *Black Spring* by Henry Miller, etc 230
86. Letter to Jack Common 233
87. Review of *Zest of Life* by Johann Wöller 234
88. Shooting an Elephant 235
89. Bookshop Memories 242
90. Review of *The Calf of Paper* by Scholem Asch, etc 247
91. In Defence of the Novel 249
92. Letter to Leonard Moore 256
93. Review of *The Novel Today* by Philip Henderson 256

1937

94. Postcard to James Hanley 263
95. Your Questions Answered 264
96. Letter to Eileen Blair 264
97. Letter to Victor Gollancz 267
98. Letter to Mr Thompson 268
99. Letter to Cyril Connolly 268
100. Spilling the Spanish Beans 269
101. Review of *The Spanish Cockpit* by Franz Borkenau, etc 276
102. Letter to Rayner Heppenstall 278
103. Letter to Geoffrey Gorer 280
104. Review of *The Men I Killed* by Brigadier-General F. P. Crozier 282
105. Letter to Geoffrey Gorer 283
106. Review of *Journey to Turkistan* by Sir Eric Teichman 286
107. Review of *Red Spanish Notebook* by Mary Low and Juan Brea, etc 287
108. Letter to Jack Common 288
109. Lettercard to Cyril Connolly 290
110. Review of *Storm over Spain* by Mairin Mitchell, etc 290

1938

111. Review of *Spanish Testament* by Arthur Koestler 295
112. Letter to Jack Common 296
113. Letter to the Editor of *Time and Tide* 297

114. Letter to Raymond Mortimer 299
115. Letter to Alec Houghton Joyce 302
116. Letter to Jack Common 303
117. Review of *Workers' Front* by Fenner Brockway 304
118. Review of *Trials in Burma* by Maurice Collis 306
119. Review of *Glimpses and Reflections* by John Galsworthy 307
120. Letter to Cyril Connolly 309
121. Letter to Jack Common 310
122. Letter to Stephen Spender 311
123. Letter to Stephen Spender 312
124. Letter to Jack Common 314
125. Letter to Geoffrey Gorer 315
126. Notes on the Spanish Militias 316
127. Letter to Cyril Connolly 328
128. Letter to Jack Common 329
129. Letter to the Editor of the *New English Weekly* 330
130. Review of *Assignment in Utopia* by Eugene Lyons 332
131. Review of *The Freedom of the Streets* by Jack Common 335
132. Why I Joined the Independent Labour Party 336
133. Letter to Jack Common 338
134. Review of *The Civil War in Spain* by Frank Jellinek 340
135. Letter to Cyril Connolly 343
136. Review of *Searchlight on Spain* by the Duchess of Atholl 344
137. Letter to Ida Mabel Blair 347
138. Review of *The Communist International* by Franz Borkenau 348
139. Letter to Jack Common 351
140. Letter to Jack Common 352
141. Letter to Jack Common 355
142. Letter to John Sceats 357
143. Letter to John Sceats 360
144. Letter to Cyril Connolly 362
145. Letter to Frank Jellinek 363
146. Letter to Jack Common 367

1939

147. Review of *Power: A New Social Analysis* by Bertrand Russell 375

148. Letter to Herbert Read 377
149. Review of *Russia under Soviet Rule* by N. de Basily 378
150. Letter to Geoffrey Gorer 381
151. Review of *Communism and Man* by F. J. Sheed 383
152. Letter to Herbert Read 385
153. Marrakech 387
154. Letter to Jack Common 393
155. Not Counting Niggers 394
156. Review of *Stendhal* by F. C. Green 398
157. Democracy in the British Army 401

1940

158. Letter to Victor Gollancz 409
159. Letter to Geoffrey Gorer 410
160. Review of *The Last Days of Madrid* by S. Casado 411
161. Letter to David H. Thomson 413
162. Charles Dickens 413
163. Boys' Weeklies and Frank Richards's Reply 460
164. Inside the Whale 493
165. Letter to Geoffrey Gorer 527
166. Letter to Humphry House 529
167. The Limit to Pessimism 533
168. My Country Right or Left 535

Appendix I: Books by or containing contributions by George Orwell 541
Appendix II: Chronology 543
Index 553

Acknowledgements

The editors wish to express their grateful thanks to the following institutions and libraries, their trustees, curators and staffs for their co-operation and valuable help and for making copies of Orwell material available: Sir Frank Francis, Director and Principal Librarian of the British Museum (for: II: 37; III: 105; IV: 8); Dr John D. Gordan, Curator of the Henry W. and Albert A. Berg Collection of the New York Public Library, Astor, Lenox and Tilden Foundations (for: I: 18, 22, 23, 31, 33, 36, 38, 48, 50–2, 54, 58, 60, 61, 73, 75, 76, 86, 92, 98, 108, 112, 116, 121, 124, 128, 133, 139, 140, 141, 146, 154; III: 53, 97, 106; IV: 29, 59, 92, 95, 100, 106, 107, 110, 115, 121, 126, 136, 137, 142, 144, 159, 164, 165); Dr Warren Roberts, Director of the Humanities Research Center, University of Texas (for: I: 65, 66, 79, 102, 122, 123, 161; II: 4, 6, 10, 50; III: 52); S. C. Sutton, Librarian and Keeper of India Office Records (for: I: 115); Robert L. Collison, Librarian of the BBC Library (for: II: 38, 39, 52); Dr G. Chandler, Librarian of Liverpool City Library (for: I: 94); Wilbur Smith, Head of the Department of Special Collections, Library of the University of California, Los Angeles (for: I: 84); Anne Abley, Librarian of St Antony's College, Oxford (for: IV: 31, 32); and J. W. Scott, Librarian of University College London, for the material in the George Orwell Archive.

We are also deeply indebted to all those recipients of letters from Orwell, or their executors, who have been kind enough to make available the correspondence published in these volumes.

We would like to thank the following publications for permission to reproduce material first published in their pages: *Commentary; Encounter;* the *Evening Standard; Forward; Life;* the *Listener;* the *London Magazine;* the *Manchester Evening News;* the *New Leader* (NY); the *New Statesman and Nation;* the *New Yorker;* the *New York Times Book Review;* the *Observer; Partisan Review; Peace*

News; the *Socialist Leader; Time and Tide; The Times; Tribune; Wiadomosci.*

We would like to thank the following for allowing us to use material whose copyright they own: the executors of the late Frank Richards for his "Reply to George Orwell" in *Horizon*; H. W. Wilson & Co. for Orwell's entry in *Twentieth Century Authors*; Professor George Woodcock and D. S. Savage for their contributions to the controversy "Pacifism and the War" in *Partisan Review*; Dr Alex Comfort for his contribution to the same controversy and for his "Letter to an American Visitor" in *Tribune*; William Collins Sons & Co. Ltd for *The English People*; the executors of the late James Agate for his contribution to the controversy in the *Manchester Evening News*; the executors of Gerard Manley Hopkins and the Oxford University Press for "Felix Randal"; Elek Books Ltd for the Introduction to Jack London's *Love of Life*; Eyre & Spottiswoode Ltd for the Introduction to Leonard Merrick's *The Position of Peggy Harper* and the executors of the late Konni Zilliacus for his letter to *Tribune*.

We would like to thank the following for their co-operation and invaluable help: Mrs Evelyn Anderson, the Hon. David Astor, Frank D. Barber, Dennis Collings, Dr Alex Comfort, Jack Common, Lettice Cooper, Stafford Cottman, Humphrey Dakin, Mrs John Deiner, Mrs William Dunn, Mrs T. S. Eliot, Dr McDonald Emslie, Faber and Faber Ltd, Mr and Mrs Francis Fierz, Roy Fuller, T. R. Fyvel, Livia Gollancz, Victor Gollancz Ltd, Mrs Arthur Goodman, A. S. F. Gow, James Hanley, Rayner Heppenstall, Inez Holden, Mrs Humphry House, Mrs Lydia Jackson, Frank Jellinek, Dr Shirley E. Jones, Jon Kimche, Denys King-Farlow, Arthur Koestler, Mrs Georges Kopp, James Laughlin, F. A. Lea, John Lehmann, John McNair, Michael Meyer, Henry Miller, Raymond Mortimer, Mrs Middleton Murry, Mrs Rosalind Obermeyer, Laurence O'Shaughnessy, *Partisan Review,* Professor R. S. Peters, Ruth Pitter, Joyce Pritchard, Philip Rahv, Sir Herbert Read, Vernon Richards, the Rev. Herbert Rogers, the Hon. Sir Steven Runciman, Brenda Salkeld, John Sceats, Roger Senhouse, Stephen Spender, Professor Gleb Struve, Julian Symons, F. J. Warburg and Professor George Woodcock. We would also like to thank: Angus Calder (for allowing us to consult his unpublished thesis on the Common Wealth Party); Howard Fink (for allowing us to consult his unpublished *Chronology of Orwell's Loci and Activities*);

and I. R. Willison (whose *George Orwell: Some Materials for a Bibliography*, School of Librarianship, London University, 1953, was indispensable).

Finally, this edition would not have been possible but for the patient and understanding editorial help of Aubrey Davis and the support and help of the Library staff of University College London, particularly that of J. W. Scott, the Librarian, Margaret Skerl, Karen Bishop, Mrs Michael Kraushaar, and Mrs Gordon Leitch.

Introduction

In 1940 George Orwell wrote to a friend: "I am very anxious to slow off and not hurry on with my next book, as I have now published eight in eight years which is too much. . . . I've now got an idea for a really big novel, I mean big in bulk, and I want to lie fallow before doing it." After his return from Burma in 1927 he wanted to be a writer in the classical sense of someone who writes books. He would have liked to have left behind him *une oeuvre*, a long shelf of uniform volumes, not all of which could be expected to be of the same literary value, but which, together, represented a life's work as do the opulent, well-bound "sets" of the complete works of nineteenth-century novelists.

In fact he only wrote nine books and published two short collections of essays before he died: but in terms of actual words he produced very much more than seems possible for someone who died at the age of forty-six, was often struggling against ill-health and poverty and had such a passion for the time-consuming country pursuits of gardening, keeping animals, fishing and carpentry. But a great many of these words, really most of his journalism, were often written against the feeling he should be writing something else—novels or essays. The first two important and characteristic essays, "Boys' Weeklies" and "Charles Dickens", were written before the war and, as he wrote to Geoffrey Gorer, he seemed pleased to have found his own way of approaching a writer he admired or an aspect of life that amused him and he looked forward to developing this side of his work. If political events had made less impact on him, he would have lived in the country, written a book—preferably a novel—a year, pursued his interest in the essay form and, when money was badly lacking, done straightforward book reviews which, he said, he enjoyed writing. He was seldom able—and certainly did not want—to concentrate on more than one piece at a time. In 1937 he wrote to

Jack Common: "It seems only yesterday that nobody would print anything I wrote, and now I get letters from all quarters saying won't I write something, and except for the thing I actually have in hand [*Homage to Catalonia*] I am as empty as a jug."

War made him a political activist—like nearly all intellectuals of his generation he had always been politically conscious—and war made him a journalist, pamphleteer and polemicist. He went to the Spanish civil war with a strong but undefined feeling of "anti-Fascism". He came out of it a committed Socialist and a dedicated anti-Communist, knowing that he had witnessed an injustice which, if he could not right, he must use his ability as a writer to record so that justice should at least be done to the memory of his comrades and their vision of Revolution. It was only after his return from Spain that he became a journalist in any serious sense.

The outbreak of war in 1939 made it impossible for him to go on living in the country on about £5 a week, took away the quiet and peace of mind he needed to work out his projected Saga and forced him into journalism to earn his living since he was rejected as medically unfit for the army. But now he was also a journalist because he wanted to be effective, to raise his voice against the folly, stupidity and despair he saw and felt, and try to keep alive his belief in the free, equal and decent society he had briefly glimpsed in the early days of the Spanish civil war. From 1939 to his death the only writings which he thought of as serious literary productions were two more novels and some essays.

Until 1945 he made extremely little money and this, combined with natural inclination, made him a very economical writer in the sense that he published everything he wrote. He was not given to keeping notebooks, diaries, sketches or outlines of projected books or work-in-progress and threw away the drafts and manuscripts of his books when they were redundant. In fact he left very few of those "papers" which writers always seem to leave, providing such marvellous hunting-grounds for critics or biographers. He left no personal papers: there is nothing either concealed or spectacularly revealed in his letters. He was certainly reserved and undemonstrative, very "English" in the conventional use of the term although he was not secretive or inhibited. Throughout his life he wrote what he thought or felt and published it in one form or another.

These four volumes are not the Complete Journalism and Letters of George Orwell, but with the novels and books they make up the definitive Collected Works. Ian Angus and I have not set out to make an academic monument because neither his work nor his personality lends itself to such treatment and the period he lived in is too recent for any real history to have been written of it.

Anything he would have considered as an essay is certainly included. We have excluded much of the journalism and many letters. The letters which are not included are of the "glad to meet you Saturday" or "would you send the proofs to the following address" kind. The journalism we have not printed is purely ephemeral and the very few surviving pieces of his youthful work are unimportant. No one could have written as much journalism as he did and kept it all on the same level, certainly not someone who was so often tired and unwell. He could make a hack review come alive sometimes by a single sentence or a joke, and Ian Angus and I have included many for the sake of one or two phrases which no one but Orwell could have written, although we realise the pieces in themselves are of no great importance. The largest excluded section is his scripts for the BBC, where he worked in the Eastern Section, broadcasting to India, from 1941 to 1943. He must have written hundreds of thousands of words during those years and, as his letters show, he tried to keep these broadcasts free from the cant of propaganda and produce honest work on an honest level, but they were oversimplified pieces, written for an audience with a different background from his own and, though not of a different kind they are of a different level from his work for an English or American highbrow magazine, where he had no need to explain his references as he went along. Ian Angus and I have only included one piece, "The Rediscovery of Europe", in Volume II to give an idea of the kind of work he did for the BBC.

As far as the letters go, he had the common habit of settling down to "write some letters", and very often he wrote identical paragraphs conveying some specific piece of news, in letters to different people written around the same date. Where this happened the paragraph has been left in in one letter and taken out of the others, where its absence is indicated by dots. The cuts in the letters represent these repetitious paragraphs, or, very rarely, a few words which might be wounding to the relatives of people he discussed.

The material is arranged chronologically for two reasons. The first and most important one is that it is extremely difficult to pigeonhole Orwell's essays and journalism: few of the pieces can readily be labelled either as political or as literary writing. Such categories overlap and merge until what we really hear is the sound of a personal voice, an individual talking at random of the things that concern him on many different levels. What made Orwell so different from other journalists is that he seldom "reported". His work had nothing in common with that of the distinguished correspondent attached to a newspaper and he never took a line other than the one he himself felt at the moment of writing. What he did as a journalist was argue out his ideas as he went along, through article after article in left-wing journal after left-wing journal, in little magazines which often paid badly, had few readers, but which he felt stood for something worthwhile, almost as if he was talking to the reader, examining his thoughts in conversation. The nearest he got to straight reporting were his "London Letters" for *Partisan Review* during the war, and although they are fascinating accounts of the time, it is typical of him that when the war was as good as won, his first reaction, in one of his last "London Letters", was to admit and discuss the fact that much of his political analysis and his prophecies as to the outcome of the war had been based on a wrong assumption.

Taken as a whole his journalism serves much the same function as do the notebooks of other writers. It was to some extent the only activity open to him when he found he could no longer write novels because of the pressures of war, but it was not a substitute for writing novels or books: it was the action of a writer who could only express himself in that particular way at that particular moment, who found in journalism the only outlet for the ideas which in better times he would have subjected to a different discipline, an essay, a novel, or a book such as *Homage to Catalonia*. Only in *Animal Farm* and *Nineteen Eighty-Four* did Orwell set out deliberately to compose political ideas into the novel form and much of his journalism from 1939 onwards discussed the ideas crystallised in these novels. For years he had been examining them in print in one context or another, arguing them out, as it were, with himself in public. It would be hard to find another journalist so prepared to contradict himself, who hammers away at an argument so as to turn it round from every angle before he felt it had been properly examined.

Because of this, reprinting his journalism does pose one big problem: he tended to discuss the same argument from different aspects and in different ways in any number of articles. This was probably due to having to write so much to get enough money, but also because once he had started worrying about a train of thought he found it hard to think of anything else. In fact the articles are seldom the same. They often seem to start with a familiar argument and then go off to discuss a completely new aspect of the affair. In *The Lion and the Unicorn* he gave his most famous description of the English national character and when, a few years later, he was asked to write *The English People*, and did so largely for money, he seems to open the second booklet with a much weaker version of the first, but quite soon they cease to have any resemblance and a whole new set of ideas is introduced. Occasionally Ian Angus and I have cut articles where an almost identical passage recurs but we have tended to leave the articles as they are since each new twist given to the argument is characteristic.

The second reason for presenting the material chronologically was to give a continuous picture of Orwell's life as well as of his work. In his will he asked that no biography of him be written. He gave no reasons for this but his friends felt that this request was probably in part due to his natural reticence but also came from the knowledge that there was so little that could be written about his life—except for "psychological interpretation"—which he had not written himself. Apart from *Animal Farm* and *Nineteen Eighty-Four* all his novels contain straight descriptions of himself or his experiences in one guise or another and a whole chapter of *The Road to Wigan Pier* suddenly turns into straight autobiography. With these present volumes the picture is as complete as it can be. Inevitably, many of the letters he wrote have been lost and many of his friends throw away letters as a matter of course. Only one to each of his wives has survived. But with the material available, I felt that arranging the letters, rather unorthodoxly, among the texts did give an idea of how his life and work developed. To him they were one.

Because of the autobiographical aspect these volumes have been divided so that each covers a distinct period of his life. The first goes up to the Second World War. The second, 1940–43, in many ways perhaps the bleakest period of his life, covers the first part of the war and the time he worked in the BBC. In 1943 the BBC released him to become literary editor of the Socialist weekly, *Tribune*, and with the series he wrote for them called "As I Please" his journalism becomes more personal and reflects the feeling of liberation he felt working at *Tribune*, which also gave him enough time to write *Animal Farm*. He had great difficulty in getting it published but when it finally appeared in 1945 he had, for the first time, enough money to abandon most of his journalistic work and write more or less what he wanted. The last volume covers the years between 1945 and his death, a period shadowed by ill-health. As there are gaps in the documentary material Ian Angus has added a brief biographical chronology to each volume.

I should particularly like to thank five of Orwell's friends, Cyril Connolly, Geoffrey Gorer, Malcolm Muggeridge, Anthony Powell and Sir Richard Rees for their unstinting help and patience in answering queries about Orwell's life and times, and I should also like to thank Professor Hugh Thomas and Michael Foot MP for so patiently and kindly answering questions about political periods on which they are experts. Above all, I must thank William Jovanovich whose friendship, encouragement and vigorous refusal to be daunted by doubts or material difficulties have been the real force behind this collection.

Sonia Orwell

A Note on the Editing

The contents are arranged in order of publication except where the time lag between writing and appearance in print is unusually large, when we have chosen the date of writing. There are one or two rare exceptions to this rule, generally made for the sake of illustrating the development in Orwell's thought, but a note at the end of each article or review states when, and in which publication, it appeared first. If it was not published or the date of writing has determined its position the date of writing is given. Where there is no mention of a periodical at the end of an article, it has never been published before. "Why I Write", written in 1946, has been placed at the beginning of Volume I, as it seems a suitable introduction to the whole collection. Where the article was reprinted in the major collections of his writing, this has been indicated and the following abbreviations used for the various books: CE, *Collected Essays;* CrE, *Critical Essays;* DD, *Dickens, Dali and Others;* EYE, *England Your England;* ITW, *Inside the Whale;* OR, *The Orwell Reader;* SE, *Shooting an Elephant;* SJ, *Such, Such Were the Joys.*

Any title in square brackets at the head of an article or review has been supplied by us. All the others are either Orwell's own or those of the editors of the publication in question. He certainly wrote his own titles for his *Tribune* pieces: some of the others read as if he had written them but with most it is hard to tell and there is no way of finally checking.

Only when the article has never been printed before have we had the manuscript to work from and none of these were revised by Orwell as they would have been had he published them. With everything else we have had to use the text as it appeared in print. As anyone who has ever done any journalism or book reviewing knows, this means the text which appears here may well be slightly, if not very, different from the text Orwell originally wrote. Editors cut, printers make errors which are not thought of as very important in journalism, and it is only when the writer wants to reprint his pieces in book form that he bothers to restore the cuts, correct the errors and generally prepare them to survive in more lasting form: the reader therefore should bear in mind that they might well be very different if Orwell himself had revised them for re-publication. Both to these previously printed essays and journalism and to the hitherto unpublished articles and diaries we have given a uniform style in spelling, quotation marks and punctuation.

The letters were written, nearly always in haste, with scant attention to style and hardly any to punctuation; but throughout them we have corrected spelling mistakes, regularised the punctuation and have put book and periodical titles in italics. In a few cases postscripts of an unimportant nature have been omitted without indication. Otherwise cuts in both the letters and the journalism have been indicated by three dots, with a fourth dot to indicate a period. The same method was used by Orwell for indicating omissions when abridging excerpts he was quoting in reviews and essays, but as we have not made cuts in any of these excerpts there should be no confusion between our cuts and Orwell's own.

Orwell's "As I Please" column often consisted of two or more sections each devoted to a specific topic. Whenever one of the self-contained sections has been entirely omitted, this has not been indicated, but any cut made within a section is indicated by the usual three or four dots.

George Orwell never legally changed his name from Eric Blair and all the friends he made when young knew him and addressed him as Eric Blair. Later on new friends and acquaintances knew him and addressed him as George Orwell. In his letters he signs himself by the name his correspondent used. His earlier articles were signed E. A. Blair or Eric Blair and we have indicated these. From the moment this name is dropped in his published writing it is entirely signed George Orwell. Where a footnote deals with a period or a situation in which he would have looked upon himself primarily as Eric Blair we have referred to him by this name.

As this is an Anglo-American edition, many of the footnotes have been provided for the benefit of American readers and contain information we know to be familiar to English readers. We have put in the minimum of footnotes. This is largely because of the great difficulty of annotating the history of the period during which he wrote.

It is still too recent for standard histories of it to exist and the events and people he discussed are often still the subjects of fierce polemic making it difficult to give an "objective" footnote. We have only footnoted the text in some details where he talks about people or events in his personal life or where there is a reference to some topic about which the reader could find nothing in any existing book of reference. The numbers in the cross-references in the footnotes refer to items, not pages.

The Editors

1. Why I Write

From a very early age, perhaps the age of five or six, I knew that when I grew up I should be a writer. Between the ages of about seventeen and twenty-four I tried to abandon this idea, but I did so with the consciousness that I was outraging my true nature and that sooner or later I should have to settle down and write books.

I was the middle child of three, but there was a gap of five years on either side, and I barely saw my father before I was eight. For this and other reasons I was somewhat lonely, and I soon developed disagreeable mannerisms which made me unpopular throughout my schooldays. I had the lonely child's habit of making up stories and holding conversations with imaginary persons, and I think from the very start my literary ambitions were mixed up with the feeling of being isolated and undervalued. I knew that I had a facility with words and a power of facing unpleasant facts, and I felt that this created a sort of private world in which I could get my own back for my failure in everyday life. Nevertheless the volume of serious—i.e. seriously intended—writing which I produced all through my childhood and boyhood would not amount to half a dozen pages. I wrote my first poem at the age of four or five, my mother taking it down to dictation. I cannot remember anything about it except that it was about a tiger and the tiger had "chair-like teeth"—a good enough phrase, but I fancy the poem was a plagiarism of Blake's "Tiger, Tiger". At eleven, when the war of 1914–18 broke out, I wrote a patriotic poem which was printed in the local newspaper, as was another, two years later, on the death of Kitchener. From time to time, when I was a bit older, I wrote bad and usually unfinished "nature poems" in the Georgian style. I also, about twice, attempted a short story which was a ghastly failure. That was the total of the would-be serious work that I actually set down on paper during all those years.

However, throughout this time I did in a sense engage in literary activities. To begin with there was the made-to-order stuff which I produced quickly, easily and without much pleasure to myself. Apart from school work, I wrote *vers d'occasion*, semi-comic poems which I could turn out at what now seems to me astonishing speed —at fourteen I wrote a whole rhyming play, in imitation of Aristophanes, in about a week—and helped to edit school magazines, both printed and in manuscript. These magazines were the most pitiful burlesque stuff that you could imagine, and I took far less trouble with them than I now would with the cheapest journalism. But side by side with all this, for fifteen years or more, I was carrying out a literary exercise of a quite different kind: this was the making up of a continuous "story" about myself, a sort of diary existing only in the mind. I believe this is a common habit of children and adolescents. As a very small child I used to imagine that I was, say, Robin Hood, and picture myself as the hero of thrilling adventures, but quite soon my "story" ceased to be narcissistic in a crude way and became more and more a mere description of what I was doing and the things I saw. For minutes at a time this kind of thing would be running through my head: "He pushed the door open and entered the room. A yellow beam of sunlight, filtering through the muslin curtains, slanted on to the table, where a matchbox, half open, lay beside the inkpot, With his right hand in his pocket he moved across to the window. Down in the street a tortoiseshell cat was chasing a dead leaf," etc etc. This habit continued till I was about twenty-five, right through my non-literary years. Although I had to search, and did search, for the right words, I seemed to be making this descriptive effort almost against my will, under a kind of compulsion from outside. The "story" must, I suppose, have reflected the styles of the various writers I admired at different ages, but so far as I remember it always had the same meticulous descriptive quality.

When I was about sixteen I suddenly discovered the joy of mere words, i.e. the sounds and associations of words. The lines from *Paradise Lost*,

> So hee with difficulty and labour hard
> Moved on: with difficulty and labour hee,

which do not now seem to me so very wonderful, sent shivers down my backbone; and the spelling "hee" for "he" was an added pleasure. As for the need to describe things, I knew all about it already. So it is clear what kind of books I wanted to write, in so far as I could be said to want to write books at that time. I wanted to write enormous naturalistic novels with unhappy endings, full of detailed descriptions and arresting similes, and also full of purple passages in which words were used partly for the sake of their sound. And in fact my first completed novel, *Burmese Days*, which I wrote when I was thirty but projected much earlier, is rather that kind of book.

I give all this background information because I do not think one can assess a writer's motives without knowing something of his early development. His subject matter will be determined by the age he lives in—at least this is true in tumultuous, revolutionary ages like our own—but before he ever begins to write he will have acquired an emotional attitude from which he will never completely escape. It is his job, no doubt, to discipline his temperament and avoid getting stuck at some immature stage, or in some perverse mood: but if he escapes from his early influences altogether, he will have killed his impulse to write. Putting aside the need to earn a living, I think there are four great motives for writing, at any rate for writing prose. They exist in different degrees in every writer, and in any one writer the proportions will vary from time to time, according to the atmosphere in which he is living. They are:

1. Sheer egoism. Desire to seem clever, to be talked about, to be remembered after death, to get your own back on grown-ups who snubbed you in childhood, etc etc. It is humbug to pretend that this is not a motive, and a strong one. Writers share this characteristic with scientists, artists, politicians, lawyers, soldiers, successful businessmen—in short, with the whole top crust of humanity. The great mass of human beings are not acutely selfish. After the age of about thirty they abandon individual ambition—in many cases, indeed, they almost abandon the sense of being individuals at all—and live chiefly for others, or are simply smothered under drudgery. But there is also the minority of gifted, wilful people who are determined to live their own lives to the end, and writers belong in this class. Serious writers, I should say, are on the whole more vain and self-centred than journalists, though less interested in money.

2. Aesthetic enthusiasm. Perception of beauty in the external world, or, on the other hand, in words and their right arrangement. Pleasure in the impact of one sound on another, in the firmness of good prose or the rhythm of a good story. Desire to share an experience which one feels is valuable and ought not to be missed. The aesthetic motive is very feeble in a lot of writers, but even a

pamphleteer or a writer of textbooks will have pet words and phrases which appeal to him for non-utilitarian reasons; or he may feel strongly about typography, width of margins, etc. Above the level of a railway guide, no book is quite free from aesthetic considerations.

3. Historical impulse. Desire to see things as they are, to find out true facts and store them up for the use of posterity.

4. Political purpose—using the word "political" in the widest possible sense. Desire to push the world in a certain direction, to alter other people's idea of the kind of society that they should strive after. Once again, no book is genuinely free from political bias. The opinion that art should have nothing to do with politics is itself a political attitude.

It can be seen how these various impulses must war against one another, and how they must fluctuate from person to person and from time to time. By nature—taking your "nature" to be the state you have attained when you are first adult—I am a person in whom the first three motives would outweigh the fourth. In a peaceful age I might have written ornate or merely descriptive books, and might have remained almost unaware of my political loyalties. As it is I have been forced into becoming a sort of pamphleteer. First I spent five years in an unsuitable profession (the Indian Imperial Police, in Burma), and then I underwent poverty and the sense of failure. This increased my natural hatred of authority and made me for the first time fully aware of the existence of the working classes, and the job in Burma had given me some understanding of the nature of imperialism: but these experiences were not enough to give me an accurate political orientation. Then came Hitler, the Spanish civil war, etc. By the end of 1935 I had still failed to reach a firm decision. I remember a little poem that I wrote at that date, expressing my dilemma:

A happy vicar I might have been
Two hundred years ago,
To preach upon eternal doom
And watch my walnuts grow;

But born, alas, in an evil time,
I missed that pleasant haven,
For the hair has grown on my upper lip
And the clergy are all clean-shaven.

And later still the times were good,
We were so easy to please,
We rocked our troubled thoughts to sleep
On the bosoms of the trees.

All ignorant we dared to own
The joys we now dissemble;
The greenfinch on the apple bough
Could make my enemies tremble.

But girls' bellies and apricots,
Roach in a shaded stream,
Horses, ducks in flight at dawn,
All these are a dream.

It is forbidden to dream again;
We maim our joys or hide them;
Horses are made of chromium steel
And little fat men shall ride them.

I am the worm who never turned,
The eunuch without a harem;
Between the priest and the commissar
I walk like Eugene Aram;

And the commissar is telling my fortune
While the radio plays,
But the priest has promised an Austin Seven,
For Duggie always pays.

I dreamed I dwelt in marble halls,
And woke to find it true;
I wasn't born for an age like this;
Was Smith? Was Jones? Were you?[1]

The Spanish war and other events in 1936–37 turned the scale and thereafter I knew where I stood. Every line of serious work that I have written since 1936 has been written, directly or indirectly, *against* totalitarianism and *for* democratic Socialism, as I understand it. It seems to me nonsense, in a period like our own, to think that one can avoid writing of such subjects. Everyone writes of them in

[1] This poem first appeared in the *Adelphi*, December 1936.

one guise or another. It is simply a question of which side one takes and what approach one follows. And the more one is conscious of one's political bias, the more chance one has of acting politically without sacrificing one's aesthetic and intellectual integrity.

What I have most wanted to do throughout the past ten years is to make political writing into an art. My starting point is always a feeling of partisanship, a sense of injustice. When I sit down to write a book, I do not say to myself, "I am going to produce a work of art." I write it because there is some lie that I want to expose, some fact to which I want to draw attention, and my initial concern is to get a hearing. But I could not do the work of writing a book, or even a long magazine article, if it were not also an aesthetic experience. Anyone who cares to examine my work will see that even when it is downright propaganda it contains much that a full-time politician would consider irrelevant. I am not able, and I do not want, completely to abandon the world-view that I acquired in childhood. So long as I remain alive and well I shall continue to feel strongly about prose style, to love the surface of the earth, and to take pleasure in solid objects and scraps of useless information. It is no use trying to suppress that side of myself. The job is to reconcile my ingrained likes and dislikes with the essentially public, non-individual activities that this age forces on all of us.

It is not easy. It raises problems of construction and of language, and it raises in a new way the problem of truthfulness. Let me give just one example of the cruder kind of difficulty that arises. My book about the Spanish civil war, *Homage to Catalonia*, is, of course, a frankly political book, but in the main it is written with a certain detachment and regard for form. I did try very hard in it to tell the whole truth without violating my literary instincts. But among other things it contains a long chapter, full of newspaper quotations and the like, defending the Trotskyists who were accused of plotting with Franco. Clearly such a chapter, which after a year or two would lose its interest for any ordinary reader, must ruin the book. A critic whom I respect read me a lecture about it. "Why did you put in all that stuff?" he said. "You've turned what might have been a good book into journalism." What he said was true, but I could not have done otherwise. I happened to know, what very few people in England had been allowed to know, that innocent men were being falsely accused. If I had not been angry about that I should never have written the book.

In one form or another this problem comes up again. The problem of language is subtler and would take too long to discuss. I will only say that of late years I have tried to write less picturesquely and more exactly. In any case I find that by the time you have perfected any style of writing, you have always outgrown it. *Animal Farm* was the first book in which I tried, with full consciousness of what I was doing, to fuse political purpose and artistic purpose into one whole. I have not written a novel for seven years, but I hope to write another fairly soon. It is bound to be a failure, every book is a failure, but I know with some clarity what kind of book I want to write.

Looking back through the last page or two, I see that I have made it appear as though my motives in writing were wholly public-spirited. I don't want to leave that as the final impression. All writers are vain, selfish and lazy, and at the very bottom of their motives there lies a mystery. Writing a book is a horrible, exhausting struggle, like a long bout of some painful illness. One would never undertake such a thing if one were not driven on by some demon whom one can neither resist nor understand. For all one knows that demon is simply the same instinct that makes a baby squall for attention. And yet it is also true that one can write nothing readable unless one constantly struggles to efface one's own personality. Good prose is like a window pane. I cannot say with certainty which of my motives are the strongest, but I know which of them deserve to be followed. And looking back through my work, I see that it is invariably where I lacked a *political* purpose that I wrote lifeless books and was betrayed into purple passages, sentences without meaning, decorative adjectives and humbug generally.

Gangrel [No. 4, Summer], 1946; SJ; EYE; OR; CE.

1920–1929

2. Letter to Steven Runciman

Grove Terrace
Polperro RSO, Cornwall
[August 1920]

My dear Runciman,[1]

I have a little spare time, & I feel I *must* tell you about my first adventure as an amateur tramp. Like most tramps, I was driven to it. When I got to a wretched little place in Devonshire,—Seaton Junction, Mynors,[2] who had to change there, came to my carriage & said that a beastly Oppidan[3] who had been perpetually plaguing me to travel in the same compartment as him was asking for me. As I was among strangers, I got out to go to him whereupon the train started off. You need two hands to enter a moving train, & I, what with kit-bag, belt etc had only one. To be brief, I was left behind. I despatched a telegram to say I would be late (it arrived next day), & about 2½ hours later got a train: at Plymouth, North Rd, I found there were no more trains to Looe[4] that night. It was too late to telephone, as the post offices were shut. I then made a consultation of my financial position. I had enough for my remaining fare & 7½d over. I could therefore either sleep at the YMCA place, price 6d, & starve, or have something to eat but nowhere to sleep. I chose the latter. I put my kit-

[1] Steven Runciman (1903–   ), Kt. 1958, historian, whose books include *A History of the Crusades*, *The Sicilian Vespers*, and *The Fall of Constantinople*.

[2] Roger Mynors (1903–   ), Kt. 1963, Corpus Christi Professor of Latin Language and Literature, Oxford, since October 1953.

[3] There are about eleven hundred boys at Eton, of whom seventy are "King's Scholars" and live in the College proper. The remainder are called "Oppidans" and live in houses supervised by Housemasters. Steven Runciman, Roger Mynors and Eric Blair were King's Scholars and entered as members of the 1916 Election. Blair saw few of his contemporaries at Eton after he left.

[4] The Blair family spent most of their summer holidays in Cornwall at either Looe or Polperro. On this particular journey Blair was returning from an Eton OTC (Officers' Training Corps) exercise and was therefore in uniform.

bag in the cloak-room & got 12 buns for 6d: half-past-nine found me sneaking into some farmer's field,—there were a few fields wedged in among rows of slummy houses. In that light I of course looked like a soldier strolling round,—on my way I had been asked whether I was demobilized yet, & I finally came to anchor in the corner of a field near some allotments. I then began to remember that people frequently got fourteen days for sleeping in somebody else's field & "having no visible means of support", particularly as every dog in the neighbourhood barked if I even so much as moved. The corner had a large tree for shelter, & bushes for concealment, but it was unendurably cold; I had no covering, my cap was my pillow, I lay "with my martial cloak (rolled cape) around me". I only dozed & shivered till about 1 oc, when I readjusted my puttees, & managed to sleep long enough to miss the first train, at 4.20 by about an hour, & to have to wait till 7.45 for another. My teeth were still chattering when I awoke. When I got to Looe I was forced to walk 4 miles in the hot sun; I am very proud of this adventure, but I would not repeat it.

Yours sincerely,
E. A. Blair

3. A Farthing Newspaper

The *Ami du Peuple* is a Paris newspaper. It was established about six months ago, and it has achieved something really strange and remarkable in the world where everything is a "sensation", by being sold at ten centimes, or rather less than a farthing the copy. It is a healthy, full-sized sheet, with news, articles, and cartoons quite up to the usual standard, and with a turn for sport, murders, nationalist sentiment and anti-German propaganda. Nothing is abnormal about it except its price.

Nor is there any need to be surprised at this last phenomenon, because the proprietors of the *Ami du Peuple* have just explained all about it, in a huge manifesto which is pasted on the walls of Paris wherever bill-sticking is not *défendu*. On reading this manifesto one learns with pleased surprise that the *Ami du Peuple* is not like other newspapers; it was the purest public spirit, uncontaminated by any base thoughts of gain, which brought it to birth. The proprietors, who hide their blushes in anonymity, are emptying their pockets for the mere pleasure of doing good by stealth. Their objects, we learn, are to make war on the great trusts, to fight for a lower cost of living, and above all to combat the powerful newspapers which are strangling free speech in France. In spite of the sinister attempts of these other newspapers to put the *Ami du Peuple* out of action, it will fight on to the last. In short, it is all that its name implies.

One would cheer this last stand for democracy a great deal louder, of course, if one did not happen to know that the proprietor of the *Ami du Peuple* is M. Coty, a great industrial capitalist, and also proprietor of the *Figaro* and the *Gaulois*. One would also regard the *Ami du Peuple* with less suspicion if its politics were not anti-radical and anti-Socialist, of the goodwill-in-industry, shake-hands-and-make-it-up species. But all that is beside the point at this moment. The important questions, obviously, are these: Does the *Ami du Peuple* pay its way? And if so, how?

The second question is the one that really matters. Since the march of progress is going in the direction of always bigger and nastier trusts, any departure is worth noticing which brings us nearer to that day when the newspaper will be simply a sheet of advertisement and propaganda, with a little well-censored news to sugar the pill. It is quite possible that the *Ami du Peuple* exists on its advertisements, but it is equally possible that it makes only an indirect profit, by putting across the sort of propaganda wanted by M. Coty and his associates. In the above-mentioned manifesto, it was declared that the proprietors might rise to an even dizzier height of philanthropy by giving away the *Ami du Peuple* free of charge. This is not so impossible as it may sound. I have seen a daily paper (in India) which was given away free for some time with apparent profit to its backers, a ring of advertisers who found a free newspaper to be a cheap and satisfactory means of blowing their own trumpet. Their paper was rather above the average Indian level, and it supplied, of course, just such news as they themselves approved, and no other. That obscure Indian paper forecast the logical goal of modern journalism; and the *Ami du Peuple* should be noticed as a new step in the same direction.

But whether its profits are direct or indirect, the *Ami du Peuple* is certainly prospering. Its circulation is already very large, and though it started out as a mere morning paper it has now produced an afternoon and late evening edition. Its proprietors speak with perfect truth when they declare that some of the other papers have done their best to crush this new champion of free speech. These others (they, too, of course, acting from the highest altruistic motives) have made a gallant attempt to have it excluded from the newsagents' shops, and have even succeeded as far as the street-corner kiosks are concerned. In some small shops, too, whose owners are Socialists, one will even see the sign "Ici on ne vend pas *l'Ami du Peuple*" exhibited in the windows. But the *Ami du Peuple* is not worrying. It is sold in the streets and the cafés with great vigour, and it is sold by barbers and tobacconists and all kinds of people who have never done any newsagency before. Sometimes it is simply left out on the boulevard in great piles, together with a tin for the two-sou pieces, and with no attendant whatever. One can see that the proprietors are determined, by hook or by crook, to make it the most widely read paper in Paris.

And supposing they succeed—what then? Obviously the *Ami du Peuple* is going to crowd out of existence one or more of the less prosperous papers—already several are feeling the pinch. In the end, they will presumably either be destroyed, or they will survive by imitating the tactics of the *Ami du Peuple*. Hence every paper of this kind, whatever its intentions, is the enemy of free speech. At present France is the home of free speech, in the press if not elsewhere. Paris alone has daily papers by the dozen, nationalist, Socialist and Communist, clerical and anti-clerical, militarist and anti-militarist, prosemitic and anti-semitic. It has the *Action Française*, a Royalist paper and still one of the leading dailies, and it has *l'Humanité*, the reddest daily paper outside Soviet Russia. It has *La Libertà*, which is written in Italian and yet may not even be sold in Italy, much less published there. Papers are printed in Paris in French, English, Italian, Yiddish, German, Russian, Polish, and languages whose very alphabets are unrecognisable by a western European. The kiosks are stuffed with papers, all different. The press combine, about which French journalists are already grumbling, does not really exist yet in France. But the *Ami du Peuple*, at least, is doing its gallant best to make it a reality.

And supposing that this kind of thing is found to pay in France, why should it not be tried elsewhere? Why should we not have our farthing, or at least our halfpenny newspaper in London? While the journalist exists merely as the publicity agent of big business, a large circulation, got by fair means or foul, is a newspaper's one and only aim. Till recently various of our newspapers achieved the desired level of "net sales" by the simple method of giving away a few thousand pounds now and again in football competition prizes. Now the football competitions have been stopped by law, and doubtless some of the circulations have come down with an ugly bump. Here, then, is a worthy example for our English press magnates. Let them imitate the *Ami du Peuple* and sell their papers at a farthing. Even if it does no other good whatever, at any rate the poor devils of the public will at last feel that they are getting the correct value for their money.

E. A. Blair

G. K.'s Weekly, 29 December 1928

4. Letter to Max Plowman

6 Rue du Pot de Fer
Paris 5
22 September 1929

Dear Sir,[1]
During August I sent you an article[2] describing a day in a casual ward. As a month has now gone by, I should be glad to hear from you about it. I have no other copy of the article, & I want to submit it elsewhere if it is no use to you—

Yours faithfully
E. A. Blair

[1] Max Plowman (1883–1941), journalist and author; worked on the *Adelphi* 1929–41; Warden of the Adelphi Centre 1938–41; ardent supporter of Peace Pledge Union from its foundation in 1934 and its General Secretary 1937–8. Publications include *Introduction to the Study of Blake*, *A Subaltern on the Somme* and *The Faith Called Pacifism*. He encouraged Eric Blair in his early writing and was one of the first to publish his work. Plowman and his wife, Dorothy, always remained friends of Orwell's.

[2] Not published at this time, but it is probable that this article, in a revised form, was published as "The Spike" in the *Adelphi*, April 1931. See 11.

1930

5. Review

Herman Melville by Lewis Mumford

This admirable book is rightly termed a biography, but its chief concern is to analyse Melville's intellect—in Mr Mumford's words, "his ideas, his feelings, his urges, his vision of life". Just enough detail is given to show the dismal quotidian round which enslaved Melville when his voyages were over. We see him as an overworked man of genius, living among people to whom he was hardly more than a tiresome, incomprehensible failure. We are shown how poverty, which threatened even when he was writing *Moby Dick*, infected him through nearly forty years with such loneliness and bitterness as to cripple his talents almost completely. Mr Mumford does not allow this background of poverty to be forgotten; but his declared aim is to expound, criticise, and—unpleasant but necessary word—interpret.

It is just this aim which is responsible for the only large fault of the book. The criticism which sets out to interpret—to be at the deepest meaning and cause of every act—is very well when applied to a man, but it is a dangerous method of approaching a work of art. Done with absolute thoroughness, it would cause art itself to vanish. And therefore when Mr Mumford is interpreting Melville himself—analysing his philosophy and psychology, his religion and sexual life—he is excellent; but he goes on to interpret Melville's poetry, and therein he is not so successful. For one can only "interpret" a poem by reducing it to an allegory—which is like eating an apple for the pips. As in the old legend of Cupid and Psyche, there are times when it is wise to accept without seeking knowledge.

It follows that Mr Mumford is least happy when he is dealing with *Moby Dick*. He is justly appreciative and nobly enthusiastic, but he has altogether too keen an eye for the inner meaning. He asks us, in effect, to take *Moby Dick* as an allegory first and a poem afterwards:

> *Moby Dick* . . . is, fundamentally, a parable on the mystery of evil and the accidental malice of the universe. The white whale stands for the brute energies of existence . . . while Ahab is the spirit of man, small and feeble, but purposive, that pits its puniness against this might, and its purpose against the blank senselessness of power . . . .

That much no one will deny, but it was a pity that Mr Mumford should pursue the allegory to the bitter end. Whaling, he continues, is the symbol of existence and livelihood, the common whales (as opposed to Moby Dick) are tractable nature, the crew of the *Pequod* are the races of mankind—and so forth. It is the old mistake of wanting to read too much between the lines. Here is an example of interpretation altogether too acute:

> In . . . Hamlet, an unconscious incest-wish incapacitates the hero for marriage with the girl he has wooed. . . .

Very ingenious, one feels, but how much better not to have said it! One is reminded of the ghosts in Fielding's underworld, who plagued Shakespeare for the meaning of "Put out the light, and then put out the light". Shakespeare himself had forgotten—and in any case who cares what it meant? It is a fine line, let it go at that. And so with *Moby Dick*. It were much better to have discoursed simply on the form, which is the stuff of poetry, and left the "meaning" alone.

It has been necessary to mention this fault at some length, but it does not seriously spoil the book, because Mr Mumford is concerned with Melville's mind as a whole rather than his mere artistry. And for that purpose the analytical, interpretative method is the best. For the first time Melville's strange and conflicting qualities are disentangled. He was, it is clear, a man as proud as Lucifer, raging against the gods like his own Ahab, and yet full of a native joy that made him embrace life even while he saw its cruelty. He was a kind of ascetic voluptuary, disciplined and (so far as one can discover) superhumanly chaste, and yet amorous of delightful things wherever he found them. More important than his strength, he had —what is implied in real strength—passionate sensitiveness; to him seas were deeper and skies vaster than to other men, and similarly beauty was more actual and pain and humiliation more agonising. Who but Melville would have seen the beauty and terror of a ridiculous beast like a whale? And who else could have written scenes like the bullying of Harry in *Redburn*, or that shocking and ludicrous account of an amputation in *White Jacket*? Such things were done by a man who felt more vividly than common men, just as a kestrel sees more vividly than a mole.

The best chapters of Mr Mumford's book are those in which he relates Melville to his times, and shows how the changing spirit of the century made and marred him. It is evident that Melville owed much to American liberty—or, it may be, the tradition of liberty; the American wildness of spirit that showed itself, though so diversely, in *Life on the Mississippi* and *Leaves of Grass*. Melville lived a wretched life, and was generally poor and harassed, but at least he had an improvident youth behind him. He had not been bred, like so many Europeans, in respectability and despair. America before the Civil War may have been a rough place for a man of culture, but it was at any rate a hard country to starve in. Young men were not always tethered to safe jobs, and they could wander—how many American artists of the nineteenth century spent their youth, like Melville, in adventurous, irresponsible, ungenteel ways. Later, when industrialism was tightening its grip, something in Melville's spirit wilted with the times. The country was being debauched by "progress", scoundrels were prospering, leisure and free thought were declining—necessarily his joy and therefore his creative power waned in such years. But the older, freer America played a part in *Moby Dick*, and still more in the inimitable freshness of *Typee* and *Redburn*.

Such a book as this should do whatever criticism can for Melville's reputation. Whoever is not queasy in the presence of strength will always love Melville, and the same kind of reader will salute Mr Mumford's book for its enthusiastic praise as well as for its discernment. It will not convert the doubtful (and what book ever does that?), but it can teach a great deal to Melville's admirers, and will certainly persuade them to go further afield among his works than the two or three successes by which he is known.

E. A. Blair

New Adelphi, March–May 1930

6. Review

Alexander Pope by Edith Sitwell, *The Course of English Classicism* by Sherard Vines

It is possible, and perhaps necessary, to divide all art into classical and romantic; to see as two separate things the trim formal garden of classicism, and the wild romantic jungle, full of stupendous beauty, and also of morasses and sickly weeds. And yet the two encroach and claim neutral ground, so that sometimes it is hard to say which is jungle and which is garden. Something of the sort occurs in the two books under review. Both touch the same subject, and both are agreed on one point, namely, that Pope was a supreme poet—in some ways *the* supreme English poet; and yet they praise him for qualities which are not only different but mutually exclusive. Mr Sherard Vines, as an upholder of the classical tradition, presents Pope as the high-water mark of classicism; Miss Sitwell, essentially a romantic, discovers romantic qualities in Pope, and praises him for those. They do agree, in a manner, about Pope, but they contradict one another on the fundamental principles of poetry.

Mr Sherard Vines gives an admirable account of the main drift of classicism. He presents the classical mind as something at once strong and elegant, noble and moderate, simple and sophisticated. It will have as much beauty as you like, but no noise, no violent novelty, no exuberance, no mystification. All the assaults on eye, ear and fancy, which from the romantic point of view *are* art, it regards simply as a kind of hitting below the emotional belt:

> "Spell" and "incantation", words that have crept into modern poetics, have nothing to do with the polite; they are merely Gothic. In *Cato*, a model of polite tragedy, there is no disturbing magic, but instead that rarer thing equilibrium, dearer to the mind of a Chinese sage than to superstitious England. . . . It is indeed a perverse age that extols *Hamlet* and ignores *Cato*. . . .

And again:

> Music has its own way of being efficient, and poetry quite another way. When they approach, it is not along the path imagined by quasi-mystical theorists, but on the broad trysting ground, the Hyde Park, may we say, of opera and oratorio. . . .

This is the reply churlish to all romantic poetry. Mr Sherard Vines is perforce hard on Shakespeare, and very rude indeed to Shelley, Coleridge and Wordsworth; he could not be otherwise, for from the classical point of view these writers broke all the rules, and their gift was largely of music, which is the foe of elegance. Poetry therefore, as Mr Sherard Vines sees it, is a thing of wit, grandeur and good sense, not of "magic" and seductive sounds; and Pope, the "unfailingly efficient" poet, who made no high flights and no lapses, is its supreme exponent.

But turn to Miss Sitwell, and we are back immediately to the spells and incantations. This is how Miss Sitwell approaches the subject of technique:

> The poet feels the poem in the palm of his sensitive hands, understanding its exact weight . . . letting the poem grow in his veins. . . . The poet knows, through his sensitive hands, the difference between the sea-cold marble of the Ode, with all its divine variation of ivy-dark veins (cold as the satyrine forests)—veins with the shape of the Aegean waves within them, veins full of the light—the difference between this and the hot velvet petals of that rose the lyric. . . .

This is not, so to say, classical talk. So far from frowning upon "magic", Miss Sitwell comes to Pope for the same enchantment as one finds in people like Francis Thompson or Gerard Manley Hopkins. She classes Pope with Shakespeare, Shelley and Coleridge—she even likens *The Dunciad* to *The Ancient Mariner*—whereas all Mr Sherard Vines says about *The Ancient Mariner* is that it "recounted improbable things of an albatross". And poetry, she says, is not to be valued primarily for its subject-matter, nor even for metrical form, but for "texture"; that is for the music, with its vast inexplicable power of pleasing or disgusting, contained in the mere impact of one syllable on another.

As a general proposition most people will agree with this, but it is disconcerting to see a writer like Pope praised chiefly for his music. Miss Sitwell is almost a fanatic in prosody; she is so minute in her examination, so sensitive to "the thick, muffled dull thud of the alliterating M's" and the "appalling deafening blows caused by the alliterative B's" and so forth, that she forgets sometimes that even melodious verse must not be hackneyed in sentiment. She will tell you for instance that such a passage as:

> 'Twas now the time when Phoebus yields to Night,
> And rising Cynthia casts her silver light,
> Wide o'er the world in solemn pomp she drew
> Her airy chariot, hung with pearly dew

has "an exquisite lightness", not noticing, apparently, that it has also an insufferable staleness and obviousness. And she finds a kind of hell-born inspiration in the very ordinary couplet,

> So watchful Bruin forms with plastic care
> Each growing lump, and brings it to a bear.

One is not accusing Miss Sitwell of exaggeration; discovering vast musical profundities in Pope, naturally she proclaims them. But when one sees such phrases as "terrible trumpet scream of rage", "smoky and appalling beauty", and the like, applied to Pope's urbane lines, one begins to wonder whether there is not something in the classical, non-musical view of poetry.

Thus, between the classicist who admires Pope because he was not like Shakespeare, and the romantic who thinks he *was* like Shakespeare, you are left in doubt. And yet, however sound are the classical arguments, what man of spirit will relinquish his Shakespeare? One remembers too that even the classical rules are only provisional. There is a passage in Mr Sherard Vines's book in which he declares that Shakespeare's use of "lads" in "golden lads and lasses" stamps him for a romantic—the proper classical word being "youths"; and it seems that other authorities say, on the contrary, that "lads" is classical and "youths" romantic; which shows how much hair-splitting is sometimes needed to define what is classical and what is not. And then it appears that Ossian, who is manifestly *not* classical, was accepted as such by some of his contemporary critics. And Mr Sherard Vines says that Fuseli was classical, if not of the purest breed; but Fuseli, one remembers, was the only man Blake ever knew who did not almost make him spew—that is, was admired by the high priest of romanticism. So, even in the formal garden, the jungle encroaches.

It remains to be added that Mr Sherard Vines has performed a difficult feat in treating such a large and crowded subject adequately in small space. Miss Sitwell's life of Pope is distinguished by her warm-hearted defence of the poet against all his detractors. Her English is queer and, one must add, precious, but there is a charm in her love of sonorous words for their own sake. Her book is finely printed, with some interesting illustrations.

E. A. Blair

New Adelphi, June–August 1930

7. Review

Angel Pavement by J. B. Priestley

Abandoning provincial life, Mr Priestley has turned his attention to London, in a novel about one Mr Golspie, an able rogue who descends upon a struggling city firm, quietly ruins it, and vanishes. The intention, more or less explicit, is to set forth the romance of London, to make a pattern of beauty from the eventless, dismal lives which interlace in a city office. Abandon, says Mr Priestley in effect, all your sneering about industrial civilisation. Remember that these clerks and typists who look so unpleasantly like ants as they stream over London Bridge at the rush hour, these clerks whom you in your superiority despise—they too are human—they too are romantic! And thus far, who will contradict him? Clerks are men and brothers, and fit material for art—applause, therefore, to the writer who can use them.

But unfortunately, a novelist is not required to have good intentions but to convey beauty. And when one has finished applauding Mr Priestley's effort to make clerks and typists interesting, one must add that the effort does not, even for a single page, come off. It is not that he writes ineptly, or is lumpishly dull, or consciously plays for cheap effects; it is simply that his writing does not touch the level at which memorable fiction begins. One compares these six hundred competent pages (and one must make the comparison, after all that has been said of Mr Priestley) with other novels of London; with Mr Arnold Bennett in *Riceyman Steps*, with Conrad in *The Secret Agent*, with Dickens in *Bleak House*; and one wonders incredulously whether anyone has really mistaken Mr Priestley for a master. His work has no damning faults, but neither has it a single gleam of beauty, nor any profundity of thought, nor even memorable humour; the book is simply a middle article spun out to six hundred pages, with all the middle article's high spirits and conscientious wit, and the same utter lack of anything intensely felt or profitably conveyed.

> Warwick's restaurant . . . might have been French or Italian or even Spanish or Hungarian; there was no telling; but it was determinedly foreign in a de-nationalised fashion, rather as if the League of Nations had invented it.

> . . . the bus stopped by the dark desolation of Lord's cricket ground, swallowed two women who were all parcels, comic hats,

and fuss (a sure sign this that Christmas was near, for you never saw these parcel-and-comic-hat women at any other time) and rolled on . . . .

The point about these two extracts is that they are as good as anything in *Angel Pavement*; there are thousands of sentences like them, seldom worse, never better, never going deeper than this beneath the skin of things. And yet consider what themes Mr Priestley is handling in this shallow and sprightly way! A cunning business swindle, dinner parties in an Earl's Court maisonette, squabbles in a Stoke Newington villa, a hospital deathbed, an attempted murder, a projected suicide! One imagines what these things might have become in other hands. One imagines, for example, Conrad brooding in his own sombre way over Turgis, the pimply and lovesick clerk; or Hardy describing the scene in which Turgis, intending suicide, has not a shilling for the gas meter; or Mr H. G. Wells, in his earlier manner, reporting the conversations of Mr Pelumpton, the boozy second-hand broker; or Mr Bennett upon the women's hostel where incipient old maids starved for adventure. But one does not get what these writers would have given, nor anything resembling it more closely than London draught beer resembles beer made with hops. What one does get is six hundred pages of middle article, quite readable and quite forgettable, with—when the plot calls for intense feeling—something like this:

> He sat there in a dream ecstasy of devotion, in which remembered kisses glittered like stars.

When a novel lacks the indefinable, unmistakable thing we call beauty, one looks in it for sound delineation of character, or humour of situation, or verbal wit. But one looks in vain in *Angel Pavement*—Mr Priestley can be clever, but he cannot be in any way memorable. All his characters—Mr Dersingham the incompetent businessman, Mr Golspie the adventurous rogue, Miss Matfield the bored typist, Mr Smeeth the desiccated accountant—are alike in their unreality, mere attenuated ghosts from the pages of Mr Hugh Walpole and Mr Arnold Bennett. All the dialogue is the same in this, that being neither incredible nor unreadable, it is not funny and has not the compelling semblance of life. All the analysis, the reflections, are alike in the ease with which they are understood, and, having been understood, are forgotten. Even the observation is suspect. Towards the end of the book there is an account of a game of bridge, and the account contains two errors which would never have been made by a careful observer. It is a small point, but it confirms the general impression that Mr Priestley's work is written altogether too easily, is not laboured upon as good fiction must be—not, in the good sense of the phrase, *worked out.*

One would not thus assail a competent and agreeable novel, if Mr Priestley had not been so extravagantly praised. He has been likened, absurdly, to Dickens, and when a novelist is likened to Dickens one must stop and ask the reason. Is it not a safe guess that Mr Priestley owes his popularity to his frank optimism? In *Angel Pavement,* it is true, he deals with gloomy subjects, but by implication—by his manner of writing—he is as cheerful as ever. He is not a professional backslapper, but he can be quoted by such, and to some of them, probably, he appears as a champion against those gloomy and obscene highbrows who are supposed to be forever corrupting English literature. It is for this reason that such a blatantly second-rate novelist has been likened to Dickens, the great master of prose, psychology and wit. Once this absurd praise is discounted, we can salute Mr Priestley for the qualities which he really possesses, and take *Angel Pavement* for what it is: an excellent holiday novel, genuinely gay and pleasant, which supplies a good bulk of reading matter for ten and sixpence.

E. A. Blair

Adelphi, October 1930

8. Letter to Max Plowman

3 Queen St
Southwold, Suffolk
1 November 1930

Dear Mr Plowman,[1]
Thank you very much for the copy of the *Adelphi,*[2] which I found an interesting one. I see that Mr Murry[3] says in his article, "Be-

[1] In September 1930 Max Plowman became co-editor of the *Adelphi.*
[2] *Adelphi,* November 1930.
[3] John Middleton Murry (1889–1957), prolific writer, critic and polemicist.

cause orthodox Christianity is exceedingly elaborate, it presents a greater appearance of unity than (childish superstition)". I know this is so, but the *why* is beyond me. It is clear that the thicker the fairy tales are piled, the more easily one can swallow them, but this seems so paradoxical that I have never been able to understand the reason for it. I don't think Roger Clarke in his article on Sex & Sin gets to [the] very bottom of the question. He says rightly that the "spiritual love" stuff fixes the desires on something unattainable, & that this leads to trouble. The point he doesn't bring out is that the "sinful lust" stuff also fixes it on something unattainable, & that attempts to realise the impossible *physical* desire are even more destructive than attempts on the spiritual side. Of course it is important to teach boys that women like Esther Summerson[1] don't exist, but it is just as important, & far harder, to teach them that women like the *Vie Parisienne* illustrations don't exist. Perhaps the writer had not the space to bring this out thoroughly. You will, I know, forgive my troubling you with my reflections, as I was interested by the questions raised.

Thanks very much for the books. I find the novel well enough, the Cayenne[2] book interesting, though it is almost certainly exaggerated. The book on Bodley[3] is more solid stuff, but I don't know that it is the kind of thing you would care to use much space on. What I suggest is doing about 1000 words altogether on the three, either in one article or separately as you prefer. I think they are worth mentioning, but not worth more than 1000 words between them. Would this do? If so, I can let you have the review in about 10 days. If you don't think it worthwhile, I will send the books back.

After having been a most effective editor of the *Athenaeum* he founded the *Adelphi* in 1923 after the death of his first wife, Katherine Mansfield, and controlled it for the next 25 years. In its origins he took a line independent of the then dominant "Bloomsbury Group". He was successively a fervent disciple of D. H. Lawrence, unorthodox Marxist, unorthodox Christian, pacifist and "back to the land" farmer, all of which creeds were proclaimed in editorials and articles in the *Adelphi*. When in 1930 Sir Richard Rees joined the *Adelphi*, both as angel and co-editor, he introduced a more political tone into the magazine and opened its pages to a less self-consciously literary type of writer.

[1] Central character and part narrator of Charles Dickens's *Bleak House*.

[2] Blair's review, signed E. A. B., of this book, *The Horrors of Cayenne* by Karl Bartz, appeared in the *Adelphi*, December 1930.

[3] He did not review either the novel or the book on Bodley.

I enclose the other article,[1] reduced to 3500 words. Thank you for giving my MS[2] to Mr Murry. I hope he understands that there is no hurry & I don't want to be a nuisance to him.

Yours sincerely
Eric A. Blair

[1] "The Spike", which appeared in the *Adelphi*, April 1931. See 11.

[2] Very likely an earlier version of the manuscript of *Down and Out in Paris and London*.

1931

9. Lettercard to Max Plowman

[Postmark: Golders Green NW11]
Monday [12 January 1931]

Dear Mr Plowman,

Thanks very much for your letter. I am in & about London at present, but when I get home I will send that article[1] & you can have a look at it. I didn't in any case suppose that you could use it yet awhile, but I thought if you liked it you might like to keep it by you. As to the review, I cannot of course let you pay for it. It was a poor piece of work, & that should be an end of it.

As to those books, I should like very much to have a try at the Carlyle book.[2] You ask what kind of thing I like reviewing. If you ever get any book (fiction or travel stuff) on India, or on low life in London, or on Villon, Swift, Smollett, Poe, Mark Twain, Zola, Anatole France or Conrad, or anything *by* M. P. Shiel or W. Somerset Maugham, I should enjoy reviewing it. Please excuse a post office pen.

Yours sincerely
Eric A. Blair

10. Review

The Two Carlyles by Osbert Burdett

This discerning, quietly able book deals chiefly with Carlyle's married life, but it is also an acute study of his intellect. It should greatly help the general reader to get Carlyle's large vague renown into focus.

[1] Probably "A Hanging", which appeared in the *Adelphi*, August 1931. See 12.
[2] *The Two Carlyles* by Osbert Burdett was reviewed by Blair in the *Adelphi*, March 1931.

Mr Burdett sums up Carlyle, finally, as an egoist, and on the literary side it is perhaps just to call him that fairly subtilised form of egoist, an orator. Only a historian, of course, can judge his historical work; but if we test him by *Heroes and Hero-Worship*—and that is fair, for it was his creed, and done in his best period—we find nothing better than oratory. There are fine panegyrics in it, fine adjectives—adjectives which, living a strange life of their own, give an air of profundity—but no real depth of thought. It is only a splendid vestment of words, draped about a few worn, rather mean ideas. Language apart, the whole purport of the book is this: that there exists some vast world-purpose, unquestionably good, and that great men (meaning *successful* men) are its instruments. The true Hero is the man who fights on the side of fate; a sort of Achilles in god-given armour, licensed to trample on mere mortals. Sincerity is the virtue we are bidden to admire in him; but we are also bidden to test his sincerity by his success. Nothing but the good prevails—and so, in the name of virtue, *vae victis!*

> I will allow a thing to struggle for itself in the world, with any sword or tongue or implement it has . . . very sure that it will, in the long run, conquer nothing which does not deserve to be conquered. What is better than itself, it cannot put away, but only what is worse.

This means no more than *vae victis*—woe to the creed that is not backed by machine-guns! But the oratory arising from this text, those fine vague sermons on Mahommed and Luther and Cromwell, are another matter.

Clearly this Great Man cult of Carlyle's was the symptom of egoism, of buried ambition. Mr Burdett points out how Carlyle's heroes grew more dominant, more grandiose, as he himself grew richer; he passed from Burns to Cromwell, from Cromwell to Frederick—from successful rebels to successful scoundrels. Briefly, his love of a conqueror, his gusto in battle scenes, was a sort of vicarious bullying. And yet one must not forget that it was *unconscious* egoism; there was a mysticism in his ugly creed. With his sense of a world-purpose ("the great deep law of the world"), he did feel that his conquering heroes served something noble, some scheme greater than their own. He had a feeling, half poetic, for the flowing of time and history; it is always at least latent in his work, and it produces his finest sentences. "The Merovingian kings, slowly wending on their bullock carts through the streets of Paris, with their long hair flowing, have all wended slowly on into Eternity." It is a simple enough idea behind the words; and yet, what splendid words! A few passages such as this are the best justification of Carlyle's opinions.

The other symptom of Carlyle's egoism was his personal unhappiness. Even if one knew nothing of his life, one could not read ten of his pages without being struck by the ill-humour, the queer, wounding adjectives ("O seagreen Prophet", and so forth), the instinctive sneer. At its worst (in his spiteful remarks about Lamb and Hazlitt, for instance, or that ugly whoop of triumph after the French defeats of 1870), his rancour suggests a man permanently soured by ill-luck. And yet Carlyle was not inevitably unhappy. His ill-health was not serious—at least, the "baleful Nessus shirt of perpetual pain" did not prevent him from living to eighty-six. His marriage was not unhappy in itself; it was merely the marriage of two unhappy people. And he was successful, even strikingly so, from early middle life onwards. The unhappiness of Mrs Carlyle, sickly and childless, is much more understandable. Nevertheless, Carlyle was nearly always desperately unhappy, and to some extent the bitter tone of his work is a reflection of this.

"Clay in his blood, Calvinism in his head, dyspepsia in his stomach," is Mr Burdett's diagnosis. He suggests that even Carlyle's occasional championship of the poor came more from a desire to thump society than from benevolence. Spleen, of course, is the exact word for Carlyle's peculiar temper; the spleen of the *unconscious* egoist, the denouncer of this and that, the discoverer of new sins. Consider the base, prying spite of this description of Marat, at the moment of Charlotte Corday's entrance:

> . . . stewing in slipper-bath; sore afflicted; ill of Revolution Fever,—of what other malady this History had rather not name. Excessively sick and worn, poor man: with precisely elevenpence-halfpenny of ready money, in paper; with slipper-bath; strong three-footed stool for writing on, the while; and a squalid—Washerwoman, one may call her. . . .

It is really an occasion for pity rather than sneers. But some obscure spite moves Carlyle to damn Marat, and so he damns him, when the facts give out, by tricks of repetition, even by punctuation; every semicolon is an insult. It will do, also, as an example of the strange impressiveness of Carlyle's abuse. No one, surely, was ever such a master of belittlement. Even at his emptiest sneer (as when he said that Whitman "thought he was a big man because he lived in a big country") the victim does seem to shrink a little. That again is the power of the orator, the man of phrases and adjectives, turned to a base use.

It should be added that almost half of Mr Burdett's book deals with the life of Carlyle and Jane Welsh before their marriage. Their love story, he says, was not an abnormal one, but it was unusual in being so well documented. As a revelation, therefore, of the frame of mind in which people get married, and of the astonishing selfishness that exists in the sincerest love, it is interesting. This book should appeal to many readers besides those specially interested in Carlyle.

Eric Blair

Adelphi, March 1931

11. The Spike

It was late afternoon. Forty-nine of us, forty-eight men and one woman, lay on the green waiting for the spike to open. We were too tired to talk much. We just sprawled about exhaustedly, with home-made cigarettes sticking out of our scrubby faces. Overhead the chestnut branches were covered with blossom, and beyond that great woolly clouds floated almost motionless in a clear sky. Littered on the grass, we seemed dingy, urban riff-raff. We defiled the scene, like sardine-tins and paper bags on the seashore.

What talk there was ran on the Tramp Major of this spike. He was a devil, everyone agreed, a tartar, a tyrant, a bawling, blasphemous, uncharitable dog. You couldn't call your soul your own when he was about, and many a tramp had he kicked out in the middle of the night for giving a back answer. When you came to be searched he fair held you upside down and shook you. If you were caught with tobacco there was hell to pay, and if you went in with money (which is against the law) God help you.

I had eightpence on me. "For the love of Christ, mate," the old hands advised me, "don't you take it in. You'd get seven days for going into the spike with eightpence!"

So I buried my money in a hole under the hedge, marking the spot with a lump of flint. Then we set about smuggling our matches and tobacco, for it is forbidden to take these into nearly all spikes, and one is supposed to surrender them at the gate. W hid them in our socks, except for the twenty or so per cent who had no socks, and had to carry the tobacco in their boots, even under their very toes. We stuffed our ankles with contraband until anyone seeing us might have imagined an outbreak of elephantiasis. But it is an unwritten law that even the sternest Tramp Majors do not search below the knee, and in the end only one man was caught. This was Scotty, a little hairy tramp with a bastard accent sired by cockney out of Glasgow. His tin of cigarette ends fell out of his sock at the wrong moment, and was impounded.

At six the gates swung open and we shuffled in. An official at the gate entered our names and other particulars in the register and took our bundles away from us. The woman was sent off to the workhouse, and we others into the spike. It was a gloomy, chilly, limewashed place, consisting only of a bathroom and dining-room and about a hundred narrow stone cells. The terrible Tramp Major met us at the door and herded us into the bathroom to be stripped and searched. He was a gruff, soldierly man of forty, who gave the tramps no more ceremony than sheep at the dipping-pond, shoving them this way and that and shouting oaths in their faces. But when he came to myself, he looked hard at me, and said:

"You are a gentleman?"

"I suppose so," I said.

He gave me another long look. "Well, that's bloody bad luck, guv'nor," he said, "that's bloody bad luck, that is." And thereafter he took it into his head to treat me with compassion, even with a kind of respect.

It was a disgusting sight, that bathroom. All the indecent secrets of our underwear were exposed; the grime, the rents and patches, the bits of string doing duty for buttons, the layers upon layers of fragmentary garments, some of them mere collections of holes held together by dirt. The room became a press of steaming nudity, the sweaty odours of the tramps competing with the sickly, sub-faecal stench native to the spike. Some of the men refused the bath, and washed only their "toe-rags", the horrid, greasy little clouts which tramps bind round their feet. Each of us had three minutes in which to bathe himself. Six greasy, slippery roller towels had to serve for the lot of us.

When we had bathed our own clothes were taken away from us, and we were dressed in the workhouse shirts, grey cotton things like nightshirts, reaching to the middle of the thigh. Then we were sent into the dining-room, where supper was set out on the deal tables. It was the invariable spike meal, always the same, whether breakfast, dinner or supper—half a pound of bread, a bit of margarine, and a pint of so-called tea. It took us five minutes to gulp down the cheap, noxious food. Then the Tramp Major served us with three cotton blankets each, and drove us off to our cells for the night. The doors were locked on the outside a little before seven in the evening, and would stay locked for the next twelve hours.

The cells measured eight feet by five, and had no lighting apparatus except a tiny, barred window high up in the wall, and a spyhole in the door. There were no bugs, and we had bedsteads and straw palliasses, rare luxuries both. In many spikes one sleeps on a wooden shelf, and in some on the bare floor, with a rolled-up coat for pillow. With a cell to myself, and a bed, I was hoping for a sound night's rest. But I did not get it, for there is always something wrong in the spike, and the peculiar shortcoming here, as I discovered immediately, was the cold. May had begun, and in honour of the season—a little sacrifice to the gods of spring, perhaps—the authorities had cut off the steam from the hot pipes. The cotton blankets were almost useless. One spent the night in turning from side to side, falling asleep for ten minutes and waking half frozen, and watching for dawn.

As always happens in the spike, I had at last managed to fall comfortably asleep when it was time to get up. The Tramp Major came marching down the passage with his heavy tread, unlocking the doors and yelling to us to show a leg. Promptly the passage was full of squalid shirt-clad figures rushing for the bathroom, for there was only one tub full of water between us all in the morning, and it was first come first served. When I arrived twenty tramps had already washed their faces. I gave one glance at the black scum on top of the water, and decided to go dirty for the day.

We hurried into our clothes, and then went to the dining-room to bolt our breakfast. The bread was much worse than usual, because the military-minded idiot of a Tramp Major had cut it into slices overnight, so that it was as hard as ship's biscuit. But we were glad of our tea after the cold, restless night. I do not know what tramps would do without tea, or rather the stuff they miscall tea. It is their food, their medicine, their panacea for all evils. Without the half gallon or so of it that they suck down a day, I truly believe they could not face their existence.

After breakfast we had to undress again for the medical inspection, which is a precaution against smallpox. It was three-quarters of an hour before the doctor arrived, and one had time now to look about him and see what manner of men we were. It was an instructive sight. We stood shivering naked to the waist in two long ranks in the passage. The filtered light, bluish and cold, lighted us up with unmerciful clarity. No one can imagine, unless he has seen such a thing, what pot-bellied, degenerate curs we looked. Shock heads, hairy, crumpled faces, hollow chests, flat feet, sagging muscles—every kind of malformation and physical rottenness were there. All were flabby and discoloured, as all tramps are under their deceptive sunburn. Two or three figures seen there stay ineradicably in my mind. Old "Daddy", aged seventy-four, with his truss, and his red, watering eyes: a herring-gutted starveling, with sparse beard and sunken cheeks, looking like the corpse of Lazarus in some primitive picture: an imbecile, wandering hither and thither with vague giggles, coyly pleased because his trousers constantly slipped down and left him nude. But few of us were greatly better than these; there were not ten decently built men among us, and half, I believe, should have been in hospital.

This being Sunday, we were to be kept in the spike over the week-end. As soon as the doctor had gone we were herded back to the dining-room, and its door shut upon us. It was a lime-washed, stone-floored room, unspeakably dreary with its furniture of deal boards and benches, and its prison smell. The windows were so high up that one could not look outside, and the sole ornament was a set of Rules threatening dire penalties to any casual who misconducted himself. We packed the room so tight that one could not move an elbow without jostling somebody. Already, at eight o'clock in the morning, we were bored with our captivity. There was nothing to talk about except the petty gossip of the road, the good and bad spikes, the charitable and uncharitable counties, the iniquities of the police and the Salvation Army. Tramps hardly ever get away from these subjects; they talk, as it were, nothing but shop. They have nothing worthy to be called conversation, because emptiness of belly leaves no speculation in their souls. The world is too much with them. Their next meal is never quite secure, and so they cannot think of anything except the next meal.

Two hours dragged by. Old Daddy, witless with age, sat silent, his back bent like a bow and his inflamed eyes dripping slowly on to the floor. George, a dirty old tramp notorious for the queer habit of sleeping in his hat, grumbled about a parcel of tommy that he had lost on the road. Bill the moocher, the best built man of us all, a Herculean sturdy beggar who smelt of beer even after twelve hours in the spike, told tales of mooching, of pints stood him in the boozers, and of a parson who had peached to the police and got him seven days. William and Fred, two young ex-fishermen from Norfolk, sang a sad song about Unhappy Bella, who was betrayed and died in the snow. The imbecile drivelled about an imaginary toff who had once given him two hundred and fifty-seven golden sovereigns. So the time passed, with dull talk and dull obscenities. Everyone was smoking, except Scotty, whose tobacco had been seized, and he was so miserable in his smokeless state that I stood him the makings of a cigarette. We smoked furtively, hiding our cigarettes like schoolboys when we heard the Tramp Major's step, for smoking, though connived at, was officially forbidden.

Most of the tramps spent ten consecutive hours in this dreary room. It is hard to imagine how they put up with it. I have come to think that boredom is the worst of all a tramp's evils, worse than hunger and discomfort, worse even than the constant feeling of being socially disgraced. It is a silly piece of cruelty to confine an ignorant man all day with nothing to do; it is like chaining a dog in a barrel. Only an educated man, who has consolations within himself, can endure confinement. Tramps, unlettered types as nearly all of them are, face their poverty with blank, resourceless minds. Fixed for ten hours on a comfortless bench, they know no way of occupying themselves, and if they think at all it is to whimper about hard luck and pine for work. They have not the stuff in them to endure the horrors of idleness. And so, since so much of their lives is spent in doing nothing, they suffer agonies from boredom.

I was much luckier than the others, because at ten o'clock the Tramp Major picked me out for the most coveted of all jobs in the spike, the job of helping in the workhouse kitchen. There was not really any work to be done there, and I was able to make off and hide in a shed used for storing potatoes, together with some workhouse paupers who were skulking to avoid the Sunday morning service.

There was a stove burning there, and comfortable packing cases to sit on, and back numbers of the *Family Herald*, and even a copy of *Raffles* from the workhouse library. It was paradise after the spike.

Also, I had my dinner from the workhouse table, and it was one of the biggest meals I have ever eaten. A tramp does not see such a meal twice in the year, in the spike or out of it. The paupers told me that they always gorged to the bursting point on Sundays, and went hungry six days of the week. When the meal was over the cook set me to do the washing-up, and told me to throw away the food that remained. The wastage was astonishing; great dishes of beef, and bucketfuls of bread and vegetables, were pitched away like rubbish, and then defiled with tea-leaves. I filled five dustbins to overflowing with good food. And while I did so my fellow tramps were sitting two hundred yards away in the spike, their bellies half filled with the spike dinner of the everlasting bread and tea, and perhaps two cold boiled potatoes each in honour of Sunday. It appeared that the food was thrown away from deliberate policy, rather than that it should be given to the tramps.

At three I left the workhouse kitchen and went back to the spike. The boredom in that crowded, comfortless room was now unbearable. Even smoking had ceased, for a tramp's only tobacco is picked-up cigarette ends, and, like a browsing beast, he starves if he is long away from the pavement-pasture. To occupy the time I talked with a rather superior tramp, a young carpenter who wore a collar and tie, and was on the road, he said, for lack of a set of tools. He kept a little aloof from the other tramps, and held himself more like a free man than a casual. He had literary tastes, too, and carried one of Scott's novels on all his wanderings. He told me he never entered a spike unless driven there by hunger, sleeping under hedges and behind ricks in preference. Along the south coast he had begged by day and slept in bathing-machines for weeks at a time.

We talked of life on the road. He criticised the system which makes a tramp spend fourteen hours a day in the spike, and the other ten in walking and dodging the police. He spoke of his own case—six months at the public charge for want of three pounds' worth of tools. It was idiotic, he said.

Then I told him about the wastage of food in the workhouse kitchen, and what I thought of it. And at that he changed his tune immediately. I saw that I had awakened the pew-renter who sleeps in every English workman. Though he had been famished along with the rest, he at once saw reasons why the food should have been thrown away rather than given to the tramps. He admonished me quite severely.

"They have to do it," he said. "If they made these places too pleasant you'd have all the scum of the country flocking into them. It's only the bad food as keeps all that scum away. These tramps are too lazy to work, that's all that's wrong with them. You don't want to go encouraging of them. They're scum."

I produced arguments to prove him wrong, but he would not listen. He kept repeating:

"You don't want to have any pity on these tramps—scum, they are. You don't want to judge them by the same standards as men like you and me. They're scum, just scum."

It was interesting to see how subtly he disassociated himself from his fellow tramps. He has been on the road six months, but in the sight of God, he seemed to imply, he was not a tramp. His body might be in the spike, but his spirit soared far away, in the pure aether of the middle classes.

The clock's hands crept round with excruciating slowness. We were too bored even to talk now, the only sound was of oaths and reverberating yawns. One would force his eyes away from the clock for what seemed an age, and then look back again to see that the hands had advanced three minutes. Ennui clogged our souls like cold mutton fat. Our bones ached because of it. The clock's hands stood at four, and supper was not till six, and there was nothing left remarkable beneath the visiting moon.

At last six o'clock did come, and the Tramp Major and his assistant arrived with supper. The yawning tramps brisked up like lions at feeding-time. But the meal was a dismal disappointment. The bread, bad enough in the morning, was now positively uneatable; it was so hard that even the strongest jaws could make little impression on it. The older men went almost supperless, and not a man could finish his portion, hungry though most of us were. When we had finished, the blankets were served out immediately, and we were hustled off once more to the bare, chilly cells.

Thirteen hours went by. At seven we were awakened, and rushed forth to squabble over the water in the bathroom, and bolt our ration of bread and tea. Our time in the spike was up, but we could not go until the doctor had examined us again, for the authorities have a terror of smallpox and its distribution by tramps. The doctor kept us waiting two hours this time, and it was ten o'clock before we finally escaped.

At last it was time to go, and we were let out into the yard. How bright everything looked, and how sweet the winds did blow, after the gloomy, reeking spike! The Tramp Major handed each man his bundle of confiscated possessions, and a hunk of bread and cheese for midday dinner, and then we took the road, hastening to get out of sight of the spike and its discipline. This was our interim of freedom. After a day and two nights of wasted time we had eight hours or so to take our recreation, to scour the roads for cigarette ends, to beg, and to look for work. Also, we had to make our ten, fifteen, or it might be twenty miles to the next spike, where the game would begin anew.

I disinterred my eightpence and took the road with Nobby, a respectable, downhearted tramp who carried a spare pair of boots and visited all the Labour Exchanges. Our late companions were scattering north, south, east and west, like bugs into a mattress. Only the imbecile loitered at the spike gates, until the Tramp Major had to chase him away.

Nobby and I set out for Croydon. It was a quiet road, there were no cars passing, the blossom covered the chestnut trees like great wax candles. Everything was so quiet and smelt so clean, it was hard to realise that only a few minutes ago we had been packed with that band of prisoners in a stench of drains and soft soap. The others had all disappeared; we two seemed to be the only tramps on the road.

Then I heard a hurried step behind me, and felt a tap on my arm. It was little Scotty, who had run panting after us. He pulled a rusty tin box from his pocket. He wore a friendly smile, like a man who is repaying an obligation.

"Here y'are, mate," he said cordially. "I owe you some fag ends. You stood me a smoke yesterday. The Tramp Major give me back my box of fag ends when we come out this morning. One good turn deserves another—here y'are."

And he put four sodden, debauched, loathly cigarette ends into my hand.

Eric Blair

Adelphi, April 1931; later reduced and reshaped to form Chapters 27 and 35 of *Down and Out in Paris and London*.

12. A Hanging

It was in Burma, a sodden morning of the rains. A sickly light, like yellow tinfoil, was slanting over the high walls into the jail yard. We were waiting outside the condemned cells, a row of sheds fronted with double bars, like small animal cages. Each cell measured about ten feet by ten and was quite bare within except for a plank bed and a pot of drinking water. In some of them brown silent men were squatting at the inner bars, with their blankets draped round them. These were the condemned men, due to be hanged within the next week or two.

One prisoner had been brought out of his cell. He was a Hindu, a puny wisp of a man, with a shaven head and vague liquid eyes. He had a thick, sprouting moustache, absurdly too big for his body, rather like the moustache of a comic man on the films. Six tall Indian warders were guarding him and getting him ready for the gallows. Two of them stood by with rifles and fixed bayonets, while the others handcuffed him, passed a chain through his handcuffs and fixed it to their belts, and lashed his arms tight to his sides. They crowded very close about him, with their hands always on him in a careful, caressing grip, as though all the while feeling him to make sure he was there. It was like men handling a fish which is still alive and may jump back into the water. But he stood quite unresisting, yielding his arms limply to the ropes, as though he hardly noticed what was happening.

Eight o'clock struck and a bugle call, desolately thin in the wet air, floated from the distant barracks. The superintendent of the jail, who was standing apart from the rest of us, moodily prodding the gravel with his stick, raised his head at the sound. He was an army doctor, with a grey toothbrush moustache and a gruff voice. "For God's sake hurry up, Francis," he said irritably. "The man ought to have been dead by this time. Aren't you ready yet?"

Francis, the head jailer, a fat Dravidian in a white drill suit and gold spectacles, waved his black hand. "Yes sir, yes sir," he bubbled. "All iss satisfactorily prepared. The hangman iss waiting. We shall proceed."

"Well, quick march, then. The prisoners can't get their breakfast till this job's over."

We set out for the gallows. Two warders marched on either side of the prisoner, with their rifles at the slope; two others marched close against him, gripping him by arm and shoulder, as though at once pushing and supporting him. The rest of us, magistrates and the like, followed behind. Suddenly, when we had gone ten yards, the procession stopped short without any order or warning. A dreadful thing had happened—a dog, come goodness knows whence, had appeared in the yard. It came bounding among us with a loud volley of barks, and leapt round us wagging its whole body, wild with glee at finding so many human beings together. It was a large woolly dog, half Airedale, half pariah. For a moment it pranced round us, and then, before anyone could stop it, it had made a dash for the prisoner, and jumping up tried to lick his face. Everyone stood aghast, too taken aback even to grab at the dog.

"Who let that bloody brute in here?" said the superintendent angrily. "Catch it, someone!"

A warder, detached from the escort, charged clumsily after the dog, but it danced and gambolled just out of his reach, taking everything as part of the game. A young Eurasian jailer picked up a handful of gravel and tried to stone the dog away, but it dodged the stones and came after us again. Its yaps echoed from the jail walls. The prisoner, in the grasp of the two warders, looked on incuriously, as though this was another formality of the hanging. It was several minutes before someone managed to catch the dog. Then we put my handkerchief through its collar and moved off once more, with the dog still straining and whimpering.

It was about forty yards to the gallows. I watched the bare brown back of the prisoner marching in front of me. He walked clumsily with his bound arms, but quite steadily, with that bobbing gait of the Indian who never straightens his knees. At each step his muscles slid neatly into place, the lock of hair on his scalp danced up and down, his feet printed themselves on the wet gravel. And once, in spite of the men who gripped him by each shoulder, he stepped slightly aside to avoid a puddle on the path.

It is curious, but till that moment I had never realised what it means to destroy a healthy, conscious man. When I saw the prisoner step aside to avoid the puddle, I saw the mystery, the unspeakable wrongness, of cutting a life short when it is in full tide. This man was not dying, he was alive just as we were alive. All the organs of his body were working—bowels digesting food, skin renewing itself, nails growing, tissues forming—all toiling away in solemn foolery. His nails would still be growing when he stood on the drop, when he was falling through the air with a tenth of a second to live. His eyes saw the yellow gravel and the grey walls, and his brain still remembered, foresaw, reasoned—reasoned even about puddles. He and we were a party of men walking together, seeing, hearing, feeling, understanding the same world; and in two minutes, with a sudden snap, one of us would be gone—one mind less, one world less.

The gallows stood in a small yard, separate from the main grounds of the prison, and overgrown with tall prickly weeds. It was a brick erection like three sides of a shed, with planking on top, and above that two beams and a crossbar with the rope dangling. The hangman, a grey-haired convict in the white uniform of the prison, was waiting beside his machine. He greeted us with a servile crouch as we entered. At a word from Francis the two warders, gripping the prisoner more closely than ever, half led, half pushed him to the gallows and helped him clumsily up the ladder. Then the hangman climbed up and fixed the rope round the prisoner's neck.

We stood waiting, five yards away. The warders had formed in a rough circle round the gallows. And then, when the noose was fixed, the prisoner began crying out on his god. It was a high, reiterated cry of "Ram! Ram! Ram! Ram!", not urgent and fearful like a prayer or a cry for help, but steady, rhythmical, almost like the tolling of a bell. The dog answered the sound with a whine. The hangman, still standing on the gallows, produced a small cotton bag like a flour bag and drew it down over the prisoner's face. But the sound, muffled by the cloth, still persisted, over and over again: "Ram! Ram! Ram! Ram! Ram!"

The hangman climbed down and stood ready, holding the lever. Minutes seemed to pass. The steady, muffled crying from the prisoner went on and on, "Ram! Ram! Ram!" never faltering for an instant. The superintendent, his head on his chest, was slowly poking the ground with his stick; perhaps he was counting the cries, allowing the prisoner a fixed number—fifty, perhaps, or a hundred. Everyone had changed colour. The Indians had gone grey like bad coffee, and one or two of the bayonets were wavering. We looked at the lashed, hooded man on the drop, and listened to his cries—each cry another second of life; the same thought was in all our minds: oh, kill him quickly, get it over, stop that abominable noise!

Suddenly the superintendent made up his mind. Throwing up his head he made a swift motion with his stick. "Chalo!" he shouted almost fiercely.

There was a clanking noise, and then dead silence. The prisoner had vanished, and the rope was twisting on itself. I let go of the dog, and it galloped immediately to the back of the gallows; but when it got there it stopped short, barked, and then retreated into a corner of the yard, where it stood among the weeds, looking timorously out at us. We went round the gallows to inspect the prisoner's body. He was dangling with his toes pointed straight downwards, very slowly revolving, as dead as a stone.

The superintendent reached out with his stick and poked the bare body; it oscillated. slightly. "*He's* all right," said the superintendent. He backed out from under the gallows, and blew out a deep breath. The moody look had gone out of his face quite suddenly. He glanced at his wrist-watch. "Eight minutes past eight. Well, that's all for this morning, thank God."

The warders unfixed bayonets and marched away. The dog, sobered and conscious of having misbehaved itself, slipped after them. We walked out of the gallows yard, past the condemned cells with their waiting prisoners, into the big central yard of the prison. The convicts, under the command of warders armed with lathis, were already receiving their breakfast. They squatted in long rows, each man holding a tin pannikin, while two warders with buckets marched round ladling out rice; it seemed quite a homely, jolly scene, after the hanging. An enormous relief had come upon us now that the job was done. One felt an impulse to sing, to break into a run, to snigger. All at once everyone began chattering gaily.

The Eurasian boy walking beside me nodded towards the way we had come, with a knowing smile: "Do you know, sir, our friend (he meant the dead man), when he heard his appeal had been dismissed, he pissed on the floor of his cell. From fright.—Kindly take one of my cigarettes, sir. Do you not admire my new silver case, sir? From the boxwallah, two rupees eight annas. Classy European style."

Several people laughed—at what, nobody seemed certain.

Francis was walking by the superintendent, talking garrulously: "Well, sir, all hass passed off with the utmost satisfactoriness. It wass all finished—flick! like that. It iss not always so—oah, no! I have known cases where the doctor wass obliged to go beneath the gallows and pull the prisoner's legs to ensure decease. Most disagreeable!"

"Wriggling about, eh? That's bad," said the superintendent.

"Ach, sir, it iss worse when they become refractory! One man, I recall, clung to the bars of hiss cage when we went to take him out.

You will scarcely credit, sir, that it took six warders to dislodge him, three pulling at each leg. We reasoned with him. 'My dear fellow,' we said, 'think of all the pain and trouble you are causing to us!' But no, he would not listen! Ach, he wass very troublesome!"

I found that I was laughing quite loudly. Everyone was laughing. Even the superintendent grinned in a tolerant way. "You'd better all come out and have a drink," he said quite genially. "I've got a bottle of whisky in the car. We could do with it."

We went through the big double gates of the prison, into the road. "Pulling at his legs!" exclaimed a Burmese magistrate suddenly, and burst into a loud chuckling. We all began laughing again. At that moment Francis's anecdote seemed extraordinarily funny. We all had a drink together, native and European alike, quite amicably. The dead man was a hundred yards away.

Eric A. Blair

Adelphi, August 1931; *New Savoy*, 1946; SE; OR; CE.

13. Letter to Dennis Collings

At 1b Oakwood Rd[1]
Golders Green NW
16 August 1931

Dear Dennis,[2]
I said I would write to you. I haven't anything of great interest to report yet about the Lower Classes, & am really writing to tell you about a ghost I saw in Walberswick cemetery. I want to get it on paper before I forget the details. See plan below.

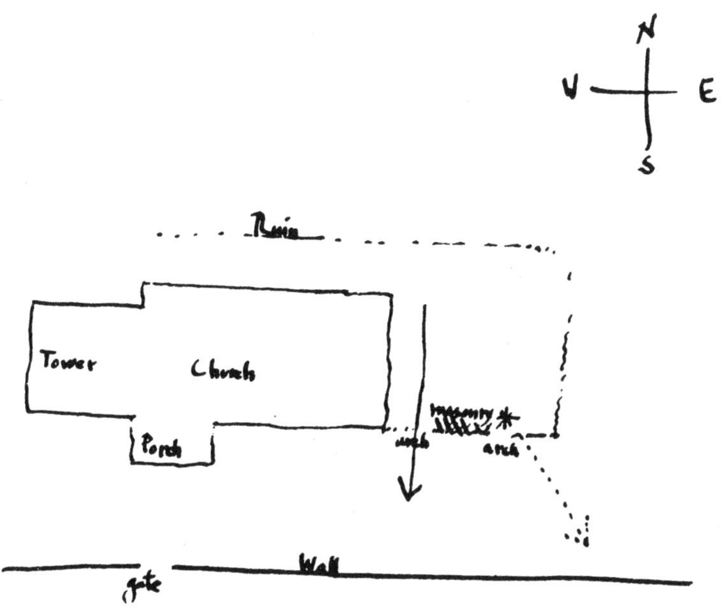

Above is W'wick church as well as I can remember it. At about 5.20 pm on 27.7.31 I was sitting at the spot marked X, looking out in the direction of the dotted arrow. I happened to glance over my

[1] The home of Mr and Mrs Francis Fierz. See 18.

[2] Dennis Collings (1905–), a friend of Eric Blair's from 1921 when the Blair family moved to Southwold and Collings's father became their family doctor. Dennis Collings grew sisal in Mozambique 1924–7, read anthropology at Cambridge 1928–31, and became assistant curator of the Raffles Museum, Singapore, when he joined the Colonial Service in 1934.

shoulder, & saw a figure pass along the line of the other arrow, disappearing behind the masonry & presumably emerging into the churchyard. I wasn't looking *directly* at it & so couldn't make out more than that it was a man's figure, small & stooping, & dressed in lightish brown; I should have said a workman. I had the impression that it glanced towards me in passing, but I made out nothing of the features. At the moment of its passing I thought nothing, but a few seconds later it struck me that the figure had made no noise, & I followed it out into the churchyard. There was no one in the churchyard, & no one within possible distance along the road—this was about 20 seconds after I had seen it; & in any case there were only 2 people in the road, & neither at all resembled the figure. I looked into the church. The only people there were the vicar, dressed in *black*, & a workman who, as far as I remember, had been sawing the whole time. In any case he was too tall for the figure. The figure had therefore vanished. Presumably an hallucination.

I have been up in town since the beginning of the month. I have made arrangements to go hop-picking, but we shan't start till the beginning of September. Meanwhile I've been busy working. I met recently one of the editors of a new paper[1] that is to start coming out in October, & I hope I shall be able to get some work from them—not enough to live on, of course, but enough to help. I've been making just a few enquiries among the tramps. Of the three friends I had before, one is believed to have been run over & killed, one has taken to drink & vanished, one is doing time in Wandsworth. I met a man today who was, till 6 weeks ago, a goldsmith. Then he poisoned his right forefinger, & had to have part of the top joint removed; that means he will be on the road for life. It is appalling what small accidents can ruin a man who works with his hands. Talking of hands, they say hop-picking disables your hands for weeks after—however, I'll describe that to you when I've done it.

Have you ever looked into the window of one of those Bible Society shops? I did today & saw huge notices "The cheapest Roman Catholic Bible 5/6d. The cheapest Protestant Bible 1/–", "The Douay version *not* stocked here" etc etc. Long may they fight, I say; so long as that spirit is in the land we are safe from the RCs —this shop, by the way, was just outside St Paul's. If you are ever near St Paul's & feel in a gloomy mood, go in & have a look at the

[1] *Modern Youth.*

statue of the first Protestant bishop of India, which will give you a good laugh. Will write again when I have news. I am sending this to S'wold.

Yours
Eric A. Blair

14. Letter to Dennis Collings

2 Windsor St
London W9
Monday night [12? October 1931]

Dear Dennis,
Herewith the narrative[1] of my adventures. Much of it repeats what I have told you before, but I wanted a full account for my own future reference. Keep it for me, will you? You will excuse carbon copy & bad typing. Please show it to Mr Pullein[2] [sic], who wanted to hear abt my experiences. Also to Eleanor Jaques[3] if she would care to see it, but don't let it go any further. Please also (I am assuming you are in S'wold) tell them both I will write to them soon.

The above will be my address till further notice. I am pretty busy, as I am getting stories etc to do for the new paper *Modern Youth*[4]. (A poisonous name for a poisonous paper—& the things I write for them are also poisonous, but one must live.)

Yours
Eric A. Blair

PS. A shop near here sells mandrakes, but I'm afraid they won't have been procured in the correct manner. Remind me sometime to tell you an interesting thing about werwolves.

[1] "Hop-Picking".

[2] Collett ("Uncle Colin") Cresswell Pulleyne, a barrister from Yorkshire; a mutual friend of Blair and Collings in Southwold.

[3] Eleanor Jaques (died 1962) came with her family from Canada to Southwold in 1921. At one time the Jaqueses were next-door neighbours of the Blairs in Stradbroke Road, Southwold. Eleanor Jaques married Dennis Collings in 1934.

[4] *Modern Youth* never appeared. It failed to pay its account with the printers, who seized the copy, including two stories by Blair. It is not known whether he succeeded in recovering them.

15. Hop-Picking

25 August 1931

On the night of the 25th I started off from Chelsea with about 14/– in hand, and went to Lew Levy's kip in Westminster Bridge Road. It is much the same as it was three years ago, except that nearly all the beds are now a shilling instead of ninepence. This is owing to interference by the LCC[1] who have enacted (in the interests of hygiene, as usual) that beds in lodging houses must be further apart. There is a whole string of laws of this type relating to lodging houses,[2] but there is not and never will be a law to say that the beds must be reasonably comfortable. The net result of this law is that one's bed is now three feet from the next instead of two feet, and threepence dearer.

26 August

The next day I went to Trafalgar Square and camped by the north wall, which is one of the recognised rendezvous of down and out people in London. At this time of year the square has a floating population of 100 to 200 people (about ten per cent of them women), some of whom actually look on it as their home. They get their food by regular begging rounds (Covent Garden at 4 am for damaged fruit, various convents during the morning, restaurants and dustbins late at night, etc) and they manage to "tap" likely-looking passers-by for enough to keep them in tea. Tea is going on the square at all hours, one person supplying a "drum", another sugar and so on. The milk is condensed milk at 2½d a tin. You jab two holes in the tin with a knife, apply your mouth to one of them and blow, whereupon a sticky greyish stream dribbles from the other. The holes are then plugged with chewed paper, and the tin is kept for days, becoming coated with dust and filth. Hot water is cadged at coffee shops, or at night boiled over watchmen's fires, but this has to be done on the sly, as the police won't allow it. Some of the people I met on the square had been there without a break for six weeks, and did not seem much the worse, except that they are all fan-

[1] London County Council.

[2] For instance, Dick's Café in Billingsgate. Dick's was one of the very few places where you could get a cup of tea for 1d, and there were fires there, so that anyone who had a penny could warm himself for hours in the early mornings. Only this last week the LCC closed it on the ground that it was unhygienic. [Author's footnote.]

tastically dirty. As always among the destitute, a large proportion of them are Irishmen. From time to time these men go home on visits, and it appears that they never think of paying their passage, but always stow away on small cargo boats, the crews conniving.

I had meant to sleep in St Martin's Church, but from what the others said it appeared that when you go in you are asked searching questions by some woman known as the Madonna, so I decided to stay the night in the square. It was not so bad as I expected, but between the cold and the police it was impossible to get a wink of sleep, and no one except a few hardened old tramps even tried to do so. There are seats enough for about fifty people, and the rest have to sit on the ground, which of course is forbidden by law. Every few minutes there would be a shout of "Look out, boys, here comes the flattie!" and a policeman would come round and shake those who were asleep, and make the people on the ground get up. We used to kip down again the instant he had passed, and this went on like a kind of game from eight at night till three or four in the morning. After midnight it was so cold that I had to go for long walks to keep warm. The streets are somehow rather horrible at that hour; all silent and deserted, and yet lighted almost as bright as day with those garish lamps, which give everything a deathly air, as though London were the corpse of a town. About three o'clock another man and I went down to the patch of grass behind the Guards' parade ground, and saw prostitutes and men lying in couples there in the bitter cold mist and dew. There are always a number of prostitutes in the square; they are the unsuccessful ones, who can't earn enough for their night's kip. Overnight one of these women had been lying on the ground crying bitterly, because a man had gone off without paying her fee, which was sixpence. Towards morning they do not even get sixpence, but only a cup of tea or a cigarette. About four somebody got hold of a number of newspaper posters, and we sat down six or eight on a bench and packed ourselves in enormous paper parcels, which kept us fairly warm till Stewart's cafe in St Martin's Lane opened. At Stewart's you can sit from five till nine for a cup of tea (or sometimes three or four people even share a cup between them) and you are allowed to sleep with your head on the table till seven; after that the proprietor wakes you. One meets a very mixed crowd there—tramps, Covent Garden porters, early business people, prostitutes—and there are constant quarrels and fights. On this occasion an old, very ugly woman, wife of a porter, was violently abusing two prostitutes, because they could afford a better breakfast than she could. As each dish was brought to them she would point at it and shout accusingly, "There goes the price of another fuck! *We* don't get kippers for breakfast, do we girls? 'Ow do you think she paid for them doughnuts? That's that there negro that 'as 'er for a tanner" etc etc, but the prostitutes did not mind much.

27 August

At about eight in the morning we all had a shave in the Trafalgar Square fountains, and I spent most of the day reading *Eugénie Grandet*, which was the only book I had brought with me. The sight of a French book produced the usual remarks—"Ah, French? That'll be something pretty warm, eh?" etc. Evidently most English people have no idea that there are French books which are not pornographic. Down and out people seem to read exclusively books of the Buffalo Bill type. Every tramp carries one of these, and they have a kind of circulating library, all swapping books when they get to the spike.

That night, as we were starting for Kent the next morning, I decided to sleep in bed and went to a lodging house in the Southwark Bridge Road. This is a sevenpenny kip, one of the few in London, and looks it. The beds are five feet long, with no pillows (you use your coat rolled up), and infested by fleas, besides a few bugs. The kitchen is a small, stinking cellar where the deputy sits with a table of flyblown jam tarts etc for sale a few feet from the door of the lavatory. The rats are so bad that several cats have to be kept exclusively to deal with them. The lodgers were dock workers, I think, and they did not seem a bad crowd. There was a youth among them, pale and consumptive-looking but evidently a labourer, who was devoted to poetry. He repeated

> A voice so thrilling ne'er was 'eard
> In Ipril from the cuckoo bird,
> Briking the silence of the seas
> Beyond the furthest 'Ebrides

with genuine feeling. The others did not laugh at him much.

28 August

The next day in the afternoon four of us started out for the hopfields. The most interesting of the men with me was a youth named Ginger, who is still my mate when I write this. He is a strong, athletic youth of twenty-six, almost illiterate and quite brainless, but daring enough for anything. Except when in prison, he has probably broken the law every day for the last five years. As a boy he did three years in Borstal, came out, married at eighteen on the strength of a successful burglary, and shortly afterwards enlisted in the artillery. His wife died, and a little while afterwards he had an accident to his left eye and was invalided out of the service. They offered him a pension or a lump sum, and of course he chose the lump sum and blued it in about a week. After that he took to burglary again, and has been in prison six times, but never for a long sentence, as they have only caught him for small jobs; he has done one or two jobs which brought him over £500. He has always been perfectly honest towards me, as his partner, but in a general way he will steal anything that is not tied down. I doubt his ever being a successful burglar, though, for he is too stupid to be able to foresee risks. It is all a great pity, for he could earn a decent living if he chose. He has a gift for street selling, and has had a lot of jobs selling on commission, but when he has had a good day he bolts instantly with the takings. He is a marvellous hand at picking up bargains and can always, for instance, persuade the butcher to give him a pound of eatable meat for twopence, yet at the same time he is an absolute fool about money, and never saves a halfpenny. He is given to singing songs of the Little Grey Home in the West type, and he speaks of his dead wife and mother in terms of the most viscid sentimentality. I should think he is a fairly typical petty criminal.

Of the other two, one was a boy of twenty named Young Ginger, who seemed rather a likely lad, but he was an orphan and had had no kind of upbringing, and had lived the last year chiefly on Trafalgar Square. The other was a little Liverpool Jew of eighteen, a thorough guttersnipe. I do not know when I have seen anyone who disgusted me so much as this boy. He was as greedy as a pig about food, perpetually scrounging round dustbins, and he had a face that recalled some low-down carrion-eating beast. His manner of talking about women, and the expression of his face when he did so, were so loathsomely obscene as to make me feel almost sick. We could never persuade him to wash more of himself than his nose and a small circle round it, and he mentioned quite casually that he had several different kinds of louse on him. He too was an orphan, and had been "on the toby" almost from infancy.

I had now about 6/–, and before starting we bought a so-called blanket for 1/6d and cadged several tins for "drums". The only reliable tin for a drum is a two-pound snuff tin, which is not very easy to come by. We had also a supply of bread and margarine and tea, and a number of knives and forks etc, all stolen at different times from Woolworth's. We took the twopenny tram as far as Bromley, and there "drummed up" on a rubbish dump, waiting for two others who were to have joined us, but who never turned up. It was dark when we finally stopped waiting for them, so we had no chance to look for a good camping place, and had to spend the night in long wet grass at the edge of a recreation ground. The cold was bitter. We had only two thin blankets between the four of us, and it was not safe to light a fire, as there were houses all round; we were also lying on a slope, so that one rolled into the ditch from time to time. It was rather humiliating to see the others, all younger than I, sleeping quite soundly in these conditions, whereas I did not close my eyes all night. To avoid being caught we had to be on the road before dawn, and it was several hours before we managed to get hot water and have our breakfast.

29 August

When we had gone a mile or two we came to an orchard, and the others at once went in and began stealing apples. I had not been prepared for this when we started out, but I saw that I must either do as the others did or leave them, so I shared the apples; I did not however take any part in the thefts for the first day, except to keep guard. We were going more or less in the direction of Sevenoaks, and by dinner time we had stolen about a dozen apples and plums and fifteen pounds of potatoes. The others also went in and tapped whenever we passed a baker's or a teashop, and we got quite a quantity of broken bread and meat. When we stopped to light a fire for dinner we fell in with two Scotch tramps who had been stealing apples from an orchard nearby, and stayed talking with them for a long time. The others all talked about sexual subjects, in a revolting manner. Tramps are disgusting when on this subject, because their poverty cuts them off entirely from women, and their minds consequently fester with obscenity. Merely lecherous people are all right, but people who would like to be lecherous, but don't get the chance, are horribly degraded by it. They remind me of the dogs that hang enviously round while two other dogs are copulating. During the conversation Young Ginger related how he and some others on Trafalgar Square had discovered one of their number to be a "Poof", or Nancy Boy. Whereupon they had instantly fallen upon him, robbed him of 12/6d, which was all he had, and spent it on themselves. Evidently they thought it quite fair to rob him, as he was a Nancy Boy.

We had been making very poor progress, chiefly because Young Ginger and the Jew were not used to walking and wanted to stop and search for scraps of food all the time. On one occasion the Jew even picked up some chipped potatoes that had been trodden on, and ate them. As it was getting on in the afternoon we decided to make not for Sevenoaks but for Ide Hill spike, which the Scotchmen had told us was better than it is usually represented. We halted about a mile from the spike for tea, and I remember that a gentleman in a car nearby helped us in the kindest manner to find wood for our fire, and gave us a cigarette each. Then we went on to the spike, and on the way picked a bunch of honeysuckle to give to the Tramp Major. We thought this might put him in a good temper and induce him to let us out next morning, for it is not usual to let tramps out of the spike on Sundays. When we got there however the Tramp Major said that he would have to keep us in till Tuesday morning. It appeared that the Workhouse Master was very keen on making every casual do a day's work, and at the same time would not hear of their working on Sunday; so we should have to be idle all Sunday and work on Monday. Young Ginger and the Jew elected to stay till Tuesday, but Ginger and I went and kipped on the edge of a park near the church. It was beastly cold, but a little better than the night before, for we had plenty of wood and could make a fire. For our supper, Ginger tapped the local butcher, who gave us the best part of two pounds of sausages. Butchers are always very generous on Saturday nights.

30 August

Next morning the clergyman coming to early service caught us and turned us out, though not very disagreeably. We went on through Sevenoaks to Seal, and a man we met advised us to try for a job at Mitchell's farm, about three miles further on. We went there, but the farmer told us that he could not give us a job, as he had nowhere where we could live, and the Government inspectors had been scouting round to see that all hop-pickers had "proper accommodation". (These inspectors,[1] by the way, managed to prevent some hundreds of

[1] Appointed by the Labour Government. [Author's footnote.]

unemployed from getting jobs in the hop-fields this year. Not having "proper accommodation" to offer to pickers, the farmers could only employ local people, who lived in their own houses.) We stole about a pound of raspberries from one of Mitchell's fields, and then went and applied to another farmer called Kronk, who gave us the same answer; we had five or ten pounds of potatoes from his fields, however. We were starting off in the direction of Maidstone when we fell in with an old Irishwoman, who had been given a job by Mitchell on the understanding that she had a lodging in Seal, which she had not. (Actually she was sleeping in a toolshed in somebody's garden. She used to slip in after dark and out before daylight.) We got some hot water from a cottage and the Irishwoman had tea with us, and gave us a lot of food that she had begged and did not want; we were glad of this, for we had now only 2½d left, and none too much food. It had now come on to rain, so we went to a farmhouse beside the church and asked leave to shelter in one of their cowsheds. The farmer and family were just starting out for evening service, and they said in a scandalised manner that of course they could not give us shelter. We sheltered instead in the lych-gate of the church, hoping that by looking draggled and tired we might get a few coppers from the congregation as they went in. We did not get anything, but after the service Ginger managed to tap a fairly good pair of flannel trousers from the clergyman. It was very uncomfortable in the lych-gate, and we were wet through and out of tobacco, and Ginger and I had walked twelve miles; yet I remember that we were quite happy and laughing all the time. The Irishwoman (she was sixty, and had been on the road all her life, evidently) was an extraordinarily cheerful old girl, and full of stories. Talking of places to "skipper" in, she told us that one cold night she had crept into a pigsty and snuggled up to an old sow, for warmth.

When night came on it was still raining, so we decided to find an empty house to sleep in, but we went first to buy half a pound of sugar and two candles at the grocer's. While I was buying them Ginger stole three apples off the counter, and the Irishwoman a packet of cigarettes. They had plotted this beforehand, deliberately not telling me, so as to use my innocent appearance as a shield. After a good deal of searching we found an unfinished house and slipped in by a window the builders had left open. The bare floor was beastly hard, but it was warmer than outside, and I managed to get two or three hours' sleep.

1 September

We got out before dawn, and by appointment met the Irishwoman in a wood nearby. It was raining, but Ginger could get a fire going in almost any circumstances, and we managed to make tea and roast some potatoes. When it was light the Irishwoman went off to work, and Ginger and I went down to Chambers's farm, a mile or two away, to ask for work. When we got to the farm they had just been hanging a cat, a thing I never heard of anyone doing before. The bailiff said that he thought he could give us a job, and told us to wait; we waited from eight in the morning till one, when the bailiff said that he had no work for us after all. We made off, stealing a large quantity of apples and damsons, and started along the Maidstone road. At about three we halted to have our dinner and make some jam out of the raspberries we had stolen the day before. Near here, I remember, they refused at two houses to give me cold water, because "the mistress doesn't allow us to give anything to tramps". Ginger saw a gentleman in a car picnicking nearby, and went up to tap him for matches, for he said that it always pays to tap from picnickers, who usually have some food left over when they are going home. Sure enough the gentleman presently came across with some butter he had not used, and began talking to us. His manner was so friendly that I forgot to put on my cockney accent, and he looked closely at me, and said how painful it must be for a man of my stamp etc. Then he said, "I say, you won't be offended, will you? Do you mind taking this?" "This" was a shilling, with which we bought some tobacco and had our first smoke that day. This was the only time in the whole journey when we managed to tap money.

We went on in the direction of Maidstone, but when we had gone a few miles it began to pour with rain, and my left boot was pinching me badly. I had not had my boots off for three days and had only had about eight hours' sleep in the last five nights, and I did not feel equal to another night in the open. We decided to make for West Malling spike, which was about eight miles distant, and if possible to get a lift part of the way. I think we hailed forty lorries before we got a lift. The lorry drivers will not give lifts nowadays, because they are not insured for third party risks and they get the sack if they have an accident. Finally we did get a lift, and were set down about two miles from the spike, getting there at eight in the evening. Outside the gates we met an old deaf tramp who was going to skipper in the pouring rain, as he had been in the spike the night before, and they would confine him for a week if he came again. He told us that Blest's farm nearby would probably give us a job, and that they would let us out of the spike early in the morning if we told them we had already got a job. Otherwise we should be confined all day, unless we went out "over the wall"—i.e. bolted when the Tramp Major was not looking. Tramps often do this, but you have to cache your possessions outside, which we could not in the heavy rain. We went in, and I found that (if West Malling is typical) spikes have improved a lot since I was last in.[1] The bathroom was clean and decent, and we were actually given a clean towel each. The food was the same old bread and marg, though, and the Tramp Major got angry when we asked in good faith whether the stuff they gave us to drink was tea or cocoa.[2] We had beds with straw palliasses and plenty of blankets, and both slept like logs.

In the morning they told us we must work till eleven, and set us to scrubbing out one of the dormitories. As usual, the work was a mere formality. (I have never done a stroke of real work in the spike, and I have never met anybody who has.) The dormitory was a room of fifty beds, close together, with that warm, faecal stink that you never seem to get away from in the workhouse. There was an imbecile pauper there, a great lump of about sixteen stone, with a tiny, snouty face and a sidelong grin. He was at work very slowly emptying chamberpots. These workhouses seem all alike, and there is something intensely disgusting in the atmosphere of them. The thought of all those grey-faced, ageing men living a very quiet, withdrawn life in a smell of WCs, and practising homosexuality, makes me feel sick. But it is not easy to convey what I mean, because it is all bound up with the smell of the workhouse.

At eleven they let us out with the usual hunk of bread and cheese, and we went on to Blest's farm, about three miles away; but we did not get there till one, because we stopped on the way and got a big haul of damsons. When we arrived at the farm the foreman told us that he wanted pickers and sent us up to the field at once. We had now only about 3d left, and that evening I wrote home asking them to send me 10/–; it came two days later, and in the meantime we should have had practically nothing to eat if the other pickers had not fed us. For nearly three weeks after this we were at work hop-picking, and I had better describe the different aspects of this individually.

[1] No: a bit worse if anything. [Author's footnote.]

[2] To this day I don't know which it was. [Author's footnote.]

2 to 19 September

Hops are trained up poles or over wires about 10 feet high, and grown in rows a yard or two apart. All the pickers have to do is to tear them down and strip the hops into a bin, keeping them as clean as possible of leaves. In practice, of course, it is impossible to keep all the leaves out, and the experienced pickers swell the bulk of their hops by putting in just as many leaves as the farmer will stand for. One soon gets the knack of the work, and the only hardships are the standing (we were generally on our feet ten hours a day), the plagues of plant lice, and the damage to one's hands. One's hands get stained as black as a negro's with the hop-juice, which only mud will remove,[1] and after a day or two they crack and are cut to bits by the stems of the vines, which are spiny. In the mornings, before the cuts had reopened, my hands used to give me perfect agony, and even at the time of typing this (October 10th) they show the marks. Most of the people who go down hopping have done it every year since they were children, and they pick like lightning and know all the tricks, such as shaking the hops up to make them lie loose in the bin etc. The most successful pickers are families, who have two or three adults to strip the vines, and a couple of children to pick up the fallen hops and clear the odd strands. The laws about child labour are disregarded utterly, and some of the people drive their children pretty hard. The woman in the next bin to us, a regular old-fashioned East Ender, kept her grandchildren at it like slaves—"Go on, Rose, you lazy little cat, pick them 'ops up. I'll warm your arse if I get up to you" etc until the children, aged from 6 to 10, used to drop down and fall asleep on the ground. But they liked the work, and I don't suppose it did them more harm than school.

As to what one can earn, the system of payment is this. Two or three times a day the hops are measured, and you are due a certain sum (in our case twopence) for each bushel you have picked. A good vine yields about half a bushel of hops, and a good picker can strip a vine in about ten minutes, so that theoretically one *might* earn about 30/– by a sixty-hour week. But in practice this is quite impossible. To begin with, the hops vary enormously. On some vines they are as large as small pears, and on others hardly bigger than peas; the bad vines take rather longer to strip than the good ones—they are generally more tangled—and sometimes it needs five or six of them

[1] Or hop-juice, funnily enough. [Author's footnote.]

to make a bushel. Then there are all kinds of delays, and the pickers get no compensation for lost time. Sometimes it rains (if it rains hard the hops get too slippery to pick), and one is always kept waiting when changing from field to field, so that an hour or two is wasted every day. And above all there is the question of measurement. Hops are soft things like sponges, and it is quite easy for the measurer to crush a bushel of them into a quart if he chooses. Some days he merely scoops the hops out, but on other days he has orders from the farmer to "take them heavy", and then he crams them tight into the basket, so that instead of getting 20 bushels for a full bin one gets only 12 or 14, i.e. a shilling or so less. There was a song about this, which the old East End woman and her grandchildren were always singing:

Our lousy hops!
Our lousy hops!
When the measurer he comes round,
Pick 'em up, pick 'em up off the ground!
When he comes to measure
He never knows where to stop;
Ay, ay, get in the bin
And take the fucking lot!

From the bin the hops are put into 10-bushel pokes which are supposed to weigh a hundredweight and are normally carried by one man. It used to take two men to hoist a full poke when the measurer had been taking them heavy.

With all these difficulties one can't earn 30/– a week or anything near it. It is a curious fact, though, that very few of the pickers were aware how little they really earned, because the piece-work system disguises the low rate of payment. The best pickers in our gang were a family of gypsies, five adults and a child, all of whom, of course, had picked hops every year since they could walk. In a little under three weeks these people earned exactly £10 between them—i.e. leaving out the child, about 14/– a week each. Ginger and I earned about 9/– a week each, and I doubt if any individual picker made over 15/– a week. A family working together can make their keep and their fare back to London at these rates, but a single picker can hardly do even that. On some of the farms nearby the tally, instead of being 6 bushels to the shilling, was 8 or 9, at which one would have a hard job to earn 10/– a week.

When one starts work the farm gives one a printed copy of rules, which are designed to reduce a picker more or less to a slave. According to these rules the farmer can sack a picker without notice and on any pretext whatever, and pay him off at 8 bushels a shilling instead of six—i.e. confiscate a quarter of his earnings. If a picker leaves his job before the picking is finished his earnings are docked the same amount. You cannot draw what you have earned and then clear off, because the farm will never pay you more than two thirds of your earnings in advance, and so are in your debt till the last day. The bin-men (i.e. foremen of gangs) get wages instead of being paid on the piece-work system, and these wages cease if there is a strike, so naturally they will raise heaven and earth to prevent one. Altogether the farmers have the hop-pickers in a cleft stick, and always will have until there is a pickers' union. It is not much use to try and form a union, though, for about half the pickers are women and gypsies, and are too stupid to see the advantages of it.

As to our living accommodation, the best quarters on the farm, ironically enough, were disused stables. Most of us slept in round tin huts about 10 feet across, with no glass in the windows, and all kinds of holes to let in the wind and rain. The furniture of these huts consisted of a heap of straw and hop-vines, and nothing else. There were four of us in our hut, but in some of them there were seven or eight—rather an advantage really, for it kept the hut warm. Straw is rotten stuff to sleep in (it is much more draughty than hay) and Ginger and I had only a blanket each, so we suffered agonies of cold for the first week; after that we stole enough pokes to keep us warm. The farm gave us free firewood, though not as much as we needed. The water tap was 200 yards away, and the latrine the same distance, but it was so filthy that one would have walked a mile sooner than use it. There was a stream where one could do some laundering, but getting a bath in the village would have been about as easy as buying a tame whale.

The hop-pickers seemed to be of three types: East Enders (mostly costermongers), gypsies, and itinerant agricultural labourers with a sprinkling of tramps. The fact that Ginger and I were tramps got us a great deal of sympathy, especially among the fairly well-to-do people. There was one couple, a coster and his wife, who were like a father and mother to us. They were the kind of people who are generally drunk on Saturday nights and who tack a "fucking" on to every noun, yet I have never seen anything that exceeded their kindness and delicacy. They gave us food over and over again. A child would come to the hut with a saucepan: "Eric, mother was going to throw this stew away, but she said it was a pity to waste it. Would you like it?" Of course they were not really going to have thrown it away, but said this to avoid the suggestion of charity. One day they gave us a whole pig's head, ready cooked. These people had been on the road several years themselves, and it made them sympathetic—"Ah, I know what it's like. Skippering in the fucking wet grass, and then got to tap the milkman in the morning before you can get a cup of tea. Two of my boys were born on the road" etc. Another man who was very decent to us was an employee in a paper factory. Before this he had been vermin man to ——, and he told me that the dirt and vermin in —— passed belief. When he worked at ——, the rats were so numerous that it was not safe to go into the kitchens at night unarmed; you had to carry a revolver. After I had mixed with these people for a few days it was too much fag to go on putting on my cockney accent, and they noticed that I talked "different". As usual, this made them still more friendly, for these people seem to think that it is especially dreadful to "come down in the world".

Out of 200 pickers at Blest's farm, 50 or 60 were gypsies. They are curiously like oriental peasants—the same heavy faces, at once dull and sly, and the same sharpness in their own line and startling ignorance outside it. Most of them could not read even a word, and none of their children seemed ever to have gone to school. One gypsy, aged about 40, used to ask me such questions as, "How far is Paris from France?" "How many days' journey by caravan to Paris?" etc. A youth, aged twenty, used to ask this riddle half a dozen times a day—"I'll tell you something you can't do?"—"What?"—"Tickle a gnat's arse with a telegraph pole." (At this, never-failing yells of laughter.) The gypsies seem to be quite rich, owning caravans, horses, etc yet they go on all the year round working as itinerant labourers and saving money. They used to say that our way of life (living in houses etc) seemed disgusting to them, and to explain how clever they had been in dodging the army during the war. Talking to them, you had the feeling of talking to people from another century. I often heard a gypsy say, "If I knew where so and so was, I'd ride my horse till it hadn't a shoe left to catch him"—not a 20th century metaphor at all. One day some gypsies were talking about a noted horse-thief called George Bigland, and one man, defending him, said: "I don't think George is as bad as you make out. I've known him to steal Gorgias' (Gentiles') horses, but he wouldn't go so far as to steal from one of us."

The gypsies call us Gorgias and themselves Romanies, but they are nicknamed Didecais (not certain of spelling). They all knew Romany, and occasionally used a word or two when they didn't want to be understood. A curious thing I noticed about the gypsies—I don't know whether it is the same everywhere—was that you would often see a whole family who were totally unlike one another. It almost seems to countenance the stories about gypsies stealing children; more likely, though, it is because it's a wise child etc.

One of the men in our hut was the old deaf tramp we had met outside West Malling spike—Deafie, he was always called. He was rather a Mr F's aunt in conversation, and he looked just like a drawing by George Belcher, but he was an intelligent, decently educated man, and no doubt would not have been on the road if he could hear. He was not strong enough for heavy work, and he had done nothing for years past except odd jobs like hopping. He calculated that he had been in over 400 different spikes. The other man, named Barrett, and a man in our gang named George, were good specimens of the itinerant agricultural labourer. For years past they had worked on a regular round: lambing in early spring, then pea-picking, strawberries, various other fruits, hops, "spud-grabbing", turnips and sugar beet. They were seldom out of work for more than a week or two, yet even this was enough to swallow up anything they could earn. They were both penniless when they arrived at Blest's farm, and I saw Barrett work certainly one day without a bite to eat. The proceeds of all their work were the clothes they stood up in, straw to sleep on all the year round, meals of bread and cheese and bacon, and I suppose one or two good drunks a year. George was a dismal devil, and took a sort of worm-like pride in being underfed and overworked, and always tobying from job to job. His line was, "It doesn't do for people like us to have fine ideas". (He could not read or write, and seemed to think even literacy a kind of extravagance.) I know this philosophy well, having often met it among the dishwashers in Paris. Barrett, who was 63, used to complain a lot about the badness of food nowadays, compared with what you could get when he was a boy—"In them days we didn't live on this fucking bread and marg, we 'ad good solid tommy. Bullock's 'eart. Bacon dumpling. Black pudden. Pig's 'ead." The glutinous, reminiscent tone in which he said "pig's 'ead" suggested decades of underfeeding.

Besides all these regular pickers there were what are called "home-dwellers", i.e. local people who pick at odd times, chiefly for the fun of it. They are mostly farmers' wives and the like, and as a rule they and the regular pickers loathe one another. One of them, however, was a very decent woman, who gave Ginger a pair of shoes and me an excellent coat and waistcoat and two shirts. Most of the local people seemed to look on us as dirt, and the shopkeepers were very insolent, though between us we must have spent several hundred pounds in the village.

One day at hop-picking was very much like another. At about a quarter to six in the morning we crawled out of the straw, put on our coats and boots (we slept in everything else) and went out to get a fire going—rather a job this September, when it rained all the time. By half past six we had made tea and fried some bread for breakfast, and then we started off for work, with bacon sandwiches and a drum of cold tea for our dinner. If it didn't rain we were working pretty steadily till about one, and then we would start a fire between the vines, heat up our tea and knock off for half an hour. After that we were at it again till half past five, and by the time we had got home, cleaned the hop-juice off our hands and had tea, it was already dark and we were dropping with sleep. A good many nights, though, we used to go out and steal apples. There was a big orchard nearby, and three or four of us used to rob it systematically, carrying a sack and getting half a hundredweight of apples at a time, besides several pounds of cobnuts. On Sundays we used to wash our shirts and socks in the stream, and sleep the rest of the day. As far as I remember I never undressed completely all the time we were down there, nor washed my teeth, and I only shaved twice a week. Between working and getting meals (and that meant fetching everlasting cans of water, struggling with wet faggots, frying in tin-lids, etc) one seemed to have not an instant to spare. I only read one book all the time I was down there, and that was a Buffalo Bill. Counting up what we spent I find that Ginger and I fed ourselves on about 5/– a week each, so it is not surprising that we were constantly short of tobacco and constantly hungry, in spite of the apples and what the others gave us. We seemed to be forever doing sums in farthings to find out whether we could afford another half ounce of shag or another two-pennorth of bacon. It wasn't a bad life, but what with standing all day, sleeping rough and getting my hands cut to bits, I felt a wreck at the end of it. It was humiliating to see that most of the people there looked on it as a holiday—in fact, it is because hopping is regarded as a holiday that the pickers will take such starvation wages. It gives one an insight into the lives of farm labourers, too, to realise that according to their standards hop-picking is hardly work at all.

One night a youth knocked at our door and said that he was a new picker and had been told to sleep in our hut. We let him in and fed him in the morning, after which he vanished. It appeared that he was not a picker at all, but a tramp, and that tramps often work this dodge in the hopping season, in order to get a kip under shelter. Another night a woman who was going home asked me to help her get her luggage to Wateringbury station. As she was leaving early they had paid her off at eight bushels a shilling, and her total earnings were only just enough to get herself and family home. I had to push a perambulator, with one eccentric wheel and loaded with huge packages, two and a half miles through the dark, followed by a retinue of yelling children. When we got to the station the last train was just coming in, and in rushing the pram across the level crossing I upset it. I shall never forget that moment—the train bearing down on us, and the porter and I chasing a tin chamberpot that was rolling up the track. On several nights Ginger tried to persuade me to come and rob the church with him, and he would have done it alone if I had not managed to get it into his head that suspicion was bound to fall on him, as a known criminal. He had robbed churches before, and he said, what surprised me, that there is generally something worth having in the Poorbox. We had one or two jolly nights, on Saturdays, sitting round a huge fire till midnight and roasting apples. One night, I remember, it came out that, of about fifteen people round the fire, everyone except myself had been in prison. There were uproarious scenes in the village on Saturdays, for the people who had money used to get well drunk, and it needed the police to get them out of the pub. I have no doubt the residents thought us a nasty vulgar lot, but I could not help feeling that it was rather good for a dull village to have this invasion of cockneys once a year.

19 September

On the last morning, when we had picked the last field, there was a queer game of catching the women and putting them in the bins. Very likely there will be something about this in the Golden Bough. It is evidently an old custom, and all harvests have some custom of this kind attached to them. The people who were illiterate or thereabouts brought their tally books to me and other "scholars" to have them reckoned up, and some of them paid a copper or two to have it done. I found that in quite a number of cases the farm cashiers had made a mistake in the addition, and invariably the mistake was in favour of the farm. Of course the pickers got the sum due when they complained, but they would not have if they had accepted the farm cashier's reckoning. Moreover, the farm had a mean little rule that anyone who was going to complain about his tally book had to wait till all the other pickers had been paid off. This meant waiting till the afternoon, so that some people who had buses to catch had to go home without claiming the sum due to them. (Of course it was only a few coppers in most cases. One woman's book, however, was added up over £1 wrong.)

Ginger and I packed our things and walked over to Wateringbury to catch the hop-pickers' train. On the way we stopped to buy tobacco, and as a sort of farewell to Kent, Ginger cheated the tobacconist's girl of fourpence, by a very cunning dodge. When we got to Wateringbury station about fifty hoppers were waiting for the train, and the first person we saw was old Deafie, sitting on the grass with a newspaper in front of him. He lifted it aside, and we saw that he had his trousers undone and was exhibiting his penis to the women and children as they passed. I was surprised—such a decent old man, really; but there is hardly a tramp who has not some sexual abnormality. The Hoppers' train was ninepence cheaper than the ordinary fare, and it took nearly five hours to get us to London—30 miles. At about 10 at night the hop-pickers poured out at London Bridge station, a number of them drunk and all carrying bunches of hops; people in the street readily bought these bunches of hops, I don't know why. Deafie, who had travelled in our carriage, asked us into the nearest pub and stood us each a pint, the first beer I had had in three weeks. Then he went off to Hammersmith, and no doubt he will be on the bum till next year's fruit-picking begins.

On adding up our tally book, Ginger and I found that we had made just 26/– each by eighteen days' work. We had drawn 8/– each in advances (or "subs" as they are called), and we had made another 6/– between us by selling stolen apples. After paying our fares we got to London with about 16/– each. So we had, after all, kept ourselves while we were in Kent and come back with a little in pocket; but we had only done it by living on the very minimum of everything.

19 September to 8 October

Ginger and I went to a kip in Tooley Street, owned by Lew Levy who owns the one in Westminster Bridge Road. It is only sevenpence a night, and it is probably the best sevenpenny one in London. There are bugs in the beds, but not many, and the kitchens, though dark and dirty, are convenient, with abundant fires and hot water. The lodgers are a pretty low lot—mostly Irish unskilled labourers, and out of work at that. We met some queer types among them. There was one man, aged 68, who worked carrying crates of fish (they weigh a hundredweight each) in Billingsgate Market. He was interested in politics, and he told me that on Bloody Sunday in '88 he had taken part in the rioting and been sworn in as a special constable on the same day. Another old man, a flower seller, was mad. Most of the time he behaved quite normally, but when his fits were on he would walk up and down the kitchen uttering dreadful beast-like yells, with an expression of agony on his face. Curiously enough, the fits only came on in wet weather. Another man was a thief. He stole from shop counters and vacant motor cars, especially commercial travellers' cars, and sold the stuff to a Jew in Lambeth Cut. Every evening you would see him smartening himself up to go "up West". He told me that he could count on £2 a week, with a big haul from time to time. He managed to swoop the till of a public house almost every Christmas, generally getting £40 or £50 by this. He had been stealing for years and only been caught once, and then was bound over. As always seems the case with thieves, his work brought him no good, for when he got a large sum he blued it instantly. He had one of the ignoblest faces I ever saw, just like a hyena's; yet he was likeable, and decent about sharing food and paying debts.

Several mornings Ginger and I worked helping the porters at Billingsgate. You go there at about five and stand at the corner of one of the streets which lead up from Billingsgate into Eastcheap. When a porter is having trouble to get his barrow up, he shouts "Up the 'ill!" and you spring forward (there is fierce competition for the jobs, of course) and shove the barrow behind. The payment is "twopence an up". They take on about one shover-up for four hundredweight, and the work knocks it out of your thighs and elbows, but you don't get enough jobs to tire you out. Standing there from five till nearly midday, I never made more than 1/6d. If you are very lucky a porter takes you on as his regular assistant, and then you make about 4/6d a morning. The porters themselves seem to make about £4 or £5 a week. There are several things worth noticing about Billingsgate. One is that vast quantities of the work done there are quite unnecessary, being due to the complete lack of any centralised transport system. What with porters, barrowmen, shovers-up etc, it now costs round about £1 to get a ton of fish from Billingsgate to one of the London railway termini. If it were done in an orderly manner, by lorries, I suppose it would cost a few shillings. Another thing is that the pubs in Billingsgate are open at the hours when other pubs are shut. And another is that the barrowmen in Billingsgate do a regular traffic in stolen fish, and you can get fish dirt cheap if you know one of them.

After about a fortnight in the lodging house I found that I was writing nothing, and the place itself was beginning to get on my nerves, with its noise and lack of privacy, and the stifling heat of the kitchen, and above all the dirt. The kitchen had a permanent sweetish reek of fish, and all the sinks were blocked with rotting fish guts which stank horribly. You had to store your food in dark corners which were infested by black beetles and cockroaches, and there were clouds of horrible languid flies everywhere. The dormitory was also disgusting, with the perpetual din of coughing and spitting—everyone in a lodging house has a chronic cough, no doubt from the foul air. I had got to write some articles, which could not be done in such surroundings, so I wrote home for money and took a room in Windsor Street near the Harrow Road. Ginger has gone off on the road again. Most of this narrative was written in the Bermondsey public library, which has a good reading room and was convenient for the lodging house.

NOTES:

New Words (i.e. words new to me) discovered this time.

Shackles: broth or gravy.
Drum, a: a billy can. (With verb to drum up meaning to light a fire.)
Toby, on the: on the tramp. (Also to toby, and a toby, meaning a tramp. Slang Dictionary gives the toby as the highroad.)
Chat, a: a louse. (Also chatty, lousy. SD gives this but not a chat.)
Get, a: ? (Word of abuse, meaning unknown.)
Didecai, a: a gypsy.
Sprowsie, a: a sixpence.
Hard-up: tobacco made from fag ends. (SD gives a hard-up as a man who collects fag ends.)
Skipper, to: to sleep out. (SD gives a skipper as a barn.)

Scrump, to: to steal.
Knock off, to: to arrest.
Jack off, to: to go away.
Jack, on his: on his own.
Clods: coppers.

Burglar's Slang

A stick, or a cane: a jemmy. (SD gives stick.)
Peter, a: a safe. (In SD.)
Bly, a: an oxy-acetylene blowlamp.[1]

Use of the word "tart" among East Enders. This word now seems absolutely interchangeable with "girl", with no implication of "prostitute". People will speak of their daughter or sister as a tart.

Rhyming slang. I thought this was extinct, but it is far from it. The hop-pickers used these expressions freely: a dig in the grave, meaning a shave. The hot cross bun, meaning the sun. Greengages, meaning wages. They also used the abbreviated rhyming slang, e.g. "Use your twopenny" for "Use your head". This is arrived at like this: Head, loaf of bread, loaf, twopenny loaf, twopenny.

Homosexual vice in London. It appears that one of the great rendezvous is Charing Cross underground station. It appeared to be taken for granted by the people on Trafalgar Square that youths could earn a bit this way, and several said to me, "I need never sleep out if I choose to go down to Charing Cross." They added that the usual fee is a shilling.

Written October 1931

[1] I forgot to mention that these lamps are hired out to burglars. Ginger said that he had paid £3.10.0 a night for the use of one. So also with other burglars' tools of the more elaborate kinds. When opening a puzzle-lock, clever safe-breakers use a stethoscope to listen for the click of the tumblers. [Author's footnote.]

16. Letter to T. S. Eliot

2 Windsor Street
London W9
30 October 1931

Dear Mr Eliot,
I am writing to you personally, as Richard Rees[1] tells me that he has spoken to you on my behalf. I have just read a rather interesting French novel called *A la Belle de Nuit*, by Jacques Roberti. It is the story of a prostitute, quite true to life so far as one can judge, & most ruthlessly told, but not a mere exploitation of a dirty subject. It seems to me worth translating, & if Messrs Faber & Faber[2] would like to try a translation I think I could do the job as well as most people. I don't pretend to have a scholarly knowledge of French, but I am used to mixing in the kind of French society described in the novel, & I know French slang, if not well, better than the majority of Englishmen. I don't know whether such a book would sell, but I believe Zola's novels sell in England, & this author seems to have some resemblances to Zola.

Perhaps you will let me know whether Messrs Faber & Faber would like to hear more of this? If they would like to see the book I can send it along, or translate a few pages as a specimen. I see that the translation rights are reserved, but I suppose that could be fixed up if it were decided to translate.

Yours truly
Eric Blair

[1] Sir Richard Rees, Bt. (1900–   ) painter, author and critic, whose writings include *George Orwell: Fugitive from the Camp of Victory*, *Simone Weil* and *A Theory of My Time*. From 1930 to 1936 he edited the *Adelphi* and met Orwell as a young contributor. They remained close friends until Orwell's death; throughout the years Rees was constant in his devotion, help and encouragement.

[2] T. S. Eliot was a director of Messrs Faber & Faber.

17. Letter to T. S. Eliot

2 Windsor St
W9
4 November 1931

Dear Mr Eliot,

Thank you for your letter. I am sending *A la Belle de Nuit*[1] under a separate cover. As I said, I think it ought to have more chance in England than most French novels. If Messrs Faber & Faber ever want any other French books translated, I should be very much obliged if they would give me a trial. I am anxious to get hold of some work of this kind, & I think I could do it as well as the average translator.

Yours truly
Eric A. Blair

[1] Neither Faber & Faber nor any other publisher commissioned this translation.

1932

18. Letter to Leonard Moore

The Hawthorns
Station Rd
Hayes, Middlesex
26 April 1932

Dear Mr Moore,[1]

Thank you for your letter. The history of the ms "Days in London and Paris" is this. About a year and a half ago I completed a book of this description, but shorter (about 35000 words), and after taking advice I sent it to Jonathan Cape. Cape's said they would like to publish it but it was too short and fragmentary (it was done in diary form), and that they might be disposed to take it if I made it longer. I then put in some things I had left out, making the ms you have, and sent it back to Cape's, who again rejected it. That was last September. Meanwhile a friend who was editor of a magazine[2] had seen the first ms, and he said that it was worth publishing and spoke about it to T. S. Eliot, who is a reader to Faber and Faber. Eliot said the same as Cape's—i.e. that the book was interesting but much too short. I left the ms you have with Mrs Sinclair Fierz[3] and asked her to throw it away, as I did not think it a good piece of work, but I suppose she sent it to you instead. I should of course be very pleased if you could sell it, and it is very kind of you to take the trouble of trying. No publishers have seen it except Faber's and Cape's. If by any chance you *do* get it accepted, will you please see that it is

[1] Leonard Moore, of Christy and Moore, literary agents for Orwell until his death.

[2] Sir Richard Rees, Bt., then editing the *Adelphi*.

[3] Mabel Sinclair Fierz, wife of Francis Ernest Fierz, an executive in a steel manufacturing firm. Born in Brazil, they made their home in England in 1908, meeting Eric Blair while on holiday in Southwold in the summer of 1930. During the early 'thirties Blair frequently stayed for week-ends at their London home. The Fierzes and Blair had many literary interests in common. Mabel Fierz wrote occasional reviews for the *Adelphi*; her husband was a great Dickens enthusiast.

published pseudonymously, as I am not proud of it. I have filled up the form you sent, but I have put in a clause that I only want an agent for dealings with publishers. The reason is this. I am now very busy teaching in a school, and I am afraid that for some months I shan't be able to get on with any work except occasional reviews or articles, and I get the commissions for these myself. But there is a novel[1] that I began some months ago and shall go on with next holidays, and I dare say it will be finished within a year: I will send it to you then. If you could get me any French or Spanish books to translate into English I would willingly pay you whatever commission you think right, for I like that kind of work. There is also a long poem describing a day in London which I am doing, and it *may* be finished before the end of this term. I will send you that too if you like, but I should not think there is any money for anybody in that kind of thing. As to those stories[2] you have I should shy them away, as they are not really worth bothering with.

Yours truly
Eric A. Blair

PS. I tried to get Chatto & Windus to give me some of Zola's novels to translate, but they wouldn't. I should think somebody might be willing to translate Zola—he has been done, but atrociously badly. Or what about Huysmans? I can't believe *Sainte Lydwine de Schiedam* has been translated into English. I also tried to get Faber's to translate a novel called *A la Belle de Nuit*, by Jacques Roberti. It is very good but appallingly indecent, & they refused it on that ground. I should think somebody might take it on—do you know anybody who isn't afraid of that kind of thing? (The book isn't pornographic, only rather sordid.) I could get hold of the copy I had and send it if necessary. I could also translate old French, at least anything since 1400 AD.

[1] *Burmese Days.*
[2] The manuscripts of these stories have not survived.

19. Review

The Spirit of Catholicism by Karl Adam

This is a notable book, and well worth reading, though it contains too many sentences of this type:

> Since the community and not the individual is the bearer of the spirit of Jesus, and since its visibility consists especially in the manifestation of this essential unity, therefore the visible organism of the Church postulates for its visibility a real principle of unity in which the supra-personal unity of all the faithful obtains perceptible expression and which supports, maintains and protects this unity.

It is hard work to dredge a meaning out of such morasses of words, but no one who is interested in the present revival of Catholicism will find the trouble wasted.

What distinguishes this book from the current drizzle of Catholic propaganda is that it is more or less non-controversial. Our English Catholic apologists are unrivalled masters of debate, but they are on their guard against saying anything genuinely informative. Few of them have any object beyond self-justification; their writings, therefore, are either a stream of cheery insult at biologists and Protestant historians, or an attempt to bluff the fundamental difficulties of faith out of existence. Father Adam does not proceed on these lines. He is not trying to prove any particular adversary a fool but rather to show what goes on inside the Catholic soul, and he hardly bothers to argue about the philosophical basis of faith. It is interesting to compare his book with some English book of similar tendency—for instance, with Father Martindale's recent book, *The Roman Faith.* The contrast between the Catholic who simply believes, and the convert who must for ever be justifying his conversion, is like the contrast between a Buddha and a performing fakir. Father Martindale, being committed to the statement that faith is essentially reasonable, can neither stand up to his difficulties nor ignore them. Consequently he evades them, with considerable nimbleness. He sails over the theory of evolution in a sort of logical balloon-flight, with common sense flung overboard for ballast; he dodges past the problem of evil like a man dodging past his creditor's doorway—and so on. Father Adam, who has started by saying that faith is not to be approached in the same spirit as "the profane sciences", has no need of these tricks. With a creed that is safe from "profane" criticism, he is in a very strong position; it gives him the chance to develop his own ideas, and to say something constructive and interesting.

What, then, can the non-Catholic learn from this book about the Catholic faith? Well, in one sense nothing, for there can be little real contact of mind between believer and unbeliever. As Father Adam says, "the Catholic of a living faith, and he alone, can make this investigation" (into the nature of Catholicism), and the others, with their ill-will or *ignorantia invincibilis* or what-not, are self-excluded. Nevertheless, in an objective way, something can be learned, or rather, re-learned, namely, the Hebrew-like pride and exclusiveness of the genuine Catholic mind. When Father Adam writes of the Communion of the Saints, one gets an impression of the Church not so much as a body of thought as of a kind of glorified family bank—a limited company paying enormous dividends, with non-members rigidly excluded from benefits. Here are Father Adam's words:

> The Saints during their mortal life amassed beyond the measure of their duty a store of wealth. . . . this wealth of the Saints is that "treasure of the Church", that sacred family inheritance, which belongs to all members of the body of Christ, and which is at the service especially of sick and feeble members.

The smallest shareholder draws his bonus on the profits made by Augustine or Aquinas. The point is missed if one forgets that the "family" means the Church and the Church alone; the rest of humanity, stray saints apart, being so much negligible matter, for whom there can be nothing save a slightly rigid pity, for *extra ecclesiam nulla salus*, and "dogmatic intolerance", as Father Adam puts it, "is a duty to the infinite truth". Father Adam allows that non-Catholics of goodwill have been known to exist here and there; but these in reality are Catholics without knowing it, since any virtue that exists outside the Church must be held to have proceeded, "invisibly", *from* the Church. And apart from special mercies, which are by no means to be counted on, "all pagans, Jews, heretics and schismatics have forfeited eternal life and are destined to everlasting fire".

This is quite straightforward, and much more impressive than what we get from our English Catholic apologists. These, with their public-school methods of controversy, have given so strong an impression of not being in earnest that hardly a soul in England bothers to hit back at them. Nearly all our anti-clerical feeling is directed at the poor, unoffending old Church of England. If ever a word is raised against Rome, it is only some absurd tale about Jesuit intrigues or babies' skeletons dug up from the floors of nunneries. Very few people, apart from the Catholics themselves, seem to have grasped that the Church is to be taken seriously. Books of this kind, therefore, written with genuine learning and free from silly-cleverness, are of great value.

[Unsigned]

New English Weekly, 9 June 1932

20. Letter to Eleanor Jaques

The Hawthorns
Hayes, Middlesex
Tuesday [14? June 1932]

Dear Eleanor,
How do things go with you? I hope your father is better, & that you have got your garden into shape. I have been teaching at the above foul place for nearly two months. I don't find the work uninteresting, but it is very exhausting, & apart from a few reviews etc I've hardly done a stroke of writing. My poor poem, which was promising not too badly, has of course stopped dead. The most disagreeable thing here is not the job itself (it is a day-school, thank God, so I have nothing to do with the brats out of school hours) but Hayes itself, which is one of the most godforsaken places I have ever struck. The population seems to be entirely made up of clerks who frequent tin-roofed chapels on Sundays & for the rest bolt themselves within doors. My sole friend is the curate—High Anglican but not a creeping Jesus & a very good fellow. Of course it means that I have to go to Church, which is an arduous job here, as the service is so popish that I don't know my way about it & feel an awful BF when I see everyone bowing & crossing themselves all round me & can't follow suit. The poor old vicar, who I suspect hates all this popery, is dressed up in cope & biretta & led round in procession with candles

etc, looking like a bullock garlanded for sacrifice. I have promised to paint one of the church idols (a quite skittish-looking BVM, half life-size, & I shall try & make her look as much like one of the illustrations in *La Vie Parisienne* as possible) & to grow a marrow for the harvest festival. I would "communicate" too, only I am afraid the bread might choke me. Have you read anything interesting lately? I read for the first time Marlowe's *Faustus*, & thought it rotten, also a mangy little book on Shakespeare trying to prove that Hamlet = Earl of Essex, also a publication called *The Enemy* of Wyndham Lewis' (not the professional RC[1]), who seems to have something in him, also something of Osbert Sitwell, also some odes of Horace, whom I wish I hadn't neglected hitherto—otherwise nothing, not having much time or energy. Mrs Carr[2] sent me two books of Catholic apologetics, & I had great pleasure in reviewing one of them for a new paper called the *New English Weekly*.[3] It was the first time I had been able to lay the bastinado on a professional RC at any length. I have got a few square feet of garden, but have had rotten results owing to rain, slugs & mice. I have found hardly any birds' nests—this place is on the outskirts of London, of course. I have also been keeping a pickle-jar aquarium, chiefly for the instruction of the boys, & we have newts, tadpoles, caddis-flies etc. If when you are passing, if you ever do, the pumping station at the beginning of the ferry-path, you see any eggs of puss moths on the poplar trees there, I should be awfully obliged if you would pick the leaves & send them me by post. I want some, & have only been able to find one or two here. Of course I don't mean make an expedition there, I only mean if you happen to be passing. What is Dennis[4] doing these days? I want to consult him about an extraordinary fungus that was dug up here, but of course he never answers letters. I may or may not come back to S'wold for the summer holidays. I want to get on with my novel[5] & if possible finish the poem I had begun, & I think perhaps it would be best for me to go to some quiet place in France, where I can live cheaply & have less temptation from the World, the Flesh & the Devil than at S'wold. . . . By the way, if you are ever to be in London

[1] D. B. Wyndham Lewis.

[2] A mutual friend in Southwold.

[3] *The Spirit of Catholicism* by Karl Adam in the *New English Weekly*, 9 June 1932. See 19.

[4] Dennis Collings.

[5] *Burmese Days*.

please let me know, as we might meet, that is if you would like to. Please remember me to your parents, also to Mr & Mrs Pullein[1] if you see them.

Yours
Eric A. Blair

21. Letter to Eleanor Jaques

The Hawthorns
Station Rd
Hayes, Middlesex
Sunday [19 June 1932]

Dear Eleanor,

I am sorry I did not after all ring up this morning, but when I did not hear from you till Saturday I arranged to take some of the boys out & your letter only arrived afterwards. Also I am not very near a telephone here. I hope you had not been counting on going out to-day. Let me know if you *are* staying in town, & if so we can arrange to go out again. Thanks so much for sending the jumping bean, which, however, got crushed in the post, poor little thing. I duly went fishing yesterday, but it was rotten—at least there were fish there, but they won't bite in this hot clear weather, & I only got one mangy little tench during the whole day. I am going to try near Uxbridge, & I believe the fishing in the Thames near Hampton Court is not so bad, & that would be nearer for you if you are staying in London. I found a few birds' nests while we were fishing, & the water-birds there were quite interesting to watch.

Let me hear from you soon,

Yours
Eric A. Blair

[1] Collett Cresswell Pulleyne and his mother.

22. Letter to Leonard Moore

The Hawthorns
Church Road
Hayes, Middx
1 July 1932

Dear Mr Moore,
Thank you for your letter. I went & saw Mr Gollancz[1] at the time named, & he gave me a full account of the alterations he wants made in the book.[2] Names are to be changed, swearwords etc cut out, and there is one passage which is to be either changed or cut out. It's a pity, as it is about the only good bit of writing in the book, but he says the circulation libraries would not stand for it. I am going to let him have the ms back in about a week. I did not say anything about the book having no commercial value as he seemed to think fairly well of it, so perhaps you will be able to get good terms from him.

Yours truly
Eric A. Blair

23. Letter to Leonard Moore

The Hawthorns
Church Road
Hayes, Middx
6 July 1932

Dear Mr Moore,
I am sending herewith the ms which I told Mr Gollancz I would let him have back in about a week. I have made the alterations of names etc that he asked for, & I think there is now nothing that can cause offence. The passage between pp. 6 and 13 that was objected to cannot be altered very radically. I have crossed out or altered the phrases that seemed to show too definitely what was happening & perhaps like this it might pass inspection. If not, I think the only thing to do is to remove Chap II in toto, as Chap III follows fairly consecutively from Chap I.

[1] Victor Gollancz (1893–1967), Kt. 1965, the publisher.

[2] *Down and Out in Paris and London.*

As to a title (Mr Gollancz said the present one will not do) I suggest putting as the start the quotation

> "The Lady Poverty was fair,
> But she hath lost her looks of late"
> (Alice Meynell)

calling the book "The Lady Poverty" or "Lady Poverty". If this will not do I will think of another title.

I think if it is all the same to everybody I would prefer the book to be published pseudonymously. I have no reputation that is lost by doing this and if the book has any kind of success I can always use the same pseudonym again.

Perhaps you will be kind enough to tell Mr Gollancz all this?

Yours truly
Eric A. Blair

24. Letter to Eleanor Jaques

The Hawthorns
Church Road
Hayes, Middx
Friday [8 July 1932]

Dear Eleanor,

Please do write & tell me you were not hurt at my not after all coming to meet you that Sunday—you did not write & I thought it might be that. I should be so sorry if you became angry with me. I would gladly have come if I could.

How is S'wold? Nothing happens here. I have had a small controversy with Fr Martindale, SJ[1] & he wrote & told Mrs Carr he would like to meet me, as I was deeply in error & he could put me right. I must meet him sometime if possible.

[1] C. C. Martindale, SJ (1879–1963), Roman Catholic theologian, a famous preacher and a member of the staff of Farm Street Church, London. His letter in the *New English Weekly*, 23 June 1932, disputing remarks Blair had made in his review of Karl Adam's *The Spirit of Catholicism* about Martindale's book, *The Roman Faith* (see 19), was replied to by Blair in the *New English Weekly*, 30 June.

Is there any hope of your coming up to town again? I *may* be in S'wold during the first week or two of the holidays—not certain. Please remember me to your parents, & write & tell me you are not incensed with me.

Yours
Eric A. Blair

25. Clink

This trip was a failure, as the object of it was to get into prison, and I did not, in fact, get more than forty-eight hours in custody; however, I am recording it, as the procedure in the police court etc was fairly interesting. I am writing this eight months after it happened, so am not certain of any dates, but it all happened a week or ten days before Xmas 1931.

I started out on Saturday afternoon with four or five shillings, and went out to the Mile End Road, because my plan was to get drunk and incapable, and I thought they would be less lenient towards drunkards in the East End. I bought some tobacco and a "Yank Mag" against my forthcoming imprisonment, and then, as soon as the pubs opened, went and had four or five pints, topping up with a quarter bottle of whisky, which left me with twopence in hand. By the time the whisky was low in the bottle I was tolerably drunk—more drunk than I had intended, for it happened that I had eaten nothing all day, and the alcohol acted quickly on my empty stomach. It was all I could do to stand upright, though my brain was quite clear—with me, when I am drunk, my brain remains clear long after my legs and speech have gone. I began staggering along the pavement in a westward direction, and for a long time did not meet any policemen, though the streets were crowded and all the people pointed and laughed at me. Finally I saw two policemen coming. I pulled the whisky bottle out of my pocket and, in their sight, drank what was left, which nearly knocked me out, so that I clutched a lamp-post and fell down. The two policemen ran towards me, turned me over and took the bottle out of my hand.

They: "'Ere, what you bin drinking?" (For a moment they may have thought it was a case of suicide.)

I: "Thass my boll whisky. You lea' me alone."

They: "Coo, 'e's fair bin bathing in it!—What you bin doing of, eh?"

I: "Bin in boozer, 'avin' bit o' fun. Christmas, ain't it?"

They: "No, not by a week it ain't. You got mixed up in the dates, you 'ave. You better come along with us. We'll look after yer."

I: "Why sh'd I come along you?"

They: "Jest so's we'll look after you and make you comfortable. You'll get run over, rolling about like that."

I: "Look. Boozer over there. Less go in 'ave drink."

They: "You've 'ad enough for one night, ole chap. You best come with us."

I: "Where you takin' me?"

They: "Jest somewhere as you'll get a nice quiet kip with a clean sheet and two blankets and all."

I: "Shall I get drink there?"

They: "Course you will. Got a boozer on the premises, we 'ave."

All this while they were leading me gently along the pavement. They had my arms in the grip (I forget what it is called) by which you can break a man's arm with one twist, but they were as gentle with me as though I had been a child. I was internally quite sober, and it amused me very much to see the cunning way in which they persuaded me along, never once disclosing the fact that we were making for the police station. This is, I suppose, the usual procedure with drunks.

When we got to the station (it was Bethnal Green, but I did not learn this till Monday) they dumped me in a chair and began emptying my pockets while the sergeant questioned me. I pretended, however, to be too drunk to give sensible answers, and he told them in disgust to take me off to the cells, which they did. The cell was about the same size as a Casual Ward cell (about 10 ft by 5 ft by 10 ft high), but much cleaner and better appointed. It was made of white porcelain bricks, and was furnished with a WC, a hot water pipe, a plank bed, a horsehair pillow and two blankets. There was a tiny barred window high up near the roof, and an electric bulb behind a guard of thick glass was kept burning all night. The door was steel, with the usual spy-hole and aperture for serving food through. The constables in searching me had taken away my money, matches, razor, and also my scarf—this, I learned afterwards, because prisoners have been known to hang themselves on their scarves.

There is very little to say about the next day and night, which were unutterably boring. I was horribly sick, sicker than I have ever been from a bout of drunkenness, no doubt from having an empty stomach. During Sunday I was given two meals of bread and marg and tea (spike quality), and one of meat and potatoes—this, I believe, owing to the kindness of the sergeant's wife, for I think only bread and marg is provided for prisoners in the lock-up. I was not allowed to shave, and there was only a little cold water to wash in. When the charge sheet was filled up I told the story I always tell, viz. my name was Edward Burton, and my parents kept a cake-shop in Blythburgh, where I had been employed as a clerk in a draper's shop; that I had had the sack for drunkenness, and my parents, finally getting sick of my drunken habits, had turned me adrift. I added that I had been working as an outside porter at Billingsgate, and having unexpectedly "knocked up" six shillings on Saturday, had gone on the razzle. The police were quite kind, and read me lectures on drunkenness, with the usual stuff about seeing that I still had some good in me etc etc. They offered to let me out on bail on my own recognisance, but I had no money and nowhere to go, so I elected to stay in custody. It was very dull, but I had my "Yank Mag", and could get a smoke if I asked the constable on duty in the passage for a light—prisoners are not allowed matches, of course.

The next morning very early they turned me out of my cell to wash, gave me back my scarf, and took me out into the yard and put me in the Black Maria. Inside, the Black Maria was just like a French public lavatory, with a row of tiny locked compartments on either side, each just large enough to sit down in. People had scrawled their names, offences and the lengths of their sentences all over the walls of my compartment; also, several times, variants on this couplet:

> Detective Smith knows how to gee;
> Tell him he's a cunt from me.

("Gee" in this context means to act as an *agent provocateur.*) We drove round to various stations picking up about ten prisoners in all, until the Black Maria was quite full. They were quite a jolly crowd inside. The compartment doors were open at the top, for ventilation, so that you could reach across, and somebody had managed to smuggle matches in, and we all had a smoke. Presently we began singing, and, as it was near Christmas, sang several carols. We drove up to Old Street Police Court singing:

Adeste, fideles, laeti, triumphantes,
Adeste, adeste ad Bethlehem etc.

which seemed to me rather inappropriate.

At the police court they took me off and put me in a cell identical with the one at Bethnal Green, even to having the same number of bricks in it—I counted in each case. There were three men in the cell besides myself. One was a smartly dressed, florid, well-set-up man of about thirty-five, whom I would have taken for a commercial traveller or perhaps a bookie, and another a middle-aged Jew, also quite decently dressed. The other man was evidently a habitual burglar. He was a short rough-looking man with grey hair and a worn face, and at this moment in such a state of agitation over his approaching trial that he could not keep still an instant. He kept pacing up and down the cell like a wild beast, brushing against our knees as we sat on the plank bed, and exclaiming that he was innocent—he was charged, apparently, with loitering with intent to commit burglary. He said that he had nine previous convictions against him, and that in these cases, which are mainly of suspicion, old offenders are nearly always convicted. From time to time he would shake his fist towards the door and exclaim "Fucking toe-rag! Fucking toe-rag!", meaning the "split" who had arrested him.

Presently two more prisoners were put into the cell, an ugly Belgian youth charged with obstructing traffic with a barrow, and an extraordinary hairy creature who was either deaf and dumb or spoke no English. Except this last all the prisoners talked about their cases with the utmost freedom. The florid, smart man, it appeared, was a public house "guv'nor" (it is a sign of how utterly the London publicans are in the claws of the brewers that they are always referred to as "governors", not "landlords"; being, in fact, no better than employees), and had embezzled the Christmas Club money. As usual, he was head over ears in debt to the brewers, and no doubt had taken some of the money in hopes of backing a winner. Two of the subscribers had discovered this a few days before the money was due to be paid out, and laid an information. The "guv'nor" immediately paid back all save £12, which was also refunded before his case came up for trial. Nevertheless, he was certain to be sentenced, as the magistrates are hard on these cases—he did, in fact, get four months later in the day. He was ruined for life, of course. The brewers would file bankruptcy proceedings and sell up all his stock and furniture, and he would never be given a pub licence again. He was trying to brazen it out in front of the rest of us, and smoking cigarettes incessantly from a stock of Gold Flake packets he had laid in—the last time in his life, I dare say, that he would have quite enough cigarettes. There was a staring, abstracted look in his eyes all the time while he talked. I think the fact that his life was at an end, as far as any decent position in society went, was gradually sinking into him.

The Jew had been a buyer at Smithfields for a Kosher butcher. After working seven years for the same employer he suddenly misappropriated £28, went up to Edinburgh—I don't know why Edinburgh—and had a "good time" with tarts, and came back and surrendered himself when the money was gone. £16 of the money had been repaid, and the rest was to be repaid by monthly instalments. He had a wife and a number of children. He told us, what interested me, that his employer would probably get into trouble at the synagogue for prosecuting him. It appears that the Jews have arbitration courts of their own, and a Jew is not supposed to prosecute another Jew, at least in a breach of trust case like this, without first submitting it to the arbitration court.

One remark made by these men struck me—I heard it from almost every prisoner who was up for a serious offence. It was, "It's not the prison I mind, it's losing my job." This is, I believe, symptomatic of the dwindling power of the law compared with that of the capitalist.

They kept us waiting several hours. It was very uncomfortable in the cell, for there was not room for all of us to sit down on the plank bed, and it was beastly cold in spite of the number of us. Several of the men used the WC, which was disgusting in so small a cell, especially as the plug did not work. The publican distributed his cigarettes generously, the constable in the passage supplying lights. From time to time an extraordinary clanking noise came from the cell next door, where a youth who had stabbed his "tart" in the stomach—she was likely to recover, we heard—was locked up alone. Goodness knows what was happening, but it sounded as though he were chained to the wall. At about ten they gave us each a mug of tea—this, it appeared, not provided by the authorities but by the police court missionaries —and shortly afterwards shepherded us along to a sort of large waiting room where the prisoners awaited trial.

There were perhaps fifty prisoners here, men of every type, but on the whole much more smartly dressed than one would expect. They were strolling up and down with their hats on, shivering with the cold. I saw here a thing which interested me greatly. When I was being taken to my cell I had seen two dirty-looking ruffians, much dirtier than myself and presumably drunks or obstruction cases, being put into another cell in the row. Here, in the waiting room these two were at work with note-books in their hands, interrogating prisoners. It appeared that they were "splits", and were put into the cells disguised as prisoners, to pick up any information that was going—for there is complete freemasonry between prisoners, and they talk without reserve in front of one another. It was a dingy trick, I thought.

All the while the prisoners were being taken by ones and twos along a corridor to the court. Presently a sergeant shouted "Come on the drunks!" and four or five of us filed along the corridor and stood waiting at the entrance of the court. A young constable on duty there advised me:

"Take your cap off when you go in, plead guilty and don't give back any answers. Got any previous convictions?"

"No."

"Six bob you'll get. Going to pay it?"

"I can't. I've only twopence."

"Ah well, it don't matter. Lucky for you Mr Brown isn't on the bench this morning. Teetotaller he is. He don't half give it to the drunks. Coo!"

The drunk cases were dealt with so rapidly that I had not even time to notice what the court was like. I only had a vague impression of a raised platform with a coat of arms over it, clerks sitting at tables below, and a railing. We filed past the railing like people passing through a turnstile, and the proceedings in each case sounded like this:

"Edward-Burton-drunk-and-incapable-Drunk?-Yes-Six-shillings-move-on-NEXT!"

All this in the space of about five seconds. At the other side of the court we reached a room where a sergeant was sitting at a desk with a ledger.

"Six shillings?" he said.

"Yes."

"Going to pay it?"

"I can't."

"All right, back you go to your cell."

And they took me back and locked me in the cell from which I had come, about ten minutes after I had left it.

The publican had also been brought back, his case having been postponed, and the Belgian youth, who, like me, could not pay his fine. The Jew was gone, whether released or sentenced we did not know. Throughout the day prisoners were coming and going, some waiting trial, some until the Black Maria was available to take them to prison. It was cold, and the nasty faecal stench in the cell became unbearable. They gave us our dinner at about two o'clock—it consisted of a mug of tea and two slices of bread and marg for each man. Apparently this was the regulation meal. One could, if one had friends outside, get food sent in, but it struck me as damnably unfair that a penniless man must face his trial with only bread and marg in his belly; also unshaven—I, at this time, had had no chance of shaving for over forty-eight hours—which is likely to prejudice the magistrates against him.

Among the prisoners who were put temporarily in the cell were two friends or partners named apparently Snouter and Charlie, who had been arrested for some street offence—obstruction with a barrow, I dare say. Snouter was a thin, red-faced, malignant-looking man, and Charlie a short, powerful, jolly man. Their conversation was rather interesting.

Charlie: "Cripes, it ain't 'alf fucking cold in 'ere. Lucky for us ole Brown ain't on today. Give you a month as soon as look at yer."

Snouter: (bored, and singing)

> "Tap, tap, tapetty tap,
> I'm a perfect devil at that;
> Tapping 'em 'ere, tapping 'em there,
> *I* bin tapping 'em everywhere—"

Charlie: "Oh, fuck off with yer tapping! Scrumping's what yer want at this time of year. All them rows of turkeys in the winders, like rows of fucking soldiers with no clo'es on—don't it make yer fucking mouth water to look at 'em. Bet yer a tanner I 'ave one of 'em afore tonight."

Snouter: "What's 'a good? Can't cook the bugger over the kip-'ouse fire, can you?"

Charlie: "Oo wants to cook it? I know where I can flog (sell) it for a bob or two, though."

Snouter: "'S no good. Chanting's the game this time of year. Carols. Fair twist their 'earts round, I can, when I get on the mournful. Old tarts weep their fucking eyes out when they 'ear me. I won't 'alf give them a doing this Christmas. I'll kip indoors if I 'ave to cut it out of their bowels."

Charlie: "Ah, *I* can sling you a bit of a carol. 'Ymns, too." (He begins singing in a good bass voice)

"Jesu, lover of my soul,
Let me to thy bosom fly—"

The Constable on duty: (looking through the grille) "Nah then, in 'ere, nah then! What yer think this is? Baptist prayer meeting?"

Charlie: (in a low voice as the constable disappears) "Fuck off, pisspot." (He hums)

"While the gathering waters roll,
While the tempest still is 'igh!

You won't find many in the 'ymnal as I can't sling you. Sung bass in the choir my last two years in Dartmoor, I did."

Snouter: "Ah? Wassit like in Dartmoor now? D'you get jam now?"

Charlie: "Not jam. Gets cheese, though, twice a week."

Snouter: "Ah? 'Ow long was you doing?"

Charlie: "Four year."

Snouter: "Four years without cunt—Cripes! Fellers inside'd go 'alf mad if they saw a pair of legs (a woman), eh?"

Charlie: "Ah well, in Dartmoor we used to fuck old women down on the allotments. Take 'em under the 'edge in the mist. Spud-grabbers they was—ole trots seventy years old. Forty of us was caught and went through 'ell for it. Bread and water, chains—every-think. I took my Bible oath as I wouldn't get no more stretches after that."

Snouter: "Yes, you! 'Ow come you got in the stir lars' time, then?"

Charlie: "You wouldn't 'ardly believe it, boy. I was narked—narked by my own sister! Yes, my own fucking sister. My sister's a cow if ever there was one. She got married to a religious maniac, and 'e's so fucking religious that she's got fifteen kids now. Well, it was 'im put 'er up to narking me. But I got it back on 'em, *I* can tell you. What do you think I done first thing, when I come out of the stir? I bought a 'ammer, and I went round to my sister's 'ouse and smashed 'er piano to fucking matchwood. I did. 'There,' I says, 'that's what you get for narking me! You mare!' I says." etc etc.

This kind of conversation went on more or less all day between these two, who were only in for some petty offence and were quite pleased with themselves. Those who were going to prison were silent and restless, and the look on some of the men's faces—respectable men under arrest for the first time—was dreadful. They took the publican out at about three in the afternoon, to be sent off to prison. He had cheered up a little on learning from the constable on duty that he was going to the same prison as Lord Kylsant.[1] He thought that by sucking up to Lord K in jail he might get a job from him when he came out.

I had no idea how long I was going to be incarcerated, and supposed that it would be several days at least. However, between four and five o'clock they took me out of the cell, gave back the things which had been confiscated, and shot me into the street forthwith. Evidently the day in custody served instead of the fine. I had only twopence and had had nothing to eat all day except bread and marg and was damnably hungry; however, as always happens when it is a choice between tobacco and food, I bought tobacco with my twopence. Then I went down to the Church Army shelter in the Waterloo Road, where you get a kip, two meals of bread and corned beef and tea and a prayer meeting, for four hours' work at sawing wood.

The next morning I went home, got some money, and went out to Edmonton. I turned up at the Casual Ward about nine at night, not downright drunk but more or less under the influence, thinking this would lead to prison—for it is an offence under the Vagrancy Act for a tramp to come drunk to the Casual Ward. The porter, however, treated me with great consideration, evidently feeling that a tramp with money enough to buy drink ought to be respected. During the next few days I made several more attempts to get into trouble by begging under the noses of the police, but I seemed to bear a charmed life—no one took any notice of me. So, as I did not want to do anything serious which might lead to investigations about my identity etc, I gave it up. The trip, therefore, was more or less a failure, but I have recorded it as a fairly interesting experience.

Written August 1932

[1] Lord Kylsant (1863–1937), Conservative MP and Chairman of The Royal Mail Steam Package Company was sentenced to twelve months' imprisonment in 1931 for circulating a false prospectus, but his personal guilt was never entirely established in the public mind.

26. Review

Byron and the Need of Fatality by Charles du Bos, translated by Ethel Colburn Mayne

This book is a study of the underlying causes of Byron's incest with his half-sister, and as far as one can judge—for only a specialist could keep track of the vast quantities of Byronic literature—an exceptionally penetrating one. M. du Bos' thesis is that Byron committed incest, besides other far worse actions, because he was one of those men who must needs feel themselves the creatures of destiny. He created a sort of myth in which he was the central character, and in which he was doomed, like Oedipus, to commit some appalling and inescapable crime. It took the form of incest, perhaps because of a family tradition of inbreeding, which M. du Bos says had always had a morbid fascination for Byron. The story is an absorbing one, and when it deals with the short married life of the Byrons—Byron hated his wife from the start, and took care to let her learn that he had committed incest—it reaches genuine tragedy. The only person whose behaviour is not fully explained is Augusta Leigh, the half-sister. She seems not to have been a vicious woman, but she must have been vague and pliable to the point of idiocy. (Her way of referring to a liaison with her half-brother was, "I have been most unfortunate in all my nearest connections.") Perhaps, at the start, she hardly understood what she was doing; at any rate, it is clear that the blame was wholly Byron's.

Nevertheless, though M. du Bos is very fair to Byron, there is one thing in his favour which he leaves unsaid. It is that the whole business of the incest was a fairly trivial matter. Byron's subsequent behaviour to his wife was abominable, but the incest *in itself* was not an outrageous case. Augusta Leigh was only Byron's half-sister —M. du Bos, after an introductory passage, refers to her throughout as "the *sister*"; this is rather misleading—and they had been brought up separately. In certain societies (among some of the ancient Greeks, for instance) marriage with non-uterine sisters has been an accepted custom; it is not, therefore, forbidden by any radical instinct. Moreover, M. du Bos' narrative makes it clear that Byron had no feeling of perversion in what he did. It is true that with his "need of fatality" he was glad of this chance to damn himself. Incest smelt of hell-fire (a great disinfectant, and, to spirited natures, a great provocative) and therefore it appealed to him; but there was evidently a quite natural attraction as well—in fact, on M. du Bos' showing Augusta was the only woman who ever did attract Byron greatly. He made a deadly sin out of his personal tastes, as normal men make a virtue out of *their* personal tastes. It is unfair, and could even prejudice sound judgement of his poetry, to regard him as a cold-blooded pervert.

This is worth remembering, because there are spiritually two Byrons, and the business of the incest obscures the one who matters to posterity. Byron, as M. du Bos says, was "born in two halves". One half is the Byron of *Manfred*—the "fated being", with his beauty, his superhuman wickedness and all the rest of it—for whose sake, according to Samuel Butler, all right-minded girls used once to weep at the mention of Missolonghi. And the other half is the Byron of *Don Juan*, with unparalleled qualities both as man and poet—unparalleled, that is, in the century since his death. For is there not something especially lacking in our own age, and especially to be honoured, in the sane, earthbound, bawdy spirit of *Don Juan*? And still better is the enthusiasm for justice and honesty which led Byron into sympathy with all rebels—with the French revolutionists, with the Luddite rioters, with Napoleon against the kings of Europe, with the Greeks against the Turks. In a far more corrupt age than Byron's, who has produced a poem anything like *The Vision of Judgement?*

> He had written praises of a regicide,
> He had written praises of all kings whatever,
> He had written for republics far and wide,
> And then against them bitterer than ever.
> For pantisocracy he once had cried
> Aloud—a scheme less moral than 'twas clever;
> Then grew a hearty anti-Jacobin—
> Had turn'd his coat—and would have turn'd his skin.

This of the then Poet Laureate, and *mutatis mutandis* it might be said of about half our modern political journalists. But how very unmodern it would be to say it! Similarly with "The Isles of Greece"—almost the only good English patriotic poem, though the *patria* in the case happens not to be England. Romantic nationalism means very little today, but the underlying mood of "The Isles of Greece", and the peculiar clear ring of its oratory, are permanently valuable. The contrast between the manliness, the fundamental decency of

Byron's best poems, and his behaviour towards women, brings out the truth of M. du Bos' remark that Byron was "born in two halves".

This is a fair-minded, discerning book, very interesting to anyone who wants to see the whole story of Byron, his wife and his half-sister thoroughly thrashed out. M. du Bos has been especially happy in his translator, herself author of a well-known life of Lady Byron.

Eric Blair

Adelphi, September 1932

27. Common Lodging Houses

Common lodging houses, of which there are several hundred in London, are night-shelters specially licensed by the LCC. They are intended for people who cannot afford regular lodgings, and in effect they are extremely cheap hotels. It is hard to estimate the lodging-house population, which varies continually, but it always runs into tens of thousands, and in the winter months probably approaches fifty thousand. Considering that they house so many people and that most of them are in an extraordinarily bad state, common lodging houses do not get the attention they deserve.

To judge the value of the LCC legislation on this subject, one must realise what life in a common lodging house is like. The average lodging house ("doss house", it used to be called) consists of a number of dormitories, and a kitchen, always subterranean, which also serves as a sitting-room. The conditions in these places, especially in southern quarters such as Southwark or Bermondsey, are disgusting. The dormitories are horrible fetid dens, packed with anything up to a hundred men, and furnished with beds a good deal inferior to those in a London casual ward. Normally these beds are about 5 ft 6 in. long by 2 ft 6 in. wide, with a hard convex mattress and a cylindrical pillow like a block of wood; sometimes in the cheaper houses, not even a pillow. The bed-clothes consist of two raw-umber-coloured sheets, supposed to be changed once a week, but actually, in many cases, left on for a month, and a cotton counterpane; in winter there may be blankets, but never enough. As often as not the beds are verminous, and the kitchens invariably swarm with cockroaches or black beetles. There are no baths, of course, and no room where any privacy is attainable. These are the normal and accepted conditions in all ordinary lodging houses. The charges paid for this kind of accommodation vary between 7d and 1/1d a night. It should be added that, low as these charges sound, the average common lodging house brings in something like £40 net profit a week to its owner.

Besides the ordinary dirty lodging houses, there are a few score, such as the Rowton Houses and the Salvation Army hostels, that are clean and decent. Unfortunately, all of these places set off their advantages by a discipline so rigid and tiresome that to stay in them is rather like being in jail. In London (curiously enough it is better in some other towns) the common lodging house where one gets both liberty and a decent bed does not exist.

The curious thing about the squalor and discomfort of the ordinary lodging house is that these exist in places subject to constant inspection by the LCC. When one first sees the murky, troglodytic cave of a common lodging-house kitchen, one takes it for a corner of the early nineteenth century which has somehow been missed by the reformers; it is a surprise to find that common lodging houses are governed by a set of minute and (in intention) exceedingly tyrannical rules. According to the LCC regulations, practically everything is against the law in a common lodging house. Gambling, drunkenness, or even the introduction of liquor, swearing, spitting on the floor, keeping tame animals, fighting—in short, the whole social life of these places—are all forbidden. Of course, the law is habitually broken, but some of the rules are enforceable, and they illustrate the dismal uselessness of this kind of legislation. To take an instance: some time ago the LCC became concerned about the closeness together of beds in common lodging houses, and enacted that these must be at least 3 ft apart. This is the kind of law that is enforceable, and the beds were duly moved. Now, to a lodger in an already overcrowded dormitory it hardly matters whether the beds are 3 ft apart or 1 ft; but it does matter to the proprietor, whose income depends upon his floor space. The sole real result of this law, therefore, was a general rise in the price of beds. Please notice that though the space between the beds is strictly regulated, nothing is said about the beds themselves—nothing, for instance, about their being fit to sleep in. The lodging-house keepers can, and do, charge 1/– for a bed less restful than a heap of straw, and there is no law to prevent them.

Another example of LCC regulations. From nearly all common

lodging houses women are strictly excluded; there are a few houses specially for women, and a very small number—too small to affect the general question—to which both men and women are admitted. It follows that any homeless man who lives regularly in a lodging house is entirely cut off from female society—indeed, cases even happen of man and wife being separated owing to the impossibility of getting accommodation in the same house. Again, some of the cheaper lodging houses are habitually raided by slumming parties, who march into the kitchen uninvited and hold lengthy religious services. The lodgers dislike these slumming parties intensely, but they have no power to eject them. Can anyone imagine such things being tolerated in a hotel? And yet a common lodging house is only a hotel at which one pays 8d a night instead of 10/6d. This kind of petty tyranny can, in fact, only be defended on the theory that a man poor enough to live in a common lodging house thereby forfeits some of his rights as a citizen.

One cannot help feeling that this theory lies behind the LCC rules for common lodging houses. All these rules are in the nature of interference-legislation—that is, they interfere, but not for the benefit of the lodgers. Their emphasis is on hygiene and morals, and the question of comfort is left to the lodging-house proprietor, who, of course, either shirks it or solves it in the spirit of organised charity. It is worth pointing out the improvements that could actually be made in common lodging houses by legislation. As to cleanliness, no law will ever enforce that, and in any case it is a minor point. But the sleeping accommodation, which is the important thing, could easily be brought up to a decent standard. Common lodging houses are places in which one pays to sleep, and most of them fail in their essential purpose, for no one can sleep well in a rackety dormitory on a bed as hard as bricks. The LCC would be doing an immense service if they compelled lodging-house keepers to divide their dormitories into cubicles and, above all, to provide comfortable beds; for instance, beds as good as those in the London casual wards. And there seems no sense in the principle of licensing all houses for "men only" or "women only" as though men and women were sodium and water and must be kept apart for fear of an explosion; the houses should be licensed for both sexes alike, as they are in some provincial towns. And the lodgers should be protected by law against various swindles which the proprietors and managers are now able to practise on them. Given these conditions, common lodging houses would serve their purpose, which is an important one, far better than they do now. After all, tens of thousands of unemployed and partially employed men have literally no other place in which they can live. It is absurd that they should be compelled to choose, as they are at present, between an easy-going pigsty and a hygienic prison.

Eric Blair

New Statesman and Nation, 3 September 1932

28. Letter to Brenda Salkeld[1] (extract)

The Hawthorns
Church Rd
Hayes, Mdx
Sunday [September? 1932]

I am writing as I promised, but can't guarantee an even coherent letter, for a female downstairs is making the house uninhabitable by playing hymn-tunes on the piano, which, in combination with the rain outside & a dog yapping somewhere down the road, is rapidly qualifying me for the mental home.

I have spent a most dismal day, first in going to Church, then in reading the *Sunday Times*, which grows duller & duller, then in trying to write a poem which won't go beyond the first stanza, then in reading through the rough draft of my novel,[2] which depresses me horribly. I really don't know which is the more stinking, the *Sunday Times* or the *Observer*. I go from one to the other like an invalid turning from side to side in bed & getting no comfort whichever way he turns. I thought the *Observer* would be a little less dull when Squire[3] stopped infesting it, but they seem deliberately to seek out

[1] Brenda Salkeld, a contemporary of Orwell, whom he met in 1928 at Southwold where she worked as gym mistress at St Felix's School for Girls, returning to her home at Bedford in the school holidays. She remained friends with Orwell until his death.

[2] *Burmese Days*.

[3] J. C. Squire (1884–1958), Kt. 1933, poet and critic. Founder of the *London Mercury* (1919–39), and its editor 1919–34. Edited the *English Men of Letters* series.

the dullest people they can get to review the dullest books. By the way, if you are by any chance wanting to impose a penance upon yourself, I should think you might try Hugh Walpole's recent 800-page novel.[1]

I hope you will read one or two of those books I mentioned to you. By the way, I forgot to mention, what I think you told me before you had not read, Dr Garnett's (not Richard or Edward Garnett) *The Twilight of the Gods*. If you haven't read that, it's a positive duty to do so. The story the title is taken from is far from being the best, but some of the others, such as "The Purple Head" are excellent. I suppose you have read Mark Twain's *Life on the Mississippi*? And J. S. Haldane's *Possible Worlds*? And Guy Boothby's *Dr Nikola*? And Mrs Sherwood's *The Fairchild Family*? All these are in different ways a little off the track (*Dr Nikola* is a boy's sixpenny thriller, but a first rate one) & I can recommend all of them. H. L. Mencken's book *In Defence of Women* would probably be amusing, but I haven't read it. I see Wyndham Lewis (*not* D. B. Wyndham Lewis, a stinking RC) has just brought out a book called *Snooty Baronet*, apparently a novel of sorts. It might be interesting. All I've ever read of his was a queer periodical called *The Enemy*, & odd articles, but he's evidently got some kick in him—whether at all a sound thinker or not, I can't be sure without further acquaintance. The copy of *The Enemy* I read was all a ferocious attack, about the length of an average novel, on Gertrude Stein—rather wasted energy, one would say.

29. Letter to Eleanor Jaques

The Hawthorns
Church Road
Hayes, Mdx
Monday [19 September 1932]

Dearest Eleanor,

You will think it very neglectful of me not to have written all this time, but I have hardly known whether I am on my head or my heels since arriving. Now, however, things have shaken down a bit. I have started the term's work, also been to church yesterday—sitting behind a moribund hag who stinks of mothballs & gin, & has to be more

[1] *The Fortress* by Hugh Walpole.

or less carried to & from the altar at communion; I suppose the truth is the poor old wretch is more or less in articulo mortis & is communicating as frequently as possible lest the Devil should happen to slip in at some moment when she is in mortal sin, & carry her off to the hottest part of Hell. I have managed to put in an hour or two at my own work, also frantically busy with a play the boys are to act at the end of the term. Also reading a book called *Belief in God* by Bishop Gore—late Bishop of Oxford, who confirmed me, & seemingly quite sound in doctrine tho' an Anglican.

How horrible & wintry the weather has turned these last two days. On the whole we had excellent weather at S'wold, & I cannot remember when I have ever enjoyed any expeditions so much as I did those with you. . . . Do come up to London soon if you can. It would make so much difference having someone like you about the place, even if we could only meet occasionally & then only walk about the streets & picture galleries. I am going to make one or two expeditions in partibus infidelium later in the winter—but nothing very interesting this time, only to see how the Embankment sleepers get on in winter.

Please remember me to your parents, also Dennis[1] & the Pulleins.[2] I will write again soon, when I have more leisure & more news.

With all my love
Eric

30. Letter to Eleanor Jaques

The Hawthorns
Church Road
Hayes, Mdx
Wed. night [19 October 1932]

Dearest Eleanor,
I am glad to hear you had a nice time on the broads, even tho' the motor boat was not too docile. I have been unutterably busy & am half exhausted already. I am going up to town for a night or two on the 28th—intend going out on to the Embankment that night to see

[1] Dennis Collings.
[2] Collett Pulleyne and his family in Southwold.

how the sleepers out get on at this time of year. Is there any chance of your being up in town by then? And when you *are* coming up, what will your address be? We simply must meet if it can be managed.

The papers this morning report quite serious rioting in Lambeth round the City Hall.[1] It was evidently *food*-rioting, as the bakers' shops were looted. That points to pretty serious conditions & there may be hell to pay in the winter if things are as bad as that already. I expect, tho', just enough will be done to prevent anything violent happening. I know the quarter where it happened so well—I dare say some of my friends took part in it.

. . . I heard from Dennis Collings the other day, asking me to go & stay with him at Cambridge at the half term. I would have liked to, but it is hard for me to get away, & there are, tho' I did not tell him so, two or three people at Cambridge whom I'm not anxious to meet. By the way, if you see the Pulleynes (*do* they spell their name like that? I'm never sure) any time, I would be awfully obliged if you would get from them an ms[2] of mine they have describing some adventures last Xmas. It's not very interesting but Brenda Salkeld is anxious to see it & I'd take it very kindly if you would send it to her—I hope it would not be too much trouble? Don't let your parents see the ms, as it has bad words in it. My novel[3] is making just a little progress. I see now more or less what will have to be done to it when the rough draft is finished, but the longness & complicatedness are terrible. I've done no other writing, except part of a mucky play the boys are to act later. I am told that there was a letter in the *New Statesman* some weeks back, attacking me for an article I'd written for them.[4] So annoying—I never saw it, & not to reply to an attack looks as tho' one admitted being wrong, which I'm sure I wasn't there in any major fact. I take in the *Church Times* regularly now & like it more every week. I do so like to see that there is life in the old dog yet—I mean in the poor old C of E. I shall have to go to Holy Communion soon, hypocritical tho' it is, because my curate friend is bound to think it funny if I always go to Church but never communicate. What is the procedure? I have almost forgotten it. As far as I remember you go up to the rail & kneel down, but I don't remem-

[1] Should be County Hall.

[2] "Clink". See 25.

[3] *Burmese Days*.

[4] Theodore Fyfe in a letter to the *New Statesman and Nation*, 17 September 1932, criticised Blair's article, "Common Lodging Houses". See 27.

ber whether there are any responses to make. You have to go fasting, do you not? And what about being in mortal sin? I wish you would prompt me. It seems rather mean to go to HC when one doesn't believe, but I have passed myself off for pious & there is nothing for it but to keep up the deception.

... Write soon & let me know your news, & above all if & when you are coming up to town. By the way, the other day I saw a man —Communist, I suppose—selling the *Daily Worker*, & I went up to him & said, "Have you the *DW*?"—He: "Yes, sir." Dear old England!

With love
Eric

31. Letter to Leonard Moore

The Hawthorns
Church Road
Hayes, Mdx
15 November 1932

Dear Mr Moore,

Many thanks for your letter & the two sets of proofs[1] which arrived yesterday. As there are *two* proofs, I do not fully understand whether I am intended to correct the one bearing reader's objections with a view to answering those objections, & the other for misprints etc, or whether I need only correct one. I have begun doing *both* corrections in the copy with the reader's remarks, & hope this will do. I can let you have the proof back in abt a week—I can't manage it before, as I am terribly rushed at present.

I have no objection to the title, but do you think that "X" is a good pseudonym? The reason I ask is that if this book doesn't flop as I anticipate, it might be better to have a pseudonym I could also use for my next one. I leave this to you and Mr Gollancz to decide.

The novel[2] is not getting on badly in the sense that I am fairly pleased with what is now done, but it moves slowly as I have practically no time to work. I did a good deal to it during the holidays & some at the beginning of the term, but at present, besides teach-

[1] Of *Down and Out in Paris and London.*

[2] *Burmese Days.*

ing, I am kept busy producing a school play, which means making costumes etc besides rehearsing. I *hope* to get the book done by the summer, but can't promise.

I hope that you & Mrs Moore are well.

Yours sincerely
Eric A. Blair

32. Letter to Eleanor Jaques

The Hawthorns
Church Rd
Hayes, Mdx
18 November 1932

Dearest Eleanor,

Thanks so much for your letter. It was so delightful to hear from you again & know that you are up in London & we can meet. My only *good* days for going up to town are Fridays & Saturdays. I could meet you on either Friday or Saturday of next week any time after 4 pm. Could you manage either of those days? If *not*, I could manage either Wednesday or Tuesday as you suggest, but it would have to be after 6 pm. Please let me know, also where you would like to meet.

I am sorry to hear about your ankle & the operation. I hope, however, that the ankle will be permanently better now? I have been having an appallingly busy time, & for several weeks past have not set pen to paper except to correct some proofs of my book.[1] Besides all the usual school work, I have had to write & produce a play—am now in the throes of rehearsing it—& what is worst of all, have had to make most of the suits of armour etc for the boys to act it. For the last few weeks I have been suffering untold agonies with glue & brown paper etc. Also painting a cigarette box for the Church Bazaar, which I very rashly undertook to gild—will never try that job again. Also suffering from a devilish cold, & correcting proofs. My book is to come out in early Jan., I think. Gollancz wants to call it "The Confessions of a Down & Out". I am protesting against this as I don't answer to the name of down & out, but I will let it go if he thinks seriously that it is a taking title.

[1] *Down and Out in Paris and London.*

By the way, I have half an idea that *Macbeth* will be on at Sadler's Wells next Sat. If they have a matinée, would you like to go to it? I so adore *Macbeth*. In a moment I will go upstairs & see if I can find the Sadler's Wells programme, & then I can find out if it is on that day. If so, I could probably get away early, as there isn't much to do on Saturdays. If there is no matinée, *perhaps* I could go to the evening performance, but it is a little difficult because it means sleeping the night in London.

I have just found the programme. It says there is a matinée of *Macbeth* on Sat. the 26th November at 2.30 at the *Old Vic*. That is rather convenient—much more get-at-able than the other theatre. Do tell me you can come. And let me know where to meet. The Old Vic is in the Waterloo Rd, some distance south of the river. Till I hear from you, au revoir.

With love
Eric

33. Letter to Leonard Moore

The Hawthorns
Church Rd
Hayes, Mdx
Sat. [19 November 1932]

Dear Mr Moore,
Many thanks for your letter. I sent off the proof with the printer's queries on it yesterday. I made a few alterations and added one or two footnotes, but I think I arranged it so that there would be no need of "over-running". I will send on the other proof as soon as possible.

As to a pseudonym, a name I always use when tramping etc is P. S. Burton, but if you don't think this sounds a probable kind of name, what about

Kenneth Miles,
George Orwell,
H. Lewis Allways.

I rather favour George Orwell.

I would rather not promise to have the other book[1] ready by the summer. I could certainly do it by then if I were not teaching, but in this life I can't *settle* to any work, & at present particularly I am rushed off my feet. I have got to produce a school play, & have not only to write it, but I have got to do all the rehearsing &, worst of all, make most of the costumes. The result is that I have practically no leisure.

I should like very much to come out and see you and Mrs Moore some time. I can get to Gerrard's Cross quite easily from here, but I have unfortunately forgotten your home address. Perhaps you could let me know it? I could come over some Sunday afternoon—Sunday the 4th Dec., for instance, if you would be at home then?

Yours sincerely,
Eric A. Blair

PS. As to the *title* of the book. Would "The Confessions of a Dish-washer" do as well? I would *rather* answer to "dishwasher" than "down & out", but if you and Mr G[2] think the present title best for selling purposes, then it is better to stick to it.

34. Letter to Eleanor Jaques

The Hawthorns
Church Rd
Hayes, Mdx
Wed. [30 November 1932]

My Dearest Eleanor,
I would have written before if I had had time, to tell you how much I enjoyed seeing you again & to ask whether you will be able to come out again. If we had even passable weather, how would it be to go out some Sunday into the country, where we could go for a long walk & then have lunch at a pub? London is depressing when one has no money. I couldn't go this Sunday, as I have to go & see some

[1] *Burmese Days.*
[2] Victor Gollancz.

people[1] at Gerrard's Cross, but some other, perhaps. Let me know.

. . . I am living in a sort of nightmare—school work, rehearsing boys for their parts in the play, making costumes, & playing football. No writing of any description, of course. The friend who was going to lend me *Ulysses* has at last got his copy back, & I shall go up to town one day to collect it, if I can manage it. If I do, I will let you know beforehand & we could meet for tea if you were anywhere in that part of London. Please send that ms[2] back sometime—no hurry though. Also that letter you cut out of the *Nation.*[3] I like to know everything that is said by my enemies.

How I wish you were here. Whatever happens you must get some kind of job in London so that we can meet from time to time. I shall be a little less penniless next term, I hope. I am so looking forward to the holidays, tho' I'm afraid I shan't have too much time. . . .

With much love
Eric

35. Letter to Eleanor Jaques

The Hawthorns
Church Rd
Hayes, Mdx
Tue. [13 December 1932]

Dearest Eleanor,

Many thanks for your last letter. I have had not an instant to write. I hope all goes well with you? Are you selling any stockings? And do your clients behave properly? I was in Trafalgar Square only yesterday, because I'd had to run up to London, but it was such short notice that I couldn't write to let you know, & I didn't know any address except your Roehampton one, otherwise we might have met. A pity.

Can you by any chance come out with me this Sunday 18th? (w.p. of course, but given even tolerable weather I should love to go

[1] Leonard Moore and his wife.

[2] "Clink". See 25.

[3] Theodore Fyfe's letter in the *New Statesman and Nation.*

for a walk somewhere.) For instance if you could take a ticket to Uxbridge from Paddington & let me know the time, I could get in at Hayes & we could go on to Uxbridge & have a good long walk, & get lunch at Denham or somewhere—I hardly know the country but could consult a map. I hope it will be possible. Also, a friend of mine in London has some time shortly coming to stay with him a person who he says is most exciting—an old man who lives the life of a vagabond in order to conform with the Sermon on the Mount. He said if the old man arrived before I went away, to come in & see him, & I said I would like to bring a friend, so if all the times fitted we might go there some evening. In any case I must try to arrange a meeting with you somehow before I leave London. I leave here about the 22nd, I think. What date are you going down? Perhaps we could travel together. Let me know your news & your plans, & your address if you have changed it. I must stop now or I shall miss the post.

With much love
Eric

PS. Thanks ever so for sending that letter from the *Nation*. A very feeble attack I thought—not worth answering.

36. Letter to Leonard Moore

36 High St
Southwold, Suffolk
Friday [23 December 1932]

Dear Mr Moore,

Thanks very much for the advance copies,[1] which have just arrived. I think the get-up is very nice, & they have shown extraordinary cleverness in making it look quite a long book. What does "a recommendation of the Book Society" on the cover mean?

I wonder if it could be arranged that one copy should be sent for review to the *Adelphi*? They know me and I write for them sometimes, so they would give it a sympathetic review, I expect.

[1] Of *Down and Out in Paris and London*.

I hope you will have a Merry Christmas. Please give my kindest wishes to Mrs Moore. The miserable school play over which I had wasted so much time went off not badly. I am now free till the 18th, & I hope in that time I'll be able to polish up a fair chunk of the novel[1] to the point where you can form an opinion on it.

Yours very sincerely
Eric A. Blair

[1] *Burmese Days.*

1933

***Down and Out in Paris and London** was published in London by Victor Gollancz on 9 January 1933 and in New York by Harper Brothers on 30 June 1933.*

37. Introduction to the French Edition of *Down and Out in Paris and London*

[A French edition of *Down and Out in Paris and London* called *La Vache Enragée* was published in Paris by Gallimard on 8 May 1935. Orwell wrote an Introduction for it of which the English original no longer exists. The following is a re-casting back into English from the French translation.]

My kind translators have asked me to write a short preface for the French edition of this book. As probably many of my French readers will wonder what chain of events brought me to Paris at the time when the incidents described in this book took place, I think it would be best to begin by giving them a few biographical details.

I was born in 1903. In 1922 I went to Burma where I joined the Indian Imperial Police. It was a job for which I was totally unsuited: so, at the beginning of 1928, while on leave in England, I gave in my resignation in the hopes of being able to earn my living by writing. I did just about as well at it as do most young people who take up a literary career—that is to say, not at all. My literary efforts in the first year barely brought me in twenty pounds.

In the spring of 1928 I set off for Paris so as to live cheaply while writing two novels[1]—which I regret to say were never published—and also to learn French. One of my Parisian friends found me a room in a cheap hotel in a working-class district which I have described briefly in the first chapter of this book, and which any sharp-witted Parisian will doubtless recognise. During the summer of 1929 I had written my two novels, which the publishers left on my hands,

[1] The manuscript of neither novel survives.

to find myself almost penniless and in urgent need of work. At that time it was not illegal—or at any rate not seriously illegal—for foreigners living in France to take jobs and it seemed more natural to me to stay in the city I was in, rather than return to England where, at that time, there were about two and a half million unemployed. So I stayed on in Paris and the events which I describe in this book took place towards the end of the autumn of 1929.

As for the truth of my story, I think I can say that I have exaggerated nothing except in so far as all writers exaggerate by selecting. I did not feel I had to describe events in the exact order in which they happened, but everything I have described did take place at one time or another. At the same time I have refrained, as far as possible, from drawing individual portraits of particular people. All the characters I have described in both parts of the book are intended more as representative types of the Parisian or Londoner of the class to which they belong than as individuals.

I should also add that this book makes no claims to giving a complete picture of life in Paris or London but only to portray one particular aspect. As almost without exception all the scenes and incidents in which I was involved have something repugnant about them it might seem that, without wishing to do so, I have given the impression that I think Paris and London are unpleasant cities. This was never my intention and if, at first sight, the reader should get this impression this is simply because the subject-matter of my book is essentially unattractive: my theme is poverty. When you haven't a penny in your pocket you are forced to see any city or country in its least favourable light and all human beings, or nearly all, appear to you either as fellow sufferers or as enemies. I want to emphasise this point particularly for my French readers because I would be distressed if they thought I have the least animosity towards a city of which I have very happy memories.

At the beginning of this preface I promised to give the reader some biographical details. So, for those it might interest, I will just add that after leaving Paris towards the end of 1929 I earned my living largely by teaching and in a small way by writing. . . .

London, 15 October 1934

38. Letter to Leonard Moore

The Hawthorns
Church Rd
Hayes, Mdx
1 February 1933

Dear Mr Moore,
I don't suppose you saw the enclosed rather snooty letter which was in the *Times* of 31st Jan. It would have been most damaging to let it go unanswered. I enclose herewith a copy of the letter I have sent in reply, and if you have time I wish you would let me know whether this was the right reply to make.

I rang up your office on Saturday on the off chance of finding you there, but they said you were away. I wanted to know what you thought of the first 100 pp. of my novel,[1] that is if you had had time to look at it. I know that as it stands it is fearful from a literary point of view, but I wanted to know whether given a proper polishing up, excision of prolixities & general tightening up, it was at all the sort of thing people want to read about. I should think that [the] fact that it is about Burma and there are so few novels with that setting, might offset the lack of action in the story—it is mostly description, I am afraid; there are to be a murder and a suicide later, but they play rather a subsidiary part.

Yours sincerely
Eric A. Blair

39. Letter to the Editor of *The Times*

Sir,
I have read a letter in your columns[2] from M. Humbert Possenti attacking the truthfulness of my book *Down and Out in London and Paris* which was reviewed in your *Literary Supplement* of 12 January. Referring to alleged dirtiness in the service quarters of a Paris hotel M. Possenti says:

> I am moved, as a *restaurateur* and *hôtelier* of 40 years' experience, to deny in the most emphatic manner possible the truth of

[1] *Burmese Days.*
[2] *The Times,* 31 January 1933.

> what the author says. Such a disgusting state of things as he describes is in such places inconceivable. The kitchens of large and "smart" restaurants have to be clean: the work has to be done in an orderly and cleanly manner or it would not get done at all. Such kitchens, I assert, are cleaner than those of most private houses, etc.

M. Possenti seems not to realise that these remarks are quite beside the point. The passages objected to in my book did not refer to Paris hotels in general, but to one particular hotel. And as M. Possenti does not know which hotel this was he has no means of testing the truth of my statements. So I am afraid that, in spite of his 40 years' experience, my evidence in this case is worth more than his.

M. Possenti adds that hotel kitchens could not be seriously dirty, because "speaking generally" it is usual to allow inspection by customers. I do not know how "general" this practice is, but I do know that in our hotel there were places which no customer could possibly have been allowed to see with any hope of retaining his custom. M. Possenti also misquotes me by saying that I had "vowed never to eat a meal in a Parisian restaurant as long as I lived." I said nothing of the kind. What I did say was that I should never again enjoy a meal in a "smart" restaurant—i.e. a restaurant in which the food, in order to make it sufficiently elegant in appearance, has to be mauled about by sweaty hands.

By the way, M. Possenti seems to think that I have some patriotic animus against French restaurants as opposed to English ones. Far from it. I wrote about a Paris hotel and restaurant because it was of those that I had direct experience. I had no wish whatever to suggest that in this matter of kitchen dirtiness the French are worse than any other nation.

Yours faithfully,
"George Orwell"

The Times, 11 February 1933

40. Letter to Eleanor Jaques

The Hawthorns
Church Rd
Hayes, Mdx
Sunday [26 February 1933]

Dearest Eleanor,

How nice to hear from you again & know that you are in the land of the living. I am sorry that job with the fashion-plate artist didn't come to anything. I do hope you will find something to suit you, & don't forget abt letting me know when you do come up to town. I am having a beastly cold—my first this winter, I think, but none the less annoying. It was very kind of Dennis to think of writing to the *Times* in my defence. They took their time about printing my letter of reply, & I have since also been criticised in the *Licensed Victuallers Gazette*,[1] but I think they are beneath answering. I think I shall be able to let the agent have the second 100 pp. of my novel by the end of this term. The other book[2] has been disposed of to Harpers—I mean the American rights—& I should think they are pretty good people to deal with. Yes, I met the old vagabond chap, & he was rather interesting. His philosophy seemed to me Buddhist rather than Christian—all about the futility of making any effort & the necessity [of] attaining peace of mind, in other words Nirvana. But he came flying back from Nirvana pretty rapidly when I said something against Carlyle (the old chap is a Scotchman) so evidently the affairs of this world still have their claws in him. He said, what struck me as a sane remark, that he did not counsel anyone else to follow his own example, for everyone must work out his salvation in the way suited to him. This fits in with the Indian saying that there are 84,000 or is it 84,000,000 ways to salvation, & I suppose abt double the number to damnation. I have just read a book called *James Joyce & the Plain Reader*[3]—weak trash, which would give the impression that J was a writer on the Walpole-Priestley level. Also Upton Sinclair's autobiography—ridiculous, but rather fun. I have dug a biggish-sized patch of my garden, but there is still a lot to do & it is difficult to find the time. I wish you were coming up to town this next week-end, as I have two or three free days on end—half-term.

With much love
Eric

[1] *Licensed Victuallers Gazette*, 17 February 1933.
[2] *Down and Out in Paris and London.*
[3] *James Joyce and the Plain Reader* by Charles Duff.

41. Poem

Sometimes in the middle autumn days,
The windless days when the swallows have flown,
And the sere elms brood in the mist,
Each tree a being, rapt, alone,

I know, not as in barren thought,
But wordlessly, as the bones know,
What quenching of my brain, what numbness,
Wait in the dark grave where I go.

And I see the people thronging the street,
The death-marked people, they and I
Goalless, rootless, like leaves drifting,
Blind to the earth and to the sky;

Nothing believing, nothing loving,
Not in joy nor in pain, not heeding the stream
Of precious life that flows within us,
But fighting, toiling as in a dream.

O you who pass, halt and remember
What tyrant holds your life in bond;
Remember the fixed, reprieveless hour,
The crushing stroke, the dark beyond.

And let us now, as men condemned,
In peace and thrift of time stand still
To learn our world while yet we may,
And shape our souls, however ill;

And we will live, hand, eye and brain,
Piously, outwardly, ever-aware,
Till all our hours burn clear and brave
Like candle flames in windless air;

So shall we in the rout of life
Some thought, some faith, some meaning save,
And speak it once before we go
In silence to the silent grave.

Eric Blair

Adelphi, March 1933

42. Letter to Brenda Salkeld (extract)

The Hawthorns
Church Rd
Hayes, Mdx
Friday night [10? March 1933]

Forgive me for not writing for so long, but I have been as usual submerged with work & in the intervals trying to break the back of my garden.

Have you seen any more of your friends who worship Bernard Shaw? Tell them that Shaw is Carlyle & water, that he ought to have been a Quaker (cocoa and commercial dishonesty), that he has squandered what talents he may have had back in the '80's in inventing metaphysical reasons for behaving like a scoundrel, that he suffers from an inferiority complex towards Shakespeare, & that he is the critic, cultured critic (not very cultured but it is what B meant) that Samuel Butler prayed to be delivered from. Say that Shaw's best work was one or two early novels & one or two criticisms he wrote for the *Saturday Review* when Harris[1] was editor, & that since then it has got steadily worse until its only function is to console fat women who yearn to be highbrows. Say also that he has slandered Ibsen in a way that must make poor old I turn in his grave. Also that Shaw cribbed the plot of *Pygmalion* from Smollett & afterwards wrote somewhere or other that Smollett is unreadable.

43. Letter to Eleanor Jaques

The Hawthorns
Church Rd
Hayes, Mdx
Thursday [25 May 1933]

Dearest Eleanor,
I write this not knowing where you are, but I shall send it to your address in Roehampton, hoping they will forward it if necessary. Do please try & come out somewhere with me when you are up in town again. It is such lovely weather, & it would be so delightful to go for a long walk in the country somewhere. If you can't manage

[1] Frank Harris (1856–1931), British-American man of letters; author of *My Life and Loves*.

a Saturday or Sunday, I can always make an excuse & get away. Or at worst we could meet in town for an afternoon. What are you doing in August? I don't know whether I'll be in S'wold or not—not, if my parents let their house. I am probably leaving this place at the end of the term, but I may go to another rather similar school in Uxbridge, which is near here. Write soon & let me know when you [are] going to be in town & if you can meet me.

With love from
Eric

44. Letter to Brenda Salkeld (extract)

The Hawthorns
Church Rd
Hayes, Mdx
Saturday [June? 1933]

I sent you about two thirds of the rough draft of my novel yesterday. I would have sent it earlier, but it has been with my agent all this time. He is quite enthusiastic about it, which is more than I am; but you are not to think that when finished it will be quite as broken-backed as at present, for with me almost any piece of writing has to be done over and over again. I wish I were one of those people who can sit down and fling off a novel in about four days. There is no news here. I am frightfully busy, suffering from the heat, and exercised about the things in my garden, which are going to dry up and die if this cursed weather doesn't change. I am growing, among other things, a pumpkin, which of course needs much more careful treatment than a marrow. I have read nothing, I think, except periodicals, all of which depress me beyond words. Do you ever see the *New English Weekly*? It is the leading Social Credit[1] paper. As a monetary scheme Social Credit is probably sound, but its promoters seem to think that they are going to take the main weapon out of the hands of the governing classes without a fight, which is an illusion. A few years ago I thought it rather fun to reflect that our civilisation is doomed, but now it fills me above all else with boredom to think of

[1] The Social Credit movement, based on the ideas of Major C. H. Douglas, claimed that prosperity could be achieved through a reform of the monetary system.

the horrors that will be happening within ten years—either some appalling calamity, with revolution and famine, or else all-round trustification and Fordification, with the entire population reduced to docile wage-slaves, our lives utterly in the hands of the bankers, and a fearful tribe of Lady Astors[1] and Lady Rhonddas[2] et hoc genus riding us like succubi in the name of Progress. Have you read *Ulysses* yet? It sums up better than any book I know the fearful despair that is almost normal in modern times. You get the same kind of thing, though only just touched upon, in Eliot's poems. With E, however, there is also a certain sniffish "I told you so" implication, because as the spoilt darling of the *Church Times* he is bound to point out that all this wouldn't have happened if we had not shut our eyes to the Light. The *CT* annoys me more and more. It is a poor satisfaction even to see them walloping the Romans, because they do it chiefly by descending to their level. I wonder whether it is true, as I have been told, that the *CT* advertisement columns are full of disguised abortion advertisements? If so it is pretty disgusting in a paper which is in constant pursuit of Bertrand Russell, Barney the Apostate,[3] etc because of their birth control propaganda. By the way did you see Barney's recent pronouncements at the Conference on I forget what, about the undesirable multiplication of the lower classes. His latest phrase is "the social problem class", meaning all those below a certain income. Really you sometimes can't help thinking these people are doing it on purpose. Write soon.

[1] Nancy Witcher Astor (1879–1964), wife of the first Viscount Astor, born in Virginia, society and political hostess at Cliveden, the Astor estate on the Thames; first woman to take her seat in the House of Commons, 1919–45; eloquent advocate of temperance and women's rights.

[2] Margaret Haig Thomas (1883–1958), second Viscountess Rhondda, highly successful business woman and ardent believer in the equality of the sexes; actively edited her own independent weekly *Time and Tide* 1928–58.

[3] Ernest William Barnes (1874–1953), mathematician and modernist churchman, Bishop of Birmingham 1924–53. His writings include *Should Such a Faith Offend?* and *Scientific Theory and Religion.*

45. Letter to Eleanor Jaques

The Hawthorns
Church Rd
Hayes, Mdx
7 July 1933

Dearest Eleanor,
It seems so long since that day I went out with you—actually, I suppose, abt a month. This "glorious" weather has been almost the death of me. However, I occasionally manage to get over to Southall & have a swim at the open-air baths, & my garden has done pretty well considering the drought. The only failures I have had were shallots & broad beans, both I fancy due to having been planted too late. I have had enormous quantities of peas, & I am a convert forever to the system of sinking a trench where you are going to grow a row of peas. I hope I shall be in S'wold for part of the summer holidays, but I am afraid it won't be long, because I am going to a new school at Uxbridge next term & they may want me to do some tutoring during the holidays. God send I'll be able to drop this foul teaching after next year. I do hope you'll be in Southwold during the holidays & perhaps we can go & picnic as we did last year. I am so pining to see the sea again. Do try to be in S'wold if you can, & keep some days free for me during the first fortnight in August. I think I shall get home about the 28th of this month. My novel will be about finished by the end of this term, but I don't like large sections of it & am going to spend some months revising it. Please write & tell me what your plans are, & remember me to your parents.

With much love
Eric

46. Letter to Eleanor Jaques

The Hawthorns
Church Rd
Hayes, Mdx
Thursday [20 July 1933]

Dearest Eleanor,
Do write & tell me if you will be in S'wold during the summer holidays. I am going to be there I think from the 29th inst. to the 18th

August, & am so wanting to see you. If you are to be there, try & keep some days free for me, & it would be so nice if we could go & bathe & make our tea like we used to do last year along the W'wick shore. Let me know.

The heat here is fearful but it is good for my marrows & pumpkins, which are swelling almost visibly. We have had lashings of peas, beans just beginning, potatoes rather poor, owing to the drought I suppose. I have finished my novel but there are wads of it that I simply hate, & am going to change. They say it will be soon enough if it is done some time at the end of the year. Please G I get a little spare time in my next job. I went over to see the prize-giving at the school & it looked pretty bloody—the girls' section of the school (which I shall have nothing to do with—perhaps it is for the best) sang the female version of Kipling's "If". I am told that there is also a female version of "Forty years on", which I would give something to get hold of. I have been reading *in* D. H. Lawrence's collected letters. Some of them very interesting—there is a quality about L that I can't define, but everywhere in his work one comes on passages of an extraordinary freshness, vividness, so that tho' I would never, even given the power, have done it quite like that myself, I feel that he has seized on an aspect of things that no one else would have noticed. In another way, which I can still less explain, he reminds me of someone from the Bronze Age. I think there are some scraps of mine in the August *Adelphi*[1]—a poem, but I am not sure it is not one you have seen. Au revoir, & write soon.

Much love from
Eric

47. Poem

A dressed man and a naked man
Stood by the kip-house fire,
Watching the sooty cooking-pots
That bubble on the wire;

[1] There was no poem by Orwell in this issue of the *Adelphi*, only his review of *Baudelaire* by Enid Starkie.

And bidding tanners up and down,
Bargaining for a deal,
Naked skin for empty skin,
Clothes against a meal.

"Ten bob it is," the dressed man said,
"These boots cost near a pound,
This coat's a blanket of itself
When you kip on the frosty ground."

"One dollar," said the naked man,
"And that's a hog too dear;
I've seen a man strip off his shirt
For a fag and a pot of beer."

"Eight and a tanner," the dressed man said,
"And my life-work is yours,
All I've earned at the end of a life
Knocking at farmers' doors;

Turnips, apples, hops and peas,
And the spike when times are slack,
Fifty years I've tobied it
For these clothes upon my back."

"Take seven," said the naked man,
"It's cold and the spikes are shut;
Better be naked here in kip
Than dressed in Lambeth Cut."

"One tanner more," the dressed man said,
"One tanner says the word,
Off comes my coat of ratcatcher
And my breeches of velvet cord;

Now pull my shirt over my head,
I'm naked sole to crown,
And that's the end of fifty years
Tobying up and down."

A minute and they had changed about,
And each had his desire;
A dressed man and a naked man
Stood by the kip-house fire.

Eric Blair

Adelphi, October 1933

48. Letter to Leonard Moore

Frays College
Harefield Rd
Uxbridge, Mdx
Sunday [26 November 1933]

Dear Mr Moore,
Will you by any chance be at home next Sunday afternoon—the second I think the date is? I finished my novel some time back and have been typing it out in what spare time I can get in this place, and I think I can get it all typed by Saturday. . . .

I am very dissatisfied with the novel, but it is all about up to the standard of what you saw, and of course I have made all the necessary corrections and tightened it up as well as I could. It will be about 375 pp.—allowing for the fact that I have used wide margins, about 85,000 words. That seems awfully long to me. If the publisher said he would take it subject to cutting I would know where to cut it, but I'd rather not have to, as I am sick of the sight of it. Let's hope the next one will be better.

Yours sincerely
Eric A. Blair

49. Letter to Brenda Salkeld (extract)

Frays College
Harefield Road
Uxbridge, Mdx
Sunday [10? December 1933]

Many thanks for your letter of some time back. I have at last a few instants in which I can sit down to reply. I am so glad you got hold of and read *Ulysses* at last. When you say "What do you think Joyce is after?" I should say several things, which it is not very easy to define shortly. In the first place one has got to decide what a novel normally sets out to do. I should say that it sets out first (I am placing these in order of difficulty, the simplest first) to display or create character, secondly to make a kind of pattern or design which any good story contains, and thirdly, if the novelist is up to it, to produce *good writing*, which can exist almost as it were in vacuo and independent of subject. This is very crudely put, but you might see what I mean by the analogy of a picture—not that I am any judge of pictures—which has in the first place a subject (e.g. it might be a portrait), secondly a design made up of lines, planes etc and lastly if the painter is really good can give one the greatest pleasure of all by its (so to speak) *texture*—the quality of the brushmarks etc. I think *Ulysses* follows this scheme fairly closely, but the queer and original thing about it is that instead of taking as his material the conventional and highly simplified version of life presented in most novels, Joyce attempts to present life more or less as it is lived. Of course he is not trying *merely* to represent life. When *Ulysses* first came out one heard it said on every side that it was an attempt to describe a day in somebody's life, leaving nothing out, etc etc. It is not that. If one thinks, a complete description of a day, or even of an hour, would be simply an enormous omnium gatherum, quite formless and probably not at all interesting, and in any case would not convey the impression of life at all. Art implies selection and there is as much selection in *Ulysses* as in *Pride and Prejudice*. Only Joyce is attempting to select and represent events and thoughts as they occur in life and not as they occur in fiction. Of course he is not altogether successful but the very way in which he sets about it is enough to show how extraordinarily original his mind is. When I first came on *Ulysses* it was some odd chapters in a review, and I happened to strike that passage where Gerty Macdowell is soliloquising. It then seemed to me a sort of elephantine joke to write the whole passage in the style of the Heartsease library, but I now see that you could not possibly display the interior of the girl's mind so well in any other way, except at much greater length. You will remember no doubt how well the horrid little narcissistic touches about her "girlish treasures" and being "lost in dreams" etc were done. Similarly Bloom, Mrs B and Dedalus are all given styles of their own, to display the different qualities of their minds. Dedalus's style is infected with Elizabethan and medieval literature, Mrs B thinks in a sort of formless mess, and Bloom thinks in a series of short phrases, except in the brothel scene, where he is too drunk to know the difference between reality and imagination. There are certain changes of style that I don't see the reason for, e.g. the frequent parodies of newspaper reports, and also of Homer or it may be of ancient Irish literature, though some of these are quite amusing. For instance you may remember when Paddy Dignam, the drunkard, is dead, Joyce suddenly breaks into mock-Homeric style with "Fleet was his foot upon the bracken, Dignam of the beamy brow". The scene where the medical students are talking in the pub seems to be done in a series of Parodies of English literature from the earliest times to the present day. This again I don't see the reason for, unless it is because a baby is being born "off" and the change of style symbolises birth, which seems to me rather elephantine. Quite apart from the different styles used to represent different manners of thought, the observation is in places marvellous. For instance, the funeral scene. Compare the thoughts which pass through Bloom's mind with those that pass through the mind of an ordinary character in fiction at a funeral. As to the design itself, so far as I understand it, it doesn't seem to me to be altogether successful. The incidents are clearly based on the *Odyssey*. You can identify a lot of them. Bloom is Odysseus, Dedalus is Telemachus, Mrs B is Penelope (complete with suitors), Gertie Macdowell is Nausicaa, Bella what's her name who keeps the brothel is Circe etc. I fancy Joyce's idea in basing it on the *Odyssey* is that he means to say "There is the Bronze Age—here is us". Nevertheless the book does seem to me to split up into a lot of unrelated or thinly related incidents.

I hope you will forgive me for lecturing you at this enormous length. After all you can always stop reading. As to the characters themselves, I think both Dedalus and Bloom are certainly self-portraits—one of Joyce at 22 and the other at 38. I think Bloom is much the more interesting as well as the more successful. Dedalus is the ordinary modern intellectual whose mind is poisoned by his inability to believe in anything, and only different from the English version of the same thing by having been brought up in a Catholic atmosphere and on monkish learning instead of the classical education you get or are supposed to get in England. Bloom on the other hand is a rather exceptionally sensitive specimen of the man in the street, and I think the especial interest of this is that the cultivated man and the man in the street so rarely meet in modern English literature. The man in the street is usually described in fiction either by writers who are themselves intellectually men in the street, tho' they may have great gifts as novelists (e.g. Trollope), or by cultivated men who describe him *from outside* (e.g. Samuel Butler, Aldous Huxley). If you read the words of almost any writer of the intellectual type, you would never guess that he also is a being capable of getting drunk, picking girls up in the street, trying to swindle somebody out of half a crown, etc. I think the interest of Bloom is that he is an ordinary uncultivated man described from within by someone who can also stand outside him and see him from another angle. Not that Bloom is an absolutely typical man in the street. He has obviously for instance a streak of intellectual curiosity, which sometimes gets him into trouble with his pub friends and his wife. Also there are his sexual abnormalities, which are not those of the average man. I am not sure that purely as a bit of character-drawing Mrs B is not the best of the lot. Buck Mulligan is good. The other minor characters don't seem to me to stand out much, but some of the pub conversations are very good.

As to the actual writing in *Ulysses*, it isn't everybody's money, but personally I think it is superb in places. If you look you will see that Joyce is continually holding himself back from breaking out into a species of verse, and at times he does so, and those are the bits I like. The bit where Bloom remembers the time he was making love to his wife on the cliffs before they were married, and where he sees the man eating in that disgusting chop-shop, and then his subsequent thoughts about the butchers' stalls at the market, and the bit in the brothel scene where Bella, who has then turned into a man, tells him about his wife (Bloom's) being unfaithful to him, and where the plaster statuette is talking about the sheet of the *Pink'un* that she was wrapped up in, have haunted me ever since reading them. If you read these aloud you will see that most of them are essentially verse. One of the most remarkable things in the book, to me, is the verse describing the thoughts of somebody's dog—you remember, it starts "The curse of my curses, Seven days every day". He seems to me there actually to have discovered a new rhythmical scheme.

Excuse this long and somewhat didactic letter. The fact is Joyce interests me so much that I can't stop talking about him once I start. I thought you would have read most of the books in that list. You ask whether I was really impressed by *The Dynasts*. I wouldn't want to read it again in toto, but I think it attains the end it sets out for, and there are some very fine passages in it. The description of the battle of Waterloo is splendid, though probably historically misleading, but you would miss some of the effect if you hadn't read the rest of the book. Of course wads of it are dull beyond words. I have read nothing lately except a smelly little pamphlet on Plato and Aristotle which doesn't tell you anything much about Plato and Aristotle. I am crushed with work as usual, but hope to be a little freer next week when the examinations we are now doing are over. My novel is with the agent. He seems hopeful about it, but personally I am sick of the sight of it. It is a fearful length—almost Priestley-size. The next one[1] will be better I hope, but I don't suppose I shall be able to start it before the holidays.

If you want to read *Portrait of the Artist*, Joyce's earlier book, you can get it out of Smith's. There are good bits in it. The part where the boy passes through a pious stage is written in a subtly loathsome style which is very clever. But it is a commonplace book compared with *Ulysses*. Write again soon.

50. Letter to Leonard Moore

Uxbridge Cottage Hospital
Thursday [28 December 1933]

Dear Mr Moore,

Now that I am stronger[2] I can thank you for your great kindness in several times dropping in & enquiring after me, also for your Christmas card. I am hoping to get up in a day or two, & perhaps leave this place in about a week, after which I am going straight down to Southwold. Of course I can't go back to school at the beginning of the term, so I am going to chuck teaching, at least for the while. It is perhaps rather imprudent, but my people are anxious that I should do so, as they are concerned about my health, & of course I shall be able to write my next novel[3] in 6 months or so if I haven't got to be teaching at the same time. I trust all will go well with the

[1] *A Clergyman's Daughter.*

[2] In December Orwell was critically ill with pneumonia.

[3] *A Clergyman's Daughter.*

one[1] now with the publisher—I suppose we shan't hear till half way through Jan. Please remember me to Mrs Moore.

Yours sincerely
Eric A. Blair

[1] *Burmese Days.*

1934

51. Letter to Leonard Moore

36 High St
Southwold, Suffolk
Saturday [27 January 1934]

Dear Mr Moore,

Many thanks for your letter. It is disappointing about Heinemann's —however, if we can find *somebody* to publish the book,[1] no matter. My best time to see Mr Sax[t]on[2] would be Wednesday at 4.30. I don't know where his office is—perhaps you could let me know? I will try and come in at your office before going to see him, but it is rather difficult to get up to London from here before, say, 2 pm.

I have just received a copy of that French book I spoke to you of,[3] and will read it before Wednesday and let you know what it is like. It is quite short, and from the glance I have taken at it, it seems to be a book of anti-materialist, anti-marxist tendency.

I am much stronger, and have begun doing a little work. By the way, I know that Harper's owe me a few royalties[4]—not much, I am afraid, but about £20 or £30. Do you think it would be possible to get anything out of them say next month? It doesn't matter now, but I may be getting rather hard up in a month or two.

Yours sincerely
Eric A. Blair

[1] On first reading *Burmese Days* Gollancz had rejected it for fear of libel. Moore then tried the manuscript on other publishers. It is not known how many, but certainly Heinemann and Cape rejected it.

[2] Eugene Saxton, chief editor of Harper Brothers, New York. He first asked for some alterations in *Burmese Days* for fear of libel, but eventually published it without these modifications.

[3] *Esquisse d'une philosophie de la dignité humaine* by Paul Gille which had been suggested to Orwell by his aunt, Nellie Adam, neé Limouzin, then living in Paris, because her husband was translating it into Esperanto. Orwell had asked Moore in a letter of 16 January 1934 about the prospects of getting a translation of the book published in England. He never did the translation.

[4] For *Down and Out in Paris and London.*

52. Letter to Leonard Moore

36 High St
Southwold, Suffolk
Thursday [8 February 1934]

Dear Mr Moore,
Many thanks for your letter, and for the exertions you have been taking over my novel[1]. As soon as I get the ms from you I will go over it very carefully and make the necessary alterations, which should not, I think, take more than three or four days at most. But with regard to Mr Saxton's remarks about the last two or three pp. of the novel, I am sorry to say I don't agree with him at all. I will cut these out if it is absolutely insisted upon, but not otherwise. I hate a novel in which the principal characters are not disposed of at the end. I will, however, cut out the offending words "it now remains to tell" etc.

Yours sincerely
Eric A. Blair

53. On a Ruined Farm near the His Master's Voice Gramophone Factory

As I stand at the lichened gate
With warring worlds on either hand—
To left the black and budless trees,
The empty sties, the barns that stand

Like tumbling skeletons—and to right
The factory-towers, white and clear
Like distant, glittering cities seen
From a ship's rail—as I stand here,

I feel, and with a sharper pang,
My mortal sickness; how I give
My heart to weak and stuffless ghosts,
And with the living cannot live.

[1] *Burmese Days.*

The acid smoke has soured the fields,
And browned the few and windworn flowers;
But there, where steel and concrete soar
In dizzy, geometric towers—

There, where the tapering cranes sweep round,
And great wheels turn, and trains roar by
Like strong, low-headed brutes of steel—
There is my world, my home; yet why

So alien still? For I can neither
Dwell in that world, nor turn again
To scythe and spade, but only loiter
Among the trees the smoke has slain.

Yet when the trees were young, men still
Could choose their path—the wingèd soul,
Not cursed with double doubts, could fly
Arrow-like to a foreseen goal;

And they who planned those soaring towers,
They too have set their spirit free;
To them their glittering world can bring
Faith, and accepted destiny;

But none to me as I stand here
Between two countries, both-ways torn,
And moveless still, like Buridan's donkey
Between the water and the corn.

Eric Blair

Adelphi, April 1934; *The Best Poems of 1934*, selected by Thomas Moult.

54. Letter to Leonard Moore

36 High Street
Southwold, Suffolk
11 April 1934

Dear Mr Moore,

Many thanks for your letter. . . . I suppose you haven't heard from Harper's whether their solicitors thought the novel[1] was all right?

[1] *Burmese Days.*

It has been foul weather here and everything is very backward. My novel[1] is not getting on badly, and I have done more than I expected to do in the time, though of course very roughly as yet.

Yours sincerely
Eric A. Blair

55. Letter to Brenda Salkeld (extract)

36 High Street
Southwold, Suffolk
27 July 1934

Many thanks for your last letter. How I wish you were here! I am so miserable, struggling in the entrails of that dreadful book[2] and never getting any further, and loathing the sight of what I have done. *Never* start writing novels, if you wish to preserve your happiness.

I had lunch yesterday with Dr Ede. He is a bit of a feminist and thinks that if a woman was brought up exactly like a man she would be able to throw a stone, construct a syllogism, keep a secret etc. He tells me that my anti-feminist views are probably due to Sadism! I have never read the Marquis de Sade's novels—they are unfortunately very hard to get hold of. Do you remember that afternoon when we had tea with Delisle Burns[3] and I asked him what was the tune of "Malbrouck s'en va-t-en guerre", and he said it was the same as "For he's a jolly good fellow"? And the other night I was passing the King's Head, and the Buffaloes, who were holding one of their secret conclaves in there, were singing it—or rather, as they seemed to be gargling it through pints of beer, what it sounded like was:

Fo-or-*ee's* a jorrigoo' fellow,
For-*ee's* a jorrigoo' fellow,
For-ee's a jorrigoo' fe-ellow—
And toori oori us!

And I could not help thinking again what very peculiar histories

[1] *A Clergyman's Daughter.*

[2] *A Clergyman's Daughter.*

[3] Cecil Delisle Burns (1879–1942), at this time Stevenson Lecturer in Citizenship, Glasgow University. His publications include *Leisure, Horizon of Experience* and *Challenge to Democracy.*

tunes have. To think that Napoleon was whistling, at I forget what battle, the same tune as the Buffaloes were singing! And it struck me that an *idea* is very like a tune in this way, that it goes through the ages remaining the same in itself but getting into such very different company. It is an idea that interests me, and I must use it in my next book. I found Vacandard's history of the Inquisition quite interesting. It is a Catholic history, so you can be sure that you are getting, so to speak, the minimum of everything. It appears, though V himself doesn't mention it, that the pendulum in Poe's story was actually used, though not at such a late date as Poe makes out. Torture was not used in the tribunals of the Inquisition after the middle of the 18th century, but the Pope did not formally abolish it till 1816. Our hedgehog has disappeared. I knew it would be so. It does occasionally come at night (it is somewhere in the next door garden, I think), but we never see it. If I were not fairly busy I should go mad here. I shall have to go up to London in October, but not before, I think, as I doubt if I can finish my novel before then. I don't know when the other[1] is coming out—I haven't had the proofs yet, and I don't know how long it will take after I have corrected the proofs. Write soon and tell me what you are doing.

56. Letter to Brenda Salkeld (extract)

36 High St
Southwold, Suffolk
Tuesday night [late August? 1934]

Many thanks for your letter. I am going up to town as soon as I have finished the book[2] I am doing, which should be at the end of October. I haven't settled yet where I am going to stay, but somewhere in the slums for choice. A friend wrote offering me the lease of part of a flat in Bayswater, but it would choke me to live in Bayswater. No, I have never seen a tortoise drinking. Darwin mentions that when he was in the Galapagos Is the big tortoises there which lived on cactuses & things on the higher ground used to come down into the valley once or twice in the year to drink, & the journey took them a day or two. They stored the water in a kind of sack in their

[1] *Burmese Days.*
[2] *A Clergyman's Daughter.*

bellies. I have been reading some books by Lafcadio Hearne—tiresome stuff, & he idolises the Japanese, who always seem to me such a boring people. I also tried to read Lord Riddell's diary of the Peace Conference & After. What tripe! It is amazing how some people can have the most interesting experiences & then have absolutely nothing to say about them. I went to the pictures last week and saw Jack Hulbert in "Jack Ahoy" which I thought very amusing, & a week or two before that there was quite a good crook film, which, however, my father ruined for me by insisting on telling me the plot beforehand. This week "The Constant Nymph" is on. I haven't been to it, of course, but even when I see the posters it makes me go hot all over to think that in my youth—I think I must have been about 23 when it was published in book form—I was affected by it almost to tears *O mihi praeteritos* etc. I should think that any *critic* who lives to a great age must have many passages in his youth that he would willingly keep dark. There must be, for instance, many critics who in the 'nineties went all mushy over Hall Caine or even Marie Corelli—though M.C isn't so absolutely bad, judging by the only book of hers I ever read. It was called *Thelma* & there was a very licentious clergyman in it who wasn't half bad. Did you, by the way, give me back those books of Swift? It doesn't matter, only I don't want to lose them. Yes, *Roughing It* does "date" a bit, but not enough —because anything worth reading always "dates". I have practically no friends here now, because now that Dennis & Eleanor are married & Dennis has gone to Singapore, it has deprived me of two friends at a single stroke. Everything is going badly. My novel about Burma made me spew when I saw it in print, & I would have rewritten large chunks of it, only that costs money and means delay as well. As for the novel I am now completing, it makes me spew even worse, & yet there *are* some decent passages in it. I don't know how it is, I can write decent passages but I can't put them together. I was rather pluming myself on having a poem in the *Best Poems of 1934*,[1] but I now learn that there are several dozen of these anthologies of the so called best poems of the year, & Ruth Pitter[2] writes to tell me that

[1] "On a Ruined Farm near the His Master's Voice Gramophone Factory". See 53.

[2] Ruth Pitter (1897–), poet, had known Orwell since the time the Blairs lived in Mall Chambers, Notting Hill Gate, just after the First World War. Her works include *Persephone in Hades* and *The Spirit Watches*, both of which he reviewed in the *Adelphi* in September 1932 and February 1940 respectively.

she is in 4 of this year's batch, including one called *Twenty Deathless Poems.*

I nearly died of cold the other day when bathing, because I had walked out to Easton Broad not intending to bathe, & then the water looked so nice that I took off my clothes & went in, & then about 50 people came up & rooted themselves to the spot. I wouldn't have minded that, but among them was a coastguard who could have had me up for bathing naked, so I had to swim up & down for the best part of half an hour, pretending to like it.

57. Letter to Brenda Salkeld (extract)

36 High St
Southwold, Suffolk
Wed. night [early September? 1934]

As you complain about the gloominess of my letters, I suppose I must try and put on what Mr Micawber called the hollow mask of mirth, but I assure you it is not easy, with the life I have been leading lately. My novel,[1] instead of going forwards, goes backwards with the most alarming speed. There are whole wads of it that are so awful that I really don't know what to do with them. And to add to my other joys, the fair, or part of it, has come back and established itself on the common just beyond the cinema, so that I have to work to the accompaniment of roundabout music that goes on till the small hours. You may think that this is red ink I am writing in, but really it is some of the bloody sweat that has been collecting round me in pools for the last few days.

I managed to get my copy of *Ulysses* through safely this time. I rather wish I had never read it. It gives me an inferiority complex. When I read a book like that and then come back to my own work, I feel like a eunuch who has taken a course in voice production and can pass himself off fairly well as a bass or a baritone, but if you listen closely you can hear the good old squeak just the same as ever. I also bought for a shilling a year's issue of a weekly paper of 1851, which is not uninteresting. They ran among other things a matrimonial agency, and the correspondence relating to this is well worth reading. "Flora is twenty one, tall, with rich chestnut hair and a silvery laugh,

[1] *A Clergyman's Daughter.*

and makes excellent light pastry. She would like to enter into correspondence with a professional gentleman between the ages of twenty and thirty, preferably with auburn whiskers and of the Established Church." The interesting thing to me is that these people, since they try to get married through a matrimonial agency, have evidently failed many times elsewhere, and yet as soon as they advertise in this paper, they get half a dozen offers. The women's descriptions of themselves are always most flattering, and I must say that some of the cases make me distinctly suspicious—for of course that was the great age of fortune-hunting. You remember that beautiful case in *Our Mutual Friend*, where both parties worked the same dodge on each other. I most particularly want to get this novel done by the end of September, and every day makes a difference. I know it sounds silly to make such a fuss for so little result, but I find that anything like changing my lodging upsets my work for a week or so. When I said that I was going to stay in a slummy part of London I did not mean that I am going to live in a common lodging house or anything like that. I only meant that I didn't want to live in a respectable quarter, because they make me sick, besides being more expensive. I dare say I shall stay in Islington. It is maddening that you cannot get unfurnished rooms in London, but I know by experience that you can't, though of course you can get a flat or some horrible thing called a maisonette. This age makes me so sick that sometimes I am almost impelled to stop at a corner and start calling down curses from Heaven like Jeremiah or Ezra or somebody—"Woe upon thee, O Israel, for thy adulteries with the Egyptians" etc etc. The hedgehogs keep coming into the house, and last night we found in the bathroom a little tiny hedgehog no bigger than an orange. The only thing I could think was that it was a baby of one of the others, though it was fully formed—I mean, it had its prickles. Write again soon. You don't know how it cheers me up to see one of your letters waiting for me.

58. Letter to Leonard Moore

36 High St
Southwold, Suffolk
3 October 1934

Dear Mr Moore,

I am sending my novel *A Clergyman's Daughter* under a separate cover. I will register it, and trust it will arrive all right. I am not at all pleased with it. It was a good idea, but I am afraid I have made a muck of it—however, it is as good as I can do for the present. There are bits of it that I don't dislike, but I am afraid it is very disconnected as a whole, and rather unreal. Possibly you will be able to find a publisher for it. I should be interested to hear your reader's opinion, and what publisher you intend to try it on. In case the point should come up, the school described in Chapter IV is totally imaginary, though of course I have drawn on my general knowledge of what goes on in schools of that type.

Yes, of course keep a copy of *Burmese Days*[1] when it arrives. By the way, I notice that that anthology of which I told you, in which there is one of my poems,[2] comes from Jonathan Cape. It might be worth mentioning that to him when we show him *Burmese Days*. But I don't think it is at all likely that he would publish that book.

Yours sincerely
Eric A. Blair

Burmese Days *was published in New York by Harper and Brothers on 25 October 1934. Orwell made slight changes in the text as a precaution against possible libel action before it was published in London by Victor Gollancz Ltd on 24 June 1935. The original text was first published in England in May 1944 by Penguin Books.*

59. My Epitaph by John Flory

[The following is an excerpt from an early unpublished draft of *Burmese Days*.]

Goodness knows where they will bury me—in their own grave yard I suppose, two feet deep in a painted coffin. There will be no mourners,

[1] The American edition.

[2] "On a Ruined Farm near the His Master's Voice Gramophone Factory". See 53.

and no rejoicers either, which seems sadder still, for the Burmese celebration of a funeral with music and gambling is nicer than our beastly mummeries. But if there were anyone here whose hand could form the letters, I would like him to carve this on the bark of some great peepul tree above my head.

JOHN FLORY
Born 1890
Died of Drink 1927

"Here lie the bones of poor John Flory;
His story was the old, old story.
Money, women, cards and gin
Were the four things that did him in.

He has spent sweat enough to swim in
Making love to stupid women;
He has known misery past thinking
In the dismal art of drinking.

O stranger, as you voyage here
And read this welcome, shed no tear;
But take the single gift I give,
And learn from me how not to live."

60. Letter to Leonard Moore

3 Warwick Mansions
Pond St
Hampstead NW3
14 November 1934

Dear Mr Moore,
Many thanks for your letter. I hope you can read my handwriting. I have left my typewriter down in the shop.[1]

I knew there would be trouble over that novel.[2] However, I am

[1] Booklovers' Corner, 1 South End Road, Hampstead, where Orwell worked in the autumn of 1934 and throughout 1935 and which he describes in "Bookshop Memories". See 89.

[2] *A Clergyman's Daughter*: Gollancz was afraid of libel in certain passages.

anxious to get it published, as there are parts of it I was pleased with, & I dare say that if I had indicated to me the sort of changes that Mr Gollancz wants, I could manage it. I am willing to admit that the part about the school, which is what seems to have roused people's incredulity, is overdrawn, but not nearly so much so as people think. In fact I was rather amused to see that they say "all that was done away with 30 or 40 years ago" etc as one always hears that any particularly crying abuse was "done away with 30 or 40 years ago". As to this part, it is possible that if Mr Gollancz agrees, a little "toning down" might meet the bill. I don't want to bother you with details about this, however.

As to the points about libel, swearwords etc they are a very small matter & could be put right by a few strokes of the pen. The book does, however, contain an inherent fault of structure which I will discuss with Mr Gollancz, & this could not be rectified in any way that I can think of. I was aware of it when I wrote the book, & imagined that it did not matter, because I did not intend it to be so realistic as people seem to think it is.

I wonder if you could be kind enough to arrange an interview for me with Mr Gollancz? I should think it would take quite an hour to talk over the various points, if he could spare me that much time. I don't particularly mind what day or time I see him, so long as I know a day beforehand so as to let them know at the shop.

I have seen one review of *Burmese Days* in the *Herald Tribune*. Rather a bad one, I am sorry to say—however, big headlines, which I suppose is what counts.

Yours sincerely
Eric A. Blair

1935

61. Letter to Leonard Moore

3 Warwick Mansions
Pond Street
Hampstead NW3
22 January 1935

Dear Mr Moore,

Many thanks for your letter. Naturally I am very pleased to hear that you have made such good terms with Gollancz for *A Clergyman's Daughter*. I am afraid he is going to lose money this time, all right. However, we must hope for the best.

I wonder if you can persuade him, if he puts "Books by the same author", or words to that effect, on the front page, to mention *Burmese Days*. He probably won't want to, as it was published in anomalous circumstances and not by him, but I want that book, if possible, not to be altogether lost sight of.

Yours sincerely
Eric A. Blair

62. Letter to Brenda Salkeld (extract)

Booklovers' Corner
1 South End Road
Hampstead NW3
16 February 1935

Isn't it sickening, I can't keep the room I am in at present for more than a few weeks.

Gollancz, who has re-read *Burmese Days*, wrote enthusiastically about it & said he was going to have it thoroughly vetted by his lawyer, after which the latter was to cross-examine me on all the doubtful points. I hope the lawyer doesn't report against it as he did last time. You notice that all this happened a year ago, & I do not know what has made G change his mind again. Perhaps some other publisher has wiped his eye by publishing a novel about India, but I don't seem to remember any this year. Rees got me a lot more signatures for you,[1] which I will send when I can find them, but at present I have mislaid them. I am living a busy life at present. My time-table is as follows: 7 am get up, dress etc, cook & eat breakfast. 8.45 go down & open the shop, & I am usually kept there till about 9.45. Then come home, do out my room, light the fire etc. 10.30 am –1 pm I do some writing. 1 pm get lunch & eat it. 2 pm–6.30 pm I am at the shop. Then I come home, get my supper, do the washing up & after that sometimes do about an hour's work. In spite [of] all this, I have got more work done in the last few days than during weeks before when I was being harried all day long. I hope G *does* publish *Burmese Days*, as apart from the money (& my agent has tied him down with a pretty good contract) it will tide over the very long interval there is going to be between *A Clergyman's Daughter* & the one[2] I am writing now. I want this one to be a work of art, & that can't be done without much bloody sweat. My mother writes me that she isn't going away after all, so I will come down to S'wold for a week-end as soon as I can, but it will have to be when my employer's wife is up & about again. Write soon.

63. Review

Caliban Shrieks by Jack Hilton

This witty and unusual book may be described as an autobiography without narrative. Mr Hilton lets us know, briefly and in passing, that he is a cotton operative who has been in and out of work for years past, that he served in France during the latter part of the war, and that he has also been on the road, been in prison, etc etc; but he wastes little time in explanations and none in description. In effect his book is a series of comments on life as it appears when one's income is two pounds a week or less. Here, for instance, is Mr Hilton's account of his own marriage:

[1] At this time Brenda Salkeld was collecting autographs of literary figures.
[2] *Keep the Aspidistra Flying.*

> Despite the obvious recognition of marriage's disabilities, the bally thing took place. With it came, not the entrancing mysteries of the bedroom, nor the passionate soul-stirring emotion of two sugar-candied Darby and Joans, but the practical resolve that, come what may, be the furnisher's dues met or no, the rent paid or spent, we—the wife and I—would commemorate our marriage by having, every Sunday morn, ham and eggs for breakfast. So it was we got one over on the poet with his madness of love, the little dove birds, etc.

There are obvious disadvantages in this manner of writing—in particular, it assumes a width of experience which many readers would not possess. On the other hand, the book has a quality which the objective, descriptive kind of book almost invariably misses. It deals with its subject *from the inside*, and consequently it gives one, instead of a catalogue of facts relating to poverty, a vivid notion of what it *feels* like to be poor. All the time that one reads one seems to hear Mr Hilton's voice, and what is more, one seems to hear the voices of the innumerable industrial workers whom he typifies. The humorous courage, the fearful realism and the utter imperviousness to middle-class ideals, which characterise the best type of industrial worker, are all implicit in Mr Hilton's way of talking. This is one of those books that succeed in conveying a frame of mind, and that takes more doing than the mere telling of a story.

Books like this, which come from genuine workers and present a genuinely working-class outlook, are exceedingly rare and correspondingly important. They are the voices of a normally silent multitude. All over England, in every industrial town, there are men by scores of thousands whose attitude to life, if only they could express it, would be very much what Mr Hilton's is. If all of them could get their thoughts on to paper they would change the whole consciousness of our race. Some of them try to do so, of course; but in almost every case, inevitably, what a mess they make of it! I knew a tramp once who was writing his autobiography. He was quite young, but he had had a most interesting life which included, among other things, a jail-escape in America, and he could talk about it entrancingly. But as soon as he took a pen in his hand he became not only boring beyond measure but utterly unintelligible. His prose style was modelled upon *Peg's Paper* ("With a wild cry I sank in a stricken heap" etc), and his ineptitude with words was so great that after wading through two pages of laboured description you could not even be certain what he was attempting to describe. Looking back upon that autobiography, and a number of similar documents that I have seen, I realise what a considerable literary gift must have gone to the making of Mr Hilton's book.

As to the sociological information that Mr Hilton provides, I have only one fault to find. He has evidently not been in the Casual Ward since the years just after the war, and he seems to have been taken in by the lie, widely published during the last few years, to the effect that casual paupers are now given a "warm meal" at midday. I could a tale unfold about those "warm meals". Otherwise, all his facts are entirely accurate so far as I am able to judge, and his remarks on prison life, delivered with an extraordinary absence of malice, are some of the most interesting that I have read.

Adelphi, March 1935

64. Letter to Brenda Salkeld (extract)

77 Parliament Hill
Hampstead NW3.[1]
7 March 1935

Just a line to thank you for your nice letter and to tell you that I sent off your copy of *A Clergyman's Daughter* last night. As you will see, it is tripe, except for chap 3, part 1, which I am pleased with, but I don't know whether *you* will like it. It is billed to come out on Monday next, so don't show it to anyone before that, will you? I am glad to say my agent has made very good terms for *Burmese Days*.

No, I *don't* feed entirely on things that don't need cooking. I have bought a small gas-stove called a Bachelor Griller, and you can grill, boil and fry on it, but not bake. As a matter of fact I can cook not too badly, and I have already given a dinner-party to three people all at once and cooked everything myself. But of course I haven't much time, because I still have to go to the shop for about an hour in the morning besides the afternoon, and it is a struggle to get

[1] Orwell had rented a furnished room at this address in the flat of Mrs Rosalind Obermeyer, who was studying for a diploma in psychology at University College London. It was she who introduced Orwell to Eileen O'Shaughnessy, his future wife, who was also studying psychology at the same college.

in three hours a day at my writing. The other night I went to the Coliseum to see the so-called Blackbirds—a troop of negro actors—and was bored stiff. I mean if I get time to go and see George Robey as Falstaff. I dare say he could do the part if he would sink his own personality. I have bought an awfully nice set of chessmen—wood, not ivory, but they are beautiful big pieces, weighted, and the white ones are real boxwood. The other day my employer was at a house buying books, and they offered him these chessmen, and he bought them for a *shilling*. We were going to put them in the window at ten shillings, but I bought them in for seven and six instead. They would cost thirty shillings new, I should say. I must say I do see some queer interiors when I go out to fetch books that we buy. The other day I went to a house inhabited by an old woman and her middle-aged daughter, and I was just about to look at the books when every light in the house fused. Of course these two women were helpless, so with that chivalry which you have so often noticed in me I spent half an hour crawling about among the rafters with candles and bits of ginger-beer wire, mending the fuse. I have been reading a lot of back numbers of the *Criterion*—a paper I don't normally see, as it costs seven and sixpence, but we bought some among some books. I must say that for pure snootiness it beats anything I have ever seen. Here is T. S. Eliot on the servant-problem as seen from the Anglo-Catholic standpoint: "I do not like the situation (i.e. of having only one servant). . . . I should prefer to employ a large staff of servants, each doing much lighter work but profiting by the benefits of the cultured and devout atmosphere of the home in which they lived." That bit about the cultured and devout atmosphere reminds me, as Samuel Butler said of a cracked church bell he heard somewhere, of the smell of a bug. I must stop now. You will see if you read *A Clergyman's Daughter* that I have employed you as a collaborator in two places.

***A Clergyman's Daughter** was published in London by Victor Gollancz Ltd on 11 March 1935 and in New York by Harper and Brothers on 17 August 1936.*

65. Letter to Rayner Heppenstall

50 Lawford Rd
Kentish Town NW
Tuesday night [September? 1935]

Dear Rayner,[1]
Many thanks for letter. I hope the enclosed MS is what you wanted. I infer from what you would no doubt call your handwriting that you were taught script at school; the result is that I can't read a single word of the manuscript part of your letter, so I may not have followed your instructions exactly.

I am suffering unspeakable torments with my serial,[2] having already been at it four days and being still at the second page. This is because I sat down and wrote what was not a bad first instalment, and then upon counting it up found it was 3500 words instead of 2000. Of course this means rewriting it entirely. I don't think I am cut out for a serial-writer. I shall be glad to get back to my good old novel[3] where one has plenty of elbow room. I have three more chapters and an epilogue to do, and then I shall spend about two months putting on the twiddly bits.

Even if my serial doesn't come to anything, and I don't expect it to, I intend taking a week or so off next month. My people have asked me to come down and stay with them, and if I can get my sister to drive me over, as I don't think I can drive her present car, I will come over and see you. I don't know that part of the country, but if it is like ours it must be nice this time of year.

I forwarded a letter this evening which had urgent proofs on it. I hope it gets to you in time, but it had already been to your old address. You ought to let editors and people know that you have changed your address.

[1] Rayner Heppenstall (1911–   ), novelist, poet and critic, whose works include *The Blaze of Noon* and *Four Absentees*, met Orwell in the spring of 1935 through Sir Richard Rees. In the summer of that year Heppenstall, Orwell and Michael Sayers, who contributed short stories and criticism to the *Adelphi*, began sharing a flat at the above address.

[2] It is not known what this serial was.

[3] *Keep the Aspidistra Flying.*

You are right about Eileen.[1] She is the nicest person I have met for a long time. However, at present alas! I can't afford a ring, except perhaps a Woolworth's one. Michael[2] was here last night with Edna and we all had dinner together. He told me he has a story in the anthology of stories that is coming out, but he seemed rather down in the mouth about something. I was over at the Fierz' place on Sunday and met Brenda[3] and Maurice[4] whom no doubt you remember, and they were full of a story apparently current among Communists to the effect that Col. Lawrence[5] is not really dead but staged a fake death and is now in Abyssinia. I did not like Lawrence, but I would like this story to be true.

Au revoir. Please remember me to the Murrys.[6]

Yours
Eric A. Blair

66. Letter to Rayner Heppenstall

50 Lawford Rd
Kentish Town NW
5 October 1935

Dear Rayner,

I managed to dig out your things, but only "après plaingtz et pleurs at angoisseux gemissements". I trust they are the right ones. I sent off my bloody serial-instalment and synopsis about a week ago, but don't expect them to accept it. It is too much out of my line. If they *do* accept, I shall take about three weeks off, and shall probably go

[1] Eileen Maud O'Shaughnessy, daughter of Laurence O'Shaughnessy, a Collector of Customs, and Marie O'Shaughnessy, was born on 25 September 1905 in South Shields and was educated at Sunderland High School. She read English at St Hugh's College, Oxford, and, after taking her degree in 1927, was successively a teacher, secretary to a business woman and journalist on a London newspaper. In September 1934 she had begun a two-year course at University College London studying for an MA in psychology.

[2] Michael Sayers.

[3] Brenda Verstone.

[4] Maurice Oughton.

[5] T. E. Lawrence (Lawrence of Arabia).

[6] Rayner Heppenstall was staying with John Middleton Murry in Norfolk.

and stay somewhere near London where I can be in country air but come up to town once a week to see to the shop.[1] If they *don't*, I shall in any case take a week off, and shall probably come down to S'wold in which case I will come over and see you. I am very happy to have got back to my novel,[2] which is going not badly. I haven't seen Michael[3] for some time. Eileen says she won't marry me as yet (of course you won't repeat these things I tell you about E etc) as she is not earning any money at present and doesn't want to be a drag on me. However, that will arrange itself later when she has finished her course[4] at London University, and besides perhaps I shall be earning more next year. On the other hand by next year we may all have been blown sky-high. I was down at Greenwich the other day and looking at the river I thought what wonders a few bombs would work among the shipping. Last night I went with Geoffrey Gorer[5] to see Greta Garbo in "Anna Karenina"—not too bad. Please remember me to the Murrys.

Yours
Eric

67. Review

Tropic of Cancer by Henry Miller

Modern man is rather like a bisected wasp which goes on sucking jam and pretends that the loss of its abdomen does not matter. It is some perception of this fact which brings books like *Tropic of Cancer* (for there will probably be more and more of them as time goes on) into being.

Tropic of Cancer is a novel, or perhaps rather a chunk of autobiography, about Americans in Paris—not the moneyed dilettante type, but the out-at-elbow, good-for-nothing type. There is much in

[1] Booklovers' Corner.

[2] *Keep the Aspidistra Flying.*

[3] Michael Sayers.

[4] Eileen O'Shaughnessy's psychology course was due to finish in June 1936.

[5] Geoffrey Gorer (1905–   ), social anthropologist, whose books include *Africa Dances, The Revolutionary Ideas of the Marquis de Sade, The American People* and *Exploring English Character*. Gorer had written Orwell a fan letter about *Burmese Days*. They met and remained friends until Orwell's death.

it that is remarkable, but its most immediately noticeable and perhaps essential feature is its descriptions of sexual encounters. These are interesting not because of any pornographic appeal (quite the contrary), but because they make a definite attempt to get at real facts. They describe sexual life from the point of view of the man in the street—but, it must be admitted, rather a debased version of the man in the street. Nearly all the characters in the book are *habitués* of the brothel. They act and describe their actions with a callous coarseness which is unparalleled in fiction, though common enough in real life. Taken as a whole, the book might even be called a vilification of human nature. As it may justly be asked what good is done by vilifying human nature, I must amplify the remark I made above.

One result of the breakdown of religious belief has been a sloppy idealisation of the physical side of life. In a way this is natural enough. For if there is no life beyond the grave, it is obviously harder to face the fact that birth, copulation, etc are in certain aspects disgusting. In the Christian centuries, of course, a pessimistic view of life was taken more or less for granted. "Man that is born of woman hath but a short time to live and is full of misery", says the Prayer Book, with the air of stating something obvious. But it is a different matter to admit that life is full of misery when you believe that the grave really finishes you. It is easier to comfort yourself with some kind of optimistic lie. Hence the tee-heeing brightness of *Punch*, hence Barrie and his bluebells, hence H. G. Wells and his Utopiae infested by nude school-marms. Hence, above all, the monstrous soppification of the sexual theme in most of the fiction of the past hundred years. A book like *Tropic of Cancer*, which deals with sex by brutally insisting on the facts, swings the pendulum too far, no doubt, but it does swing it in the right direction. Man is not a Yahoo, but he is rather like a Yahoo and needs to be reminded of it from time to time. All one asks of a book of this kind is that it shall do its job competently and without snivelling—conditions that are satisfied in this case, I think.

Probably, although he chooses to describe ugly things, Mr Miller would not answer to the name of pessimist. He even has passages of rather Whitmanesque enthusiasm for the process of life. What he seems to be saying is that if one stiffens oneself by the contemplation of ugliness, one ends by finding life not less but more worth living. From a literary point of view his book is competent, though not dazzlingly so. It is firmly done, with very few lapses into the typical modern slipshoddy [sic]. If it attracts critical attention it will no doubt be coupled with *Ulysses*, quite wrongly. *Ulysses* is not only a vastly better book, but also quite different in intention. Joyce is primarily an artist; Mr Miller is a discerning though hardboiled person giving his opinions about life. I find his prose difficult to quote, because of the unprintable words which are scattered all over it, but here is one sample:

> When the tide is on the ebb and only a few syphilitic mermaids are left stranded in the muck the Dôme looks like a shooting gallery that's been struck by a cyclone. Everything is slowly dribbling back to the sewer. For about an hour there is a death-like calm during which the vomit is mopped up. Suddenly the trees begin to screech. From one end of the boulevard to the other a demented song rises up. It is the signal that announces the close of the exchange. What hopes there were are swept up. The moment has come to void the last bagful of urine. The day is sneaking in like a leper. . . .

There is a fine rhythm to that. The American language is less flexible and refined than the English, but it has more life in it, perhaps. I do not imagine that in *Tropic of Cancer* I have discovered the great novel of the century, but I do think it a remarkable book, and I strongly advise anyone who can get hold of a copy to have a look at it.

New English Weekly, 14 November 1935

1936

68. [On Kipling's Death]

Rudyard Kipling was the only popular English writer of this century who was not at the same time a thoroughly bad writer. His popularity was, of course, essentially middle-class. In the average middle-class family before the War, especially in Anglo-Indian families, he had a prestige that is not even approached by any writer of today. He was a sort of household god with whom one grew up and whom one took for granted whether one liked him or whether one did not. For my own part I worshipped Kipling at thirteen, loathed him at seventeen, enjoyed him at twenty, despised him at twenty-five, and now again rather admire him. The one thing that was never possible, if one had read him at all, was to forget him. Certain of his stories, for instance "The Strange Ride", "Drums of the Fore and Aft" and "The Mark of the Beast", are about as good as it is possible for that kind of story to be. They are, moreover, exceedingly well told. For the vulgarity of his prose style is only a surface fault; in the less obvious qualities of construction and economy he is supreme. It is, after all (see the *Times Literary Supplement*), much easier to write inoffensive prose than to tell a good story. And his verse, though it is almost a byword for badness, has the same peculiarly memorable quality.

> I've lost Britain, I've lost Gaul,
> I've lost Rome, and, worst of all,
> I've lost Lalage!

may be only a jingle, and "The Road to Mandalay" may be something worse than a jingle, but they do "stay by one". They remind one that it needs a streak of genius even to become a byword.

What is much more distasteful in Kipling than sentimental plots or vulgar tricks of style, is the imperialism to which he chose to lend his genius. The most one can say is that when he made it the choice was more forgivable than it would be now. The imperialism of the 'eighties and 'nineties was sentimental, ignorant and dangerous, but it was not entirely despicable. The picture then called up by the word "empire" was a picture of overworked officials and frontier skirmishes, not of Lord Beaverbrook and Australian butter. It was still possible to be an imperialist and a gentleman, and of Kipling's *personal* decency there can be no doubt. It is worth remembering that he was the most widely popular English writer of our time, and yet that no one, perhaps, so consistently refrained from making a vulgar show of his personality.

If he had never come under imperialist influences, and if he had developed, as he might well have done, into a writer of music-hall songs, he would have been a better and more lovable writer. In the rôle he actually chose, one was bound to think of him, after one had grown up, as a kind of enemy, a man of alien and perverted genius. But now that he is dead, I for one cannot help wishing that I could offer some kind of tribute—a salute of guns, if such a thing were available—to the story-teller who was so important to my childhood.

New English Weekly, 23 January 1936

69. Review

The Lively Lady by Kenneth Roberts, *War Paint* by F. V. Morley, *Long Shadows* by Lady Sanderson, *Who Goes Home?* by Richard Curle, *Gaudy Night* by Dorothy Sayers

When is a novel not a novel?

Take almost any serial from *Peg's Paper* or *Violet's Paper*, paragraph it in a civilised manner, give it a sophisticated title (this is done by choosing a title that ought to have a "the" in it and then leaving out the "the"), and it will be found to be quite indistinguishable from four-fifths of the things that pass as novels nowadays. As a matter of fact, several of the books on my present list are rather worse than *Peg's Paper*, because they are just as infantile and vulgar and have much less vitality. However, with ten books[1] to review I have no space for a jeremiad on the present state of English fiction. So here goes.

The Lively Lady and *War Paint* are both of them historical novels

[1] This extract covers only five of the ten books.

dealing with approximately the same period—the period of the Napoleonic War. *The Lively Lady* is written by an American. It is blood-and-thundery stuff about privateering in the war of 1812, and is chiefly interesting as showing that the old-fashioned nineteenth-century type of American bumptiousness ("The libation of freedom must sometimes be quaffed in blood" etc) is still going strong. *War Paint*, though written by an Englishman, is also about Americans. It is an exceedingly naïve adventure story, and at the same time a sort of Chelsea Hospital for superannuated jokes. For my own part I don't object to old jokes—indeed, I reverence them. When sea-sickness and adultery have ceased to be funny, western civilisation will have ceased to exist. But with the plot of a story it is a rather different matter; there, I think, we have a right to expect something new. I would like to draw Mr Morley's attention to a certain chapter in the middle of his book and to a certain story of Conan Doyle's entitled "The Striped Chest".

After this we take a dive into the sewers of literature. I see no reason to be polite to a book like *Long Shadows*. It is tripe. One quotation should be enough:

> . . . the house was folded in the silence of night, while towards it, all unseen in the darkness, came the spirit of the past, stirred from its long rest and bringing who can say what joy and sorrow to those on whom its shadow should fall?

Who Goes Home? is perhaps a very little better. It is a mystery-story, and it does work up a faint flicker of interest as to what is going to happen. But what English! It is amazing that people can go on turning out books year after year and yet continue to write so badly. Here for example is a sentence (it has points of interest for the social historian) explaining why the villain was a villain:

> Gore's background was austere and bourgeois, but perhaps long ago there had been some frustrated poet in the family, to say nothing of some would-be swindler or worse, and perhaps their influence had mysteriously fused in him.

The moral would seem to be, never frustrate a poet.

I do not share the opinion expressed in the *Observer* that *Gaudy Night* puts Miss Sayers "definitely among the great writers", but there is no doubt that as far as literary ability goes she is out of the class of the other writers I am considering here. Yet even she, if one looks closely, is not so far removed from *Peg's Paper* as might appear at a casual glance. It is, after all, a very ancient trick to write novels with a lord for a hero. Where Miss Sayers has shown more astuteness than most is in perceiving that you can carry that kind of thing off a great deal better if you pretend to treat it as a joke. By being, on the surface, a little ironical about Lord Peter Wimsey and his noble ancestors, she is enabled to lay on the snobbishness ("his lordship" etc.) much thicker than any overt snob would dare to do. Also, her slickness in writing has blinded many readers to the fact that her stories, considered as detective stories, are very bad ones. They lack the minimum of probability that even a detective story ought to have, and the crime is always committed in a way that is incredibly tortuous and quite uninteresting. In *Gaudy Night* Harriet Vane has at last succumbed to Lord Peter's advances. So it is time that Lord Peter, who is now forty-five, settled down and gave up detection. But needless to say he won't. He and his title are a lot too profitable for that. A little bird in a yellow jacket[1] has just whispered to me that next year there will be another corpse in the library and Lord Peter and Harriet (Viscountess Wimsey?) will be off on a fresh quest.

New English Weekly, 23 January 1936

70. Letter to Cyril Connolly

Warrington Lane
Wigan, Lancashire
14 February 1936

Dear Connolly,[2]
I was sorry I missed seeing you again before leaving London. When is your novel[3] coming out? I will write to the Obelisk Press[4] (by the

[1] Gollancz's books had yellow dust-jackets.

[2] Cyril Connolly, (1903–), the author and critic, editor of *Horizon* (1940–50). A contemporary of Orwell's at St Cyprian's and Eton, he remained a friend until Orwell's death. In a conversation with Denys King-Farlow Orwell said, "Without Connolly's help I don't think I would have got started as a writer when I came back from Burma."

[3] *The Rock Pool*. See 83.

[4] The Obelisk Press was a publishing house run from Paris between the wars by Jack Kahane. He published books in English for the continental market, many of which were considered too risky for English publishers to handle, and many of which later became "classics".

way you might tell me their address) & ask for a copy, & then I expect I can either review it or get it reviewed for the *New English Weekly*. Not that that gives one much of a boost, but every little helps. Possibly also the *Adelphi*, but this I doubt, as they now fight shy of everything that hasn't a political implication.

I am living here with a family of coal-miners, employed & unemployed.[1] After staying a month in Lancs. I intend to go on to Yorkshire or Durham or both & have a look at the mines & miners there. I haven't been down any coal mines yet but am arranging to do so. The miners here are very nice people, very warm-hearted & willing to take me for granted. I would like to stay a good long time in the north, 6 months or a year, only it means being away from my girl & also I shall have to come back & do some work after about a couple of months. I am just correcting the proofs of my novel,[2] which should be out in about a month I suppose; otherwise not doing any work, as it is impossible in these surroundings.

I suppose you heard about Alan Clutton-Brock's wife?[3] A bad job, & he has two small kids, too.

Yours
Eric A. Blair

PS. This address will find me for abt 3 weeks, not longer.

Encounter, January 1962

71. Letter to Sir Richard Rees, Bt.

Darlington Street
Wigan, Lancs.
29 February 1936

Dear Richard,

I thought you might like a line to hear how I am getting on in partibus infidelium. Your introductions were of the greatest value to me, especially that to Meade,[4] who put me in touch with a friend

[1] Victor Gollancz had commissioned Orwell to write a book about working-class conditions in the north of England. It was published under the title *The Road to Wigan Pier*.

[2] *Keep the Aspidistra Flying*.

[3] Alan Clutton-Brock, art critic and contemporary of Orwell at Eton. His wife had been killed in a motor accident.

[4] Frank Meade, of Longsight, Manchester: an official of the Amalgamated Society of Woodworkers. He ran the Manchester office of the *Adelphi* and was

at Wigan who was exactly what I wanted. I have been here nearly three weeks and have collected reams of notes and statistics, though in what way I shall use them I haven't made up my mind yet. I have been living and associating almost entirely with miners, largely unemployed of course. The lads at the NUWM[1] have been of great service to me and everyone has been most willing to answer questions and show me over their houses. I have gone into the housing question rather minutely, because it is a very urgent one here and I gather in most places in the north. I have only been down one coal mine so far but hope to go down some more in Yorkshire. It was for me a pretty devastating experience and it is a fearful thought that the labour of crawling as far as the coal face (about a mile in this case but as much as 3 miles in some mines), which was enough to put my legs out of action for four days, is only the beginning and ending of a miner's day's work, and his real work comes in between. Have you ever been down a mine? I don't think I shall ever feel quite the same about coal again.

I went over and saw the Deiners[2] and Garrett[3] earlier this week. Unfortunately I was ill while there and so not at my best, but I had some long talks with G and was greatly impressed by him. Had I known before that he was "Matt Low", I should have taken steps to meet him earlier. I am leaving Wigan on Monday, going to stay a couple of nights at Sheffield to meet your friend Brown,[4] then on to Leeds to stay a day or two with my sister[5] till I can find some miner's house to stay at in Barnsley. I may also go up to Durham for a little while but I am not sure—the trouble is that the travelling is rather expensive. I am coming back to town about the end of March and then perhaps may be able to do some work again—impossible, of course, in these surroundings. I am arranging to take a cottage at Wallington near Baldock in Herts, rather a pig in a poke because

---

business manager of *Labour's Northern Voice*, the organ of the Independent Socialist Party.

[1] National Unemployed Workers' Movement.

[2] John Stanley Deiner, telephone engineer, and his wife May, who lived in Liverpool and were connected with John Middleton Murry and the *Adelphi*.

[3] George Garrett, of Liverpool, seaman, Marxist, short story writer and critic who also wrote under the name of Matt Low for Middleton Murry's *Adelphi*.

[4] William Brown, an unemployed man in Sheffield, who contributed Marxist articles to the *Adelphi*.

[5] Marjorie, married to Humphrey Dakin, a civil servant at the National Savings Committee.

I have never seen it, but I am trusting the friends who have chosen it for me, and it is very cheap, only 7/6 a week. My novel[1] ought to be out in a few weeks. There was the usual last-minute stew about libel, this time, unfortunately after it was in proof so that I had to spoil a whole chapter with alterations. This business of libel is becoming a nightmare—it appears that there now exist firms of crook solicitors who make a regular income by blackmailing publishers. However I hope I may get an American edition of my novel printed unmutilated.

Meade said something about your coming up north a little later, but I expect it will be after I have returned home. Let me know about your movements.

Yours
Eric A. Blair

Encounter, January 1962

72. Review of Penguin Books

Esther Waters by George Moore, *Our Mr Wrenn* by Sinclair Lewis, *Dr Serocold* by Helen Ashton, *The Owls' House* by Crosbie Garstin, *Hangman's House* by Donn Byrne, *Odd Craft* by W. W. Jacobs, *Naval Occasions* by Bartimeus, *My Man Jeeves* by P. G. Wodehouse, *Autobiography* (Vol. I) by Margot Asquith, *Autobiography* (Vol. II) by Margot Asquith. All published by John Lane, The Bodley Head in the Penguin Library, Third Series, at sixpence.

The Penguin Books are splendid value for sixpence, so splendid that if the other publishers had any sense they would combine against them and suppress them. It is, of course, a great mistake to imagine that cheap books are good for the book trade. Actually it is just the other way about. If you have, for instance, five shillings to spend and the normal price of a book is half-a-crown, you are quite likely to spend your whole five shillings on two books. But if books are sixpence each you are not going to buy ten of them, because you don't want as many as ten; your saturation-point will have been reached long before that. Probably you will buy three sixpenny books and spend the rest of your five shillings on seats at the "movies". Hence the cheaper books become, the less money is spent on books. This

[1] *Keep the Aspidistra Flying.*

is an advantage from the reader's point of view and doesn't hurt trade as a whole, but for the publisher, the compositor, the author and the bookseller it is a disaster.

As for the present batch of Penguin Books—the third batch of ten —far and away the best of them, of course, is *Esther Waters.* I do not know Moore's work very well, but I cannot believe that he ever did anything better than this. It was written by a man whose fingers were all thumbs and who had not learned some of the most elementary tricks of the novelist, for instance, how to introduce a new character, but the book's fundamental sincerity makes its surface faults almost negligible. Moore's great advantage as a novelist lay in not having an over-developed sense of pity; hence he could resist the temptation to make his characters more sensitive than they would be in real life. *Esther Waters* is in the same class as *Of Human Bondage* —both of them books which are stuffed full of literary faults but which are not likely to drop out of favour.

Sinclair Lewis's *Our Mr Wrenn* is a weak early work which hardly seems worth reprinting. Presumably it was chosen because the copyright of *Babbitt* or *Elmer Gantry* would have been too expensive. *Dr Serocold* is good of its kind—it describes a day in the life of a country doctor—and must not be judged by its appalling last sentence. According to Miss E. M. Delafield, the only cases that doctors in fiction ever attend are confinements. Miss Ashton, who is a doctor herself, has evidently noticed this tendency and avoided it. Crosbie Garstin I cannot do with, nor with Donn Byrne—the latter, I think, still has a biggish reputation, but he was too like a professional Irishman for my taste. It would be interesting to know whether W. W. Jacobs keeps his popularity. On his low level he is as good a short story writer as we have had. His stories look as though they grew together. But their range is tiny, and they depend upon the Punch-like notion that a working-class person, as such, is a figure of fun and possesses no sense of honour. I should expect a Communist to describe *Odd Craft* as ideologically poisonous, which indeed it is.

I suppose I ought not to be rude to *Naval Occasions,* which I greatly enjoyed when I was a little boy just before the war. Those were the great days of the Navy's popularity. Small boys wore sailor suits, and everyone belonged to something called the Navy League and had a bronze medal which cost a shilling, and the popular slogan was "We want eight (dreadnoughts) and we won't wait!" Bartimeus, I fancy, aspired to be the Kipling of the Navy and merely succeeded in being a rather more naïve and likeable Ian Hay. It was a pity not to choose a better Wodehouse book than *My Man Jeeves*, which was the first of its series and contains at least one story which has since been reissued in a better form. Still, it was a great day for Mr Wodehouse when he created Jeeves, and thus escaped from the realm of comedy, which in England always stinks of virtue, into the realm of pure farce. The great charm of Jeeves is that (although he did pronounce Nietzsche to be "fundamentally unsound") he is beyond good and evil.

Finally, there are the two volumes of Lady Asquith's autobiography. This, I admit, I have never been able to read *in toto*, either now or when it first appeared. If you are born into one of our governing families and spend your life in political circles, you are bound to meet interesting people, but you don't, it seems, necessarily learn to write decent English. I remember that some French novelist, describing a letter he had received from a lady of title, said: "Her style was that of a concierge."

In my capacity as reader I applaud the Penguin Books; in my capacity as writer I pronounce them anathema. Hutchinson are now bringing out a very similar edition, though only of their own books, and if the other publishers follow suit, the result may be a flood of cheap reprints which will cripple the lending libraries (the novelist's foster-mother) and check the output of new novels. This would be a fine thing for literature, but it would be a very bad thing for trade, and when you have to choose between art and money—well, finish it for yourself.

New English Weekly, 5 March 1936

73. Letter to Jack Common

Agnes Terrace
Barnsley, Yorks.
17 March 1936

Dear Common,[1]

Would you like a short review of Alec Browne's [sic] book *The Fate of the Middle Classes*?[2] Or is someone else doing it for you? I have scrounged a free copy and it seems not an uninteresting book, at any rate it is on an important subject, and I thought I might, e.g. do a few lines for the *Adelphi* Forum[3] on it.

I have been in these barbarous regions for about two months and have had a very interesting time and picked up a lot of ideas for my next book,[4] but I admit I am beginning to pine to be back in the languorous South and also to start doing some work again, which of course is impossible in the surroundings I have been in. My next novel[5] ought to be out shortly. It would have been out a month ago only there was one of those fearful last-minute scares about libel and I was made to alter it to the point of ruining it utterly. What particularly stuck in my gizzard was that the person who dictated the alterations to me was that squirt Norman Collins.[6] Do you want a copy sent to the *Adelphi*? If you think you could get it reviewed I will have them send a copy, but not if you haven't space to spare. I went to the *Adelphi* offices[7] in Manchester and saw Higginbottom

[1] Jack Common (1903–), writer and editor, of working-class origin. Had worked in a solicitor's office, in a shoe shop and as a mechanic. In June 1930 he joined the *Adelphi* as circulation pusher. Became assistant editor 1932; editor 1935–6. His publications include *The Freedom of the Streets*, *Seven Shifts* (edited and with a preface), *Kiddar's Luck* and *The Ampersand*. He met Orwell as a young contributor to the *Adelphi* and they remained friends.

[2] Orwell's review of *The Fate of the Middle Classes* by Alec Brown appeared in the *Adelphi*, May 1936.

[3] The *Adelphi* Forum was described by the editor as being "open for short topical comments and for the expression of opinion which may be entirely different from our own".

[4] *The Road to Wigan Pier*.

[5] *Keep the Aspidistra Flying*.

[6] Norman Collins (1907–), author of *London Belongs To Me* (published in the United States as *Dulcimer Street*) and *Children of the Archbishop*. Deputy Chairman of Victor Gollancz Ltd 1934–41; Controller Light Programme BBC 1946–47.

[7] On the initiative of a number of Middleton Murry's northern admirers, the printing and publishing organisation of the *Adelphi* had been taken over by the

[sic][1] several times, also Meade with whom I stayed several days. I may tell you in case you don't know that there are fearful feuds and intrigues going on among the followers of the *Adelphi* and I will tell you about these when I see you. I didn't say anything of this to Rees when I wrote, because I thought his feelings might be hurt.

What about the international situation? Is it war? I think not, because if the government have any sense at all they must realise that they haven't got the country behind them. I think things will remain uneasily in statu quo and the war will break out later, possibly this autumn. If you notice wars tend to break out in the autumn, perhaps because continental governments don't care to mobilise until they have got the harvest in.

I heard Mosley[2] speak here on Sunday. It sickens one to see how easily a man of that type can win over and bamboozle a working class audience. There was some violence by the Blackshirts, as usual, and I am going to write to the *Times*, about it, but what hope of their printing my letter?[3]

I shall be at the above address till about the 25th, after that returning to London, by sea if I can manage it. Hoping to see you some time after that,

Yours
Eric A. Blair

Workers' Northern Publishing Society in Manchester. In the early 'thirties Murry found himself at the head of a breakaway segment of the Independent Labour Party, known as the Independent Socialist Party—a short-lived phenomenon. It was from these *Adelphi* supporters that, when Orwell was commissioned by Gollancz to write a book on working-class conditions in the north, Richard Rees gave him names as contacts.

[1] Sam Higenbottam, a contributor to the *Adelphi*, a Socialist, and author of *Our Society's History*, a history of the Amalgamated Society of Woodworkers.

[2] Sir Oswald Mosley, Bt. (1896–), politician, successively Conservative, Independent and Labour Member of Parliament. In 1931 he broke away from the Labour Party to form the "New Party". Later he became fanatically pro-Hitler and turned his party into the British Union of Fascists. His followers were known as Blackshirts.

[3] Orwell wrote the letter, but *The Times* did not publish it.

74. *The Road to Wigan Pier* Diary 31 January–25 March 1936

[This is a typescript diary found among Orwell's papers which, with other notes, formed the basis for *The Road to Wigan Pier.*]

31 January

To Coventry by train as arranged, arriving about 4 pm. Bed and Breakfast house, very lousy, 3/6d. Framed certificate in hall setting forth that (John Smith) had been elected to the rank of Primo Buffo. Two beds in room—charge for room to yourself 5/–. Smell as in common lodging houses. Half-witted servant girl with huge body, tiny head and rolls of fat at back of neck curiously recalling ham-fat.

1 February

Lousy breakfast with Yorkshire commercial traveller. Walked 12 miles to outskirts of Birmingham, took bus to Bull Ring (very like Norwich Market) and arrived 1 pm. Lunch in Birmingham and bus to Stourbridge. Walked 4–5 miles to Clent Youth Hostel. Red soil everywhere. Birds courting a little, cock chaffinches and bullfinches very bright and cock partridge making mating call. Except for village of Meriden, hardly a decent house between Coventry and Birmingham. West of Birmingham the usual villa-civilisation creeping out over the hills. Raining all day, on and off.

Distance walked, 16 miles. Spent on conveyances, 1/4d. On food, 2/3d.

2 February

Comfortable night in hostel, which I had to myself. One-storey wooden building with huge coke stove which kept it very hot. You pay 1/– for bed, 2d for the stove and put pennies in the gas for cooking. Bread, milk, etc on sale at hostel. You have to have your own sleeping bag but get blankets, mattress and pillows. Tiring evening because the warden's son, I suppose out of kindness, came across and played ping-pong with me till I could hardly stand on my feet. In the morning long talk with the warden who keeps poultry and collects glass and pewter. He told me how in France in 1918, on the heels of the retreating Germans, he looted some priceless glass which was discovered and looted from him in turn by his divisional general. Also showed me some nice pieces of pewter and some very curious Japanese pictures, showing clear traces of European influence, looted by his father in some naval expedition about 1860.

Left 10 am, walked to Stourbridge, took bus to Wolverhampton, wandered about slummy parts of Wolverhampton for a while, then had lunch and walked 10 miles to Penkridge. Wolverhampton seems frightful place. Everywhere vistas of mean little houses still enveloped in drifting smoke, though this was Sunday, and along the railway line huge banks of clay and conical chimneys ("pot-banks"). Walk from W'ton to Penkridge very dull and raining all the way. Villa-civilisation stretches almost unbroken between the two towns. In Penkridge about 4.30 halted for cup of tea. A tiny frowzy parlour with a nice fire, a little wizened oldish man and an enormous woman about 45, with tow-coloured bobbed hair and no front teeth. Both of them thought me a hero to be walking on such a day. Had tea with them en famille. About 5.15 left and walked another couple of miles, then caught bus the remaining 4 miles to Stafford. Went to Temperance Hotel thinking this would be cheap, but bed and breakfast 5/–. The usual dreadful room and twill sheets greyish and smelly as usual. Went to bathroom and found commercial traveller developing snapshots in bath. Persuaded him to remove them and had bath, after which I find myself very footsore.

Distance walked, about 16 miles. Spent on conveyances, 1/5d. On food, 2/8½d.

3 February

Left 9 am and took bus to Hanley. Walked round Hanley and part of Burslem. Frightfully cold, bitter wind, and it had been snowing in the night; blackened snow lying about everywhere. Hanley and Burslem about the most dreadful places I have seen. Labyrinths of tiny blackened houses and among them the pot-banks like monstrous burgundy bottles half buried in the soil, belching forth smoke. Signs of poverty everywhere and very poor shops. In places enormous chasms delved out, one of them about 200 yards wide and about as deep, with rusty iron trucks on a chain railway crawling up one side, and here and there on the almost perpendicular face of the other, a few workmen hanging like samphire-gatherers, cutting into the face with their picks apparently aimlessly, but I suppose digging out clay. Walked on to Eldon and lunch at pub there. Frightfully cold. Hilly country, splendid views, especially when one gets further east and hedges give way to stone walls. Lambs here seem much more backward than down south. Walked on to Rudyard Lake.

Rudyard Lake (really a reservoir, supplying the pottery towns) very depressing. In the summer it is a pleasure resort. Cafés, house-boats and pleasure-boats every ten yards, all deserted and flyblown, this being the off-season. Notices relating to fishing, but I examined the water and it did not look to me as though it had any fish in it. Not a soul anywhere and bitter wind blowing. All the broken ice had been blown up to the south end, and the waves were rocking it up and down, making a clank-clank, clank-clank—the most melancholy noise I ever heard. (Mem. to use in novel some time and to have an empty Craven A packet bobbing up and down among the ice.)

Found hostel, about 1 mile further on, with difficulty. Alone again. A most peculiar place this time. A great draughty barrack of a house, built in the sham-castle style—somebody's Folly—about 1860. All but three or four of the rooms quite empty. Miles of echoing stone passages, no lighting except candles and only smoky little oilstoves to cook on. Terribly cold.

Only 2/8d left, so tomorrow must go into Manchester (walk to Macclesfield, then bus) and cash cheque.

Distance walked, 12 miles. Spent on conveyances 1/8d. On food, 2/8½d.

4 February

Got out of bed so cold that I could not do up any buttons and had to [go] down and thaw my hands before I could dress. Left about 10.30 am. A marvellous morning. Earth frozen hard as iron, not a breath of wind and the sun shining brightly. Not a soul stirring. Rudyard Lake (about 1½ miles long) had frozen over during the night. Wild ducks walking about disconsolately on the ice. The sun coming up and the light slanting along the ice the most wonderful red-gold colour I have ever seen. Spent a long time throwing stones over the ice. A jagged stone skimming across ice makes exactly the same sound as a redshank whistling.

Walked to Macclesfield, 10 or 11 miles, then bus to Manchester. Went and collected letters, then to bank to cash cheque but found they were shut—they shut at 3 pm here. Very awkward as I had only 3d in hand. Went to Youth Hostel headquarters and asked them to cash cheque, but they refused, then to Police Station to ask them to introduce me to a solicitor who would cash a cheque, but they also refused. Frightfully cold. Streets encrusted with mounds of dreadful black stuff which was really snow frozen hard and blackened by smoke. Did not want to spend night in streets. Found my way to poor quarter (Chester Street), went to pawnshop and tried to pawn raincoat but they said they did not take them any longer. Then it occurred to me my scarf was pawnable, and they gave me 1/11d on it. Went to common lodging house, of which there were three close together in Chester Street.

Long letter from Rees advising me about people to go and see, one of them, luckily, in Manchester.

Distance walked, about 13 miles. Spent on conveyances, 2/–. On food, 10d.

5 February

Went and tried to see Meade but he was out. Spent day in common lodging house. Much as in London. 11d for bed, cubicles not dormitories. The "deputy" a cripple as they seem so often to be. Dreadful method here of making tea in tin bowls. Cashed cheque in morning but shall stay tonight in lodging house and go and see Meade tomorrow.

6–10 February

Staying with the Meades at 49 Brynton Rd, Longsight, Manchester. Brynton Rd is in one of the new building estates. Very decent houses with bathrooms and electric light, rent I suppose about 12/– or 14/–. Meade is some kind of Trade Union Official and has something to do with the editing of *Labour's Northern Voice*—these are the people who do the publishing side of the *Adelphi*. The Ms have been very decent to me. Both are working-class people, speak with Lancashire accents and have worn the clogs in their childhood, but the atmosphere in a place like this is entirely middle-class. Both the Ms were faintly scandalised to hear I had been in the common lodging house in Manchester. I am struck again by the fact that as soon as a working man gets an official post in the Trade Union or goes into Labour politics, he becomes middle-class whether he will or no, i.e. by fighting against the bourgeoisie he becomes bourgeois. The fact is that you *cannot help* living in the manner appropriate and developing the ideology appropriate to your income (in M's case I suppose about £4 a week). The only quarrel I have with the Ms is that they call me "comrade". Mrs M, as usual, does not understand much about politics but has adopted her husband's views as a wife ought to; she pronounces the word "comrade" with manifest discomfort.

Am struck by the difference of manners even as far north as this. Mrs M is surprised and not altogether approving when I get up when she enters the room, offer to help with the washing-up, etc. She says, "Lads up here expect to be waited on."

M sent me across to Wigan to see Joe Kennan, an electrician who takes a prominent part in the Socialist movement. Kennan also lives in a decent Corporation house (Beech Hill Building Estate) but is more definitely a working man. A very short, stout, powerful man with an extraordinarily gentle, hospitable manner and very anxious to help. His elder child was upstairs in bed (scarlet fever suspected), the younger on the floor playing with soldiers and a toy cannon. Kennan smiles and says, "You see—and I'm supposed to be a pacifist." He sent me to the NUWM shelter with a letter to the secretary asking him to find me a lodging in Wigan. The shelter is a dreadful ramshackle little place but a godsend to these unemployed men as it is warm and there are newspapers etc there. The secretary, Paddy Grady, an unemployed miner. A tall lean man about 35, intelligent and well-informed and very anxious to help. He is a single man getting 17/– a week and is in a dreadful state physically from years of underfeeding and idleness. His front teeth are almost entirely rotted away. All the men at the NUWM very friendly and anxious to supply me with information as soon as they heard I was a writer and collecting facts about working-class conditions. I cannot get them to treat me precisely as an equal, however. They call me either "Sir" or "Comrade".

11 February

Staying at Warrington Lane, Wigan. Board and lodging 25/– a week. Share room with another lodger (unemployed railwayman), meals in kitchen and wash at scullery sink. Food all right but indigestible and in monstrous quantities. Lancashire method of eating tripe (cold with vinegar) horrible.

The family. Mr H, aged 39, has worked in the pit since he was 13. Now out of work for nine months. A largish, fair, slow-moving, very mild and nice-mannered man who considers carefully before he answers when you ask him a question, and begins, "In my estimation". Has not much accent. Ten years ago he got a spurt of coal dust in his left eye and practically lost the sight of it. Was put to work "on top" for a while but went back to the pit as he could earn more there. Nine months ago his other eye went wrong (there is something called "nyastygmus" or some such name that miners suffer from) and he can only see a few yards. Is on "compensation" of 29/– a week, but they are talking of putting him on "partial compensation" of 14/– a week. It all depends whether the doctor passes him as fit for work, though of course there would not be any work, except perhaps a job "on top", but there are very few of these. If he is put on partial compensation he can draw the dole until his stamps are exhausted.

Mrs H. Four years older than her husband. Less than 5 feet tall. Toby-jug figure. Merry disposition. Very ignorant—adds up 27 and 10 and makes it 31. Very broad accent. There seem to be 2 ways of dealing with the "the" here. Before consonants it is often omitted altogether ("Put joog on table" etc); before vowels it is often incorporated with the word, e.g. "My sister's in thospital"—th as in thin.

The son "our Joe", just turned 15 and has been working in the pit a year. At present is on night shift. Goes to work about 9 pm returns between 7 and 8 am, has breakfast and promptly goes to bed in bed vacated by another lodger. Usually sleeps till 5 or 6 pm. He started work on 2/8d a day, was raised to 3/4d, i.e. £1 a week. Out of this 1/8d a week comes off for stoppages (insurance etc) and 4d a day for his tram fares to and from the pit. So his net wage, working full time, is 16/4d a week. In summer, however, he will only be working short-time. A tallish, frail, deadly pale youth, obviously much exhausted by his work, but seems fairly happy.

Tom, Mrs H's cousin, unmarried and lodging there—paying 25/– a week. A very hairy man with a hare-lip, mild disposition and very simple. Also on night shift.

Joe, another lodger, single. Unemployed on 17/–[1] a week. Pays 6/– a week for his room and sees to his own food. Gets up about 8 to give his bed up to "our Joe" and remains out of doors, in Public Library etc most of day. A bit of an ass but has some education and enjoys a resounding phrase. Explaining why he never married, he says portentously, "Matrimonial chains is a big item". Repeated this sentence a number of times, evidently having an affection for it. Has been totally unemployed for 7 years. Drinks when he gets the chance, which of course he never does nowadays.

The house has two rooms and scullery downstairs, 3 rooms upstairs, tiny back yard and outside lavatory. No hot water laid on. Is

[1] 15/–? [Author's footnote.]

in bad repair—front wall is bulging. Rent 12/– and with rates 15/–. The total income of the Hs is:

Mr H's compensation	29/– a week.
Joe's wages	16/4d ,,
Tom's weekly payment	25/– ,,
Joe's ditto	6/– ,,
Total	£3–16–4d.

Payment of rent and rates leaves £3–2–4d. This has to feed 4 people and clothe and otherwise provide for 3.[1] Of course at present there is my own contribution as well but that is an abnormality.

Wigan in the centre does not seem as bad as it has been represented—distinctly less depressing than Manchester. Wigan Pier said to have been demolished. Clogs commonly worn here and general in the smaller places outside such as Hindley. Shawl over head commonly worn by older women, but girls evidently only do it under pressure of dire poverty. Nearly everyone one sees very badly dressed and youths on the corners markedly less smart and rowdy than in London, but no very obvious signs of poverty except the number of empty shops. One in three of registered workers said to be unemployed.

Last night to Co-Op hall with various people from the NUWM to hear Wal Hannington speak. A poor speaker, using all the padding and clichés of the Socialist orator, and with the wrong kind of cockney accent (once again, though a Communist entirely a bourgeois), but he got the people well worked up. Was surprised by the amount of Communist feeling here. Loud cheers when Hannington announced that if England and USSR went to war USSR would win. Audience very rough and all obviously unemployed (about 1 in 10 of them women) but very attentive. After the address a collection taken for expenses—hire of hall and H's train-fare from London. £1–6–0d raised—not bad from about 200 unemployed people.

You can always tell a miner by the blue tattooing of coal dust on the bridge of his nose. Some of the older men have their foreheads veined with it like Roquefort cheese.

12 February

Terribly cold. Long walk along the canal (one-time site of Wigan Pier) towards some slag-heaps in the distance. Frightful landscape

[1] The Hs are well off by local standards. [Author's footnote.]

of slag-heaps and belching chimneys. Some of the slag-heaps almost like mountains—one just like Stromboli. Bitter wind. They have had to send a steamer to break the ice in front of the coal barges on the canal. The bargemen were muffled to the eyes in sacks. All the "flashes" (stagnant pools made by the subsidence of disused pits) covered with ice the colour of raw umber. Beards of ice on the lock gates. A few rats running slowly through the snow, very tame, presumably weak with hunger.

13 February

Housing conditions in Wigan terrible. Mrs H tells me that at her brother's house (he is only 25, so I think he must be her half brother, but he has already a child of 8), 11 people, 5 of them adults, belonging to 3 different families, live in 4 rooms, "2 up 2 down".

All the miners I meet have either had serious accidents themselves or have friends or relatives who have. Mrs H's cousin had his back broken by a fall of rock—"And he lingered seven year afore he died and it were a-punishing of him all the while"—and her brother-in-law fell 1200 feet down the shaft of a new pit. Apparently he bounced from side to side, so was presumably dead before he got to the bottom. Mrs H adds: "They wouldn't never have collected t'pieces only he were wearing a new suit of oilskins."

15 February

Went with NUWM collectors on their rounds with a view to collecting facts about housing conditions, especially in the caravans. Have made notes on these, q.v. What chiefly struck me was the expression on some of the women's faces, especially those in the more crowded caravans. One woman had a face like a death's head. She had a look of absolutely intolerable misery and degradation. I gathered that she felt as I would feel if I were coated all over with dung. All the people however seemed to take these conditions quite for granted. They have been promised houses over and over again but nothing has come of it and they have got into the way of thinking that a livable house is something absolutely unattainable.

Passing up a horrible squalid side-alley, saw a woman, youngish but very pale and with the usual draggled exhausted look, kneeling by the gutter outside a house and poking a stick up the leaden waste-pipe, which was blocked. I thought how dreadful a destiny it was to be kneeling in the gutter in a back-alley in Wigan, in the bitter cold, prodding a stick up a blocked drain. At that moment she looked up and caught my eye, and her expression was as desolate as I have ever seen; it struck me that she was thinking just the same thing as I was.

Changing lodgings as Mrs H is ill with some mysterious malady and ordered into hospital. They have found lodgings for me at Darlington Rd, over a tripe shop where they take in lodgers. The husband an ex-miner (age 58), the wife ill with a weak heart, in bed on sofa in kitchen. Social atmosphere much as at the Hs but house appreciably dirtier and very smelly. A number of other lodgers. An old ex-miner, age about 75, on old age pension plus half a crown weekly from parish (12/6d in all). Another, said to be of superior type and "come down in the world", more or less bedridden. An Irish ex-miner who had [a] shoulder blade and several ribs crushed by a fall of stone a few years ago and lives on disability pension of about 25/– a week. Of distinctly superior type and started off as a clerk but went "down pit" because he was big and strong and could earn more as a miner (this was before the war). Also some newspaper canvassers. Two for *John Bull*,[1] distinctly motheaten, ages about 40 and 55, one quite young and was for four years in rubber firm in Calcutta. Cannot quite make this lad out. He puts on [a] Lancashire accent when talking to the others (he belongs locally) but to me talks in the usual "educated" accent. The family apart from the Fs themselves consists of a fat son who is at work somewhere and lives nearby, his wife Maggie who is in the shop nearly all day, their two kids, and Annie, fiancée of the other son who is in London. Also a daughter in Canada (Mrs F says "at Canada"). Maggie and Annie do practically the whole work of the house and shop. Annie very thin, overworked (she also works in a dress-sewing place) and obviously unhappy. I gather that the marriage is by no means certain to take place but that Mrs F treats Annie as a relative all the same and that Annie groans under her tyranny. Number of rooms in the house exclusive of shop premises, 5 or 6 and a bathroom–WC. Nine people sleeping here. Three in my room besides myself.

Struck by the astonishing ignorance about and wastefulness of food among the working class people here—more even than in the south, I think. One morning when washing in the Hs' scullery made an inventory of the following food: A piece of bacon about 5 pounds. About 2 pounds of shin of beef. About a pound and a half of liver

[1] A popular weekly paper containing topical articles of a sensational nature and with competitions offering large prizes.

(all of these uncooked). The wreck of a monstrous meat pie (Mrs H when making a pie always made it in an enamelled *basin* such as is used for washing up in. Ditto with puddings). A dish containing 15 or 20 eggs. A number of small cakes. A flat fruit pie and a "cake-a-pie" (pastry with currants in it). Various fragments of earlier pies. 6 large loaves and 12 small ones (I had seen Mrs H cook these the night before). Various odds and ends of butter, tomatoes, opened tins of milk etc. There was also more food keeping warm in the oven in the kitchen. Everything except bread habitually left about uncovered and shelves filthy. Food here consists almost entirely of bread and starch. A typical day's meals at the Hs. Breakfast (about 8 am.): two fried eggs and bacon, bread (no butter) and tea. Dinner (about 12.30 pm): a monstrous plate of stewed beef, dumplings and boiled potatoes (equal to about 3 Lyons portions) and a big helping of rice pudding or suet pudding. Tea (about 5 pm): plate of cold meat, bread and butter, sweet pastries and tea. Supper (about 11 pm): fish and chips, bread and butter and tea.

16 February

Great excitement because a couple who stayed here for a month about Xmas have been arrested (at Preston) as coiners and it is believed they were making their false coins while here. The police inspector here for about an hour asking questions. Mrs F tells of snooping round their room while they were out and finding a lump of something like solder under the mattress and some little pots like egg-cups only larger. Mrs F agreed instantly to everything the police inspector suggested, and when he was upstairs searching the room I made two suggestions and she agreed to those too. I could see she had made up her mind they were guilty on hearing they were unmarried. When the inspector had written out her statement it came out that she could not read or write (except her signature), though her husband can read a little.

One of the canvassers' beds is jammed across the foot of mine. Impossible to stretch my legs out straight as if I do so my feet are in the small of his back. It seems a long time since I slept between linen sheets. Twill sheets even at the Ms. Theirs (the Ms') was the only house I have been in since leaving London that did not smell.

17 February

The newspaper-canvassers are rather pathetic. Of course it is a quite desperate job. I fancy what *John Bull* do is to take on people who make frantic efforts and work up a little more or less spurious business for a while, then sack them and take on more, and so on. I should judge these men each make £2 or £3 a week. Both have families and one is a grandfather. They are so hard up that they cannot pay for full board but pay something for their rooms and have a squalid little cupboard of food in the kitchen, from which they take out bread, packets of marg etc and cook themselves meals in a shamefaced manner. They are allocated so many houses each day and have to knock at every door and book a minimum number of orders. They are at present working some swindle on behalf of *John Bull* by which you get a "free" tea set by sending two shillings worth of stamps and twenty four coupons. As soon as they have had their food they start filling up blank forms for the next day, and presently the older one falls asleep in his chair and begins snoring loudly.

Am struck, though, by their knowledge of working-class conditions. They can tell you all about housing, rents, rates, state of trade, etc in every town in the north of England.

18 February

In the early morning the mill girls clumping down the cobbled street, all in clogs, make a curiously formidable sound, like an army hurrying into battle. I suppose this is the typical sound of Lancashire. And the typical imprint in the mud the outline of a clog-iron, like one half of a cow's hoof. Clogs are very cheap. They cost about 5/– a pair and need not wear out for years because all they need is new irons costing a few pence.

As always and everywhere, the dress peculiar to the locality is considered plebeian. A very down in the mouth respectable woman, at one of the houses I visited with the NUWM collectors, said: "I've always kept myself decent-like. I've never worn a shawl over my head—I wouldn't be seen in such a thing. I've worn a hat since I was a girl. But it don't do you much good. At Christmas time we was that hard put to it that I thought I'd go up and try for a well-wisher. (Hamper given away by some charitable organisation.) When I got up there the clergyman says to me, '*You* don't want no well-wisher,' he says. 'There's plenty worse than you. We knows many a one that's living on bread and jam,' he says. 'And how do you know what *we're* living on?' I says. He says, 'You can't be so bad if you can dress as well as that,' he says—meaning my hat. I didn't get no well-wisher.

If I'd ha' gone up with a shawl over my head I'd ha' got it. That's what you get for keeping yourself respectable."

19 February

When a "dirt-heap" sinks, as it does ultimately, it leaves a hummocky surface which is made more so by the fact that in times of strikes the miners dig into some of these places in search of small coals. One which is used as a playground looks like a choppy sea suddenly frozen. It is called locally "the flock mattress". The soil over them is grey and cindery and only an evil-looking brownish grass grows on them.

This evening to a social the NUWM had got up in aid of Thaelmann's[1] defence-fund. Admission and refreshments (cup of tea and meat pie) 6d. About 200 people, preponderantly women, largely members of the Co-Op, in one of whose rooms it was held, and I suppose for the most part living directly or indirectly on the dole. Round the back a few aged miners sitting looking on benevolently, a lot of very young girls in front. Some dancing to the concertina (many of the girls confessed that they could not dance, which struck me as rather pathetic) and some excruciating singing. I suppose these people represented a fair cross-section of the more revolutionary element in Wigan. If so, God help us. Exactly the same sheeplike crowd—gaping girls and shapeless middle-aged women dozing over their knitting—that you see everywhere else. There is no *turbulence* left in England. One good song, however, by an old woman, I think a cockney, who draws the old age pension and makes a bit by singing at pubs, with the refrain:

For you can't do that there 'ere,
No, you can't do that there 'ere;
Anywhere else you can do that there,
But you can't do that there 'ere.

20 February

This afternoon with Paddy Grady to see the unemployed miners

[1] Ernst Thaelmann (1886–1944), a transport worker who became Chairman of the German Communist Party from 1925 onwards. A member of the Reichstag 1924–33, he ran for Presidency in 1932 against Hindenburg and polled five million votes. Arrested in 1933, the date for his trial was postponed several times and in October 1936 Berlin announced that he would be detained for life without one. Officially reported killed in an air raid, he was shot by the Nazis in August 1944 at Buchenwald.

robbing the "dirt-train", or, as they call it, "scrambling for the coal". A most astonishing sight. We went by the usual frightful routes along the colliery railway line to Fir Tree Sidings, on our way meeting various men and women with sacks of stolen coal which they had slung over bicycles. I would like to know where they got these bicycles—perhaps made of odd parts picked off rubbish dumps. None had mudguards, few had saddles and some had not even tyres. When we got to the big dirt-heap where the trainloads of shale from that pit are discharged, we found about 50 men picking over the dirt, and they directed us to the place further up the line where the men board the train. When we got there we found not less than 100 men, a few boys, waiting, each with a sack and coal hammer strapped under his coat tails. Presently the train hove in sight, coming round the bend at about 20 mph. 50 or 70 men rushed for it, seized hold of the bumpers etc and hoisted themselves onto the trucks. It appears that each truck is regarded as the property of the men who have succeeded in getting onto it while it is moving. The engine ran the trucks up onto the dirt-heap, uncoupled them and came back for the remaining trucks. There was the same wild rush and the second train was boarded in the same manner, only a few men failing to get onto it. As soon as the trucks had been uncoupled the men on top began shovelling the stuff out to their women and other supporters below, who rapidly sorted out the dirt and put all the coal (a considerable amount but all small, in lumps about the size of eggs) into their sacks. Further down the "broo" were the people who had failed to get onto either train and were collecting the tiny fragments of coal that came sliding down from above. You do not, of course, when you are boarding the train, know whether you are getting onto a good truck or not, and what kind of truck you get is entirely luck. Thus some of the trucks, instead of being loaded with the dirt from the floor of the mine, which of course contains a fair quantity of coal, were loaded entirely with shale. But it appears, what I had never heard of before, that among the shale, at any rate in some mines, there occurs an inflammable rock called "cannel" (not certain of spelling) which makes fairly good fuel. It is not commercially valuable because it is hard to work and burns too fast, but for ordinary purposes is good enough. Those who were on the shale trucks were picking out the "cannel", which is almost exactly like the shale except that it is a little darker and is known by splitting horizontally, almost like slate. I watched the people working until they had almost emptied the trucks. There were twenty trucks and something over 100 people were at work on them. Each, so far as I could judge, got about ½ cwt of either coal or "cannel". This performance sometimes happens more than once a day when several dirt-trains are sent out, so it is evident that several tons of fuel are stolen every day.

The economics and ethics of the whole business are rather interesting. In the first place, robbing the dirt-train is of course illegal, and one is technically trespassing by being on the dirt-heap at all. Periodically people are prosecuted—in fact in this morning's *Examiner* there was a report of 3 men being fined for it. But no notice is taken of the prosecutions, and in fact one of the men fined was there this afternoon. But at the same time the coal company have no intention of using the coal etc that is thrown out among the dirt, because it would not repay the cost of sorting. If not stolen, therefore, it would be wasted. Moreover, this business saves the company the expense of emptying the trucks, because by the time the coal-pickers have done with them they are empty. Therefore they connive at the raiding of the train—I noticed that the engine-driver took no notice of the men clambering onto the trucks. The reason for the periodical prosecutions is said to be that there are so many accidents. Only recently a man slipped under the train and had both legs cut off. Considering the speed the train goes at, it is remarkable that accidents do not happen oftener.

The most curious vehicle I saw used for carrying away coal was a cart made of a packing case and the wheels from two kitchen mangles.

Some of this coal that is stolen is said to be on sale in the town at 1/6d a bag.

21 February

The squalor of this house is beginning to get on my nerves. Nothing is ever cleaned or dusted, the rooms not done out till 5 in the afternoon, and the cloth never even removed from the kitchen table. At supper you still see the crumbs from breakfast. The most revolting feature is Mrs F being always in bed on the kitchen sofa. She has a terrible habit of tearing off strips of newspaper, wiping her mouth with them and then throwing them onto the floor. Unemptied chamberpot under the table at breakfast this morning. The food is dreadful, too. We are given those little twopenny ready-made steak and kidney pies out of stock. I hear horrible stories, too, about the cellars where the tripe is kept and which are said to swarm with black beetles. Apparently they only get in fresh supplies of tripe at long intervals. Mrs F dates events by this. "Let me see, now. I've had in three lots of froze (frozen tripe) since then," etc. I judge they get in a consignment of "froze" about once in a fortnight. Also it is very tiring being unable to stretch my legs straight out at night.

24 February

Yesterday went down Crippen's mine with Jerry Kennan, another electrician friend of his, two small sons of the latter, two other electricians and an engineer belonging to the pit, who showed us round. The depth to the cage bottom was 300 yards. We went down at 10.30 and came up at 1.30, having covered, according to the engineer who showed us round, about 2 miles.

As the cage goes down you have the usual momentary qualm in your belly, then a curious stuffed-up feeling in your ears. In the middle of its run the cage works up a tremendous speed (in some of the deeper mines they are said to touch 60 mph or more) then slows down so abruptly that it is difficult to believe you are not going upwards again. The cages are tiny—about 8 feet long by 3½ wide by 6 high. They are supposed to hold 10 men or (I think) about a ton and a half of coal. There were only six of us and two boys, but we had difficulty in packing in and it is important to face in the direction you are going to get out the other end.

Down below it was lighter than I expected, because apart from the lamps we all carried there were electric lights in the main roads. But what I had not expected, and what for me was the most important feature all through, was the lowness of the roof. I had vaguely imagined wandering about in places rather like the tunnels of the Underground; but as a matter of fact there were very few places where you could stand upright. In general the roof was about 4 ft or 4 ft 6 ins high, sometimes much lower, with every now and again a beam larger than the others under which you had to duck especially low. In places the walls were quite neatly built up, almost like the stone walls in Derbyshire, with slabs of shale. There were pit-props, almost all of wood, every yard or so overhead. They are made of small larch trees sawn to the appropriate length (from the quantity used I see now why people laying down plantations almost always plant larch) and are simply laid on the ends of the upright props, which are laid on slabs of wood, and not fixed in any way. The bottom slabs gradually sink into the floor, or, as the miners put it, "the floor comes up", but the weight overhead keeps the whole thing in place. By the way the steel girders used here and there instead of wooden props had buckled, you got an idea of the weight of the roof. Underfoot is thick stone dust and the rails, about 2½ ft wide, for the trolleys. When the path is downhill miners often slide down these on their clogs, which, being hollow underneath, more or less fit onto the rails.

After a few hundred yards of walking doubled up and once or twice having to crawl, I began to feel the effects in a violent pain all down my thighs. One also gets a bad crick in the neck, because though stooping one has to look up for fear of knocking into the beams, but the pain in the thighs is the worst. Of course as we got nearer the coal face the roads tended to get lower. Once we crawled through a temporary tunnel which was like an enlarged rat hole, with no props, and in one place there had been a fall of stone during the night—3 or 4 tons[1] of stuff, I should judge. It had blocked up the entire road except for a tiny aperture near the roof which we had to crawl through without touching any timber. Presently I had to stop for a minute to rest my knees, which were giving way, and then after a few hundred yards more we came to the first working. This was only a small working with a machine worked by two men, much like an enlarged version of the electric drills used for street mending. Nearby was the dynamo (or whatever it is called) which supplied the power through cables to this and the other machines; also the comparatively small drills (but they weigh 50 lbs each and have to be hoisted onto the shoulder) for drilling holes for blasting charges; also bundles of miners' tools locked together on wires like bundles of keys, which is always done for fear of losing them.

We went a few hundred yards further and came to one of the main workings. The men were not actually working here, but a shift was just coming down to start work about 250 yards further on. Here there was one of the larger machines which have a crew of 5 men to work them. This machine has a revolving wheel on which there are teeth about a couple of inches long set at various angles; in principle it is rather like an immensely thickened circular saw with the teeth much further apart, and running horizontally instead of vertically. The machine is dragged into position by the crew and the front part of it can be swivelled round in any direction and pressed

[1] Jerry Kennan said 20 or 30. I don't know which of us would be best judge. [Author's footnote.]

against the coal face by the man working it. Two men called "scufters" shovel the coal onto a rubber-belt conveyor which carries it through a tunnel to the tubs on the main road, where it is hauled by steam haulage to the cages. I had not realised before that the men operating the coal-cutter are working in a place rather less than a yard high. When we crawled in under the roof to the coal face we could at best kneel, and then not kneel upright, and I fancy the men must do most of their work lying on their bellies. The heat also was frightful—round about 100 degrees F so far as I could judge. The crew keep burrowing into the coal face, cutting a semi-circular track, periodically hauling the machine forward and propping as they go. I was puzzled to know how that monstrous machine—flat in shape, of course, but 6 or 8 feet long and weighing several tons, and only fitted with skids, not wheels—could have been got into position through that mile or so of passages. Even to drag the thing forward as the seam advances must be a frightful labour, seeing that the men have to do it practically lying down. Up near the coal face we saw a number of mice, which are said to abound there. They are said to be commonest in pits where there are or have been horses. I don't know how they get down into the mine in the first place. Probably in the cages, but possibly by falling down the shaft, as it is said that a mouse (owing to its surface area being large relative to its weight) can drop any distance uninjured.

On the way back my exhaustion grew so great that I could hardly keep going at all, and towards the end I had to stop and rest every fifty yards. The periodical effort of bending and raising oneself at each successive beam was fearful, and the relief when one could stand upright, usually owing to a hole in the roof, was enormous. At times my knees simply refused to lift me after I had knelt down. It was made worse by the fact that at the lowest parts the roof is usually on a slope, so that besides bending you have to walk more or less sideways. We were all pretty distressed except the engineer taking us round, who was used to it, and the two small boys, who did not have to bend to any extent; but I was by a good deal the worst, being the tallest. I would like to know whether any miners are as tall as I am, and if so, whether they suffer for it. The few miners whom we met down the pit could move with extraordinary agility, running about on all fours among the props almost like dogs.

After we had at last emerged and washed off the more obtrusive dirt and had some beer, I went home and had dinner and then soaked myself for a long time in a hot bath. I was surprised at the quantity of dirt and the difficulty of getting it off. It had penetrated to every inch of my body in spite of my overalls and my clothes underneath those. Of course very few miners have baths in their homes—only a tub of water in front of the kitchen fire. I should say it would be quite impossible to keep clean without a proper bathtub.

In the room where we changed our clothes there were several cages of canaries. These have to be kept there by law, to test the air in cases of explosion. They are sent down in the cage, and, if they do not faint, the air is all right.

The Davy lamps give out a fair amount of light. There is an air intake at the top but the flame is cut off from this by a fine gauze. Flame cannot pass through holes of less than a certain diameter. The gauze therefore lets the air in to sustain the flame but will not let the flame out to explode dangerous gases. Each lamp when full will burn for 8–12 hours, and they are locked, so that if they go out down the pit they cannot be relighted. Miners are searched for matches before going down the pit.

27 February

On Wednesday (25th) went over to Liverpool to see the Deiners and Garrett. I was to have come back the same night, but almost as soon as I got to Liverpool I felt unwell and was ignominiously sick, so the Deiners insisted on putting me to bed and then on my staying the night. I came back yesterday evening.

I was very greatly impressed by Garrett. Had I known before that it is he who writes under the pseudonym of Matt Low in the *Adelphi* and one or two other places, I would have taken steps to meet him earlier. He is a biggish hefty chap of about 36, Liverpool-Irish, brought up a Catholic but now a Communist. He says he has had about 9 months' work in (I think) about the last 6 years. He went to sea as a lad and was at sea about 10 years, then worked as a docker. During the war he was torpedoed on a ship that sank in 7 minutes, but they had expected to be torpedoed and had got their boats ready, and were all saved except the wireless operator, who refused to leave his post until he had got an answer. He also worked in an illicit brewery in Chicago during Prohibition, saw various hold-ups, saw Battling Siki immediately after he had been shot in a street brawl, etc etc. All this however interests him much less than Communist politics. I urged him to write his autobiography, but as usual, living in about 2 rooms on the dole with a wife (who I gather objects to his writing) and a number of kids, he finds it impossible to settle to any long work and can only do short stories. Apart from the enormous unemployment in Liverpool it is almost impossible for him to get work because he is blacklisted everywhere as a Communist.

He took me down to the docks to see dockers being taken on for an unloading job. When we got there we found about 200 men waiting in a ring and police holding them back. It appeared that there was a fruit ship which needed unloading and, on the news that there were jobs going, there had been a fight between the dockers which the police had to intervene to stop. After a while the agent of the company (known as the stevedore, I think) emerged from a shed and began calling out the names or rather numbers of gangs whom he had engaged earlier in the day. Then he needed about 10 men more, and walked round the ring picking out a man here and there. He would pause, select a man, take him by the shoulder and haul him forward, exactly as at a sale of cattle. Presently he announced that that was all. A sort of groan went up from the remaining dockers, and they trailed off, about 50 men having been engaged out of 200. It appears that unemployed dockers have to sign on twice a day, otherwise they are presumed to have been working (as their work is mainly casual labour, by the day) and their dole docked for that day.

I was impressed by the fact that Liverpool is doing much more in the way of slum-clearance than most towns. The slums are still very bad but there are great quantities of Corporation houses and flats at low rents. Just outside Liverpool there are quite considerable towns consisting entirely of Corporation houses, which are really quite livable and decent to look at, but having as usual the objection that they take people a long way from their work. In the centre of the town there are huge blocks of workers' flats imitated from those in Vienna. They are built in the form of an immense ring, five storeys high, round a central courtyard about 60 yards across, which forms a playground for children. Round the inner side run balconies, and there are wide windows on each side so that everyone gets some sunlight. I was not able to get inside any of these flats, but I gather each has either 2 or 3 rooms,[1] kitchenette and bathroom with hot water. The rents vary from about 7/– at the top to 10/– at the bottom. (No lifts, of course.) It is noteworthy that the people in Liverpool have got used to the idea of flats (or tenements, as they call them) whereas

[1] Presumably 3—living room and 2 bedrooms. [Author's footnote.]

in a place like Wigan the people, though realising that flats solve the problem of letting people live near their work, all say they would rather have a house of their own, however bad it was.

There are one or two interesting points here. The re-housing is almost entirely the work of the Corporation, which is said to be entirely ruthless towards private ownership and to be even too ready to condemn slum houses without compensation. Here therefore you have what is in effect Socialist legislation, though it is done by a local authority. But the Corporation of Liverpool is almost entirely Conservative. Moreover, though the re-housing from the public funds is, as I say, in effect a Socialist measure, the actual work is done by private contractors, and one may assume that here as elsewhere the contractors tend to be the friends, brothers, nephews etc of those on the Corporation. Beyond a certain point therefore Socialism and Capitalism are not easy to distinguish, the State and the capitalist tending to merge into one. On the other side of the river, the Birkenhead side (we went through the Mersey tunnel) you have Port Sunlight, a city within a city, all built and owned by the Leverhulme soap works. Here again are excellent houses at fairly low rents, but, as with publicly-owned property, burdened by restrictions. Looking at the Corporation buildings on the one side, and Lord Leverhulme's buildings on the other, you would find it hard to say which was which.

Another point is this. Liverpool is practically governed by Roman Catholics. The Roman Catholic ideal, at any rate as put forward by the Chesterton-Beachcomber[1] type of writer, is always in favour of private ownership and against Socialist legislation and "progress" generally. The Chesterton type of writer wants to see a free peasant or other small-owner living in his own privately owned and probably insanitary cottage; not a wage-slave living in an excellently appointed Corporation flat and tied down by restrictions as to sanitation etc. The RCs in Liverpool, therefore, are going against the supposed implications of their own religion. But I suppose that if the Chestertons *et hoc genus* grasped that it is possible for the RCs to capture the machinery of local and other government, even when it is called Socialist, they would change their tune.

[1] "Beachcomber", a column in the *Daily Express*, started in 1924 by J. B. Morton, a Roman Catholic. Throughout his journalism Orwell makes pejorative references to it. See III, 46 for a fuller description of his objections.

No clogs or shawl over head in Liverpool. Returning by car, noticed how abruptly this custom stops a little west of Wigan.[1]

Am trying to arrange to return to London by sea if G can get me a passage on a cargo boat.

Bought two brass candlesticks and a ship in a bottle. Paid 9/- for the candlesticks. G considered I was swindled but they are quite nice brass.

2 March

At Wallace Road, Sheffield. Thick snow everywhere on the hills as I came along. Stone boundaries between the fields running across the snow like black piping across a white dress. Warm and sunny, however. For the first time in my life saw rooks copulating. On the ground, not in a tree. The manner of courtship was peculiar. The female stood with her beak open and the male walked round her and it appeared as though he was feeding her.

Memories of Wigan: slagheaps like mountains, smoke, rows of blackened houses, sticky mud criss-crossed by imprints of clogs, heavy-set young women standing at street corners with their babies wrapped in their shawls, immense piles of broken chocolate in cut-price confectioners' windows.

3 March

This house: two up two down, living room about 14′ by 12′, parlour rather smaller. Sink and copper in living room, no gas fire, outside WC. Rent with rates about 8/6d. 2 cellars as well. Husband is out of work (PAC[2]—was previously store-keeper at a factory which closed down and discharged its whole staff), wife works as a char at 6d an hour. One kid aged 5.

B: age 45 but looks less. Has malformed right hand, also one foot. This was inherited and he fears it is transmissible, so will not marry. Owing to this has never had much in the way of regular work. Was with a circus for some years as groom, clown and "Wild West" rider —he could apparently handle the bridle with his damaged hand.

[1] It is said by everyone in Wigan that clogs are going out. Yet in the poorer quarters 1 person in 2 seems to me to wear clogs, and there are (I think) 10 shops which sell nothing else. [Author's footnote.]

[2] Drawing the dole from the Public Assistance Committee of the local authority.

Now lives alone and for some reason gets no dole, only something from the parish and help from his brother. Has a single room with only an open fireplace—no oven—to cook on. Is terribly embittered and declares that feeling of actual hatred for the bourgeoisie, even personal hatred of individuals, is necessary to any genuine Socialist. Is nevertheless a good fellow and very anxious to help. Mixed up with his political feelings is the usual local patriotism of the Yorkshireman and much of his conversation consists of comparison between London and Sheffield to the detriment of the former. Sheffield is held to lead London in everything, e.g. on the one hand the new housing schemes in Sheffield are immensely superior, and on the other hand the Sheffield slums are more squalid than anything London can show. I notice that apart from the usual hatred between the Northerner and the Southerner, there is also hatred between the Yorkshireman and the Lancashireman, and also internecine hatred between the various Yorkshire towns. No one up here seems to have heard of any place in the south of England except London. If you come from the south you are assumed to be a cockney however often you deny it. At the same time as the Northerner despises the Southerner he has an uneasy feeling that the latter knows more of the arts of life and is very anxious to impress him.

Had a very long and exhausting day (I am now continuing this March 4th) being shown every quarter of Sheffield on foot and by tram. I have now traversed almost the whole city. It seems to me, by daylight, one of the most appalling places I have ever seen. In whichever direction you look you see the same landscape of monstrous chimneys pouring forth smoke which is sometimes black and sometimes of a rosy tint said to be due to sulphur. You can smell the sulphur in the air all the while. All buildings are blackened within a year or two of being put up. Halting at one place I counted the factory chimneys I could see and there were 33. But it was very misty as well as smoky—there would have been many more visible on a clear day. I doubt whether there are any architecturally decent buildings in the town. The town is very hilly (said to be built on seven hills, like Rome) and everywhere streets of mean little houses blackened by smoke run up at sharp angles, paved with cobbles which are purposely set unevenly to give horses etc a grip. At night the hilliness creates fine effects because you look across from one hillside to the other and see the lamps twinkling like stars. Huge jets of flame shoot periodically out of the roofs of the foundries (many working night shifts at present) and show a splendid rosy colour through the smoke and steam. When you get a glimpse inside you see enormous fiery serpents of red-hot and white-hot (really lemon-coloured) iron being rolled out into rails. In the central slummy part of the town are the small workshops of the "little bosses", i.e. smaller employers who are making chiefly cutlery. I don't think I ever in my life saw so many broken windows. Some of these workshops have hardly a pane of glass in their windows and you would not believe they were inhabitable if you did not see the employees, mostly girls, at work inside.

The town is being torn down and rebuilt at an immense speed. Everywhere among the slums are gaps with squalid mounds of bricks where condemned houses have been demolished and on all the outskirts of the town new estates of Corporation houses are going up. These are much inferior, at any rate in appearance, to those at Liverpool. They are in terribly bleak situations, too. One estate just behind where I am living now, at the very summit of a hill, on horrible sticky clay soil and swept by icy winds. Notice that the people going into these new houses from the slums will always be paying higher rents, and also will have to spend much more on fuel to keep themselves warm. Also, in many cases, will be further from their work and therefore spend more on conveyances.

In the evening was taken to a Methodist Church where some kind of men's association (they call it a Brotherhood) meet once a week to listen to a lecture and have discussions. Next week a Communist is speaking, to the evident dismay of the clergyman who made the announcements. This week a clergyman who spoke on "Clean and Dirty Water". His lecture consisted of incredibly silly and disconnected ramblings about Shaw's *Adventures of Black Girl* etc. Most of the audience did not understand a word of it and in fact hardly listened, and the talk and the questions afterwards were so unbearable that B and I slipped out with his friend Binns to see the latter's back to back house, on which I took notes. B says that most of the members of this Brotherhood are unemployed men who will put up with almost anything in order to have a warm place where they can sit for a few hours.

Accent in Sheffield not so broad as in Lancashire. A very few people, mostly miners I think, wear clogs.

5 March

At 21 Estcourt Avenue, Headingley, Leeds.[1] I left Sheffield at 10.30 this morning, and in spite of its being such a frightful place and of the relief of getting back into a comfortable house, I was quite sorry to leave the Searles. I have seldom met people with more natural decency. They were as kind to me as anyone could possibly be, and I hope and trust they liked me. Of course I got their whole life-history from them by degrees. Searle is 33 and was an only child. When a youth he joined the Army and was in the Ordnance Corps (or whatever it is called) with the army of occupation in Palestine and in Egypt. He has vivid memories of Egypt and wishes he was back there. Since then he has only had short-lived jobs, e.g. as store-keeper and check-weighman at various works, also as railway (outside) porter. Mrs S comes from a somewhat more prosperous family, as her father till only a few weeks ago[2] was in a good job at £5 a week and also made something on the side by making fishing rods. But it was a very large family (11) and she went into service. She married S when he was on the dole, against the opposition of her family. At first they could not get a house, and lived in a single room, in which two children were born and one died. They told me they had only one bed for the family and had to "lay out" the dead baby in the perambulator. Finally, after frightful difficulty (one reason for this is that private landlords are not too keen on letting to people on the dole and there is a certain amount of bribery of agents) they got this house, of which the rent is about 8/6d. Mrs S earns about 9/– a week from her charing. Exactly what deduction is made for this from S's dole I don't know, but their total income is 32/6d. In spite of which I had great difficulty in getting them to accept enough for my keep while there—they wanted to charge only 6/– for full board and lodging from Monday night to Thursday morning. They keep the house very clean and decent, have a bit of garden, though they can't do much with it, as it has factory chimneys on one side and the gas works on the other, besides being poor soil, and are very fond of one another. I was surprised by Mrs S's grasp of the economic situation and also of abstract ideas—quite unlike most working-class women in this, though she is I think not far from illiterate. She does not

[1] The home of Orwell's elder sister, Marjorie, and her husband, Humphrey Dakin.

[2] He died very suddenly and his wife has now no resources except the old age pension. [Author's footnote.]

seem resentful against the people who employ her—indeed she says they are kind to her—but sees quite clearly the essential facts about domestic service. She told me how the other day as she waited at the lunch table she calculated the price of the food on the table (for 5 persons for one meal) and it came to 6/3d—as much as the PAC allows her child for a fortnight.

B was very good and took my request to "show me over Sheffield" even too seriously, so that from morning to night I was being rushed from place to place, largely on foot, to see public buildings, slums, housing estates etc. But he is a tiresome person to be with, being definitely disgruntled and too conscious of his Communist convictions. In Rotherham we had to have lunch at a slightly expensive restaurant because there didn't seem to be any others except pubs (B is TT), and when in there he was sweating and groaning about the "bourgeois atmosphere" and saying he could not eat this kind of food. As he declares that it is necessary to literally hate the bourgeoisie, I wondered what he thought of me, because he told me at the very start I was a bourgeois and remarked on my "public school twang". However, I think he was disposed to treat me as a sort of honorary proletarian, partly because I had no objection to washing in the sink etc but more because I seemed interested in Sheffield. He was very generous and though I had told him at the start that I was going to pay for his meals etc while we were together, he would always go out of his way to spare me expense. It seems that he lives on 10/– a week—I had this from Searle: exactly where B's 10/– comes from I don't know—and the rent of his room is 6/–. Of course it would not be possible to subsist on the remainder, allowing for fuel. You could only keep alive on 4/– a week[1] if you spent nothing on fuel and nothing on tobacco or clothes. I gather B gets meals from time to time from the Ss and other friends, also from his brother who is in comparatively good employ. His room is decent and even cultured-looking, as it has bits of "antique" furniture which he has made himself, and some crude but not disagreeable pictures, mostly of circuses, which he has painted. Much of his bitterness obviously comes from sexual starvation. His deformity handicaps him with women, his fear of transmitting it has stopped him from marrying (he says he would only marry a woman past the childbearing age), and his inability to earn money makes it more impossible still. However, at one of the *Adelphi* summer schools he picked up with some

[1] See opposite page.

school-mistress (aged 43) who I gather is his mistress when opportunities permit and who is willing to marry him, only her parents oppose it. The Searles say he has improved greatly since taking up with this woman—before that he used to have fits occasionally.

We had an argument one evening in the Searles' house because I helped Mrs S with the washing-up. Both of the men disapproved of this, of course. Mrs S seemed doubtful. She said that in the North working-class men never offered any courtesies to women (women are allowed to do all the house-work unaided, even when the man is unemployed, and it is always the man who sits in the comfortable chair), and she took this state of things for granted, but did not see why it should not be changed. She said that she thought the women now-a-days, especially the younger women, would like it if men opened doors for them etc. The position now-a-days is anomalous. The man is practically always out of work, whereas the woman occasionally is working. Yet the woman continues to do all the housework and the man not a hand's-turn, except carpentering and gardening. Yet I think it is instinctively felt by both sexes that the man would lose his manhood if, merely because he was out of work, he became a "Mary Ann".

---

[1] LIVING ON 4s A WEEK: MAN'S DESCRIPTION OF HOW HE DOES IT. Following the disclosures in the *News of the World* of parents who have to bring up big families on tiny incomes, a correspondent draws our attention to the case of a man who spend less than 4s a week on food.

His week's supply and its cost is as follows:—

	s.	d.
3 Wholemeal loaves	1	0
½lb. Margarine		2½
½lb. Dripping		3
1lb. Cheese		7
1lb. Onions		1½
1lb. Carrots		1½
1lb. Broken biscuits		4
2 lb. Dates		6
1 Tin evaporated milk		5
10 Oranges		5
Total cost	3	11½

The man, Mr W. Leach, of Lilford Road, London, S.E., adds that he would prefer to boil the carrots to eating them raw "but, of course, to boil the water would cost too much." *News of the World*, 1 March 1936. Also in *New Statesman and Nation*. [Newspaper cutting kept by Orwell among his notes.]

One particular picture of Sheffield stays by me. A frightful piece of waste ground (somehow, up here a piece of waste ground attains a squalor that would be impossible even in London), trampled quite bare of grass and littered with newspaper, old saucepans etc. To the right, an isolated row of gaunt four-room houses, dark red, blackened by smoke. To the left an interminable vista of factory chimneys, chimney behind chimney, fading away into a dim blackish haze. Behind me a railway embankment made from the slag of furnaces. In front, across the piece of waste ground, a cubical building of dingy red and yellow brick, with the sign, "John Grocock, Haulage Contractor".

Other memories of Sheffield: stone walls blackened by smoke, a shallow river yellow with chemicals, serrated flames, like circular saws, coming out from the cowls of the foundry chimneys, thump and scream of steam hammers (the iron seems to scream under the blow), smell of sulphur, yellow clay, backsides of women wagging laboriously from side to side as they shove their perambulators up the hills. . . .

7 March

Staying till next Wed. with M[arjorie] and H[umphrey] at 21 Estcourt Avenue, Headingley. Conscious all the while of difference in atmosphere between middle-class home even of this kind and working-class home. The essential difference is that here there is *elbow-room*, in spite of there being 5 adults and 3 children, besides animals, at present in the house. The children make peace and quiet difficult, but if you definitely want to be alone you can be so—in a working-class house *never*, either by night or day.

One of the kinds of discomfort inseparable from a working man's life is *waiting about*. If you receive a salary it is paid into your bank and you draw it out when you want it. If you receive *wages*, you have to go and get them in somebody else's time and are probably kept hanging about and probably expected to behave as though being paid your wages at all was a favour. When Mr H at Wigan went to the mine to draw his compensation, he had to go, for some reason I did not understand, on two separate days each week, and was kept waiting in the cold for about an hour before he was paid. In addition the four tram journeys to and from the mine cost him 1/–, reducing his compensation from 29/– weekly to 28/–. He took this for granted, of course. The result of long training in this kind of thing is that whereas the bourgeois goes through life expecting to get what he wants, within limits, the working man always feels himself the slave of a more or less mysterious authority. I was impressed by the fact that when I went to Sheffield Town Hall to ask for certain statistics, both B and Searle—both of them people of much more forcible character than myself—were nervous, would not come into the office with me, and assumed that the Town Clerk would refuse information. They said, "He might give it to *you*, but he wouldn't to *us*." Actually the Town Clerk was snooty and I did not get all the information I asked for. But the point was that I assumed my questions would be answered, and the other two assumed the contrary.

It is for this reason that in countries where the class hierarchy exists, people of the higher class always tend to come to the front in times of stress, though not really more gifted than the others. That they will do so seems to be taken for granted always and everywhere. NB. to look up the passage in Lissagaray's *History of the Commune* describing the shootings after the Commune had been suppressed. They were shooting the ringleaders without trial, and as they did not know who the ringleaders were, they were picking them out on the principle that those of better class than the others would be the ringleaders. One man was shot because he was wearing a watch, another because he "had an intelligent face". NB. to look up this passage.

Yesterday with H and M to Haworth Parsonage, home of the Brontës and now a museum. Was chiefly impressed by a pair of Charlotte Brontë's cloth-topped boots, very small, with square toes and lacing up at the sides.

9 March

Yesterday with H and M to their cottage at Middlesmoor, high up on the edge of the moors. Perhaps it is only the time of year, but even up there, miles from any industrial towns, the smoky look peculiar to this part of the country seems to hang about anything. Grass dull-coloured, streams muddy, houses all blackened as though by smoke. There was snow everywhere, but thawing and slushy. Sheep very dirty—no lambs, apparently. The palm was out and primroses putting out new shoots; otherwise nothing moving.

11 March

On the last two evenings to "discussion groups"—societies of people who meet once a week, listen-in to some talk on the radio and then discuss it. Those at the one on Monday were chiefly unemployed men and I believe these "discussion groups" were started or at any rate suggested by the Social Welfare people who run the unemployed occupational centres. That on Monday was decorous and rather dull. Thirteen people including ourselves (one woman besides M) and we met in a room adjoining a public library. The talk was on Galsworthy's play *The Skin Game* and the discussion kept to the subject until most of us adjourned to a pub for bread and cheese and beer afterwards. Two people dominated the assembly, one a huge bull-headed man named Rowe who contradicted whatever the last speaker had said and involved himself in the most appalling contradictions, the other a youngish, very intelligent and extremely well-informed man named Creed. From his refined accent, quiet voice and apparent omniscience, I took him for a librarian. I find he keeps a tobacconist's shop and was previously a commercial traveller. During the war he was imprisoned as a conscientious objector. The other meeting was at a pub and the people were of higher standing. The arrangement is that M and H go there taking the portable radio, and the publican, who is a member of the group, lets them have a room for the evening. On this occasion the talk was called "If Plato lived Today", but actually no one listened-in except M and myself—H has gone to Bedford. When the talk was over the publican, a Canadian with a very bald head, a market gardener who was already the worse for drink, and another man rolled in and there began an orgy of drinking from which we escaped with difficulty about an hour later. Much of the talk on both nights about the European situation and most people saying (some of them with ill-dissembled hope) that war is certain. With two exceptions all pro-German.

Today to Barnsley to fix up about a place to stay. Wilde, secretary of the South Yorkshire Branch of the Working Men's Club & Institute Union, has fixed it all up for me. The address is Agnes Avenue. The usual 2 up 2 down house, with sink in living room, as at Sheffield. The husband is a miner and was away at work when we got there. House very disorganised as it was washing day, but seemed clean. Wilde, though kind and helpful, was a very vague person. He was a working miner till 1924 but as usual has been bourgeois-ified. Smartly dressed with gloves and umbrella and very little accent—I would have taken him for a solicitor from his appearance.

Barnsley is slightly smaller than Wigan—about 70,000 inhabitants —but distinctly less poverty-stricken, at any rate in appearance. Much better shops and more appearance of business being done. Many miners coming home from the morning shift. Mostly wearing clogs but of a square-toed pattern different from the Lancashire ones.

13 March

At Agnes Terrace, Barnsley.

This house is bigger than I had imagined. Two rooms and tiny larder under the stairs downstairs, 3 or 4[1] rooms upstairs. Eight people in the house—5 adults and 3 children. Front room which should be parlour is used as bedroom. Living room, about 14′ by 12′, has the usual kitchener, sink and copper. No gas stove. Electric light in all rooms save one. Outside WC.

The Family. Mr G, a short powerful man, age about 45, with coarse features, enlarged nose and a very fatigued, pale look. He is rather bald, has his own teeth (unusual in a working-class person of that age) but they are very discoloured. A bit deaf, but very ready to talk, especially about technicalities of mining. Has worked in the pit ever since a small boy. On one occasion was buried by a fall of earth or stone—no bones broken, but it took ten minutes to dig him out and two hours to drag him to the cage. He tells me no machinery (stretchers etc) exists for conveying injured men away from the scene of accidents. Obviously some kind of stretcher running on the trolley rails could be contrived, but this would involve stopping all the haulage of coal while it was being done. So injured men have to be carried to the cage by helpers who are themselves bending double and can only get them along very slowly. Mr G works at removing the coal onto the trucks after it is cut—"scufting" I think it is called. He and his mate are paid piece-work 2/2d per ton—1/1d each. On full time his wages average £2–10–0d a week. His stoppages amount to 6/11d. He works at Darton, about 4 miles away and goes there by bus. Journeys cost 6d a day. So his net wages on full time are about £2–0–0d a week.

Mrs G is about 10 years younger,[2] motherly type, always cooking and cleaning, accent less broad than her husband's. Two little girls, Doreen and Ireen (spelling?) aged 11 and 10. The other lodgers are a widowed joiner, employed on the woodwork at the new dog-track, and his son aged about 11, and a professional singer who is going to sing at one of the pubs. All the larger pubs in Barnsley employ

[1] 3. [Author's footnote.]

[2] Actually their ages are 50 and 38. [Author's footnote.]

singers and dancers (some of these very immoral according to Mrs G) more or less constantly.

The house is very clean and decent and my room the best I have had in lodgings up here. Flannelette sheets this time.

14 March

Much talk last night with Mr G about his war experiences. Especially about the malingering he saw going on when he was invalided with some injury to his leg, and the astute ways the doctors had of detecting it. One man feigned complete deafness and successfully kept it up during tests lasting two hours. Finally he was told by signs that he would be discharged and could go, and just as he was passing through the door the doctor said casually "Shut that door after you, would you?" The man turned and shut it, and was passed for active service. Another man feigned insanity and got away with it. For days he was going round with a bent pin on a bit of string, pretending to be catching fish. Finally he was discharged, and on parting with G he held up his discharge papers and said "This is what I was fishing for." I was reminded of the malingering I saw in the Hôpital Cochin in Paris, where unemployed men used to remain for months together on pretence of being ill.[1]

Beastly cold again. Sleet this morning. But yesterday as I came on the train they were ploughing and the earth looked much more spring-like; especially in one field where the earth was very black, not like the usual clay soil hereabouts, and as the ploughshare turned it over it looked like chocolate fudge being sliced up with a knife.

I am very comfortable in this house but do not think I shall pick up much of interest in Barnsley. I know no one here except Wilde, who is thoroughly vague. Cannot discover whether there is a branch of the NUWM here. The public library is no good. There is no proper reference library and it seems no separate directory of Barnsley is published.

15 March

Last night with Wilde and others to the general meeting of the South Yorkshire Branch of the Working Men's Club & Institute Union, held at one of the clubs in Barnsley. About 200 people there, all busily tucking into beer and sandwiches, though it was only 4.30 pm —they had got an extension for the day. The club was a big building,

[1] See IV, 58.

really an enlarged pub with one big hall which could be used for concerts etc and in which the meeting was held. It was a bit stormy in parts, but Wilde and the chairman had them pretty well in hand and were complete masters of all the usual platform phraseology and procedure. I notice from the balance sheet that W's salary is £260 per annum. Before this I had never realised the number and importance of these working men's clubs, especially in the North and especially in Yorkshire. Those at this meeting consisted of pairs of delegates sent by all the clubs in South Yorkshire. There would have been I should say 150 delegates, representing therefore 75 clubs and probably about 10,000 members. That is in South Yorkshire alone. After the meeting I was taken to have tea in the committee room with about 30 of what were, I gathered, some of the more important delegates. We had cold ham, bread and butter, cakes and whisky which everyone poured into their tea. After that with W and the others went down to the Radical and Liberal Club in the middle of the town, where I have been before. There was a sort of smoking concert going on, as these clubs, like the pubs, all engage singers etc for the weekends. There was quite a good knockabout comedian whose jokes were of the usual twins-mother-in-law-kippers type, and pretty steady boozing. Wilde's accent becomes much broader when he is in these surroundings. It appears that these clubs were first started as a kind of charitable concern in the mid-nineteenth century, and were, of course, Temperance. But they escaped by becoming financially self-supporting and have developed, as I say, into sort of glorified co-operative pubs. G, who belongs to the Radical and Liberal Club, tells me his subscription is 1/6d a quarter and all drinks are 1d or 2d a pint cheaper than at the pubs. Youths under 21 are not admitted and (I think) women cannot be members but can go there with their husbands. Most of the clubs are avowedly non-political, and in this and in the fact that the members are mostly of the more prosperous working-class type—comparatively few unemployed—one can foresee the germs of a danger that they will be politically mobilised for anti-Socialist purposes.

Talking with a man who was previously a miner but now works as a labourer for the Corporation. He was telling me about the housing conditions in Barnsley in his childhood. He grew up in a back to back house in which there were 11 people (two bedrooms, I suppose) and you not only had to walk 200 yards to get to the lavatory, but shared it with, in all, 36 people.

Have arranged to go down the Grimethorpe pit next Saturday. This is a very up-to-date pit and possesses certain machinery that does not exist anywhere else in England. Also to go down a "day hole" pit on Thursday afternoon. The man I spoke to told me it was a mile to the coal face, so if the "travelling" is bad I shan't go the whole way—I only want to see what a "day hole" is like and am not going to incapacitate myself like last time.

When G comes back from the pit he washes before having his food. I don't know whether this is usual, but I have often seen miners sitting down to eat with Christy Minstrel faces—completely black except very red lips which become clean by eating. When G arrives he is as black as ink, especially his scalp—for this reason miners usually wear their hair short. He pours out a large basin of hot water, strips to the waist and washes himself very methodically, first his hands, then his upper arms, then his forearms, then his chest and shoulders, then his face and head. Then he dries himself and his wife washes his back. His navel is still a nest of coal-dust. I suppose from the waist down he must normally be quite black. There are public baths and the miners go to them but as a rule not more than once a week—one cannot be surprised at this, as a miner has not much time between working and sleeping. Miners' houses with bathrooms, other than the new Corporation ones, are practically unknown. Only a few colliery companies have baths at the pit-heads.

I notice that G does not eat very much. At present, working on the afternoon shift, he has the same breakfast as I have (an egg and bacon, bread—no butter—and tea) and has a light lunch, such as bread and cheese, about half past twelve. He says he cannot do his work if he has eaten too much. All he takes with him to the pit is some bread and dripping and cold tea. This is the usual thing. The men do not want much in the stifling air down there, and besides, they are not allowed any time off for eating. He gets home between 10 and 11 pm and it is then that he has his only heavy meal of the day.

16 March

Last night to hear Mosley speak at the Public Hall, which is in structure a theatre. It was quite full—about 700 people I should say. About 100 Blackshirts on duty, with two or three exceptions weedy-looking specimens, and girls selling *Action*[1] etc. Mosley spoke for an hour and a half and to my dismay seemed to have the meeting

[1] The journal of the British Union of Fascists.

mainly with him. He was booed at the start but loudly clapped at the end. Several men who tried at the beginning to interject questions were thrown out, one of them—who as far as I could see was only trying to get a question answered—with quite unnecessary violence, several Blackshirts throwing themselves upon him and raining blows on him while he was still sitting down and had not attempted any violence. M is a very good speaker. His speech was the usual clap-trap—Empire free trade, down with the Jew and the foreigner, higher wages and shorter hours all round, etc etc. After the preliminary booing the (mainly) working-class audience was easily bamboozled by M speaking from as it were a Socialist angle, condemning the treachery of successive governments towards the workers. The blame for everything was put upon mysterious international gangs of Jews who are said to be financing, among other things, the British Labour Party and the Soviet. M's statement re the international situation: "We fought Germany before in a British quarrel; we are not going to fight them now in a Jewish one" was received with loud applause. Afterwards there were questions as usual, and it struck me how easy it is to bamboozle an uneducated audience if you have prepared beforehand a set of repartees with which to evade awkward questions, e.g. M kept extolling Italy and Germany, but when questioned about concentration camps etc always replied, "We have no foreign models; what happens in Germany need not happen here." To the question, "How do you know that your own money is not used to finance cheap foreign labour?" (M having denounced the Jewish financiers who are supposed to do this), M replied, "All my money is invested in England," and I suppose comparatively few of the audience realised that this means nothing.

At the beginning M said that anyone ejected would be charged under the Public Meetings Act. I don't know whether this was actually done, but presumably the power to do so exists. In connection with this the fact that there are no police on duty *inside the building* is of great importance. Anyone who interrupts can be assaulted and thrown out and then charged into the bargain, and of course the stewards, i.e. M himself, are the judges of what constitutes an interruption. Therefore one is liable to get both a hammering and a fine for asking a question which M finds it difficult to answer.

At the end of the meeting a great crowd collected outside, as there was some public indignation about the men who had been thrown out. I waited for a long time in the crowd to see what would happen, but M and party did not emerge. Then the police managed to split the crowd and I found myself at the front, whereupon a policeman ordered me away, but quite civilly. I went round to the back of the crowd and waited again, but still M did not appear and I concluded he had been sneaked out by a back door, so went home. In the morning at the *Chronicle* office, however, I was told that there had been some stone-throwing and two men had been arrested and remanded.

G changed this morning onto the early morning shift. He gets up at 3.45 am and has to be at work, i.e. at the coal face, at 6. He gets home about 2.30 pm. His wife does not get up to get his breakfast and he says few miners will allow their wives to do so. Also that there are still some miners who if they meet a woman on their way to work will turn back and go home. It is considered bad luck to see a woman before going to work. I presume this only applies to the early morning shift.

18 March

The Barnsley public baths are very bad. Old-fashioned bathtubs, none too clean, and not nearly enough of them. I judged by the appearance of the place there were at most 50 baths[1]—this in a town of 70–80 thousand inhabitants, largely miners, not one of whom has a bath in his own house, except in the new Corporation houses.

Some curious coincidences. When I went to see Len Kaye he recommended me to see Tommy Degnan, to whom I had also been recommended by Paddy Grady at Wigan. But what was more curious still, D was one of the men who were thrown out at Mosley's meeting, though not the one I actually saw thrown out. I went round to see D last night and had some difficulty in finding him. He lives in a dreadful barn of a place called Garden House, which is an old almost ruinous house which half a dozen unemployed men have taken and made a sort of lodging house of. D himself is not unemployed, though at the moment "playing" because a few days before the hammering he got at M's meeting he was slightly crushed by a fall of stone in the mine. We went out to look for the man whom I actually saw thrown out, as I want to get particulars and see his bruises before writing to the papers about it, but couldn't find him, and I am to see him today. Then in the street we ran across another man whom I saw thrown out. The latter's ejection was an interesting instance of the

[1] Actually 19! [Author's footnote.]

way any upset can be misrepresented and turned to advantage by a demagogue of the type of Mosley. At the time of the uproar at the back of the hall, this last man—name Hennessey,[1] I think—was seen to rush on to the stage, and everyone thought he had gone there to shout something out and interrupt M's speech. It struck me at the time as curious that though on the stage he didn't shout anything out, and the next moment, of course, the Blackshirts on the platform seized him and bundled him out. M shouted out, "A typical example of Red tactics!" It now appears what happened was this. Hennessey saw the Blackshirts at the back of the hall bashing D, and couldn't get to him to help him because there is no aisle up the middle; but there was an aisle up the right hand side, and the only way he could get to this was over the stage. D after being thrown out was charged under the Public Meetings Act, but H not. I don't know yet whether the other man, Marshall, was. The woman who was thrown out—this was somewhere at the back and I didn't see it—was hit on the head with a trumpet and was a day in hospital. D and H were in the Army together and H was wounded in the leg and D taken prisoner when the Vth Army was defeated in 1918. D, being a miner, was sent to work in the Polish mines. He said all of them had pit-head baths. H says the French ones have them too.

G told me a dreadful story of how a friend of his, a "dataller", was buried alive. He was buried under a fall of small stone, and they rushed to him and, though they could not get him out completely, they got his head and shoulders free so that he could breathe. He was alive and spoke to them. At this moment they saw that the roof was coming down again and had to take to flight themselves. Once again he was buried, and once again they managed to get to him and uncover his head, and again he was alive and spoke to them. Then the roof came down again, and this time they did not get him out for some hours, after which, of course, he was dead. But the real point of the story, from G's point of view, was that this man had known beforehand that this part of the mine was unsafe and likely to bury him: "And it worked on his mind to that extent that he kissed his wife before he went to work. And she told me afterwards that it was the first time in years he'd kissed her."

There is a very old woman—a Lancashire woman—living near

[1] His name is Firth. I got it as Hennessey because he was introduced to me as Hellis Firth. (*E*llis Firth—people here very capricious about their H's.) [Author's footnote.]

here who in her day has worked down the pit, dragging tubs of coal with a harness and chain. She is 83, so I suppose this would be in the 'seventies.

19 March

In frightful exhaustion after going down the "day hole", as, of course, when the time came I had not the strength of mind to say I did not want to go as far as the coal face.

I went down with the "deputy" (Mr Lawson) about 3 pm and came up about 6.15 pm. L said we had covered not quite 2 miles. I must say that I got on perceptibly better than at Wigan, either because the going was a little better, as I think it was—probably one could stand upright about one third of the way—or because L, who is an old man, moderated his pace to mine. The chief feature of this pit, apart from its being a "day hole", is that it is infernally wet in most places. There were quite considerable streams running here and there, and two enormous pumps have to be kept running all day and most of the night. The water is pumped up to ground level and has made a considerable pool, but curiously enough it is clear, clean water—even drinkable, L said—and the pool was quite ornamental with water-hens swimming about on it. We went down when the morning shift came up, and there are comparatively few men on the afternoon shift for some reason I did not understand. When we got to the coal face the men were there with the coal-cutter, which was not running at the moment, but they set it running to show me. The teeth on a revolving chain—in principle it is an enormously tough and powerful bandsaw—cut in underneath the coal face, after which huge boulders of coal can be easily tumbled out and broken up with picks before being loaded onto the tubs. Some of these boulders of coal, not yet broken up, were about 8 feet long by two thick by four high—the seam is four feet six, I think—and must have weighed many tons.[1] As it cuts the machine travels backwards or forwards, as desired, along the coal face, on its own power. The place where these men, and those loading the broken coal onto the tubs, were working was like hell. I had never thought of it before, but of course as the machine works it sends forth clouds of coal dust which almost stifle one and make it impossible to see more than a few feet. No lamps except Davy lamps of an old-fashioned pattern, not more than two or three candle-power, and it puzzled one to see how these men

[1] A cubic yard of coal is said to weigh 27 cwt. [Author's footnote.]

can see to work, except when there are a number of them together. To get from one part of the coal face to another you had to crawl along awful tunnels cut through the coal, a yard high by two feet wide, and then to work yourself on your bottom over mountainous boulders of coal. Of course in doing this I dropped my lamp and it went out. L called to one of the men working and he gave me his lamp. Then L said "You'd better cut yourself a bit of coal as a memento" (visitors always do this), and while I was cutting out a piece of coal with the pick, I knocked my second lamp over and put that out too. We had to go about a quarter of a mile with only one lamp between the two of us, which was disconcerting and brought it home to me how easily you could lose yourself down there if you didn't happen to know the roads.

We passed tubs, carrying props etc, going to and fro on the endless belt, which is worked by electricity. The tubs only move at 1½ miles an hour. All the miners at this pit seem to carry sticks, and they gave me one which was a great help. They are about two foot six long and hollowed out just below the knob. At moderate heights (4 ft to 5 ft) you keep your hand on the knob, and when you have to bend really low you grip the stick by the hollow. The ground underfoot was as mucky as a farmyard in many places. They say the best way to go is to keep one foot on the trolley-rail and the other on the sleepers, if you can find them. The miners going down the roads *run*, bent double of course, in places where I could barely stagger. They say it is easier to run than walk when you have the hang of it. It was rather humiliating that coming back, which we did by the most direct route, took me three quarters of an hour and only takes the miners a quarter of an hour. But we had gone to the nearest working, only about half way to the end. Those who work at the furthest working take nearly an hour to get to their work. This time I was given one of the new crash helmets which many, though not all, miners now wear. To look at they are very like a French or Italian tin hat, and I had always imagined they were made of metal. Actually they are of a kind of compressed fibre and very light. Mine was a bore because it was too small and fell off when I bent very low. But how glad of it I was! Coming back when I was tired and could not bend much I must have bashed my head twenty times—once hard enough to bring down a huge chunk of stone—but felt absolutely nothing.

Walked home with L to Dodworth as I could get the bus more easily there. He has a two-mile walk with some pretty stiff hills going to and from work, in addition to the walk inside the mine when he gets there. But I suppose as "deputy" he doesn't do much manual work. He has worked in this mine 22 years and says he knows it so well that he never needs to look up to see when there is a beam coming.

Birds all singing. Tiny pink buds on the elms that I had never noticed before. Many female flowers on the hazels. But I suppose as usual the old maids will be cutting them all off for Easter decorations.

When I sit typing the family, especially Mrs G and the kids, all gather round to watch absorbedly, and appear to admire my prowess almost as much as I admire that of the miners.

20 March

Talking with Firth. He gets 32/– a week from the UAB.[1] Mrs F is a Derbyshire woman. Two kids, ages 2 years 5 months and 10 months. They are fairly sturdy as yet and it is evidently the case that these kids do much better in infancy than later, as for about their first three years they get help from the Infants' Welfare Clinic. Mrs F gets three packets of baby's food (dried milk) a week and also a little Nestle's milk. On one occasion she got an allowance of 2/– a week for a month to buy eggs for the elder child. While there we sent out for some beer. I noted both the Fs let the children drink a little beer out of their glasses. Another kid was in and out of the house mothering the F baby. Her father was murdered four years ago. The widowed mother gets an allowance of 22/– a week, I do not know from what source, on which she has to keep herself and 4 children.

I did not know before, what F told me, that when the mines have baths at the pit-head these are built not by the company but by the miners themselves, out of the Welfare Fund to which every miner subscribes. This is the case at any rate round here—must try and find out if it is so everywhere. It is by the way another argument against the statement that miners do not want or appreciate baths. One reason why not all pits have baths is that when a pit is anywhere near being worked out it is not considered worth while to build baths.

I forgot to mention that in the "day hole" at Wentworth the pit props, owing to the damp, had strange fungi exactly like cotton wool growing on them. If you touched them they went all to nothing, leaving a nasty smell. It appears that a Lancashire miner, instead of

[1] Unemployment Assistance Board.

slinging his lamp round his neck, has a band above the elbow and hangs the lamp from that.

Today G earned little or nothing. The coal-cutter had broken down so there was no coal for him to fill into the tubs. When this happens those on piece-work get no compensation, except a shilling or two for odd jobs called bye-work.

I see the *Manchester Guardian* has not printed my letter re Mosley and I suppose they never will. I hardly expected *The Times* to print it, but I think the *MG* might, considering their reputation.

21 March

This morning went down the Grimethorpe pit. Not exhausting this time, because in order not to clash with the visit of some students from the Technical College we went to the nearest working, only about ¼ mile and little bending.

The depth of the mine, at least at the part we went to, is a little over 400 yards. The young engineer who took me thought the cages *average* 60 mph when going down, in which case they must touch 80 or more at their fastest. I think this must be an exaggeration, but they certainly travel faster than the average railway train. The especial feature of this pit is the "skip wagon", by which the coal is sent straight up in special cages instead of being sent up, much more laboriously, in tubs. The full tubs come slowly along an inclined rail and are controlled by men at the sides with brakes. Each tub halts for a moment on a weighing machine and its weight is entered up, then the tubs move on and move two at a time into a kind of container which grips them underneath. The container then turns right over, spilling the coal down a chute into the cage below. When the cage has got 8 tons, i.e. about 16 tubs, in it, it goes out and the coal is spilt down a similar chute on the surface. Then it goes along conveyor belts and over screens which automatically sort it, and is washed as well. The coal which is being sold to factories etc is shot straight into goods trucks on the railway line below and then weighed truck and all, the weight of the truck being known. This is the only pit in England which works this system—all others send the coal up in the tubs, which takes much more time and needs more tubs. The system has been worked for a long time in Germany and USA. The Grimethorpe pit turns out about 500 tons of coal a day.

This time I saw the fillers actually working at the coal face, and now having seen the different operations of coal-getting, except blasting, in progress separately, I understand more or less how it is done. The coal-cutter travels along the face cutting into the bottom of the ledge of coal to the depth of 5 feet. Then the coal can be tumbled out in boulders with picks, or—as here, the Grimethorpe coal being very hard—is first loosened with blasting charges and then extracted. Then the fillers (who have also extracted it) load it onto the conveyor belt which runs behind them and carries it to a chute from which it runs into the tubs. As far as possible the three operations are done in three separate shifts. The coal cutter works on the afternoon shift, the blasting is done on the night shift (when the minimum number of people are in the pit), and the fillers extract the coal on the morning shift. Each man has to clear a space 4 or 5 yards wide. So, as the seam of coal is about a yard high and the cutter has undermined it to a depth of 5 feet, each man has to extract and load onto the belt (say) 14 × 5 × 3 cubic feet of coal, equals 210 cubic feet, equals nearly 8 cubic yards of coal. If it is really the case that a cubic yard of coal weighs 27 cwt, this would be well over 10 tons—i.e. each man has to shift nearly a ton and a half an hour. When the job is done the coal face has advanced 5 feet, so during the next shift the conveyor belt is taken to pieces, moved 5 feet forward and reassembled, and fresh props are put in.

The place where the fillers were working was fearful beyond description. The only thing one could say was that, as conditions underground go, it was not particularly hot. But as the seam of coal is only a yard high or a bit more, the men can only kneel or crawl to their work, never stand up. The effort of constantly shovelling coal over your left shoulder and flinging it a yard or two beyond, while in a kneeling position, must be very great even to men who are used to it. Added to this there are the clouds of coal dust which are flying down your throat all the time and which make it difficult to see any distance. The men were all naked except for trousers and knee-pads. It was difficult to get through the conveyor belt to the coal face. You had to pick your moment and wriggle through quickly when the belt stopped for a moment. Coming back we crawled onto the belt while it was moving; I had not been warned of the difficulty of doing this and immediately fell down and had to be hauled off before the belt dashed me against the props etc which were littered about further down. Added to the other discomforts of the men working there, there is the fearful din of the belt which never stops for more than a minute or so.

Electric lights this time—no Davy lamps used in the pit except for testing for gas. They can detect the presence of gas by the flame turning blue. By the height to which the flame can be turned while still remaining blue, they have a rough test of the percentage of gas in the atmosphere. All the roads we went through, except one or two galleries used for short cuts, were high and well-built and even paved underfoot in places. I have at last grasped the reason for the doors one passes through from time to time. The air is sucked out of one entry by fans and goes in of its own accord at another entry. But if not prevented it will come back by the shortest route instead of going all round the mine. Hence the doors, which stop it from taking short cuts.

Excellent baths at the pit. They have no less than 1000 h & c shower baths. Each miner has two lockers, one for his pit clothes and one for his ordinary clothes (so that the pit clothes shall not dirty the others.) Thus he can come and go clean and decent. According to the engineer, the baths were built partly by the Miners' Welfare, partly by the royalty owners, and the company also contributed.

During this week G has had two narrow escapes from falls of stone, one of which actually grazed him on its way down. These men would not last long if it were not that they are used to the conditions and know when to stand from under. I am struck by the difference between the miners when you see them underground and when you see them in the street etc. Above ground, in their thick ill-fitting clothes, they are ordinary-looking men, usually small and not at all impressive and indeed not distinguishable from other people except by their distinctive walk (clumping tread, shoulders very square) and the blue scars on their noses. Below, when you see them stripped, all, old and young, have splendid bodies, with every muscle defined and wonderfully small waists. I saw some miners going into their baths. As I thought, they are quite black from head to foot. So the ordinary miner, who has not access to a bath, must be black from the waist down six days a week at least.

I have been wondering about what people like the Firths have to eat. Their total income is 32/– a week. Rent 9/0½d. Gas say 1/3d. Coal (say 3 cwt @ 9d) 2/3d. Other minor expenses (e.g. F keeps up his Union payments) say 1/–. That leaves 18/6d. But Mrs F gets a certain amount of baby-food free from the Clinic, so say the baby only costs 1/– a week beyond this. That leaves 17/6d. F smokes at any rate some cigarettes, say 1/– (6 packets of Woodbines a week).

That leaves 16/6d a week to feed 2 adults and a girl aged 2 years, or about 5/6d per week per head. And this takes no account of clothes, soap, matches, etc etc. Mrs F said they fed chiefly on bread and jam. If I can do so delicately I must ask F to give me a fairly exact account of their meals for one day.

22 March

Kaye says his father, a collier (now too old for work), always washed the top half of his body and his feet and legs to above the knees. The rest of his body was only washed at very long intervals, the old man believing that washing all over led to lumbago.

Communist meeting in the Market Place disappointing. The trouble with all these Communist speakers is that instead of using the popular idiom they employ immensely long sentences full of "despite" and "notwithstanding" and "be that as it may" etc in the Garvin[1] strain—and this in spite of always speaking with broad provincial or cockney accents—Yorkshire in this case. I suppose they are given set speeches which they learn by heart. After the visiting speaker Degnan got up to speak and was a much more effective speaker—he speaks very broad Lancashire and though he can talk like a leading article if he wants to he doesn't choose. The usual crowd of men of all ages gaping with entirely expressionless faces and the usual handful of women a little more animated than the men—I suppose because no woman would go to a political meeting unless exceptionally interested in politics. About 150 people. Collection taken for the defence of the young men arrested in the Mosley affair and realised 6/–.

Wandering round Barnsley Main Colliery and the glassworks along the canal with F and another man whose name I did not get. The latter's mother had just died and was lying dead at home. She was 89 and had been a midwife for 50 years. I noted the lack of hypocrisy with which he was laughing and joking and came into the pub to have a drink etc. The monstrous slag-heaps round Barnsley Main are all more or less on fire under the surface. In the darkness you can see long serpentine fires creeping all over them, not only red but very sinister blue flames (from sulphur) which always seem on the point of going out and then flicker up again.

I notice that the word "spink" (for a great tit, I think, but at any rate some small bird) is in use here as well as in Suffolk.

[1] J. L. Garvin (1868–1947), right-wing editor of the *Observer*, 1908 to 1942.

23 March

At Mapplewell. Houses about the worst I have seen, though we did not manage to get into the very worst ones, which were one-roomed or two-roomed cabins of stone, about 20′ by 15′ by 15′ high, or even less, and practically ruinous. Rent of these, some of which are property of colliery, said to be about 3/–. In the row called Spring Gardens we found public indignation because the landlords have served about half the row with notices to quit for arrears of, in some cases, only a few shillings. (Firth, in Barnsley, has a notice to quit though only about 5/– in arrear and paying this off at 3d per week.) The people took us in and insisted on our seeing their houses. Frightful interiors. In the first one old father, out of work of course, obviously horribly bewildered by his notice to quit after 22 years tenancy and turning anxiously to F and me with some idea that we could help him. The mother rather more self-possessed. Two sons aged about 24, fine big men with powerful well-shaped bodies, narrow faces and red hair, but thin and listless from obvious under-nourishment and with dull brutalised expressions. Their sister, a little older and very like them, with prematurely lined face, glancing from F to me, again with the idea that perhaps we might help. One of the sons, taking no notice of our presence, all the while slowly peeling off his socks in front of the fire; his feet almost black with sticky dirt. The other son was at work. The house terribly bare—no bed-clothes except overcoats etc—but fairly clean and tidy. At the back children playing about in the muck, some of them, aged 5 or 6, bare-foot and naked except for a sort of shift. F told the tenants if the notice to quit was persisted with to come into Barnsley and see him and Degnan. I told them the landlord was only bluffing and to hold their ground and if he threatened taking it to court to threaten in return to sue him for lack of repairs. Hope I did the right thing.

I have glanced at B's novel. It is b——s.

25 March

Men along the private line leading to Gauber pit unloading trucks of slack. They say the mine "can't get shut o' t'slack" and are laying it by. This is regarded as a sinister sign. If the pits are storing slack already they will soon be running short time. The men get 4d a ton for unloading the slack. A truck holds about 10 tons, so they have to unload 3 trucks to make a day's wage.

I think in the dirtiest interiors I see, more than any of the various kinds of squalor—the piles of unwashed crocks, the scraps of miscellaneous food all over the lino-topped table, the dreadful rag mats with the crumbs of years trodden into them—the things that oppress me most are the scraps of newspaper that are scattered all over the floor.

G is quite badly ill with bronchitis. He stayed away from work yesterday, then this morning, when still obviously ill, insisted on going to work.

Returning to Leeds tomorrow, then on to London on Monday.

75. Letter to Jack Common

The Stores
Wallington
3 April 1936

Dear Common,

I received an unsigned letter which from internal evidence I decided must be from you. I moved into the above yesterday and find myself pretty comfortable, so I think I shall dig myself in, that is if the landlord doesn't raise the rent on me. Of course it isn't what you might call luxurious, but it is as good as one could expect for 7/6 a week so near London. The garden is potentially good but has been left in the most frightful state I have ever seen. I am afraid it will be a year before I can get it nice. As you see by the address this used to be the village shop. The people who had it went bankrupt over a model farm and there has been no shop in the village for a year, so I am thinking of reopening it. Of course there couldn't be much profit in a village of 50–100 inhabitants, especially as vans come from Baldock (three miles away) several times a week, but I don't think I could actually lose money as I have got to pay the rent of the house in any case. At present I am sending out feelers, on the one hand trying to make sure my landlord doesn't double the rent the day after I have bought a new bacon-slicer, on the other making enquiries among the villagers to see whether they would like to have a shop here again. I am a bit vague about how one gets in touch with the wholesalers for a "general" shop, but I suppose it isn't more complicated than a bookshop. If I do open it will be only for certain stated hours so as not to interfere with my work.

I'll send along a review of Brown's book[1] as soon as I can settle to work again, also I'll see that the *Adelphi* get a copy of my novel.[2] It ought to be out in a few weeks and would have been out a month ago if it had not been for all that bollox about libel. I collected some interesting material for my new book[3] while in Yorkshire and Lancashire, and only hope I shall be able to make use of it. It is a pity I just missed Rees, who is now in Lancashire somewhere I believe. The feuds I observed among the *Adelphi* followers seemed to centre round two causes. One was that people in each area in the north seem to be savagely jealous of people from other areas and their jealousy takes the form of declaring that theirs is the only genuine distressed area and the others don't know what poverty means. Besides this Brown at Sheffield told me that at the *Adelphi* summer schools people from the middle classes and genuine working-class people didn't get on together and he and other working-class people were annoyed by patronising airs put on by some of the others. How much truth there was in this I can't say. . . .

When I have got the house and garden into some kind of trim and started to do a little work again, I will come over and see you—I'll give you plenty of notice beforehand. It is a cross-country journey but not far if one did it on a push-bike. Have you got a car or anything nowadays? I would like it if you come over here some time.

Yours
Eric A. Blair

76. Letter to Jack Common

The Stores
Wallington, Nr Baldock
Thursday [16? April 1936]

Dear Common,

Thanks for yours. I have now seen my landlord and it is OK about the rent, so I have definitely decided to open the shop and have spread the news among the villagers to some extent. I should certainly be very obliged if you would find out about the wholesalers.

[1] *The Fate of the Middle Classes* by Alec Brown.

[2] *Keep the Aspidistra Flying.*

[3] *The Road to Wigan Pier.*

I didn't know you had your shop still. I believe there are some wholesalers of the kind at Watford, Kingford or Kingston or some such name. I don't know whether, seeing that I shall only want tiny amounts at a time (apart from the smallness of the village I haven't much storage room), they will make any trouble about delivery. I intend, at first at any rate, to stock nothing perishable except children's sweets. Later on I might start butter and marg but it would mean getting a cooler. I am not going to stock tobacco because the pubs here (two to about 75 inhabitants!) stock it and I don't want to make enemies, especially as one pub is next door to me. I am beginning to make out lists, though whether any one wholesaler will cover the lot I am not certain. I suppose what I shall start off [with] will be about twenty quids' worth of stuff. Are these people good about giving credit? What I would like to do would be to give a deposit of about £5 and then pay quarterly. I suppose my bank would give me a reference. It is a pity in view of this that I have just changed my branch because the Hampstead branch were getting quite trustful and told me I could overdraw, though I never asked them. I shall want besides stock one or two articles of shop equipment, such as scales, a bell etc. There are some that go with this place but my landlord has them and he is the sort of person who takes a year before he hands anything over. I have got to tidy up the shop premises and repaint, but if I can click with a wholesalers I should be ready to open up in about 3 weeks.

Yes, this business of class-breaking is a bugger. The trouble is that the socialist bourgeoisie, most of whom give me the creeps, will not be realistic and admit that there are a lot of working-class habits which they don't like and don't want to adopt. E.g. the typical middle-class socialist not only doesn't eat with his knife but is still slightly horrified by seeing a working man do so. And then so many of them are the sort of eunuch type with a vegetarian smell who go about spreading sweetness and light and have at the back of their minds a vision of the working class all TT, well washed behind the ears, readers of Edward Carpenter[1] or some other pious sodomite and talking with BBC accents. The working classes are very patient under it all. All the two months I was up north, when I spent my entire time in asking people questions about how much dole they got, what they had to eat etc I was never once socked on the jaw and only

[1] Edward Carpenter (1844–1929), writer and social reformer, whose works include *Towards Democracy* and *The Intermediate Sex*.

once told to go to hell, and then by a woman who was deaf and thought I was a rate-collector. This question has been worrying me for a long time and part of my next book[1] is to be about it.

I will get over when I have a bike or something. If you come over here, either let me know so that there shall be food, or take your chance—but there'll always be *something*, of course. The garden is still Augean (I have dug up twelve boots in two days) but I am getting things straight a little. It is awful to think that for nearly three months I have not done a stroke of work. Getting and spending we lay waste our powers. However I have wads of notes which give me the illusion of not having wasted my time.

Yours
Eric A. Blair

77. Letter to Sir Richard Rees, Bt.

The Stores
Wallington
Nr Baldock, Herts.
20 April 1936

Dear Richard,

Thanks for your card. Clitheroe, which I vaguely associate with cotton shirts, seems rather a melancholy place to spend the summer in, but everyone to his taste. I have been here about a fortnight, and as you see by the address it has been the village store, and as there is now no shop here (only a tiny village of about 50–75 inhabitants) I am going to reopen it as a "general" shop when I have fixed up with some wholesalers. Jack Common, who has something to do with a shop of the kind I believe, is going to advise me. I haven't as yet done much about it because I have been too busy battling with the garden, which though small has been left in an unspeakable state. It will be about a year before I can make it really nice. It is quite a nice cottage and very cheap, but no conveniences; I shall put these in by degrees if I stay, as I think I shall. I intend opening the shop in the afternoons only, so as to leave me my mornings to work in. I don't expect to make much out of it but I ought to make my rent and a bit over. Wallington is about 35 or 40 miles from town but you can get there fairly quickly if you bike to Hitchin.

[1] *The Road to Wigan Pier.*

I haven't begun my new book[1] yet but am all set to do so. It is not going to be a novel this time. Do you know John Strachey[2] personally? I was at school about the same time as him but didn't know him. I would like to have a talk about Mosley with him some time if I run across him. I heard Mosley speak in Barnsley and his speech though delivered with an excellent platform technique was the most unutterable bollox, but I heard Strachey state in a speech once that Mosley was a very able man. I suppose Strachey has known Mosley intimately, and I would like to know whether M is sincere in what he says or whether he is deliberately bamboozling the public.

I am going to bike over and see Common some day this week. It is about 8–10 miles. I asked them to send a copy of my new book[3] to the *Adelphi*—don't know whether they have done so. I also sent a copy to Mrs Meade because I had promised them a copy and M asked me privately to send it to his wife, but this is troubling me, because I feel she might think herself obliged to read it and it might bore her. If you are with them you could drop a hint to the effect that presentation copies are not meant to be read. It is still beastly cold and everything very late. I have found no nests except thrushes and blackbirds and have not heard the cuckoo or seen a swallow—I usually see my first about the 14th. The blackthorn is out and there are plenty of primroses and cowslips but the hedges are still very bare. If you want to be quiet some time come and stay here, because it is a good place to be quiet if you don't mind the primitiveness, which is bearable at any rate in summer, and there is a nice room you could have.

Yours
Eric A. Blair

Encounter, January 1962

[1] *The Road to Wigan Pier.*

[2] John Strachey (1901–63), politician and political theorist, Labour MP 1929–31, in which year he stood as a candidate for Mosley's New Party, but shortly after abandoned it and became caught up in the new, widespread enthusiasm for Communism. His book *The Coming Struggle for Power*, 1932, was the most influential exercise in Marxism produced by the English Left. In 1945 he joined the Labour Government as Minister of Food 1945–50. He was Secretary of State for War 1950–1.

[3] *Keep the Aspidistra Flying.*

***Keep the Aspidistra Flying** was published in London by Victor Gollancz Ltd on 20 April 1936, and in New York by Harcourt, Brace in 1956.*

78. Review

Bastard Death by Michael Fraenkel, *Fast One* by Paul Cain

Some time ago I reviewed a very unusual book called *Tropic of Cancer*, and I suggested that its particular attitude to life derived ultimately from the modern notion that death is an *end* and not the gateway to a new lease of life. The book I have before me this week, also by an American, deals more directly with the same subject—in fact, death is its avowed theme.

Unfortunately, I find *Bastard Death*, as a whole, almost unintelligible. *Tropic of Cancer*, apart from a certain discursiveness, was cast more or less in ordinary novel form. *Bastard Death* is hardly a novel at all. It consists of a series of separate paragraphs with no very apparent connection between them—in effect, tiny essays—which are perhaps the bones of a possible novel. Here are two or three of them taken at random:

> I hurry through the streets stark, my sight swollen—an ancient blight upon me. I dare not look into the faces of things . . . of men, women, children, dogs, cats, birds, trees, water, houses. For suffering has conceived indecently.
>
> The light thins and shrinks, it walks over the hills, nostalgia rankling in it—the pain of distance, of otherness.
>
> To be strong, to remain in this strength now, the depth cannot be plumbed, the mystery, the sacredness. Now is self-realisation, self-completion, death.

This, you see, is difficult, and it is not made easier by the explanatory notes, like chapter headings, that are placed here and there in the margin. I wish I could say that I understood more of this book than individual passages here and there, but I do not. What the author seems to me to be attempting is, in the first place, to reach a fuller awareness of death—a completer realisation of death as an absolute (the only absolute we know); secondly, to strip his mind of ordinary mental processes until a point is reached at which thought can begin anew. That is about all I can say—in fact my only function as reviewer is to point this book out to people with minds more abstract than my own. I will take a chance and say that it *is* a remarkable book, and the opinion of Henry Miller, whose writing I do understand and who contributes an introductory letter to this book, confirms me in this.

Fast One is also an American book, but of a somewhat different type. The blurb describes it as "a whirlwind of doublecrossing, ambush and murder". Here is a specimen paragraph:

> The little man came into the room quickly and kicked the side of Kells' head very hard. Kells relaxed his grip on Rose and Rose stood up. He brushed himself and went over and kicked Kells' head and face several times. His face was dark and composed and he was breathing hard. He kicked Kells very carefully, drawing his foot back and aiming, and then kicking very accurately and hard.

This kind of disgusting rubbish (hailed as "genius" when it comes in a slightly more refined form from Hemingway) is growing commoner and commoner. Some of the threepenny "Yank Mags" which you buy at Woolworth's now consist of nothing else. Please notice the sinister change that has come over an important sub-department of English fiction. There was, God knows, enough physical brutality in the novels of Fielding, Meredith, Charles Reade, etc, but

> our masters then
> Were still, at least, our countrymen.

In the old-style English novel you knocked your man down and then chivalrously waited for him to get up before knocking him down again; in the modern American version he is no sooner down than you take the opportunity of jumping on his face. Unfortunately I have not space here to discuss this question of assault and battery in English fiction. I can only state in passing that it is not, as Bernard Shaw seems to suggest in the preface to *Cashel Byron's Profession*, traceable to sadism, but to a subtler and more ignoble cause.

New English Weekly, 23 April 1936

79. Letter to John Lehmann

The Stores
Wallington
Near Baldock, Herts.
27 May 1936

Dear Mr Lehmann,[1]

I waited before answering your letter, as a friend in London was endeavouring to get me a copy of *New Writing*, but evidently she hasn't succeeded yet. What I was going to say was, I am writing a book at present & the only other thing I have in mind is a sketch,[2] (it would be abt 2000–3000 words), describing the shooting of an elephant. It all came back to me very vividly the other day & I would like to write it, but it may be that it is quite out of your line. I mean it might be too low brow for your paper & I doubt whether there is anything anti-Fascist in the shooting of an elephant! Of course you can't say in advance that you would like it, but perhaps you could say tentatively whether it is at all likely to be in your line or not. If not, then I won't write it; if you think it might interest you I will do it & send it along for you to consider. I am sorry to be so vague but without seeing a copy of *New Writing* I can't tell what sort of stuff it uses.

Yours very truly
George Orwell

80. Letter to Geoffrey Gorer

The Stores
Wallington
Nr Baldock, Herts.
Sat. [May? 1936]

Dear Gorer,

Many thanks for your kind offices re *Time & Tide*. They gave me some novels to review. I would have written to you before only as

[1] John Lehmann (1907–   ), writer and publisher, founder and editor of *New Writing*, a literary magazine committed to anti-Fascism, 1936–46, and later first editor of the *London Magazine* 1954.

[2] "Shooting an Elephant", which Lehmann published in the second number of *New Writing*, Autumn 1936. See 88.

usual I lost your letter with the address & it didn't turn up till this morning. I have had the shop open nearly a fortnight. I took 19/– the first week, this week will be 25/– or 30/–. That is turnover & the profit on it abt pays the rent. I think the business could be worked up to £3 or so. It is very little trouble & no hanging about like in a bookshop. In a grocer's shop people come in to buy something, in a bookshop they come in to make a nuisance of themselves.

I am getting married very shortly[1]—it is fixed for June 9th at the parish church here. This is as it were in confidence because we are telling as few people as possible till the deed is done, lest our relatives combine against us in some way & prevent it. It is very rash of course but we have talked it over & decided I should never be economically justified in marrying so might as well be unjustified now as later. I expect we shall rub along all right—as to money I mean—but it will always be hand to mouth as I don't see myself ever writing a best-seller. I have made a fairly good start on my new book.[2]

I was glad to see your book[3] got such good reviews. I saw a very good one in the *Times*. The book itself I haven't seen yet. When you were in that part of the world did you go to Singapore by any chance? I have a great friend there at the Raffles Museum, Dennis Collings his name is, an anthropologist & very gifted in various strange ways—for instance he can do things like forging a medieval sword so that you can't tell it from a real one. I read your "Notes by the Way"[4] with great interest. What you say about trying to study our own customs from an anthropological point of view opens up a lot of fields of thought, but one thing to notice about ourselves is that people's habits etc are formed not only by their upbringing & so forth but also very largely by books. I have often thought it would be very interesting to study the conventions etc of *books* from an anthropological point of view. I don't know if you ever read Elmer Rice's *A Voyage to Purilia*. It contains a most interesting analysis of certain conventions—taken for granted & never even mentioned—existing in the ordinary film. It would be interesting & I believe valuable to work out the underlying beliefs & general imaginative background of a writer like Edgar Wallace. But of course that's the kind of thing nobody will ever print.

[1] To Eileen O'Shaughnessy.
[2] *The Road to Wigan Pier.*
[3] *Bali and Angkor.*
[4] "Notes on the Way", *Time and Tide*, 23 May 1936.

Thank God it has rained at last, after 3 weeks drought, & my vegetables are doing fairly well.

Yours
Eric A. Blair

81. Letter to Anthony Powell

The Stores
Wallington
Nr Baldock, Herts.
8 June 1936

Dear Mr Powell,[1]
I must apologise for not writing earlier to thank you for your letter & *Caledonia.*[2] I liked the latter very much. It is so rare nowadays to find anyone hitting back at the Scotch cult. I am glad to see you make a point of calling them "Scotchmen", not "Scotsmen" as they like to be called. I find this a good easy way of annoying them.

Yes, the reviewers are awful, so much so that in a general way I prefer the ones who lose their temper & call me names to the silly asses who mean so well & never bother to discover what you are writing about.

Please forgive me for not writing earlier. I have been away, but even so I delayed.

Yours truly
George Orwell

[1] Anthony Powell (1905–), novelist, whose early works include *Afternoon Men, From a View to a Death,* etc; since 1951 he has been writing the series *A Dance to the Music of Time.* When *Keep the Aspidistra Flying* was published he wrote to Orwell saying he liked it. In 1941 they met and remained friends until Orwell's death.

[2] Verses in pastiche of an eighteenth-century satire, of which about 100 copies, with a frontispiece by Edward Burra, were printed by a friend in 1934 as a wedding present for the Powells.

82. Letter to Denys King-Farlow

The Stores
Wallington
Nr. Baldock, Herts.
9 June 1936

Dear King-Farlow,[1]

Of course I remember you. But have you changed your name back to King-Farlow? It was Nettleton most of the time you were at Eton. I only got your letter this morning. It was forwarded by Cyril Connolly, who has been away. I'm afraid I can't possibly come along on the 11th, much as I would like to, first of all because it's always difficult for me to get away from here, secondly because like the chap in the *NT* I have married a wife and therefore I cannot come. Curiously enough I am getting married this very morning—in fact I am writing this with one eye on the clock and the other on the Prayer Book, which I have been studying for some days past in hopes of steeling myself against the obscenities of the wedding service. When exactly I'll be up in town I don't know. This place as you see by the address used to be the village "general" shop, and when I came here I re-opened it as such—the usual little shop stocking groceries, sweets, packets of aspirins, etc. It doesn't bring in much but it does pay my rent for me, and for a literary gent that is a consideration. On the other hand it makes it very difficult to get away from here. But if you are ever passing anywhere near, do drop in. It's not much off your track if you are going anywhere in a north-easterly direction or e.g. to Cambridge. I should always be at home, except on Saturday afternoons and sometimes on Sundays, and should love to see you again.

I am not in touch with many of the Etonians of our time. Connolly came to see me once in town and he has been very kind in reviewing my books. I used to see Alan Clutton-Brock in 1928—just recently his wife was killed in a motor smash. It was sad abt poor Godfrey Meynell.[2] I went and stayed at Cambridge with

[1] Hugh St Denys Nettleton King-Farlow, MBE (1902–), King's Scholar at Eton at the same time as Eric Blair. After Cambridge and Princeton he worked with Royal Dutch Shell in Canada, the United States and Europe. At school he and Blair were great friends and together they produced the hand-written magazine, *Election Times*.

[2] Godfrey Meynell, a contemporary of Blair at Eton, had joined the Army and was killed on the North West Frontier of India leading his native troops in action. He was posthumously awarded the VC.

Gow[1] when I came back from Burma at the end of '27, but though he was very kind it seemed to me I had moved out of his orbit and he out of mine. I suppose most of the others we knew are dons, civil servants and barristers. I hear you have been in the USA a long time and are very rich and flourishing. I have had a bloody life a good deal of the time but in some ways an interesting one. Please excuse this untidy scrawl.

Yours,
Eric A. Blair

[The original of this letter has been lost and the text given here is reproduced from *Encounter*, January 1962, where it was first printed.]

83. Review

The Rock Pool by Cyril Connolly, *Almayer's Folly* by Joseph Conrad

As Mr Cyril Connolly is almost the only novel reviewer in England who does not make me sick, I opened this, his first novel, with a lively interest.

The usual thing to say about a first novel is that it shows great promise but the author has not got his subject-matter completely under control. With Mr Connolly's novel I should say it is just the other way about. The treatment is mature and skilful—the book looks as if had been worked at over a period of years—but the subject-matter, especially considering that this is a first novel, is tiresome. The story is a kind of modernisation of the myth of Hylas. A young Englishman of the su-superior, moneyed and cultured type, an Old Wykehamist and a thoroughly ineffectual ass—a 1930 version, really, of the Bernard Shaw Englishman—lands up in one of those dreadful colonies of expatriates calling themselves artists which were dotted all over France during the nineteen-twenties. He decides that he will study them in a detached, scientific way, as one might study the fauna of a rock pool. But behold! detachment is not so easy as he thinks. Almost instantly he has fallen into the pool and been dragged down to the level of its inhabitants, or even lower if that were possible. Before long he is drinking, cadging and lechering exactly like the rest

[1] A. S. F. Gow (1886–   ), classical scholar, assistant master at Eton 1914–25 and Orwell's classical tutor.

of them, and on the last page he is left gazing at the world through a mist of Pernod but dimly feeling that his present degradation is better than respectable life in England.

There are two reasons why subject-matter such as this is unsatisfactory. In the first place one can hardly approach a novel about artists' colonies on the Mediterranean without reflecting that Norman Douglas and Aldous Huxley did that kind of thing a long time ago and probably better. A more serious objection is that even to want to write about so-called artists who spend on sodomy what they have gained by sponging betrays a kind of spiritual inadequacy. For it is clear that Mr Connolly rather admires the disgusting beasts he depicts, and certainly he prefers them to the polite and sheeplike Englishman; he even compares them, in their ceaseless war against decency, to heroic savage tribes struggling against western civilisation. But this, you see, only amounts to a distaste for normal life and common decency, and one might equally well express it, as so many do, by scuttling beneath the moulting wing of Mother Church. Obviously, modern mechanised life becomes dreary if you let it. The awful thraldom of money is upon everyone and there are only three immediately obvious escapes. One is religion, another is unending work, the third is the kind of sluttish antinomianism—lying in bed till four in the afternoon, drinking Pernod—that Mr Connolly seems to admire. The third is certainly the worst, but in any case the essential evil is to think in terms of *escape*. The fact to which we have got to cling, as to a life-belt, is that it *is* possible to be a normal decent person and yet to be fully alive. Mr Connolly seems to suggest that there are only two alternatives: lie in bed till four in the afternoon, drinking Pernod, or you will infallibly surrender to the gods of Success and become a London social-cum-literary backstairs-crawler. The orthodox Christian tries to pitchfork you with a very similar dilemma. But both dilemmas are false and unnecessarily depressing.

I criticise Mr Connolly's subject-matter because I think he could write a better novel if he would concern himself with more ordinary people. But I do not mean to imply that this book is not worth reading. Actually, during the past year I have only read about two *new* books that interested me more, and I doubt if I have read even one that was more amusing. Presumably it was refused publication in England because of the law of libel—there is no indecency in it. The Obelisk Press do a great service by publishing the books that cannot be published over here. It is a pity they think it necessary to pretend in their blurbs and catalogues that they are specialists in pornography.

This time the Penguin Books have not been so well selected as formerly. Out of all Conrad's books, why choose *Almayer's Folly*? There is nothing memorable in it except a certain underlying feeling which one might not detect unless one had lived in the East. It was written when Conrad's English was far from perfect—it is not merely that he employs the foreign idioms that persisted in his prose till far later, but that he had not yet grasped the vulgarity of certain cliché expressions, so that the book teems with phrases like "that astute individual". At present Conrad is out of fashion, ostensibly because of his florid style and redundant adjectives (for my part I like a florid style: if your motto is "Cut out the adjectives", why not go a bit further and revert to a system of grunts and squeals, like the animals?), but actually, I suspect, because he was a gentleman, a type hated by the modern intelligentsia. He is pretty certain to come back into favour. One of the surest signs of his genius is that women dislike his books. But *Almayer's Folly* is only indirectly interesting, because it was Conrad's first book and because of the anecdote about Galsworthy which I suppose is not worth repeating.

New English Weekly, 23 July 1936

84. Letter to Henry Miller

The Stores
Wallington
Nr Baldock, Herts.
26 August 1936

Dear Miller,

Many thanks for your letter. It made me feel rather bad all the same, because I had been meaning for weeks to write to you and had been putting it off. Well, *Black Spring* arrived all right and I liked part of it very much, especially the opening chapters, but I do think, and shall say in reviewing it, that a book like *Tropic of Cancer*, dealing with events that happened or might have happened in the ordinary three-dimensional world, is more in your line. I liked *Tropic of Cancer* especially for three things, first of all a peculiar rhythmic quality in your English, secondly the fact that you dealt with facts well known to everybody but never mentioned in print (e.g. when the chap is supposed to be making love to the woman but is dying for a piss all the while), thirdly the way in which you would wander off into a kind of reverie where the laws of ordinary reality were slipped just a little but not too much. You do this also in *Black Spring*, e.g. I like very much your meditation beginning in a public urinal on pp. 60–64, but I think on the whole you have moved too much away from the ordinary world into a sort of Mickey Mouse universe where things and people don't have to obey the rules of space and time. I dare say I am wrong and perhaps have missed your drift altogether, but I have a sort of belly-to-earth attitude and always feel uneasy when I get away from the ordinary world where grass is green, stones hard etc. It is also, I know, pretty bloody when you have written one unusual book to be blamed for not writing another exactly like it. But I don't want you to think there wasn't a lot in *Black Spring* that I enjoyed. The quality of the prose is fine too, especially that passage I referred to before about the dung and the angels. When I read a piece like that I feel as you feel when you are galloping a really good horse over ground where you don't have to look out for rabbit holes. I will do what I can in the way of reviews. The *Adelphi* told me I could do a short bit on it, but they are soon going to become a quarterly, and I shall also do it for the *New English*, but they have shut up shop for August as they always do, so the reviews[1] will be a bit late I expect, but I suppose in your case that doesn't matter so much as with the ordinary twopenny-halfpenny novel that is genius for a week and then is sold off as a remainder. I have got to go and milk the goat now but will continue this letter when I come back.

27.8.1936. I am glad you managed to get hold of a copy of *Down and Out*. I haven't one left and it is out of print, and I was going to send you a copy of the French translation (I suppose it was the English version you saw) when I got your letter. Yes, it was published in America too but didn't sell a great deal. I don't know what sort of reviews it got in France—I only saw about two, either because the press-cutting people didn't get them or because I hadn't arranged to have copies sent out with flattering letters to leading critics, which I am told you should do in France. Some others of my

[1] Orwell's review of Miller's *Black Spring* appeared only in the *New English Weekly*, 24 September 1936.

books have also been published in America. My second book, *Burmese Days*, was published there before being published in England, because my publisher was afraid the India Office might take steps to have it suppressed. A year later my English publisher brought out a version of it with various names etc altered, so the American edition of it is the proper one. That is the only one of my books that I am pleased with—not that it is any good qua novel, but the descriptions of scenery aren't bad, only of course that is what the average reader skips. My third book, *A Clergyman's Daughter*, which came out in England about a year ago, was published in America last week. That book is bollox, but I made some experiments in it that were useful to me. My last book, *Keep the Aspidistra Flying*, won't, I imagine be published in America, because it is a domestic sort of story with an entirely English theme and the American public are getting restive about what I believe is called "British sissy-stuff". I noticed also when I worked in the bookshop that it is harder and harder to sell American books in England. The two languages are drifting further and further apart.

Yes, I agree about English poverty. It is awful. Recently I was travelling among the worst parts of the coal areas in Lancashire and Yorkshire—I am doing a book[1] about it now—and it is dreadful to see how the people have collapsed and lost all their guts in the last ten years. I reviewed Connolly's novel for the *NEW*, but though it amused me I didn't think a lot of it. It surprised me that he should be in such a stew about the book "dating"—as though every book worth reading didn't "date"! I see from the blurb on *Black Spring* that you got a pretty good write-up from Eliot & Co., also that I am mentioned among them. That is a step up for me—the first time I have been on anybody else's blurb. So no doubt I shall be Sir Eric Blair yet.

Write if or when you feel inclined.

Yours
Eric A. Blair

[1] *The Road to Wigan Pier.*

85. Review

Black Spring by Henry Miller, *A Passage to India* by E. M. Forster, *Death of a Hero* by Richard Aldington, *The Jungle* by Upton Sinclair, *A Hind Let Loose* by C. E. Montague, *A Safety Match* by Ian Hay

When Henry Miller's *Tropic of Cancer* appeared a year ago I approached it with caution because, like a lot of other people, I did not wish to seem or to be impressed by mere obscenity. But I realise now, from the intensity with which it has stayed in my mind, that I underpraised it, and I would like to mention it again before dealing with his new novel, *Black Spring*.

The interest of *Tropic of Cancer* was that it cast a kind of bridge across the frightful gulf which exists, in fiction, between the intellectual and the man-in-the-street. English fiction on its higher levels is for the most part written by literary gents about literary gents for literary gents; on its lower levels it is generally the most putrid "escape" stuff—old maids' fantasies about Ian Hay male virgins, or little fat men's visions of themselves as Chicago gangsters. Books about ordinary people behaving in an ordinary manner are extremely rare, because they can only be written by someone who is capable of standing both inside and outside the ordinary man, as Joyce for instance stands inside and outside Bloom; but this involves admitting that you yourself *are* an ordinary person for nine-tenths of the time, which is exactly what no intellectual ever wants to do. *Tropic of Cancer* was a smaller book than *Ulysses*. It was not primarily a work of art and it made no attempt to analyse different states of consciousness. But in one way it bridged the gap between the thinking and the unthinking man more successfully than *Ulysses*, in that it was not complicated by feelings of horror and repentance. The average sensual man was not used as a kind of confession-box like Eliot's Sweeney, but taken for granted. The book's standpoint was really that of Whitman, but without Whitman's American puritanism (which escapes notice because disguised as a kind of nudist uplift) or his American bumptiousness. It was a notable effort to get the thinking man down from his chilly perch of superiority and back into contact with the man-in-the-street; it was only incidentally a pity, perhaps, that the street in question should be the Rue de la Harpe.

Black Spring is a book of different scope. It no longer deals with recognisable events of ordinary life, or rather it uses them only as nuclei round which spins a kind of Mickey Mouse universe where things do not have to happen according to the ordinary laws of space and time. Each chapter or each passage starts off with a fragment of reality which is so to speak blown out into a balloon of fantasy. I take one example more or less at random:

> . . . Men and women promenading on the sidewalks: curious beasts, half-human, half-celluloid. Walking up and down the Avenue half-crazed, their teeth polished, their eyes glazed. The women in beautiful garbs, each one equipped with a cold-storage smile. . . . Smiling through life with that demented, glazed look in the eyes, the flags unfurled, the sex flowing sweetly through the sewers. I had a gat with me and when we got to Forty-Second Street I opened fire. Nobody paid any attention. I mowed them down right and left, but the crowd got no thinner. The living walked over the dead, smiling all the while to advertise their beautiful white teeth.

You see here how something that is or might be a description of ordinary reality slides away into pure dream There is no need to get bogged up in metaphysical discussions about the meaning of "reality". The point is that words are here being used to invade what is really the province of the film. A Mickey Mouse film breaks the rules of common sense more violently than any book ever written, yet because it is seen it is perfectly intelligible. Try to describe it in words and you will fail; worse, nobody, will listen to you. The truth is that the written word loses its power if it departs too far, or rather if it stays away too long, from the ordinary world where two and two make four. A tendency to put his day-dreams on paper was apparent in Henry Miller's earlier book, and I think he has been led further in that direction by the remarkable power over words which enables him to slide from reality to fantasy and from urinals to angels without the smallest appearance of effort or incongruity. From a technical point of view this book is an advance on the other. At worst his prose can be flat and full of rhymes, like the passage I quoted above, but at its best it is astonishing. As usual I cannot quote any of the best passages, because of the unprintable words, but if you can get hold of a copy, have a look at the passage between pages 50 and 64, for instance. It is the kind of prose which, when I read it, makes me feel that I should like to fire a salute of twenty-one guns.

I advise anyone who can get hold of this book to read it, and if you happen to have a copy of the first edition, hold it tight, for it may be worth money some day. But I still prefer the earlier book, and I wish that Mr Miller would chronicle some more of the adventures of his disreputable friends, for which task he seems so admirably suited.

There is some good stuff in the last issue of the Penguin Library. *A Passage to India* is not the perfect novel about India, but it is the best we have ever had and the best we are likely to get, for it is only by some improbable accident that anyone capable of writing a decent novel can be got to stay in India long enough to absorb the atmosphere. I was too young to fight in the war and therefore my opinion about it is valueless, but *Death of a Hero* has always seemed to me to be much the best of the English war books, at least of those describable as novels. The Soviet Government seem to have thought the same when they authorised its translation into Russian. It is a tribute to the book's vitality that the realistic descriptions of the fighting do not clash too violently with the preposterous burlesque of the first part. *The Jungle* is good if you like facts—and you can be sure they are authentic facts, for no one has ever got away with a libel action against Upton Sinclair. *A Hind Let Loose*, on the other hand, like all Montague's books, is tiresome and empty. He was one of those "deliciously witty" writers who are all sparkle and no taste, like soda-water.

I shan't quote from *A Safety Match*, but I will quote from the blurb, what the late Professor Saintsbury wrote to the author on its publication: "Let me congratulate you on *A Safety Match. I have read nothing so good for a long time.*" My italics. Please notice that Saintsbury was probably the most widely read man in Europe. This shows you what happens to professors of literature when they are so unwise as to write about contemporary books.

New English Weekly, 24 September 1936

86. Letter to Jack Common

The Stores
Wallington
Nr Baldock, Herts.
5 October 1936

Dear Comrade Common,[1]
(I hope by the way you share my prejudice against that accursed word "comrade", which has kept many a likely recruit away from the Socialist movement), thanks for yours. I thought *Walls Have Mouths* was very good and have given it the best review[2] I could manage in the length, because I thought 800 words was probably the maximum you would have room for. I also take the liberty of sending a poem[3] I had by me and thought you might be able to use. I want some time to do a short note on Henry Miller the American novelist, who in my opinion is something out of the common. I have done reviews of his books in the *New English Weekly*, but would like to give him a boost anywhere I am allowed, which of course is not in the commercial press, as he comes from a non-advertising publisher.

Yes, do come across any time you feel up to the effort. We are practically always at home, except sometimes on Saturday and Sunday afternoons, and at the end of this month when we are going to stay with my people for a week. It is a pity it is so difficult to get here. Of course you probably *could* get here by bus if you took some circuitous route, e.g. via Royston, as there is at any rate occasionally a bus from Royston to Sandon, which is only a couple of miles from here.

Things are prospering tolerably. I have just finished the rough draft of my book and begun on the revision, which will take me till some time in December. It is not a novel this time but a sort of book of essays, but I am afraid I have made rather a muck of parts of it. The goat is giving a quart of milk a day and some of the hens have begun laying. The shop is not doing a great deal but is just about paying our rent for us. I haven't heard from Rees for ages and I want to write to him. Where is he now? Is he still at the Centre?[4] I enjoyed

[1] Or, "fellow-worker before the Dawn." [Author's note on letter.]

[2] Orwell's review of *Walls Have Mouths* by W. F. R. Macartney appeared in the *Adelphi*, November 1936.

[3] "A Happy Vicar I might have been . . .", published in the *Adelphi*, December 1936. See 1.

[4] The Adelphi Centre, an offshoot of the *Adelphi* magazine, was founded in the summer of 1936 at Langham, Essex, to be a small self-supporting community

my very short trip there and met some interesting people, and I wished I could have stayed longer especially to hear Holdaway[1] and John Strachey lecture. I was greatly impressed by Large,[2] whom no doubt you know, and my wife almost fell in love with him when he came to tea here.

Please remember me to your wife.

Yours
Eric A. Blair

87. Review

Zest for Life by Johann Wöller, translated from the Danish by Claude Napier

Roughly speaking, no one capable of describing the atmosphere of the tropics is willing to stay there long enough to absorb it. Hence the rarity of good novels about the Far East, which can only be written by people who are in some way anomalous, like Joseph Conrad.

Mr Wöller is not in the same class as Conrad, but he has points in common with him. He is a Dane who has spent thirty years in the Dutch service in the East Indies, he is sodden with memories of Java and Sumatra, and he writes about them from the angle of someone in touch with European culture. Not completely in touch, or he would hardly describe Sigrid Undset and G. K. Chesterton as "two of the most considerable nordic intellects" (incidentally, how Mr Chesterton would have hated to be called "nordic"!), but too much so, probably, to have been quite at home with his fellow-officials over a gin sling. The underlying theme of the book is the peculiar double homesickness which is the punishment for deserting your native land. It is really a mistake to travel—or rather, one should travel only as a sailor or a nomad travels, not sending roots into foreign places. Live

---

which would maintain a guest-house for Summer Schools and conferences to promote Socialist studies.

[1] N. A. Holdaway, schoolmaster, Marxist theorist, member of the Independent Socialist Party, a contributor to the *Adelphi* and a director of the Adelphi Centre.

[2] E. C. Large, a plant chemist, author of *The Advance of the Fungi*, who also wrote two novels, *Sugar in the Air* and *Asleep in the Afternoon*.

among palm trees and mosquitoes in savage sunshine, in the smell of garlic and the creaking of bullock-cart wheels, and you pine for Europe until the time comes when you would exchange the whole of the so-called beauties of the East for the sight of a single snowdrop, or a frozen pond, or a red pillar-box. Come back to Europe, and all you can remember is the blood-red flowers of the hibiscus and the flying foxes streaming overhead. Yet it seems somehow a pity that the very concept of homesickness is presently going to be abolished by the machine civilisation which makes one part of the world indistinguishable from another.

By far the best thing in the book is a memory from the author's youth, an incident—imaginary, but typical of real facts—in the Dutch colonial war of 1900–12. It describes the torture of a villager who knew, or was supposed to know, where a rebel chieftain was hiding. Apart from the depth of imagination with which the scene is pictured, it brings home as a thousand political pamphlets could not do the inherent evil of imperialism. For the dreadful thing about the kind of brutalities here described, is that they are quite unavoidable. When a subject population rises in revolt you have got to suppress it, and you can only do so by methods which make nonsense of any claim for the superiority of western civilisation. In order to rule over barbarians, you have got to become a barbarian yourself. According to Mr Wöller, the Dutch are the most humane of the imperialist powers. If so, God knows what the others can be like.

This is an interesting but rather fragmentary book, and it gives, sometimes unintentionally, a good picture of what happens to the mind of a sensitive man when he strays away from the centres of civilisation.

Time and Tide, 17 October 1936

88. Shooting an Elephant

In Moulmein, in Lower Burma, I was hated by large numbers of people—the only time in my life that I have been important enough for this to happen to me. I was sub-divisional police officer of the town, and in an aimless, petty kind of way anti-European feeling was very bitter. No one had the guts to raise a riot, but if a European woman went through the bazaars alone somebody would probably spit betel juice over her dress. As a police officer I was an obvious target and was baited whenever it seemed safe to do so. When a nimble Burman tripped me up on the football field and the referee (another Burman) looked the other way, the crowd yelled with hideous laughter. This happened more than once. In the end the sneering yellow faces of young men that met me everywhere, the insults hooted after me when I was at a safe distance, got badly on my nerves. The young Buddhist priests were the worst of all. There were several thousands of them in the town and none of them seemed to have anything to do except stand on street corners and jeer at Europeans.

All this was perplexing and upsetting. For at that time I had already made up my mind that imperialism was an evil thing and the sooner I chucked up my job and got out of it the better. Theoretically—and secretly, of course—I was all for the Burmese and all against their oppressors, the British. As for the job I was doing, I hated it more bitterly than I can perhaps make clear. In a job like that you see the dirty work of Empire at close quarters. The wretched prisoners huddling in the stinking cages of the lock-ups, the grey, cowed faces of the long-term convicts, the scarred buttocks of the men who had been flogged with bamboos—all these oppressed me with an intolerable sense of guilt. But I could get nothing into perspective. I was young and ill-educated and I had had to think out my problems in the utter silence that is imposed on every Englishman in the East. I did not even know that the British Empire is dying, still less did I know that it is a great deal better than the younger empires that are going to supplant it. All I knew was that I was stuck between my hatred of the empire I served and my rage against the evil-spirited little beasts who tried to make my job impossible. With one part of my mind I thought of the British Raj as an unbreakable tyranny, as something clamped down, *in saecula saeculorum*, upon the will of prostrate peoples; with another part I thought that the greatest joy in the world would be to drive a bayonet into a Buddhist priest's guts. Feelings like these are the normal by-products of imperialism; ask any Anglo-Indian official, if you can catch him off duty.

One day something happened which in a roundabout way was enlightening. It was a tiny incident in itself, but it gave me a better glimpse than I had had before of the real nature of imperialism—the real motives for which despotic governments act. Early one morning the sub-inspector at a police station the other end of the town rang me up on the phone and said that an elephant was ravaging the bazaar. Would I please come and do something about it? I did not know what I could do, but I wanted to see what was happening and I got on to a pony and started out. I took my rifle, an old ·44 Winchester and much too small to kill an elephant, but I thought the noise might be useful *in terrorem*. Various Burmans stopped me on the way and told me about the elephant's doings. It was not, of course, a wild elephant, but a tame one which had gone "must". It had been chained up as tame elephants always are when their attack of "must" is due, but on the previous night it had broken its chain and escaped. Its mahout, the only person who could manage it when it was in that state, had set out in pursuit, but he had taken the wrong direction and was now twelve hours' journey away, and in the morning the elephant had suddenly reappeared in the town. The Burmese population had no weapons and were quite helpless against it. It had already destroyed somebody's bamboo hut, killed a cow and raided some fruit-stalls and devoured the stock; also it had met the municipal rubbish van, and, when the driver jumped out and took to his heels, had turned the van over and inflicted violence upon it.

The Burmese sub-inspector and some Indian constables were waiting for me in the quarter where the elephant had been seen. It was a very poor quarter, a labyrinth of squalid bamboo huts, thatched with palm-leaf, winding all over a steep hillside. I remember that it was a cloudy stuffy morning at the beginning of the rains. We began questioning the people as to where the elephant had gone, and, as usual, failed to get any definite information. That is invariably the case in the East; a story always sounds clear enough at a distance, but the nearer you get to the scene of events the vaguer it becomes. Some of the people said that the elephant had gone in one direction, some said that he had gone in another, some professed not even to have heard of any elephant. I had almost made up my mind that the whole story was a pack of lies, when we heard yells a little distance away. There was a loud, scandalised cry of "Go away, child! Go away this instant!" and an old woman with a switch in her hand came round the corner of a hut, violently shooing away a crowd of naked children. Some more women followed, clicking their tongues and exclaiming; evidently there was something there that the children ought not to have seen. I rounded the hut and saw a man's dead body sprawling in the mud. He was an Indian, a black Dravidian coolie, almost naked, and he could not have been dead many minutes. The people said that the elephant had come suddenly upon him round the corner of the hut, caught him with its trunk, put its foot on his back and ground him into the earth. This was the rainy season and the ground was soft, and his face had scored a trench a foot deep and a couple of yards long. He was lying on his belly with arms crucified and head sharply twisted to one side. His face was coated with mud, the eyes wide open, the teeth bared and grinning with an expression of unendurable agony. (Never tell me, by the way, that the dead look peaceful. Most of the corpses I have seen looked devilish.) The friction of the great beast's foot had stripped the skin from his back as neatly as one skins a rabbit. As soon as I saw the dead man I sent an orderly to a friend's house nearby to borrow an elephant rifle. I had already sent back the pony, not wanting it to go mad with fright and throw me if it smelled the elephant.

The orderly came back in a few minutes with a rifle and five cartridges, and meanwhile some Burmans had arrived and told us that the elephant was in the paddy fields below, only a few hundred yards away. As I started forward practically the whole population of the quarter flocked out of their houses and followed me. They had seen the rifle and were all shouting excitedly that I was going to shoot the elephant. They had not shown much interest in the elephant when he was merely ravaging their homes, but it was different now that he was going to be shot. It was a bit of fun to them, as it would be to an English crowd; besides, they wanted the meat. It made me vaguely uneasy. I had no intention of shooting the elephant—I had merely sent for the rifle to defend myself if necessary—and it is always unnerving to have a crowd following you. I marched down the hill, looking and feeling a fool, with the rifle over my shoulder and an ever-growing army of people jostling at my heels. At the bottom, when you got away from the huts, there was a metalled road and beyond that a miry waste of paddy fields a thousand yards across, not yet ploughed but soggy from the first rains and dotted with coarse grass. The elephant was standing eighty yards from the road, his left side towards us. He took not the slightest notice of the crowd's approach. He was tearing up bunches of grass, beating them against his knees to clean them and stuffing them into his mouth.

I had halted on the road. As soon as I saw the elephant I knew with perfect certainty that I ought not to shoot him. It is a serious matter to shoot a working elephant—it is comparable to destroying a huge and costly piece of machinery—and obviously one ought not to do it if it can possibly be avoided. And at that distance, peacefully eating, the elephant looked no more dangerous than a cow. I thought then and I think now that his attack of "must" was already passing off; in which case he would merely wander harmlessly about until the mahout came back and caught him. Moreover, I did not in the least want to shoot him. I decided that I would watch him for a little while to make sure that he did not turn savage again, and then go home.

But at that moment I glanced round at the crowd that had followed me. It was an immense crowd, two thousand at the least and growing every minute. It blocked the road for a long distance on either side. I looked at the sea of yellow faces above the garish clothes—faces all happy and excited over this bit of fun, all certain that the elephant was going to be shot. They were watching me as they would watch a conjuror about to perform a trick. They did not like me, but with the magical rifle in my hands I was momentarily worth watching. And suddenly I realised that I should have to shoot the elephant after all. The people expected it of me and I had got to do it; I could feel their two thousand wills pressing me forward, irresistibly. And it was at this moment, as I stood there with the rifle in my hands, that I first grasped the hollowness, the futility of the white man's dominion in the East. Here was I, the white man with his gun, standing in front of the unarmed native crowd—seemingly the leading actor of the piece; but in reality I was only an absurd puppet pushed to and fro by the will of those yellow faces behind. I perceived in this moment that when the white man turns tyrant it is his own freedom that he destroys. He becomes a sort of hollow, posing dummy, the conventionalised figure of a sahib. For it is the condition of his rule that he shall spend his life in trying to impress the "natives" and so in every crisis he has got to do what the "natives" expect of him. He wears a mask, and his face grows to fit it. I had got to shoot the elephant. I had committed myself to doing it when I sent for the rifle. A sahib has got to act like a sahib; he has got to appear resolute, to know his own mind and do definite things. To come all that way, rifle in hand, with two thousand people marching at my heels, and then to trail feebly away, having done nothing—no, that was impossible. The crowd would laugh at me. And my whole life, every white man's life in the East, was one long struggle not to be laughed at.

But I did not want to shoot the elephant. I watched him beating his bunch of grass against his knees, with that preoccupied grandmotherly air that elephants have. It seemed to me that it would be murder to shoot him. At that age I was not squeamish about killing animals, but I had never shot an elephant and never wanted to. (Somehow it always seems worse to kill a *large* animal.) Besides, there was the beast's owner to be considered. Alive, the elephant was worth at least a hundred pounds; dead, he would only be worth the value of his tusks—five pounds, possibly. But I had got to act quickly. I turned to some experienced-looking Burmans who had been there when we arrived, and asked them how the elephant had been behaving. They all said the same thing: he took no notice of you if you left him alone, but he might charge if you went too close to him.

It was perfectly clear to me what I ought to do. I ought to walk up to within, say, twenty-five yards of the elephant and test his behaviour. If he charged I could shoot, if he took no notice of me it would be safe to leave him until the mahout came back. But also I knew that I was going to do no such thing. I was a poor shot with a rifle and the ground was soft mud into which one would sink at every step. If the elephant charged and I missed him, I should have about as much chance as a toad under a steam-roller. But even then I was not thinking particularly of my own skin, only the watchful yellow faces behind. For at that moment, with the crowd watching me, I was not afraid in the ordinary sense, as I would have been if I had been alone. A white man mustn't be frightened in front of "natives"; and so, in general, he isn't frightened. The sole thought in my mind was that if anything went wrong those two thousand Burmans would see me pursued, caught, trampled on and reduced to a grinning corpse like that Indian up the hill. And if that happened it was quite probable that some of them would laugh. That would never do. There was only one alternative. I shoved the cartridges into the magazine and lay down on the road to get a better aim.

The crowd grew very still, and a deep, low, happy sigh, as of people who see the theatre curtain go up at last, breathed from innumerable throats. They were going to have their bit of fun after all. The rifle was a beautiful German thing with cross-hair sights. I did not then know that in shooting an elephant one should shoot to cut an imaginary bar running from ear-hole to ear-hole. I ought therefore, as the elephant was sideways on, to have aimed straight at his ear-hole; actually I aimed several inches in front of this, thinking the brain would be further forward.

When I pulled the trigger I did not hear the bang or feel the kick—one never does when a shot goes home—but I heard the devilish roar of glee that went up from the crowd. In that instant, in too short a time, one would have thought, even for the bullet to get there, a mysterious, terrible change had come over the elephant. He neither stirred nor fell, but every line of his body had altered. He looked suddenly stricken, shrunken, immensely old, as though the frightful impact of the bullet had paralysed him without knocking him down. At last, after what seemed a long time—it might have been five seconds, I dare say—he sagged flabbily to his knees. His mouth slobbered. An enormous senility seemed to have settled upon him. One could have imagined him thousands of years old. I fired again into the same spot. At the second shot he did not collapse but climbed with desperate slowness to his feet and stood weakly upright, with legs sagging and head drooping. I fired a third time. That was the shot that did for him. You could see the agony of it jolt his whole body and knock the last remnant of strength from his legs. But in falling he seemed for a moment to rise, for as his hind legs collapsed beneath him he seemed to tower upwards like a huge rock toppling, his trunk reaching skyward like a tree. He trumpeted, for the first and only time. And then down he came, his belly towards me, with a crash that seemed to shake the ground even where I lay.

I got up. The Burmans were already racing past me across the mud. It was obvious that the elephant would never rise again, but he was not dead. He was breathing very rhythmically with long rattling gasps, his great mound of a side painfully rising and falling. His mouth was wide open—I could see far down into caverns of pale pink throat. I waited a long time for him to die, but his breathing did not weaken. Finally I fired my two remaining shots into the spot where I thought his heart must be. The thick blood welled out of him like red velvet, but still he did not die. His body did not even jerk when the shots hit him, the tortured breathing continued without a pause. He was dying, very slowly and in great agony, but in some world remote from me where not even a bullet could damage him further. I felt that I had got to put an end to that dreadful noise. It seemed dreadful to see the great beast lying there, powerless to move and yet powerless to die, and not even to be able to finish him. I sent back for my small rifle and poured shot after shot into his heart and down his throat. They seemed to make no impression. The tortured gasps continued as steadily as the ticking of a clock.

In the end I could not stand it any longer and went away. I heard later that it took him half an hour to die. Burmans were arriving with dahs and baskets even before I left, and I was told they had stripped his body almost to the bones by the afternoon.

Afterwards, of course, there were endless discussions about the shooting of the elephant. The owner was furious, but he was only an Indian and could do nothing. Besides, legally I had done the right thing, for a mad elephant has to be killed, like a mad dog, if its owner fails to control it. Among the Europeans opinion was divided. The older men said I was right, the younger men said it was a damn shame to shoot an elephant for killing a coolie, because an elephant was worth more than any damn Coringhee coolie. And afterwards I was very glad that the coolie had been killed; it put me legally in the right and it gave me a sufficient pretext for shooting the elephant. I often wondered whether any of the others grasped that I had done it solely to avoid looking a fool.

New Writing, No. 2, Autumn 1936; *Penguin New Writing*, No. 1, [November] 1940; broadcast in the BBC Home Service, 12 October 1948; SE; OR; CE.

89. Bookshop Memories

When I worked in a second-hand bookshop—so easily pictured, if you don't work in one, as a kind of paradise where charming old gentlemen browse eternally among calf-bound folios—the thing that chiefly struck me was the rarity of really bookish people. Our shop had an exceptionally interesting stock, yet I doubt whether ten per cent of our customers knew a good book from a bad one. First edition snobs were much commoner than lovers of literature, but oriental students haggling over cheap textbooks were commoner still, and vague-minded women looking for birthday presents for their nephews were commonest of all.

Many of the people who came to us were of the kind who would be a nuisance anywhere but have special opportunities in a bookshop. For example, the dear old lady who "wants a book for an invalid" (a very common demand, that), and the other dear old lady who read such a nice book in 1897 and wonders whether you can find her a copy. Unfortunately she doesn't remember the title or the author's name or what the book was about, but she does remember that it had a red cover. But apart from these there are two well-known types of pest by whom every second-hand bookshop is haunted. One is the decayed person smelling of old breadcrusts who comes every day, sometimes several times a day, and tries to sell you worthless books. The other is the person who orders large quantities of books for which he has not the smallest intention of paying. In our shop we sold nothing on credit, but we would put books aside, or order them if necessary, for people who arranged to fetch them away later. Scarcely half the people who ordered books from us ever came back. It used to puzzle me at first. What made them do it? They would come in and demand some rare and expensive book, would make us promise over and over again to keep it for them, and then would vanish never to return. But many of them, of course, were unmistakable paranoiacs. They used to talk in a grandiose manner about themselves and tell the most ingenious stories to explain how they had happened to come out of doors without any money—stories which, in many cases, I am sure they themselves believed. In a town like London there are always plenty of not quite certifiable lunatics walking the streets, and they tend to gravitate towards bookshops, because a bookshop is one of the few places where you can hang about for a long time without spending any money. In the end one gets to know these people almost at a glance. For all their big talk there is something moth-eaten and aimless about them. Very often, when we were dealing with an obvious paranoiac, we would put aside the books he asked for and then put them back on the shelves the moment he had gone. None of them, I noticed, ever attempted to take books away without paying for them; merely to order them was enough—it gave them, I suppose, the illusion that they were spending real money.

Like most second-hand bookshops we had various sidelines. We sold second-hand typewriters, for instance, and also stamps—used stamps, I mean. Stamp-collectors are a strange, silent, fish-like breed, of all ages, but only of the male sex; women, apparently, fail to see the peculiar charm of gumming bits of coloured paper into albums. We also sold sixpenny horoscopes compiled by somebody who claimed to have foretold the Japanese earthquake. They were in sealed envelopes and I never opened one of them myself, but the people who bought them often came back and told us how "true" their horoscopes had been. (Doubtless any horoscope seems "true" if it tells you that you are highly attractive to the opposite sex and your worst fault is generosity.) We did a good deal of business in children's books, chiefly "remainders". Modern books for children are rather horrible things, especially when you see them in the mass. Personally I would sooner give a child a copy of Petronius Arbiter than *Peter Pan*, but even Barrie seems manly and wholesome compared with some of his later imitators. At Christmas time we spent a feverish ten days struggling with Christmas cards and calendars, which are tiresome things to sell but good business while the season lasts. It used to interest me to see the brutal cynicism with which Christian sentiment is exploited. The touts from the Christmas card firms used to come round with their catalogues as early as June. A phrase from one of their invoices sticks in my memory. It was: "2 doz. Infant Jesus with rabbits".

But our principal sideline was a lending library—the usual "twopenny no-deposit" library of five or six hundred volumes, all fiction. How the book thieves must love those libraries! It is the easiest crime in the world to borrow a book at one shop for twopence, remove the label and sell it at another shop for a shilling. Nevertheless booksellers generally find that it pays them better to have a certain number of books stolen (we used to lose about a dozen a month) than to frighten customers away by demanding a deposit.

Our shop stood exactly on the frontier between Hampstead and Camden Town, and we were frequented by all types from baronets to bus-conductors. Probably our library subscribers were a fair cross-section of London's reading public. It is therefore worth noting that of all the authors in our library the one who "went out" the best was —Priestley? Hemingway? Walpole? Wodehouse? No, Ethel M. Dell, with Warwick Deeping a good second and Jeffery Farnol, I should say, third. Dell's novels, of course, are read solely by women, but by women of all kinds and ages and not, as one might expect, merely by wistful spinsters and the fat wives of tobacconists. It is not true that men don't read novels, but it is true that there are whole branches of fiction that they avoid. Roughly speaking, what one might call the *average* novel—the ordinary, good-bad, Galsworthy-and-water stuff which is the norm of the English novel—seems to exist only for women. Men read either the novels it is possible to respect, or detective stories. But their consumption of detective stories is terrific. One of our subscribers to my knowledge read four or five detective stories every week for over a year, besides others which he got from another library. What chiefly surprised me was that he never read the same book twice. Apparently the whole of that frightful torrent of trash (the pages read every year would, I calculated, cover nearly three-quarters of an acre) was stored for ever in his memory. He took no notice of titles or author's names, but he could tell by merely glancing into a book whether he had "had it already".

In a lending library you see people's real tastes, not their pretended ones, and one thing that strikes you is how completely the "classical" English novelists have dropped out of favour. It is simply useless to put Dickens, Thackeray, Jane Austen, Trollope, etc into the ordinary lending library; nobody takes them out. At the mere sight of a nineteenth-century novel people say "Oh, but that's *old!*" and shy away immediately. Yet it is always fairly easy to *sell* Dickens, just as it is always easy to sell Shakespeare. Dickens is one of those authors whom people are "always meaning to" read, and, like the Bible, he is widely known at second hand. People know by hearsay that Bill Sikes was a burglar and that Mr Micawber had a bald head, just as they know by hearsay that Moses was found in a basket of bulrushes and saw the "back parts" of the Lord. Another thing that is very noticeable is the growing unpopularity of American books. And another—the publishers get into a stew about this every two or three years—is the unpopularity of short stories. The kind of person who asks the librarian to choose a book for him nearly always starts by saying "I don't want short stories", or "I do not desire little stories", as a German customer of ours used to put it. If you ask them why, they sometimes explain that it is too much fag to get used to a new set of characters with every story; they like to "get into" a novel which demands no further thought after the first chapter. I believe, though, that the writers are more to blame here than the readers. Most modern short stories, English and American, are utterly lifeless and worthless, far more so than most novels. The short stories which *are* stories are popular enough, *vide* D. H. Lawrence, whose short stories are as popular as his novels.

Would I like to be a bookseller *de métier*? On the whole—in spite of my employer's kindness to me, and some happy days I spent in the shop—no.

Given a good pitch and the right amount of capital, any educated person ought to be able to make a small secure living out of a bookshop. Unless one goes in for "rare" books it is not a difficult trade to learn, and you start at a great advantage if you know anything about the insides of books. (Most booksellers don't. You can get their measure by having a look at the trade papers where they advertise their wants. If you don't see an ad for Boswell's *Decline and Fall* you are pretty sure to see one for *The Mill on the Floss* by T. S. Eliot.) Also it is a humane trade which is not capable of being vulgarised beyond a certain point. The combines can never squeeze the small independent bookseller out of existence as they have squeezed the grocer and the milkman. But the hours of work are very long—I was only a part-time employee, but my employer put in a 70-hour week, apart from constant expeditions out of hours to buy books—and it is an unhealthy life. As a rule a bookshop is horribly cold in winter, because if it is too warm the windows get misted over, and a bookseller lives on his windows. And books give off more and nastier dust than any other class of objects yet invented, and the top of a book is the place where every bluebottle prefers to die.

But the real reason why I should not like to be in the book trade for life is that while I was in it I lost my love of books. A bookseller has to tell lies about books, and that gives him a distaste for them; still worse is the fact that he is constantly dusting them and hauling them to and fro. There was a time when I really did love books—loved the sight and smell and feel of them, I mean, at least if they were fifty or more years old. Nothing pleased me quite so much as to buy a job lot of them for a shilling at a country auction. There is a peculiar flavour about the battered unexpected books you pick up in that kind of collection: minor eighteenth-century poets, out of date gazetteers, odd volumes of forgotten novels, bound numbers of ladies' magazines of the 'sixties. For casual reading—in your bath, for instance, or late at night when you are too tired to go to bed, or in the odd quarter of an hour before lunch—there is nothing to touch a back number of the *Girl's Own Paper*. But as soon as I went to work in the bookshop I stopped buying books. Seen in the mass, five or ten thousand at a time, books were boring and even slightly sickening. Nowadays I do buy one occasionally, but only if it is a book that I want to read and can't borrow, and I never buy junk. The sweet smell of decaying paper appeals to me no longer. It is too closely associated in my mind with paranoiac customers and dead bluebottles.

Fortnightly, November 1936

90. Review

The Calf of Paper by Scholem Asch, *Midnight*, by Julian Green

The huge sociological novels which come to us from eastern Europe cannot be criticised except as historical documents, because their authors, consciously or unconsciously, tend to avoid the real problems of the novelist. On the other hand they do an extremely useful work by presenting contemporary history in a readable form, and they can hardly have too much publicity, because anything that brings it home to the Englishman that foreigners really exist and are alive and kicking, especially kicking, is to be welcomed.

I don't think *The Calf of Paper* ought properly to be described as a novel, but I found it immensely interesting and in spite of its length I finished it at a very few sittings. It is a sort of panorama of German society in the hideous period of the inflation. The French are in the Ruhr, the mark is rising like a rocket, speculators are growing rich (they have a beautifully simple system of buying on credit and not paying till the value of the mark falls), the starving people are eating food that would be disdained by pigs, and Hitler and his first small gang of bravos are just beginning to be talked about. All this is presented, *more* Zola, through the histories of two or three more or less interrelated families. The reason why such a book cannot be approached as a work of art is that its method is in reality extremely perfunctory. The author is writing what is essentially a textbook, and he puts in the characters he thinks appropriate very much as one puts ingredients into a cake. He seems to be saying, "Antisemitism is just beginning—so we must put in a few families of Jews. And the Nazis are coming up over the horizon—so we'll have a few Nazis. And then, of course, there is the food-shortage—so we'll put in some food speculators and a starving postman", and so on and so on; but there is not a single scene, character or piece of dialogue which is there because it has forced itself upon him as material *ought* to force itself upon a novelist. This is not an inherent fault of the sociological novel—in fact probably a majority of the novels worth reading are novels-with-a-purpose. Compare Zola, for instance. The scenes of violence Zola describes in *Germinal* and *La Débâcle* are supposed to symbolise capitalist corruption, but they are also scenes. At his best, Zola is not synthetic. He works under a sense of compulsion, and not like an amateur cook following the instructions on a packet of Crestona cake-flour.

Nevertheless, as I have said, *The Calf of Paper* deserves to be read by everybody, if only because it makes clear why the Nazis triumphed and were probably bound to triumph. The only point upon which the author, who is presumably a Jew himself, seems to be in doubt, is the real reason for antisemitism. But curiously enough, he supplies a clue, unconsciously, in one of the very few scenes in which a Jew (a young Bolshevik military officer) is held up for our admiration. This scene is a reminder that if you want antisemitism explained the best book to read is the Old Testament.

Turn to *Midnight*, and you might as well be in a different universe. Here is the most complete and careful avoidance of any contemporary problem—even the time, though vaguely "the present", is not pinned down to any particular decade. In spite of a veneer of naturalism over many of the scenes, the story has about as much relation to real life as one of those German films in which all the actors are silhouettes cut out of black paper.

Here is the plot, if you can call it a plot. In the first chapter there is a meaningless suicide, and a girl of twelve, named Elizabeth, the daughter of the woman who has killed herself, is left homeless. She spends a few hours successively in the houses of three more or less insane aunts, the last of them a sort of Chinese monster, then takes to flight in terror and meets in the street a kind-hearted elderly man who adopts her into his family. There is a lapse of three years, and then Elizabeth is again adopted, this time by a man who has been the lover of her dead mother. The final episode occupies more than half the book and covers a time which is apparently about two days. This episode is pure nightmare all the way through. The house to which Elizabeth has come is a ruinous place in the forest, a sort of appalling asylum inhabited by lunatics of the most varied kinds. The nightmare effect is heightened by the fact that the child has not the vaguest idea how many people the house contains. In the dead of night, overcome about equally by terror and curiosity, she creeps all over the house, peering through keyholes and softly turning door-handles, and encountering some fresh monstrosity in each room. Finally, she meets the only sane person the house contains, a ruffianly peasant boy of about seventeen, and immediately agrees to fly with him. There is a brief burst of pornography, or something approaching it, in which he seduces her, then a murder, an accidental death, another suicide, and the story ends.

If this kind of thing were written at the level of the ordinary

English novel you would stop reading after a couple of chapters. But as Mr Green's mind has in it an unmistakable touch of distinction, you read to the end and then ask yourself, "What the devil is it all *about*?" I think the answer must be that, finally, it is about nothing.

Obviously it is an attempt to work up an Edgar Allen Poe atmosphere, and in a measure it is successful. At any rate, the feeling of horror and mystery is attained. But there is this important difference, that though Poe is fantastic he is never arbitrary. Even his least naturalistic stories ("The Black Cat", "The Fall of the House of Usher", etc) are psychologically correct, in the sense that they deal with perfectly intelligible motives. In *Midnight* this is not the case—there is never the slightest reason why any of the things in it should happen. It is, I think, the product of a gifted mind, it contains absolutely no vulgarity or sentimentality, and I am willing to believe that it was written in admirable French; but it is quite meaningless.

I had never before read a novel by Julian Green, and I am glad to have done so, because I feel now that I have his measure. The naturalistic touches in this book are good enough to suggest that he might have been a good novelist along Flaubert-Maupassant lines. As it is he seems to have missed his vocation, probably by being too anxious to fly to the opposite extreme from books like *The Calf of Paper*. The truth is that ours is not an age for mysterious romances about lunatics in ruined châteaux, because it is not an age in which one can be unaware of contemporary reality. You can't ignore Hitler, Mussolini, unemployment, aeroplanes and the radio; you can only pretend to do so, which means lopping off a large chunk of your consciousness. To turn away from everyday life and manipulate black paper silhouettes with the pretence that you are really interested in them, is a sort of game of make-believe, and therefore faintly futile, like telling ghost stories in the dark.

New English Weekly, 12 November 1936

91. In Defence of the Novel

It hardly needs pointing out that at this moment the prestige of the novel is extremely low, so low that the words "I never read novels", which even a dozen years ago were generally uttered with a hint of apology, are now *always* uttered in a tone of conscious pride. It is true that there are still a few contemporary or roughly contemporary novelists whom the intelligentsia consider it permissible to read; but the point is that the ordinary good-bad novel is habitually ignored while the ordinary good-bad book of verse or criticism is still taken seriously. This means that if you write novels you automatically command a less intelligent public than you would command if you had chosen some other form. There are two quite obvious reasons why this must presently make it impossible for good novels to be written. Even now the novel is visibly deteriorating, and it would deteriorate much faster if most novelists had any idea who reads their books. It is, of course, easy to argue (*vide* for instance Belloc's queerly rancorous essay) that the novel is a contemptible form of art and that its fate does not matter. I doubt whether that opinion is even worth disputing. At any rate, I am taking it for granted that the novel is worth salvaging and that in order to salvage it you have got to persuade intelligent people to take it seriously. It is therefore worth while to analyse one of the main causes—in my opinion, *the* main cause—of the novel's lapse in prestige.

The trouble is that the novel is being shouted out of existence. Question any thinking person as to why he "never reads novels", and you will usually find that, at bottom, it is because of the disgusting tripe that is written by the blurb-reviewers. There is no need to multiply examples. Here is just one specimen, from last week's *Sunday Times*: "If you can read this book and not shriek with delight, your soul is dead." That or something like it is now being written about *every* novel published, as you can see by studying the quotes on the blurbs. For anyone who takes the *Sunday Times* seriously, life must be one long struggle to catch up. Novels are being shot at you at the rate of fifteen a day, and every one of them an unforgettable masterpiece which you imperil your soul by missing. It must make it so difficult to choose a book at the library, and you must feel so guilty when you fail to shriek with delight. Actually, however, no one who matters is deceived by this kind of thing, and the contempt into which novel reviewing has fallen is extended to novels themselves. When *all* novels are thrust upon you as works of genius, it is quite natural to assume that all of them are tripe. Within the literary intelligentsia this assumption is now taken for granted. To admit that you like novels is nowadays almost equivalent to admitting that you have a hankering after coconut ice or prefer Rupert Brooke to Gerard Manley Hopkins.

All this is obvious. What I think is rather less obvious is the way in which the present situation has arisen. On the face of it, the book-ramp is a quite simple and cynical swindle. Z writes a book which is published by Y and reviewed by X in the *Weekly W*. If the review is a bad one Y will remove his advertisement, so X has to hand out "unforgettable masterpiece" or get the sack. Essentially that *is* the position, and novel reviewing has sunk to its present depth largely because every reviewer has some publisher or publishers twisting his tail by proxy. But the thing is not so crude as it looks. The various parties to the swindle are not consciously acting together, and they have been forced into their present position partly against their will.

To begin with, one ought not to assume, as is so often done (see for instance Beachcomber's column, *passim*), that the novelist enjoys and is even in some way responsible for the reviews he gets. Nobody *likes* being told that he has written a palpitating tale of passion which will last as long as the English language; though, of course, it is disappointing not to be told that, because all novelists are being told the same, and to be left out presumably means that your books won't sell. The hack review is in fact a sort of commercial necessity, like the blurb on the dust-jacket, of which it is merely an extension. But even the wretched hack reviewer is not to be blamed for the drivel he writes. In his special circumstances he could write nothing else. For even if there were no question of bribery, direct or indirect, there can be no such thing as good novel criticism so long as it is assumed that *every novel is worth reviewing*.

A periodical gets its weekly wad of books and sends off a dozen of them to X, the hack reviewer, who has a wife and family and has got to earn his guinea, not to mention the half-crown per vol which he gets by selling his review copies. There are two reasons why it is totally impossible for X to tell the truth about the books he gets. To begin with, the chances are that eleven out of the twelve books will fail to rouse in him the faintest spark of interest. They are not more than ordinarily bad, they are merely neutral, lifeless and pointless. If he were not paid to do so he would never read a line of any of them, and in nearly every case the only truthful review he could write would be: "This book inspires in me no thoughts whatever." But will anyone pay you to write that kind of thing? Obviously not. As a start, therefore, X is in the false position of having to manufacture, say, three hundred words about a book which means nothing to him whatever. Usually he does it by giving a brief résumé of the plot (incidentally betraying to the author the fact that he hasn't read the book) and handing out a few compliments which for all their fulsomeness are about as valuable as the smile of a prostitute.

But there is a far worse evil than this. X is expected not only to say what a book is about but to give his opinion as to whether it is good or bad. Since X can hold a pen he is probably not a fool, at any rate not such a fool as to imagine that *The Constant Nymph* is the most terrific tragedy ever written. Very likely his own favourite novelist, if he cares for novels at all, is Stendhal, or Dickens, or Jane Austen, or D. H. Lawrence, or Dostoievski—or at any rate, someone immeasurably better than the ordinary run of contemporary novelists. He has got to start, therefore, by immensely lowering his standards. As I have pointed out elsewhere, to apply a decent standard to the ordinary run of novels is like weighing a flea on a spring-balance intended for elephants. On such a balance as that a flea would simply fail to register; you would have to start by constructing another balance which revealed the fact that there are big fleas and little fleas. And this approximately is what X does. It is no use monotonously saying, of book after book, "This book is tripe," because, once again, no one will pay you for writing that kind of thing. X has got to discover something which is *not* tripe, and pretty frequently, or get the sack. This means sinking his standards to a depth at which, say, Ethel M. Dell's *Way of an Eagle* is a fairly good book. But on a scale of values which makes *The Way of an Eagle* a good book, *The Constant Nymph* is a superb book, and *The Man of Property* is—what? A palpitating tale of passion, a terrific, soul-shattering masterpiece, an unforgettable epic which will last as long as the English language, and so on and so forth. (As for any *really* good book, it would burst the thermometer.) Having started with the assumption that all novels are good, the reviewer is driven ever upwards on a topless ladder of adjectives. And *sic itur ad* Gould.[1] You can see reviewer after reviewer going the same road. Within two years of starting out with at any rate moderately honest intentions, he is proclaiming with maniacal screams that Miss Barbara Bedworthy's *Crimson Night* is the most terrific, trenchant, poignant, unforgettable, of the earth earthy and so forth masterpiece which has ever, etc etc etc. There is no way out of it when you have once com-

[1] Gerald Gould, at the time an influential novel reviewer for the *Observer*.

mitted the initial sin of pretending that a bad book is a good one. But you cannot review novels for a living without committing that sin. And meanwhile every intelligent reader turns away, disgusted, and to despise novels becomes a kind of snobbish duty. Hence the queer fact that it is possible for a novel of real merit to escape notice, merely because it has been praised in the same terms as tripe.

Various people have suggested that it would be all to the good if no novels were reviewed at all. So it would, but the suggestion is useless, because nothing of the kind is going to happen. No paper which depends on publishers' advertisements can afford to throw them away, and though the more intelligent publishers probably realise that they would be no worse off if the blurb-review were abolished, they cannot put an end to it for the same reason as the nations cannot disarm—because nobody wants to be the first to start. For a long time yet the blurb-reviews are going to continue, and they are going to grow worse and worse; the only remedy is to contrive in some way that they shall be disregarded. But this can only happen if somewhere or other there is decent novel reviewing which will act as a standard of comparison. That is to say, there is need of just *one* periodical (one would be enough for a start) which makes a speciality of novel reviewing but refuses to take any notice of tripe, and in which the reviewers *are* reviewers and not ventriloquists' dummies clapping their jaws when the publisher pulls the string.

It may be answered that there are such periodicals already. There are quite a number of highbrow magazines, for instance, in which the novel reviewing, what there is of it, is intelligent and not suborned. Yes, but the point is that periodicals of that kind do not make a speciality of novel reviewing, and certainly make no attempt to keep abreast of the current output of fiction. They belong to the highbrow world, the world in which it is already assumed that novels, as such, are despicable. But the novel is a popular form of art, and it is no use to approach it with the *Criterion-Scrutiny* assumption that literature is a game of back-scratching (claws in or claws out according to circumstances) between tiny cliques of highbrows. The novelist is primarily a story teller, and a man may be a very good story teller (*vide* for instance Trollope, Charles Reade, Mr Somerset Maugham) without being in the narrow sense an "intellectual". Five thousand novels are published every year, and Ralph Straus[1] implores you to

[1] Ralph Straus (1882–1950), chief fiction reviewer for the *Sunday Times* from 1928 until his death.

read all of them, or would if he had all of them to review. The *Criterion* probably deigns to notice a dozen. But between the dozen and the five thousand there may be a hundred or two hundred or even five hundred which at different levels have genuine merit, and it is on these that any critic who cares for the novel ought to concentrate.

But the first necessity is some method of *grading*. Great numbers of novels never ought to be mentioned at all (imagine for instance the awful effects on criticism if every serial in *Peg's Paper* had to be solemnly reviewed!), but even the ones that are worth mentioning belong to quite different categories. *Raffles* is a good book, and so is *The Island of Dr Moreau*, and so is *La Chartreuse de Parme*, and so is *Macbeth;* but they are "good" at very different levels. Similarly, *If Winter Comes* and *The Well-Beloved* and *An Unsocial Socialist* and *Sir Lancelot Greaves* are all bad books, but at different levels of "badness". This is the fact that the hack reviewer has made it his special business to obscure. It ought to be possible to devise a system, perhaps quite a rigid one, of grading novels into classes A, B, C and so forth, so that whether a reviewer praised or damned a book, you would at least know how seriously he meant it to be taken. As for the reviewers, they would have to be people who really cared for the art of the novel (and that means, probably, neither highbrows nor lowbrows nor midbrows, but elastic-brows), people interested in technique and still more interested in discovering what a book is *about*. There are plenty of such people in existence; some of the very worst of the hack reviewers, though now past praying for, started like that, as you can see by glancing at their earlier work. Incidentally, it would be a good thing if more novel reviewing were done by amateurs. A man who is not a practised writer but has just read a book which has deeply impressed him is more likely to tell you what it is *about* than a competent but bored professional. That is why American reviews, for all their stupidity, are better than English ones; they are more amateurish, that is to say, more serious.

I believe that in some such way as I have indicated the prestige of the novel could be restored. The essential need is a paper that would keep abreast of current fiction and yet refuse to sink its standards. It would have to be an obscure paper, for the publishers would not advertise in it; on the other hand, once they had discovered that somewhere there was praise that was real praise, they would be ready enough to quote it on their blurbs. Even if it were a very obscure paper it would probably cause the general level of novel reviewing to rise, for the drivel in the Sunday papers only continues because there is nothing with which to contrast it. But even if the blurb reviewers continued exactly as before, it would not matter so long as there also existed decent reviewing to remind a few people that serious brains can still occupy themselves with the novel. For just as the Lord promised that he would not destroy Sodom if ten righteous men could be found there, so the novel will not be utterly despised while it is known that somewhere or other there is even a handful of novel reviewers with no straws in their hair.

At present, if you care about novels and still more if you write them, the outlook is depressing in the extreme. The word "novel" calls up the words "blurb", "genius" and "Ralph Straus" as automatically as "chicken" calls up "bread sauce". Intelligent people avoid novels almost instinctively; as a result, established novelists go to pieces and beginners who "have something to say" turn in preference to almost any other form. The degradation that must follow is obvious. Look for instance at the fourpenny novelettes that you see piled up on any cheap stationer's counter. These things are the decadent offspring of the novel, bearing the same relation to *Manon Lescaut* and *David Copperfield* as the lap-dog bears to the wolf. It is quite likely that before long the average novel will be not much different from the fourpenny novelette, though doubtless it will still appear in a seven and sixpenny binding and amid a flourish of publishers' trumpets. Various people have prophesied that the novel is doomed to disappear in the near future. I do not believe that it will disappear, for reasons which would take too long to set forth but which are fairly obvious. It is much likelier, if the best literary brains cannot be induced to return to it, to survive in some perfunctory, despised and hopelessly degenerate form, like modern tomb-stones, or the Punch and Judy show.

New English Weekly, 12 and 19 November, 1936

92. Letter to Leonard Moore

The Stores
Wallington
Nr Baldock, Herts.
15 December 1936

Dear Mr Moore,

Herewith the MS of *The Road to Wigan Pier*. Parts of it I am fairly pleased with, but I should think the chances of Gollancz choosing it as a Left Book Club[1] selection are small, as it is too fragmentary and, on the surface, not very left-wing. Perhaps if it were sent on to him more or less at once he might have a look at it or get someone else to do so before the Xmas holiday, but I suppose we are not likely to hear from him before I leave for Spain,[2] which should be in about a week. . . .

Yours sincerely
Eric A. Blair

93. Review

The Novel Today by Philip Henderson

Mr Philip Henderson's book, *The Novel Today*, is a survey of the contemporary novel from a Marxist standpoint. It is not a very good book, in fact it can be described as a weaker version of Mirsky's *Intelligentsia of Great Britain*, written by someone who has got to live in England and cannot afford to insult too many people, but it is of some interest because it raises the question of art and propaganda which now rumbles like a sort of "noises off" round every critical discussion.

On the last occasion when *Punch* produced a genuinely funny joke, which was only six or seven years ago, it was a picture of an intoler-

[1] The Left Book Club, founded by Victor Gollancz in May 1936, and published by him, was anti-Fascist, pro-Soviet and for the Popular Front. Subscribers had to accept the monthly choice of the Selection Committee consisting of Victor Gollancz, Harold Laski and John Strachey. By this time the membership had reached 40,000.

[2] The Spanish civil war had broken out in July 1936 and, as an anti-Fascist, Orwell decided to go to Spain as soon as he had finished *The Road to Wigan Pier*.

able youth telling his aunt that when he came down from the University he intended to "write". "And what are you going to write about, dear?" his aunt enquires. "My dear aunt," the youth replies crushingly, "one doesn't write *about* anything, one just *writes.*" This was a perfectly justified criticism of current literary cant. At that time, even more than now, art for art's sake was going strong, though the phrase itself had been discarded as ninety-ish; "art has nothing to do with morality" was the favourite slogan. The artist was conceived as leaping to and fro in a moral, political and economic void, usually in pursuit of something called "Beauty", which was always one jump ahead. And the critic was supposed to be completely "impartial", i.e. to deal in abstract aesthetic standards which were completely unaffected by his other prejudices. To admit that you liked or disliked a book because of its moral or religious tendency, even to admit noticing that it *had* a tendency, was too vulgar for words.

This is still the official attitude, but it is in process of being abandoned, and especially by the extremists at the opposite poles of thought, the Communist and the Catholic. Both the Communist and the Catholic usually believe, though unfortunately they do not often say, that abstract aesthetic standards are all bunkum and that a book is only a "good" book if it preaches the right sermon. To the Communist, good literature means "proletarian" literature. (Mr Henderson is careful to explain, however, that this does not mean literature written by proletarians; which is just as well, because there isn't any.) In Henri Barbusse's *One Looks at Russia,* for instance, it is stated almost in so many words that a novel about "bourgeois" characters cannot be a good novel. So expressed this is an absurdity, but in some ways it is not a bad position to take up. Any critic who stuck to it consistently would at least do useful work by dragging into the light the (often quite unaesthetic) reasons for which books are liked or disliked. But unfortunately the notion of art for art's sake, though discredited, is too recent to be forgotten, and there is always a temptation to revert to it in moments of difficulty. Hence the frightful intellectual dishonesty which can be observed in nearly all propagandist critics. They are employing a double set of values and dodging from one to the other according as it suits them. They praise or dispraise a book *because* its tendency is Communist, Catholic, Fascist or what-not; but at the same time, they pretend to be judging it on purely aesthetic grounds. Few people have the guts to say outright that art and propaganda are the same thing.

You can see this at its crudest in the so-called book-reviews in some of the Roman Catholic papers, and indeed in religious papers generally. The editorial staff of the *Church Times* gnash their false teeth and quake in their galoshes at the mention of "modern" (i.e. post-Tennysonian) poetry, but strange to say they make an exception of T. S. Eliot. Eliot is a declared Anglo-Catholic, and therefore his poetry, though "modern", has got to be praised. And the Communist critic is hardly more honest. Most of the time Mr Henderson is keeping up a pretence of strict critical impartiality, but it is strange how invariably his aesthetic judgements coincide with his political ones. Proust, Joyce, Wyndham Lewis, Virginia Woolf, Aldous Huxley, Wells, E. M. Forster (all of them "bourgeois" novelists) are patted on the head with varying degrees of contempt; Lawrence (proletarian turned bourgeois, which is worse) is viciously attacked; Hemingway, on the other hand, is treated rather respectfully (because Hemingway, you see, is rumoured to be toying with Communism); Barbusse is bowed down to; and a huge wad of mediocre stuff called *Daughters of Albion*, by Mr Alec Brown, gets pages and pages of praise all to itself, because here at last you have real "proletarian" literature—written, like all other "proletarian" literature, by a member of the middle classes.

This kind of thing is very depressing to anyone who cares for the cause of Socialism. For what is it except the most ordinary chauvinism turned upside down? It simply gives you the feeling that the Communist is no better than his opposite number. Nevertheless, these books of Marxist literary criticism have their value for anyone who wants to study the Marxist mind. The basic trouble with all orthodox Marxists is that, possessing a system which appears to explain everything, they never bother to discover what is going on inside other people's heads. That is why in every western country, during the last dozen years, they have played straight into the hands of their adversaries. In a book of literary criticism, unlike a tract on economics, the Marxist cannot take cover behind his favourite polysyllables; he has got to come out into the open and you can see just what kind of blinkers he is wearing.

I do not recommend this particular book, which is badly written and thoroughly dull all through, but to anyone who has not yet read it I do recommend Mirsky's *Intelligentsia of Great Britain*, which was published in 1935. It is a terribly malignant but very able book, and in a distorted way it performs a remarkable feat of synthesis. It is the archetype of Marxist literary criticism. And when you read it you understand—though this, of course, is not what the author intends—why Fascism arose, and why even a quite intelligent outsider can be taken in by the vulgar lie, now so popular, that "Communism and Fascism are the same thing".

New English Weekly, 31 December 1936

1937

94. Postcard to James Hanley

Juventud Communist Iberica
Monte Oscurio
Alcubierre, Huesca
Commandante Kopp.[1]
[Postmark 13 February 1937.]

Dear Mr Hanley,[2]
Many thanks for your letter. I dare say my wife has already acknowledged it, as it reached me open & she is dealing with my correspondence while I am away. I'm sorry I cannot write much of a letter —I am not in very comfortable circumstances here—but anyway it was kind of you to write & I am glad you found the book[3] interesting. It is due out about March 10th I believe, but I shall probably still be in the line here when it comes out, so shan't know how it gets on. Gollancz thought parts of it might give offence in certain quarters but that it was worth risking.

Yours sincerely
Eric Blair ("George Orwell")

[1] Georges Kopp (1902–51), a Belgian engineer, commander of the third regiment, Lenin Division, [i.e. the POUM militia] in which Orwell was serving on the Aragon front. After being imprisoned in a GPU jail in Spain, Kopp got to England in January 1939 where he was nursed by Laurence and Gwen O'Shaughnessy, Eileen Blair's brother and his wife. He joined the French Foreign Legion in September 1939 and was captured by the Germans south of the Marne in June 1940. He escaped from a French military hospital and worked as a civil engineer in France at the same time as working for British Naval Intelligence until betrayed to the Gestapo. The British managed to fly him out in September 1943. Previously married to Germaine Warnotte, by whom he had six sons and two daughters, in 1944 he married Doreen Hunton, sister of Gwen O'Shaughnessy. He died in 1951 from his war wounds. Unfortunately no letters from Orwell to Kopp survive, but they and their families remained friends.

[2] James Hanley (1901–), novelist and short-story writer, whose publications include *Boy*, *The Furys* and *Broken Water*.

[3] *The Road to Wigan Pier*.

The Road to Wigan Pier *was published in London by Victor Gollancz Ltd in a Left Book Club edition and in a public edition on 8 March 1937. It was published in New York by Harcourt, Brace in 1958.*

95. Your Questions Answered

[In the BBC Programme "Your Questions Answered", broadcast on 2 December 1943, Orwell was asked: "How long is the Wigan Pier and what is the Wigan Pier?"]

"Well, I am afraid I must tell you that Wigan Pier doesn't exist. I made a journey specially to see it in 1936, and I couldn't find it. It did exist once, however, and to judge from the photographs it must have been about twenty feet long.

Wigan is in the middle of the mining areas, and though it's a very pleasant place in some ways its scenery is not its strong point. The landscape is mostly slag-heaps, looking like the mountains of the moon, and mud and soot and so forth. For some reason, though it's not worse than fifty other places, Wigan has always been picked on as a symbol of the ugliness of the industrial areas. At one time, on one of the little muddy canals that run round the town, there used to be a tumble-down wooden jetty; and by way of a joke someone nicknamed this Wigan Pier. The joke caught on locally, and then the music-hall comedians got hold of it, and they are the ones who have succeeded in keeping Wigan Pier alive as a byword, long after the place itself had been demolished."

96. Letter to Eileen Blair

[Hospital, Monflorite]
Monday [5? April 1937]

Dearest,[1]

You really are a wonderful wife. When I saw the cigars my heart melted away. They will solve all tobacco problems for a long time to

[1] In order to be near her husband, Eileen Blair had gone out to Barcelona in mid-February 1937 and worked as John McNair's secretary.

come. McNair[1] tells me you are all right for money, as you can borrow & then repay when B.E[2] brings some pesetas, but don't go beggaring yourself, & above all don't go short of food, tobacco etc. I hate to hear of your having a cold & feeling run down. Don't let them overwork you either, & don't worry about me, as I am much better & expect to go back to the lines tomorrow or the day after. Mercifully the poisoning in my hand didn't spread, & it is now almost well, tho' of course the wound is still open. I can use it fairly well & intend to have a shave today, for the first time in abt 5 days. The weather is much better, real spring most of the time, & the look of the earth makes me think of our garden at home & wonder whether the wallflowers are coming out & whether old Hatchett is sowing the potatoes. Yes, Pollitt's review[3] was pretty bad, tho' of course good as publicity. I suppose he must have heard I was serving in the Poum[4]

[1] John McNair (1887–1968) a Tynesider who was an indefatigable worker for the cause of Socialism all his life. He left school at twelve, but ran into trouble with employers because of his left-wing sympathies and in order to find work went to France where he stayed for twenty-five years, becoming a leather merchant, founding a French football club with eight teams, and lecturing on English poets at the Sorbonne. Returning to England in 1936 he rejoined the Independent Labour Party, becoming its General Secretary 1939–55. The first British worker to go to Spain, where he remained from August 1936 to June 1937, he was the representative in Barcelona of the ILP. A constant contributor to the *New Leader*, the weekly organ of the ILP (later the *Socialist Leader*), he wrote the official biography of James Maxton, the leader of the ILP, called *The Beloved Rebel*, 1955.

[2] Robert (Bob) Edwards (1906–), since 1955 Labour and Co-operative MP. Stood unsuccessfully as ILP Parliamentary candidate in 1935. In January 1937 was Captain of the ILP contingent in Spain, linked to the POUM. Left Spain at the end of March to attend the ILP Conference at Glasgow, but was unable to return because of the ban imposed by the British Government—due to its non-intervention policy—preventing British nationals from participating in the Spanish civil war.

[3] Harry Pollitt (1890–1960), a Lancashire boiler-maker and a founder-member of the Communist Party of Great Britain in 1920, became its General Secretary in 1929 and, together with Rajani Palme Dutt, led the party until his death. He was, however, removed from the leadership from the autumn of 1939 until Germany's invasion of Russia in July 1941 for his temporary advocacy of a war of democracy against Fascism. His review of *The Road to Wigan Pier* appeared in the *Daily Worker*, 17 March 1937.

[4] POUM, *Partido Obrero de Unificacion Marxista* (Workers' Party of Marxist Unification), a small party with not much influence outside Catalonia, and chiefly important because it contained an unusually high proportion of politically-conscious members, mostly Anarchists.

militia. I don't pay much attention to the *Sunday Times* reviews,[1] as G[2] advertises so much there that they daren't down his books, but the *Observer*[1] was an improvement on last time. I told McNair that when I came on leave I would do the *New Leader* an article, as they wanted one, but it will be such a come-down after B.E's that I don't expect they'll print it. I'm afraid it is not much use expecting leave before about the 20th April. This is rather annoying in my own case as it comes abt through my having exchanged from one unit to another—a lot of the men I came to the front with are now going on leave. If they suggested that I should go on leave earlier I don't think I would say no, but they are not likely to & I am not going to press them. There are also some indications—I don't know how much one can rely on these—that they expect an action hereabouts, & I am not going on leave just before that comes off if I can help it. Everyone has been very good to me while I have been in hospital, visiting me every day etc. I think now that the weather is getting better I can stick out another month without getting ill, & then what a rest we will have, & go fishing too if it is in any way possible.

As I write this Michael, Parker & Buttonshaw[3] have just come in, & you should have seen their faces when they saw the margarine. As to the photos, of course there are lots of people who want copies, & I have written the numbers wanted on the backs, & perhaps you can get reproductions. I suppose it doesn't cost too much—I shouldn't like to disappoint the Spanish machine-gunners etc. Of course some of the photos were a mess. The one which has Buttonshaw looking very blurred in the foreground is a photo of a shell-burst, which you can see rather faintly on the left, just beyond the house.

I shall have to stop in a moment, as I am not certain when McNair is going back & I want to have this letter ready for him. Thanks ever so much for sending the things, dear, & do keep well & happy. I told McNair I would have a talk with him abt the situation when I came on leave, & you might at some opportune moment say something to him abt my wanting to go to Madrid etc. Goodbye, love. I'll write again soon.

With all my love
Eric

[1] *The Road to Wigan Pier* was reviewed by Edward Shanks and by Hugh Massingham in the *Sunday Times* and the *Observer* respectively, 14 March 1937.

[2] Victor Gollancz.

[3] Michael Wilton also known as Milton (English), Buck Parker (South African) and Buttonshaw (American): three members of the same unit as Orwell.

97. Letter to Victor Gollancz

Hotel Continental
Barcelona
9 May 1937

Dear Mr Gollancz,

I didn't get an opportunity earlier to write and thank you for the introduction you wrote to *Wigan Pier*, in fact I didn't even see the book, or rather the B[ook] C[lub] edition of it, till about 10 days ago when I came on leave, and since then I have been rather occupied. I spent my first week of leave in being slightly ill, then there was 3 or 4 days of street-fighting in which we were all more or less involved, in fact it was practically impossible to keep out of it. I liked the introduction very much, though of course I could have answered some of the criticisms you made. It was the kind of discussion of what one is really talking about that one always wants and never seems to get from the professional reviewers. I have had a lot of reviews sent on to me, some of them very hostile but I should think mostly good from a publicity point of view. Also great numbers of letters from readers.

I shall be going back to the front probably in a few days and barring accidents I expect to be there till about August. After that, I think I shall come home as it will be about time I started on another book. I greatly hope I come out of this alive if only to write a book about it. It is not easy here to get hold of any facts outside the circle of one's own experience, but with that limitation I have seen a great deal that is of immense interest to me. Owing partly to an accident I joined the POUM militia instead of the International Brigade,[1] which was a pity in one way because it meant that I have never seen the Madrid front; on the other hand it has brought me into contact with Spaniards rather than Englishmen and especially with genuine revolutionaries. I hope I shall get a chance to write the truth about what I have seen. The stuff appearing in the English papers is largely the most appalling lies—more I can't say, owing to the censorship. If I can get back in August I hope to have a book ready for you about the beginning of next year.

Yours sincerely,
Eric A. Blair

[1] The International Brigades were composed of foreign volunteers, mostly Communist, and played an important part in the defence of Madrid.

98. Letter to Mr Thompson

Sanatori Maurin
Sarria, Barcelona
8 June 1937

Dear Mr Thompson,[1]
Please forgive me for only now answering your letter dated 12.3.37. I have been in Spain since the beginning of the year, most of that time at the front, & my letters have only got to me at long intervals. I got yours abt a fortnight ago, I think. You kindly said that you intended reviewing my last book,[2] & I thought that if it was not too late I would write & warn you that from your point of view I am on the wrong side of the fence, as I have been fighting for what you call "the Caballero[3] clique of capitalists." However I have got a Fascist bullet in me now, if that is any consolation to you, & shall probably have to come home shortly. I just thought I would tell you lest you should think I am a sympathiser with your viewpoint, which on the whole I am not. But thanks very much for writing.

Yours sincerely
George Orwell

99. Letter to Cyril Connolly

Sanatori Maurin
Sarria, Barcelona
8 June 1937

Dear Cyril,
. . . If I can get my discharge papers I ought to be home in abt a fortnight. I have been nastily wounded, not really a very bad wound, a bullet through the throat which of course ought to have killed me but has merely given me nervous pains in the right arm & robbed me of most of my voice. The doctors here don't seem certain whether I shall get my voice back or not. Personally I believe I shall, as some days it is much better than others, but in any case I want to get home

[1] Not identified.
[2] *The Road to Wigan Pier.*
[3] Francisco Largo Caballero, a left-wing Socialist, who headed a coalition government of Socialists, Communists, Anarchists and some liberal Republicans from September 1936 to May 1937.

& be properly treated. I was just reading one of your articles on Spain in a February *New Statesman*. It is a credit to the *New Statesman* that it is the only paper, apart from a few obscure ones such as the *New Leader*, where any but the Communist viewpoint has ever got through. Liston Oak's article[1] recently on the Barcelona troubles was very good & well balanced. I was all through that business & know what lies most of the stuff in the papers was. Thanks also for recently telling the public that I should probably write a book on Spain, as I shall, of course, once this bloody arm is right. I have seen wonderful things & at last really believe in Socialism, which I never did before. On the whole, though I am sorry not to have seen Madrid, I am glad to have been on a comparatively little-known front among Anarchists & Poum people instead of in the International Brigade, as I should have been if I had come here with CP credentials instead of ILP ones. A pity you didn't come up to our position & see me when you were in Aragon. I would have enjoyed giving you tea in a dugout.

Yours
Eric Blair

Encounter, January 1962

100. Spilling the Spanish Beans

The Spanish war has probably produced a richer crop of lies than any event since the Great War of 1914–1918, but I honestly doubt, in spite of all those hecatombs of nuns who have been raped and crucified before the eyes of *Daily Mail* reporters, whether it is the pro-Fascist newspapers that have done the most harm. It is the left-wing papers, the *News Chronicle* and the *Daily Worker*, with their far subtler methods of distortion, that have prevented the British public from grasping the real nature of the struggle.

The fact which these papers have so carefully obscured is that the Spanish Government (including the semi-autonomous Catalan Government) is far more afraid of the revolution than of the Fascists. It is now almost certain that the war will end with some kind of compromise, and there is even reason to doubt whether the Government,

[1] "Behind Barcelona's Barricades", by Liston M. Oak, in the *New Statesman & Nation*, 15 May 1937.

which let Bilbao fall without raising a finger, wishes to be too victorious; but there is no doubt whatever about the thoroughness with which it is crushing its own revolutionaries. For some time past a reign of terror—forcible suppression of political parties, a stifling censorship of the press, ceaseless espionage and mass imprisonment without trial—has been in progress. When I left Barcelona in late June the jails were bulging; indeed, the regular jails had long since overflowed and the prisoners were being huddled into empty shops and any other temporary dump that could be found for them. But the point to notice is that the people who are in prison now are not Fascists but revolutionaries; they are there not because their opinions are too much to the Right, but because they are too much to the Left. And the people responsible for putting them there are those dreadful revolutionaries at whose very name Garvin quakes in his galoshes—the Communists.

Meanwhile the war against Franco continues, but, except for the poor devils in the front-line trenches, nobody in Government Spain thinks of it as the real war. The real struggle is between revolution and counter-revolution; between the workers who are vainly trying to hold on to a little of what they won in 1936, and the Liberal-Communist bloc who are so successfully taking it away from them. It is unfortunate that so few people in England have yet caught up with the fact that Communism is now a counter-revolutionary force; that Communists everywhere are in alliance with bourgeois reformism and using the whole of their powerful machinery to crush or discredit any party that shows signs of revolutionary tendencies. Hence the grotesque spectacle of Communists assailed as wicked "Reds" by right-wing intellectuals who are in essential agreement with them. Mr Wyndham Lewis, for instance, ought to love the Communists, at least temporarily. In Spain the Communist-Liberal alliance has been almost completely victorious. Of all that the Spanish workers won for themselves in 1936 nothing solid remains, except for a few collective farms and a certain amount of land seized by the peasants last year; and presumably even the peasants will be sacrificed later, when there is no longer any need to placate them. To see how the present situation arose, one has got to look back to the origins of the civil war.

Franco's bid for power differed from those of Hitler and Mussolini in that it was a military insurrection, comparable to a foreign invasion, and therefore had not much mass backing, though Franco has since been trying to acquire one. Its chief supporters, apart from certain sections of Big Business, were the land-owning aristocracy and the huge, parasitic Church. Obviously a rising of this kind will array against it various forces which are not in agreement on any other point. The peasant and the worker hate feudalism and clericalism; but so does the "liberal" bourgeois, who is not in the least opposed to a more modern version of Fascism, at least so long as it isn't called Fascism. The "liberal" bourgeois is genuinely liberal up to the point where his own interests stop. He stands for the degree of progress implied in the phrase "la carrière ouverte aux talents". For clearly he has no chance to develop in a feudal society where the worker and the peasant are too poor to buy goods, where industry is burdened with huge taxes to pay for bishops' vestments, and where every lucrative job is given as a matter of course to the friend of the catamite of the duke's illegitimate son. Hence, in the face of such a blatant reactionary as Franco, you get for a while a situation in which the worker and the bourgeois, in reality deadly enemies, are fighting side by side. This uneasy alliance is known as the Popular Front (or, in the Communist press, to give it a spuriously democratic appeal, People's Front). It is a combination with about as much vitality, and about as much right to exist, as a pig with two heads or some other Barnum and Bailey monstrosity.

In any serious emergency the contradiction implied in the Popular Front is bound to make itself felt. For even when the worker and the bourgeois are both fighting against Fascism, they are not fighting for the same things; the bourgeois is fighting for bourgeois democracy, i.e. capitalism, the worker, in so far as he understands the issue, for Socialism. And in the early days of the revolution the Spanish workers understood the issue very well. In the areas where Fascism was defeated they did not content themselves with driving the rebellious troops out of the towns; they also took the opportunity of seizing land and factories and setting up the rough beginnings of a workers' government by means of local committees, workers' militias, police forces, and so forth. They made the mistake, however (possibly because most of the active revolutionaries were Anarchists with a mistrust of all parliaments), of leaving the Republican Government in nominal control. And, in spite of various changes in personnel, every subsequent Government had been of approximately the same bourgeois-reformist character. At the beginning this seemed not to matter, because the Government, especially in Catalonia, was almost powerless and the bourgeoisie had to lie low or even (this was still happening when I reached Spain in December) to disguise themselves as workers. Later, as power slipped from the hands of the Anarchists into the hands of the Communists and right-wing Socialists, the Government was able to reassert itself, the bourgeoisie came out of hiding and the old division of society into rich and poor reappeared, not much modified. Henceforward every move, except a few dictated by military emergency, was directed towards undoing the work of the first few months of revolution. Out of the many illustrations I could choose, I will cite only one, the breaking-up of the old workers' militias, which were organised on a genuinely democratic system, with officers and men receiving the same pay and mingling on terms of complete equality, and the substitution of the Popular Army (once again, in Communist jargon, "People's Army"), modelled as far as possible on an ordinary bourgeois army, with a privileged officer-caste, immense differences of pay, etc etc. Needless to say, this is given out as a military necessity, and almost certainly it does make for military efficiency, at least for a short period. But the undoubted purpose of the change was to strike a blow at equalitarianism. In every department the same policy has been followed, with the result that only a year after the outbreak of war and revolution you get what is in effect an ordinary bourgeois State, with, in addition, a reign of terror to preserve the *status quo*.

This process would probably have gone less far if the struggle could have taken place without foreign interference. But the military weakness of the Government made this impossible. In the face of Franco's foreign mercenaries they were obliged to turn to Russia for help, and though the quantity of arms supplied by Russia has been greatly exaggerated (in my first three months in Spain I saw only one Russian weapon, a solitary machine-gun), the mere fact of their arrival brought the Communists into power. To begin with, the Russian aeroplanes and guns, and the good military qualities of the International Brigades (not necessarily Communist but under Communist control), immensely raised the Communist prestige. But, more important, since Russia and Mexico were the only countries openly supplying arms, the Russians were able not only to get money for their weapons, but to extort terms as well. Put in their crudest form, the terms were: "Crush the revolution or you get no more arms." The reason usually given for the Russian attitude is that if Russia appeared to be abetting the revolution, the Franco-Soviet pact (and the hoped-for alliance with Great Britain) would be imperilled; it may be, also, that the spectacle of a genuine revolution in Spain would rouse unwanted echoes in Russia. The Communists, of course, deny that any direct pressure has been exerted by the Russian Government. But this, even if true, is hardly relevant, for the Communist Parties of all countries can be taken as carrying out Russian policy; and it is certain that the Spanish Communist Party, plus the right-wing Socialists whom they control, plus the Communist press of the whole world, have used all their immense and ever-increasing influence upon the side of counter-revolution.

In the first half of this article I suggested that the real struggle in Spain, on the Government side, has been between revolution and counter-revolution; that the Government, though anxious enough to avoid being beaten by Franco, has been even more anxious to undo the revolutionary changes with which the outbreak of war was accompanied.

Any Communist would reject this suggestion as mistaken or wilfully dishonest. He would tell you that it is nonsense to talk of the Spanish Government crushing the revolution, because the revolution never happened; and that our job at present is to defeat Fascism and defend democracy. And in this connection it is most important to see just how the Communist anti-revolutionary propaganda works. It is a mistake to think that this has no relevance in England, where the Communist Party is small and comparatively weak. We shall see its relevance quickly enough if England enters into an alliance with the USSR; or perhaps even earlier, for the influence of the Communist Party is bound to increase—visibly is increasing—as more and more of the capitalist class realise that latter-day Communism is playing their game.

Broadly speaking, Communist propaganda depends upon terrifying people with the (quite real) horrors of Fascism. It also involves pretending—not in so many words, but by implication—that Fascism has nothing to do with capitalism. Fascism is just a kind of meaningless wickedness, an aberration, "mass sadism", the sort of thing that would happen if you suddenly let loose an asylumful of homicidal maniacs. Present Fascism in this form, and you can mobilise public opinion against it, at any rate for a while, without provoking any revolutionary movement. You can oppose Fascism by bourgeois "democracy", meaning capitalism. But meanwhile you have got to get rid of the troublesome person who points out that

Fascism and bourgeois "democracy" are Tweedledum and Tweedledee. You do it at the beginning by calling him an impracticable visionary. You tell him that he is confusing the issue, that he is splitting the anti-Fascist forces, that this is not the moment for revolutionary phrase-mongering, that for the moment we have got to fight against Fascism without enquiring too closely what we are fighting *for*. Later, if he still refuses to shut up, you change your tune and call him a traitor. More exactly, you call him a Trotskyist.

And what is a Trotskyist? This terrible word—in Spain at this moment you can be thrown into jail and kept there indefinitely, without trial, on the mere rumour that you are a Trotskyist—is only beginning to be bandied to and fro in England. We shall be hearing more of it later. The word "Trotskyist" (or "Trotsky-Fascist") is generally used to mean a disguised Fascist who poses as an ultra-revolutionary in order to split the left-wing forces. But it derives its peculiar power from the fact that it means three separate things. It can mean one who, like Trotsky, wished for world revolution; or a member of the actual organisation of which Trotsky is head (the only legitimate use of the word); or the disguised Fascist already mentioned. The three meanings can be telescoped one into the other at will. Meaning No 1 may or may not carry with it meaning No 2, and meaning No 2 almost invariably carries with it meaning No 3. Thus: "XY has been heard to speak favourably of world revolution; therefore he is a Trotskyist; therefore he is a Fascist." In Spain, to some extent even in England, *anyone* professing revolutionary Socialism (i.e. professing the things the Communist Party professed until a few years ago) is under suspicion of being a Trotskyist in the pay of Franco or Hitler.

The accusation is a very subtle one, because in any given case, unless one happened to know the contrary, it might be true. A Fascist spy probably *would* disguise himself as a revolutionary. In Spain, everyone whose opinions are to the Left of those of the Communist Party is sooner or later discovered to be a Trotskyist, or at least, a traitor. At the beginning of the war the POUM, an opposition Communist party roughly corresponding to the English ILP, was an accepted party and supplied a minister to the Catalan Government; later it was expelled from the Government; then it was denounced as Trotskyist; then it was suppressed, every member that the police could lay their hands on being flung into jail.

Until a few months ago the Anarcho-Syndicalists were described as "working loyally" beside the Communists. Then the Anarcho-Syndicalists were levered out of the Government; then it appeared that they were not working so loyally; now they are in the process of becoming traitors. After that will come the turn of the left-wing Socialists. Caballero, the left-wing Socialist ex-premier, until May 1937 the idol of the Communist press, is already in outer darkness, a Trotskyist and "enemy of the people". And so the game continues. The logical end is a régime in which every opposition party and newspaper is suppressed and every dissentient of any importance is in jail. Of course, such a régime will be Fascism. It will not be the same as the Fascism Franco would impose, it will even be better than Franco's Fascism to the extent of being worth fighting for, but it will be Fascism. Only, being operated by Communists and Liberals, it will be called something different.

Meanwhile, can the war be won? The Communist influence has been against revolutionary chaos and has therefore, apart from the Russian aid, tended to produce greater military efficiency. If the Anarchists saved the Government from August to October 1936, the Communists have saved it from October onwards. But in organising the defence they have succeeded in killing enthusiasm (inside Spain, not outside). They made a militarised conscript army possible, but they also made it necessary. It is significant that as early as January of this year voluntary recruiting had practically ceased. A revolutionary army can sometimes win by enthusiasm, but a conscript army has got to win with weapons, and it is unlikely that the Government will ever have a large preponderance of arms unless France intervenes or unless Germany and Italy decide to make off with the Spanish colonies and leave Franco in the lurch. On the whole, a deadlock seems the likeliest thing.

And does the Government seriously intend to win? It does not intend to lose, that is certain. On the other hand, an outright victory, with Franco in flight and the Germans and Italians driven into the sea, would raise difficult problems, some of them too obvious to need mentioning. There is no real evidence and one can only judge by the event, but I suspect that what the Government is playing for is a compromise that would leave the war situation essentially in being. All prophecies are wrong, therefore this one will be wrong, but I will take a chance and say that though the war may end quite soon or may drag on for years, it will end with Spain divided up, either by actual frontiers or into economic zones. Of course, such a compromise might be claimed as a victory by either side, or by both.

All that I have said in this article would seem entirely commonplace in Spain, or even in France. Yet in England, in spite of the intense interest the Spanish war has aroused, there are very few people who have even heard of the enormous struggle that is going on behind the Government lines. Of course, this is no accident. There has been a quite deliberate conspiracy (I could give detailed instances) to prevent the Spanish situation from being understood. People who ought to know better have lent themselves to the deception on the ground that if you tell the truth about Spain it will be used as Fascist propaganda.

It is easy to see where such cowardice leads. If the British public had been given a truthful account of the Spanish war they would have had an opportunity of learning what Fascism is and how it can be combated. As it is, the *News Chronicle* version of Fascism as a kind of homicidal mania peculiar to Colonel Blimps bombinating in the economic void has been established more firmly than ever. And thus we are one step nearer to the great war "against Fascism" (cf 1914, "against militarism") which will allow Fascism, British variety, to be slipped over our necks during the first week.

New English Weekly, 29 July and 2 September 1937

101. Review

The Spanish Cockpit by Franz Borkenau, *Volunteer in Spain* by John Sommerfield

Dr Borkenau has performed a feat which is very difficult at this moment for anyone who knows what is going on in Spain; he has written a book about the Spanish war without losing his temper. Perhaps I am rash in saying that it is the best book yet written on the subject, but I believe that anyone who has recently come from Spain will agree with me. After that horrible atmosphere of espionage and political hatred it is a relief to come upon a book which sums the situation up as calmly and lucidly as this.

Dr Borkenau is a sociologist and not connected with any political party. He went to Spain with the purpose of doing some "field work" upon a country in revolution, and he made two trips, the first in August, the second in January. In the difference between those two periods, especially the difference in the social atmosphere, the essential history of the Spanish revolution is contained. In August the Government was almost powerless, local soviets were functioning everywhere and the Anarchists were the main revolutionary force; as a result everything was in terrible chaos, the churches were still smouldering and suspected Fascists were being shot in large numbers, but there was everywhere a belief in the revolution, a feeling that the bondage of centuries had been broken. By January power had passed, though not so completely as later, from the Anarchists to the Communists, and the Communists were using every possible method, fair and foul, to stamp out what was left of the revolution. The pre-revolutionary police forces had been restored, political espionage was growing keener and keener, and it was not long before Dr Borkenau found himself in jail. Like the majority of political prisoners in Spain, he was never told what he was accused of; but he was luckier than most in being released after a few days, and even (very few people have managed this lately) saving his documents from the hands of the police. His book ends with a series of essays upon various aspects of the war and the revolution. Anyone who wants to understand the Spanish situation should read the really brilliant final chapter, entitled "Conclusions".

The most important fact that has emerged from the whole business is that the Communist Party is now (presumably for the sake of Russian foreign policy) an anti-revolutionary force. So far from pushing the Spanish Government further towards the Left, the Communist influence has pulled it violently towards the Right. Dr Borkenau, who is not a revolutionary himself,[1] does not particularly regret this fact; what he does object to is that it is being deliberately concealed. The result is that public opinion throughout Europe still regards the Communists as wicked Reds or heroic revolutionaries as the case may be, while in Spain itself:

> It is at present impossible . . . to discuss openly even the basic facts of the political situation. The fight between the revolutionary and non-revolutionary principle, as embodied in Anarchists and Communists respectively, is inevitable, because fire and water cannot mix. . . . But as the Press is not even

[1] See 138.

> allowed to mention it, nobody is fully aware of the position, and the political antagonism breaks through, not in open fight to win over public opinion, but in backstairs intrigues, assassinations by Anarchist bravos, legal assassinations by Communist police, subdued allusions, rumours. . . . The concealment of the main political facts from the public and the maintenance of this deception by means of censorship and terrorism carries with it far-reaching detrimental effects, which will be felt in the future even more than at present.

If that was true in February, how much truer it is now! When I left Spain in late June the atmosphere in Barcelona, what with the ceaseless arrests, the censored newspapers and the prowling hordes of armed police, was like a nightmare.

Mr Sommerfield was a member of the International Brigade and fought heroically in the defence of Madrid. *Volunteer in Spain* is the record of his experiences. Seeing that the International Brigade is in some sense fighting for all of us—a thin line of suffering and often ill-armed human beings standing between barbarism and at least comparative decency—it may seem ungracious to say that this book is a piece of sentimental tripe; but so it is. We shall almost certainly get some good books from members of the International Brigade, but we shall have to wait for them until the war is over.

Time and Tide, 31 July 1937

102. Letter to Rayner Heppenstall

The Stores
Wallington
Nr Baldock, Herts.
31 July 1937

Dear Rayner,
Thanks so much for your letter. I was glad to hear from you. I hope Margaret[1] is better. It sounds dreadful, but from what you say I gather that she is at any rate up and about.

We had an interesting but thoroughly bloody time in Spain. Of course I would never have allowed Eileen to come nor probably

[1] Mrs Rayner Heppenstall.

gone myself if I had foreseen the political developments, especially the suppression of the POUM, the party in whose militia I was serving. It was a queer business. We started off by being heroic defenders of democracy and ended by slipping over the border with the police panting on our heels. Eileen was wonderful, in fact actually seemed to enjoy it. But though we ourselves got out all right nearly all our friends and acquaintances are in jail and likely to be there indefinitely, not actually charged with anything but suspected of "Trotskyism". The most terrible things were happening even when I left, wholesale arrests, wounded men dragged out of hospitals and thrown into jail, people crammed together in filthy dens where they have hardly room to lie down, prisoners beaten and half starved etc etc. Meanwhile it is impossible to get a word about this mentioned in the English press, barring the publications of the ILP, which is affiliated to the POUM. I had a most amusing time with the *New Statesman* about it. As soon as I got out of Spain I wired from France asking if they would like an article and of course they said yes, but when they saw my article was on the suppression of the POUM they said they couldn't print it. To sugar the pill they sent me to review a very good book which appeared recently, *The Spanish Cockpit*, which blows the gaff pretty well on what has been happening. But once again when they saw my review they couldn't print it as it was "against editorial policy", but they actually offered to pay for the review all the same—practically hush-money. I am also having to change my publisher, at least for this book. Gollancz is of course part of the Communism-racket, and as soon as he heard I had been associated with the POUM and Anarchists and had seen the inside of the May riots in Barcelona, he said he did not think he would be able to publish my book, though not a word of it was written yet. I think he must have very astutely foreseen that something of the kind would happen, as when I went to Spain he drew up a contract undertaking to publish my fiction but not other books. However I have two other publishers on my track and I think my agent is being clever and has got them bidding against one another. I have started my book[1] but of course my fingers are all thumbs at present.

My wound was not much, but it was a miracle it did not kill me. The bullet went clean through my neck but missed everything except one vocal cord, or rather the nerve governing it, which is paralysed. At first I had no voice at all, but now the other vocal cord is

[1] *Homage to Catalonia.*

compensating and the damaged one may or may not recover. My voice is practically normal but I can't shout to any extent. I also can't sing, but people tell me this doesn't matter. I am rather glad to have been hit by a bullet because I think it will happen to us all in the near future and I am glad to know that it doesn't hurt to speak of. What I saw in Spain did not make me cynical but it does make me think that the future is pretty grim. It is evident that people can be deceived by the anti-Fascist stuff exactly as they were deceived by the gallant little Belgium stuff, and when war comes they will walk straight into it. I don't, however, agree with the pacifist attitude, as I believe you do. I still think one must fight for Socialism and against Fascism, I mean fight physically with weapons, only it is as well to discover which is which. I want to meet Holdaway and see what he thinks about the Spanish business. He is the only more or less orthodox Communist I have met whom I could respect. It will disgust me if I find he is spouting the same defence of democracy and Trotsky-Fascist stuff as the others.

I would like much to see you, but I honestly don't think I shall be in London for some time, unless absolutely obliged to go up on business. I am just getting going with my book, which I want to get done by Xmas, also very busy trying to get the garden etc in trim after being so long away. Anyway keep in touch and let me know your address. I can't get in touch with Rees. He was on the Madrid front and there was practically no communication. I heard from Murry[1] who seemed in the weeps about something. Au revoir.

Yours
Eric

103. Letter to Geoffrey Gorer

The Stores
Wallington
Nr Baldock, Herts.
16 August 1937

Dear Geoffrey,
How are things? I gather from your stuff in *Time and Tide* that you are back in England. Can't you come out and see us some time?

[1] John Middleton Murry.

We can always put you up, except perhaps during the next week or so when my wife's mother will be in our midst. We got back from Spain about six weeks ago, having had a pretty bloody time and finally sneaking over the border with the police just one jump behind. You cannot conceive the awfulness of the things that are happening in Spain. It is a real reign of terror, Fascism being imposed under the pretence of resisting Fascism, people being flung into jail literally by hundreds and kept there for months without trial, newspapers suppressed, etc etc. The most disgusting thing of all is the way the so-called anti-Fascist press in England has covered it up. I wonder if you saw my review in *Time and Tide* of a book called *The Spanish Cockpit* (which by the way you ought to read)? The author wrote and told me that I was the only reviewer who had mentioned the essential point of the book, i.e. that the Communist Party is now the chief anti-revolutionary party. But the interesting thing was that I had also reviewed it for the *New Statesman* and was, of course, able to treat it more seriously than for *Time and Tide*. But the *NS* having previously refused an article of mine on the suppression of the POUM on the ground that it would "cause trouble", also refused to print the review as it "controverted editorial policy", or in other words blew the gaff on the Communist Party. They then offered to pay for the review, though unprinted, then asked me by telegram to review another book. They were evidently very anxious to prevent me giving away the fact that they are covering up important pieces of news. However they will get a nasty jar when my book on Spain comes out, as I intend to do an appendix on the lies and suppressions in the English press. Whatever you do don't believe a word you read in the *News Chronicle* or *Daily Worker*. The only daily paper I have seen in which a gleam of truth sometimes gets through is the [*Daily*] *Express*—their reports are silly and full of mistakes, of course, but seem honest in intention.

I got wounded by a sniper outside Huesca. It wasn't much but it ought to have killed me, in fact for a few minutes I thought it had, which was an interesting experience. The bullet went through my neck from front to back but skidded round both the carotid artery and the backbone in the most remarkable way. I have one vocal cord paralysed so I can't shout loud or sing, but my voice is pretty normal. I am getting pretty well going with my book and we are very busy trying to do something about the garden, which was in a ghastly mess when we got back and is now empty of everything.

We are going to get some more hens. We have some young ducks but they didn't do well, owing I think to improper feeding in their first week, and we lost several.

Let us know how you are getting on and if you can come and see us. I shall be in town some time next month I think. Eileen sends love.

Yours
Eric A. Blair

104. Review

The Men I Killed by Brigadier-General F. P. Crozier, CB, CMG, DSO

General Crozier is a professional soldier and by his own showing spent the years between 1899 and 1921 in almost ceaseless slaughter of his fellow creatures; hence as a pacifist he makes an impressive figure, like the reformed burglar at a Salvation Army meeting. Everyone will remember his earlier books, with their clipped telegram-like style and their tales of colonial wars in which eager young officers smack their chops over the prospect of "real slaughter". In parts these books were disgusting, but they were completely straightforward and were of great value as illustrating the spirit in which the dirty little wars of that period were waged. Evidently when you are twenty years old it is great fun to turn a machine-gun on a crowd of unarmed "natives". But European war is a different matter, and after much experience of both kinds General Crozier has decided that the only remedy is complete refusal to fight in any circumstances. The only question is, can he advance any argument which will drive the general public an inch farther in the direction of active resistance to war?

Here, on the whole, the book fails. It is a rambling, incoherent book, circling vaguely round two anti-war arguments, one of them good so far as it goes, the other doubtful. The first is the fact that the actual process of war consists in doing things which are instinctively felt to be disgusting, such as shooting your own men to prevent them running away. It is right to insist upon this kind of thing, for war still remains "glorious" in the secret imaginations of most people who have not fought. The other is the fact that all known methods of defence against the aeroplane are more or less useless and that the German bombers could probably reduce England to chaos and starvation in a few weeks. It is doubtful whether this has much value as an argument against war; though true, it amounts to scare-mongering and, coupled with the consciousness of German re-armament, it simply induces in most people a desire to see England "stronger" (i.e. possessed of more bombing planes) than ever. The two facts which even now are not very widely grasped, and which should be made the centre of all anti-war agitation, are quite different from these. General Crozier is aware of them, but only intermittently aware. They are:

1. That war against a foreign country only happens when the moneyed classes think they are going to profit from it.

2. That every war when it comes, or before it comes, is represented not as a war but as an act of self-defence against a homicidal maniac ("militarist" Germany in 1914, "Fascist" Germany next year or the year after).

The essential job is to get people to recognise war propaganda when they see it, especially when it is disguised as peace propaganda.

The test for any pacifist is, does he differentiate between foreign war and civil war? If he does not, he is simply saying in effect that violence may be used by the rich against the poor but not by the poor against the rich. This test General Crozier passes, and if not a completely logical pacifist he is at least a very engaging one. As a living contradiction of the widespread notion that every pacifist is a Creeping Jesus, he should be of great value to his cause.

New Statesman and Nation, 28 August 1937

105. Letter to Geoffrey Gorer

The Stores
Wallington
Nr Baldock, Herts.
15 September 1937

Dear Geoffrey,

Thanks so much for your letter. I am glad you are enjoying yourself in Denmark, though, I must admit, it is one of the few countries I have never wanted to visit. I rang you up when I was in town, but of course you weren't there. I note you are coming back about the 24th. We shall be here till the 10th October, then we are going down to Suffolk to stay at my parents' place for some weeks. But if you can manage it any time between the 24th and the 10th, just drop us a line and then come down and stay. We can always put you up without difficulty.

What you say about not letting the Fascists in owing to dissensions between ourselves is very true so long as one is clear what one means by Fascism, also who or what it is that is making unity impossible. Of course all the Popular Front stuff that is now being pushed by the Communist press and party, Gollancz and his paid hacks etc etc only boils down to saying that they are in favour of British Fascism (prospective) as against German Fascism. What they are aiming to do is to get British capitalist-imperialism into an alliance with the USSR and thence into a war with Germany. Of course they piously pretend that they don't want the war to come and that a French-British-Russian alliance can prevent it on the old balance of power system. But we know what the balance of power business led to last time, and in any case it is manifest that the nations are arming with the intention of fighting. The Popular Front boloney boils down to this: that when the war comes the Communists, labourites etc, instead of working to stop the war and overthrow the Government, will be on the side of the Government provided that the Government is on the "right" side, i.e. against Germany. But everyone with any imagination can foresee that Fascism, not of course called Fascism, will be imposed on us as soon as the war starts. So you will have Fascism with Communists participating in it, and, if we are in alliance with the USSR, taking a leading part in it. This is what has happened in Spain. After what I have seen in Spain I have come to the conclusion that it is futile to be "anti-Fascist" while attempting to preserve capitalism. Fascism after all is only a development of capitalism, and the mildest democracy, so-called, is liable to turn into Fascism when the pinch comes. We like to think of England as a democratic country, but our rule in India, for instance, is just as bad as German Fascism, though outwardly it may be less irritating. I do not see how one can oppose Fascism except by working for the overthrow of capitalism, starting, of course, in one's own country. If one collaborates with a capitalist-imperialist government in a struggle "against Fascism", i.e. against a rival imperialism, one is simply letting Fascism in by the back door. The whole struggle in Spain, on the Government side, has turned upon this. The revolutionary parties, the Anarchists, POUM, etc wanted to complete the revolution, the others wanted to fight the Fascists in the name of "democracy", and, of course, when they felt sure enough of their position and had tricked the workers into giving up their arms, re-introduce capitalism. The grotesque feature, which very few people outside Spain have yet grasped, is that the Communists stood furthest of all to the Right, and were more anxious even than the liberals to hunt down the revolutionaries and stamp out all revolutionary ideas. For instance, they have succeeded in breaking up the workers' militias, which were based on the trade unions and in which all ranks received the same pay and were on a basis of equality, and substituting an army on bourgeois lines where a colonel is paid eight times as much as a private etc. All these changes, of course, are put forward in the name of military necessity and backed up by the "Trotskyist" racket, which consists of saying that anyone who professes revolutionary principles is a Trotskyist and in Fascist pay. The Spanish Communist press has for instance declared that Maxton[1] is in the pay of the Gestapo. The reason why so few people grasp what has happened in Spain is because of the Communist command of the press. Apart from their own press they have the whole of the capitalist anti-Fascist press (papers like the *News Chronicle*) on their side, because the latter have got onto the fact that official Communism is now anti-revolutionary. The result is that they have been able to put across an unprecedented amount of lies and it is almost impossible to get anyone to print anything in contradiction. The accounts of the Barcelona riots in May, which I had the misfortune to be involved in, beat everything I have ever seen for lying. Incidentally the *Daily Worker* has been following me personally with the most filthy libels, calling me pro-Fascist etc, but I asked Gollancz to silence them, which he did, not very willingly I imagine. Queerly enough I am still contracted to write a number of books for him, though he refused to publish the book I am doing on Spain before a word of it was written.

I should like to meet Edith Sitwell very much, some time when I am in town. It surprised me very much to learn that she had heard of me and liked my books. I don't know that I ever cared much for her poems, but I liked very much her life of Pope.

Try and come down here some time. I hope your sprue is gone.

Yours
Eric

[1] James Maxton (1885–1946), Independent Labour MP 1922–46; Chairman of the Independent Labour Party (ILP) 1926–31, 1934–39.

106. Review

Journey to Turkistan by Sir Eric Teichman

Sir Eric Teichman's journey across Sinkiang began and ended in the same places as that of Mr Fleming and Mlle Maillart earlier in the year, but he followed a more northerly route and travelled the greater part of the distance in Ford trucks, one of which broke down and had to be abandoned on the way. From Kashgar onwards he travelled by yak, pony and aeroplane.

On the whole, this is a less interesting book than those of Mlle Maillart and Mr Fleming,[1] the reason is probably that the author was travelling with a definite official purpose and, like all people in such positions, says less than he knows. Obviously, though he does not say so, he was sent to Sinkiang to report upon the extent and nature of the Russian influence. From what he says it is evident that though the Russians have not officially absorbed Sinkiang they are in a position to do so whenever it suits them. Economically the province is dominated by the USSR—as, for geographical reasons, it must be and ought to be—and the weak Chinese administration is only kept in place by the aid of Russian troops. It is also evident from what Sir Eric does *not* say that this state of affairs is acceptable to Great Britain. From our point of view this is the important fact.

Ten years ago the news that the USSR was in virtual control of Chinese Turkistan would have been greeted with a howl of dismay. Now—though Sir Eric has an anti-Communist prejudice which he scarcely conceals—Soviet expansion is regarded with a friendly smile, or something that is meant to look like a friendly smile. The reason, we need not doubt, is that British policy is ceasing to be anti-Russian because Russia is a potential ally against Germany and Japan. And for any thinking person this is a very sinister fact. For if our ruling class is becoming pro-Russian, it is certainly not becoming pro-Socialist. It may be that we are headed for a military alliance with the USSR which would give the National Government, or some faked-up Popular Front government, the one perfect alibi for an imperialist war. Moreover, the mere fact that British imperialism can regard Soviet expansion without dismay gives one a hint of the immense changes that are taking place, not in British policy but in Russian policy. . . .

Time and Tide, 25 September 1937

[1] *News from Tartary* by Peter Fleming, and *Forbidden Journey* by Ella K. Maillart.

107. Review

Red Spanish Notebook by Mary Low and Juan Brea, *Heroes of the Alcazar* by R. Timmermans

Red Spanish Notebook gives a vivid picture of Loyalist Spain, both at the front and in Barcelona and Madrid, in the earlier and more revolutionary period of the war. It is admittedly a partisan book, but probably it is none the worse for that. The joint authors were working for the POUM, the most extreme of the revolutionary parties, since suppressed by the Government. The POUM has been so much vilified in the foreign, and especially the Communist press, that a statement of its case was badly needed.

Up till May of this year the situation in Spain was a very curious one. A mob of mutually hostile political parties were fighting for their lives against a common enemy, and at the same time quarrelling bitterly among themselves as to whether this was or was not a revolution as well as a war. Definitely revolutionary events had taken place—land had been seized by the peasants, industries collectivised, big capitalists killed or driven out, the Church practically abolished—but there had been no fundamental change in the structure of government. It was a situation capable of developing either towards Socialism or back to capitalism; and it is now clear that, given a victory over Franco, some kind of capitalist republic will emerge. But at the same time there was occurring a revolution of ideas that was perhaps more important than the short-lived economic changes. For several months large blocks of people believed that all men are equal and were able to act on their belief. The result was a feeling of liberation and hope that is difficult to conceive in our money-tainted atmosphere. It is here that *Red Spanish Notebook* is valuable. By a series of intimate day-to-day pictures (generally small things: a boot-black refusing a tip, a notice in the brothels saying, "Please treat the women as comrades") it shows you what human beings are like when they are trying to behave as human beings and not as cogs in the capitalist machine. No one who was in Spain during the months when people still believed in the revolution will ever forget that strange and moving experience. It has left something behind that no dictatorship, not even Franco's, will be able to efface.

In every book written by a political partisan one has got to be on the look-out for one or another class of prejudice. The authors of this book are Trotskyists—I gather that they were sometimes an embarrassment to the POUM, which was not a Trotskyist body, though for a while it had Trotskyists working for it—and therefore their prejudice is against the official Communist Party, to which they are not always strictly fair. But is the Communist Party always strictly fair to the Trotskyists? Mr C. L. R. James, author of that very able book *World Revolution*, contributes an introduction.

Heroes of the Alcazar re-tells the story of the siege last autumn, when a garrison mainly of cadets and Civil Guards held out for seventy-two days against terrible odds, until Toledo was relieved by Franco's troops. There is no need because one's sympathies are on the other side to pretend that this was not a heroic exploit. And some of the details of siege-life are very interesting; I particularly liked the account of the ingenious way in which a motor-bicycle engine was hitched on to a hand-mill to grind corn for the garrison. But the book is poorly written, in a glutinous style, full of piety and denunciations of the "Reds". There is an introduction by Major Yeats Brown, who generously concedes that not *all* the "Red Militia" were "cruel and treacherous". The photographs of groups of defenders bring home one of the most pathetic aspects of the civil war. They are so like groups of Government militiamen that if they were changed round no one would know the difference.

Time and Tide, 9 October 1937

108. Letter to Jack Common

The Stores
Wallington
Nr Baldock, Herts.
Tuesday [October? 1937]

Dear Jack,
I was so glad to hear from you. I had tried and failed to get your address. Had I known you were still in Datchworth I could probably have evolved it out of my inner consciousness, but I had vaguely heard you had gone to London. Do come across any time you can summon the energy. Of course it is a bloody cross-country journey. Have you got a bike? We can always put you up. As I remember it it isn't the kind of journey one wants to make twice in one day.

Comc any time except this week-end, when someone else is coming, which uses up our only spare room.

I would like to do something for the Penguin people very much, only the devil of it is that at present I simply can't write about anything but Spain and am struggling with a bloody book on it which I have contracted to do by the end of the year. Of course I could detach something from the book—I think there is at any rate one chapter that would do—but that mightn't be the kind of thing they want and also I don't know that my publishers would want it. It is a devil of a business. It seems only yesterday that nobody would print anything I wrote, and now I get letters from all quarters saying won't I write something, and except for the thing I actually have on hand I am as empty as a jug. Of course I never could and never have written short stories proper. This Spain business has upset me so that I really can't write about anything else, and unfortunately what one has to write about is not picturesque stuff but a blasted complicated story of political intrigue between a lot of cosmopolitan Communists, Anarchists etc. Beyond the book I am not doing anything except the usual hack-work of reviews which I don't count as writing.

We had a devil of a time in Spain but very interesting. I had the bad luck to be heavily mixed up in the political business owing to serving in the POUM militia via the ILP, so I was also mixed up in the Barcelona fighting in May and finally had to flee from Spain with the police in hot pursuit. Had I gone to Spain with no political affiliations at all I should probably have joined the International Column and should no doubt by this time have had a bullet in the back for being "politically unreliable", or at least have been in jail. If I had understood the situation a bit better I should probably have joined the Anarchists. As it was I went there with ILP papers and was thus drafted into the POUM militia, so am being denounced from time to time as a Fascist, Trotskyist, etc in the *Daily Worker*, also have had to change my publisher as Gollancz won't have any more to do with me now I am a Trotskyist. I got badly wounded at Huesca but had a very lucky escape and am now perfectly all right. . . . I haven't seen Richard Rees yet but have heard from him and I hope he will come down here later. He got back about a month ago. I gather he got somehow mixed up in the political business too, I really don't know how, as he was with the Communist Party, but of course we are all Trotskyists nowadays.

Come across when you feel like it. Might be better to drop a card in advance but it doesn't matter very greatly as we are generally here. Please remember me to your wife.

Yours
Eric Blair

109. Lettercard to Cyril Connolly

At. 56 Upper Park Rd[1]
Hampstead NW3
[Postmark: 1 December 1937]

Dear Cyril,
Thanks, I would like to come to lunch on Friday very much. I would also like to meet Stephen Spender if he is free. I've often said rude things abt him in print etc, but I daresay he won't know or won't mind.

Yours
Eric Blair

Encounter, January 1962

110. Review

Storm Over Spain by Mairin Mitchell, *Spanish Rehearsal* by Arnold Lunn, *Catalonia Infelix* by E. Allison Peers

Storm over Spain sounds like a war book, but though it covers a period that includes the civil war the author says very little about the war itself—a subject which is obviously distasteful to her. As she very truly remarks, the atrocity stories that are so eagerly circulated by both sides are an indictment not of Right or Left, but simply of war.

Her book is valuable for a number of reasons, but especially because, unlike almost all English writers on Spain, she gives a fair deal to the Spanish Anarchists. The Anarchists and Syndicalists have been persistently misrepresented in England, and the average English person still retains his eighteen-ninetyish notion that Anarchism is the same thing as anarchy. Anyone who wants to know what Spanish Anarchism stands for, and the remarkable things it achieved,

[1] The address of Sir Richard Rees, Bt.

especially in Catalonia, during the first few months of the revolution, should read Chapter VII of Miss Mitchell's book. The pity is that so much of what the Anarchists achieved has already been undone, ostensibly because of military necessity, actually in order to prepare the way for the return of capitalism when the war is over.

Mr Arnold Lunn writes as a supporter of General Franco and believes life in "red" Spain (which he has not visited) to be one continuous massacre. On the authority of Mr Arthur Bryant, who, "as an historian, is well accustomed to weigh evidence", he puts the number of non-combatants massacred by the "reds" since the beginning of the war as 350,000. It would appear, also, that "the burning of a nun in petrol or the sawing off of a Conservative tradesman's legs" are "the commonplaces of 'democratic' Spain".

Now, I was about six months in Spain, almost exclusively among Socialists, Anarchists and Communists, and if I remember rightly I never even once sawed off a Conservative tradesman's legs. I am almost certain I should remember doing such a thing, however commonplace it may seem to Mr Lunn and Mr Bryant. But will Mr Lunn believe me? No, he will not. And meanwhile stories every bit as silly as this are being manufactured on the other side, and people who were sane two years ago are swallowing them eagerly. That, apparently, is what war, even war in other countries, does to the human mind.

Professor Allison Peers is the leading English authority on Catalonia. His book is a history of the province, and naturally, at the present moment, the most interesting chapters are those towards the end, describing the war and the revolution. Unlike Mr Lunn, Professor Peers understands the internal situation on the Government side, and Chapter XIII of his book gives an excellent account of the strains and stresses between the various political parties. He believes that the war may last for years, that Franco is likely to win, and that there is no hope of democracy in Spain when the war is over. All of them depressing conclusions, but the first two are quite probably correct and the last is most assuredly so.

Time and Tide, 11 December 1937

1938

111. Review

Spanish Testament by Arthur Koestler

Mr Arthur Koestler, a *News Chronicle* correspondent, stayed in Malaga when the Republican troops had departed—a bold thing to do for he had already published a book containing some very unfriendly remarks about General Queipo de Llano. He was thrown into jail by the rebels, and suffered what must have been the fate of literally tens of thousands of political prisoners in Spain. That is to say, he was condemned to death without trial and then kept in prison for months, much of the time in solitary confinement, listening at his keyhole night after night for the roar of rifle-fire as his fellow-prisoners were shot in batches of six or a dozen. As usual—for it really does seem to be quite usual—he knew that he was under sentence of death without knowing with any certainty what he was accused of.

The prison part of the book is written mainly in the form of a diary. It is of the greatest psychological interest—probably one of the most honest and unusual documents that have been produced by the Spanish war. The earlier part is more ordinary and in places even looks rather as though it had been "edited" for the benefit of the Left Book Club. Even more than Mr Steer's,[1] this book lays bare the central evil of modern war—the fact that, as Nietzsche puts it, "he who fights against dragons becomes a dragon himself."

Mr Koestler says:

> I can no longer pretend to be objective.... Anyone who has lived through the hell of Madrid with his eyes, his nerves, his heart, his stomach—and then pretends to be objective, is a liar. If those who have at their command printing machines and printer's ink for the expression of their opinions, remain neutral and objective in the face of such bestiality, then Europe is lost.

[1] *The Tree of Gernika* by G. L. Steer.

I quite agree. You cannot be objective about an aerial torpedo. And the horror we feel of these things has led to this conclusion: if someone drops a bomb on your mother, go and drop two bombs on his mother. The only apparent alternatives are to smash dwelling houses to powder, blow out human entrails and burn holes in children with lumps of thermite, or to be enslaved by people who are more ready to do these things than you are yourself; as yet no one has suggested a practicable way out.

Time and Tide, 5 February 1938

112. Letter to Jack Common

The Stores
Wallington
Nr Baldock, Herts.
5 February 1938

Dear Jack,
I'm bloody sorry, but Max[1] got it wrong about my having any sort of job. At least all it was was this. I had to have some help with heavy digging and various other things I couldn't do unaided, so had to have a chap stay here a week and give me a hand. He is gone now. I enclose cheque for £2. God knows I wish it was more but perhaps it will pay some bill or other. It is a pity you are so far away. There [are] a lot of things I would like to talk about. If you ever manage to come over here again, come so that you can stay. It seems a pity to come all that way just for a day. My book thank God is done and gone to press. It ought to be out in March. I think the title will be *Homage to Catalonia*, because we couldn't think of a better one. I'm not starting another for a few weeks. Please remember me to the wife and kid.

Yours
Eric Blair

[1] Max Plowman.

113. Letter to the Editor of *Time and Tide*

Sir,

In "Time-Tide Diary" of 22 January, Sirocco remarks upon the "unnatural agreement" of Left Book Club writers, and adds, "Why are there no orange volumes[1] by Anarchists? Who publishes the perorations of those nice young Trotskyites one meets at parties?"

As a matter of fact, a certain number of political books written from a left-wing but non-Communist standpoint do get published, in particular by Messrs Secker & Warburg, who are coming to be known rather inaccurately as "the Trotskyist publishers". I have had the honour of reviewing several books of this type, dealing with the Spanish war, in your columns. One was *Red Spanish Notebook*, which was written actually by Trotskyists. I thought it, as I said at the time, a prejudiced book, but interesting in detail and giving a good picture of Catalonia in the early months of the war. Another was Mairin Mitchell's *Storm Over Spain*, written by a Catholic, but very sympathetic to the Spanish Anarchists. And above all there was Franz Borkenau's *The Spanish Cockpit* (published by Faber's), which was written from a strictly non-party standpoint, except in so much that the author was pro-Government and anti-Franco. This in my opinion is by a long way the ablest book that has yet appeared on the Spanish war or is likely to appear until the dust of conflict has died down. But the sequel to my review of it is rather interesting, and gives one a glimpse of the kind of censorship under which we are now suffering and of which the Left Book Club is a symptom.

Shortly after my review of *The Spanish Cockpit* appeared in *Time and Tide*, the author wrote and thanked me, saying that though the book had been widely praised I was the only reviewer who had drawn attention to one of its central themes, i.e. to the real part played by the Communist Party in Spain. Simultaneously I had had the book to review for another well-known weekly paper, and had said much the same as I said in *Time and Tide*, but at greater length. My review was refused publication on the ground that it "controverted editorial policy". Meanwhile I had already discovered that it was almost impossible to get any publicity in the English press for a truthful account of what had been happening in Catalonia in May-June 1937. A number of people had said to me with varying degrees of frankness that one must not tell the truth about what was hap-

[1] The Left Book Club members' copies were bound in limp orange covers.

pening in Spain, and the part played by the Communist Party, because to do so would be to prejudice public opinion against the Spanish Government and so aid Franco. I do not agree with this view, because I hold the outmoded opinion that in the long run it does not pay to tell lies, but in so far as it was dictated by a desire to help the Spanish Government, I can respect it. But what I think is interesting is this. The pro-Government papers covered up the disreputable happenings in Spain, the mass imprisonments without trial, assassinations by the secret police, etc; but so did the pro-Franco papers. The huge "Trotsky-Fascist" plot which the Communist press claimed to have discovered was given wide publicity; the fact that Prieto and other members of the Government denied that there was any truth whatever in the "plot" story, and said roundly that the police were practically an independent body under Communist control, was carefully unmentioned. It will be seen, therefore, that the pro-Communist censorship extends a great deal further than the Left Book Club. The newspapers of the Right, although professing to lump all "reds" together and to be equally hostile to all of them, are in fact perfectly well aware which parties and individuals are or are not dangerous to the structure of capitalism. Ten years ago it was almost impossible to get anything printed in favour of Communism: today it is almost impossible to get anything printed in favour of Anarchism or "Trotskyism". Did not Miss Ellen Wilkinson remark in your number of 22 January that in Paris "one can meet a Pertinax and a former Chef du Cabinet, Poincaré, at a lunch with Communist leaders without any sense of strain"? And does she really see no more in this than that Pertinax and Thorez are both frightened of Hitler?

George Orwell

Time and Tide, 5 February 1938

114. Letter to Raymond Mortimer

The Stores
Wallington
Nr Baldock, Herts
9 February 1938

Dear Mortimer,[1]

With reference to your letter of February 8th. I am extremely sorry if I have hurt your or anybody else's feelings, but before speaking of the general issues involved, I must point out that what you say in it is not quite correct. You say, "Your review of *The Spanish Cockpit* was refused, because it gave a most inadequate and misleading description of the book. You used the review merely to express your own opinions and to present facts which you thought should be known. Moreover, last time I saw you, you acknowledged this. Why then do you now suggest, quite mistakenly, that the review was refused because it 'controverted editorial policy'? Are you confusing the review with the previous refusal of an article, which you submitted, and which the editor turned down because we had just printed three articles on the same subject?"

I attach a copy of Kingsley Martin's letter. You will see from this that the review *was* refused because it "controverts the political policy of the paper" (I should have said "political policy", not "editorial policy".) Secondly, you say that my previous article had

[1] On reading Orwell's letter to the Editor of *Time and Tide* Raymond Mortimer, the critic, then literary editor of the *New Statesman and Nation*, and one of the best that paper has had, wrote to Orwell on 8 February 1938 in protest, saying: "It is possible of course that the 'well known weekly paper' to which you refer is not the *New Statesman*, but I take this as a reference to us, and so no doubt will the majority of those who read your letter." The offices of the *New Statesman* were bombed during the war so all the correspondence of that time has been lost. But among his papers Orwell kept the originals of Kingsley Martin's—editor of the *New Statesman* 1931–60—and Raymond Mortimer's letters and a carbon copy, which we print here, of his reply to Mortimer, quoting from their letters. In reply to his letter Raymond Mortimer sent a handwritten note saying, "Dear Orwell, Please accept my humble apologies. I did not know Kingsley Martin had written to you in those terms. My own reasons for refusing the review were those that I gave. I should be sorry for you not to write for us, and I should like to convince you from past reviews that there is no premium here on Stalinist orthodoxy."

Orwell did book reviews for the literary pages of the *New Statesman* from July 1940 to August 1943 but, as is recorded in conversation with his friends, he never forgave Kingsley Martin for his "line" over the Spanish civil war.

been turned down "because we had just printed three articles on the same subject." Now, the article I sent in was on the suppression of the POUM, the alleged "Trotsky-Fascist" plot, the murder of Nin, etc. So far as I know the *New Statesman* has never published any article on this subject. I certainly did and do admit that the review I wrote was tendentious and perhaps unfair, but it was not returned to me on those grounds, as you see from the letter attached.

Nothing is more hateful to me than to get mixed up in these controversies and to write, as it were, against people and newspapers that I have always respected, but one has got to realise what kind of issues are involved and the very great difficulty of getting the truth ventilated in the English press. So far as one can get at the figures, not less than 3000 political prisoners (i.e. anti-Fascists) are in the Spanish jails at present, and the majority of them have been there six or seven months without any kind of trial or charge, in the most filthy physical conditions, as I have seen with my own eyes. A number of them have been bumped off, and there is not much doubt that there would have been a wholesale massacre if the Spanish Government had not had the sense to disregard the clamour in the Communist press. Various members of the Spanish Government have said over and over again to Maxton, McGovern,[1] Félicien Challaye[2] and others that they wish to release these people but are unable to do so because of Communist pressure. What happens in Loyalist Spain is largely governed by outside opinion, and there is no doubt that if there had [been] a general protest from foreign Socialists the anti-Fascist prisoners would have been released. Even the protests of a small body like the ILP have had some effect. But a few months back when a petition was got up for the release of the anti-Fascist prisoners, nearly all the leading English Socialists refused to sign it. I do not doubt that this was because, though no doubt they disbelieved the tale about a "Trotsky-Fascist" plot, they had gathered a general impression that the Anarchists and the POUM were working against the Government, and, in particular, had believed the lies that were published in the English press about the fighting in Barcelona in May

[1] John McGovern (1887–1968), ILP Member of Parliament 1930–47, Labour MP 1947–59. In 1934 he led a hunger march from Glasgow to London.

[2] Félicien Challaye, French left-wing politician, member of the committee of "la Ligue des droits des hommes", a liberal, anti-Fascist movement to protect civil liberty throughout the world; he resigned from "la Ligue" in November 1937, along with seven other members, in protest against what they took to be the movement's cowardly subservience to Stalinist tyranny.

1937. To mention an individual instance, Brailsford[1] in one of his articles in the *New Statesman* was allowed to state that the POUM had attacked the Government with stolen batteries of guns, tanks etc. I was in Barcelona during the fighting, and as far as one can ever prove a negative I can prove by eye-witnesses etc that this tale was absolutely untrue. At the time of the correspondence over my review I wrote to Kingsley Martin to tell him it was untrue, and more recently I wrote to Brailsford to ask him what was the source of the story. He had to admit that he had had it on what amounted to no authority whatever. (Stephen Spender has his letter at present, but I could get it for you if you wanted to see it.) Yet neither the *New Statesman* nor Brailsford has published any retraction of this statement, which amounts to an accusation of theft and treachery against numbers of innocent people. I do not think you can blame me if I feel that the *New Statesman* has its share of blame for the one-sided view that has been presented.

Once again, let me say how sorry I am about this whole business but I have got to do what little I can to get justice for people who have been imprisoned without trial and libelled in the press, and one way of doing so is to draw attention to the pro-Communist censorship that undoubtedly exists. I would keep silent about the whole affair if I thought it would help the Spanish Government (as a matter of fact, before we left Spain some of the imprisoned people asked us *not* to attempt any publicity abroad because it might tend to discredit the Government), but I doubt whether it helps in the long run to cover things up as has been done in England. If the charges of espionage etc that were made against us in the Communist papers had been given a proper examination at the time in the foreign press, it would have been seen that they were nonsense and the whole business might have been forgotten. As it was, the rubbish about a Trotsky-Fascist plot was widely circulated and no denial of it was published except in very obscure papers and, very half-heartedly, in the [*Daily*] *Herald* and *Manchester Guardian*. The result was that there was no protest from abroad and all these thousands of people have stayed in prison, and a number have been murdered, the effect

[1] H. N. Brailsford (1873–1958), Socialist intellectual, author and political journalist. Leader writer for the *Manchester Guardian*, *Daily News* and the *Nation*. Joined the ILP in 1907; editor of the *New Leader*, weekly organ of the ILP, 1922–26. Publications include *The War of Steel and Gold*; *Shelley, Godwin and their Circle*; *Voltaire* and *Subject India*.

being to spread hatred and dissension all through the Socialist movement.

I am sending back the books you gave me to review. I think it would be better if I did not write for you again. I am terribly sorry about this whole affair, but I have got to stand by my friends, which may involve attacking the *New Statesman* when I think they are covering up important issues.

Yours sincerely
[George Orwell]

115. Letter to Alec Houghton Joyce

The Stores
Wallington
Nr Baldock, Herts.
12 February 1938

Dear Mr Joyce,[1]
The *Pioneer* newspaper (Lucknow) recently wrote asking me to take up an appointment with them for a year or two years, and in case there should be any difficulty about my entry into India they advised me to consult you. For the purpose of any enquiries you might have to make, perhaps it will be simpler if I give you full particulars about myself, my political record etc.

I was born in 1903 (by mistake this has been entered as 1902 on my passport), educated at Eton 1917–1921, served in the Indian Imperial Police in Burma 1922–1927 and resigned at the beginning of 1928 because the work was not suited to me. During 1928–9 I lived in Paris, was then teaching in England for about four years, and since about 1933 have earned my living by writing. At the end of 1936 I went to Spain, joined the militia and was serving until June 1937, when I was wounded and returned to England. I have never been a member of any political party, but I am of Socialist sympathies, have been associated to some extent with the ILP, and when in Spain was with the ILP contingent on the Aragon front.

The books I have published are as follows: *Down and Out in Paris and London*, *Burmese Days*, *A Clergyman's Daughter*, *Keep the Aspidistra Flying* and *The Road to Wigan Pier*. All these were published by Victor Gollancz. *The Road to Wigan Pier* was the Left Book

[1] Information Officer at the India Office.

Club choice for March 1937. My next book, *Homage to Catalonia*, is to be published in March by Secker and Warburg. I have also contributed to the *New Statesman, Time and Tide*, the *Listener*, the *New English Weekly* and other papers.

My object in going to India is, apart from the work on the *Pioneer*, to try and get a clearer idea of political and social conditions in India than I have at present. I shall no doubt write some book on the subject afterwards, and if I can arrange it I shall probably contribute occasional articles on Indian affairs to *Time and Tide* or some other English paper.

I hope these notes may be of use to you. I am very sorry to put you to inconvenience and greatly obliged to you for your help.

Yours sincerely
Eric Blair

PS. I should have said that I usually write under the name of "George Orwell".

116. Letter to Jack Common

The Stores
Wallington
Nr Baldock, Herts.
16 February 1938

Dear Jack,

About Saturday. How about meeting in Hitchin on Saturday at 3.30 pm which will be in comfortable time for tea which might stretch out till pub-opening time and then I can take the late bus home. I think the best place to meet would be Woolworth's, so unless I hear from you to the contrary will look out for you at Woolworth's (inside) at 3.30 pm Saturday.

As to taking a book to Gollancz, if you do do so, keep it dark that you have one coming out with Secker.[1] So long as that fact is hidden until it is too late, i.e. until the book has gone to press. G is, of course, very enterprising about "left" stuff, and as he is not too bright intellectually doesn't necessarily see Trotskyist or other heretical implications if they are not on the surface. I think myself

[1] Secker & Warburg.

it is rather a good idea to have a foot in both the Gollancz and the Secker camps. Warburg,[1] of course, doesn't mind, and on the other hand if Gollancz has your name on his list and one of your books appearing shortly, it is liable to make his hirelings pull their punches a bit when the Secker book appears. . . . Unless the India Office take steps to prevent it, I am in all probability going to India for about a year quite shortly. It is a frightful bore and I have seldom wanted to do anything less, but I feel that it is an opportunity to see interesting things and that I should afterwards curse myself if I didn't go. I wish it didn't come at this moment, because I particularly wanted to vegetate for a few months, look after the garden etc and think about my next novel.[2] I am afraid I don't just at the moment see how exactly you connect up with the *Aryan Path*. I always had a vague idea it had to do with theosophy. The only bit of advice I can give is that on a number of occasions when someone suddenly turned the light up the ectoplasm turned out to be butter-muslin. But I have always thought there might be a lot of cash in starting a new religion, and we'll talk it over some time. Looking forward to seeing you on Saturday. . . .

Yours
Eric Blair

117. Review

Workers' Front by Fenner Brockway

For the past year or two every Socialist, whether he likes it or not, has been involved in the savage controversy that rages over the policy of the Popular Front. Hateful in every way as this controversy has become, it raises questions that are too important to be ignored, not merely by Socialists but also by those who are outside or even hostile to the whole Socialist movement.

Mr Brockway's book is written from the standpoint that it is now usual to denounce as "Trotskyist". His plea is that a Popular Front (i.e., a line-up of capitalist and proletarian for the ostensible purpose of opposing Fascism) is simply an alliance of enemies and

[1] F. J. Warburg, managing director of Secker & Warburg.
[2] *Coming Up for Air.*

must always, in the long run, have the effect of fixing the capitalist class more firmly in the saddle. There is very little doubt that this is true, and a short time ago few people would have bothered to deny it. Until about 1933 any Socialist, or any anti-Socialist in an unbuttoned moment, would have told you that the whole history of class-collaboration (and "Popular Front" or "People's Front" is only a polite name for this) is summed up in the limerick about the young lady of Niger. But unfortunately the menacing rise of Hitler has made it very difficult to view the situation objectively. Rubber truncheons and castor oil have scared people of the most diverse kinds into forgetting that Fascism and capitalism are at bottom the same thing. Hence the Popular Front—an unholy alliance between the robbers and the robbed. In England the Popular Front is as yet only an idea, but it has already produced the nauseous spectacle of bishops, Communists, cocoa-magnates, publishers, duchesses and Labour MPs marching arm in arm to the tune of "Rule Britannia" and all tensing their muscles for a rush to the bomb-proof shelter when and if their policy begins to take effect.

Against all this Mr Brockway urges that Fascism can only be combatted by attacking capitalism in its non-Fascist as well as its Fascist forms; and that therefore the only real enemy Fascism has to face is the class that does not benefit from capitalism, i.e. the working class. It is a pity that he tends to use the expression "working class" in a rather narrow and restricted sense, being, like nearly all Socialist writers, too much dominated by the concept of a "proletarian" as a manual labourer. In all western countries there now exists a huge middle class whose interests are identical with those of the proletariat but which is quite unaware of this fact and usually sides with its capitalist enemy in moments of crisis. There is no doubt that this is partly due to the tactlessness of Socialist propaganda. Perhaps the best thing one can wish the Socialist movement at this moment is that it should shed some of its nineteenth-century phraseology.

Much of Mr Brockway's book is taken up in criticising the tactics of the Communist Party—necessarily so, because the whole manoeuvre of the Popular Front is bound up with the Franco-Russian Alliance and the volte-face performed by the Comintern in the past few years. Underlying this is a much larger question, always more or less present when the Popular Front is discussed, though it is seldom brought into the foreground. This is the question of the huge though inscrutable changes that are occurring in the USSR. As the destinies of all of us are involved here, directly or indirectly, this book, written from what is at the moment the most unpopular angle, ought not to be neglected even by those who are hostile to its main implications.

New English Weekly, 17 February 1938

118. Review

Trials in Burma by Maurice Collis

This is an unpretentious book, but it brings out with unusual clearness the dilemma that faces every official in an empire like our own. Mr Collis was District Magistrate of Rangoon in the troubled period round about 1930. He had to try cases which were a great deal in the public eye, and he soon discovered the practical impossibility of keeping to the letter of the law and pleasing European opinion at the same time. Finally, for having sentenced a British army officer to three months' imprisonment for criminal negligence in driving a car, he was reprimanded and hurriedly transferred to another post. For the same offence a native would have been imprisoned as a matter of course.

The truth is that every British magistrate in India is in a false position when he has to try a case in which European and native interests clash. In theory he is administering an impartial system of justice; in practice he is part of a huge machine which exists to protect British interests, and he has often got to choose between sacrificing his integrity and damaging his career. Nevertheless, owing to the exceptionally high traditions of the Indian Civil Service, the law in India is administered far more fairly than might be expected—and incidentally, far too fairly to please the business community. Mr Collis grasps the essential situation clearly enough; he recognises that the Burman has profited very little from the huge wealth that has been extracted from his country, and that the hopeless rebellion of 1931 had genuine grievances behind it. But he is also a good imperialist, and it was precisely his concern for the good name of English justice that got him into hot water with his fellow countrymen on more than one occasion.

In 1930 he had to try Sen Gupta, one of the leaders of the Congress Party and at that time Mayor of Calcutta, who had paid a flying visit to Rangoon and made a seditious speech. The account of the trial makes curious reading—an Indian crowd roaring outside, Mr Collis wondering whether he would be knocked on the head the next moment, and the prisoner sitting in the dock reading a newspaper to make it clear that he did not recognise the jurisdiction of an English court. Mr Collis's sentence was ten days' imprisonment—a wise sentence, for it deprived Sen Gupta of a chance of martyrdom. Afterwards the two men were able to meet privately and talk the affair over. The description of the Indian and the Englishman meeting in perfect amity, each fully aware of the other's motives, each regarding the other as an honourable man and yet, in the last resort, as an enemy, is strangely moving and makes one wish that politics nearer home could be conducted in an equally decent spirit.

[Unsigned]

Listener, 9 March 1938

119. Review

Glimpses and Reflections by John Galsworthy

John Galsworthy was an Old Harrovian with one skin too few, and towards the end of his life the missing skin renewed itself. It is a process almost drearily normal, but interesting in Galsworthy's case because of the fact that the bitterness of his earlier vision of life gave his books an undeniable power.

Glimpses and Reflections is a collection of short essays and letters to the press, largely on such subjects as the caging of songbirds and the traffic in worn-out horses. No one would guess that the man who wrote them once wrote books which were considered dangerously subversive and which were, in fact, morbidly pessimistic. Much of Galsworthy's later writing is tripe, but some of the early plays and novels (*The Man of Property*, *The Country House*, *Justice*, *Fraternity*, and some others) do at least leave behind them a kind of flavour, an atmosphere—a rather unwholesome atmosphere of frustration and exaggerated pity, mixed up with country scenery and dinners in Mayfair. The picture he was trying to build up was a picture of a money-ruled world of unspeakable cruelty—a world in which an obtuse, beef-eating race of squires, lawyers, bishops, judges and stockbrokers squatted *in saecula saeculorum* on the backs of a hypersensitive race of slum-dwellers, servants, foreigners, fallen women and artists. It was not an altogether untrue picture of the Edwardian days when English capitalism still seemed unassailable. But quite suddenly something happened; Galsworthy's private quarrel with society (whatever it may have been) came to an end, or perhaps it was merely that the oppressed classes began to seem less oppressed. From then on it was obvious that he was in no essential way different from the people he had made his name by attacking.

In the letters and essays in this book he emerges as the perfect Dumb Friends' Leaguer, seeing virtually nothing wrong in contemporary society except over-population and cruelty to animals. His solution for all economic troubles is emigration—abolish unemployment by getting the unemployed out of sight; he goes into frenzies over the suffering of pit ponies, but is conspicuously less sorry for coal miners: he quotes Adam Lindsay Gordon's "Life is mostly froth and bubble", and states that it is his "philosophic and religious motto". And it is interesting to note that he seems anxious to explain away the apparent revolutionary implications of some of his plays.

Probably many people, opening this book at random and coming upon the quotation from Adam Lindsay Gordon or an essay entitled "Playing the Game with Birds and Animals", would turn away in disgust, thanking God that they are post-war and post-Eliot. But there is more to it than that. Galsworthy was a bad writer, and some inner trouble, sharpening his sensitiveness, nearly made him into a good one; his discontent healed itself, and he reverted to type. It is worth pausing to wonder in just what form the thing is happening to oneself.

New Statesman and Nation, 12 March 1938

120. Letter to Cyril Connolly

The Stores
Wallington
Nr Baldock, Herts.
14 March 1938

Dear Cyril,

I see from the *NS & N* list that you have a book[1] coming out sometime this spring. If you can manage to get a copy sent me I'll review it for the *New English* [*Weekly*], possibly also *Time & Tide.* I arranged for Warburg to send you a copy of my Spanish book[2] (next month) hoping you may be able to review it. You scratch my back, I'll scratch yours.

I am writing this in bed. I may not be going to India after all & any way not before the autumn. The doctors don't think I ought to go. I've been spitting blood again, it always turns out to be not serious, but it's alarming when it happens & I am going to a Sanatorium in Kent to be X rayed. I've no doubt they'll find as before that I am OK but any way it's a good excuse for not going to India, which I never wanted to. This bloody mess-up in Europe has got me so that I really can't write anything. I see Gollancz has already put my next novel on his list tho' I haven't written a line or even sketched it out. It seems to me we might as well all pack our bags for the concentration camp. King-Farlow was here the other day & I am going to stay next week-end with him after leaving the Sanatorium. When in town I'll try & look you up. Could you be kind enough to write me a line to 24 Croom's Hill, Greenwich SE10,[3] to let me know your telephone address, which of course I've lost again, & then if occasion arises I can ring you up. Please remember me to your wife.

Yours
Eric Blair

Encounter, January, 1962

[1] *Enemies of Promise.*

[2] *Homage to Catalonia.*

[3] Home of Eileen Blair's brother, Laurence (Eric) O'Shaughnessy, a chest and heart surgeon.

121. Letter to Jack Common

Jellicoe Ward
Preston Hall
Aylesford, Kent
Wed. [late March? 1938]

Dear Jack,
Warburg has just sent me along a copy of *Seven Shifts*,[1] which I know I shall read with great interest. He also asked me to give it a bit of a boost. I'll do so, but I admit this business of sending out books to be boosted, which W has now done to me 3 or 4 times, makes me a bit uneasy. The trouble is I've always got at the back of my mind a picture of myself as a sort of Gerald Gould selling my intellectual virtue at constantly-decreasing prices. A year or two ago Eileen said I should never be quoted in a blurb because what I said about people's books was always too offensive, & though it wasn't meant as such I took this as a compliment. But now I've been on two blurbs, one of them one of W's, & I don't want to become a sort of fixture on the backs of his dust-covers with "'Genius'—George Orwell" kept permanently in type. The trouble is that everyone in writing is torn between three motives, *i.* Art for art's saking in the ivory tower, *ii.* political propaganda & *iii.* pulling in the dough. But any way I'll say what I can about the book & I'll also see if I can review it for the *New Leader*.

I expect Eileen wrote & told you I was in this place. I'm afraid I'll have to be here about another two months. I don't think there's really much wrong with me: evidently I have an old lesion in one lung which has been there at any rate 10 years & was never discovered before because I am non-infectious, i.e. no bacteria to show. The bore is that I can't work, & what with having slacked for abt 2 months on the strength of finishing my last book,[2] my next,[3] which Gollancz has hopefully put on his list, I see, will be some time coming along. I am studying botany in a very elementary way, otherwise mainly doing crossword puzzles. It is a very nice place & everyone is very good to me.

Please remember me to the wife & Peter.[4] I hope all goes well with

[1] Edited and with a preface by Jack Common.
[2] *Homage to Catalonia.*
[3] *Coming Up for Air.*
[4] Jack Common's son.

you. I'm going to send this to care of Warburg because I'm not certain whether you've changed your address.

Yours
Eric Blair

PS. Where is Rees? Is he in Spain? I hope to Christ he'll get out before Franco gets to the coast. No doubt they wouldn't shoot him if he's only with an ambulance, but there's bound to be some unpleasantness.

122. Letter to Stephen Spender

Jellicoe Ward
Preston Hall
Aylesford, Kent
2 April 1938

Dear Spender,

I hope things go well with you. I really wrote to say I hoped you'd read my Spanish book (title *Homage to Catalonia*) when it comes out, which should be shortly. I have been afraid that having read those two chapters you would carry away the impression that the whole book was Trotskyist propaganda, whereas actually only abt half of it or less is controversial. I hate writing that kind of stuff and am much more interested in my own experiences, but unfortunately in this bloody period we are living in one's only experiences *are* being mixed up in controversies, intrigues etc. I sometimes feel as if I hadn't been properly alive since abt the beginning of 1937. I remember on sentry-go in the trenches near Alcubierre I used to do Hopkins's poem "Felix Randal", I expect you know it, over and over to myself to pass the time away in that bloody cold, & that was abt the last occasion when I had any feeling for poetry. Since then it's gone right out of my head. I don't know that I can give you a copy of my book because I've already had to order about 10 extra ones & it's so damned expensive, but you can always get it out of the library.

I have been in this place abt 3 weeks. I am afraid from what they say it is TB all right but evidently a very old lesion and not serious. They say I am to stay in bed and rest completely for abt 3 months & then I shall probably be OK. It means I can't work & is rather a bore, but perhaps is all for the best.

The way things are going in Spain simply desolates me. All those towns & villages I knew smashed abt, & I suppose the wretched peasants who used to be so decent to us being chased to & fro & their landlords put back onto them. I wonder if we shall ever be able to go back to Spain if Franco wins. I suppose it would mean getting a new passport anyway. I notice that you and I are both on the board of sponsors or whatever it is called of the SIA.[1] So also is Nancy Cunard,[2] all rather comic because it was she who previously sent me that bloody rot which was afterwards published in book form (called *Authors Take Sides*). I sent back a very angry reply in which I'm afraid I mentioned you uncomplimentarily, not knowing you personally at that time. However I'm all for this SIA business if they are really doing anything to supply food etc, not like that damned rubbish of signing manifestos to say how wicked it all is.

Write some time if you get time. I'd like to meet again when I get out of here. Perhaps you will be able to come and stay with us some time.

Yours
Eric Blair

Encounter, January 1962

123. Letter to Stephen Spender

Jellicoe Pavilion
Preston Hall
Aylesford, Kent
Friday [15? April 1938]

Dear Spender,
Thank you very much for your letter & the copy of your play.[3] I waited to read the latter before replying. It interested me, but I'm not quite sure what I think abt it. I think with a thing like that one wants to see it acted, because in writing you obviously had different

[1] Solidaridad Internacional Antifascista.

[2] Nancy Cunard (1896–1965), daughter of the shipowner; poet and writer of literary reminiscences, devoted to Socialist causes and especially the causes and arts of the Negro.

[3] *Trial of a Judge.*

scenic effects, supplementary noises, etc in mind which would determine the beat of the verse. But there's a lot in it that I'd like to discuss with you when next I see you.

You ask how it is that I attacked you not having met you, & on the other hand changed my mind after meeting you. I don't know that I had exactly attacked you, but I had certainly in passing made offensive remarks abt "parlour Bolsheviks such as Auden & Spender" or words to that effect. I was willing to use you as a symbol of the parlour Bolshie because *a.* your verse, what I had read of it, did not mean very much to me, *b.* I looked upon you as a sort of fashionable successful person, also a Communist or Communist sympathiser, & I have been very hostile to the CP since about 1935, & *c.* because not having met you I could regard you as a type & also an abstraction. Even if when I met you I had not happened to like you, I should still have been bound to change my attitude, because when you meet anyone in the flesh you realise immediately that he is a human being & not a sort of caricature embodying certain ideas. It is partly for this reason that I don't mix much in literary circles, because I know from experience that once I have met & spoken to anyone I shall never again be able to show any intellectual brutality towards him, even when I feel that I ought to, like the Labour MPs who get patted on the back by dukes & are lost forever more.

It is very kind of you to review my Spanish book. But don't go & get into trouble with your own party—it's not worth it. However, of course you can disagree with all my conclusions, as I think you would probably do anyway, without actually calling me a liar. If you would come & see me some time I would like it very much, if it's not too much of an inconvenience. I am not infectious. I don't think this place is very difficult to get to, because the Green Line buses stop at the gate. I am quite happy here & they are very nice to me, but of course it's a bore not being able to work & I spend most of my time doing crossword puzzles.

Yours
Eric Blair

Encounter, January 1962

124. Letter to Jack Common

Jellicoe Pavilion
Preston Hall
Aylesford, Kent
20 April 1938

Dear Jack,

Thanks so much for yours. I'm really writing to say that I liked *Seven Shifts* very much, especially Watson's contribution.[1] I wrote Secker's a note some of which might be used for a blurb & I've also asked the *New Leader* if they'd like it reviewed. Of course it's very difficult for a small publishing firm like that ever to score a thumping success, tho' I suppose by specialising along certain lines they can at any rate keep going. It's not only that without thousands to whack abt you can't advertise, but that if you don't advertise no one will review you decently if at all. Then again with S & W's[2] there's the political issue & Communists sabotaging their books as far as they can manage it. My own book I have no doubt will be ignored in a number of places on that issue, but I've pulled a few strings which may ring a bell here & there. As to the great proletarian novel, I really don't see how it's to come into existence. The stuff in *Seven Shifts* is written from a prole point of view, but of course as literature it's bourgeois literature. The thing is that all of us talk & write two different languages, & when a man from, say, Scotland or even Yorkshire writes in standard English he's writing something quite as different from his own tongue as Spanish is from Italian. I think the first real prole novel that comes along will be spoken over the radio.

I'm glad to hear Richard's[3] coming home. From your saying so I gather he's in Catalonia—I thought he'd be at Madrid again, in which case it wouldn't be so easy to get away.

Love to all
Yours
Eric Blair

[1] One of the seven contributions was "The Big Chimney" by J. H. Watson.
[2] Secker & Warburg.
[3] Sir Richard Rees, Bt.

125. Letter to Geoffrey Gorer

Jellicoe Pavilion
Preston Hall
Aylesford, Kent
18 April 1938

Dear Geoffrey,

I must write to thank you for your marvellous review. I kept pinching myself to make sure I was awake, but I shall also have to pinch myself if *T & T*[1] print it—I'm afraid they'll think it's too long & laudatory. I don't think they'll bother abt the subject-matter, as they've been very good about the Spanish war. But even if they cut it, thanks ever so for the intention. There were just one or two points. One is that you say the fighting in Barcelona was started by the Assault Guards. Actually it was Civil Guards. There weren't any Assault Guards there then, & there is a difference, because the Civil Guards are the old Spanish Gendarmerie dating from the early 19th century & in reality a more or less pro-Fascist body, i.e. they have always joined the Fascists where it was possible. The Assault Guards are a new formation dating from the Republic of 1931, pro-Republican & not hated by the working people to the same extent. The other is that if you are obliged to shorten or otherwise alter the review, it doesn't particularly matter to insist, as you do now, that I only took part in the Barcelona fighting to the extent of doing sentry. I did, as it happens, but if I had been ordered to actually fight I would have done so, because in the existing chaos there didn't seem anything one could do except obey one's own party & immediate military superiors. But I'm so glad you liked the book. Various people seem to have received review copies, but I haven't had any myself yet and I am wondering uneasily what the dust-jacket is like. Warburg talked of decorating it with the Catalan colours, which are easily mistaken for *a.* the Spanish royalist colours or *b.* the MCC.[2]

Hope all goes well with you. I am much better, in fact I really doubt whether there is anything wrong with me. Eileen is battling with the chickens etc alone but comes down once a fortnight.

Yours
Eric Blair

[1] Geoffrey Gorer's review of *Homage to Catalonia* appeared in *Time and Tide*, 30 April 1938.

[2] Marylebone Cricket Club.

***Homage to Catalonia* was published in London by Secker and Warburg Ltd on 25 April 1938, and in New York by Harcourt, Brace in 1952.**

126. Notes[1] on the Spanish Militias[2]

[These notes were found among Orwell's papers after his death. He had never mentioned them and it is extremely difficult to know when they were written, although it is clear they were written after he had left Spain. It is likely they were not written until some time in 1939 when he was in Morocco but they are placed here as they could well serve as an appendix to *Homage to Catalonia.*]

I joined the POUM militia at the end of 1936. The circumstances of my joining this militia rather than any other were the following. I had intended going to Spain to gather materials for newspaper articles etc, and had also some vague idea of fighting if it seemed worth while, but was doubtful about this owing to my poor health and comparatively small military experience. Just before I started someone told me I should not be able to cross the frontier unless

[1] NB. that these notes refer only to the POUM militia, exceptional because of the internal political struggle, but in actual composition etc. probably not very dissimilar from the other militias in Catalonia in the first year of war. [Author's footnote.]

[2] . . . "From the point of view of political theory there were only three parties that mattered, the PSUC the POUM and the CNT [Confederacion Nacional de Trabajadores]—FAI [Federacion Anarquista Iberica], loosely described as the Anarchists. I take the PSUC first, as being the most important; it was the party that finally triumphed. . . .

It is necessary to explain that when one speaks of the PSUC 'line' one really means the Communist Party 'line'. The PSUC (Partido Socialista Unificado de Catalunya) was the Socialist Party of Catalonia; it had been formed at the beginning of the war by the fusion of various Marxist parties, including the Catalan Communist Party, but it was now entirely under Communist control and was affiliated to the Third International. Elsewhere in Spain no formal unification between Socialists and Communists had taken place, but the Communist viewpoint and the right-wing Socialist viewpoint could everywhere be regarded as identical. Roughly speaking, the PSUC was the political organ of the UGT (Unión General de Trabajadores), the Socialist trade unions. . . . They contained many sections of the manual workers, but since the outbreak of war they had also been swollen by a large influx of middle-class members. . . .

The PSUC 'line' which was preached in the Communist and pro-Communist press throughout the world, was approximately this: 'At present nothing matters except winning the war; without victory in the war all else is meaningless. There-

I had papers from some left-wing organisation (this was untrue at that time although party cards etc undoubtedly made it easier). I applied to John Strachey who took me to see Pollitt. P after questioning me evidently decided that I was politically unreliable and refused to help me, also tried to frighten me out of going by talking a lot about Anarchist terrorism. Finally he asked whether I would undertake to join the International Brigade. I said I could not undertake to join anything until I had seen what was happening. He then

---

fore this is not the moment to talk of pressing forward with the revolution.... At this stage we are not fighting for the dictatorship of the proletariat, we are fighting for parliamentary democracy. Whoever tries to turn the civil war into a social revolution is playing into the hands of the Fascists and is in effect, if not in intention, a traitor.'

The POUM 'line' differed from this on every point except, of course, the importance of winning the war. The POUM was one of those dissident Communist parties which have appeared in many countries in the last few years as a result of the opposition to 'Stalinism'.... It was made up partly of ex-Communists and partly of an earlier party, the Workers' and Peasants' Bloc. Numerically it was a small party, with not much influence outside Catalonia, and chiefly important because it contained an unusually high proportion of politically conscious members.... It did not represent any block of trade unions. The POUM militiamen were mostly CNT members, but the actual party-members generally belonged to the UGT. It was, however, only in the CNT that the POUM had any influence. The POUM 'line' was approximately this: 'It is nonsense to talk of opposing Fascism by bourgeois "democracy". Bourgeois "democracy" is only another name for capitalism, and so is Fascism; to fight against Fascism on behalf of "democracy" is to fight against one form of capitalism on behalf of a second which is liable to turn into the first at any moment. The only real alternative to Fascism is workers' control. If you set up any less goal than this, you will either hand the victory to Franco, or, at best, let in Fascism by the back door. ... The war and the revolution are inseparable.' " From *Homage to Catalonia*, Chap. V.

Professor Hugh Thomas, author of *The Spanish Civil War* (Eyre & Spottiswoode 1961) in a letter to the editors, comments: "... first that the CNT and FAI were actually different organisations of which the latter was, broadly speaking, the leadership of the former, having been set up in the 'twenties to keep the CNT from revisionism. Secondly, where George Orwell said in *Homage to Catalonia* that the Communist's viewpoint and the right-wing Socialists' viewpoint could everywhere be regarded as identical, this was only the case for quite a short time, since Prieto, the leading right-wing Socialist, moved over into a very strong anti-Communist position quite soon. Thirdly, it is only very 'roughly speaking' that the PSUC was the political organ of the UGT. Indeed, this is nearer a mistake than any of the other points, because the UGT was the nationwide labour organisation, admittedly led by Socialists, whereas the PSUC was simply confined to Catalonia."

refused to help me but advised me to get a safe-conduct from the Spanish Embassy in Paris, which I did. Just before leaving England I also rang up the ILP, with which I had some slight connections, mainly personal, and asked them to give me some kind of recommendation. They sent me a letter to Paris addressed to John McNair at Barcelona. When I crossed the frontier the passport people and others, at that time Anarchists, did not pay much attention to my safe-conduct but seemed impressed by the letter with ILP heading, which they evidently knew by sight. It was this that made me decide to produce my letter to McNair (whom I did not know) and through this that I joined the POUM militia. After one glimpse of the troops in Spain I saw that I had relatively a lot of training as a soldier and decided to join the militia. At that time I was only rather dimly aware of the differences between the political parties, which had been covered up in the English left-wing press. Had I had a complete understanding of the situation I should probably have joined the CNT militia.

At this time the militias, though theoretically being re-cast on an ordinary army basis, were still organised in column, centuria, seccion, the centuria of about 100 men more or less centring round some individual and often being called "So-and-so's bandera". The commander of the centuria ranked more or less as captain, but below that there was no well-defined rank except corporal and private. People wore stripes etc of rank in Barcelona but it was "not done" to wear them at the front. Theoretically promotion was by election, but actually the officers and NCOs were appointed from above. As I shall point out later this does not in practice make much difference. One peculiar feature however was that a man could choose which section he should belong to and as a rule could also change to another bandera if he wanted to. At that time men were being sent into the line with only a few days' training and that of a parade-ground kind, and in many cases without ever having fired a rifle. I had brought with me ordinary British army ideas and was appalled by the lack of discipline. It is of course always difficult to get recruits to obey orders and becomes much more so when they find themselves thrust into trenches and having to put up with cold etc which they are not accustomed to. If they have not had a chance to familiarise themselves with firearms they are often much more afraid of bullets than they need be and this is an added source of indiscipline. (Incidentally a lot of harm was done by the lies published in the left-wing papers to the effect that the Fascists were using explosive bullets. So far as I know there is no such thing as an explosive bullet, and certainly the Fascists weren't using them.) At the beginning one had to get orders obeyed (a) by appealing to party loyalty and (b) by force of personality, and for the first week or two I made myself thoroughly unpopular. After about a week a man flatly refused to go to a certain place which he declared was exposed to fire, and I made him do so by force—always a mistake, of course, and doubly so with a Spaniard. I was immediately surrounded by a ring of men calling me a Fascist. There was a tremendous argument; however most of the men took my side and I found that people rather competed to join my section. After this, for some weeks or months, both among the Spaniards and the few English who were on this front, this kind of argument recurred over and over again, i.e. indiscipline, arguments as to what was justifiable and what was "revolutionary", but in general a consensus of opinion that one must have strict discipline combined with social equality. There was always a lot of argument as to whether it was justifiable to shoot men for desertion and disobedience and in general people agreed that it was, though some would never do so. Much later, about March, near Huesca, some 200 CNT troops suddenly decided to walk out of the line. One could hardly blame them as they had been there about five months, but obviously such a thing could not be allowed and there was a call for some POUM troops to go and stop them. I volunteered though not feeling very happy about it. Fortunately they were persuaded to go back by their political delegates or somebody, so it never came to violence. There was a lot of argument about this, but again the majority agreed that it would be justifiable to use one's rifle against men doing this if necessary. Throughout this period, i.e. January–April 1937, the gradual improvement in discipline was brought about almost entirely by "diffusion of revolutionary consciousness", i.e. endless arguments and explanations as to *why* such and such a thing was necessary. Everyone was fanatically keen on keeping social equality between officers and men, no military titles and no differences of food etc and this was often carried to lengths that were rather ridiculous, though they seemed less ridiculous in the line where minute differences of comfort were very appreciable. When the militias were theoretically incorporated in the Popular Army[1] all officers were expected to pay their extra pay, i.e. anything

[1] Popular Army: . . . "Since February [1937] the entire armed forces had

over 10 pesetas a day, into the Party funds, and everyone agreed to do so, though whether this actually happened I don't know, because I am not certain whether anyone actually began drawing extra pay before the POUM militia was redistributed. Punishments for disobedience were, however, being used even at the time when I first reached the front. It is extremely difficult to punish men who are already in the front line, because short of killing them it is hard to make them more uncomfortable than they are already. The usual punishment was double hours of sentry-go—very unsatisfactory because everyone is already short of sleep. Occasionally men were shot. One man who attempted to cross to the Fascist lines and was clearly a spy was shot. Another caught stealing from other militiamen was sent back supposedly to be shot, though I don't think he actually was. Courts Martial were supposed to consist of one officer, one NCO and one militiaman, though I never saw one in action.

Periodically political delegates used to be sent round by the Party to visit the men in the line and, when possible, deliver [some] sort of political discourses. In addition every centuria had one or more men in its own ranks who were called its political delegates. I never grasped what the function of these men had originally been—they had evidently at the beginning had some function for which there was afterwards no need. When with the ILP English I was appointed their political delegate, but this time the political delegate was simply a go-between who was sent to headquarters to complain about rations etc and therefore so far as the English were concerned it was simply a question of choosing among the few men who spoke Spanish. The English were stricter than the Spaniards about electing officers and in one or two cases changed an NCO by election. They also appointed a committee of 5 men who were supposed to regulate all the affairs of the section. Although I was voted on to the committee myself I opposed its formation on the ground that we were now part of an army being commanded from above in more or less the ordinary way, and therefore such a committee had no function. Actually it had no important function but was occasionally useful for regulating very small matters. Contrary to what is generally believed the political leaders of the POUM were very hostile to this committee idea and

---

theoretically been incorporated in the Popular Army [by the Government], and the militias were, on paper, reconstructed along Popular Army lines . . ." From *Homage to Catalonia*, Chap. IX.

were anxious to prevent the idea spreading from the English to the Spaniards.

Before joining the English I was some weeks in a Spanish bandera, and of about 80 men in it some 60 were completely raw recruits. In these weeks the discipline improved a good deal, and from then on till the end of April there was a slow but fairly steady improvement in discipline throughout the militia. By April a militia unit when it had to march anywhere still *looked* like a retreat from Moscow, but this was partly because the men had been experienced solely in trench warfare. But by this time there was no difficulty in getting an order obeyed and no fear that it would be disobeyed as soon as your back was turned. Outwardly the special "revolutionary" characteristics remained the same till the end of May, but in fact certain differences were showing themselves by this time. In May when I was commanding a seccion (which now meant a platoon) the younger Spaniards called me "usted". I pulled them up about it but the word was evidently coming back, and no doubt the universal use of "tu" in the early months of the war was an affectation and would seem most unnatural to a Latin people. One thing that seemed to stop abruptly about March was the shouting of revolutionary slogans to the Fascists. This was not practised at Huesca, though in many cases the trenches were very close together. On the Zaragoza front it had been practised regularly and probably had its share in bringing in the deserters who were very numerous there (at one time about 15 a week on a section of front held by about 1000 men). But the universal use of "camarada" and the notion that we were all supposed to be equals persisted until the militia was redistributed.[1] It was noticeable that the first drafts of the Popular Army who came up to the line conformed with this. Between the POUM and PSUC militias, up to the time when I last saw the latter at the beginning of March, there was no perceptible difference in state of discipline and social atmosphere.

The general organisation was in some ways very good but in others quite unnecessarily incompetent. One striking feature about this war was the good food organisation. Up till May 1937 when certain things began to give out the food was always good, and it was always regular, a thing not easy to arrange even in a very stationary war. The cooks were very devoted, sometimes bringing food up under

[1] My medical discharge-ticket, signed by a doctor at Monzon (a long way behind the line) about 18th June refers to me as "Comrade Blair". [Author's footnote.]

heavy fire. I was impressed by the food-organisation behind the lines and the way in which the peasants had been got to co-operate. The men's clothes were laundered from time to time, but it was not done very well or very regularly. The postal arrangements were good and letters which had started from Barcelona always got to the front promptly, though an extraordinary number of letters sent into Spain went astray somewhere on the way to Barcelona. Ideas of sanitation practically did not exist and no doubt only the dry climate prevented epidemics. There was no medical service worth mentioning till one got about 10 miles behind the lines. This did not matter so long as there was only a small trickle of casualties, but even so many lives were lost unnecessarily. Trenches were at the beginning extremely primitive but about March a labour battalion was organised. This was very efficient and able to construct long sections of trench very rapidly and without noise. Nevertheless up to about May there was not much idea of communication-trenches, even where the front line was near the enemy, and it was not possible, e.g. to get wounded men away without carrying them under fire. No effort was made to keep the roads behind the line in repair, although, no doubt, the labour to do so was available. The POUM Red Aid, to which it was voluntary-compulsory to subscribe, were very good about looking after wounded men in hospital etc. In regard to stores, there was probably some peculation and favouritism, but I think extremely little. When cigarettes began to run short the little English section received rather more than their fair share, a tribute to the Spanish character. The grand and inexcusable mistake made in this war, at any rate on the Aragon front, was to keep the men in the line for unnecessarily long periods. By Xmas 1936 the war was almost entirely stationary and for long periods during the next six months there was little fighting. It should therefore have been perfectly possible to organise the four days in four days out, or even four days in two days out, system. On this arrangement men do not actually get more hours of rest but they do periodically get a few nights in bed or at any rate with the chance to take their clothes off. As it was men were sometimes kept as long as five months in the line continuously. It sometimes happened that trenches were a long way from the enemy, say 1000 yards, but this is more boring and therefore worse for morale than being at 50–100 yards. Meanwhile they were sleeping in trenches in intolerable discomfort, usually lousy and up till April almost always cold. Moreover even when one is

1000 yards from the enemy one is under rifle and occasional shell fire, causing a trickle of casualties and therefore fear which is cumulative. In these circumstances it is difficult to do more than keep on keeping on. During February–March, the period when there was little fighting round Huesca, attempts were made to train the men in various things, use of the machine-gun, signalling, open-order work (advancing by rushes) etc. These were mainly a failure because everyone was suffering from lack of sleep and too exhausted to learn. I myself at this time tried to master the mechanism of the Hotchkiss machine-gun and found that lack of sleep had simply deprived me of the power to learn. In addition it would no doubt have been feasible to grant leave at shorter intervals, but the failure to do so probably had reasons other than incompetence. But it would have been quite easy to take the men in and out of trenches as I have indicated, and to provide some kind of amenities for the troops not in the line. Even as far back as Barbastro the life of the troops was much drearier than it need have been. With a little organisation it would have been possible to arrange immediately behind the lines for hot baths, delousing, entertainments of some kind, cafés (actually there were some very feeble attempts at these) and also women. The very few women who were in or near the line and were get-atable were simply a source of jealousy. There was a certain amount of sodomy among the younger Spaniards. I doubt whether troops can simultaneously engage in trench warfare and be trained for mobile warfare, but more training would certainly have been possible if more care had been devoted to resting the men. As it was they were exhausted for nothing at a period when the war was stagnant. Looking back I see that they stood it extremely well, and even at the time it was the fact that they did *not* disintegrate or show mutinous tendencies under these intolerable conditions that converted me (to some extent) to the notion of "revolutionary discipline". Nevertheless the strain that was put upon them was partly unnecessary.

As to jealousies between the different militias, so far as the rank and file were concerned I myself did not see serious signs of these till May 1937. To what extent the Aragon front was sabotaged from political motives I suppose we shall learn sooner or later. I do not know how important the capture of Huesca would have been, but there is little doubt that it could have been taken in February or March with adequate artillery. As it was it was surrounded except for one gap about a km wide, and this with so little artillery that preliminary bombardments were an impossibility, as they would only have served as a warning. This meant that attacks could only be surprise attacks delivered by a few hundred men at most. By the beginning of April Huesca appeared to be doomed, but the gap was never closed, the attacks petered out and a little later it became clear that the Fascist trenches were more strongly held and that they had improved their defences. At the end of June the big attack on Huesca was staged, clearly from political motives, to provide the Popular Army with a victory and discredit the CNT militia. The result was what could have been foreseen—heavy losses and an actual worsening of the position. But as far as the rank and file were concerned party-feeling did not usually get beyond vague rumours that "they", usually meaning the PSUC, had stolen guns etc meant for ourselves. On the Zaragoza front where POUM and PSUC militia were distributed more or less alternately relations were good. When the POUM took over a sector from the PSUC at Huesca there were signs of jealousy, but this I think was purely military, the PSUC troops having failed to take Huesca and the POUM boasting that they were going to do so. The Guadalajara victory in February could be regarded as, and in fact was, a Communist victory, but everyone was unaffectedly glad and in fact enthusiastic. A little later than this one of our aeroplanes, presumably Russian, dropped a bomb in the wrong place and killed a number of POUM militamen. Later, no doubt, it would have been said that this was "done on purpose", but at the time this did not occur to anybody. About May, perhaps following on the Barcelona trouble, relations worsened. In Lerida, where large numbers of the new Popular Army formations were in training, when detachments of Popular Army marched past, I saw militiamen of I do not know what militia giving them raspberries and bleating in imitation of sheep. As to victimisation of men known to have served with the POUM, I doubt whether it began until after the alleged espionage discoveries. Immediately after these there appear to have been one or two serious incidents. About the end of June it seems that a detachment of PSUC militia were sent or came of their own accord to attack one of the POUM positions outside Huesca, and the men at the latter had to defend themselves with their machine-guns. I have not either the exact date or more than general facts of this, but the source from which I had it leaves me in no doubt that it happened. It was no doubt the result of irresponsible statements in the press about espionage, desertion, etc which had caused or almost caused trouble on earlier occasions.

The fact that the militias were organised by and owed loyalty to different parties had bad effects after a certain date. At the beginning, when everyone was full of enthusiasm, inter-party rivalry was perhaps not a bad thing—this impression at least I derived from those who were in the earlier fighting when Sietamo etc were taken. But when the militias were dwindling as against the Popular Army the effect was to make every party anxious to keep its strength up at no matter what cost. I believe that this was one reason for the fact, noted above, that leave was not granted as often as it might have been. Up till about June there was in reality no way of making a man who had gone on leave rejoin his unit, and conscription into the Popular Army, [when] passed into law (I forget when exactly it was passed) was completely ineffective. Therefore a militiaman once on leave could simply go home, and he had the more motive to do so as he had just drawn a big wad of back-pay, or he could join another organisation, which was often done at that time. In practice most men returned from leave, but some did not, so that every spell of leave meant a dwindling of numbers. In addition, I am certain that anxiety to keep up numbers made local commanders over-anxious not to incur casualties when they could not gain *éclat* by incurring them. On the Zaragoza front valuable minor opportunities—the kind of thing that would not have got into the papers but would have made a certain difference—were lost owing to this, while such casualties as did occur were completely pointless. Also the useless riff-raff, amounting to five or ten per cent, who are to be found in all bodies of troops and who should be got rid of ruthlessly, were seldom or never got rid of. In January when I complained about the state of discipline a higher-up officer gave me his opinion that all the militias competed in slackness of discipline in order to detach recruits from the others. I don't know whether this was true or said owing to momentary fed-upness.

As to the personnel of the POUM militia, I doubt whether it was much different from the others. In standard of physique, which is a rough test, they were about equal to the PSUC. The POUM did not ask party affiliation from their militiamen, doubtless because being a minority party they found it hard to attract recruits. When the men were in the line efforts were made to get them to join the party, but it is fair to say that there was no kind of pressure. There was the usual proportion of riff-raff, and in addition a certain number of very ignorant peasants and people of no particular political alignment who had probably joined the POUM militia more or less by accident. In addition there was a certain number of people who had simply joined for the sake of a job. The fact that in December 1936 there was already a serious bread shortage in Barcelona and militiamen got bread in plenty had a lot to do with this. Nevertheless some of these nondescripts afterwards turned into quite good soldiers. Apart from a rather large number of refugee Germans there was a sprinkling of foreigners of many races, even including a few Portuguese. Putting aside the Germans, the best soldiers were usually the machine-gunners, who were organised in crews of six and kept rather apart from the others. The fetichistic attitude which men in this position develop towards their gun, rather as towards a household god, is interesting and should be studied. A few of the machine-gunners were old soldiers who had done their service over and over again owing to the Spanish substitute system, but most of them were "good party men", some of them men of extremely high character and intelligence. I came to the conclusion, somewhat against my will, that in the long run "good party men" make the best soldiers. The detachment of in all about 30 English and Americans sent out by the ILP were divided rather sharply between old soldiers of no particular political affiliations and "good party men" with no military experience. As I am nearer to the first type myself I am probably not prejudiced in saying that I believe the second to be superior. Old soldiers are of course more useful at the beginning of a campaign, and they are all right when there is any fighting, but they have more tendency to go to pieces under inaction and physical exhaustion. A man who has fully identified with some political party is reliable in *all* circumstances. One would get into trouble in left-wing circles for saying so, but the feeling of many Socialists towards their party is very similar to that of the thicker-headed type of public-school man towards his old school. There are individuals who have no particular political feelings and are completely reliable, but they are usually of bourgeois origin. In the POUM militia there was a slight but perceptible tendency for people of bourgeois origin to be chosen as officers. Given the existing class-structure of society I regard this as inevitable. Middle-class and upper-class people have usually more self-confidence in unfamiliar circumstances, and in countries where conscription is not in force they usually have more military tradition than the working class. This is notably the case in England. As to age, 20 to 35 seems to be the proper age for front-line soldiers. Above 35 I would not trust anybody in the line as a common soldier or junior officer unless he is of known political reliability. As for the younger limit, boys as young as 14 are often very brave and reliable, but they simply cannot stand the lack of sleep. They will even fall asleep standing up.

As to treachery, fraternisation, etc there were just enough rumours about this to suggest that such things happened occasionally, and in fact they are inevitable in civil war. There were vague rumours that at some time pre-arranged truces had been held in no man's land for exchange of newspapers. I do not know of an instance of this but once saw some Fascist papers which might have been procured in this manner. The stories circulated in the Communist press about non-aggression pacts and people coming and going freely between our lines and the Fascists were lies. There was undoubtedly treachery among the peasants. The reason why no attack on this front ever came off at the time scheduled was no doubt partly incompetence, but it was also said that if the time was fixed more than a few hours ahead it was invariably known to the Fascists. The Fascists always appeared to know what troops they had opposite them, whereas we only knew what we could infer from patrols etc. I do not know what method was used by spies for getting messages into Huesca, but the method of sending messages out was flash-lamp signalling. There were morse code signals at a certain hour every night. These were always recorded, but except for slogans such as "Viva Franco" they were always in cipher. I don't know whether they were successfully deciphered. The spies behind the lines were never caught, in spite of many attempts. Desertions were very rare, though up to May 1937 it would have been easy to walk out of the line, or with a little risk, across to the Fascists. I knew of a few desertions among our men and a few among the PSUC, but the whole number would have been tiny. It is noticeable that men in a force of this type retain political feeling against the enemy as they would not in an ordinary army. When I first reached the front it was taken for granted that officer-prisoners taken by us must be shot, and the Fascists were said to shoot all prisoners—a lie, no doubt, but the significant thing was that people believed it. As late as March 1937 I heard credibly of an officer-prisoner taken by us being shot—again the significant thing is that no one seemed to think this wrong.

As to the actual performance of the POUM militia, I know of

this chiefly from others, as I was at the front during the most inactive period of the war. They took part in the taking of Sietamo and the advance on Huesca, and after this the division was split up, some at Huesca, some on the Zaragoza front and a few at Teruel. I believe there was also a handful on the Madrid front. In late February the whole division was concentrated on the eastern side of Huesca. Tactically this was the less important side, and during March–April the part played by the POUM was only raids and holding attacks, affairs involving at most two hundred men and a few score casualties. In some of these they did well, especially the refugee Germans. In the attack on Huesca at the end of June the division lost heavily, 4–600 killed. I was not in this show but heard from others who were that the POUM troops behaved well. By this time the campaigns in the press had begun to produce a certain amount of disaffection. By April even the politically uninterested had grasped that except in their own press and that of the Anarchists no good would be reported of them, whatever their actual performance might be. At the time this produced only a certain irritation, but I know that later, when the division was redistributed, some men who were able to dodge the conscription did so and got civilian jobs on the ground that they were tired of being libelled. A number of men who were in the Huesca attack assured me that General Pozas deliberately withheld the artillery to get as many POUM troops killed as possible—doubtless untrue, but showing the effect of campaigns like that conducted by the Communist press. I do not know what happened to the division after being redistributed, but believe they mostly went to the 26th division. Considering the circumstances and their opportunities, I should say that the performance of the POUM militia was respectable though in no way brilliant.

Written February 1939?

127. Letter to Cyril Connolly

Jellicoe Pavilion
Preston Hall
Aylesford, Kent
27 April 1938

Dear Cyril,
Thanks for your letter. I'm glad you weren't shot in Spain. It's a bloody mess down there, the game's up I'm afraid. I wish I were

there. The ghastly thing is that if the war is lost it will simply lead to an intensification of the policy that caused the Spanish Govt to be let down, & before we know where we are we shall be in the middle of another war to save democracy.

Did you manage to get my book to review, or did they give it to someone else? It came out on Monday.

I have been here abt 5 or 6 weeks & I am afraid I shall have to be here another 8 or 10. There isn't really anything very wrong, evidently an old TB lesion which has partly healed itself & which I must have had 10 years or more. I think if it had been serious the exposure in Spain would have done for me, whereas I came out of that business feeling very well & actually putting on weight until I was wounded. I can't work, of course, which is a bore & will put my next novel back till 1939. I heard from Stephen Spender, who sent me a copy of his play & says he'll come & see me some time. Funny, I had always used him & the rest of that gang as symbols of the pansy Left, & in fact I don't care for his poems to speak of, but when I met him in person I liked him so much & was sorry for the things I had said about him.

Please remember me to your wife.

Yours
Eric Blair

No, don't come & visit me. I know it would depress you—this place I mean—& it's probably a tiresome journey.

Encounter, January 1962

128. Letter to Jack Common

Jellicoe Pavilion
Preston Hall
Aylesford Kent
Sunday [May? 1938]

Dear Jack,

Warburg sent me a copy of your book[1] yesterday, & I think it's bloody good, though there's a lot you say that I don't agree to. I'll do a review of it for the *New English Weekly*, also send Warburg a note on it as he asked for blurb purposes. As I told you before I'm frankly opposed to this blurb business even when one admires the

[1] *The Freedom of the Streets.*

book in question, because the only way one can get any hearing worth having for one's critical opinions is by being the sort of person who *can't* be quoted on blurbs. Is that your first published book, apart from *Seven Shifts*? Isn't it a grand feeling when you see your thoughts taking shape at last in a solid lump? I don't know if Eileen remembered to send you a copy of my Spanish book, but if not she will when she gets back home on Monday. I don't know how it's sold, but I haven't had as many reviews as usual so I suppose it's been boycotted a bit. Of course apart from any political back-stabbing there is the usual reviewing ramp, i.e. the number & favourableness of the reviews you get is directly dependent on the amount your publisher spends on advertising. I think if I was a publisher I wouldn't even do it in such a roundabout way as that, but simply pay the leading hack-reviewers a monthly retaining fee to keep my books to the fore. I hope things go well with you. I am much better though not out of bed yet so I suppose I shall be here another month or two months. It's a bore not being able either to work or to get home & try & salvage what is left of the garden after this bloody weather, but undoubtedly the rest has done me good & incidentally has made me keen to get started with my next novel,[1] though when I came here I had been thinking that what with Hitler, Stalin & the rest of them the day of novel-writing was over. As it is if I start it in August I daresay I'll have to finish it in the concentration camp.

All the best to Mary[2] & Peter.

Yours
Eric Blair

129. Letter to the Editor of the *New English Weekly*

Sir,
May I suggest the following considerations to your correspondent, Mr Romney Green?[3]

[1] *Coming Up for Air.*

[2] Mrs Jack Common.

[3] Romney Green's letter in the *New English Weekly*, 12 May 1938, was part of a correspondence arising out of Green's article "Delinquent Stars" on Aldous Huxley in the *New English Weekly*, 14 April 1938.

1. He says: "(pacifist) theories are just sufficiently plausible to put to rest the consciences of those well-to-do intellectuals who are rather worried by the social problem but who, if war can otherwise be averted, don't really want to see it solved. It is these people who have the pacifist stars on all their drawing-room tables, and who, since nothing can be done about the social problem till war is abolished, may clearly feel quite justified in doing nothing about it."

Is anything of this kind happening? Is it really pacifist literature that we see on every drawing-room table—is it not, on the contrary, so-called "anti-Fascist" literature? Pacifism is so far from being fashionable, or acceptable to the possessing class, that all the big daily newspapers unite to boycott all news of pacifist activities. Virtually the whole of the left-wing intelligentsia, via their mouthpieces in the *News Chronicle*, the *New Statesman*, *Reynolds*, etc, are clamouring for a Popular Front government as a prelude to war against Germany. It is true that they are usually too mealy-mouthed to say openly that they wish for war, but that is what they mean, and in private they will often admit that war is "inevitable", by which they mean desirable.

2. He also says: "I seriously doubt either the intelligence or the sincerity of anyone who goes about England with his eyes open . . . and who . . . professes to think that nothing can be done about the social problem until war is abolished."

The implication is that pacifism is somehow being used, or could be used, as an excuse for blocking social reform. Once again, where is this happening, and how could it happen? In every country except those which are definitely outside the war-orbit, the supposed necessity to prepare for war is being systematically used to prevent every kind of social advance. It goes without saying that this happens in the Fascist countries, but "guns before butter" also rules in the democracies. We have seen how, in the space of two years, the French working class have been swindled out of every advantage they won in 1936, and always by means of the same catchword—"All Frenchmen must unite against Hitler". The truth is that any real advance, let alone any genuinely revolutionary change, can only begin when the mass of the people definitely refuse capitalist-imperialist war and thus make it clear to their rulers that a war policy is not practicable. So long as they show themselves willing to fight "in defence of democracy", or "against Fascism", or for any other flyblown slogan, the same trick will be played upon them again and again: "You can't have a rise in wages *now*, because we have got to prepare for war. Guns before butter!"

Meanwhile there is considerable possibility of producing an effective anti-war movement in England. It is a question of mobilising the dislike of war that undoubtedly exists in ordinary decent people, as opposed to the hack-journalists and the pansy left. The fact that a book like Mr Huxley's[1] contains a certain amount of self-righteousness (we are all self-righteous in different ways), and is written too much from the standpoint of a middle-class intellectual, is beside the point. Anyone who helps to put peace on the map is doing useful work. The real enemies of the working class are not those who talk to them in a too highbrow manner; they are those who try to trick them into identifying their interests with those of their exploiters, and into forgetting what every manual worker inwardly knows—that modern war is a racket.

George Orwell

New English Weekly, 26 May 1938

130. Review

Assignment in Utopia by Eugene Lyons

To get the full sense of our ignorance as to what is really happening in the USSR, it is worth trying to translate the most sensational Russian event of the past two years, the Trotskyist trials, into English terms. Make the necessary adjustments, let Left be Right and Right be Left, and you get something like this:

Mr Winston Churchill, now in exile in Portugal, is plotting to overthrow the British Empire and establish Communism in England. By the use of unlimited Russian money he has succeeded in building up a huge Churchillite organisation which includes members of Parliament, factory managers, Roman Catholic bishops and practically the whole of the Primrose League. Almost every day some dastardly act of sabotage is laid bare—sometimes a plot to blow up the House of Lords, sometimes an outbreak of foot and mouth disease in the Royal racing-stables. Eighty per cent of the Beefeaters at the Tower are discovered to be agents of the Comintern. A high official of the Post Office admits brazenly to having embezzled postal orders to the tune of £5,000,000 and also to having committed *lèse*

[1] *Ends and Means* by Aldous Huxley.

majesté by drawing moustaches on postage stamps. Lord Nuffield, after a 7-hour interrogation by Mr Norman Birkett, confesses that ever since 1920 he has been fomenting strikes in his own factories. Casual half-inch paras in every issue of the newspapers announce that fifty more Churchillite sheep-stealers have been shot in Westmorland or that the proprietress of a village shop in the Cotswolds has been transported to Australia for sucking the bull's-eyes and putting them back in the bottle. And meanwhile the Churchillites (or Churchillite-Harmsworthites as they are called after Lord Rothermere's execution) never cease from proclaiming that it is *they* who are the real defenders of capitalism and that Chamberlain and the rest of his gang are no more than a set of Bolsheviks in disguise.

Anyone who has followed the Russian trials knows that this is scarcely a parody. The question arises, could anything like this happen in England? Obviously it could not. From our point of view the whole thing is not merely incredible as a genuine conspiracy, it is next door to incredible as a frame-up. It is simply a dark mystery, of which the only seizable fact—sinister enough in its way—is that Communists over here regard it as a good advertisement for Communism.

Meanwhile the truth about Stalin's régime, if we could only get hold of it, is of the first importance. Is it Socialism, or is it a peculiarly vicious form of state-capitalism? All the political controversies that have made life hideous for two years past really circle round this question, though for several reasons it is seldom brought into the foreground. It is difficult to go to Russia, once there it is impossible to make adequate investigations, and all one's ideas on the subject have to be drawn from books which are so fulsomely "for" or so venomously "against" that the prejudice stinks a mile away. Mr Lyons's book is definitely in the "against" class, but he gives the impression of being much more reliable than most. It is obvious from his manner of writing that he is not a vulgar propagandist, and he was in Russia a long time (1928–34) as correspondent for the United Press Agency, having been sent there on Communist recommendation. Like many others who have gone to Russia full of hope he was gradually disillusioned, and unlike some others he finally decided to tell the truth about it. It is an unfortunate fact that any hostile criticism of the present Russian régime is liable to be taken as propaganda *against Socialism;* all Socialists are aware of this, and it does not make for honest discussion.

The years that Mr Lyons spent in Russia were years of appalling hardship, culminating in the Ukraine famine of 1933, in which a number estimated at not less than three million people starved to death. Now, no doubt, after the success of the Second Five Year Plan, the physical conditions have improved, but there seems no reason for thinking that the social atmosphere is greatly different. The system that Mr Lyons describes does not seem to be very different from Fascism. All real power is concentrated in the hands ot two or three million people, the town proletariat, theoretically the heirs of the revolution, having been robbed even of the elementary right to strike; more recently, by the introduction of the internal passport system, they have been reduced to a status resembling serfdom. The GPU are everywhere, everyone lives in constant terror of denunciation, freedom of speech and of the press are obliterated to an extent we can hardly imagine. There are periodical waves of terror, sometimes the "liquidation" of kulaks or Nepmen, sometimes some monstrous state trial at which people who have been in prison for months or years are suddenly dragged forth to make incredible confessions, while their children publish articles in the newspapers saying "I repudiate my father as a Trotskyist serpent." Meanwhile the invisible Stalin is worshipped in terms that would have made Nero blush. This—at great length and in much detail—is the picture Mr Lyons presents, and I do not believe he has misrepresented the facts. He does, however, show signs of being embittered by his experiences, and I think he probably exaggerates the amount of discontent prevailing among the Russians themselves.

He once succeeded in interviewing Stalin, and found him human, simple and likeable. It is worth noticing that H. G. Wells said the same thing, and it is a fact that Stalin, at any rate on the cinematograph, has a likeable face. Is it not also recorded that Al Capone was the best of husbands and fathers, and that Joseph Smith (of brides in the bath fame) was sincerely loved by the first of his seven wives and always returned to her between murders?

New English Weekly, 9 June 1938

131. Review

The Freedom of the Streets by Jack Common

Jack Common, a writer who is at present not so well known as he might be but who is potentially a sort of Chesterton of the Left, approaches the subject of Socialism from an interesting and unfamiliar angle.

He is of proletarian origin, and much more than most writers of this kind he preserves his proletarian viewpoint. In doing so he puts his finger on one of the chief difficulties of the Socialist movement—the fact that the word "Socialism" means something quite different to a working man from what it means to a middle-class Marxist. To those who actually have the destiny of the Socialist movement in their hands, virtually everything that a manual worker means when he says "Socialism" is either irrelevant or heretical. As Mr Common shows in a series of separate but connected essays, the manual workers in a machine civilisation have certain characteristics forced upon them by the circumstances in which they live: loyalty, improvidence, generosity, hatred of privilege. It is out of these that they evolve their vision of a future society, so that the mystique of proletarian Socialism is the idea of equality. This is a very different vision from that of the middle-class Socialist who accepts Marx as his prophet—literally a prophet, a tipster who not only tells you which horse to back, but also provides the reason why the horse didn't win.

The spirit in which Mr Common writes is the mixture of messianic hope and cheerful pessimism that is sometimes to be found in the quieter corners of the four-ale bar on a Saturday night. He thinks that we are all going to be blown to hell by bombs, but that the dictatorship of the proletariat is really going to happen:

> A time is coming when even the comparatively comfortable will suffer under the terror of lawless governments, created in their own choice or by their acquiescence. The about-to-be-bombed need not fear Communism. They will be Communists themselves by the time the bombing is over, if they survive. . . . For it only needs a turn of the screw, an increase of tension, and the fragile and rather imaginary partitions by which the masses of all the world are allowed to cherish their divisions will blow away.

Yes: but if there were any certainty that this will happen, would it not be the duty of every Socialist to hope and work for war? And dare any thinking person do that nowadays?

There must be very many minds in which that hackneyed phrase, "dictatorship of the proletariat", has been successively a nightmare, a hope and a chimaera. One starts off—for after all, that is how most middle-class people *do* start—by thinking "God help us all when it happens!" and one ends up by thinking "What a pity it can't happen!" Mr Common writes all the while as though the dictatorship of the proletariat were just round the corner—a pious hope, but the facts do not seem to give much warrant for it. It would seem that what you get over and over again is a movement of the proletariat which is promptly canalised and betrayed by astute people at the top, and then the growth of a new governing class. The one thing that never arrives is equality. The mass of the people never get the chance to bring their innate decency into the control of affairs, so that one is almost driven to the cynical thought that men are only decent when they are powerless.

Meanwhile this is an interesting book, which tells you much less about Socialism as an economic theory and much more about it as a body of belief, one might almost say a way of life, than the average textbook. I particularly recommend the two essays called "The Judgement of the Vulgar" and "Fascism in Men of Good Will". Allowing for the fact that it has found literary expression—which in itself is slightly abnormal—this is the authentic voice of the ordinary man, the man who might infuse a new decency into the control of affairs if only he could get there, but who in practice never seems to get much further than the trenches, the sweatshop and the jail.

New English Weekly, 16 June 1938

132. Why I Joined the Independent Labour Party

Perhaps it will be frankest to approach it first of all from the personal angle.

I am a writer. The impulse of every writer is to "keep out of politics". What he wants is to be left alone so that he can go on writing books in peace. But unfortunately it is becoming obvious that this ideal is no more practicable than that of the petty shopkeeper who hopes to preserve his independence in the teeth of the chain-stores.

To begin with, the era of free speech is closing down. The freedom of the press in Britain was always something of a fake, because in the last resort, money controls opinion; still, so long as the legal right to say what you like exists, there are always loopholes for an unorthodox writer. For some years past I have managed to make the capitalist class pay me several pounds a week for writing books against capitalism. But I do not delude myself that this state of affairs is going to last for ever. We have seen what has happened to the freedom of the press in Italy and Germany, and it will happen here sooner or later. The time is coming—not next year, perhaps not for ten or twenty years, but it is coming—when every writer will have the choice of being silenced altogether or of producing the dope that a privileged minority demands.

I have got to struggle against that, just as I have got to struggle against castor oil, rubber truncheons and concentration camps. And the only régime which, in the long run, will dare to permit freedom of speech is a Socialist régime. If Fascism triumphs I am finished as a writer—that is to say, finished in my only effective capacity. That of itself would be a sufficient reason for joining a Socialist party.

I have put the personal aspect first, but obviously it is not the only one.

It is not possible for any thinking person to live in such a society as our own without wanting to change it. For perhaps ten years past I have had some grasp of the real nature of capitalist society. I have seen British imperialism at work in Burma, and I have seen something of the effects of poverty and unemployment in Britain. In so far as I have struggled against the system, it has been mainly by writing books which I hoped would influence the reading public. I shall continue to do that, of course, but at a moment like the present writing books is not enough. The tempo of events is quickening; the dangers which once seemed a generation distant are staring us in the face. One has got to be actively a Socialist, not merely sympathetic to Socialism, or one plays into the hands of our always-active enemies.

Why the ILP more than another?

Because the ILP is the only British party—at any rate the only one large enough to be worth considering—which aims at anything I should regard as Socialism.

I do not mean that I have lost all faith in the Labour Party. My most earnest hope is that the Labour Party will win a clear majority in the next General Election. But we know what the history of the

Labour Party has been, and we know the terrible temptation of the present moment—the temptation to fling every principle overboard in order to prepare for an imperialist war. It is vitally necessary that there should be in existence some body of people who can be depended on, even in the face of persecution, not to compromise their Socialist principles.

I believe that the ILP is the only party which, as a party, is likely to take the right line either against imperialist war or against Fascism when this appears in its British form. And meanwhile the ILP is not backed by any moneyed interest, and is systematically libelled from several quarters. Obviously it needs all the help it can get, including any help I can give it myself.

Finally, I was with the ILP contingent in Spain. I never pretended, then or since, to agree in every detail with the policy the POUM put forward and the ILP supported, but the general course of events has borne it out. The things I saw in Spain brought home to me the fatal danger of mere negative "anti-Fascism". Once I had grasped the essentials of the situation in Spain I realised that the ILP was the only British party I felt like joining—and also the only party I could join with at least the certainty that I would never be led up the garden path in the name of capitalist democracy.

New Leader (London), 24 June 1938

133. Letter to Jack Common

New Hostel
Preston Hall
Aylesford, Kent
5 July 1938

Dear Jack,

You know I have to go abroad for the winter,[1] probably for abt 6 months starting abt end of August. Well, would you like to have our cottage rent-free & in return look after the animals? I'll tell you all the facts & you can work out the pros & cons for yourself.

i. The doctors say I must live somewhere further south. That means giving up the cottage when we come back at latest. But I

[1] The doctors in the hospital in Aylesford advised Orwell to spend the winter in a warm climate for the sake of his lungs.

don't want to scrap the livestock, because we have now worked the flock of fowls up to abt 30, which can be worked up to abt 100 next year, & it would also mean selling the hen-houses, which cost a lot but which you don't get much for if you sell them. We have therefore the choice of getting someone to inhabit the cottage, or of paying someone to look after the animals, which plus storage of furniture works out at abt the same expense as keeping on the rent of the cottage.

ii. You know what our cottage is like. It's bloody awful. Still it's more or less livable. There is one room with a double bed & one with a single, & I fancy there is enough linen etc to do for 2 people & a kid. When there is sudden rain in winter the kitchen tends to flood, otherwise the house is passably dry. The living room fire, you may remember, smokes, but I think the chimney will have been seen to before we leave—anyway it doesn't need anything very drastic doing to it. There is water laid on, but no hot, of course. There is a Calor Gas stove, which is expensive (the gas, I mean), but there is also a little oil oven that can be resuscitated. As to produce, there won't be many vegetables, as of course Eileen alone couldn't cope with all of the garden, but at any rate there will be potatoes enough to see you through the winter. There'll also be milk, about a quart a day, as the goat has just kidded. A lot of people are prejudiced against goats' milk but really it's no different from cow & is said to be good for kids.

iii. As to the looking after animals. This means feeding etc abt 30 fowls & feeding & milking the goats. I'll leave careful instructions abt food etc & arrange for the corn merchant to deliver supplies & send the bill on to me. You could also sell the eggs (the butcher who calls twice a week buys any quantity) & put the money aside for us. There won't be many eggs at first, as most of the birds are young pullets hatched this year, but by early spring they should be laying abt 100 a week.

Let me know would you whether you would like to take this on. It would suit us, & for you at any rate I dare say it would be a quiet place to work in.

All the best to Mary & Peter.

Yours
Eric Blair

134. Review

The Civil War in Spain by Frank Jellinek

Frank Jellinek's book on the Paris Commune had its faults, but it revealed him as a man of unusual mind. He showed himself able to grasp the real facts of history, the social and economic changes that underlie spectacular events, without losing touch with the picturesque aspect which the bourgeois historian generally does so much better. On the whole his present book bears out the promise of the other. It shows signs of haste, and it contains some misrepresentations which I will point out later, but it is probably the best book on the Spanish war from a Communist angle that we are likely to get for some time to come.

Much the most useful part of the book is the earlier part, describing the long chain of causes that led up to the war and the fundamental issues at stake. The parasitic aristocracy and the appalling condition of the peasants (before the war 65 per cent of the population of Spain held 6·3 per cent of the land, while 4 per cent held 60 per cent of it), the backwardness of Spanish capitalism and the dominance of foreign capitalists, the corruption of the Church, and the rise of the Socialist and Anarchist labour movements—all these are treated in a series of brilliant chapters. The short biography which Mr Jellinek gives of Juan March, the old tobacco-smuggler who is one of the men behind the Fascist rebellion (although, queerly enough, he is believed to be a Jew), is a wonderful story of corruption. It would be fascinating reading if March were merely a character in Edgar Wallace; unfortunately he happens to be a real man.

The chapter on the Church does not leave much doubt as to why practically all the churches in Catalonia and eastern Aragon were burnt at the outbreak of war. Incidentally, it is interesting to learn that, if Mr Jellinek's figures are correct, the world organisation of Jesuits only numbers about 22,000 people. For sheer efficiency they must surely have all the political parties in the world beaten hollow. But the Jesuits' "man of affairs" in Spain is, or was, on the board of directors of forty-three companies!

At the end of the book there is a well-balanced chapter on the social changes that took place in the first few months of the war, and an appendix on the collectivisation decree in Catalonia. Unlike the majority of British observers, Mr Jellinek does not under-rate the Spanish Anarchists. In his treatment of the POUM however, there is no doubt that he is unfair, and—there is not much doubt of this either—intentionally unfair.

Naturally I turned first of all to the chapter describing the fighting in Barcelona in May 1937, because both Mr Jellinek and myself were in Barcelona at the time, and this gave me a measure of checking his accuracy. His account of the fighting is somewhat less propagandist than those that appeared in the Communist press at the time, but it is certainly one-sided and would be very misleading to anyone who knew nothing of the facts. To begin with, he appears at times to accept the story that the POUM was really a disguised Fascist organisation, and refers to "documents" which "conclusively proved" this and that, without telling us any more about these mysterious documents—which, in fact, have never been produced. He even refers to the celebrated "N" document (though admitting the "N" probably did not stand for Nin),[1] and ignores the fact that Irujo, the Minister of Justice, declared this document to be "worthless", i.e. a forgery. He states merely that Nin was "arrested", and does not mention that Nin disappeared and was almost certainly murdered. Moreover, he leaves the chronology uncertain and—whether intentionally or not—gives the impression that the alleged discovery of a Fascist plot, the arrest of Nin, etc took place *immediately after* the May fighting.

This point is important. The suppression of the POUM did *not* occur immediately after the May fighting. There was a five weeks' interval. The fighting ended on 7 May and Nin was arrested on 15 June. The suppression of the POUM only occurred after, and almost certainly as a result of, the change in the Valencia Government. I have noticed several attempts in the press to obscure these dates. The reason is obvious enough; however, there can be no doubt about the matter, for all the main events were recorded in the newspapers at the time.

Curiously enough, about 20 June, the *Manchester Guardian* correspondent in Barcelona sent here a despatch[2] in which he contradicted the absurd accusations against the POUM—in the circumstances a

[1] The "N" document, a forged letter purported by the Communists to be from Andreas Nin, a prominent member of the POUM, to Franco, on which they based their charges of conspiracy between the POUM and Franco to justify their suppression of the POUM. Nin was later murdered in prison by the Communists.

[2] "Barcelona after the Rising", from our Special Correspondent, in the *Manchester Guardian*, 26 June 1937. See 145.

very courageous action. This correspondent must almost certainly have been Mr Jellinek himself. What a pity that for propaganda purposes he should now find it necessary to repeat a story which after this lapse of time seems even more improbable.

His remarks on the POUM occupy a considerable share of the book, and they have an air of prejudice which would be obvious even to anyone who knew nothing whatever about the Spanish political parties. He thinks it necessary to denigrate even useful work such as that done by Nin as Councillor of Justice, and is careful not to mention that the POUM took any serious part either in the first struggles against the Fascist rising or at the front. And in all his remarks about the "provocative attitude" of the POUM newspapers it hardly seems to occur to him that there was any provocation on the other side. In the long run this kind of thing defeats its own object. Its effect on me, for instance, is to make me think: "If I find that this book is unreliable where I happen to know the facts, how can I trust it where I don't know the facts?" And many others will think the same.

Actually I am quite ready to believe that in the main Mr Jellinek is strictly fair besides being immensely well-informed. But in dealing with "Trotskyism" he writes as a Communist, or Communist partisan, and it is no more possible for a Communist today to show common sense on this subject than on the subject of "Social Fascism" a few years ago. Incidentally, the speed with which the angels in the Communist mythology turn into devils has its comic side. Mr Jellinek quotes approvingly a denunciation of the POUM by the Russian Consul in Barcelona, Antonov Ovseenko, now on trial as a Trotskyist!

All in all, an excellent book, packed full of information and very readable. But one has got to treat it with a certain wariness, because the author is under the necessity of showing that though other people may sometimes be right, the Communist Party is always right. It does not greatly matter that nearly all books by Communists are propaganda. Most books are propaganda, direct or indirect. The trouble is that Communist writers are obliged to claim infallibility for their Party chiefs. As a result Communist literature tends more and more to become a mechanism for explaining away mistakes.

Unlike most of the people who have written of the Spanish war, Mr Jellinek really knows Spain: its language, its people, its territories, and the political struggle of the past hundred years. Few men are better qualified to write an authoritative history of the Spanish war. Perhaps some day he will do so. But it will probably be a long time hence, when the "Trotsky-Fascist" shadow-boxing has been dropped in favour of some other hobby.

New Leader (London), 8 July 1938

135. Letter to Cyril Connolly

New Hostel
Preston Hall
Aylesford, Kent
8 July 1938

Dear Cyril,

Thanks so much for your letter. I am rather taking you at your word in the matter of asking advice about the S. of France, but don't answer till you feel fit. What I want to know is, can one rent small furnished cottages in small villages? I suppose thousands of people have small summer villas in those parts which they'd be willing to let, but are such places livable in winter? I don't want to go to a pension if I can help it, I hate the places & I must have a place of my own to work in, also I'd rather stay in a very small village which generally don't have pensions in them. I don't of course want you to arrange anything for me, only to let me know whether it is feasible to take such a place as I suggest & what kind of rent.

I'm glad you liked the book,[1] & thanks for recommending it to people. I had better reviews than I expected but of course all the best ones in obscure papers. I had Jellinek's book to review for several papers. I thought it was pretty bloody, the usual CP stuff of course & obviously written in haste, but he is really very good in a way. I suppose it's true what you say abt people not revising their stuff nowadays, though it's incomprehensible to me. What you say about finding old letters of mine makes me apprehensive. I wonder how you can write abt St Cyprian's.[2] It's all like an awful nightmare to me, & sometimes I think I can still taste the porridge (out of those pewter bowls, do you remember?) If you have written about Eton as I should think you might, you'd better watch out you don't get horsewhipped on the steps of your club, if you belong to one....

[1] *Homage to Catalonia.*

[2] The private school at which Orwell and Connolly were pupils together. At this time Cyril Connolly was writing about it in *Enemies of Promise*.

Today is the start of the Eton & Harrow match[1] & it has poured steadily all day. I am much better, & most of the day out of doors. I still haven't done a stroke of work but keep toying with the idea of starting my novel.[2] One good effect the rest has had on me is that it has made me feel I can write a novel again, whereas when I came here I felt my novel-writing days were over.

Please remember me to your wife.

Yours
Eric Blair

Encounter, January 1962

136. Review

Searchlight on Spain by the Duchess of Atholl

At this time of day it is hardly necessary to point out that there are not merely two versions of the Spanish war. Even among Government partisans there are three at least, the Communist version, the Anarchist, and the "Trotskyist". In England we have learnt a little of the "Trotskyist" version and next to nothing of the Anarchist version, while the Communist version is, so to speak, the official one. The Duchess of Atholl's book follows the familiar lines—in fact, with the excision of not very many sentences it could pass as having been written by a Communist. I doubt whether it contains anything that has not been said before, and therefore, rather than discuss the book itself, perhaps it is more useful to stop and reflect just why it is that books like this are appearing.

There is, of course, nothing surprising nowadays in a pro-Communist Duchess. Nearly all moneyed people who enter the left-wing movement follow the "Stalinist" line as a matter of course. Neither Anarchism nor "Trotskyism" has much appeal for anyone with more than £500 a year. But the real question is not why moneyed people are "Stalinists" but why they enter the left-wing movement at all. They did not do so a few years ago. Why does the Duchess back the Spanish Government and not Franco? It is not as though she were a lonely eccentric. Plenty of other people deeply embedded

[1] An annual cricket match between the two schools, taking place in early July at Lord's cricket ground, London.

[2] *Coming Up for Air.*

in the British capitalist system, peers, newspaper proprietors and the higher clergy, have taken the same line. Why? When all is said and done the Spanish war is essentially a class war, and Franco is the defender of the moneyed class. How is it that these people manage to be such good Socialists abroad and such good Conservatives at home?

At first sight it looks easy: because the Fascist powers menace the British Empire. The Duchess herself supplies this answer in her chapter "What it means to us", in which the dangers of a Fascist domination of Spain are set forth. Germany and Italy will be astride our route to India, France will have another frontier to defend, etc etc. Here "anti-Fascism", of a kind, and British imperialism join hands. Incidentally, several books pointing this moral have appeared in this same series. It would seem that whoever defends the British Empire also defends democracy—which, to anyone who knows anything about the actual running of the Empire, appears to have a catch in it.

But it is not so simple as that. For though a fairly large section of the British governing class are anti-Franco, the majority are pro-Franco, subjectively and objectively. By a combination of meanness and hypocrisy that would take a lot of beating, Chamberlain and his friends have allowed the Spanish Republic to be slowly strangled. How is one to explain the apparent contradiction? If one believes that the duchesses and deans who quack about "anti-Fascism" are really worrying about British dividends, one has apparently got to believe also that Chamberlain is *not* worrying about British dividends—which is incredible.

It may be that behind the apparent split in governing-class opinion there is a conflict of financial interests. But I think another explanation is possible. Between the "anti-Reds" and the moneyed "anti-Fascists" there is no fundamental difference. They are all part of the same system and many of them are in the same political party. They will show their essential agreement in any really important crisis—above all, they will show it when England goes to war. When the guns begin to shoot, Chamberlain and the Duchess of Atholl, Lloyd George and Lord Rothermere, will meet on the same recruiting platform. It is quite possible, therefore, that this strange phenomenon of anti-Fascism in high life is simply a part of the national war-preparation.

Chamberlain is preparing for war against Germany. Rearmament, the military understanding with France, ARP[1] and various sinister mumbles about conscription, cannot be explained in any other way. It is quite likely that he has made a mess of things and allowed the strategic situation to worsen, and that this has happened partly because he fears a Russian-controlled Spain as much as Mussolini does; nevertheless, he is preparing for war. And while the Government makes the *physical* preparations for war, the so-called Left, by constantly stirring up a spirit of hatred and self-righteousness, looks after the mental side. The armament factories build the guns, and papers like the *News Chronicle* create the will to use them. We all remember what happened when Delilah said "The Philistines be upon thee, Samson". The first real threat to British interests has turned nine out of ten British Socialists into jingoes.

And what is the function of the Conservative anti-Fascists? They are the liaison officers. The average English left-winger is now a good imperialist, but he is still theoretically hostile to the English ruling class. The people who read the *New Statesman* dream of war with Germany, but they also think it necessary to laugh at Colonel Blimp. However, when the war begins they will be forming fours on the barrack square under Colonel Blimp's boiled blue eye. It is necessary to effect a reconciliation beforehand. That, I think, is the real function of books like this of the Duchess of Atholl's, and Mr G. T. Garratt's *Mussolini's Roman Empire*, and the prophetic utterances of Madame Tabouis, and various others of the same kind. These people are forming—not consciously, of course—the link between Left and Right which is absolutely necessary for the purpose of war. The war in Spain—indeed, the whole situation since the Abyssinia crisis, but especially the war in Spain—has had a catalytic effect upon English opinion, bringing into being combinations which no one could have foreseen a few years ago. There is much that is not yet clear, but I do not see how patriotic Communists and communistic duchesses can be explained except on the supposition that the ranks are being closed for war.

New English Weekly, 21 July 1938

[Below is excerpt from Orwell's review of the same book in *Time and Tide*, 16 July 1938.]

... In her final chapter, "What it means to us", she points out the probable consequence of a Fascist victory in Spain—that England

[1] Air Raid Precautions.

may lose the command of the Mediterranean and France may be faced with another hostile frontier. This raises what is perhaps the most mysterious question of the whole Spanish war. Why has our Government behaved as it has done? Without any doubt the British Cabinet has behaved as though it wished Franco to win; and yet if Franco wins it may—to put it at its worst—mean the loss of India. The Duchess of Atholl states the facts but does not offer any explanation of Mr Chamberlain's attitude. Other writers have been less cautious. The real meaning of British foreign policy in the last two years will not become clear until the war in Spain is over; but in trying to divine it I believe it is much safer to assume that the British Cabinet are not fools and that they have no intention of giving anything away....

137. Letter to Ida Mabel Blair

New Hostel
Preston Hall
Aylesford, Kent
8 August 1938

Darling Mum,
I hope all goes well. As I haven't heard from you for some days I infer that Father is at any rate not worse and that they haven't decided to operate. We will come down to Southwold before going away, but I am not certain yet of the date, as I have to arrange that with the doctors. Eileen thinks it would be better to come down fairly soon, e.g. the week-end after next, and then come back here before going away, which I think we are to do about the end of the month. We'll stay at the Swan or somewhere. Eileen was down for the week-end, now has gone back to town, but next week-end is coming back and I think is going to stay in Aylesford. Our friends have taken over the cottage. She has left me Marx,[1] who sleeps in a shed with a puppy belonging to Dr McDougall. It is a very large golden retriever puppy, almost as large as Marx, and last night they fought fiercely at feeding time, but I think they are settling down a bit. We have at last had some rain which has freshened things up, and in spite of the drought the corn seems good and the fruit not

[1] The Orwells' dog.

bad. Eileen says at home we had hardly any fruit owing to the late frosts. I am very much better, in fact I really don't think I have anything wrong with me, and I am anxious to get away and start working, which I can't here. My next novel will be very late of course, but I dare say I'll get it done in time to come out about next March. We have more or less settled to go to Morocco, but haven't decided about what place or how to get there. I am writing to Marjorie[1] to ask her if she'll have Marx, and as I have lost her Bristol address I am sending the letter for you to forward. I hope Jane[2] is going along all right. Let me know how Father is getting on and whether it will be all right for you if we come down about the week after next. We won't be any nuisance in the house anyway, as we'll stay out.

Much love to all
Eric

138. Review

The Communist International by Franz Borkenau

When Dr Borkenau's *The Spanish Cockpit*[3] appeared the Spanish war was about a year old and the book dealt only with the events of the first six or seven months. Nevertheless it remains the best book on the subject and, what is more, it is a book different in *kind* from nearly all that have appeared on either side. As soon as one opened it one was aware that here at last, amid the shrieking horde of propagandists, was a grown-up person, a man capable of writing dispassionately even when he knew the facts. It is unfortunate that political books nowadays are almost invariably written either by fools or by ignoramuses. If a writer on a political subject manages to preserve a detached attitude, it is nearly always because he does not know what he is talking about. To understand a political movement one has got to be involved in it, and as soon as one is involved one becomes a propagandist. Dr Borkenau, however, apart from his intellectual gifts, is in the very unusual position of having been for eight years a member of the German Communist Party and for some time an official of the Comintern, and of having finally reverted to a

[1] Orwell's sister, Marjorie Dakin.
[2] Marjorie Dakin's daughter.
[3] See 101.

belief in liberalism and democracy. This is a development about as uncommon as being converted from Catholicism to Protestantism, but a sociologist could hardly have a better background.

In the twenty years' history of the Comintern Dr Borkenau traces three more or less separate periods. In the first period, the immediate post-war years, there is a genuine revolutionary ferment in Europe, and in consequence the Comintern is an organisation sincerely aiming at world revolution and not entirely under Russian influence. In the second phase it becomes an instrument in Stalin's struggles first against the Trotsky-Zinoviev group, later against the Bukharin-Rykov group. In the third phase, the one we are in now, it becomes more or less openly an instrument of Russian foreign policy. Meanwhile there are the alternate swings of Comintern policy to "left" and "right". As Dr Borkenau points out, the earlier changes were comparatively insignificant, the more recent ones catastrophic. The swing-over in Communist policy that took place between 1934 and 1936 was in fact so extraordinary that the general public has as yet failed to grasp it. In the "ultra-left" phase of 1928–34, the "Social Fascist" phase, revolutionary purity was so pure that every labour leader was declared to be in capitalist pay, the Russian sabotage trials "proved" that M. Blum and other leaders of the Second International were plotting the invasion of Russia, and anyone who advocated a united front of Socialists and Communists was denounced as a traitor, Trotskyist, mad dog, hyena and all the other items in the Communist vocabulary.

Social democracy was declared to be the real enemy of the working class, Fascism was dismissed as something utterly without importance, and this insane theory was kept up even *after* Hitler had come to power. But then came German rearmament and the Franco-Russian pact. Almost overnight Communist policy in the non-Fascist countries swung round to the Popular Front and "defence of democracy", and anyone who cavilled at lining up with liberals and Catholics was once again a traitor, Trotskyist, mad dog, hyena and so forth. Of course such changes of policy are only possible because every Communist Party outside the USSR gets a new membership every few years. Whether there will be another corresponding swing to the "left" seems doubtful. Dr Borkenau thinks that Stalin may ultimately be compelled to dissolve the Comintern as the price of a secure alliance with the western democracies. On the other hand it is worth remembering that the rulers of the democracies, so called, are not fools, they are aware that Communist agitation even in its "left" phases is not a serious danger, and they may prefer to keep in being an organisation which plays almost invariably into their hands.

In so far as it aims—and it still professes rather vaguely to aim—at world revolution, the Comintern has been a complete failure. Nevertheless it has done an immense amount of mischief and has been, in Dr Borkenau's opinion, one the the chief causes of the growth of Fascism. In every Communist Party only about five per cent of the membership—that is to say, a framework of party officials—remains constant; but in each phase of policy there pass through the party some thousands or tens of thousands of people who emerge having learnt nothing save a contempt for democratic methods. They do not emerge with a belief in Socialism, but they do emerge with a belief in violence and double-crossing. Consequently when the critical moment comes they are at the mercy of the man who really specialises in violence and double-crossing, in other words, the Fascist.

Dr Borkenau thinks that the root cause of the vagaries of Comintern policy is the fact that revolution as Marx and Lenin predicted it and as it happened, more or less, in Russia, is not thinkable in the advanced western countries, at any rate at present. Here I believe he is right. Where I part company from him is when he says that for the western democracies the choice lies between Fascism and an orderly reconstruction through the co-operation of all classes. I do not believe in the second possibility, because I do not believe that a man with £50,000 a year and a man with fifteen shillings a week either can, or will, co-operate. The nature of their relationship is, quite simply, that the one is robbing the other, and there is no reason to think that the robber will suddenly turn over a new leaf. It would seem, therefore, that if the problems of western capitalism are to be solved, it will have to be through a third alternative, a movement which is genuinely revolutionary, i.e. willing to make drastic changes and to use violence if necessary, but which does not lose touch, as Communism and Fascism have done, with the essential values of democracy. Such a thing is by no means unthinkable. The germs of such a movement exist in numerous countries, and they are capable of growing. At any rate, if they don't, there is no real exit from the pigsty we are in.

This is a profoundly interesting book. I have not enough specialised knowledge to judge its accuracy, but I think it is safe to say that it is as little coloured by prejudice as a book on a controversial subject can be. Probably the best way to test its value as a historical work would be to watch its reception in the Communist press—on the principle of "the worse the better", I need hardly say. I hope that Dr Borkenau will not only go on writing, but that he will find imitators. It is a most encouraging thing to hear a human voice when fifty thousand gramophones are playing the same tune.

New English Weekly, 22 September 1938

139. Letter to Jack Common

Chez Madame Vellat
Rue Edmond Doutte
Medinah
Marrakech, French Morocco
26 September 1938

Dear Jack,

After October 15th my address will actually be Villa Simont, Sidahan, Route de Casablanca, Marrakech, but in case of doubt better write to the address I am at at present, as the house we're taking is some way out of the town and I'm not certain about their delivering letters.

I don't know whether or not you will be fitting on your gas mask by the time this gets to you, but things look pretty bad and are perhaps even worse than I think because I don't see the English papers and the local French ones are inclined to minimise things. If war does break out it is utterly impossible to foresee what will happen, but unless I am kicked out I don't think I shall come home, at any rate until the time I was supposed to be coming, i.e. early next spring. The whole thing seems to me so utterly meaningless that I think I shall just concentrate on remaining alive. In a mess of this kind it's just a case of sauve qui peut, so in the event of war breaking out you must do what you think fit about the cottage and the animals. The bank any way will pay the rent for the next six months, and if you are just keeping out of it you would probably be as safe there as any where, I don't think anyone will drop a bomb on Wallington and it might even be profitable to expand the fowl industry a bit, as eggs are sure to be scarce and sought after, at any rate until chicken food gets even scarcer. On the other hand if you feel impelled either to join the army or go to jail or for any other reason to leave Wallington, will you communicate with my brother-in-law and put the matter in his hands? His name and address are Laurence O'Shaughnessy, 24 Crooms Hill, Greenwich. He will see to the disposal of the cottage, which could perhaps be let furnished to bomb-dodgers. And in the interim, if you left and the house hadn't a tenant for the time being, he will arrange for the Hatchetts and Andersons[1] to look after the animals. I just make these arrangements because it is as well to be prepared for the worst and if the worst does happen communication by letter may become difficult almost immediately. But I suppose there is still hope that all may be well. The next week or two will show any way. Hope all is going well with you and all are in good health and not finding the primitive conditions too much of a bore. I don't care much for this country and am already pining to be back in England, always supposing there isn't a war there. Love to Mary and Peter.

Yours
Eric

140. Letter to Jack Common

Chez Madame Vellat
Rue Edmond Doutte
Marrakech, French Morocco
29 September 1938

Dear Jack,

I wrote yesterday making suggestions as to what you should do in case of war, then this morning received your letter in which you didn't sound as though war were really likely, so write now in a more normal mood. At this end of the world I can't make out about this war business. The troops are standing by more or less in full kit, the artillery is trained on the proletarian end of the town "in case of trouble" and this afternoon we had some kind of air-raid practice which I couldn't get the hang of, but meanwhile the French population is utterly uninterested and evidently doesn't believe that war is coming. Of course they are out of all danger here, except for the young ones who will be mobilised, and perhaps that affects their

[1] Neighbours at Wallington.

attitude. The whole thing is so utterly insane that it just sickens me. One thing I am certain of. Unless there is some tremendous loss of prestige, such as Hitler seizing the whole of Czechoslovakia while England and France do nothing, and perhaps at the same time painting the British ambassador's arse green and sending him back to England, Chamberlain is safe to win the next election with a big majority. The so-called left parties have played straight into his hands by their idiotic policy. . . .

It makes me sad to hear you say you've never been out of England, especially when I think of the bastards who do travel, simply going from hotel to hotel and never seeing any difference anywhere except in the temperature. At the same time I'm not sure how much good travel does to anyone. One thing I have always believed, and that is that one really learns nothing from a foreign country unless one works in it, or does something that really involves one with the inhabitants. This trip is something quite new to me, because for the first time I am in the position of a tourist. The result is that it is quite impossible, at any rate at present, to make any contact with the Arabs, whereas if I were here, say, on a gun-running expedition, I should immediately have the entrée to all kinds of interesting society, in spite of the language difficulty. I have often been struck by how easy it is to get people to take you for granted if you and they are really in the same boat, and how difficult otherwise. For instance, when I was with the tramps, merely because they assumed that I was on the bum it didn't make a damn's worth of difference to them that I had a middle-class accent and they were willing to be actually more intimate than I wanted. Whereas if, say, you brought a tramp into the house and tried to get him to talk to you it would just be a patron-client relationship and quite meaningless. I am as usual taking careful notes of everything I see, but am not certain what use I shall be able to make of them afterwards. Here in Marrakech it is in some ways harder to find out about conditions in Morocco than it would be in a less typical Arab town. In a town like Casablanca you have a huge French population and a white proletariat, and consequently local branches of the Socialist Party and so forth. Here with not very important differences it is very like Anglo-Indian society and you are more or less obliged to be a pukka sahib or suffer the consequences. We're staying in the town itself for another two or three weeks, then we're taking a villa outside. That will be slightly more expensive but quieter to work in and I simply have to have a bit of garden and a few animals. I shall also be interested to see a little of how the Arab peasants live. Here in the town conditions are pretty frightful, wages generally work out at about 1d or 2d an hour and it's the first place I've seen where beggars do literally beg for bread and eat it greedily when given it. It's still pretty hot but getting better and we're both pretty well in health. There's nothing wrong with me really, but much as I resent the waste of time it's probably done me good to lay off work for seven months. People who don't write think that writing isn't work, but you and I know the contrary. Thank God I've just begun to work again and made a start on my new novel, which was billed for this autumn but might appear in the spring perhaps. Of course if war comes God knows if the publishing of books will even continue. To me the idea of war is a pure nightmare. Richard Rees was talking as though even war couldn't be worse than the present conditions, but I think what this really means is that he doesn't see any peace-time activity for himself which he feels to be useful. A lot of intellectuals feel like this, which I think is one explanation of why the so-called left-wingers are now the jingoes. But I personally do see a lot of things that I want to do and to continue doing for another thirty years or so, and the idea that I've got to abandon them and either be bumped off or depart to some filthy concentration camp just infuriates me. Eileen and I have decided that if war does come the best thing will be to just stay alive and thus add to the number of sane people.

The above address will find me for a bit. I'll give you the new one when I have it—probably a poste restante address, as I don't think they will deliver letters where we are going to. Best love to Mary and Peter. Eileen also sends love.

Yours
Eric

PS. Yes, I did once just meet Alec Henderson at a party. The village people are really very nice, especially the Hatchetts, Mrs Anderson, Titley, Keefe, Edie (Mrs Ridley's daughter) and her husband Stanley, and Albert, Mrs R's other son-in-law. I don't know what one can really do for old H except occasionally to give him eggs when his hens don't lay. He is a dear old man. Tell them all you've heard from me and I wanted to be remembered to them.

141. Letter to Jack Common

Chez Madame Vellat
Rue Edmond Doutte
Medinah
Marrakech, French Morocco
12 October 1938

Dear Jack,

Thanks for yours. There were several important items I wanted to talk to you about but they were chased out of my mind by the European situation. The first is, I think we forgot to warn you not to use thick paper in the WC. It sometimes chokes the cesspool up, with disastrous results. The best to use is Jeyes paper which is 6d a packet. The difference of price is negligible, and on the other hand a choked cesspool is a misery. Secondly, if you find the sitting room fire smokes intolerably, I think you can get a piece of tin put in the chimney, which is what it needs, for a very small sum. Brookers in Hitchin would tell you all about it. Or you could probably do it yourself. I was always meaning to but put it off. Thirdly, I enclose cheque for £3. Could you some time get this cashed and pay £2 to Field, the postmaster at Sandon, for the rent of the field. It's a lot overdue as a matter of fact but F never remembers about it. Field goes past in his grey car, which he uses to carry cattle in, every Tuesday on his way to Hitchin Market, and one can sometimes stop him if one jumps into the middle of the road and waves. As to the remaining £1, could you some time in the winter get some or, if possible, all of the ground in the vegetable garden dug over? Old H[1] is getting so old that I don't really like asking him to do that kind of work, but he's always glad of it and, of course, willing to work for very low rates. There's no hurry, it's just a question of getting the vacant ground turned over some time in the winter and preferably some manure (the goat's stuff is quite good if there isn't too much straw in it) dug in. The official theory is that we are to give up the cottage next spring, so I suppose on good business principles one ought to exhaust the soil by taking an enormous crop of Brussels off it and then let it go to hell. But I hate starving soil and in addition I'm not so certain of giving up the cottage. As I expect you've discovered by this time it's truly a case of be it never so humble, but the fact is that it's a roof and moving is so damned expensive besides being a misery. I think I would rather feel I had the cottage there to

[1] Hatchett, a neighbour at Wallington.

move into next April, even if when the time comes we don't actually do it, because I don't know what my financial situation will be next year. I don't believe my book on Spain sold at all, and if I have to come back to England and start on yet another book with about £50 in the world I would rather have a roof over my head from the start. It's a great thing to have a roof over your head even if it's a leaky one. When Eileen and I were first married, when I was writing *Wigan Pier*, we had so little money that sometimes we hardly knew where the next meal was coming from, but we found we could rub along in a remarkable manner with spuds and so forth. I hope the hens have begun laying. Some of them have by this time, I expect, at any rate they ought to. We've just bought the hens for our house, which we're moving into on Saturday. The hens in this country are miserable little things like the Indian ones, about the size of bantams, and what is regarded as a good laying hen, i.e. it lays once a fortnight, costs less than a shilling. They ought only to cost about 6d, but at this time of year the price goes up because after Yom Kippur every Jew, of whom there are 13000 in this town, eats a whole fowl to recompense him for the strain of fasting 12 hours.

Well, the mortal moon hath her eclipse endured till 1941, I suppose. I don't think one need be surprised at Chamberlain's stock slumping a bit after the danger is over. Judging from the letters I get from home I should say people feel as you feel when you are just going to dive off the springboard and then think better of it. The real point is what will happen at the election, and unless the Conservative Party splits right up I prophesy they will win hands down. Because the other bloody fools can't produce any policy except "We want war", and however ashamed people may feel *after* we've let down Czechoslovakia, or whoever it may be, they'll shy away from war when it comes to a show-down. The only hope of Labour getting in is for some downright disaster to happen, or alternatively, for the elections to be held a year hence with another million unemployed. I think now we're in for a period of slow fascisation, the sort of Dollfuss-Schussnig Fascism which is what Chamberlain and Co would presumably introduce, but I would sooner have that than have the Left parties identified in the public mind as the war party. The only hope is that if Chamberlain wins and then begins seriously to prepare for war with Germany, as of course he will, the LP[1] will be driven back to an anti-war policy in which they will be able to

[1] The Labour Party.

exploit the discontent with conscription etc. The policy of simultaneously shouting for a war policy and pretending to denounce conscription, rearmament etc is utter nonsense and the general public aren't such bloody fools as not to see it. As to the results if war comes, although *some* kind of revolutionary situation will no doubt arise, I do not see how it can lead to anything except Fascism *unless* the Left has been anti-war from the outset. I have nothing but contempt for the fools who think that they can first drive the nation into a war for democracy and then when people are a bit fed up suddenly turn round and say "Now we'll have the revolution." What sickens me about left-wing people, especially the intellectuals, is their utter ignorance of the way things actually happen. I was always struck by this when I was in Burma and used to read anti-imperialist stuff. Did you see Kingsley Martin's[1] ("Critic") article in last week's *NS* about the conditions on which the LP should support the Government in war. As though the Government would allow any conditions. The bloody fool seems to think war is a cricket match. I wish someone would print my anti-war pamphlet[2] I wrote earlier this year, but of course no one will.

All the best. Love to Mary and Peter. E sends love.

Yours
Eric

142. Letter to John Sceats

Boite Postale 48
Gueliz
Marrakech, French Morocco
26 October 1938

Dear Sceats,[3]
I hope all goes well with you. I had meant to look you up before leaving England, but as it turned out I went almost straight from the

[1] Kingsley Martin (1897–), left-wing writer and journalist, editor of *The New Statesman & Nation* 1931–60.

[2] All efforts to find a copy of this pamphlet, which is alleged to have been published in mimeographed form, have so far been fruitless.

[3] John Sceats (1912–), insurance agent, had written some articles in *Controversy* that Orwell admired leading him to invite Sceats to visit him in the summer of 1938. *Controversy*, 1936–9, was a Socialist monthly edited by C. A. Smith,

sanatorium to the boat and only had one day in London, which of course was pretty full. I'm writing to you now for some expert advice. The chap in the novel[1] I'm writing is supposed to be an insurance agent. His job isn't in the least important to the story, I merely wanted him to be a typical middle-aged bloke with about £5 a week and a house in the suburbs, and he's also rather thoughtful and fairly well-educated, even slightly bookish, which is more plausible with an insurance agent than, say, a commercial traveller. But I want any mention that is made of his job to be correct. And meanwhile I have only very vague ideas as to what an insurance agent does. I want him to be a chap who travels round and gets part of his income from commissions, not merely an office employee. Does such a chap have a "district" and a regular round like a commercial traveller? Does he have to go touting round for orders, or just go round and sign the people up when they want to be insured? Would he spend all his time in travelling or part of it in the office? Would he have an office of his own? Do the big insurance companies have branch offices all over the place (this chap lives in a suburb which might be Hayes or Southall) or do they only have the head office and send all the agents out from there? And would such a man do valuations of property, and would the same man do life insurance and property insurance? I'd be very glad of some elucidation on these points. My picture of this chap is this. He spends about two days a week in the branch office in his suburb and the rest of the time in travelling round in a car over a district of about half a county, interviewing people who've written in to say that they want to be insured, making valuations of houses, stock and so forth, and also touting for orders on which he gets an extra commission, and that by this he is earning round about £5 a week after being with the firm 18 years (having started very much at the bottom). I want to know if this is plausible.

Well, "The mortal moon hath her eclipse endured and the sad augurs mock their own presage", and some of them are very sad indeed to judge by the *New Statesman*. However, I suppose they'll get the war they're longing for in about two years. The real attitude

---

dedicated to the realisation of a classless society; it offered a forum for the public discussion of the different methods and tactics which divided the parties of the Left. It became the *Left Forum*, June–September 1939, then *Left*, October 1939–May 1950.

[1] *Coming Up for Air.*

of the governing class to this business is summed up in the remark I overheard from one of the Gibraltar garrison the moment I set foot there: "It's pretty clear Hitler's going to have Czechoslovakia. Much better let him have it. We shall be ready in 1941." Meanwhile the net result will be a sweeping win for the Conservatives at the General Election. I judge from letters from more or less conservative relatives at home that now that it is all over people are a bit fed up and saying "What a pity we didn't hold on a bit longer and Hitler would have backed down." And from this the bloody fools of the LP infer that after all the English people *do* want another war to make the world safe for democracy and that their best line is to exploit the anti-fascist stuff. They don't seem to see that the election will revive the spirit of the crisis, the word will be Chamberlain and Peace, and if the LP go round saying "We want war", which is how ordinary people, quite rightly, interpret the firm line with Hitler stuff, they will just be eaten up. I think a lot of people in the last two years have been misled by phenomena like the Left Book Club. Here you have about 50,000 people who are willing to make a noise about Spain, China etc and because the majority of people are normally silent this gives the impression that the Left Bookmongers are the voice of the nation instead of being a tiny minority. No one seems to reflect that what matters is not what a few people say when all is quiet but what the majority do in moments of crisis. The only hope is that if the LP gets a knock at the election, as it's almost certain to do, this will gradually force them back to their proper policy. But I am afraid it may be a year or two years before this happens.

I've got to go down to a meal that's getting cold, so au revoir. I'd be enormously obliged if you'd let me know about those points some time, but there's no immediate hurry.

Yours
Eric Blair

143. Letter to John Sceats

Boite Postale 48
Gueliz
Marrakech, French Morocco
24 November 1938

Dear Sceats,

Thanks so much for your letter with the very useful information about insurance offices. I see that my chap will have to be a Representative and that I underrated his income a little. I've done quite a lot of work, but unfortunately after wasting no less than a fortnight doing articles for various papers fell slightly ill so that properly speaking I've done no work for 3 weeks. It's awful how the time flies by. What with all this illness I've decided to count 1938 as a blank year and sort of cross it off the calendar. But meanwhile the concentration camp looms ahead and there is so much one wants to do. I've got to the point now when I feel I could write a good novel if I had five years peace and quiet, but at present one might as well ask for five years in the moon.

This is on the whole rather a dull country. Some time after Xmas we want to go for a week into the Atlas mountains which are 50 or 100 miles from here and look rather exciting. Down here it's flat dried-up country rather like a huge allotment patch that's been let "go back", and practically no trees except olives and palms. The poverty is something frightful, though of course it's always a little more bearable for people in a hot climate. The people have tiny patches of ground which they cultivate with implements which would have been out of date in the days of Moses. One can get a sort of idea of the prevailing hunger by the fact that in the whole country there are practically no wild animals, everything edible being eaten by human beings. I don't know how it would compare with the poorer parts of India, but Burma would seem like a paradise compared to it, so far as standard of living goes. The French are evidently squeezing the country pretty ruthlessly. They absorb most of the fertile land as well as the minerals, and the taxes seem fairly heavy considering the poverty of the people. On the surface their administration looks better than ours and certainly rouses less animosity in the subject race, because they have very little colour-prejudice. But I think underneath it is much the same. So far as I can judge there is no anti-French movement of any size among the Arabs, and if there were one it would almost certainly be nationalist rather than

Socialist, as the great majority of the people are at the feudal stage and the French, I fancy, intend them to remain so. I can't tell anything about the extent of the local Socialist movement, because it has for some time only existed illegally. I asked the ILP to get the French Socialist party to put me in touch with any Socialist movement existing here, if only because I could thus learn more about local conditions, but they haven't done so, perhaps because it's too dangerous. The local French, though they're quite different from the British population in India, mostly petty traders and even manual workers, are stuffily conservative and mildly pro-Fascist. I wrote two articles on local conditions for the *Quarterly* which I hope they'll print, as they were I think not too incorrect and subtly Trotskyist. I hope by the way that *Controversy* has not succumbed. It would be a disaster if it did and still more if the *N*[*ew*] *L*[*eader*] had to turn into a monthly. As to *Controversy* I'm sure the sale could be worked up with a little energy and a certain willingness to distribute back numbers, and I'll do what I can in my nearest town when I get back.

Have you heard any rumours about the General Election? The only person I can make contact with here who might conceivably know something is the British consul, who thinks the Government are going to defer the election as long as possible and that attempts may also be made to resuscitate the old Liberal party. Personally I don't think anything can prevent Chamberlain winning unless there is some unforeseen scandal. Labour may win a few by-elections, but the general election will be fought in a completely different emotional atmosphere. The best one can hope is that it may teach Labour a lesson. I only get English papers rather intermittently and haven't seen the results of some of the by-elections. I see Labour won Dartford but gather the Conservatives won Oxford.

Let me have a line some time to hear how things are going.

Yours
E. A. Blair

144. Letter to Cyril Connolly

Boite Postale 48
Gueliz
Marrakech, French Morocco
14 December 1938

Dear Cyril,

I see your book[1] is out. Send me a copy, won't you? I can't get English books here. The *New English* were going to send it to me to review, but they haven't done so, perhaps haven't had a copy. I have been in this place about three months, as it is supposed to do my lungs good to spend the winter here. I have less than no belief in theories about certain climates being "good for" you; on enquiry they always turn out to be a racket run by tourist agencies and local doctors, but now I am here I suppose I shall stay till about April. Morocco seems to me a beastly dull country, no forests and literally no wild animals, and the people anywhere near a big town utterly debauched by the tourist racket and their poverty combined, which turn them into a race of beggars and curio-sellers. Some time next month we are going into the Atlas for a bit, which may be more interesting. I am getting on with my novel which was listed to come out in the autumn but, owing to this bloody illness, didn't get it started till two or three months ago. Of course I shall have to rush it as I must get it done in time for the spring. It's a pity, really, as it's a good idea, though I don't think you'll like it if you see it. Everything one writes now is overshadowed by this ghastly feeling that we are rushing towards a precipice and, though we shan't actually prevent ourselves or anyone else from going over, must put up some sort of fight. I suppose actually we have about two years before the guns begin to shoot. I am looking forward to seeing your book, I gather from the reviews that a lot of it is about Eton, and it will interest me very much to see whether the impressions you retain are anything like my own. Of course you were in every way much more of a success at school than I, and my own position was complicated and in fact dominated by the fact that I had much less money than most of the people about me, but as far as externals go we had very much the same experiences from 1912 to 1921. And our literary development impinged at certain points, too. Do you remember one or other of us getting hold of H. G. Wells's *Country of the Blind* about 1914, at St Cyprian's, and being so enthralled with it that we were constantly

[1] *Enemies of Promise.*

pinching it off each other? It's a very vivid memory of mine, stealing along the corridor at about four o'clock on a midsummer morning into the dormitory where you slept and pinching the book from beside your bed. And do you remember at about the same time my bringing back to school a copy of Compton Mackenzie's *Sinister Street*, which you began to read, and then . . . Mrs Wilkes found out and there was a fearful row about bringing a "book of that kind" (though at the time I didn't even know what "sinister" meant) into the school. I'm always meaning one of these days to write a book about St Cyprian's.[1] I've always held that the public schools aren't so bad, but people are wrecked by those filthy private schools long before they get to public school age.

Please give all the best to your wife. I hope I'll see you when I get back.

Yours
E. A. Blair

PS. I suppose the Quintin Hogg who won the Oxford election was the little squirt who was a fag when I left school.

Encounter, January 1962

145. Letter to Frank Jellinek

Boite Postale 48
Gueliz
Marrakech, French Morocco
20 December 1938

Dear Jellinek,

Many thanks for your letter. I am extremely sorry that I attributed that note in the *Manchester Guardian* to you,[2] but my reason for doing so was that the *MG* had not denied it. The facts were these. I was apparently semi-disabled by my wound (though actually it got all right soon afterwards) and had decided to go back to England, and on June 15 I went up to Sietamo to get my discharge-papers, which for some reason unknown to me one had to go up to the front to do. When I got there the POUM troops besides the others in Sietamo were being got ready for an action which actually took place

[1] See IV, 86.
[2] See 134.

some days later, and it was only by a bit of luck that I did not get involved in the battle, though at the time I could hardly use my right arm. When I managed to get back to Barcelona on June 20, it was to find that the POUM had been suppressed, everyone I knew was in jail or in hiding, I had to sleep two nights in the streets, and the police had been interfering with my wife in the most revolting manner. What really angered me about all this was that it had carefully been kept secret from the men at the front and even from people in Lerida (where I had been on June 20). On I forget which day I saw you in a café near the Hotel Oriente. I was going to cross the road and speak to you, but at this time, as was not unnatural in the circumstances, I was ready to believe that every Communist was a spy, and I simply walked on. Then later in England, when I went through the files of the *MG*, I saw the note saying that the POUM were not Fascists (or words to that effect), which I naturally attributed to you. I was greatly touched and wrote to the *MG* congratulating them and asking for your address. I suppose the man who replied didn't know who had sent that message, and he merely said that you were in Mexico and they didn't know your address. I am going to send a note to the *New Leader*[1] saying I was wrong about who sent the message. If they don't insert it, please believe it is only for lack of space. They are quite honest, though often no doubt mistaken, but with only 8 pages per week one hasn't much space to spare.

I am writing at the same time as this asking my agent to send you a copy of my book on the Spanish war. Parts of it might interest you. I have no doubt I have made a lot of mistakes and misleading statements, but I have tried to indicate all through that the subject is very complicated and that I am extremely fallible as well as biassed. Without answering in detail all the points in your letter, I might indicate more clearly than I could do in the book my position on one or two questions that inevitably come up in a controversy of this kind. I entirely agree with you that the whole business about the POUM has had far too much fuss made about it and that the net result of this kind of thing is to prejudice people against the Spanish Government. But my position has always been that this kind of controversy could die a natural death and cause comparatively little harm if people would refrain from telling lies in the beginning. The sequence of events is approximately this. The POUM preach a "line" which may or may not make it more difficult to secure military

[1] "A Mistake Corrected", *New Leader* (London), 13 January 1939.

efficiency for the Spanish Government, and which is also rather too like what the CP were saying in 1930. The CP feel that they have got to silence this at all costs, and therefore begin stating in the press that the POUM are Fascists in disguise. This kind of accusation is infinitely more resented than any ordinary polemic could be, with the result that the various people and parties who could be described as "Trotskyist" tend to develop into mere anti-Communists. What complicates it and enormously increases the feeling of bitterness it causes is that the capitalist press will on the whole throw its weight on the Communist side of the controversy. I know that Communists don't as a rule believe this, because they have got into the habit of feeling that they are persecuted and have hardly noticed that since about 1936 (i.e. since the change of "line") the attitude towards them in the democratic countries is very different. Communist doctrine in its present form appeals to wealthy people, at least some wealthy people, and they have a very strong footing in the press in both England and France. In England, for instance, the *News Chronicle* and *New Statesman* are under direct Communist influence, there is a considerable press which is actually official CP and certain influential papers which are bitterly *anti-Socialist* nevertheless prefer "Stalinism" to "Trotskyism". On the other side, of course, there is nothing, because what is now called "Trotskyism" (using the word very widely) has no appeal to anyone with over £500 a year. The result is that the most appalling lies can be printed and except in a few papers like the *MG* which keep up the old traditions it is quite impossible to answer them. One's only resort is to start miserable little rags like the ones the Trotskyists run, which, necessarily, are nothing but anti-Communist papers. There is no question that appalling lies were published about the POUM, not only by the official CP press, but by papers like the *NC* and *NS & N*, which after publishing refuse to print any answers in their correspondence columns. I don't know whether you have yet seen the accounts of the POUM trial. The trial made it clear, as it was bound to do if fairly conducted, that there was no truth in the accusations of espionage, which were for the most part merely silly. One accusation, for instance, had been that several miles of the Aragon front had been entirely deserted for two months—this at a time when I was there myself. This witness broke down in the box. Similarly, after all the statements in papers of the type of the *Daily Worker* about "two hundred signed confessions" etc, there was complete failure to produce any evidence whatever. Although the trial was conducted more or less in camera, *Solidaridad Obrera*[1] was allowed afterwards to print a report, and it was made quite clear that the charges of espionage were dismissed and the four men who were sentenced were only convicted of taking part in the May fighting in Barcelona. In the face of all this the CP press printed reports that they had been condemned for espionage. In addition this was also done by some pro-CP papers, which significantly enough are also pro-Fascist papers. E.g. the *Observer* reported the verdict in such a way as to let it appear that the verdict was one of espionage, and the French press of this country, which of course is pro-Franco, reported the accusation, stated that it had been "proved" and then failed to report the verdict. You must agree that this kind of thing is likely to cause resentment, and though in the heat of the moment it may seem "realistic" to say "These people are obstructing us—therefore they might as well be Fascists—there[fore] we'll say they *are* Fascists", in the end it may do more harm than good. I am not a Marxist and I don't hold with all this stuff that boils down to saying "Anything is right which advances the cause of the Party". On the title page of my book you will find two texts from Proverbs which sum up the two prevailing theories of how to combat Fascism, and I personally agree with the first and not the second.[2]

I think you'll find answers in my book to some of what you say. Actually I've given a more sympathetic account of the POUM "line" than I actually felt, because I always told them they were wrong and refused to join the party. But I had to put it as sympathetically as possible, because it has had no hearing in the capitalist press and nothing but libels in the left-wing press. Actually, considering the way things have gone in Spain, I think there was something in what they said, though no doubt their way of saying it was tiresome and provocative in the extreme.

I got over the wound with no ill-effects but now my lungs have been giving trouble and they sent me to spend the winter in this country. I think it's doing me good, and I expect to be back in England in April.

Yours
Eric Blair ("George Orwell")

[1] A Spanish Anarchist daily newspaper of the time.

[2] "Answer not a fool according to his folly, lest thou be like unto him."
"Answer a fool according to his folly, lest he be wise in his own conceit." Proverbs 26: 4–5.

PS. I don't agree with you that there was no persecution of POUM militiamen. There was a lot—even, later on, in hospitals, as I learned from a man who was wounded later than I. I have today heard from George Kopp, who was my commandant at the front, and who has just got out of Spain after 18 months in jail. Making all allowance for exaggerations, and I know people who have been in those circumstances always exaggerate, there is no question he has been shamefully treated, and there were probably some hundreds of others in the same case.

The chap who told you something about the ILP militiamen signing some kind of statement was probably a man named Parker. If so it was probably a lie. Ditto if it was a man named Frankfort. If it was a man named Hiddlestone[1] it was probably not a lie but might have been some kind of mistake. I know nothing about it as I came to Spain quite independently of them.

146. Letter to Jack Common

Boite Postale 48
Gueliz
Marrakech, French Morocco
26 December 1938

Dear Jack,

... In a few days I'll try and send you a few quid (I'm afraid at best it'll have to be a few) towards ex[pens]es. I've written recently to my bank to know whether I've got any money left, and I'll get their reply in a few days. Of course this journey, which at any rate was made on borrowed money,[2] has been very expensive and I don't think I'll have any money to speak of coming in for three or four months. The novel ought to be done beginning of April. It's really a mess but parts of it I like and it's suddenly revealed to me a

[1] Buck Parker, Frank Frankfort, Reg Hiddlestone, members of the ILP Contingent linked to the 3rd Regiment, Division Lenin, POUM, of which Orwell had also been a member.

[2] The novelist L. H. Myers, an admirer of Orwell's work, had given Dorothy Plowman £300 to give to Orwell so that he could make the journey, but asked her not to reveal his identity.

big subject which I'd never really touched before and haven't time to work out properly now. I can't tell you how deeply I wish to keep alive, out of jail, and out of money-worries for the next few years. I suppose after this book I shall write some kind of pot-boiler, but I have very dimly in my mind the idea for an enormous novel in several volumes and I want several years to plan it out in peace. Of course when I say peace I don't mean absence of war, because actually you can be at peace when you're fighting, but I don't think what I mean by peace is compatible with modern totalitarian war. Meanwhile the Penguin people are making moves towards reprinting one or other of my books,[1] and I hope they'll do so, because though I don't suppose there's much dough in it it's the best possible advert. Besides it's damned annoying to see your books out of print. One of mine, *Down and Out*, is so completely out of print that neither I nor anyone else known to me except my mother possesses a copy —this in spite of the fact that it was the most-taken-out book in the library at Dartmoor. I'm glad Warburg has struck it lucky with at any rate one book. I must say for him that he has enterprise and has published a wider range of stuff than almost anyone. My Spain book sold damn all, but it didn't greatly matter as my agent had got the money out of him in advance and the reviews were OK.

God knows when that parcel will turn up. From what I know of French post offices it wouldn't surprise me if it was just in time for Xmas 1939. Actually I left it and a lot of others to be sent off by the shopkeeper, because I was fatigued by a long afternoon of shopping, which is really tiring in this country as in most oriental countries. Arabs are even greater bargainers than Indians and one is obliged to conclude that they like it. If the price of an article is a shilling, the shopman starts by demanding two shillings and the buyer starts by offering threepence, and they may well take half an hour to agree on the shilling, though both know from the start that this is the right price. One thing that greatly affects one's contacts in foreign countries is that English people's nerves are not so durable as those of some other races, they can't stand noise, for instance. I like the Arabs, they're very friendly and, considering their position, not at all servile, but I've made no real contact, partly because they mostly speak a kind of bastard French and so I've been

[1] *Down and Out in Paris and London* was published by Penguin Books in 1940.

too lazy to learn any Arabic. The French in this country seem dull and stodgy beyond all measure, far worse than Anglo-Indians. I doubt whether there's any real political movement among the Arabs. The left-wing parties have all been suppressed (by the Popular Front) but I don't think they can ever have amounted to much. The people are entirely in the feudal stage and most of them seem to think they are still ruled by the Sultan, which by a fiction they are. There've been no echoes of the Tunis business except in the French press. If a big Arab movement ever arises I think it's bound to be pro-Fascist. I am told the Italians in Libya treat them atrociously, but their main oppressors have been the democracies, so-called. The attitude of the so-called left-wing in England and France over this imperialism business simply sickens me. If they went on in the same vein they would end by turning every thinking coloured person into a Fascist. Underlying this is the fact that the working class in England and France have absolutely no feeling of solidarity with the coloured working class.

You asked where Marrakech was. It's somewhere near the top left hand corner of Africa and immediately north of the Atlas Mountains. Funnily enough we've been having the cold snap even here and on Xmas eve there was a heavy frost—don't know whether that is usual here, but judging by the vegetation I don't think it can be. I had the queer and rather pleasant experience of seeing the oranges and lemons on the trees frosted all over, which apparently didn't damage them. The effects of the frost were very curious. Some nasturtiums I had sown earlier were withered up by it, but the cactuses and the Bougainvillea, which is a tropical plant from the South Pacific, weren't affected. The mountains have been covered with snow even on their lower slopes for some time past. As soon as I've done the rough draft of my novel we're going to take a week off and go into the mountains. The Romans thought they were the end of the world, and they certainly look as if they might be. It's generally fine and bright in the daytime, but we have fires all the time. The only fuel is olive wood, because there simply isn't a wild tree for miles and miles. This is one of those countries which are very nearly desert and which just exactly support a small population of men and beasts who eat every eatable thing and burn every burnable thing on the surface, so that if there were one more person there'd be a famine. And to think that in Roman times North Africa was full of magnificent forests full of lions and elephants. There are now practically no wild animals bigger than a hare, and I suppose even the human population is smaller. I've just been reading about approximately these parts in Flaubert's *Salammbô*, a book which for some reason I'd always steered clear of but which is simply stunning.

I'm not surprised at J.M.M entering the Church.[1] But he won't stay in it long. I suppose in the near future there will be a book called *The Necessity of Fascism*. But I think it's really time someone began looking into Fascism seriously. There must be more to it than one would gather from the Left press. Mussolini has been "just about to" collapse ever since 1926.

The French hardly celebrate Xmas, only the New Year. The Arabs probably celebrate the New Year, but it may not be the same as ours. They are pretty strict Mahomedans, except that owing to poverty they are not overscrupulous about what they eat. We simply haven't celebrated Xmas yet, but shall when we get a pudding that is coming from England. Eileen was ill on Xmas day and I actually forgot till the evening what day it was. It's all very gloomy, because my father is very ill and my sister who was to come out here consequently can't. Two friends have just got back from Spain. One is a chap called Robert Williams[2] who has come out with his guts full of bits of shell. He says Barcelona is smashed out of recognition, everyone is half starved and you can get 900 pesetas for a £. The other is George Kopp, a Belgian, whom there is a lot about in my book. He has just escaped after 18 months in a GPU jail, in which he lost seven stone in weight. They were bloody fools to let him go after what they have done to him, but I suppose they couldn't help themselves. It's evident from several things that the Communists have lost most of their power and the GPU only exists unofficially.

My love to Mary and Peter. Eileen sends love and thanks Mary for the letter. I'll write again when I hear from the bank. I hope the cold will let up. It can be bloody in a small cottage. About February we'll have to think of getting Muriel[3] mated, but there's no hurry. Whatever happens don't let her go to that broken-down old wreck of Mr Nicholls's,[4] who is simply worn out by about

[1] John Middleton Murry had become a communicating member of the Church of England.

[2] A fellow member of the POUM militia.

[3] A goat owned by the Blairs.

[4] A neighbour at Wallington.

twenty years of fucking his own sisters, daughters, grand-daughters and great-grand-daughters.

Yours
Eric

PS. Were you giving the pullets a forcing mash? Clarke's stuff is pretty good.

1939

147. Review

Power: A New Social Analysis by Bertrand Russell

If there are certain pages of Mr Bertrand Russell's book, *Power*, which seem rather empty, that is merely to say that we have now sunk to a depth at which the restatement of the obvious is the first duty of intelligent men. It is not merely that at present the rule of naked force obtains almost everywhere. Probably that has always been the case. Where this age differs from those immediately preceding it is that a liberal intelligentsia is lacking. Bully-worship, under various disguises, has become a universal religion, and such truisms as that a machine-gun is still a machine-gun even when a "good" man is squeezing the trigger—and that in effect is what Mr Russell is saying—have turned into heresies which it is actually becoming dangerous to utter.

The most interesting part of Mr Russell's book is the earlier chapters in which he analyses the various types of power—priestly, oligarchical, dictatorial and so forth. In dealing with the contemporary situation he is less satisfactory, because like all liberals he is better at pointing out what is desirable than at explaining how to achieve it. He sees clearly enough that the essential problem of today is "the taming of power" and that no system except democracy can be trusted to save us from unspeakable horrors. Also that democracy has very little meaning without approximate economic equality and an educational system tending to promote tolerance and tough-mindedness. But unfortunately he does not tell us how we are to set about getting these things; he merely utters what amounts to a pious hope that the present state of things will not endure. He is inclined to point to the past; all tyrannies have collapsed sooner or later, and "there is no reason to suppose (Hitler) more permanent than his predecessors."

Underlying this is the idea that common sense always wins in the end. And yet the peculiar horror of the present moment is that we cannot be sure that this is so. It is quite possible that we are descending into an age in which two and two will make five when the Leader says so. Mr Russell points out that the huge system of organised lying upon which the dictators depend keeps their followers out of contact with reality and therefore tends to put them at a disadvantage as against those who know the facts. This is true so far as it goes, but it does not prove that the slave-society at which the dictators are aiming will be unstable. It is quite easy to imagine a state in which the ruling caste deceive their followers without deceiving themselves. Dare anyone be sure that something of the kind is not coming into existence already? One has only to think of the sinister possibilities of the radio, state-controlled education and so forth, to realise that "the truth is great and will prevail" is a prayer rather than an axiom.

Mr Russell is one of the most readable of living writers, and it is very reassuring to know that he exists. So long as he and a few others like him are alive and out of jail, we know that the world is still sane in parts. He has rather an eclectic mind, he is capable of saying shallow things and profoundly interesting things in alternate sentences, and sometimes, even in this book, he is less serious than his subject deserves. But he has an essentially *decent* intellect, a kind of intellectual chivalry which is far rarer than mere cleverness. Few people during the past thirty years have been so consistently impervious to the fashionable bunk of the moment. In a time of universal panic and lying he is a good person to make contact with. For that reason this book, though it is not so good as *Freedom and Organisation*, is very well worth reading.

Adelphi, January 1939

148. Letter to Herbert Read

Boite Postale 48
Gueliz
Marrakech, French Morocco
4 January 1939

Dear Read,

Thanks for your letter and the manifesto.[1] Funnily enough I'd already seen it in *La Flêche* and had thoughts of making further enquiries. I'll certainly sign it, though if you merely want a few names to represent England you could get some much better-known people. But any way use my name for anything it is worth. You asked if I wanted to suggest any changes in the manifesto. The only point I am a bit doubtful about, though I don't press it, is this. On p. 2 you say "To make Russia safe for bureaucracy, first the German workers, then the Spanish workers, then the Czechoslovakian workers, have been left in the lurch". I've no doubt this is true, but is it strategically wise for people in our position to raise the Czech question at this moment? No doubt the Russians *did* leave the Czechs in the soup, but it does not seem to me that they behaved worse or very differently from the British and French Governments, and to suggest by implication that they ought to have gone to war to defend the Czechs is to suggest that Britain and France ought to have gone to war too, which is just what the Popular Frontiersmen would say and what I don't believe to be true. I don't press this point, I merely suggest it, and any way add my name to the manifesto.

I am spending the winter here for the sake of my lungs, which I think it is doing a little good to. Owing to this blasted health business I have had what is practically a wasted year, but the long rest has done me good and I am getting on with a new novel, whereas a year ago, after that awful nightmare in Spain, I had seriously thought I would never be able to write a novel again. Meanwhile, curiously enough, I had for some time past been contemplating writing to you about a matter which is much on my mind. It is this:

I believe it is vitally necessary for those of us who intend to oppose the coming war to start organising for illegal anti-war activities.

[1] *Towards a Free Revolutionary Art*, calling for the formation of the International Federation of Independent Revolutionary Art, signed by André Breton, founder and leader of the Surrealist movement, and Diego Rivera, painter of the Mexican revolution, when they rejected the Third International politically and culturally. *La Clé* was its monthly bulletin.

It is perfectly obvious that any open and legal agitation will be impossible not only when war has started but when it is imminent, and that if we do not make ready *now* for the issue of pamphlets etc we shall be quite unable to do so when the decisive moment comes. At present there is considerable freedom of the press and no restriction on the purchase of printing presses, stocks of paper etc, but I don't believe for an instant that this state of affairs is going to continue. If we don't make preparations we may find ourselves silenced and absolutely helpless when either war or the pre-war fascising processes begin. It is difficult to get people to see the danger of this, because most English people are constitutionally incapable of believing that anything will ever change. In addition, when one has to deal with actual pacifists, one generally finds that they have a sort of lingering moral objection to illegality and underground work. I quite agree that people, especially people who have any kind of notoriety, can get the best results by fighting in the open, but we might find it extremely useful to have an underground organisation *as well.* It seems to me that the commonsense thing to do would be to accumulate the things we should need for the production of pamphlets, stickybacks etc, lay them by in some unobtrusive place and not use them until it became necessary. For this we should need organisation and, in particular, money, probably 3 or 4 hundred pounds, but this should not be impossible with the help of the people one could probably rope in by degrees. Would you drop me a line and let me know whether you are interested in this idea? But even if you are not, don't speak of it to anyone, will you?

I enclose the manifesto, which I have signed.

Yours
Eric Blair

PS. I'm keeping the leaflet of *Clé* & will send in a subscription as soon as I can get into Marrakech & buy a money-order.

149. Review

Russia under Soviet Rule by N. de Basily

Russia under Soviet Rule falls definitely into the "anti" class of books on the USSR, but for once it is not Trotskyist. The author—

an exile, of course—holds approximately the same opinions as Kerensky and the others of the Provisional Government of 1917, with which he was associated in an official capacity. He is therefore attacking the Bolshevik experiment not from a Socialist but from a liberal-capitalist standpoint, rather as Gaetano Salvemini attacks the Fascist experiment of Italy. His book might almost, in fact, be a companion volume to *Under the Axe of Fascism*. In the last analysis it is doubtful whether any liberal criticism of a totalitarian system is really relevant; it is rather like accusing the Pope of being a bad Protestant. However, as the dictators are generally dishonest enough to claim the liberal virtues on top of the totalitarian ones, they certainly lay themselves open to attacks of this kind.

The author, it should be noticed, though hostile to the Bolshevik régime, does not think that it is going to collapse in the near future. His main thesis is that it has functioned inefficiently and that the loss of liberty and enormous suffering which it has caused were largely unnecessary. The modernisation of industry and agriculture which Stalin has undertaken is, according to Mr de Basily, simply a continuation of something that was already happening in pre-war Russia, and the rate of progress has actually been slowed down rather than advanced by the Revolution. It is of course obvious that a statement of this kind cannot be finally proved or disproved. Even to begin to examine it is to sink into a bog of statistics—and incidentally this book contains more figures, mainly from Soviet sources, and longer footnotes than any book I have read for years. But it is worth being reminded that Russia was already being fairly rapidly modernised in the ten years or so preceding the Revolution. It is now, perhaps, beginning to be possible to see the Russian revolution in some kind of historical perspective, and the hitherto accepted version of a barbarous feudal country turning overnight into a sort of super-America is something that will probably have to be revised.

But is life—life for the ordinary person—any better in Russia than it was before? That is the thing that it seems almost impossible for an outsider to be certain about. Statistics, even when they are honestly presented (and how often does that happen nowadays?) are almost always misleading, because one never knows what factors they leave out of account. To give a crude illustration, it would be easy to show, by stating the figures for fuel-consumption and saying nothing about the temperature, that everyone in Central Africa is suffering from cold. Who does not know those Soviet statistics, published by Mr Gollancz and others, in which the curve of everything except mortality goes up and up and up? And how much do they really tell one? Mr de Basily's statistics, naturally, point a different moral, but, without in the least questioning the accuracy of his figures, I would not infer too much from them. As far as the material side of life goes, all that seems to emerge fairly certainly is this: that the standard of living was rising during the NEP period, dropped during the period 1928–33, and is now rising again but is still low by western European standards. This is denied by Soviet apologists, but not very convincingly. The average wage in 1936 was only 225 roubles a month—the purchasing-power of the rouble being about threepence. Moreover, it is well known that it is next door to impossible for a Soviet citizen, unless on some kind of official mission, to visit any foreign country—a silent admission that life is more comfortable elsewhere.

If Mr de Basily were merely claiming that twenty years of Bolshevik rule had failed to raise the general standard of living, his criticism would be hardly worth making. After all, one could not reasonably expect an experiment on such a scale to work perfectly at the beginning. Economically the Bolsheviks have been far more successful than any outsider would have prophesied in 1918. But the intellectual, moral and political developments—the ever-tightening Party dictatorship, the muzzled press, the purges, the oriental worship of Stalin—are a different matter. Mr de Basily devotes a good many chapters to this. He is, nevertheless, comparatively optimistic, because, as a liberal, he takes it for granted that the "spirit of freedom" is bound to revive sooner or later. He even believes that this is happening already:

> The thirst for liberty, the notion of self-respect . . . all these features and characteristics of the old Russian élite are beginning to be appropriated by the intellectuals of to-day. . . . The moment the Soviet élite opens its fight for the emancipation of the human individual, the vast popular masses will be at its side.

But will they? The terrifying thing about the modern dictatorships is that they are something entirely unprecedented. Their end cannot be foreseen. In the past every tyranny was sooner or later overthrown, or at least resisted, because of "human nature", which as a matter of course desired liberty. But we cannot be at all certain that "human nature" is constant. It may be just as possible to produce a breed of men who do not wish for liberty as to produce a breed of hornless cows. The Inquisition failed, but then the Inquisition had not the resources of the modern state. The radio, press-censorship, standardised education and the secret police have altered everything. Mass-suggestion is a science of the last twenty years, and we do not yet know how successful it will be.

It is noticeable that Mr de Basily does not attribute all the shortcomings of the present Russian régime to Stalin's personal wickedness. He thinks that they were inherent from the very start in the aims and nature of the Bolshevik Party. It is probably a good thing for Lenin's reputation that he died so early. Trotsky, in exile, denounces the Russian dictatorship, but he is probably as much responsible for it as any man now living, and there is no certainty that as a dictator he would be preferable to Stalin, though undoubtedly he has a much more interesting mind. The essential act is the rejection of democracy—that is, of the underlying values of democracy; once you have decided upon that, Stalin—or at any rate someone *like* Stalin—is already on the way. I believe this opinion is gaining ground, and I hope it will continue to do so. If even a few hundred thousand people can be got to grasp that it is useless to overthrow Tweedledum in order to set up Tweedledee, the talk of "democracy versus Fascism" with which our ears are deafened may begin to mean something.

New English Weekly, 12 January 1939

150. Letter to Geoffrey Gorer

Boite Postale 48
Gueliz
Marrakech, French Morocco
20 January 1939

Dear Geoffrey,

I've been meaning to write to you for ages, & here I am doing it at last. We have been in this country ever since September & I think it has done my lungs a good deal of good. I don't cough much now & have put on abt ½ a stone. Eileen is also thriving. In September the climate was foul, unbearably hot & every kind of insect pest, but as winter comes on it gets to be a lovely clear kind of weather like spring in England. I am writing this 5 or 6 thousand feet up in the Atlas. I'd finished the rough draft of my novel & wanted to take a week off, so we came up here. It's wonderful country, enormous limestone gorges & ravines full of frozen snow, & little Berber villages of mud huts with flat tops. The Berbers—the kind round here are called Chleuh—are fascinating people, often more or less white with red cheeks, & the women have the most wonderful eyes. But what fascinates me about them most of all is that they are so dirty. You will see exquisitely beautiful women walking abt with their necks almost invisible under dirt. Of course the poverty is such as you would expect & you have only to produce a packet of cigarettes to be more or less buried under a pile of people of all ages & both sexes. But that seems to be the same everywhere in Morocco. It is funny that all hill people have a certain resemblance, perhaps in their walk, & there is something about the people here that slightly reminds me of the Kachins in Burma.

I hope your book[1] on the Lepchas went off all right. I'm not displeased with parts of my novel, which I hope to have finished by the beginning of April. I don't know what I shall do next. Nelson's wanted me to do a book[2] for that series they are bringing out, then it fell through owing to my being ill, but if I can connect up with them again I should like to do that before doing another novel. I have an idea for a very big novel, in fact 3 in series, making something abt the size of *War and Peace*, but I want another year to think over the first part. I suppose it's a sign of approaching senile decay when one starts projecting a Saga, but in my case it may merely be another way of saying that I hope war won't break out, because I don't think I could write a Saga in the middle of a war, certainly not in the concentration camp. I must say we were very glad to be out of England for the war crisis. One gets so fed up with arguing with people about this war business, & everything that could conceivably be said has been said already. I think you are a bit younger than me & probably don't remember the great war very vividly, but I have a very retentive memory & often when I hear people tirading against Hitler nowadays I often think the clock has somehow slipped back twenty years. In Morocco the French simply paid no attention & obviously didn't

[1] *Himalayan Village*, 1938.

[2] In June 1938 Orwell had been negotiating with the publishers, Thomas Nelson and Sons, about writing a book for them to be called *Poverty in Practice*, but his ill-health prevented him from doing it.

think war conceivable. I think the absolutely bottomless selfishness of the French may help to save the situation, because it is obvious that they would not fight unless French soil is invaded & the higher-ups presumably know this. What a mess in Spain! A friend who recently came out tells me that Barcelona is smashed out of recognition, all the children are hungry & you could buy 900 pesetas for an English pound note. I keep hearing in roundabout ways of Spaniards I knew, always that they are killed. It does seem so meaningless. George Kopp, whom you may remember reading abt in my book on the war, recently escaped, having lost 7 stone of weight thanks to what the GPU had done to him during 18 months. I hope he publishes his experiences, because it is time this kind of thing was put a stop to.

I have no idea where you are, but shall send this to Highgate, of course. I hope you'll be in England in the spring & that we'll see you when we get back. Eileen sends love.

Yours
Eric

151. Review

Communism and Man by F. J. Sheed

This book—a refutation of Marxian Socialism from the Catholic standpoint—is remarkable for being written in a good temper. Instead of employing the abusive misrepresentation which is now usual in all major controversies, it gives a fairer exposition of Marxism and Communism than most Marxists could be trusted to give of Catholicism. If it fails, or at any rate ends less interestingly than it begins, this is probably because the author is less ready to follow up his own intellectual implications than those of his opponents.

As he sees clearly enough, the radical difference between Christian and Communist lies in the question of personal immortality. Either this life is a preparation for another, in which case the individual soul is all-important, or there is no life after death, in which case the individual is merely a replaceable cell in the general body. These two theories are quite irreconcilable, and the political and economic systems founded upon them are bound to be antagonistic.

What Mr Sheed is not ready to admit, however, is that acceptance of the Catholic position implies a certain willingness to see the present injustices of society continue. He seems to claim that a truly Catholic society would contain all or most of what the Socialist is aiming at—which is a little too like "having it both ways".

Individual salvation implies liberty, which is always extended by Catholic writers to include the right to private property. But in the stage of industrial development which we have now reached, the right to private property means the right to exploit and torture millions of one's fellow creatures. The Socialist would argue, therefore, that one can only defend property if one is more or less indifferent to economic justice.

The Catholic's answer to this is not very satisfactory. It is not that the Church condones the injustices of capitalism—quite the contrary. Mr Sheed is quite right in pointing out that several Popes have denounced the capitalist system very bitterly, and that Socialists usually ignore this. But at the same time the Church refuses the only solution that is likely to make any real difference. Private property is to remain, the employer-employee relationship is to remain, even the categories "rich" and "poor" are to remain—but there is to be justice and fair distribution. In other words, the rich man is not to be expropriated, he is merely to be told to behave himself.

> (The Church) does not see men primarily as exploiters and exploited, with the exploiters as people whom it is her duty to overthrow . . . from her point of view the rich man as sinner is the object of her most loving care. Where others see a strong man in the pride of success, she sees a poor soul in danger of hell. . . . Christ has told her that the souls of the rich are in special danger; and care for souls is her primary work.

The objection to this is that *in practice* it makes no difference. The rich man is called to repentance, but he never repents. In this matter Catholic capitalists do not seem to be perceptibly different from the others.

It is obvious that any economic system would work equitably if men could be trusted to behave themselves but long experience has shown that in matters of property only a tiny minority of men will behave any better than they are compelled to do. This does not mean that the Catholic attitude toward property is untenable, but it does mean that it is very difficult to square with economic justice. In practice, accepting the Catholic standpoint means accepting exploitation, poverty, famine, war and disease as part of the natural order of things.

It would seem, therefore, that if the Catholic Church is to regain its spiritual influence, it will have to define its position more boldly. Either it will have to modify its attitude toward private property, or it will have to say clearly that its kingdom is not of this world and that feeding bodies is of very small importance compared with saving souls.

In effect it does say something of the kind, but rather uneasily, because this is not the message that modern men want to hear. Consequently for some time past the Church has been in an anomalous position, symbolised by the fact [that] the Pope almost simultaneously denounces the capitalist system and confers decorations on General Franco.

Meanwhile this is an interesting book, written in a simple style and remarkably free from malice and cheap witticisms. If all Catholic apologists were like Mr Sheed, the Church would have fewer enemies.

Peace News, 27 January 1939

152. Letter to Herbert Read

Boite Postale 48
Gueliz
Marrakech, French Morocco
5 March 1939

Dear Read,

Thanks so much for your letter. I am probably leaving this country about the 22nd or 23rd of March and should be in England by the end of the month. I shall probably be in London a few days and I'll try and arrange to come and see you. If I could help with *Revolt*[1] I'd like to, though till I've seen what kind of paper it is to be I don't know whether I could be of any use. The trouble is that if I am writing a book as I generally am I find it almost impossible to do any other creative work, but on the other hand I *like* doing reviews, if they would want anything in that line. If we could keep a left-wing

[1] *Revolt*, edited by Vernon Richards in London, ran for six issues from 11 February to 3 June 1939, and aimed at presenting the Spanish civil war from an anti-Stalinist point of view.

but non-Stalinist review in existence (it's all a question of money, really) I believe a lot of people would be pleased. People aren't all fools, they must begin soon to see through this "anti-fascist" racket. A thought that cheers me a lot is that each generation, which in literature means about ten years, is in revolt against the last, and just as the Audens etc rose in revolt against the Squires and Drinkwaters,[1] there must be another gang about due to rise against the Audens.

About the press business. I quite agree that it's in a way absurd to start preparing for an underground campaign unless you know who is going to campaign and what for, but the point is that if you don't make some preparations beforehand you will be helpless when you want to start, as you are sure to sooner or later. I cannot believe that the time when one can buy a printing press with no questions asked will last for ever. To take an analogous case. When I was a kid you could walk into a bicycle-shop or ironmonger's and buy any firearm you pleased, short of a field gun, and it did not occur to most people that the Russian revolution and the Irish civil war would bring this state of affairs to an end. It will be the same with printing presses etc. As for the sort of thing we shall find ourselves doing, the way I see the situation is like this. The chances of Labour or any Left combination winning the election are in my opinion nil, and in any case if they did get in I doubt whether they'd be better than or much different from the Chamberlain lot. We are therefore in either for war in the next two years, or for prolonged war-preparation, or possibly only for sham war-preparations designed to cover up other objects, but in any of these cases for a fascising process leading to an authoritarian régime, i.e. some kind of austro-fascism. So long as the objective, real or pretended, is war against Germany, the greater part of the Left will associate themselves with the fascising process, which will ultimately mean associating themselves with wage-reductions, suppression of free speech, brutalities in the colonies etc. Therefore the revolt against these things will have to be against the Left as well as the Right. The revolt will form itself into two sections, that of the dissident lefts like ourselves, and that of the fascists, this time the idealistic Hitler-fascists, in England more or less represented by Mosley. I don't know whether Mosley will have the sense and guts to stick out against war with Germany, he might decide to cash in on the patriotism business, but in that case someone else will

[1] John Drinkwater (1882–1937), dramatist, poet and biographer who had great popular acclaim but little success among intellectuals.

take his place. If war leads to disaster and revolution, the official Left having already sold out and been identified in the public mind with the war-party, the fascists will have it all their own way unless there is in being some body of people who are both anti-war and anti-fascist. Actually there will be such people, probably very great numbers of them, but their being able to do anything will depend largely on their having some means of expression during the time when discontent is growing. I doubt whether there is much hope of saving England from fascism of one kind or another, but clearly one must put up a fight, and it seems silly to be silenced when one might be making a row merely because one had failed to take a few precautions beforehand. If we laid in printing presses etc in some discreet place we could then cautiously go to work to get together a distributing agency, and we could then feel "Well, if trouble does come we are ready." On the other hand if it doesn't come I should be so pleased that I would not grudge a little wasted effort. As to money, I shall probably be completely penniless for the rest of this year unless something unexpected happens. Perhaps if we definitely decided on a course of action your friend Penrose[1] might put up something, and I think there are others who could be got to see the necessity. What about Bertrand Russell, for instance? I suppose he has some money, and he would fall in with the idea fast enough if he could be persuaded that free speech is menaced.

When I get back I'll write or ring up and try and arrange to meet. If you're going to be in town about the beginning of April, or on the other hand going to be away or something, could you let me know? But better not write to the above as the letter might miss me. Write to: at 24 Croom's Hill, Greenwich SE10.

Yours
Eric Blair

153. Marrakech

As the corpse went past the flies left the restaurant table in a cloud and rushed after it, but they came back a few minutes later.

The little crowd of mourners—all men and boys, no women—

[1] Roland Penrose (1900–), Kt. 1966, painter and writer who used his independent means to help many painters and artistic and left-wing projects.

threaded their way across the market-place between the piles of pomegranates and the taxis and the camels, wailing a short chant over and over again. What really appeals to the flies is that the corpses here are never put into coffins, they are merely wrapped in a piece of rag and carried on a rough wooden bier on the shoulders of four friends. When the friends get to the burying-ground they hack an oblong hole a foot or two deep, dump the body in it and fling over it a little of the dried-up, lumpy earth, which is like broken brick. No gravestone, no name, no identifying mark of any kind. The burying-ground is merely a huge waste of hummocky earth, like a derelict building-lot. After a month or two no one can even be certain where his own relatives are buried.

When you walk through a town like this—two hundred thousand inhabitants, of whom at least twenty thousand own literally nothing except the rags they stand up in—when you see how the people live, and still more how easily they die, it is always difficult to believe that you are walking among human beings. All colonial empires are in reality founded upon that fact. The people have brown faces—besides, there are so many of them! Are they really the same flesh as yourself? Do they even have names? Or are they merely a kind of undifferentiated brown stuff, about as individual as bees or coral insects? They rise out of the earth, they sweat and starve for a few years, and then they sink back into the nameless mounds of the graveyard and nobody notices that they are gone. And even the graves themselves soon fade back into the soil. Sometimes, out for a walk, as you break your way through the prickly pear, you notice that it is rather bumpy underfoot, and only a certain regularity in the bumps tells you that you are walking over skeletons.

I was feeding one of the gazelles in the public gardens.

Gazelles are almost the only animals that look good to eat when they are still alive, in fact, one can hardly look at their hindquarters without thinking of mint sauce. The gazelle I was feeding seemed to know that this thought was in my mind, for though it took the piece of bread I was holding out it obviously did not like me. It nibbled rapidly at the bread, then lowered its head and tried to butt me, then took another nibble and then butted again. Probably its idea was that if it could drive me away the bread would somehow remain hanging in mid-air.

An Arab navvy working on the path nearby lowered his heavy

hoe and sidled towards us. He looked from the gazelle to the bread and from the bread to the gazelle, with a sort of quiet amazement, as though he had never seen anything quite like this before. Finally he said shyly in French:

"*I* could eat some of that bread."

I tore off a piece and he stowed it gratefully in some secret place under his rags. This man is an employee of the Municipality.

When you go through the Jewish quarters you gather some idea of what the medieval ghettoes were probably like. Under their Moorish rulers the Jews were only allowed to own land in certain restricted areas, and after centuries of this kind of treatment they have ceased to bother about overcrowding. Many of the streets are a good deal less than six feet wide, the houses are completely windowless, and sore-eyed children cluster everywhere in unbelievable numbers, like clouds of flies. Down the centre of the street there is generally running a little river of urine.

In the bazaar huge families of Jews, all dressed in the long black robe and little black skull-cap, are working in dark fly-infested booths that look like caves. A carpenter sits cross-legged at a prehistoric lathe, turning chair-legs at lightning speed. He works the lathe with a bow in his right hand and guides the chisel with his left foot, and thanks to a lifetime of sitting in this position his left leg is warped out of shape. At his side his grandson, aged six, is already starting on the simpler parts of the job.

I was just passing the coppersmiths' booths when somebody noticed that I was lighting a cigarette. Instantly, from the dark holes all round, there was a frenzied rush of Jews, many of them old grandfathers with flowing grey beards, all clamouring for a cigarette. Even a blind man somewhere at the back of one of the booths heard a rumour of cigarettes and came crawling out, groping in the air with his hand. In about a minute I had used up the whole packet. None of these people, I suppose, works less than twelve hours a day, and every one of them looks on a cigarette as a more or less impossible luxury.

As the Jews live in self-contained communities they follow the same trades as the Arabs, except for agriculture. Fruit-sellers, potters, silversmiths, blacksmiths, butchers, leather-workers, tailors, water-carriers, beggars, porters—whichever way you look you see nothing but Jews. As a matter of fact there are thirteen thousand of them, all living in the space of a few acres. A good job Hitler isn't here. Perhaps he is on his way, however. You hear the usual dark rumours about the Jews, not only from the Arabs but from the poorer Europeans.

"Yes, *mon vieux*, they took my job away from me and gave it to a Jew. The Jews! They're the real rulers of this country, you know. They've got all the money. They control the banks, finance—everything."

"But," I said, "isn't it a fact that the average Jew is a labourer working for about a penny an hour?"

"Ah, that's only for show! They're all moneylenders really. They're cunning, the Jews."

In just the same way, a couple of hundred years ago, poor old women used to be burned for witchcraft when they could not even work enough magic to get themselves a square meal.

All people who work with their hands are partly invisible, and the more important the work they do, the less visible they are. Still, a white skin is always fairly conspicuous. In northern Europe, when you see a labourer ploughing a field, you probably give him a second glance. In a hot country, anywhere south of Gibraltar or east of Suez, the chances are that you don't even see him. I have noticed this again and again. In a tropical landscape one's eye takes in everything except the human beings. It takes in the dried-up soil, the prickly pear, the palm-tree and the distant mountain, but it always misses the peasant hoeing at his patch. He is the same colour as the earth, and a great deal less interesting to look at.

It is only because of this that the starved countries of Asia and Africa are accepted as tourist resorts. No one would think of running cheap trips to the Distressed Areas. But where the human beings have brown skins their poverty is simply not noticed. What does Morocco mean to a Frenchman? An orange-grove or a job in government service. Or to an Englishman? Camels, castles, palm-trees, Foreign Legionnaires, brass trays and bandits. One could probably live here for years without noticing that for nine-tenths of the people the reality of life is an endless, back-breaking struggle to wring a little food out of an eroded soil.

Most of Morocco is so desolate that no wild animal bigger than a hare can live on it. Huge areas which were once covered with forest have turned into a treeless waste where the soil is exactly like broken-up brick. Nevertheless a good deal of it is cultivated, with frightful labour. Everything is done by hand. Long lines of women, bent double like inverted capital Ls, work their way slowly across the fields, tearing up the prickly weeds with their hands, and the peasant gathering lucerne for fodder pulls it up stalk by stalk instead of reaping it, thus saving an inch or two on each stalk. The plough is a wretched wooden thing, so frail that one can easily carry it on one's shoulder, and fitted underneath with a rough iron spike which stirs the soil to a depth of about four inches. This is as much as the strength of the animals is equal to. It is usual to plough with a cow and a donkey yoked together. Two donkeys would not be quite strong enough, but on the other hand two cows would cost a little more to feed. The peasants possess no harrows, they merely plough the soil several times over in different directions, finally leaving it in rough furrows, after which the whole field has to be shaped with hoes into small oblong patches, to conserve water. Except for a day or two after the rare rainstorms there is never enough water. Along the edges of the fields channels are hacked out to a depth of thirty or forty feet to get at the tiny trickles which run through the subsoil.

Every afternoon a file of very old women passes down the road outside my house, each carrying a load of firewood. All of them are mummified with age and the sun, and all of them are tiny. It seems to be generally the case in primitive communities that the women, when they get beyond a certain age, shrink to the size of children. One day a poor old creature who could not have been more than four feet tall crept past me under a vast load of wood. I stopped her and put a five-sou piece (a little more than a farthing) into her hand. She answered with a shrill wail, almost a scream, which was partly gratitude but mainly surprise. I suppose that from her point of view, by taking any notice of her, I seemed almost to be violating a law of nature. She accepted her status as an old woman, that is to say as a beast of burden. When a family is travelling it is quite usual to see a father and a grown-up son riding ahead on donkeys, and an old woman following on foot, carrying the baggage.

But what is strange about these people is their invisibility. For several weeks, always at about the same time of day, the file of old women had hobbled past the house with their firewood, and though they had registered themselves on my eyeballs I cannot truly say that I had seen them. Firewood was passing—that was how I saw it. It was only that one day I happened to be walking behind them, and the curious up-and-down motion of a load of wood drew my attention to the human being underneath it. Then for the first time I noticed the poor old earth-coloured bodies, bodies reduced to bones and leathery skin, bent double under the crushing weight. Yet I suppose I had not been five minutes on Moroccan soil before I noticed the overloading of the donkeys and was infuriated by it. There is no question that the donkeys are damnably treated. The Moroccan donkey is hardly bigger than a St Bernard dog, it carries a load which in the British army would be considered too much for a fifteen-hands mule, and very often its pack-saddle is not taken off its back for weeks together. But what is peculiarly pitiful is that it is the most willing creature on earth, it follows its master like a dog and does not need either bridle or halter. After a dozen years of devoted work it suddenly drops dead, whereupon its master tips it into the ditch and the village dogs have torn its guts out before it is cold.

This kind of thing makes one's blood boil, whereas—on the whole—the plight of the human beings does not. I am not commenting, merely pointing to a fact. People with brown skins are next door to invisible. Anyone can be sorry for the donkey with its galled back, but it is generally owing to some kind of accident if one even notices the old woman under her load of sticks.

As the storks flew northward the Negroes were marching southward—a long, dusty column, infantry, screw-gun batteries and then more infantry, four or five thousand men in all, winding up the road with a clumping of boots and a clatter of iron wheels.

They were Senegalese, the blackest Negroes in Africa, so black that sometimes it is difficult to see whereabouts on their necks the hair begins. Their splendid bodies were hidden in reach-me-down khaki uniforms, their feet squashed into boots that looked like blocks of wood, and every tin hat seemed to be a couple of sizes too small. It was very hot and the men had marched a long way. They slumped under the weight of their packs and the curiously sensitive black faces were glistening with sweat.

As they went past a tall, very young Negro turned and caught my eye. But the look he gave me was not in the least the kind of look you might expect. Not hostile, not contemptuous, not sullen, not even inquisitive. It was the shy, wide-eyed Negro look, which actually is a look of profound respect. I saw how it was. This wretched boy, who is a French citizen and has therefore been dragged from the forest to scrub floors and catch syphilis in garrison towns, actually has feelings of reverence before a white skin. He has been taught that the white race are his masters, and he still believes it.

But there is one thought which every white man (and in this connection it doesn't matter twopence if he calls himself a Socialist) thinks when he sees a black army marching past. "How much longer can we go on kidding these people? How long before they turn their guns in the other direction?"

It was curious, really. Every white man there has this thought stowed somewhere or other in his mind. I had it, so had the other onlookers, so had the officers on their sweating chargers and the white NCOs marching in the ranks. It was a kind of secret which we all knew and were too clever to tell; only the Negroes didn't know it. And really it was almost like watching a flock of cattle to see the long column, a mile or two miles of armed men, flowing peacefully up the road, while the great white birds drifted over them in the opposite direction, glittering like scraps of paper.

Written [Spring] 1939

New Writing, Christmas 1939: SJ; EYE; CE

154. Letter to Jack Common

36 High St
Southwold, Suffolk
Sunday [9 April 1939]

Dear Jack,
Many thanks for yours, which has been forwarded from London, & please excuse delay both in answering & putting in an appearance. I *was* to have come down to Wallington last Wed. (5th) after making a hasty visit here, then no sooner got here than I became ill again & have spent a week in bed. It's nothing serious, mainly due to the change of temperature no doubt, & Eileen's had a cold too, probably from the same cause. We are coming down to Wallington on Tuesday (the 11th) but probably shan't arrive till 6 or 7 pm. I think Eileen's mother is being dropped there earlier & Mrs Anderson[1] has been informed, so doubtless all will be well. I'm sorry if we've thrown you out with this late arrival. . . . I hope you're all flourishing & more

[1] A neighbour at Wallington.

or less finished with winter colds etc. If you're in one of the Council houses you're no doubt finding it a lot more sanitary than our cottage. We intend to stay the summer, then move. I finished my novel[1] just before we got back & dumped it but haven't heard any repercussions yet. Gollancz was anxious that I shouldn't "leave" him as they call it & by contract he's supposed to publish my next 3 fictions, but if he tries to bugger me abt I think I shall leave him, & then there'll be long complications abt who else to go to. Love to Mary & Peter—looking forward to seeing you in the near future.

Yours
Eric

Coming Up for Air *was published in London by Victor Gollancz Ltd on 12 June 1939, and in New York by Harcourt, Brace in 1950.*

155. Not Counting Niggers

A dozen years ago anyone who had foretold the political line-up of today would have been looked on as a lunatic. And yet the truth is that the present situation—not in detail, of course, but in its main outlines—ought to have been predictable even in the golden age before Hitler. Something like it was bound to happen as soon as British security was seriously threatened.

In a prosperous country, above all in an imperialist country, left-wing politics are always partly humbug. There can be no real reconstruction that would not lead to at least a temporary drop in the English standard of life, which is another way of saying that the majority of left-wing politicians and publicists are people who earn their living by demanding something that they don't genuinely want. They are red-hot revolutionaries as long as all goes well, but every real emergency reveals instantly that they are shamming. One threat to the Suez Canal, and "anti-Fascism" and "defence of British interests" are discovered to be identical.

It would be very shallow as well as unfair to suggest that there is *nothing* in what is now called "anti-Fascism" except a concern

[1] *Coming Up for Air.*

for British dividends. But it is a fact that the political obscenities of the past two years, the sort of monstrous harlequinade in which everyone is constantly bounding across the stage in a false nose—Quakers shouting for a bigger army, Communists waving Union Jacks, Winston Churchill posing as a democrat—would not have been possible without this guilty consciousness that we are all in the same boat. Much against their will the British governing class have been forced into the anti-Hitler position. It is still possible that they will find a way out of it, but they are arming in the obvious expectation of war and they will almost certainly fight when the point is reached at which the alternative would be to give away some of their own property instead of, as hitherto, other people's. And meanwhile the so-called opposition, instead of trying to stop the drift to war, are rushing ahead, preparing the ground and forestalling any possible criticism. So far as one can discover the English people are still extremely hostile to the idea of war, but in so far as they are becoming reconciled to it, it is not the militarists but the "anti-militarists" of five years ago who are responsible. The Labour Party keeps up a pettifogging grizzle against conscription at the same time as its own propaganda makes any real struggle against conscription impossible. The Bren machine-guns pour from the factories, books with titles like *Tanks in the Next War*, *Gas in the Next War*, etc pour from the press, and the warriors of the *New Statesman* gloze over the nature of the process by means of such phrases as "Peace Bloc", "Peace Front", "Democratic Front", and, in general, by pretending that the world is an assemblage of sheep and goats, neatly partitioned off by national frontiers.

In this connection it is well worth having a look at Mr Streit's much-discussed book, *Union Now.*[1] Mr Streit, like the partisans of the "Peace Bloc", wants the democracies to gang up against the dictatorships, but his book is outstanding for two reasons. To begin with he goes further than most of the others and offers a plan which, even it it is startling, is constructive. Secondly, in spite of a rather nineteen-twentyish American naïveté, he has an essentially decent cast of mind. He genuinely loathes the thought of war, and he does not sink to the hypocrisy of pretending that any country which can be bought or bullied into the British orbit instantly becomes a democracy. His book therefore presents a kind of test case. In it you are seeing the sheep-and-goats theory at its *best*. If you can't accept

[1] By Clarence K. Streit.

it in that form you will certainly never accept it in the form handed out by the Left Book Club.

Briefly, what Mr Streit suggests is that the democratic nations, starting with fifteen which he names, should voluntarily form themselves into a union—not a league or an alliance, but a union similar to the United States, with a common government, common money and complete internal free trade. The initial fifteen states are, of course, the USA, France, Great Britain, the self-governing dominions of the British Empire, and the smaller European democracies, not including Czechoslovakia, which still existed when the book was written. Later, other states could be admitted to the Union when and if they "proved themselves worthy". It is implied all along that the state of peace and prosperity existing within the Union would be so enviable that everyone else would soon be pining to join it.

It is worth noticing that this scheme is not so visionary as it sounds. Of course it is not going to happen, nothing advocated by well-meaning literary men ever happens, and there are certain difficulties which Mr Streit does not discuss; but it is of the order of things which *could* happen. Geographically the USA and the western European democracies are nearer to being a unit than, for instance, the British Empire. Most of their trade is with one another, they contain within their own territories everything they need, and Mr Streit is probably right in claiming that their combined strength would be so great as to make any attack on them hopeless, even if the USSR joined up with Germany. Why then does one see at a glance that this scheme has something wrong with it? What is there about it that smells—for it *does* smell, of course?

What it smells of, as usual, is hypocrisy and self-righteousness. Mr Streit himself is not a hypocrite, but his vision is limited. Look again at his list of sheep and goats. No need to boggle at the goats (Germany, Italy and Japan), they are goats right enough, and billies at that. But look at the sheep! Perhaps the USA will pass inspection if one does not look too closely. But what about France? What about England? What about even Belgium and Holland? Like everyone of his school of thought, Mr Streit has coolly lumped the huge British and French empires—in essence nothing but mechanisms for exploiting cheap coloured labour—under the heading of democracies!

Here and there in the book, though not often, there are references to the "dependencies" of the democratic states. "Dependencies" means subject races. It is explained that they are to go on being dependencies, that their resources are to be pooled among the states of the Union, and that their coloured inhabitants will lack the right to vote in Union affairs. Except where the tables of statistics bring it out, one would never for a moment guess what *numbers* of human beings are involved. India, for instance, which contains more inhabitants than the whole of the "fifteen democracies" put together, gets just a page and a half in Mr Streit's book, and that merely to explain that as India is not yet fit for self-government the *status quo* must continue. And here one begins to see what would really be happening if Mr Streit's scheme were put into operation. The British and French empires, with their six hundred million disenfranchised human beings, would simply be receiving fresh police forces; the huge strength of the USA would be behind the robbery of India and Africa. Mr Streit is letting cats out of bags, but *all* phrases like "Peace Bloc", "Peace Front", etc contain some such implication; all imply a tightening-up of the existing structure. The unspoken clause is always "not counting niggers". For how can we make a "firm stand" against Hitler if we are simultaneously weakening ourselves at home? In other words, how can we "fight Fascism" except by bolstering up a far vaster injustice?

For of course it *is* vaster. What we always forget is that the overwhelming bulk of the British proletariat does not live in Britain, but in Asia and Africa. It is not in Hitler's power, for instance, to make a penny an hour a normal industrial wage; it is perfectly normal in India, and we are at great pains to keep it so. One gets some idea of the real relationship of England and India when one reflects that the *per capita* annual income in England is something over £80, and in India about £7. It is quite common for an Indian coolie's leg to be thinner than the average Englishman's arm. And there is nothing racial in this, for well-fed members of the same races are of normal physique; it is due to simple starvation. This is the system which we all live on and which we denounce when there seems to be no danger of its being altered. Of late, however, it has become the first duty of a "good anti-Fascist" to lie about it and help to keep it in being.

What real settlement, of the slightest value, can there be along these lines? What meaning would there be, even if it were successful, in bringing down Hitler's system in order to stabilise something that is far bigger and in its different way just as bad?

But apparently, for lack of any real opposition, this is going to be our objective. Mr Streit's ingenious ideas will not be put into operation, but something resembling the "Peace Bloc" proposals probably will. The British and Russian governments are still haggling, stalling and uttering muffled threats to change sides, but circumstances will probably drive them together. And what then? No doubt the alliance will stave off war for a year or two. Then Hitler's move will be to feel for a weak spot or an unguarded moment; then our move will be more armaments, more militarisation, more propaganda, more war-mindedness—and so on, at increasing speed. It is doubtful whether prolonged war-preparation is morally any better than war itself; there are even reasons for thinking that it may be slightly worse. Only two or three years of it, and we may sink almost unresisting into some local variant of austro-Fascism. And perhaps a year or two later, in reaction against this, there will appear something we have never had in England yet—a real Fascist movement. And because it will have the guts to speak plainly it will gather into its ranks the very people who ought to be opposing it.

Further than that it is difficult to see. The downward slide is happening because nearly all the Socialist leaders, when it comes to the pinch, are merely His Majesty's Opposition, and nobody else knows how to mobilise the decency of the English people, which one meets with everywhere when one talks to human beings instead of reading newspapers. Nothing is likely to save us except the emergence within the next two years of a real mass party whose first pledges are to refuse war and to right imperial injustice. But if any such party exists at present, it is only as a possibility, in a few tiny germs lying here and there in unwatered soil.

Adelphi, July 1939

156. Review

Stendhal by F. C. Green

Stendhal, by Professor F. C. Green, is said to be the first book on Stendhal written in English for over sixty years. What this probably demonstrates is that the biographer and the novelist need different material to work on. Stendhal's life was of the kind that is absorbingly interesting when one sees it from the inside, as one does in certain passages in his novels, but not particularly suited to biography, because he lived more or less in obscurity and had periods of years on end when nothing particular was happening. He was never a popular idol or a resounding scandal, never even starved in a garret or wrote masterpieces in a debtors' prison. In a fairly active life of fifty-nine years (1783–1843) his experiences seem to have been, on the whole, the kind of experiences that happen to ordinary unsuccessful people.

One of them was to see war at close quarters. For some years Stendhal held a responsible position in the supplies department of Napoleon's army, and he was in the retreat from Moscow, which in itself would be quite enough adventure for one normal lifetime. It was the kind of thing that would never happen to an even potentially successful writer, but undoubtedly it was a bit of luck for all of us that it happened to Stendhal. He seems to have written little or nothing about the Moscow campaign, but without that large scale demonstration of the boringness of war he might never have written his celebrated description of Waterloo, which must be one of the earliest pieces of *truthful* battle literature in existence. As a soldier and later as a consular agent Stendhal seems to have been both brave and competent, but it is evident that like most sensitive people he found action boring. Among the flames of Moscow he read an English translation of *Paul et Virginie*, and during the revolution of 1830 he sat listening to the gunfire in the streets without, apparently, feeling any impulse to join in. The things that seem to have moved him most deeply were scenery and, of course, an endless succession of love affairs, in which he was passably successful. He also caught syphilis, a thing that must have affected his outlook to some extent, though, as Professor Green points out, before Ibsen and Brieux had done their worst syphilis was merely a disease like any other.

As a writer Stendhal is in a peculiar position, because everyone has read two of his books and nobody except a small circle of admirers has read any of the others. Professor Green gives long and interesting analyses of his four principal novels, but finds it as difficult as it always is to explain just where Stendhal's charm lies. For of course with Stendhal it is above all a question of *charm*. There is something about him, a kind of mental climate, that makes it possible for him to get away with all the vices that ruin the ordinary sensitive novel. As for the besetting sin of novelists, narcissism, he is able to wallow in it without ever once giving offence. Of the two novels that everyone knows, it is easier to see why *Le Rouge et le Noir* leaves a lasting impression behind, because it has what the other at first sight seems to lack, a central unifying theme. As Professor Green rightly says, its theme is class-hatred. Julien Sorel, the clever, ambitious peasant-boy, at a time when reaction has triumphed and right-thinking is synonymous with stupidity, enters the Church with quite deliberate hypocrisy, because the Church is the only profession in which one can rise. As a poor hanger-on in aristocratic families, he loathes from the bottom of his heart the snobbish halfwits who surround him. But what gives the book its tone is that his hatred is mixed up with envy, as it would be in real life, of course. Julien is in fact the type of the revolutionary, and nine times out of ten a revolutionary is merely a climber with a bomb in his pocket. After all, the hated aristocrats are deeply fascinating. Mathilde de la Mole is all the *more* fascinating because of her atrocious pride and egoism. "What a frightful character!" Julien thinks, and instantly her frightfulness makes her twice as desirable as before. It is interesting to compare *Le Rouge et le Noir* with another epic of snobbishness, *Great Expectations.* Here the whole thing is happening on a lower social level, but there is a certain similarity of theme. Once again it is the fascination of something felt and known to be rotten. The one flaw in *Le Rouge et le Noir* is the shooting of Madame de Rênal, which brings Julien to the guillotine. Professor Green maintains that this too can be explained in terms of class-hatred. It may be so, and yet few people can have read the book without feeling that this is a peculiarly meaningless outrage and has only been put in because Julien has got to die in the limelight. A comparatively probable ending would have been to have him killed in a duel by some jealous relative of Mathilde. Perhaps this would have struck Stendhal as too obvious.

La Chartreuse de Parme does not seem at first sight to have an equally seizable theme, and yet one cannot read it without feeling that it *has* a theme, if only because Stendhal is peculiarly adept at producing what Professor Green calls "unity of tone". Without his very delicate feeling for proportion he could not deal so freely in improbabilities. Actually the theme of *La Chartreuse de Parme* is magnanimity. Unlike people in real life, the principal characters in it are spiritually decent. Apart from the Waterloo episode the whole book is an escape from time and space into a sort of Shakespearean never-never land. Admittedly it is a queer kind of magnanimity that the characters show, but that is just where Stendhal's genius comes in. For what one is obliged to feel is not merely that the Duchess of Sanseverina is superior to the ordinary "good" woman, but that she herself *is* a good woman, in spite of a few trifles like murder, incest, etc. She and Fabrice and even Mosca are incapable of acting *meanly*, a thing that carries no weight in the Judaeo-Christian scheme of morals. Like several other novelists of the first rank, Stendhal has discovered a new kind of sensitiveness. He is deeply sentimental and completely adult, and it is perhaps this unlikely combination that is the basis of his peculiar flavour.

In parts, at any rate in the opening chapters, Professor Green's is not an easy book to read, but it must have been a lot harder to write. Apart from the labour of research it needed a very difficult interweaving of biography and criticism. I doubt whether this could have been more skilfully or conscientiously done than it is here, and what is especially to be praised is the way in which Professor Green has avoided the Maurois touch and ignored the picturesqueness of Stendhal's background—the Revolution, Napoleon, etc etc. He sticks to his subject, and when he is doubtful about the facts he says so. The book was certainly needed, and it deserves to become the standard English biography of Stendhal.

New English Weekly, 27 July 1939

157. Democracy in the British Army

When the Duke of Wellington described the British army as "the scum of the earth, enlisted for drink", he was probably speaking no more than the truth. But what is significant is that his opinion would have been echoed by any non-military Englishman for nearly a hundred years subsequently.

The French Revolution and the new conception of "national" war changed the character of most continental armies, but England was in the exceptional position of being immune from invasion and of being governed during most of the nineteenth century by a non-military bourgeoisie. Consequently its army remained, as before, a small professional force more or less cut off from the rest of the nation. The war-scare of the 'sixties produced the Volunteers, later to develop into the Territorials, but it was not till a few years before the Great War that there was serious talk of universal service. Until the late nineteenth century the total number of white troops, even in wartime, never reached a quarter of a million men, and it is probable that every great British land battle between Blenheim and Loos was fought mainly by foreign soldiers.

In the nineteenth century the British common soldier was usually a farm labourer or slum proletarian who had been driven into the army by brute starvation. He enlisted for a period of at least seven years—sometimes as much as twenty-one years—and he was inured to a barrack life of endless drilling, rigid and stupid discipline, and degrading physical punishments. It was virtually impossible for him to marry, and even after the extension of the franchise he lacked the right to vote. In Indian garrison towns he could kick the "niggers" with impunity, but at home he was hated or looked down upon by the ordinary population, except in wartime, when for brief periods he was discovered to be a hero. Obviously such a man had severed his links with his own class. He was essentially a mercenary, and his self-respect depended on his conception of himself not as a worker or a citizen but simply as a fighting animal.

Since the war the conditions of army life have improved and the conception of discipline has grown more intelligent, but the British army has retained its special characteristics—small size, voluntary enlistment, long service and emphasis on regimental loyalty. Every regiment has its own name (not merely a number, as in most armies), its history and relics, its special customs, traditions, etc etc, thanks to which the whole army is honeycombed with snobberies which are almost unbelievable unless one has seen them at close quarters. Between the officers of a "smart" regiment and those of an ordinary infantry regiment, or still more a regiment of the Indian army, there is a degree of jealousy almost amounting to a class difference. And there is no question that the long-term private soldier often identifies with his own regiment almost as closely as the officer does. The effect is to make the narrow "non-political" outlook of the mercenary come more easily to him. In addition, the fact that the British army is rather heavily officered probably diminishes class friction and thus makes the lower ranks less accessible to "subversive" ideas.

But the thing which above all else forces a reactionary viewpoint on the common soldier is his service in overseas garrisons. An infantry regiment is usually quartered abroad for eighteen years consecutively, moving from place to place every four or five years, so that many soldiers serve their entire term in India, Africa, China, etc. They are only there to hold down a hostile population and the fact is brought home to them in unmistakable ways. Relations with the "natives" are almost invariably bad, and the soldiers—not so much the officers as the men—are the obvious targets for anti-British feeling. Naturally they retaliate, and as a rule they develop an attitude towards the "niggers" which is far more brutal than that of the officials or businessmen. In Burma I was constantly struck by the fact that the common soldiers were the best-hated section of the white community, and, judged simply by their behaviour, they certainly deserved to be. Even as near home as Gibraltar they walk the streets with a swaggering air which is directed at the Spanish "natives". And in practice some such attitude is absolutely necessary; you could not hold down a subject empire with troops infected by notions of class-solidarity. Most of the dirty work of the French Empire, for instance, is done not by French conscripts but by illiterate Negroes and by the Foreign Legion, a corps of pure mercenaries.

To sum up: in spite of the technical advances which do not allow the professional officer to be quite such an idiot as he used to be, and in spite of the fact that the common soldier is now treated a little more like a human being, the British army remains essentially the same machine as it was fifty years ago. A little while back any Socialist would have admitted this without argument. But we happen to be at a moment when the rise of Hitler has scared the official leaders of the Left into an attitude not far removed from jingoism. Large numbers of left-wing publicists are almost openly agitating for war. Without discussing this subject at length, it can be pointed out that a left-wing party which, within a capitalist society, becomes a war party, has already thrown up the sponge, because it is demanding a policy which can only be carried out by its opponents. The Labour leaders are intermittently aware of this—witness their shufflings on the subject of conscription. Hence, in among the cries of "Firm front!" "British prestige!" etc there mingles a quite contradictory line of talk. It is to the effect that "this time" things are going to be "different". Militarisation is not going to mean militarisation. Colonel Blimp is no longer Colonel Blimp. And in the more soft-boiled left-wing papers a phrase is bandied to and fro—"democratising the army". It is worth considering what it implies.

"Democratising" an army, if it means anything, means doing away with the predominance of a single class and introducing a less mechanical form of discipline. In the British army this would mean an entire reconstruction which would rob the army of efficiency for five to ten years. Such a process is only doubtfully possible while the

British Empire exists, and quite unthinkable while the simultaneous aim is to "stop Hitler". What will actually happen during the next couple of years, war or no war, is that the armed forces will be greatly expanded, but the new units will take their colour from the existing professional army. As in the Great War, it will be the same army, only bigger. Poorer sections of the middle class will be drawn on for the supply of officers, but the professional military caste will retain its grip. As for the new militias, it is probably quite a mistake to imagine that they are the nucleus of a "democratic army" in which all classes will start from scratch. It is fairly safe to prophesy that even if there is no class-favouritism (as there will be, presumably), militiamen of bourgeois origin will tend to be promoted first. Hore-Belisha and others have already hinted as much in a number of speeches. A fact not always appreciated by Socialists is that in England the whole of the bourgeoisie is to some extent militarised. Nearly every boy who has been to a public school has passed through the OTC (theoretically voluntary but in practice compulsory), and though this training is done between the ages of 13 and 18, it ought not to be despised. In effect the militiaman with an OTC training behind him will start with several months' advantage of the others. In any case the Military Training Act is only an experiment, aimed partly at impressing opinion abroad and partly at accustoming the English people to the idea of conscription. Once the novelty has worn off some method will be devised of keeping proletarians out of positions of command.

It is probable that the nature of modern war has made "democratic army" a contradiction in terms. The French army, for instance, based on universal service, is hardly more democratic than the British. It is just as much dominated by the professional officer and the long-service NCO and the French officer is probably rather more "Prussian" in outlook than his British equivalent. The Spanish Government militias during the first six months of war—the first year, in Catalonia—were a genuinely democratic army, but they were also a very primitive type of army, capable only of defensive actions. In that particular case a defensive strategy, coupled with propaganda, would probably have had a better chance of victory than the methods casually adopted. But if you want military efficiency in the ordinary sense, there is no escaping from the professional soldier, and so long as the professional soldier is in control he will see to it that the army is not democratised. And what is true within the armed forces is true of the nation as a whole; every increase in the strength of the military machine means more power for the forces of reaction. It is possible that some of our left-wing jingoes are acting with their eyes open. If they are, they must be aware that the *News Chronicle* version of "defence of democracy" leads directly *away* from democracy, even in the narrow nineteenth-century sense of political liberty, independence of the trade unions and freedom of speech and the press.

Left Forum, September 1939

1940

158. Letter to Victor Gollancz

The Stores
Wallington
Nr Baldock, Herts.
8 January 1940

Dear Mr Gollancz,

I cannot *at this moment* lend you *Tropic of Cancer*, because my copy has been seized. While I was writing my last book two detectives suddenly arrived at my house with orders from the public prosecutor to seize all books which I had "received through the post". A letter of mine addressed to the Obelisk Press had been seized and opened in the post. The police were only carrying out orders and were very nice about it, and even the public prosecutor wrote and said that he understood that as a writer I might have a need for books which it was illegal to possess. On these grounds he sent me back certain books, e.g. *Lady Chatterley's Lover*, but it appears that Miller's books have not been in print long enough to have become respectable. However, I know that Cyril Connolly has a copy of *Tropic of Cancer*. He is down with flu at present, but when I can get in touch with him again I will borrow the book and pass it on to you.

As to your remarks on my book.[1] I am glad you liked it. You are perhaps right in thinking I am over-pessimistic. It is quite possible that freedom of thought etc may survive in an economically totalitarian society. We can't tell until a collectivised economy has been tried out in a western country. What worries me at present is the uncertainty as to whether the ordinary people in countries like England grasp the difference between democracy and despotism well enough to want to defend their liberties. One can't tell until they see themselves menaced in some quite unmistakable manner. The intellectuals who are at present pointing out that democracy and fascism are the same thing etc depress me horribly. However, per-

[1] The manuscript of *Inside the Whale*.

haps when the pinch comes the common people will turn out to be more intelligent than the clever ones. I certainly hope so.

Yours sincerely
Eric Blair

159. Letter to Geoffrey Gorer

The Stores
Wallington
Nr Baldock, Herts.
10 January 1940

Dear Geoffrey,
It seems an age since I saw you or heard from you. I wonder what hemisphere you are in at the moment, but anyway I'll send this to Highgate trusting it'll be forwarded. I rang you up at about the beginning of the war & your brother answered & said you were in America.

We got back from Morocco in the spring & I began on another book,[1] then I'm sorry to say my father died,[2] all very painful & upsetting but I was glad when the poor old man went because he was 82 & had suffered a lot his last few months. Then I got going on the book again & then the war threw me out of my stride, so in the end a very short book that was meant to take 4 months took me 6 or 7. It ought to come out in March & I think parts of it might interest you. I have so far completely failed to serve HM government in any capacity, though I want to, because it seems to me that now we are in this bloody war we have got to win it & I would like to lend a hand. They won't have me in the army, at any rate at present, because of my lungs. Eileen has got a job in a government department,[3] which as usual she got by knowing somebody who knew somebody, etc etc. I also want a job because I want to lay off writing for a bit, I feel I have written myself out & ought to lie fallow. I am sort of incubating an enormous novel, the family saga sort of thing, only I don't want to begin it before I'm all set. It is frightfully bad for one, this feeling of the publisher's wingèd chariot hurrying near all the time. Have you

[1] *Inside the Whale.*
[2] Richard Blair died at Southwold on 28 June 1939.
[3] In the Censorship Department.

seen the new monthly magazine, *Horizon*, that Cyril Connolly & Stephen Spender are running? They are trying to get away from the bloody political squirrel-cage, & about time too. I saw Gollancz recently & he is furious with his Communist late-friends, owing to their lies etc, so perhaps the Left Book Club may become quite a power for good again, if it manages to survive. I believe there is going to be a bad paper-shortage some time next year & the number of books published will be curtailed. At the moment however the publishers are rather chirpy because the war makes people read more. Let me know how you are getting on, whether you're in England or when you're likely to be, & if you *can* indicate any wire I could pull to get a job, of course I'd be obliged. Eileen would send love if she were here.

Yours
Eric

160. Review

The Last Days of Madrid by S. Casado

Although not many people outside Spain had heard of him before the beginning of 1939, Colonel Casado's name will always be among those that are remembered in connection with the Spanish civil war. He it was who overthrew the Negrin Government and negotiated the surrender of Madrid—and, considering the actual military situation and the sufferings of the Spanish people, it is difficult not to feel that he was right. The truly disgraceful thing, as Mr Croft-Cooke says forcibly in his introduction, was that the war was ever allowed to continue so long. Colonel Casado and those associated with him were denounced all over the world in the left-wing press as traitors, crypto-Fascists, etc etc, but these accusations came very badly from people who had saved their own skins long before Franco entered Madrid. Besteiro, who took part in the Casado administration and afterwards stayed behind to face the Fascists, was also denounced as "pro-Franco". Besteiro was given thirty years' imprisonment! The Fascists certainly have a strange way of treating their friends.

Perhaps the chief interest of Colonel Casado's book is the light it throws on the Russian intervention in Spain and the Spanish reaction to it. Although well-meaning people denied it at the time, there is little doubt that from the middle of 1937 until nearly the end of the war the Spanish Government was directly under the control of Moscow. The ultimate motives of the Russians are uncertain, but at any rate they aimed at setting up in Spain a government obedient to their own orders, and in the Negrin Government they had one. But the bid that they had made for middle-class support produced unforeseen complications. In the earlier part of the war the main adversaries of the Communists in their fight for power had been the Anarchists and left-wing Socialists, and the emphasis of Communist propaganda was therefore on a "moderate" policy. The effect of this was to put power into the hands of "bourgeois Republican" officers and officials, of whom Colonel Casado became the leader. But these people were first and foremost Spaniards and resented the Russian interference almost as much as that of the Germans and Italians. Consequently the Communist-Anarchist struggle was followed by another struggle of Communists against Republicans, in which the Negrin Government was finally overthrown and many Communists lost their lives.

The very important question that this raises is whether a western country can in practice be controlled by Communists acting under Russian orders. It is a question that will probably come to the front again in the event of a revolution of the Left in Germany. The inference from Colonel Casado's book seems to be that a western or westernised people will not for any length of time allow itself to be governed from Moscow. Making all allowance for the prejudice he undoubtedly feels against the Russians and their local Communist agents, his account leaves very little doubt that the Russian domination was widely and deeply resented in Spain. He also suggests that it was the knowledge of the Russian intervention that decided Britain and France to leave the Spanish Government to its fate. This seems more doubtful. If the British and French Governments had really wanted to counter the Russian influence, by far the quickest way was to supply the Spanish Government with arms, for it had been obvious from the start that any country that supplied arms could control Spanish policy. One must conclude that the British and French Governments not only wanted Franco to win, but would in any case have preferred a Russian-controlled government to a Socialist-Anarchist combination under some such leader as Caballero.

Time and Tide, 20 January 1940

161. Letter to David H. Thomson

The Stores,
Wallington
Nr Baldock, Herts.
8 March 1940

Dear Mr Thomson,[1]

Many thanks for your letter. I am glad you enjoyed the article.[2] The whole problem of children's papers is very difficult, because I am convinced that children need this rubbish and lose something if they don't get it (merely from a literary point of view I am sure it is better to start life on penny dreadfuls than on "good" books), but at the same time it is inevitably poisoned at the source because of the special way in which the press in England is owned. The number of letters I have received about this brings it home to me that a lot of people have been thinking about this lately, and perhaps it is not too much to hope that some paper like the *News Chronicle* may some time start as a sideline a run of children's papers or women's papers with a more up-to-date ideology. I am sure the public for it exists. The immediate success of papers like *Picture Post* and the *News Review* shows how very much more thoughtful and also "left-wing" the non-highbrow public has grown during the last few years.

By the way, as the article interested you [you] might like the book it is included in (*Inside the Whale*). It is coming out on Monday and would no doubt be procurable from the library. The article had to be abridged a little for publication in *Horizon.*

Yours sincerely
George Orwell

***Inside the Whale**, a Book of Essays* ("*Charles Dickens*", "*Boys' Weeklies*" *and* "*Inside the Whale*") *was published in London by Victor Gollancz Ltd on 11 March 1940.*

162. Charles Dickens

I

Dickens is one of those writers who are well worth stealing. Even the burial of his body in Westminster Abbey was a species of theft, if you come to think of it.

[1] Deputy Regional Officer, National Council of Social Service.

[2] "Boys' Weeklies". See 163.

When Chesterton wrote his Introductions to the Everyman Edition of Dickens's works, it seemed quite natural to him to credit Dickens with his own highly individual brand of medievalism, and more recently a Marxist writer, Mr T. A. Jackson,[1] has made spirited efforts to turn Dickens into a bloodthirsty revolutionary. The Marxist claims him as "almost" a Marxist, the Catholic claims him as "almost" a Catholic, and both claim him as a champion of the proletariat (or "the poor", as Chesterton would have put it). On the other hand, Nadezhda Krupskaya, in her little book on Lenin, relates that towards the end of his life Lenin went to see a dramatised version of *The Cricket on the Hearth*, and found Dickens's "middle-class sentimentality" so intolerable that he walked out in the middle of a scene.

Taking "middle-class" to mean what Krupskaya might be expected to mean by it, this was probably a truer judgement than those of Chesterton and Jackson. But it is worth noticing that the dislike of Dickens implied in this remark is something unusual. Plenty of people have found him unreadable, but very few seem to have felt any hostility towards the general spirit of his work. Some years ago Mr Bechhofer Roberts published a full-length attack on Dickens in the form of a novel (*This Side Idolatry*), but it was a merely personal attack, concerned for the most part with Dickens's treatment of his wife. It dealt with incidents which not one in a thousand of Dickens's readers would ever hear about, and which no more invalidate his work than the second-best bed invalidates *Hamlet*. All that the book really demonstrated was that a writer's literary personality has little or nothing to do with his private character. It is quite possible that in private life Dickens was just the kind of insensitive egoist that Mr Bechhofer Roberts makes him appear. But in his published work there is implied a personality quite different from this, a personality which has won him far more friends than enemies. It might well have been otherwise, for even if Dickens was a bourgeois, he was certainly a subversive writer, a radical, one might truthfully say a rebel. Everyone who has read widely in his work has felt this. Gissing, for instance, the best of the writers on Dickens, was anything but a radical himself, and he disapproved of this strain in Dickens and wished it were not there, but it never occurred to him to deny it. In *Oliver Twist*, *Hard Times*, *Bleak House*, *Little Dorrit*, Dickens attacked English institutions with a ferocity that has never since been ap-

[1] *Charles Dickens: The Progress of a Radical* by T. A. Jackson, 1937.

proached. Yet he managed to do it without making himself hated, and, more than this, the very people he attacked have swallowed him so completely that he has become a national institution himself. In its attitude towards Dickens the English public has always been a little like the elephant which feels a blow with a walking-stick as a delightful tickling. Before I was ten years old I was having Dickens ladled down my throat by schoolmasters in whom even at that age I could see a strong resemblance to Mr Creakle, and one knows without needing to be told that lawyers delight in Serjeant Buzfuz and that *Little Dorrit* is a favourite in the Home Office. Dickens seems to have succeeded in attacking everybody and antagonising nobody. Naturally this makes one wonder whether after all there was something unreal in his attack upon society. Where exactly does he stand, socially, morally and politically? As usual, one can define his position more easily if one starts by deciding what he was *not*.

In the first place he was *not*, as Messrs Chesterton and Jackson seem to imply, a "proletarian" writer. To begin with, he does not write about the proletariat, in which he merely resembles the overwhelming majority of novelists, past and present. If you look for the working classes in fiction, and especially English fiction, all you find is a hole. This statement needs qualifying, perhaps. For reasons that are easy enough to see, the agricultural labourer (in England a proletarian) gets a fairly good showing in fiction, and a great deal has been written about criminals, derelicts and, more recently, the working-class intelligentsia. But the ordinary town proletariat, the people who make the wheels go round, have always been ignored by novelists. When they do find their way between the covers of a book, it is nearly always as objects of pity or as comic relief. The central action of Dickens's stories almost invariably takes place in middle-class surroundings. If one examines his novels in detail one finds that his real subject-matter is the London commercial bourgeoisie and their hangers-on—lawyers, clerks, tradesmen, innkeepers, small craftsmen and servants. He has no portrait of an agricultural worker, and only one (Stephen Blackpool in *Hard Times*) of an industrial worker. The Plornishes in *Little Dorrit* are probably his best picture of a working-class family—the Peggottys, for instance, hardly belong to the working class—but on the whole he is not successful with this type of character. If you ask any ordinary reader which of Dickens's proletarian characters he can remember, the three he is almost certain to mention are Bill Sikes, Sam Weller and Mrs Gamp. A burglar, a valet and a drunken midwife—not exactly a representative cross-section of the English working class.

Secondly, in the ordinarily accepted sense of the word, Dickens is not a "revolutionary" writer. But his position here needs some defining.

Whatever else Dickens may have been, he was not a hole-and-corner soul-saver, the kind of well-meaning idiot who thinks that the world will be perfect if you amend a few by-laws and abolish a few anomalies. It is worth comparing him with Charles Reade, for instance. Reade was a much better informed man than Dickens, and in some ways more public-spirited. He really hated the abuses he could understand, he showed them up in a series of novels which for all their absurdity are extremely readable, and he probably helped to alter public opinion on a few minor but important points. But it was quite beyond him to grasp that, given the existing form of society, certain evils *cannot* be remedied. Fasten upon this or that minor abuse, expose it, drag it into the open, bring it before a British jury, and all will be well—that is how he sees it. Dickens at any rate never imagined that you can cure pimples by cutting them off. In every page of his work one can see a consciousness that society is wrong somewhere at the root. It is when one asks "Which root?" that one begins to grasp his position.

The truth is that Dickens's criticism of society is almost exclusively moral. Hence the utter lack of any constructive suggestion anywhere in his work. He attacks the law, parliamentary government, the educational system and so forth, without ever clearly suggesting what he would put in their places. Of course it is not necessarily the business of a novelist, or a satirist, to make constructive suggestions, but the point is that Dickens's attitude is at bottom not even *de*structive. There is no clear sign that he wants the existing order to be overthrown, or that he believes it would make very much difference if it *were* overthrown. For in reality his target is not so much society as "human nature". It would be difficult to point anywhere in his books to a passage suggesting that the economic system is wrong *as a system*. Nowhere, for instance, does he make any attack on private enterprise or private property. Even in a book like *Our Mutual Friend*, which turns on the power of corpses to interfere with living people by means of idiotic wills, it does not occur to him to suggest that individuals ought not to have this irresponsible power. Of course one can draw this inference for oneself, and one can draw it again from the remarks about Bounderby's will at the end of *Hard Times*, and indeed from the whole of Dickens's work one can infer the evil of *laissez-faire* capitalism; but Dickens makes no such inference himself. It is said that Macaulay refused to review *Hard Times* because he disapproved of its "sullen Socialism". Obviously Macaulay is here using the word "Socialism" in the same sense in which, twenty years ago, a vegetarian meal or a Cubist picture used to be referred to as "Bolshevism". There is not a line in the book that can properly be called Socialistic; indeed, its tendency if anything is pro-capitalist, because its whole moral is that capitalists ought to be kind, not that workers ought to be rebellious. Bounderby is a bullying windbag and Gradgrind has been morally blinded, but if they were better men, the system would work well enough—that, all through, is the implication. And so far as social criticism goes, one can never extract much more from Dickens than this, unless one deliberately reads meanings into him. His whole "message" is one that at first glance looks like an enormous platitude: If men would behave decently the world would be decent.

Naturally this calls for a few characters who are in positions of authority and who *do* behave decently. Hence that recurrent Dickens figure, the Good Rich Man. This character belongs especially to Dickens's early optimistic period. He is usually a "merchant" (we are not necessarily told what merchandise he deals in), and he is always a superhumanly kind-hearted old gentleman who "trots" to and fro, raising his employees' wages, patting children on the head, getting debtors out of jail and, in general, acting the fairy godmother. Of course he is a pure dream figure, much further from real life than, say, Squeers or Micawber. Even Dickens must have reflected occasionally that anyone who was so anxious to give his money away would never have acquired it in the first place. Mr Pickwick, for instance, had "been in the city", but it is difficult to imagine him making a fortune there. Nevertheless this character runs like a connecting thread through most of the earlier books. Pickwick, the Cheerybles, old Chuzzlewit, Scrooge—it is the same figure over and over again, the good rich man, handing out guineas. Dickens does however show signs of development here. In the books of the middle period the good rich man fades out to some extent. There is no one who plays this part in *A Tale of Two Cities*, nor in *Great Expectations*—*Great Expectations* is, in fact, definitely an attack on patronage—and in *Hard Times* it is only very doubtfully played by Gradgrind after his reformation. The character reappears in a rather different form as Meagles in *Little Dorrit* and John Jarndyce in *Bleak House*—one might perhaps add Betsy Trotwood in *David Copperfield.* But in these books the good rich man has dwindled from a "merchant" to a *rentier.* This is significant. A *rentier* is part of the possessing class, he can and, almost without knowing it, does make other people work for him, but he has very little direct power. Unlike Scrooge or the Cheerybles, he cannot put everything right by raising everybody's wages. The seeming inference from the rather despondent books that Dickens wrote in the 'fifties is that by that time he had grasped the helplessness of well-meaning individuals in a corrupt society. Nevertheless in the last completed novel, *Our Mutual Friend* (published 1864–5), the good rich man comes back in full glory in the person of Boffin. Boffin is a proletarian by origin and only rich by inheritance, but he is the usual *deus ex machina,* solving everybody's problems by showering money in all directions. He even "trots" like the Cheerybles. In several ways *Our Mutual Friend* is a return to the earlier manner, and not an unsuccessful return either. Dickens's thoughts seem to have come full circle. Once again, individual kindliness is the remedy for everything.

One crying evil of his time that Dickens says very little about is child labour. There are plenty of pictures of suffering children in his books, but usually they are suffering in schools rather than in factories. The one detailed account of child labour that he gives is the description in *David Copperfield* of little David washing bottles in Murdstone & Grinby's warehouse. This, of course, is autobiography. Dickens himself, at the age of ten, had worked in Warren's blacking factory in the Strand, very much as he describes it here. It was a terribly bitter memory to him, partly because he felt the whole incident to be discreditable to his parents, and he even concealed it from his wife till long after they were married. Looking back on this period, he says in *David Copperfield*:

> It is a matter of some surprise to me, even now, that I can have been so easily thrown away at such an age. A child of excellent abilities and with strong powers of observation, quick, eager, delicate, and soon hurt bodily or mentally, it seems wonderful to me that nobody should have made any sign in my behalf. But none was made; and I became, at ten years old, a little labouring hind in the service of Murdstone & Grinby.

And again, having described the rough boys among whom he worked:

> No words can express the secret agony of my soul as I sunk into this companionship . . . and felt my hopes of growing up to be a learned and distinguished man crushed in my bosom.

Obviously it is not David Copperfield who is speaking, it is Dickens himself. He uses almost the same words in the autobiography that he began and abandoned a few months earlier. Of course Dickens is right in saying that a gifted child ought not to work ten hours a day pasting labels on bottles, but what he does not say is that *no* child ought to be condemned to such a fate, and there is no reason for inferring that he thinks it. David escapes from the warehouse, but Mick Walker and Mealy Potatoes and the others are still there, and there is no sign that this troubles Dickens particularly. As usual, he displays no consciousness that the *structure* of society can be changed. He despises politics, does not believe that any good can come out of Parliament—he had been a parliamentary shorthand writer, which was no doubt a disillusioning experience—and he is slightly hostile to the most hopeful movement of his day, trade unionism. In *Hard Times* trade unionism is represented as something not much better than a racket, something that happens because employers are not sufficiently paternal. Stephen Blackpool's refusal to join the union is rather a virtue in Dickens's eyes. Also, as Mr Jackson has pointed out, the apprentices' association in *Barnaby Rudge*, to which Sim Tappertit belongs, is probably a hit at the illegal or barely legal unions of Dickens's own day, with their secret assemblies, passwords and so forth. Obviously he wants the workers to be decently treated, but there is no sign that he wants them to take their destiny into their own hands, least of all by open violence.

As it happens, Dickens deals with revolution in the narrower sense in two novels, *Barnaby Rudge* and *A Tale of Two Cities*. In *Barnaby Rudge* it is a case of rioting rather than revolution. The Gordon Riots of 1780, though they had religious bigotry as a pretext, seem to have been little more than a pointless outburst of looting. Dickens's attitude to this kind of thing is sufficiently indicated by the fact that his first idea was to make the ringleaders of the riots three lunatics escaped from an asylum. He was dissuaded from this, but the principal figure of the book is in fact a village idiot. In the chapters dealing with the riots Dickens shows a most profound horror of mob violence. He delights in describing scenes in which the "dregs" of the population behave with atrocious bestiality. These chapters are of great psychological interest, because they show how deeply he had brooded on this subject. The things he describes can only have come out of his imagination, for no riots on anything like the same scale had happened in his lifetime. Here is one of his descriptions, for instance:

> If Bedlam gates had been flung open wide, there would not have issued forth such maniacs as the frenzy of that night had made. There were men there who danced and trampled on the beds of flowers as though they trod down human enemies, and wrenched them from their stalks, like savages who twisted human necks. There were men who cast their lighted torches in the air, and suffered them to fall upon their heads and faces, blistering the skin with deep unseemly burns. There were men who rushed up to the fire, and paddled in it with their hands as if in water; and others who were restrained by force from plunging in, to gratify their deadly longing. On the skull of one drunken lad—not twenty, by his looks—who lay upon the ground with a bottle to his mouth, the lead from the roof came streaming down in a shower of liquid fire, white hot, melting his head like wax. . . . But of all the howling throng not one learnt mercy from, or sickened at, these sights; nor was the fierce, besotted, senseless rage of one man glutted.

You might almost think you were reading a description of "red" Spain by a partisan of General Franco. One ought, of course, to remember that when Dickens was writing, the London "mob" still existed. (Nowadays there is no mob, only a flock.) Low wages and the growth and shift of population had brought into existence a huge, dangerous slum-proletariat, and until the early middle of the nineteenth century there was hardly such a thing as a police force. When the brickbats began to fly there was nothing between shuttering your windows and ordering the troops to open fire. In *A Tale of Two Cities* he is dealing with a revolution which was really *about* something, and Dickens's attitude is different, but not entirely different. As a matter of fact, *A Tale of Two Cities* is a book which tends to leave a false impression behind, especially after a lapse of time.

The one thing that everyone who has read *A Tale of Two Cities* remembers is the Reign of Terror. The whole book is dominated by the guillotine—tumbrils thundering to and fro, bloody knives, heads bouncing into the basket, and sinister old women knitting as they watch. Actually these scenes only occupy a few chapters, but they are written with terrible intensity, and the rest of the book is rather slow going. But *A Tale of Two Cities* is not a companion volume to *The Scarlet Pimpernel.* Dickens sees clearly enough that the French Revolution was bound to happen and that many of the people who were executed deserved what they got. If, he says, you behave as the French aristocracy had behaved, vengeance will follow. He repeats this over and over again. We are constantly being reminded that while "my lord" is lolling in bed, with four liveried footmen serving his chocolate and the peasants starving outside, somewhere in the forest a tree is growing which will presently be sawn into planks for the platform of the guillotine, etc etc etc. The inevitability of the Terror, given its causes, is insisted upon in the clearest terms:

> It was too much the way . . . to talk of this terrible Revolution as if it were the only harvest ever known under the skies that had not been sown—as if nothing had ever been done, or omitted to be done, that had led to it—as if observers of the wretched millions in France, and of the misused and perverted resources that should have made them prosperous, had not seen it inevitably coming, years before, and had not in plain terms recorded what they saw.

And again:

> All the devouring and insatiate monsters imagined since imagination could record itself, are fused in the one realisation, Guillotine. And yet there is not in France, with its rich variety of soil and climate, a blade, a leaf, a root, a sprig, a peppercorn, which will grow to maturity under conditions more certain than those that have produced this horror. Crush humanity out of shape once more, under similar hammers, and it will twist itself into the same tortured forms.

In other words, the French aristocracy had dug their own graves. But there is no perception here of what is now called historic necessity. Dickens sees that the results are inevitable, given the causes, but he thinks that the causes might have been avoided. The Revolution is something that happens because centuries of oppression have made the French peasantry sub-human. If the wicked nobleman could somehow have turned over a new leaf, like Scrooge, there would have been no Revolution, no *jacquerie*, no guillotine—and so much the better. This is the opposite of the "revolutionary" attitude. From the "revolutionary" point of view the class-struggle is the main source of progress, and therefore the nobleman who robs the peasant and goads him to revolt is playing a necessary part, just as much as the Jacobin who guillotines the nobleman. Dickens never writes anywhere a line that can be interpreted as meaning this. Revolution as he sees it is merely a monster that is begotten by tyranny and always ends by devouring its own instruments. In Sydney Carton's vision at the foot of the guillotine, he foresees Defarge and the other leading spirits of the Terror all perishing under the same knife—which, in fact, was approximately what happened.

And Dickens is very sure that revolution *is* a monster. That is why everyone remembers the revolutionary scenes in *A Tale of Two Cities*; they have the quality of nightmare, and it is Dickens's own nightmare. Again and again he insists upon the meaningless horrors of revolution—the mass-butcheries, the injustice, the ever-present terror of spies, the frightful blood-lust of the mob. The descriptions of the Paris mob—the description, for instance, of the crowd of murderers struggling round the grindstone to sharpen their weapons before butchering the prisoners in the September massacres—outdo anything in *Barnaby Rudge*. The revolutionaries appear to him simply as degraded savages—in fact, as lunatics. He broods over their frenzies with a curious imaginative intensity. He describes them dancing the "Carmagnole", for instance:

> There could not be fewer than five hundred people, and they were dancing like five thousand demons. . . . They danced to the popular Revolution song, keeping a ferocious time that was like a gnashing of teeth in unison. . . . They advanced, retreated, struck at one another's hands, clutched at one another's heads, spun round alone, caught one another, and spun round in pairs, until many of them dropped. . . . Suddenly they stopped again, paused, struck out the time afresh, forming into lines the width of the public way, and, with their heads low down and their hands high up, swooped screaming off. No fight could have been half so terrible as this dance. It was so emphatically a fallen sport—a something, once innocent, delivered over to all devilry.

He even credits some of these wretches with a taste for guillotining children. The passage I have abridged above ought to be read in full. It and others like it show how deep was Dickens's horror of revolutionary hysteria. Notice, for instance, that touch, "with their heads low down and their hands high up" etc, and the evil vision it conveys. Madame Defarge is a truly dreadful figure, certainly Dickens's most successful attempt at a *malignant* character. Defarge and others are simply "the new oppressors who have risen on the destruction of the old", the revolutionary courts are presided over by "the lowest, cruellest and worst populace", and so on and so forth. All the way through Dickens insists upon the nightmare insecurity of a revolutionary period, and in this he shows a great deal of prescience. "A law of the suspected, which struck away all security for liberty or life, and delivered over any good and innocent person to any bad and guilty one; prisons gorged with people who had committed no offence, and could obtain no hearing"—it would apply pretty accurately to several countries today.

The apologists of any revolution generally try to minimise its horrors; Dickens's impulse is to exaggerate them—and from a historical point of view he has certainly exaggerated. Even the Reign of Terror was a much smaller thing than he makes it appear. Though he quotes no figures, he gives the impression of a frenzied massacre lasting for years, whereas in reality the whole of the Terror, so far as the number of deaths goes, was a joke compared with one of Napoleon's battles. But the bloody knives and the tumbrils rolling to and fro create in his mind a special, sinister vision which he has succeeded in passing on to generations of readers. Thanks to Dickens, the very word "tumbril" has a murderous sound; one forgets that a tumbril is only a sort of farm-cart. To this day, to the average Englishman, the French Revolution means no more than a pyramid of severed heads. It is a strange thing that Dickens, much more in sympathy with the ideas of the Revolution than most Englishmen of his time, should have played a part in creating this impression.

If you hate violence and don't believe in politics, the only major remedy remaining is education. Perhaps society is past praying for, but there is always hope for the individual human being, if you can catch him young enough. This belief partly accounts for Dickens's preoccupation with childhood.

No one, at any rate no English writer, has written better about childhood than Dickens. In spite of all the knowledge that has accumulated since, in spite of the fact that children are now comparatively sanely treated, no novelist has shown the same power of entering into the child's point of view. I must have been about nine years old when I first read *David Copperfield.* The mental atmosphere of the opening chapters was so immediately intelligible to me that I vaguely imagined they had been written *by a child.* And yet when one re-reads the book as an adult and sees the Murdstones, for instance, dwindle from gigantic figures of doom into semi-comic monsters, these passages lose nothing. Dickens has been able to stand both inside and outside the child's mind, in such a way that the same scene can be wild burlesque or sinister reality, according to the age at which one reads it. Look, for instance, at the scene in which David Copperfield is unjustly suspected of eating the mutton chops; or the scene in which Pip, in *Great Expectations,* coming back from Miss Havisham's house and finding himself completely unable to describe what he has seen, takes refuge in a series of outrageous lies—which, of course, are eagerly believed. All the isolation of childhood is there. And how accurately he has recorded the mechanisms of the child's mind, its visualising tendency, its sensitiveness to certain kinds of impression. Pip relates how in his childhood his ideas about his dead parents were derived from their tombstones:

> The shape of the letters on my father's, gave me an odd idea that he was a square, stout, dark man, with curly black hair. From the character and turn of the inscription, "ALSO GEORGIANA, WIFE OF THE ABOVE", I drew a childish conclusion that my mother was freckled and sickly. To five little stone lozenges, each about a foot and a half long, which were arranged in a neat row beside their grave, and were sacred to the memory of five little brothers of mine . . . I am indebted for a belief I religiously entertained that they had all been born on their backs with their hands in their trouser-pockets, and had never taken them out in this state of existence.

There is a similar passage in *David Copperfield.* After biting Mr Murdstone's hand, David is sent away to school and obliged to wear on his back a placard saying, "Take care of him. He bites". He looks at the door in the playground where the boys have carved their names, and from the appearance of each name he seems to know in just what tone of voice the boy will read out the placard:

> There was one boy—a certain J. Steerforth—who cut his name

> very deep and very often, who, I conceived, would read it in a rather strong voice, and afterwards pull my hair. There was another boy, one Tommy Traddles, who I dreaded would make game of it, and pretend to be dreadfully frightened of me. There was a third, George Demple, who I fancied would sing it.

When I read this passage as a child, it seemed to me that those were exactly the pictures that those particular names would call up. The reason, of course, is the sound-associations of the words (Demple—"temple"; Traddles—probably "skedaddle"). But how many people, before Dickens, had ever noticed such things? A sympathetic attitude towards children was a much rarer thing in Dickens's day than it is now. The early nineteenth century was not a good time to be a child. In Dickens's youth children were still being "solemnly tried at a criminal bar, where they were held up to be seen", and it was not so long since boys of thirteen had been hanged for petty theft. The doctrine of "breaking the child's spirit" was in full vigour, and *The Fairchild Family*[1] was a standard book for children till late into the century. This evil book is now issued in pretty-pretty expurgated editions, but it is well worth reading in the original version. It gives one some idea of the lengths to which child-discipline was sometimes carried. Mr Fairchild, for instance, when he catches his children quarrelling, first thrashes them, reciting Doctor Watts's "Let dogs delight to bark and bite" between blows of the cane, and then takes them to spend the afternoon beneath a gibbet where the rotting corpse of a murderer is hanging. In the earlier part of the century scores of thousands of children, aged sometimes as young as six, were literally worked to death in the mines or cotton mills, and even at the fashionable public schools boys were flogged till they ran with blood for a mistake in their Latin verses. One thing which Dickens seems to have recognised, and which most of his contemporaries did not, is the sadistic sexual element in flogging. I think this can be inferred from *David Copperfield* and *Nicholas Nickleby*. But mental cruelty to a child infuriates him as much as physical, and though there is a fair number of exceptions, his schoolmasters are generally scoundrels.

Except for the universities and the big public schools, every kind of education then existing in England gets a mauling at Dickens's hands. There is Doctor Blimber's Academy, where little boys are

[1] *The History of the Fairchild Family* by May M. Sherwood, 3 parts, 1818–47.

blown up with Greek until they burst, and the revolting charity schools of the period, which produced specimens like Noah Claypole and Uriah Heep, and Salem House, and Dotheboys Hall, and the disgraceful little dame-school kept by Mr Wopsle's great-aunt. Some of what Dickens says remains true even today. Salem House is the ancestor of the modern "prep school", which still has a good deal of resemblance to it; and as for Mr Wopsle's great-aunt, some old fraud of much the same stamp is carrying on at this moment in nearly every small town in England. But, as usual, Dickens's criticism is neither creative nor destructive. He sees the idiocy of an educational system founded on the Greek lexicon and the wax-ended cane; on the other hand, he has no use for the new kind of school that is coming up in the 'fifties and 'sixties, the "modern" school, with its gritty insistence on "facts". What, then, *does* he want? As always, what he appears to want is a moralised version of the existing thing—the old type of school, but with no caning, no bullying or underfeeding, and not quite so much Greek. Doctor Strong's school, to which David Copperfield goes after he escapes from Murdstone & Grinby's, is simply Salem House with the vices left out and a good deal of "old grey stones" atmosphere thrown in:

> Doctor Strong's was an excellent school, as different from Mr Creakle's as good is from evil. It was very gravely and decorously ordered, and on a sound system; with an appeal, in everything, to the honour and good faith of the boys . . . which worked wonders. We all felt that we had a part in the management of the place, and in sustaining its character and dignity. Hence, we soon became warmly attached to it—I am sure I did for one, and I never knew, in all my time, of any boy being otherwise—and learnt with a good will, desiring to do it credit. We had noble games out of hours, and plenty of liberty; but even then, as I remember, we were well spoken of in the town, and rarely did any disgrace, by our appearance or manner, to the reputation of Doctor Strong and Doctor Strong's boys.

In the woolly vagueness of this passage one can see Dickens's utter lack of any educational theory. He can imagine the *moral* atmosphere of a good school, but nothing further. The boys "learnt with a good will", but what did they learn? No doubt it was Doctor Blimber's curriculum, a little watered down. Considering the attitude to society that is everywhere implied in Dickens's novels, it comes as rather a shock to learn that he sent his eldest son to Eton and sent all his children through the ordinary educational mill. Gissing seems to think that he may have done this because he was painfully conscious of being under-educated himself. Here perhaps Gissing is influenced by his own love of classical learning. Dickens had had little or no formal education, but he lost nothing by missing it, and on the whole he seems to have been aware of this. If he was unable to imagine a better school than Doctor Strong's, or, in real life, than Eton, it was probably due to an intellectual deficiency rather different from the one Gissing suggests.

It seems that in every attack Dickens makes upon society he is always pointing to a change of spirit rather than a change of structure. It is hopeless to try and pin him down to any definite remedy, still more to any political doctrine. His approach is always along the moral plane, and his attitude is sufficiently summed up in that remark about Strong's school being as different from Creakle's "as good is from evil". Two things can be very much alike and yet abysmally different. Heaven and Hell are in the same place. Useless to change institutions without a "change of heart"—that, essentially, is what he is always saying.

If that were all, he might be no more than a cheer-up writer, a reactionary humbug. A "change of heart" is in fact *the* alibi of people who do not wish to endanger the *status quo.* But Dickens is not a humbug, except in minor matters, and the strongest single impression one carries away from his books is that of a hatred of tyranny. I said earlier that Dickens is not *in the accepted sense* a revolutionary writer. But it is not at all certain that a merely moral criticism of society may not be just as "revolutionary"—and revolution, after all, means turning things upside down—as the politico-economic criticism which is fashionable at this moment. Blake was not a politician, but there is more understanding of the nature of capitalist society in a poem like "I wander through each charter'd street" than in three-quarters of Socialist literature. Progress is not an illusion, it happens, but it is slow and invariably disappointing. There is always a new tyrant waiting to take over from the old—generally not quite so bad, but still a tyrant. Consequently two viewpoints are always tenable. The one, how can you improve human nature until you have changed the system? The other, what is the use of changing the system before you have improved human nature? They appeal to different individuals, and they probably show a tendency to alternate in point of time. The moralist and the revolutionary are constantly undermining one another. Marx exploded a hundred tons of dynamite beneath the moralist position, and we are still living in the echo of that tremendous crash. But already, somewhere or other, the sappers are at work and fresh dynamite is being stamped in place to blow Marx at the moon. Then Marx, or somebody like him, will come back with yet more dynamite, and so the process continues, to an end we cannot yet foresee. The central problem—how to prevent power from being abused—remains unsolved. Dickens, who had not the vision to see that private property is an obstructive nuisance, had the vision to see that. "If men would behave decently the world would be decent" is not such a platitude as it sounds.

II

More completely than most writers, perhaps, Dickens can be explained in terms of his social origin, though actually his family history was not quite what one would infer from his novels. His father was a clerk in government service, and through his mother's family he had connections with both the army and the navy. But from the age of nine onwards he was brought up in London in commercial surroundings, and generally in an atmosphere of struggling poverty. Mentally he belongs to the small urban bourgeoisie, and he happens to be an exceptionally fine specimen of this class, with all the "points", as it were, very highly developed. That is partly what makes him so interesting. If one wants a modern equivalent, the nearest would be H. G. Wells, who has had a rather similar history and who obviously owes something to Dickens as a novelist. Arnold Bennett was essentially of the same type, but, unlike the other two, he was a midlander, with an industrial and Nonconformist rather than commercial and Anglican background.

The great disadvantage, and advantage, of the small urban bourgeois is his limited outlook. He sees the world as a middle-class world, and everything outside these limits is either laughable or slightly wicked. On the one hand, he has no contact with industry or the soil; on the other, no contact with the governing classes. Anyone who has studied Wells's novels in detail will have noticed that though he hates the aristocrat like poison, he has no particular objection to the plutocrat, and no enthusiasm for the proletarian. His most hated types, the people he believes to be responsible for all human ills, are kings, landowners, priests, nationalists, soldiers, scholars and peasants. At first sight a list beginning with kings and ending with peasants looks like a mere omnium gatherum, but in reality all these people have a common factor. All of them are archaic types, people who are governed by tradition and whose eyes are turned towards the past—the opposite, therefore, of the rising bourgeois who has put his money on the future and sees the past simply as a dead hand.

Actually, although Dickens lived in a period when the bourgeoisie was really a rising class, he displays this characteristic less strongly than Wells. He is almost unconscious of the future and has a rather sloppy love of the picturesque (the "quaint old church" etc). Nevertheless his list of most hated types is like enough to Wells's for the similarity to be striking. He is vaguely on the side of the working class—has a sort of generalised sympathy with them because they are oppressed—but he does not in reality know much about them; they come into his books chiefly as servants, and comic servants at that. At the other end of the scale he loathes the aristocrat and—going one better than Wells in this—loathes the big bourgeois as well. His real sympathies are bounded by Mr Pickwick on the upper side and Mr Barkis on the lower. But the term "aristocrat", for the type Dickens hates, is vague and needs defining.

Actually Dickens's target is not so much the great aristocracy, who hardly enter into his books, as their petty offshoots, the cadging dowagers who live up mews in Mayfair, and the bureaucrats and professional soldiers. All through his books there are countless hostile sketches of these people, and hardly any that are friendly. There are practically no friendly pictures of the land-owning class, for instance. One might make a doubtful exception of Sir Leicester Dedlock; otherwise there is only Mr Wardle (who is a stock figure—the "good old squire") and Haredale in *Barnaby Rudge*, who has Dickens's sympathy because he is a persecuted Catholic. There are no friendly pictures of soldiers (i.e. officers), and none at all of naval men. As for his bureaucrats, judges and magistrates, most of them would feel quite at home in the Circumlocution Office. The only officials whom Dickens handles with any kind of friendliness are, significantly enough, policemen.

Dickens's attitude is easily intelligible to an Englishman, because it is part of the English puritan tradition, which is not dead even at this day. The class Dickens belonged to, at least by adoption, was growing suddenly rich after a couple of centuries of obscurity. It had grown up mainly in the big towns, out of contact with agriculture, and politically impotent; government, in its experience, was something which either interfered or persecuted. Consequently it was a class with no tradition of public service and not much tradition of usefulness. What now strikes us as remarkable about the new moneyed class of the nineteenth century is their complete irresponsibility; they see everything in terms of individual success, with hardly any consciousness that the community exists. On the other hand, a Tite Barnacle, even when he was neglecting his duties, would have some vague notion of what duties he was neglecting. Dickens's attitude is never irresponsible, still less does he take the money-grubbing Smilesian line; but at the back of his mind there is usually a half-belief that the whole apparatus of government is unnecessary. Parliament is simply Lord Coodle and Sir Thomas Doodle, the Empire is simply Major Bagstock and his Indian servant, the army is simply Colonel Chowser and Doctor Slammer, the public services are simply Bumble and the Circumlocution Office—and so on and so forth. What he does not see, or only intermittently sees, is that Coodle and Doodle and all the other corpses left over from the eighteenth century *are* performing a function which neither Pickwick nor Boffin would ever bother about.

And of course this narrowness of vision is in one way a great advantage to him, because it is fatal for a caricaturist to see too much. From Dickens's point of view "good" society is simply a collection of village idiots. What a crew! Lady Tippins! Mrs Gowan! Lord Verisopht! The Honourable Bob Stables! Mrs Sparsit (whose husband was a Powler)! The Tite Barnacles! Nupkins! It is practically a case-book in lunacy. But at the same time his remoteness from the landowning-military-bureaucratic class incapacitates him for full-length satire. He only succeeds with this class when he depicts them as mental defectives. The accusation which used to be made against Dickens in his lifetime, that he "could not paint a gentleman", was an absurdity, but it is true in this sense, that what he says against the "gentleman" class is seldom very damaging. Sir Mulberry Hawk, for instance, is a wretched attempt at the wicked-baronet type. Harthouse in *Hard Times* is better, but he would be only an ordinary achievement for Trollope or Thackeray. Trollope's thoughts hardly move outside the "gentleman" class, but Thackeray has the great advantage of having a foot in two moral camps. In some ways his outlook is very similar to Dickens's. Like Dickens, he identifies with the puritanical moneyed class against the card-playing, debt-bilking aristocracy. The eighteenth century, as he sees it, is sticking out into the nineteenth in the person of the wicked Lord Steyne. *Vanity Fair* is a full-length version of what Dickens did for a few chapters in *Little Dorrit.* But by origins and upbringing Thackeray happens to be somewhat nearer to the class he is satirising. Consequently he can produce such comparatively subtle types as, for instance, Major Pendennis and Rawdon Crawley. Major Pendennis is a shallow old snob, and Rawdon Crawley is a thick-headed ruffian who sees nothing wrong in living for years by swindling tradesmen; but what Thackeray realises is that according to their tortuous code they are neither of them bad men. Major Pendennis would not sign a dud cheque, for instance. Rawdon certainly would, but on the other hand he would not desert a friend in a tight corner. Both of them would behave well on the field of battle—a thing that would not particularly appeal to Dickens. The result is that at the end one is left with a kind of amused tolerance for Major Pendennis and with something approaching respect for Rawdon; and yet one sees, better than any diatribe could make one, the utter rottenness of that kind of cadging, toadying life on the fringes of smart society. Dickens would be quite incapable of this. In his hands both Rawdon and the Major would dwindle to traditional caricatures. And, on the whole, his attacks on "good" society are rather perfunctory. The aristocracy and the big bourgeoisie exist in his books chiefly as a kind of "noises off", a haw-hawing chorus somewhere in the wings, like Podsnap's dinner-parties. When he produces a really subtle and damaging portrait, like John Dorrit or Harold Skimpole, it is generally of some rather middling, unimportant person.

One very striking thing about Dickens, especially considering the time he lived in, is his lack of vulgar nationalism. All peoples who have reached the point of becoming nations tend to despise foreigners, but there is not much doubt that the English-speaking races are the worst offenders. One can see this from the fact that as soon as they become fully aware of any foreign race, they invent an insulting nickname for it. Wop, Dago, Froggy, Squarehead, Kike, Sheeny, Nigger, Wog, Chink, Greaser, Yellowbelly—these are merely a selection. Any time before 1870 the list would have been shorter, because the map of the world was different from what it is now, and there were only three or four foreign races that had fully entered into the

English consciousness. But towards these, and especially towards France, the nearest and best-hated nation, the English attitude of patronage was so intolerable that English "arrogance" and "xenophobia" are still a legend. And of course they are not a completely untrue legend even now. Till very recently nearly all English children were brought up to despise the southern European races, and history as taught in schools was mainly a list of battles won by England. But one has got to read, say, the *Quarterly Review* of the 'thirties to know what boasting really is. Those were the days when the English built up their legend of themselves as "sturdy islanders" and "stubborn hearts of oak" and when it was accepted as a kind of scientific fact that one Englishman was the equal of three foreigners. All through nineteenth-century novels and comic papers there runs the traditional figure of the "Froggy"—a small ridiculous man with a tiny beard and a pointed top-hat, always jabbering and gesticulating, vain, frivolous and fond of boasting of his martial exploits, but generally taking to flight when real danger appears. Over against him was John Bull, the "sturdy English yeoman", or (a more public-school version) the "strong, silent Englishman" of Charles Kingsley, Tom Hughes and others.

Thackeray, for instance, has this outlook very strongly, though there are moments when he sees through it and laughs at it. The one historical fact that is firmly fixed in his mind is that the English won the battle of Waterloo. One never reads far in his books without coming upon some reference to it. The English, as he sees it, are invincible because of their tremendous physical strength, due mainly to living on beef. Like most Englishmen of his time, he has the curious illusion that the English are larger than other people (Thackeray, as it happened, *was* larger than most people), and therefore he is capable of writing passages like this:

> I say to you that you are better than a Frenchman. I would lay even money that you who are reading this are more than five feet seven in height, and weigh eleven stone; while a Frenchman is five feet four and does not weigh nine. The Frenchman has after his soup a dish of vegetables, where you have one of meat. You are a different and superior animal—a French-beating animal (the history of hundreds of years has shown you to be so), etc etc.

There are similar passages scattered all through Thackeray's works. Dickens would never be guilty of anything of the kind. It would be an exaggeration to say that he nowhere pokes fun at foreigners, and of course, like nearly all nineteenth-century Englishmen, he is untouched by European culture. But never anywhere does he indulge in the typical English boasting, the "island race", "bulldog breed", "right little, tight little island" style of talk. In the whole of *A Tale of Two Cities* there is not a line that could be taken as meaning, "Look how these wicked Frenchmen behave!" The one place where he seems to display a normal hatred of foreigners is in the American chapters of *Martin Chuzzlewit*. This, however, is simply the reaction of a generous mind against cant. If Dickens were alive today he would make a trip to Soviet Russia and come back with a book rather like Gide's *Retour de l'URSS*. But he is remarkably free from the idiocy of regarding nations as individuals. He seldom even makes jokes turning on nationality. He does not exploit the comic Irishman and the comic Welshman, for instance, and not because he objects to stock characters and ready-made jokes, which obviously he does not. It is perhaps more significant that he shows no prejudice against Jews. It is true that he takes it for granted (*Oliver Twist* and *Great Expectations*) that a receiver of stolen goods will be a Jew, which at the time was probably justified. But the "Jew joke", endemic in English literature until the rise of Hitler, does not appear in his books, and in *Our Mutual Friend* he makes a pious though not very convincing attempt to stand up for the Jews.

Dickens's lack of vulgar nationalism is in part the mark of a real largeness of mind, and in part results from his negative, rather unhelpful political attitude. He is very much an Englishman, but he is hardly aware of it—certainly the thought of being an Englishman does not thrill him. He has no imperialist feeling, no discernible views on foreign politics, and is untouched by the military tradition. Temperamentally he is much nearer to the small Nonconformist tradesman who looks down on the "red-coats" and thinks that war is wicked—a one-eyed view, but, after all, war *is* wicked. It is noticeable that Dickens hardly writes of war, even to denounce it. With all his marvellous powers of description, and of describing things he had never seen, he never describes a battle, unless one counts the attack on the Bastille in *A Tale of Two Cities*. Probably the subject would not strike him as interesting, and in any case he would not regard a battlefield as a place where anything worth settling could be settled. It is one up to the lower-middle-class, puritan mentality.

III

Dickens had grown up near enough to poverty to be terrified of it, and in spite of his generosity of mind, he is not free from the special prejudices of the shabby-genteel. It is usual to claim him as a "popular" writer, a champion of the "oppressed masses". So he is, so long as he thinks of them as oppressed; but there are two things that condition his attitude. In the first place, he is a south of England man, and a cockney at that, and therefore out of touch with the bulk of the real oppressed masses, the industrial and agricultural labourers. It is interesting to see how Chesterton, another cockney, always presents Dickens as the spokesman of "the poor", without showing much awareness of who "the poor" really are. To Chesterton "the poor" means small shopkeepers and servants. Sam Weller, he says, "is the great symbol in English literature of the populace peculiar to England"; and Sam Weller is a valet! The other point is that Dickens's early experiences have given him a horror of proletarian roughness. He shows this unmistakably whenever he writes of the very poorest of the poor, the slum-dwellers. His descriptions of the London slums are always full of undisguised repulsion:

> The ways were foul and narrow; the shops and houses wretched; and people half naked, drunken, slipshod and ugly. Alleys and archways, like so many cesspools, disgorged their offences of smell, and dirt, and life, upon the straggling streets; and the whole quarter reeked with crime, and filth, and misery, etc etc.

There are many similar passages in Dickens. From them one gets the impression of whole submerged populations whom he regards as being beyond the pale. In rather the same way the modern doctrinaire Socialist contemptuously writes off a large block of the population as "lumpenproletariat". Dickens also shows less understanding of criminals than one would expect of him. Although he is well aware of the social and economic causes of crime, he often seems to feel that when a man has once broken the law he has put himself outside human society. There is a chapter at the end of *David Copperfield* in which David visits the prison where Littimer and Uriah Heep are serving their sentences. Dickens actually seems to regard the horrible "model" prisons, against which Charles Reade delivered his memorable attack in *It Is Never Too Late to Mend*, as too humane. He complains that the food is too good! As soon as he comes up against crime or the worst depths of poverty, he shows traces of the "I've always kept myself respectable" habit of mind. The attitude of Pip (obviously the attitude of Dickens himself) towards Magwitch in *Great Expectations* is extremely interesting. Pip is conscious all along of his ingratitude towards Joe, but far less so of his ingratitude towards Magwitch. When he discovers that the person who has loaded him with benefits for years is actually a transported convict, he falls into frenzies of disgust. "The abhorrence in which I held the man, the dread I had of him, the repugnance with which I shrank from him, could not have been exceeded if he had been some terrible beast", etc etc. So far as one can discover from the text, this is not because when Pip was a child he had been terrorised by Magwitch in the churchyard; it is because Magwitch is a criminal and a convict. There is an even more "kept-myself-respectable" touch in the fact that Pip feels as a matter of course that he cannot take Magwitch's money. The money is not the product of a crime, it has been honestly acquired; but it is an ex-convict's money and therefore "tainted". There is nothing psychologically false in this, either. Psychologically the latter part of *Great Expectations* is about the best thing Dickens ever did; throughout this part of the book one feels "Yes, that is just how Pip would have behaved." But the point is that in the matter of Magwitch, Dickens identifies with Pip, and his attitude is at bottom snobbish. The result is that Magwitch belongs to the same queer class of characters as Falstaff and, probably, Don Quixote—characters who are more pathetic than the author intended.

When it is a question of the non-criminal poor, the ordinary, decent, labouring poor, there is of course nothing contemptuous in Dickens's attitude. He has the sincerest admiration for people like the Peggottys and the Plornishes. But it is questionable whether he really regards them as equals. It is of the greatest interest to read Chapter XI of *David Copperfield* and side by side with it the autobiographical fragment (parts of this are given in Forster's *Life*), in which Dickens expresses his feelings about the blacking-factory episode a great deal more strongly than in the novel. For more than twenty years afterwards the memory was so painful to him that he would go out of his way to avoid that part of the Strand. He says that to pass that way "made me cry, after my eldest child could speak." The text makes it quite clear that what hurt him most of all, then and in retrospect, was the enforced contact with "low" associates:

> No words can express the secret agony of my soul as I sunk into this companionship; compared these everyday associates with those of my happier childhood. . . . But I held some station at the blacking warehouse too. . . . I soon became at least as expeditious and as skilful with my hands as either of the other boys. Though perfectly familiar with them, my conduct and manners were different enough from theirs to place a space between us. They, and the men, always spoke of me as "the young gentleman." A certain man . . . used to call me "Charles" sometimes in speaking to me; but I think it was mostly when we were very confidential. . . . Poll Green uprose once, and rebelled against the "young-gentleman" usage; but Bob Fagin settled him speedily.

It was as well that there should be "a space between us", you see. However much Dickens may admire the working classes, he does not wish to resemble them. Given his origins, and the time he lived in, it could hardly be otherwise. In the early nineteenth century class-animosities may have been no sharper than they are now, but the surface differences between class and class were enormously greater. The "gentleman" and the "common man" must have seemed like different species of animal. Dickens is quite genuinely on the side of the poor against the rich, but it would be next door to impossible for him not to think of a working-class exterior as a stigma. In one of Tolstoy's fables the peasants of a certain village judge every stranger who arrives from the state of his hands. If his palms are hard from work, they let him in; if his palms are soft, out he goes. This would be hardly intelligible to Dickens; all his heroes have soft hands. His younger heroes—Nicholas Nickleby, Martin Chuzzlewit, Edward Chester, David Copperfield, John Harmon—are usually of the type known as "walking gentlemen". He likes a bourgeois exterior and a bourgeois (not aristocratic) accent. One curious symptom of this is that he will not allow anyone who is to play a heroic part to speak like a working man. A comic hero like Sam Weller, or a merely pathetic figure like Stephen Blackpool, can speak with a broad accent, but the *jeune premier* always speaks the then equivalent of BBC. This is so, even when it involves absurdities. Little Pip, for instance, is brought up by people speaking broad Essex, but talks upper-class English from his earliest childhood; actually he would have talked the same dialect as Joe, or at least as Mrs Gargery. So also with Biddy Wopsle, Lizzie Hexam,

Sissie Jupe, Oliver Twist—one ought perhaps to add Little Dorrit. Even Rachel in *Hard Times* has barely a trace of Lancashire accent, an impossibility in her case.

One thing that often gives the clue to a novelist's real feelings on the class question is the attitude he takes up when class collides with sex. This is a thing too painful to be lied about, and consequently it is one of the points at which the "I'm-not-a-snob" pose tends to break down.

One sees that at its most obvious where a class-distinction is also a colour-distinction. And something resembling the colonial attitude ("native" women are fair game, white women are sacrosanct) exists in a veiled form in all-white communities, causing bitter resentment on both sides. When this issue arises, novelists often revert to crude class-feelings which they might disclaim at other times. A good example of "class-conscious" reaction is a rather forgotten novel, *The People of Clopton*, by Andrew Barton. The author's moral code is quite clearly mixed up with class-hatred. He feels the seduction of a poor girl by a rich man to be something atrocious, a kind of defilement, something quite different from her seduction by a man in her own walk of life. Trollope deals with this theme twice (*The Three Clerks* and *The Small House at Allington*) and, as one might expect, entirely from the upper-class angle. As he sees it, an affair with a barmaid or a landlady's daughter is simply an "entanglement" to be escaped from. Trollope's moral standards are strict, and he does not allow the seduction actually to happen, but the implication is always that a working-class girl's feelings do not greatly matter. In *The Three Clerks* he even gives the typical class-reaction by noting that the girl "smells". Meredith (*Rhoda Fleming*) takes more the "class-conscious" viewpoint. Thackeray, as often, seems to hesitate. In *Pendennis* (Fanny Bolton) his attitude is much the same as Trollope's; in *A Shabby Genteel Story* it is nearer to Meredith's.

One could divine a good deal about Trollope's social origin, or Meredith's, or Barton's, merely from their handling of the class-sex theme. So one can with Dickens, but what emerges, as usual, is that he is more inclined to identify himself with the middle class than with the proletariat. The one incident that seems to contradict this is the tale of the young peasant-girl in Doctor Manette's manuscript in *A Tale of Two Cities*. This, however, is merely a costume-piece put in to explain the implacable hatred of Madame Defarge, which Dickens does not pretend to approve of. In *David Copperfield*, where he is dealing with a typical nineteenth-century seduction, the class-issue does not seem to strike him as paramount. It is a law of Victorian novels that sexual misdeeds must not go unpunished, and so Steerforth is drowned on Yarmouth sands, but neither Dickens, nor old Peggotty, nor even Ham, seems to feel that Steerforth has added to his offence by being the son of rich parents. The Steerforths are moved by class-motives, but the Peggottys are not—not even in the scene between Mrs Steerforth and old Peggotty; if they were, of course, they would probably turn against David as well as against Steerforth.

In *Our Mutual Friend* Dickens treats the episode of Eugene Wrayburn and Lizzie Hexam very realistically and with no appearance of class bias. According to the "unhand me, monster" tradition, Lizzie ought either to "spurn" Eugene or to be ruined by him and throw herself off Waterloo Bridge; Eugene ought to be either a heartless betrayer or a hero resolved upon defying society. Neither behaves in the least like this. Lizzie is frightened by Eugene's advances and actually runs away from them, but hardly pretends to dislike them; Eugene is attracted by her, has too much decency to attempt seducing her and dare not marry her because of his family. Finally they are married and no one is any the worse, except perhaps Mr Twemlow, who will lose a few dinner engagements. It is all very much as it might have happened in real life. But a "class-conscious" novelist would have given her to Bradley Headstone.

But when it is the other way about—when it is a case of a poor man aspiring to some woman who is "above" him—Dickens instantly retreats into the middle-class attitude. He is rather fond of the Victorian notion of a woman (woman with a capital W) being "above" a man. Pip feels that Estella is "above" him, Esther Summerson is "above" Guppy, Little Dorrit is "above" John Chivery, Lucy Manette is "above" Sydney Carton. In some of these the "above"-ness is merely moral, but in others it is social. There is a scarcely mistakable class-reaction when David Copperfield discovers that Uriah Heep is plotting to marry Agnes Wickfield. The disgusting Uriah suddenly announces that he is in love with her:

> "Oh, Master Copperfield, with what a pure affection do I love the ground my Agnes walks on."
>
> I believe I had the delirious idea of seizing the red-hot poker out of the fire, and running him through with it. It went from me with a shock, like a ball fired from a rifle: but the image of Agnes,

> outraged by so much as a thought of this red-headed animal's, remained in my mind (when I looked at him, sitting all awry as if his mean soul griped his body) and made me giddy. . . . "I believe Agnes Wickfield to be as far above *you* (David says later on), and as far removed from all *your* aspirations, as that moon herself."

Considering how Heep's general lowness—his servile manners, dropped aitches and so forth—has been rubbed in throughout the book, there is not much doubt about the nature of Dickens's feelings. Heep, of course, is playing a villainous part, but even villains have sexual lives; it is the thought of the "pure" Agnes in bed with a man who drops his aitches that really revolts Dickens. But his usual tendency is to treat a man in love with a woman who is "above" him as a joke. It is one of the stock jokes of English literature, from Malvolio onwards. Guppy in *Bleak House* is an example, John Chivery is another, and there is a rather ill-natured treatment of this theme in the "swarry" in *Pickwick Papers*. Here Dickens describes the Bath footmen as living a kind of fantasy-life, holding dinner-parties in imitation of their "betters" and deluding themselves that their young mistresses are in love with them. This evidently strikes him as very comic. So it is, in a way, though one might question whether it is not better for a footman even to have delusions of this kind than simply to accept his status in the spirit of the catechism.

In his attitude toward servants Dickens is not ahead of his age. In the nineteenth century the revolt against domestic service was just beginning, to the great annoyance of everyone with over £500 a year. An enormous number of the jokes in nineteenth-century comic papers deal with the uppishness of servants. For years *Punch* ran a series of jokes called "Servant Gal-isms", all turning on the then astonishing fact that a servant is a human being. Dickens is sometimes guilty of this kind of thing himself. His books abound with the ordinary comic servants; they are dishonest (*Great Expectations*), incompetent (*David Copperfield*), turn up their noses at good food (*Pickwick Papers*) etc etc—all rather in the spirit of the suburban housewife with one down-trodden cook-general. But what is curious, in a nineteenth-century radical, is that when he wants to draw a sympathetic picture of a servant, he creates what is recognisably a feudal type. Sam Weller, Mark Tapley, Clara Peggotty are all of them feudal figures. They belong to the genre of the "old family retainer"; they identify themselves with their master's family and are at once doggishly faithful and completely familiar. No doubt Mark Tapley and Sam Weller are derived to some extent from Smollett, and hence from Cervantes; but it is interesting that Dickens should have been attracted by such a type. Sam Weller's attitude is definitely medieval. He gets himself arrested in order to follow Mr Pickwick into the Fleet, and afterwards refuses to get married because he feels that Mr Pickwick still needs his services. There is a characteristic scene between them:

> "Vages or no vages, board or no board, lodgin' or no lodgin', Sam Veller, as you took from the old inn in the Borough, sticks by you, come what may. . . ."
>
> "My good fellow," said Mr Pickwick, when Mr Weller had sat down again, rather abashed at his own enthusiasm, "you are bound to consider the young woman also."
>
> "I do consider the young 'ooman, sir," said Sam. "I have considered the young 'ooman. I've spoke to her. I've told her how I'm sitivated; she's ready to vait till I'm ready, and I believe she vill. If she don't, she's not the young 'ooman I take her for, and I give her up with readiness."

It is easy to imagine what the young woman would have said to this in real life. But notice the feudal atmosphere. Sam Weller is ready as a matter of course to sacrifice years of life to his master, and he can also sit down in his master's presence. A modern manservant would never think of doing either. Dickens's views on the servant question do not get much beyond wishing that master and servant would love one another. Sloppy in *Our Mutual Friend*, though a wretched failure as a character, represents the same kind of loyalty as Sam Weller. Such loyalty, of course, is natural, human and likeable; but so was feudalism.

What Dickens seems to be doing, as usual, is to reach out for an idealised version of the existing thing. He was writing at a time when domestic service must have seemed a completely inevitable evil. There were no labour-saving devices, and there was huge inequality of wealth. It was an age of enormous families, pretentious meals and inconvenient houses, when the slavey drudging fourteen hours a day in the basement kitchen was something too normal to be noticed. And given the *fact* of servitude, the feudal relationship is the only tolerable one. Sam Weller and Mark Tapley are dream figures, no less than the Cheerybles. If there have got to be masters and servants, how much better that the master should be Mr Pickwick and the servant should be Sam Weller. Better still, of course, if servants did not exist at all—but this Dickens is probably unable to imagine. Without a high level of mechanical development, human equality is not practically possible; Dickens goes to show that it is not imaginable either.

IV

It is not merely a coincidence that Dickens never writes about agriculture and writes endlessly about food. He was a cockney, and London is the centre of the earth in rather the same sense that the belly is the centre of the body. It is a city of consumers, of people who are deeply civilised but not primarily useful. A thing that strikes one when one looks below the surface of Dickens's books is that, as nineteenth-century novelists go, he is rather ignorant. He knows very little about the way things really happen. At first sight this statement looks flatly untrue, and it needs some qualification.

Dickens had had vivid glimpses of "low life"—life in a debtor's prison, for example—and he was also a popular novelist and able to write about ordinary people. So were all the characteristic English novelists of the nineteenth century. They felt at home in the world they lived in, whereas a writer nowadays is so hopelessly isolated that the typical modern novel is a novel about a novelist. Even when Joyce, for instance, spends a decade or so in patient efforts to make contact with the "common man", his "common man" finally turns out to be a Jew, and a bit of a highbrow at that. Dickens at least does not suffer from this kind of thing. He has no difficulty in introducing the common motives, love, ambition, avarice, vengeance and so forth. What he does not noticeably write about, however, is *work*.

In Dickens's novels anything in the nature of work happens offstage. The only one of his heroes who has a plausible profession is David Copperfield, who is first a shorthand writer and then a novelist, like Dickens himself. With most of the others, the way they earn their living is very much in the background. Pip, for instance, "goes into business" in Egypt; we are not told what business, and Pip's working life occupies about half a page of the book. Clennam has been in some unspecified business in China, and later goes into another barely specified business with Doyce. Martin Chuzzlewit is an architect, but does not seem to get much time for practising. In no case do their adventures spring directly out of their work. Here the contrast between Dickens and, say, Trollope is startling. And one reason for this is undoubtedly that Dickens knows very little about the professions his characters are supposed to follow. What exactly went on in Gradgrind's factories? How did Podsnap make his money? How did Merdle work his swindles? One knows that Dickens could never follow up the details of parliamentary elections and Stock Exchange rackets as Trollope could. As soon as he has to deal with trade, finance, industry or politics he takes refuge in vagueness, or in satire. This is the case even with legal processes, about which actually he must have known a good deal. Compare any lawsuit in Dickens with the lawsuit in *Orley Farm*, for instance.

And this partly accounts for the needless ramifications of Dickens's novels, the awful Victorian "plot". It is true that not all his novels are alike in this. *A Tale of Two Cities* is a very good and fairly simple story, and so in its different way is *Hard Times*; but these are just the two which are always rejected as "not like Dickens"—and incidentally they were not published in monthly numbers.[1] The two first-person novels are also good stories, apart from their sub-plots. But the typical Dickens novel, *Nicholas Nickleby, Oliver Twist, Martin Chuzzlewit, Our Mutual Friend*, always exists round a framework of melodrama. The last thing anyone ever remembers about these books is their central story. On the other hand, I suppose no one has ever read them without carrying the memory of individual pages to the day of his death. Dickens sees human beings with the most intense vividness, but he sees them always in private life, as "characters", not as functional members of society; that is to say, he sees them statically. Consequently his greatest success is *The Pickwick Papers*, which is not a story at all, merely a series of sketches; there is little attempt at development—the characters simply go on and on, behaving like idiots, in a kind of eternity. As soon as he tries to bring his characters into action, the melodrama begins. He cannot make the action revolve round their ordinary occupations; hence the crossword puzzle of coincidences, intrigues, murders, disguises,

[1] *Hard Times* was published as a serial in *Household Words* and *Great Expectations* and *A Tale of Two Cities* in *All the Year Round.* Forster says that the shortness of the weekly instalments made it "much more difficult to get sufficient interest into each." Dickens himself complained of the lack of "elbow-room". In other words, he had to stick more closely to the story. [Author's footnote.]

buried wills, long-lost brothers, etc etc. In the end even people like Squeers and Micawber get sucked into the machinery.

Of course it would be absurd to say that Dickens is a vague or merely melodramatic writer. Much that he wrote is extremely factual, and in the power of evoking visual images he has probably never been equalled. When Dickens has once described something you see it for the rest of your life. But in a way the concreteness of his vision is a sign of what he is missing. For, after all, that is what the merely casual onlooker always sees—the outward appearance, the non-functional, the surfaces of things. No one who is really involved in the landscape ever sees the landscape. Wonderfully as he can describe an *appearance*, Dickens does not often describe a *process*. The vivid pictures that he succeeds in leaving in one's memory are nearly always the pictures of things seen in leisure moments, in the coffee-rooms of country inns or through the windows of a stage-coach; the kind of things he notices are inn-signs, brass door-knockers, painted jugs, the interiors of shops and private houses, clothes, faces and, above all, food. Everything is seen from the consumer-angle. When he writes about Coketown he manages to evoke, in just a few paragraphs, the atmosphere of a Lancashire town as a slightly disgusted southern visitor would see it. "It had a black canal in it, and a river that ran purple with evil-smelling dye, and vast piles of buildings full of windows where there was a rattling and a trembling all day long, and where the piston of the steam-engine worked monotonously up and down, like the head of an elephant in a state of melancholy madness." That is as near as Dickens ever gets to the machinery of the mills. An engineer or a cotton-broker would see it differently; but then neither of them would be capable of that impressionistic touch about the heads of the elephants.

In a rather different sense his attitude to life is extremely unphysical. He is a man who lives through his eyes and ears rather than through his hands and muscles. Actually his habits were not so sedentary as this seems to imply. In spite of rather poor health and physique, he was active to the point of restlessness; throughout his life he was a remarkable walker, and he could at any rate carpenter well enough to put up stage scenery. But he was not one of those people who feel a need to use their hands. It is difficult to imagine him digging at a cabbage-patch, for instance. He gives no evidence of knowing anything about agriculture, and obviously knows nothing about any kind of game or sport. He has no interest in pugilism, for instance. Considering the age in which he was writing, it is astonishing how little physical brutality there is in Dickens's novels. Martin Chuzzlewit and Mark Tapley, for instance, behave with the most remarkable mildness towards the Americans who are constantly menacing them with revolvers and bowie-knives. The average English or American novelist would have had them handing out socks on the jaw and exchanging pistol-shots in all directions. Dickens is too decent for that; he sees the stupidity of violence, and also he belongs to a cautious urban class which does not deal in socks on the jaw, even in theory. And his attitude towards sport is mixed up with social feelings. In England, for mainly geographical reasons, sport, especially field-sports, and snobbery are inextricably mingled. English Socialists are often flatly incredulous when told that Lenin, for instance, was devoted to shooting. In their eyes shooting, hunting, etc are simply snobbish observances of the landed gentry; they forget that these things might appear differently in a huge virgin country like Russia. From Dickens's point of view almost any kind of sport is at best a subject for satire. Consequently one side of nineteenth-century life—the boxing, racing, cock-fighting, badger-digging, poaching, rat-catching side of life, so wonderfully embalmed in Leech's illustrations to Surtees—is outside his scope.

What is more striking, in a seemingly "progressive" radical, is that he is not mechanically minded. He shows no interest either in the details of machinery or in the things machinery can do. As Gissing remarks, Dickens nowhere describes a railway journey with anything like the enthusiasm he shows in describing journeys by stage-coach. In nearly all of his books one has a curious feeling that one is living in the first quarter of the nineteenth century, and in fact, he does tend to return to this period. *Little Dorrit*, written in the middle 'fifties, deals with the late 'twenties; *Great Expectations* (1861) is not dated, but evidently deals with the 'twenties and 'thirties. Several of the inventions and discoveries which have made the modern world possible (the electric telegraph, the breech-loading gun, india-rubber, coal gas, wood-pulp paper) first appeared in Dickens's lifetime, but he scarcely notes them in his books. Nothing is queerer than the vagueness with which he speaks of Doyce's "invention" in *Little Dorrit*. It is represented as something extremely ingenious and revolutionary, "of great importance to his country and his fellow-creatures", and it is also an important minor link in the book; yet we are never told what the "invention" is! On the other hand, Doyce's physical appearance is hit off with the typical Dickens touch; he has a peculiar way of moving his thumb, a way characteristic of engineers. After that, Doyce is firmly anchored in one's memory; but, as usual, Dickens has done it by fastening on something external.

There are people (Tennyson is an example) who lack the mechanical faculty but can see the social possibilities of machinery. Dickens has not this stamp of mind. He shows very little consciousness of the future. When he speaks of human progress it is usually in terms of *moral* progress—men growing better; probably he would never admit that men are only as good as their technical development allows them to be. At this point the gap between Dickens and his modern analogue, H. G. Wells, is at its widest. Wells wears the future round his neck like a millstone, but Dickens's unscientific cast of mind is just as damaging in a different way. What it does is to make any *positive* attitude more difficult for him. He is hostile to the feudal, agricultural past and not in real touch with the industrial present. Well, then, all that remains is the future (meaning science, "progress" and so forth), which hardly enters into his thoughts. Therefore, while attacking everything in sight, he has no definable standard of comparison. As I have pointed out already, he attacks the current educational system with perfect justice, and yet, after all, he has no remedy to offer except kindlier schoolmasters. Why did he not indicate what a school *might* have been? Why did he not have his own sons educated according to some plan of his own, instead of sending them to public schools to be stuffed with Greek? Because he lacked that kind of imagination. He has an infallible moral sense, but very little intellectual curiosity. And here one comes upon something which really is an enormous deficiency in Dickens, something that really does make the nineteenth century seem remote from us—that he has no ideal of *work*.

With the doubtful exception of David Copperfield (merely Dickens himself), one cannot point to a single one of his central characters who is primarily interested in his job. His heroes work in order to make a living and to marry the heroine, not because they feel a passionate interest in one particular subject. Martin Chuzzlewit, for instance, is not burning with zeal to be an architect; he might just as well be a doctor or a barrister. In any case, in the typical Dickens novel, the *deus ex machina* enters with a bag of gold in the last chapter and the hero is absolved from further struggle. The feeling, "This is what I came into the world to do. Everything else is uninteresting. I will do this even if it means starvation", which turns men of differing temperaments into scientists, inventors, artists, priests, explorers and revolutionaries—this motif is almost entirely absent from Dickens's books. He himself, as is well known, worked like a slave and believed in his work as few novelists have ever done. But there seems to be no calling except novel-writing (and perhaps acting) towards which he can imagine this kind of devotion. And, after all, it is natural enough, considering his rather negative attitude towards society. In the last resort there is nothing he admires except common decency. Science is uninteresting and machinery is cruel and ugly (the heads of the elephants). Business is only for ruffians like Bounderby. As for politics—leave that to the Tite Barnacles. Really there is no objective except to marry the heroine, settle down, live solvently and be kind. And you can do that much better in private life.

Here, perhaps, one gets a glimpse of Dickens's secret imaginative background. What did he think of as the most desirable way to live? When Martin Chuzzlewit had made it up with his uncle, when Nicholas Nickleby had married money, when John Harmon had been enriched by Boffin—what did they *do*?

The answer evidently is that they did nothing. Nicholas Nickleby invested his wife's money with the Cheerybles and "became a rich and prosperous merchant", but as he immediately retired into Devonshire, we can assume that he did not work very hard. Mr and Mrs Snodgrass "purchased and cultivated a small farm, more for occupation than profit". That is the spirit in which most of Dickens's books end—a sort of radiant idleness. Where he appears to disapprove of young men who do not work (Harthouse, Harry Gowan, Richard Carstone, Wrayburn before his reformation), it is because they are cynical and immoral or because they are a burden on somebody else; if you are "good", and also self-supporting, there is no reason why you should not spend fifty years in simply drawing your dividends. Home life is always enough. And, after all, it was the general assumption of his age. The "genteel sufficiency", the "competence", the "gentleman of independent means" (or "in easy circumstances")—the very phrases tell one all about the strange, empty dream of the eighteenth- and nineteenth-century middle bourgeoisie. It was a dream of *complete idleness*. Charles Reade conveys its spirit perfectly in the ending of *Hard Cash*. Alfred Hardie, hero of *Hard Cash*, is the typical nineteenth-century novel hero (public-school style), with gifts which Reade describes as amounting to "genius". He is an old Etonian and a scholar of Oxford, he knows most of the Greek and Latin classics by heart, he can box with prize-fighters and win the Diamond Sculls at Henley. He goes through incredible adventures in which, of course, he behaves with faultless heroism, and then, at the age of twenty-five, he inherits a fortune, marries his Julia Dodd and settles down in the suburbs of Liverpool, in the same house as his parents-in-law:

> They all lived together at Albion Villa, thanks to Alfred. . . . Oh, you happy little villa! You were as like Paradise as any mortal dwelling can be. A day came, however, when your walls could no longer hold all the happy inmates. Julia presented Alfred with a lovely boy; enter two nurses and the villa showed symptoms of bursting. Two months more, and Alfred and his wife overflowed into the next villa. It was but twenty yards off; and there was a double reason for the migration. As often happens after a long separation, Heaven bestowed on Captain and Mrs Dodd another infant to play about their knees, etc etc etc.

This is the type of the Victorian happy ending—a vision of a huge, loving family of three or four generations, all crammed together in the same house and constantly multiplying, like a bed of oysters. What is striking about it is the utterly soft, sheltered, effortless life that it implies. It is not even a violent idleness, like Squire Western's. That is the significance of Dickens's urban background and his non-interest in the blackguardly-sporting-military side of life. His heroes, once they had come into money and "settled down", would not only do no work; they would not even ride, hunt, shoot, fight duels, elope with actresses or lose money at the races. They would simply live at home in feather-bed respectability, and preferably next door to a blood-relation living exactly the same life:

> The first act of Nicholas, when he became a rich and prosperous merchant, was to buy his father's old house. As time crept on, and there came gradually about him a group of lovely children, it was altered and enlarged; but none of the old rooms were ever pulled down, no old tree was ever rooted up, nothing with which there was any association of bygone times was ever removed or changed.
>
> Within a stone's-throw was another retreat enlivened by children's pleasant voices too; and here was Kate . . . the same

true, gentle creature, the same fond sister, the same in the love of all about her, as in her girlish days.

It is the same incestuous atmosphere as in the passage quoted from Reade. And evidently this is Dickens's ideal ending. It is perfectly attained in *Nicholas Nickleby*, *Martin Chuzzlewit* and *Pickwick*, and it is approximated to in varying degrees in almost all the others. The exceptions are *Hard Times* and *Great Expectations*—the latter actually has a "happy ending", but it contradicts the general tendency of the book, and it was put in at the request of Bulwer Lytton.

The ideal to be striven after, then, appears to be something like this: a hundred thousand pounds, a quaint old house with plenty of ivy on it, a sweetly womanly wife, a horde of children, and no work. Everything is safe, soft, peaceful and, above all, domestic. In the moss-grown churchyard down the road are the graves of the loved ones who passed away before the happy ending happened. The servants are comic and feudal, the children prattle round your feet, the old friends sit at your fireside, talking of past days, there is the endless succession of enormous meals, the cold punch and sherry negus, the feather beds and warming-pans, the Christmas parties with charades and blind man's buff; but nothing ever happens, except the yearly childbirth. The curious thing is that it is a genuinely happy picture, or so Dickens is able to make it appear. The thought of that kind of existence is satisfying to him. This alone would be enough to tell one that more than a hundred years have passed since Dickens's first book was written. No modern man could combine such purposelessness with so much vitality.

V

By this time anyone who is a lover of Dickens, and who has read as far as this, will probably be angry with me.

I have been discussing Dickens simply in terms of his "message", and almost ignoring his literary qualities. But every writer, especially every novelist, *has* a "message", whether he admits it or not, and the minutest details of his work are influenced by it. All art is propaganda. Neither Dickens himself nor the majority of Victorian novelists would have thought of denying this. On the other hand, not all propaganda is art. As I said earlier, Dickens is one of those writers who are felt to be worth stealing. He has been stolen by Marxists, by

Catholics and, above all, by Conservatives. The question is, What is there to steal? Why does anyone care about Dickens? Why do *I* care about Dickens?

That kind of question is never easy to answer. As a rule, an aesthetic preference is either something inexplicable or it is so corrupted by non-aesthetic motives as to make one wonder whether the whole of literary criticism is not a huge network of humbug. In Dickens's case the complicating factor is his familiarity. He happens to be one of those "great authors" who are ladled down everyone's throat in childhood. At the time this causes rebellion and vomiting, but it may have different after-effects in later life. For instance, nearly everyone feels a sneaking affection for the patriotic poems that he learned by heart as a child, "Ye Mariners of England", "The Charge of the Light Brigade" and so forth. What one enjoys is not so much the poems themselves as the memories they call up. And with Dickens the same forces of association are at work. Probably there are copies of one or two of his books lying about in an actual majority of English homes. Many children begin to know his characters by sight before they can even read, for on the whole Dickens was lucky in his illustrators. A thing that is absorbed as early as that does not come up against any critical judgement. And when one thinks of this, one thinks of all that is bad and silly in Dickens—the cast-iron "plots", the characters who don't come off, the *longueurs*, the paragraphs in blank verse, the awful pages of "pathos". And then the thought arises, when I say I like Dickens, do I simply mean that I like thinking about my childhood? Is Dickens merely an institution?

If so, he is an institution that there is no getting away from. How often one really thinks about any writer, even a writer one cares for, is a difficult thing to decide; but I should doubt whether anyone who has actually read Dickens can go a week without remembering him in one context or another. Whether you approve of him or not, he is *there*, like the Nelson Column. At any moment some scene or character, which may come from some book you cannot even remember the name of, is liable to drop into your mind. Micawber's letters! Winkle in the witness box! Mrs Gamp! Mrs Wititterly and Sir Tumley Snuffim! Todgers's! (George Gissing said that when he passed the Monument it was never of the Fire of London that he thought, always of Todgers's.) Mrs Leo Hunter! Squeers! Silas Wegg and the Decline and Fall-off of the Russian Empire! Miss Mills and the Desert of Sahara! Wopsle acting Hamlet! Mrs Jellyby! Mantalini! Jerry Cruncher! Barkis! Pumblechook! Tracy Tupman! Skimpole! Joe Gargery! Pecksniff!—and so it goes on and on. It is not so much a series of books, it is more like a world. And not a purely comic world either, for part of what one remembers in Dickens is his Victorian morbidness and necrophilia and the blood-and-thunder scenes—the death of Sikes, Krook's spontaneous combustion, Fagin in the condemned cell, the women knitting round the guillotine. To a surprising extent all this has entered even into the minds of people who do not care about it. A music-hall comedian can (or at any rate could quite recently) go on the stage and impersonate Micawber or Mrs Gamp with a fair certainty of being understood, although not one in twenty of the audience had ever read a book of Dickens's right through. Even people who affect to despise him quote him unconsciously.

Dickens is a writer who can be imitated, up to a certain point. In genuinely popular literature—for instance, the Elephant and Castle version of *Sweeney Todd*—he has been plagiarised quite shamelessly. What has been imitated, however, is simply a tradition that Dickens himself took from earlier novelists and developed, the cult of "character", i.e. eccentricity. The thing that cannot be imitated is his fertility of invention, which is invention not so much of characters, still less of "situations", as of turns of phrase and concrete details. The outstanding, unmistakable mark of Dickens's writing is the *unnecessary detail.* Here is an example of what I mean. The story given below is not particularly funny, but there is one phrase in it that is as individual as a fingerprint. Mr Jack Hopkins, at Bob Sawyer's party, is telling the story of the child who swallowed its sister's necklace:

> Next day, child swallowed two beads; the day after that, he treated himself to three, and so on, till in a week's time he had got through the necklace—five-and-twenty beads in all. The sister, who was an industrious girl and seldom treated herself to a bit of finery, cried her eyes out at the loss of the necklace; looked high and low for it; but I needn't say, didn't find it. A few days afterwards, the family were at dinner—baked shoulder of mutton and potatoes under it—the child, who wasn't hungry, was playing about the room, when suddenly there was heard the devil of a noise, like a small hailstorm. "Don't do that, my boy," says the father. "I ain't a-doin' nothing," said the child. "Well,

don't do it again," said the father. There was a short silence, and then the noise began again, worse than ever. "If you don't mind what I say, my boy," said the father, "you'll find yourself in bed, in something less than a pig's whisper." He gave the child a shake to make him obedient, and such a rattling ensued as nobody ever heard before. "Why, dam' me, it's *in* the child," said the father; "he's got the croup in the wrong place!" "No, I haven't, father," said the child, beginning to cry, "it's the necklace; I swallowed it, father." The father caught the child up, and ran with him to the hospital, the beads in the boy's stomach rattling all the way with the jolting; and the people looking up in the air, and down in the cellars, to see where the unusual sound came from. "He's in the hospital now," said Jack Hopkins, "and he makes such a devil of a noise when he walks about, that they're obliged to muffle him in a watchman's coat, for fear he should wake the patients."

As a whole, this story might come out of any nineteenth-century comic paper. But the unmistakable Dickens touch, the thing nobody else would have thought of, is the baked shoulder of mutton and potatoes under it. How does this advance the story? The answer is that it doesn't. It is something totally unnecessary, a florid little squiggle on the edge of the page; only, it is by just these squiggles that the special Dickens atmosphere is created. The other thing one would notice here is that Dickens's way of telling a story takes a long time. An interesting example, too long to quote, is Sam Weller's story of the obstinate patient in Chapter XLIV of *The Pickwick Papers*. As it happens, we have a standard of comparison here, because Dickens is plagiarising, consciously or unconsciously. The story is also told by some ancient Greek writer. I cannot now find the passage, but I read it years ago as a boy at school, and it runs more or less like this:

> A certain Thracian, renowned for his obstinacy, was warned by his physician that if he drank a flagon of wine it would kill him. The Thracian thereupon drank the flagon of wine and immediately jumped off the house-top and perished. "For," said he, "in this way I shall prove that the wine did not kill me."

As the Greek tells it, that is the whole story—about six lines. As Sam Weller tells it, it takes round about a thousand words. Long before getting to the point we have been told all about the patient's clothes, his meals, his manners, even the newspapers he reads, and about the peculiar construction of the doctor's carriage, which conceals the fact that the coachman's trousers do not match his coat. Then there is the dialogue between the doctor and the patient. " 'Crumpets is wholesome, sir,' said the patient. 'Crumpets is *not* wholesome, sir,' says the doctor, wery fierce," etc etc. In the end the original story has been buried under the details. And in all of Dickens's most characteristic passages it is the same. His imagination overwhelms everything, like a kind of weed. Squeers stands up to address his boys, and immediately we are hearing about Bolder's father who was two pounds ten short, and Mobbs's stepmother who took to her bed on hearing that Mobbs wouldn't eat fat and hoped Mr Squeers would flog him into a happier state of mind. Mrs Leo Hunter writes a poem, "Expiring Frog"; two full stanzas are given. Boffin takes a fancy to pose as a miser, and instantly we are down among the squalid biographies of eighteenth-century misers, with names like Vulture Hopkins and the Rev. Blewberry Jones, and chapter headings like "The Story of the Mutton Pies" and "The Treasures of a Dunghill". Mrs Harris, who does not even exist, has more detail piled on to her than any three characters in an ordinary novel. Merely in the middle of a sentence we learn, for instance, that her infant nephew has been seen in a bottle at Greenwich Fair, along with the pink-eyed lady, the Prussian dwarf and the living skeleton. Joe Gargery describes how the robbers broke into the house of Pumblechook, the corn and seed merchant—"and they took his till, and they took his cashbox, and they drinked his wine, and they partook of his wittles, and they slapped his face, and they pulled his nose, and they tied him up to his bedpust, and they give him a dozen, and they stuffed his mouth full of flowering annuals to perwent his crying out." Once again the unmistakable Dickens touch, the flowering annuals; but any other novelist would only have mentioned about half of these outrages. Everything is piled up and up, detail on detail, embroidery on embroidery. It is futile to object that this kind of thing is rococo—one might as well make the same objection to a wedding-cake. Either you like it or you do not like it. Other nineteenth-century writers, Surtees, Barham, Thackeray, even Marryat, have something of Dickens's profuse, overflowing quality, but none of them on anything like the same scale. The appeal of all these writers now depends partly on period-flavour, and though Marryat is still officially a "boys' writer" and Surtees has a sort of legendary fame among hunting men, it is probable that they are read mostly by bookish people.

Significantly, Dickens's most successful books (not his *best* books) are *The Pickwick Papers*, which is not a novel, and *Hard Times* and *A Tale of Two Cities*, which are not funny. As a novelist his natural fertility greatly hampers him, because the burlesque which he is never able to resist is constantly breaking into what ought to be serious situations. There is a good example of this in the opening chapter of *Great Expectations*. The escaped convict, Magwitch, has just captured the six-year-old Pip in the churchyard. The scene starts terrifyingly enough, from Pip's point of view. The convict, smothered in mud and with his chain trailing from his leg, suddenly starts up among the tombs, grabs the child, turns him upside down and robs his pockets. Then he begins terrorising him into bringing food and a file:

> He held me by the arms in an upright position on the top of the stone, and went on in these fearful terms:
>
> "You bring me, tomorrow morning early, that file and them wittles. You bring the lot to me, at that old Battery over yonder. You do it, and you never dare to say a word or dare to make a sign concerning your having seen such a person as me, or any person sumever, and you shall be let to live. You fail, or you go from my words in any partickler, no matter how small it is, and your heart and liver shall be tore out, roasted and ate. Now, I ain't alone, as you may think I am. There's a young man hid with me, in comparison with which young man I am a Angel. That young man hears the words I speak. That young man has a secret way pecooliar to himself, of getting at a boy, and at his heart, and at his liver. It is in wain for a boy to attempt to hide himself from that young man. A boy may lock his door, may be warm in bed, may tuck himself up, may draw the clothes over his head, may think himself comfortable and safe, but that young man will softly creep and creep his way to him and tear him open. I am keeping that young man from harming you at the present moment, but with great difficulty. I find it wery hard to hold that young man off of your inside. Now, what do you say?"

Here Dickens has simply yielded to temptation. To begin with, no starving and hunted man would speak in the least like that. Moreover, although the speech shows a remarkable knowledge of the way in which a child's mind works, its actual words are quite out of tune with what is to follow. It turns Magwitch into a sort of pantomime wicked uncle, or, if one sees him through the child's eyes, into an appalling monster. Later in the book he is to be represented as neither, and his exaggerated gratitude, on which the plot turns, is to be incredible because of just this speech. As usual, Dickens's imagination has overwhelmed him. The picturesque details were too good to be left out. Even with characters who are more of a piece than Magwitch he is liable to be tripped up by some seductive phrase. Mr Murdstone, for instance, is in the habit of ending David Copperfield's lessons every morning with a dreadful sum in arithmetic. "If I go into a cheesemonger's shop, and buy five thousand double-Gloucester cheeses at fourpence halfpenny each, present payment," it always begins. Once again the typical Dickens detail, the double-Gloucester cheeses. But it is far too human a touch for Murdstone; he would have made it five thousand cashboxes. Every time this note is struck, the unity of the novel suffers. Not that it matters very much, because Dickens is obviously a writer whose parts are greater than his wholes. He is all fragments, all details—rotten architecture, but wonderful gargoyles—and never better than when he is building up some character who will later on be forced to act inconsistently.

Of course it is not usual to urge against Dickens that he makes his characters behave inconsistently. Generally he is accused of doing just the opposite. His characters are supposed to be mere "types", each crudely representing some single trait and fitted with a kind of label by which you recognise him. Dickens is "only a caricaturist"—that is the usual accusation, and it does him both more and less than justice. To begin with, he did not think of himself as a caricaturist, and was constantly setting into action characters who ought to have been purely static. Squeers, Micawber, Miss Mowcher,[1] Wegg, Skimpole, Pecksniff and many others are finally involved in "plots" where they are out of place and where they behave quite incredibly. They start off as magic-lantern slides and they end by getting mixed up in a third-rate movie. Sometimes one can put one's finger on a single sentence in which the original illusion is destroyed. There is such a

[1] Dickens turned Miss Mowcher into a sort of heroine because the real woman whom he had caricatured had read the earlier chapters and was bitterly hurt. He had previously meant her to play a villainous part. But *any* action by such a character would seem incongruous. [Author's footnote.]

sentence in *David Copperfield.* After the famous dinner-party (the one where the leg of mutton was underdone), David is showing his guests out. He stops Traddles at the top of the stairs:

> "Traddles," said I, "Mr Micawber don't mean any harm, poor fellow: but if I were you I wouldn't lend him anything."
>
> "My dear Copperfield," returned Traddles smiling, "I haven't got anything to lend."
>
> "You have got a name, you know," I said.

At the place where one reads it this remark jars a little, though something of the kind was inevitable sooner or later. The story is a fairly realistic one, and David is growing up; ultimately he is bound to see Mr Micawber for what he is, a cadging scoundrel. Afterwards, of course, Dickens's sentimentality overcomes him and Micawber is made to turn over a new leaf. But from then on the original Micawber is never quite recaptured, in spite of desperate efforts. As a rule, the "plot" in which Dickens's characters get entangled is not particularly credible, but at least it makes some pretence at reality, whereas the world to which they belong is a never-never land, a kind of eternity. But just here one sees that "only a caricaturist" is not really a condemnation. The fact that Dickens is always thought of as a caricaturist, although he was constantly trying to be something else, is perhaps the surest mark of his genius. The monstrosities that he created are still remembered as monstrosities, in spite of getting mixed up in would-be probable melodramas. Their first impact is so vivid that nothing that comes afterwards effaces it. As with the people one knew in childhood, one seems always to remember them in one particular attitude, doing one particular thing. Mrs Squeers is always ladling out brimstone and treacle, Mrs Gummidge is always weeping, Mrs Gargery is always banging her husband's head against the wall, Mrs Jellyby is always scribbling tracts while her children fall into the area—and there they all are, fixed for ever like little twinkling miniatures painted on snuff-box lids, completely fantastic and incredible, and yet somehow more solid and infinitely more memorable than the efforts of serious novelists. Even by the standards of his time Dickens was an exceptionally artificial writer. As Ruskin said, he "chose to work in a circle of stage fire." His characters are even more distorted and simplified than Smollett's. But there are no rules in novel writing, and for any work of art there is only one test worth bothering about—survival. By this test Dickens's characters have succeeded, even if the people who remember them hardly think of them as human beings. They are monsters, but at any rate they *exist.*

But all the same there is a disadvantage in writing about monsters. It amounts to this, that it is only certain moods that Dickens can speak to. There are large areas of the human mind that he never touches. There is no poetic feeling anywhere in his books, and no genuine tragedy, and even sexual love is almost outside his scope. Actually his books are not so sexless as they are sometimes declared to be, and considering the time in which he was writing, he is reasonably frank. But there is not a trace in him of the feeling that one finds in *Manon Lescaut, Salammbô, Carmen, Wuthering Heights.* According to Aldous Huxley, D. H. Lawrence once said that Balzac was "a gigantic dwarf", and in a sense the same is true of Dickens. There are whole worlds which he either knows nothing about or does not wish to mention. Except in a rather roundabout way, one cannot *learn* very much from Dickens. And to say this is to think almost immediately of the great Russian novelists of the nineteenth century. Why is it that Tolstoy's grasp seems to be so much larger than Dickens's—why is it that he seems able to tell you so much more *about yourself*? It is not that he is more gifted, or even, in the last analysis, more intelligent. It is because he is writing about people who are growing. His characters are struggling to make their souls, whereas Dickens's are already finished and perfect. In my own mind Dickens's people are present far more often and far more vividly than Tolstoy's, but always in a single unchangeable attitude, like pictures or pieces of furniture. You cannot hold an imaginary conversation with a Dickens character as you can with, say, Pierre Bezukhov. And this is not merely because of Tolstoy's greater seriousness, for there are also comic characters that you can imagine yourself talking to —Bloom, for instance, or Pécuchet, or even Wells's Mr Polly. It is because Dickens's characters have no mental life. They say perfectly the thing that they have to say, but they cannot be conceived as talking about anything else. They never learn, never speculate. Perhaps the most meditative of his characters is Paul Dombey, and his thoughts are mush. Does this mean that Tolstoy's novels are "better" than Dickens's? The truth is that it is absurd to make such comparisons in terms of "better" and "worse". If I were forced to compare Tolstoy with Dickens, I should say that Tolstoy's appeal will probably be wider in the long run, because Dickens is scarcely intelligible outside the English-speaking culture; on the other hand, Dickens is able to reach simple people, which Tolstoy is not. Tolstoy's characters can cross a frontier, Dickens's can be portrayed on a cigarette-card.[1] But one is no more obliged to choose between them than between a sausage and a rose. Their purposes barely intersect.

VI

If Dickens had been *merely* a comic writer, the chances are that no one would now remember his name. Or at best a few of his books would survive in rather the same way as books like *Frank Fairlegh, Mr Verdant Green* and *Mrs Caudle's Curtain Lectures,*[2] as a sort of hangover of the Victorian atmosphere, a pleasant little whiff of oysters and brown stout. Who has not felt sometimes that it was "a pity" that Dickens ever deserted the vein of *Pickwick* for things like *Little Dorrit* and *Hard Times*? What people always demand of a popular novelist is that he shall write the same book over and over again, forgetting that a man who would write the same book twice could not even write it once. Any writer who is not utterly lifeless moves upon a kind of parabola, and the downward curve is implied in the upward one. Joyce has to start with the frigid competence of *Dubliners* and end with the dream-language of *Finnegans Wake*, but *Ulysses* and *Portrait of the Artist* are part of the trajectory. The thing that drove Dickens forward into a form of art for which he was not really suited, and at the same time caused us to remember him, was simply the fact that he was a moralist, the consciousness of "having something to say". He is always preaching a sermon, and that is the final secret of his inventiveness. For you can only create if you can *care*. Types like Squeers and Micawber could not have been produced by a hack writer looking for something to be funny about. A joke worth laughing at always has an idea behind it, and usually a subversive idea. Dickens is able to go on being funny because he is in revolt against authority, and authority is always there to be laughed at. There is always room for one more custard pie.

His radicalism is of the vaguest kind, and yet one always knows that it is there. That is the difference between being a moralist and a politician. He has no constructive suggestions, not even a clear grasp

[1] Messrs John Player and Sons issued two series of cigarette cards entitled "Characters from Dickens" in 1913; they reissued them as a single series in 1923.

[2] *Frank Fairlegh* by F. E. Smedley, 1850; *The Adventures of Mr Verdant Green* by Cuthbert Bede (pseud. of Edward Bradley), 1853; *Mrs Caudle's Curtain Lectures* by Douglas Jerrold (reprinted from *Punch*, 1846).

of the nature of the society he is attacking, only an emotional perception that something is wrong. All he can finally say is, "Behave decently," which, as I suggested earlier, is not necessarily so shallow as it sounds. Most revolutionaries are potential Tories, because they imagine that everything can be put right by altering the *shape* of society; once that change is effected, as it sometimes is, they see no need for any other. Dickens has not this kind of mental coarseness. The vagueness of his discontent is the mark of its permanence. What he is out against is not this or that institution, but, as Chesterton put it, "an expression on the human face". Roughly speaking, his morality is the Christian morality, but in spite of his Anglican upbringing he was essentially a Bible-Christian, as he took care to make plain when writing his will. In any case he cannot properly be described as a religious man. He "believed", undoubtedly, but religion in the devotional sense does not seem to have entered much into his thoughts.[1] Where he is Christian is in his quasi-instinctive siding with the oppressed against the oppressors. As a matter of course he is on the side of the underdog, always and everywhere. To carry this to its logical conclusion one has got to change sides when the underdog becomes an upperdog, and in fact Dickens does tend to do so. He loathes the Catholic Church, for instance, but as soon as the Catholics are persecuted (*Barnaby Rudge*) he is on their side. He loathes the aristocratic class even more, but as soon as they are really overthrown (the revolutionary chapters in *A Tale of Two Cities*) his sympathies swing round. Whenever he departs from this emotional attitude he goes astray. A well-known example is at the ending of *David Copperfield*, in which everyone who reads it feels that something has gone wrong. What is wrong is that the closing chapters are pervaded, faintly but noticeably, by the cult of success. It is the gospel according to Smiles, instead of the gospel according to Dickens. The attractive, out-at-elbow characters are got rid of,

[1] From a letter to his youngest son (in 1868): "You will remember that you have never at home been harassed about religious observances, or mere formalities. I have always been anxious not to weary my children with such things, before they are old enough to form opinions respecting them. You will therefore understand the better that I now most solemnly impress upon you the truth and beauty of the Christian Religion, as it came from Christ Himself, and the impossibility of your going far wrong if you humbly but heartily respect it. . . . Never abandon the wholesome practice of saying your own private prayers, night and morning. I have never abandoned it myself, and I know the comfort of it." [Author's footnote.]

Micawber makes a fortune, Heep gets into prison—both of these events are flagrantly impossible—and even Dora is killed off to make way for Agnes. If you like, you can read Dora as Dickens's wife and Agnes as his sister-in-law, but the essential point is that Dickens has "turned respectable" and done violence to his own nature. Perhaps that is why Agnes is the most disagreeable of his heroines, the real legless angel of Victorian romance, almost as bad as Thackeray's Laura.

No grown-up person can read Dickens without feeling his limitations, and yet there does remain his native generosity of mind, which acts as a kind of anchor and nearly always keeps him where he belongs. It is probably the central secret of his popularity. A good-tempered antinomianism rather of Dickens's type is one of the marks of western popular culture. One sees it in folk-stories and comic songs, in dream-figures like Mickey Mouse and Popeye the Sailor (both of them variants of Jack the Giant-Killer), in the history of working-class Socialism, in the popular protests (always ineffective but not always a sham) against imperialism, in the impulse that makes a jury award excessive damages when a rich man's car runs over a poor man; it is the feeling that one is always on the side of the under-dog, on the side of the weak against the strong. In one sense it is a feeling that is fifty years out of date. The common man is still living in the mental world of Dickens, but nearly every modern intellectual has gone over to some or other form of totalitarianism. From the Marxist or Fascist point of view, nearly all that Dickens stands for can be written off as "bourgeois morality". But in moral outlook no one could be more "bourgeois" than the English working classes. The ordinary people in the western countries have never entered, mentally, into the world of "realism" and power politics. They may do so before long, in which case Dickens will be as out of date as the cab-horse. But in his own age and ours he has been popular chiefly because he was able to express in a comic, simplified and therefore memorable form the native decency of the common man. And it is important that from this point of view people of very different types can be described as "common". In a country like England, in spite of its class-structure there does exist a certain cultural unity. All through the Christian ages, and especially since the French Revolution, the western world has been haunted by the idea of freedom and equality; it is only an *idea*, but it has penetrated to all ranks of society. The most atrocious injustices, cruelties, lies, snobberies exist everywhere, but there are not many people who can regard these things with the same indifference as, say, a Roman slave-owner. Even the millionaire suffers from a vague sense of guilt, like a dog eating a stolen leg of mutton. Nearly everyone, whatever his actual conduct may be, responds emotionally to the idea of human brotherhood. Dickens voiced a code which was and on the whole still is believed in, even by people who violate it. It is difficult otherwise to explain why he could be both read by working people (a thing that has happened to no other novelist of his stature) and buried in Westminster Abbey.

When one reads any strongly individual piece of writing, one has the impression of seeing a face somewhere behind the page. It is not necessarily the actual face of the writer. I feel this very strongly with Swift, with Defoe, with Fielding, Stendhal, Thackeray, Flaubert, though in several cases I do not know what these people looked like and do not want to know. What one sees is the face that the writer *ought* to have. Well, in the case of Dickens I see a face that is not quite the face of Dickens's photographs, though it resembles it. It is the face of a man of about forty, with a small beard and a high colour. He is laughing, with a touch of anger in his laughter, but no triumph, no malignity. It is the face of a man who is always fighting against something, but who fights in the open and is not frightened, the face of a man who is *generously angry*—in other words, of a nineteenth-century liberal, a free intelligence, a type hated with equal hatred by all the smelly little orthodoxies which are now contending for our souls.

Written 1939

ITW; (slightly revised) CrE; DD; CE.

163. Boys' Weeklies

You never walk far through any poor quarter in any big town without coming upon a small newsagent's shop. The general appearance of these shops is always very much the same: a few posters for the *Daily Mail* and the *News of the World* outside, a poky little window with sweet-bottles and packets of Players, and a dark interior smelling of liquorice allsorts and festooned from floor to ceiling with vilely printed twopenny papers, most of them with lurid cover illustrations in three colours.

Except for the daily and evening papers, the stock of these shops hardly overlaps at all with that of the big newsagents. Their main selling line is the twopenny weekly, and the number and variety of these are almost unbelievable. Every hobby and pastime—cage-birds, fretwork, carpentering, bees, carrier-pigeons, home conjuring, philately, chess—has at least one paper devoted to it, and generally several. Gardening and livestock-keeping must have at least a score between them. Then there are the sporting papers, the radio papers, the children's comics, the various snippet papers such as *Tit-Bits*, the large range of papers devoted to the movies and all more or less exploiting women's legs, the various trade papers, the women's story-papers (the *Oracle*, *Secrets*, *Peg's Paper*, etc etc), the needlework papers—these so numerous that a display of them alone will often fill an entire window—and in addition the long series of "Yank Mags" (*Fight Stories*, *Action Stories*, *Western Short Stories*, etc), which are imported shop-soiled from America and sold at twopence-halfpenny or threepence. And the periodical proper shades off into the fourpenny novelette, the *Aldine Boxing Novels*, the *Boys' Friend Library*, the *Schoolgirls' Own Library* and many others.

Probably the contents of these shops is the best available indication of what the mass of the English people really feels and thinks. Certainly nothing half so revealing exists in documentary form. Best-seller novels, for instance, tell one a great deal, but the novel is aimed almost exclusively at people above the £4-a-week level. The movies are probably a very unsafe guide to popular taste, because the film industry is virtually a monopoly, which means that it is not obliged to study its public at all closely. The same applies to some extent to the daily papers, and most of all to the radio. But it does not apply to the weekly paper with a smallish circulation and specialised subject-matter. Papers like the *Exchange and Mart*, for instance, or *Cage-Birds*, or the *Oracle*, or *Prediction*, or the *Matrimonial Times*, only exist because there is a definite demand for them, and they reflect the minds of their readers as a great national daily with a circulation of millions cannot possibly do.

Here I am only dealing with a single series of papers, the boys' twopenny weeklies, often inaccurately described as "penny dreadfuls". Falling strictly within this class there are at present ten papers, the *Gem*, *Magnet*, *Modern Boy*, *Triumph* and *Champion*, all owned by the Amalgamated Press, and the *Wizard*, *Rover*, *Skipper*, *Hotspur* and *Adventure*, all owned by D. C. Thomson & Co. What the circulations of these papers are, I do not know. The editors and proprietors refuse to name any figures, and in any case the circulation of a paper carrying serial stories is bound to fluctuate widely. But there is no question that the combined public of the ten papers is a very large one. They are on sale in every town in England, and nearly every boy who reads at all goes through a phase of reading one or more of them. The *Gem* and *Magnet*, which are much the oldest of these papers, are of rather different type from the rest, and they have evidently lost some of their popularity during the past few years. A good many boys now regard them as old-fashioned and "slow". Nevertheless I want to discuss them first, because they are more interesting psychologically than the others, and also because the mere survival of such papers into the nineteen-thirties is a rather startling phenomenon.

The *Gem* and *Magnet* are sister-papers (characters out of one paper frequently appear in the other), and were both started more than thirty years ago. At that time, together with *Chums* and the old *B[oy's] O[wn] P[aper]*, they were the leading papers for boys, and they remained dominant till quite recently. Each of them carries every week a fifteen- or twenty-thousand word school story, complete in itself, but usually more or less connected with the story of the week before. The *Gem* in addition to its school story carries one or more adventure serials. Otherwise the two papers are so much alike that they can be treated as one, though the *Magnet* has always been the better known of the two, probably because it possesses a really first-rate character in the fat boy, Billy Bunter.

The stories are stories of what purports to be public-school life, and the schools (Greyfriars in the *Magnet* and St Jim's in the *Gem*) are represented as ancient and fashionable foundations of the type of Eton or Winchester. All the leading characters are fourth-form boys aged fourteen or fifteen, older or younger boys only appearing in very minor parts. Like Sexton Blake and Nelson Lee, these boys continue week after week and year after year, never growing any older. Very occasionally a new boy arrives or a minor character drops out, but in at any rate the last twenty-five years the personnel has barely altered. All the principal characters in both papers—Bob Cherry, Tom Merry, Harry Wharton, Johnny Bull, Billy Bunter and the rest of them—were at Greyfriars or St Jim's long before the Great War, exactly the same age as at present, having much the same kind of adventures and talking almost exactly the same dialect.

And not only the characters but the whole atmosphere of both the *Gem* and *Magnet* has been preserved unchanged, partly by means of very elaborate stylisation. The stories in the *Magnet* are signed "Frank Richards" and those in the *Gem* "Martin Clifford", but a series lasting thirty years could hardly be the work of the same person every week.[1] Consequently they have to be written in a style that is easily imitated—an extraordinary, artificial, repetitive style, quite different from anything else now existing in English literature. A couple of extracts will do as illustrations. Here is one from the *Magnet*:

> Groan!
>
> "Shut up, Bunter!"
>
> Groan!
>
> Shutting up was not really in Billy Bunter's line. He seldom shut up, though often requested to do so. On the present awful occasion the fat Owl of Greyfriars was less inclined than ever to shut up. And he did not shut up! He groaned, and groaned, and went on groaning.
>
> Even groaning did not fully express Bunter's feeling. His feelings, in fact, were inexpressible.
>
> There were six of them in the soup! Only one of the six uttered sounds of woe and lamentation. But that one, William George Bunter, uttered enough for the whole party and a little over.
>
> Harry Wharton & Co. stood in a wrathy and worried group. They were landed and stranded, diddled, dished and done! etc etc etc.

Here is one from the *Gem*:

> "Oh cwumbs!"
>
> "Oh gum!"
>
> "Oooogh!"
>
> "Urrggh!"
>
> Arthur Augustus sat up dizzily. He grabbed his handkerchief and pressed it to his damaged nose. Tom Merry sat up, gasping for breath. They looked at one another.
>
> "Bai Jove! This is a go, deah boy!" gurgled Arthur Augustus.

[1] This is quite incorrect. These stories have been written throughout the whole period by "Frank Richards" and "Martin Clifford", who are one and the same person! See articles in *Horizon*, May 1940, and *Summer Pie*, summer 1944. [Author's footnote 1945.]

"I have been thwown into quite a fluttah! Oogh! The wottahs! The wuffians! The feahful outsidahs! Wow!" etc etc etc.

Both of these extracts are entirely typical; you would find something like them in almost every chapter of every number, today or twenty-five years ago. The first thing that anyone would notice is the extraordinary amount of tautology (the first of these two passages contains a hundred and twenty-five words and could be compressed into about thirty), seemingly designed to spin out the story, but actually playing its part in creating the atmosphere. For the same reason various facetious expressions are repeated over and over again; "wrathy", for instance, is a great favourite, and so is "diddled, dished and done". "Oooogh!", "Grooo!" and "Yaroo!" (stylised cries of pain) recur constantly, and so does "Ha! ha! ha!", always given a line to itself, so that sometimes a quarter of a column or thereabouts consists of "Ha! ha! ha!" The slang ("Go and eat coke!" "What the thump!", "You frabjous ass!", etc etc) has never been altered, so that the boys are now using slang which is at least thirty years out of date. In addition, the various nicknames are rubbed in on every possible occasion. Every few lines we are reminded that Harry Wharton & Co. are "the Famous Five", Bunter is always "the fat Owl" or "the Owl of the Remove", Vernon-Smith is always "the Bounder of Greyfriars", Gussy (the Honourable Arthur Augustus D'Arcy) is always "the swell of St Jim's", and so on and so forth. There is a constant, untiring effort to keep the atmosphere intact and to make sure that every new reader learns immediately who is who. The result has been to make Greyfriars and St Jim's into an extraordinary little world of their own, a world which cannot be taken seriously by anyone over fifteen, but which at any rate is not easily forgotten. By a debasement of the Dickens technique a series of stereotyped "characters" has been built up, in several cases very successfully. Billy Bunter, for instance, must be one of the best-known figures in English fiction; for the mere number of people who know him he ranks with Sexton Blake, Tarzan, Sherlock Holmes and a handful of characters in Dickens.

Needless to say, these stories are fantastically unlike life at a real public school. They run in cycles of rather differing types, but in general they are the clean-fun, knockabout type of story, with interest centring round horseplay, practical jokes, ragging masters, fights, canings, football, cricket and food. A constantly recurring story is one in which a boy is accused of some misdeed committed by another and is too much of a sportsman to reveal the truth. The "good" boys are "good" in the clean-living Englishman tradition—they keep in hard training, wash behind their ears, never hit below the belt, etc etc—and by way of contrast there is a series of "bad" boys, Racke, Crooke, Loder and others, whose badness consists in betting, smoking cigarettes and frequenting public houses. All these boys are constantly on the verge of expulsion, but as it would mean a change of personnel if any boy were actually expelled, no one is ever caught out in any really serious offence. Stealing, for instance, barely enters as a motif. Sex is completely taboo, especially in the form in which it actually arises at public schools. Occasionally girls enter into the stories, and very rarely there is something approaching a mild flirtation, but it is always entirely in the spirit of clean fun. A boy and a girl enjoy going for bicycle rides together—that is all it ever amounts to. Kissing, for instance, would be regarded as "soppy". Even the bad boys are presumed to be completely sexless. When the *Gem* and *Magnet* were started, it is probable that there was a deliberate intention to get away from the guilty sex-ridden atmosphere that pervaded so much of the earlier literature for boys. In the 'nineties the *Boy's Own Paper*, for instance, used to have its correspondence columns full of terrifying warnings against masturbation, and books like *St Winifred's* and *Tom Brown's Schooldays* were heavy with homosexual feeling, though no doubt the authors were not fully aware of it. In the *Gem* and *Magnet* sex simply does not exist as a problem. Religion is also taboo; in the whole thirty years' issue of the two papers the word "God" probably does not occur, except in "God save the King". On the other hand, there has always been a very strong "temperance" strain. Drinking and, by association, smoking are regarded as rather disgraceful even in an adult ("shady" is the usual word), but at the same time as something irresistibly fascinating, a sort of substitute for sex. In their moral atmosphere the *Gem* and *Magnet* have a great deal in common with the Boy Scout movement, which started at about the same time.

All literature of this kind is partly plagiarism. Sexton Blake, for instance, started off quite frankly as an imitation of Sherlock Holmes, and still resembles him fairly strongly; he has hawk-like features, lives in Baker Street, smokes enormously and puts on a dressing-gown when he wants to think. The *Gem* and *Magnet* probably owe something to the school story writers who were flourishing when they began, Gunby Hadath, Desmond Coke and the rest, but they owe more to nineteenth-century models. In so far as Greyfriars and St Jim's are like real schools at all, they are much more like Tom Brown's Rugby than a modern public school. Neither school has an OTC for instance, games are not compulsory, and the boys are even allowed to wear what clothes they like. But without doubt the main origin of these papers is *Stalky & Co.* This book has had an immense influence on boys' literature, and it is one of those books which have a sort of traditional reputation among people who have never even seen a copy of it. More than once in boys' weekly papers I have come across a reference to *Stalky & Co.* in which the word was spelt "Storky". Even the name of the chief comic among the Greyfriars masters, Mr Prout, is taken from *Stalky & Co.* and so is much of the slang: "jape", "merry", "giddy", "bizney" (business), "frabjous", "don't" for "doesn't"—all of them out of date even when *Gem* and *Magnet* started. There are also traces of earlier origins. The name "Greyfriars" is probably taken from Thackeray, and Gosling, the school porter in the *Magnet*, talks in an imitation of Dickens's dialect.

With all this, the supposed "glamour" of public-school life is played for all it is worth. There is all the usual paraphernalia—lock-up, roll-call, house matches, fagging, prefects, cosy teas round the study fire, etc etc—and constant reference to the "old school", the "old grey stones" (both schools were founded in the early sixteenth century), the "team spirit" of the "Greyfriars men". As for the snob-appeal, it is completely shameless. Each school has a titled boy or two whose titles are constantly thrust in the reader's face; other boys have the names of well-known aristocratic families, Talbot, Manners, Lowther. We are for ever being reminded that Gussy is the Honourable Arthur A. D'Arcy, son of Lord Eastwood, that Jack Blake is heir to "broad acres", that Hurree Jamset Ram Singh (nicknamed Inky) is the Nabob of Bhanipur, that Vernon-Smith's father is a millionaire. Till recently the illustrations in both papers always depicted the boys in clothes imitated from those of Eton; in the last few years Greyfriars has changed over to blazers and flannel trousers, but St Jim's still sticks to the Eton jacket, and Gussy sticks to his top-hat. In the school magazine which appears every week as part of the *Magnet*, Harry Wharton writes an article discussing the pocket-money received by the "fellows in the Remove", and reveals that some of them get as much as five pounds a week! This kind of thing is a perfectly deliberate incitement to wealth-fantasy. And here it is worth noticing a rather curious fact, and that is that the school story is a thing peculiar to England. So far as I know, there are extremely few school stories in foreign languages. The reason, obviously, is that in England education is mainly a matter of status. The most definite dividing-line between the petite bourgeoisie and the working class is that the former pay for their education, and within the bourgeoisie there is another unbridgeable gulf between the "public" school and the "private" school. It is quite clear that there are tens and scores of thousands of people to whom every detail of life at a "posh" public school is wildly thrilling and romantic. They happen to be outside that mystic world of quadrangles and house-colours, but they yearn after it, day-dream about it, live mentally in it for hours at a stretch. The question is, Who are these people? Who reads the *Gem* and *Magnet*?

Obviously one can never be quite certain about this kind of thing. All I can say from my own observation is this. Boys who are likely to go to public schools themselves generally read the *Gem* and *Magnet*, but they nearly always stop reading them when they are about twelve; they may continue for another year from force of habit, but by that time they have ceased to take them seriously. On the other hand, the boys at very cheap private schools, the schools that are designed for people who can't afford a public school but consider the Council schools "common", continue reading the *Gem* and *Magnet* for several years longer. A few years ago I was a teacher at two of these schools myself. I found that not only did virtually all the boys read the *Gem* and *Magnet*, but that they were still taking them fairly seriously when they were fifteen or even sixteen. These boys were the sons of shopkeepers, office employees and small business and professional men, and obviously it is this class that the *Gem* and *Magnet* are aimed at. But they are certainly read by working-class boys as well. They are generally on sale in the poorest quarters of big towns, and I have known them to be read by boys whom one might expect to be completely immune from public school "glamour". I have seen a young coal miner, for instance, a lad who had already worked a year or two underground, eagerly reading the *Gem*. Recently I offered a batch of English papers to some British legionaries of the French Foreign Legion in North Africa; they picked out the *Gem* and *Magnet* first. Both papers are much read by girls,[1]

[1] There are several corresponding girls' papers. The *Schoolgirl* is companion-paper to the *Magnet* and has stories by "Hilda Richards". The characters are

and the Pen Pals' department of the *Gem* shows that it is read in every corner of the British Empire, by Australians, Canadians, Palestine Jews, Malays, Arabs, Straits Chinese, etc etc. The editors evidently expect their readers to be aged round about fourteen, and the advertisements (milk chocolate, postage stamps, water pistols, blushing cured, home conjuring tricks, itching-powder, the Phine Phun Ring which runs a needle into your friend's hand, etc etc) indicate roughly the same age; there are also the Admiralty advertisements, however, which call for youths between seventeen and twenty-two. And there is no question that these papers are also read by adults. It is quite common for people to write to the editor and say that they have read every number of the *Gem* or *Magnet* for the past thirty years. Here, for instance, is a letter from a lady in Salisbury:

> I can say of your splendid yarns of Harry Wharton & Co. of Greyfriars, that they never fail to reach a high standard. Without doubt they are the finest stories of their type on the market today, which is saying a good deal. They seem to bring you face to face with Nature. I have taken the *Magnet* from the start, and have followed the adventures of Harry Wharton & Co. with rapt interest. I have no sons, but two daughters, and there's always a rush to be the first to read the grand old paper. My husband, too, was a staunch reader of the *Magnet* until he was suddenly taken away from us.

It is well worth getting hold of some copies of the *Gem* and *Magnet*, especially the *Gem*, simply to have a look at the correspondence columns. What is truly startling is the intense interest with which the pettiest details of life at Greyfriars and St Jim's are followed up. Here, for instance, are a few of the questions sent in by readers:

> "What age is Dick Roylance?" "How old is St Jim's?" "Can you give me a list of the Shell and their studies?" "How much did D'Arcy's monocle cost?" "How is it fellows like Crooke are in the Shell and decent fellows like yourself are only in the Fourth?" "What are the Form captain's three chief duties?" "Who is the chemistry master at St Jim's?" (From a girl) "Where is St Jim's situated? *Could* you tell me how to get there,

interchangeable to some extent. Bessie Bunter, Billy Bunter's sister, figures in the *Schoolgirl*. [Author's footnote.]

as I would love to see the building? Are you boys just 'phoneys', as I think you are?"

It is clear that many of the boys and girls who write these letters are living a complete fantasy-life. Sometimes a boy will write, for instance, giving his age, height, weight, chest and biceps measurements and asking which member of the Shell or Fourth Form he most exactly resembles. The demand for a list of the studies on the Shell passage, with an exact account of who lives in each, is a very common one. The editors, of course, do everything in their power to keep up the illusion. In the *Gem* Jack Blake is supposed to write the answers to correspondents, and in the *Magnet* a couple of pages is always given up to the school magazine (the *Greyfriars Herald*, edited by Harry Wharton), and there is another page in which one or other character is written up each week. The stories run in cycles, two or three characters being kept in the foreground for several weeks at a time. First there will be a series of rollicking adventure stories, featuring the Famous Five and Billy Bunter; then a run of stories turning on mistaken identity, with Wibley (the make-up wizard) in the star part; then a run of more serious stories in which Vernon-Smith is trembling on the verge of expulsion. And here one comes upon the real secret of the *Gem* and *Magnet* and the probable reason why they continue to be read in spite of their obvious out-of-dateness.

It is that the characters are so carefully graded as to give almost every type of reader a character he can identify himself with. Most boys' papers aim at doing this, hence the boy-assistant (Sexton Blake's Tinker, Nelson Lee's Nipper, etc) who usually accompanies the explorer, detective or what-not on his adventures. But in these cases there is only one boy, and usually it is much the same type of boy. In the *Gem* and *Magnet* there is a model for very nearly everybody. There is the normal, athletic, high-spirited boy (Tom Merry, Jack Blake, Frank Nugent), a slightly rowdier version of this type (Bob Cherry), a more aristocratic version (Talbot, Manners), a quieter, more serious version (Harry Wharton), and a stolid, "bull-dog" version (Johnny Bull). Then there is the reckless, dare-devil type of boy (Vernon-Smith), the definitely "clever", studious boy (Mark Linley, Dick Penfold), and the eccentric boy who is not good at games but possesses some special talent (Skinner, Wibley). And there is the scholarship-boy (Tom Redwing), an important figure in this class of story because he makes it possible for boys from very poor homes to project themselves into the public-school atmosphere. In addition there are Australian, Irish, Welsh, Manx, Yorkshire and Lancashire boys to play upon local patriotism. But the subtlety of characterisation goes deeper than this. If one studies the correspondence columns one sees that there is probably *no* character in the *Gem* and *Magnet* whom some or other reader does not identify with, except the out-and-out comics, Coker, Billy Bunter, Fisher T. Fish (the money-grubbing American boy) and, of course, the masters. Bunter, though in his origin he probably owed something to the fat boy in *Pickwick*, is a real creation. His tight trousers against which boots and canes are constantly thudding, his astuteness in search of food, his postal order which never turns up, have made him famous wherever the Union Jack waves. But he is not a subject for day-dreams. On the other hand, another seeming figure of fun, Gussy (the Honourable Arthur A. D'Arcy, "the swell of St Jim's"), is evidently much admired. Like everything else in the *Gem* and *Magnet*, Gussy is at least thirty years out of date. He is the "knut" of the early twentieth century or even the "masher" of the 'nineties ("Bai Jove, deah boy!" and "Weally, I shall be obliged to give you a feahful thwashin'!"), the monocled idiot who made good on the fields of Mons and Le Cateau. And his evident popularity goes to show how deep the snob-appeal of this type is. English people are extremely fond of the titled ass (cf Lord Peter Wimsey) who always turns up trumps in the moment of emergency. Here is a letter from one of Gussy's girl admirers:

> I think you're too hard on Gussy. I wonder he's still in existence, the way you treat him. He's my hero. Did you know I write lyrics? How's this—to the tune of "Goody Goody"?
>
> Gonna get my gas-mask, join the A.R.P.
> 'Cos I'm wise to all those bombs you drop on me.
> Gonna dig myself a trench
> Inside the garden fence;
> Gonna seal my windows up with tin
> So that the tear gas can't get in;
> Gonna park my cannon right outside the kerb
> With a note to Adolf Hitler: 'Don't disturb!'
> And if I never fall in Nazi hands
> That's soon enough for me
> Gonna get my gas-mask, join the A.R.P.
>
> P.S.—Do you get on well with girls?

I quote this in full because (dated April 1939) it is interesting as being probably the earliest mention of Hitler in the *Gem*. In the *Gem* there is also a heroic fat boy, Fatty Wynn, as a set-off against Bunter. Vernon-Smith, "the Bounder of the Remove", a Byronic character, always on the verge of the sack, is another great favourite. And even some of the cads probably have their following. Loder, for instance, "the rotter of the Sixth", is a cad, but he is also a highbrow and given to saying sarcastic things about football and the team spirit. The boys of the Remove only think him all the more of a cad for this, but a certain type of boy would probably identify with him. Even Racke, Crooke and Co. are probably admired by small boys who think it diabolically wicked to smoke cigarettes. (A frequent question in the correspondence column: "What brand of cigarettes does Racke smoke?")

Naturally the politics of the *Gem* and *Magnet* are Conservative, but in a completely pre-1914 style, with no Fascist tinge. In reality their basic political assumptions are two: nothing ever changes, and foreigners are funny. In the *Gem* of 1939 Frenchmen are still Froggies and Italians are still Dagoes. Mossoo, the French master at Greyfriars, is the usual comic-paper Frog, with pointed beard, pegtop trousers, etc. Inky, the Indian boy, though a rajah, and therefore possessing snob-appeal, is also the comic babu of the *Punch* tradition. ("'The rowfulness is not the proper caper, my esteemed Bob,' said Inky. 'Let dogs delight in the barkfulness and bitefulness, but the soft answer is the cracked pitcher that goes longest to a bird in the bush, as the English proverb remarks.'")? Fisher T. Fish is the old-style stage Yankee ("'Waal, I guess,'" etc) dating from a period of Anglo-American jealousy. Wun Lung, the Chinese boy (he has rather faded out of late, no doubt because some of the *Magnet's* readers are Straits Chinese), is the nineteenth-century pantomime Chinaman, with saucer-shaped hat, pigtail and pidgin-English. The assumption all along is not only that foreigners are comics who are put there for us to laugh at, but that they can be classified in much the same way as insects. That is why in all boys' papers, not only the *Gem* and *Magnet*, a Chinese is invariably portrayed with a pigtail. It is the thing you recognise him by, like the Frenchman's beard or the Italian's barrel-organ. In papers of this kind it occasionally happens that when the setting of a story is in a foreign country some attempt is made to describe the natives as individual human beings, but as a rule it is assumed that foreigners of any one race are all alike and will conform more or less exactly to the following patterns:

> FRENCHMAN: Excitable. Wears beard, gesticulates wildly.
> SPANIARD, MEXICAN etc: Sinister, treacherous.
> ARAB, AFGHAN etc: Sinister, treacherous.
> CHINESE: Sinister, treacherous. Wears pigtail.
> ITALIAN: Excitable. Grinds barrel-organ or carries stiletto.
> SWEDE, DANE etc: Kind hearted, stupid.
> NEGRO: Comic, very faithful.

The working classes only enter into the *Gem* and *Magnet* as comics or semi-villains (race-course touts etc.). As for class-friction, trade unionism, strikes, slumps, unemployment, Fascism and civil war—not a mention. Somewhere or other in the thirty years' issue of the two papers you might perhaps find the word "Socialism", but you would have to look a long time for it. If the Russian Revolution is anywhere referred to, it will be indirectly, in the word "Bolshy" (meaning a person of violent disagreeable habits). Hitler and the Nazis are just beginning to make their appearance, in the sort of reference I quoted above. The war crisis of September 1938 made just enough impression to produce a story in which Mr Vernon-Smith, the Bounder's millionaire father, cashed in on the general panic by buying up country houses in order to sell them to "crisis scuttlers". But that is probably as near to noticing the European situation as the *Gem* and *Magnet* will come, until the war actually starts.[1] That does not mean that these papers are unpatriotic—quite the contrary! Throughout the Great War the *Gem* and *Magnet* were perhaps the most consistently and cheerfully patriotic papers in England. Almost every week the boys caught a spy or pushed a conchy into the army, and during the rationing period "EAT LESS BREAD" was printed in large type on every page. But their patriotism has nothing whatever to do with power politics or "ideological" warfare. It is more akin to family loyalty, and actually it gives one a valuable clue to the attitude of ordinary people, especially the huge untouchable block of the middle class and the better-off working class. These people are patriotic to the middle of their bones, but they do not feel that what happens in foreign countries is any of their

[1] This was written some months before the outbreak of war. Up to the end of September 1939 no mention of the war has appeared in either paper. [Author's footnote.]

business. When England is in danger they rally to its defence as a matter of course, but in between times they are not interested. After all, England is always in the right and England always wins, so why worry? It is an attitude that has been shaken during the past twenty years, but not so deeply as is sometimes supposed. Failure to understand it is one of the reasons why left-wing political parties are seldom able to produce an acceptable foreign policy.

The mental world of the *Gem* and *Magnet*, therefore, is something like this:

The year is 1910—or 1940, but it is all the same. You are at Greyfriars, a rosy-cheeked boy of fourteen in posh, tailor-made clothes, sitting down to tea in your study on the Remove passage after an exciting game of football which was won by an odd goal in the last half-minute. There is a cosy fire in the study, and outside the wind is whistling. The ivy clusters thickly round the old grey stones. The King is on his throne and the pound is worth a pound. Over in Europe the comic foreigners are jabbering and gesticulating, but the grim grey battleships of the British Fleet are steaming up the Channel and at the outposts of Empire the monocled Englishmen are holding the niggers at bay. Lord Mauleverer has just got another fiver and we are all settling down to a tremendous tea of sausages, sardines, crumpets, potted meat, jam and doughnuts. After tea we shall sit round the study fire having a good laugh at Billy Bunter and discussing the team for next week's match against Rookwood. Everything is safe, solid and unquestionable. Everything will be the same for ever and ever. That approximately is the atmosphere.

But now turn from the *Gem* and *Magnet* to the more up-to-date papers which have appeared since the Great War. The truly significant thing is that they have more points of resemblance to the *Gem* and *Magnet* than points of difference. But it is better to consider the differences first.

There are eight of these newer papers, the *Modern Boy*, *Triumph*, *Champion*, *Wizard*, *Rover*, *Skipper*, *Hotspur* and *Adventure*. All of these have appeared since the Great War, but except for the *Modern Boy* none of them is less than five years old. Two papers which ought also to be mentioned briefly here, though they are not strictly in the same class as the rest, are the *Detective Weekly* and the *Thriller*, both owned by the Amalgamated Press. The *Detective Weekly* has taken over Sexton Blake. Both of these papers admit a certain amount of sex-interest into their stories, and though certainly read by boys, they are not aimed at them exclusively. All the others are boys' papers pure and simple, and they are sufficiently alike to be considered together. There does not seem to be any notable difference between Thomson's publications and those of the Amalgamated Press.

As soon as one looks at these papers one sees their technical superiority to the *Gem* and *Magnet*. To begin with, they have the great advantage of not being written entirely by one person. Instead of one long complete story, a number of the *Wizard* or *Hotspur* consists of half a dozen or more serials, none of which goes on for ever. Consequently there is far more variety and far less padding, and none of the tiresome stylisation and facetiousness of the *Gem* and *Magnet*. Look at these two extracts, for example:

> Billy Bunter groaned.
>
> A quarter of an hour had elapsed out of the two hours that Bunter was booked for extra French.
>
> In a quarter of an hour there were only fifteen minutes! But every one of those minutes seemed inordinately long to Bunter. They seemed to crawl by like tired snails.
>
> Looking at the clock in Class-room No. 10 the fat Owl could hardly believe that only fifteen minutes had passed. It seemed more like fifteen hours, if not fifteen days!
>
> Other fellows were in extra French as well as Bunter. They did not matter. Bunter did! (*Magnet.*)

> After a terrible climb, hacking out handholds in the smooth ice every step of the way up, Sergeant Lionheart Logan of the Mounties was now clinging like a human fly to the face of an icy cliff, as smooth and treacherous as a giant pane of glass.
>
> An Arctic blizzard, in all its fury, was buffeting his body, driving the blinding snow into his face, seeking to tear his fingers loose from their handholds and dash him to death on the jagged boulders which lay at the foot of the cliff a hundred feet below.
>
> Crouching among those boulders were eleven villainous trappers who had done their best to shoot down Lionheart and his companion, Constable Jim Rogers—until the blizzard had blotted the two Mounties out of sight from below. (*Wizard.*)

The second extract gets you some distance with the story, the first takes a hundred words to tell you that Bunter is in the detention class. Moreover, by not concentrating on school stories (in point of numbers the school story slightly predominates in all these papers, except the *Thriller* and *Detective Weekly*), the *Wizard, Hotspur*, etc have far greater opportunities for sensationalism. Merely looking at the cover illustrations of the papers which I have on the table in front of me, here are some of the things I see. On one a cowboy is clinging by his toes to the wing of an aeroplane in mid-air and shooting down another aeroplane with his revolver. On another a Chinese is swimming for his life down a sewer with a swarm of ravenous-looking rats swimming after him. On another an engineer is lighting a stick of dynamite while a steel robot feels for him with its claws. On another a man in airman's costume is fighting bare-handed against a rat somewhat larger than a donkey. On another a nearly naked man of terrific muscular development has just seized a lion by the tail and flung it thirty yards over the wall of an arena, with the words, "Take back your blooming lion!" Clearly no school story can compete with this kind of thing. From time to time the school buildings may catch fire or the French master may turn out to be the head of an international anarchist gang, but in a general way the interest must centre round cricket, school rivalries, practical jokes, etc. There is not much room for bombs, death-rays, sub-machine-guns, aeroplanes, mustangs, octopuses, grizzly bears or gangsters.

Examination of a large number of these papers shows that, putting aside school stories, the favourite subjects are Wild West, Frozen North, Foreign Legion, crime (always from the detective's angle), the Great War (Air Force or Secret Service, not the infantry), the Tarzan motif in varying forms, professional football, tropical exploration, historical romance (Robin Hood, Cavaliers and Roundheads, etc) and scientific invention. The Wild West still leads, at any rate as a setting, though the Red Indian seems to be fading out. The one theme that is really new is the scientific one. Death-rays, Martians, invisible men, robots, helicopters and interplanetary rockets figure largely; here and there there are even far-off rumours of psychotherapy and ductless glands. Whereas the *Gem* and *Magnet* derive from Dickens and Kipling, the *Wizard, Champion, Modern Boy*, etc owe a great deal to H. G. Wells, who, rather than Jules Verne, is the father of "Scientifiction". Naturally it is the magical, Martian aspect of science that is most exploited, but one or two papers include serious articles on scientific subjects, besides quantities of informative snippets. (Examples: "A Kauri tree in Queensland, Australia, is over 12,000 years old"; "Nearly 50,000 thunderstorms occur every day"; "Helium gas costs £1 per

1,000 cubic feet"; "There are over 500 varieties of spiders in Great Britain"; "London firemen use 14,000,000 gallons of water annually", etc etc.) There is a marked advance in intellectual curiosity and, on the whole, in the demand made on the reader's attention. In practice the *Gem* and *Magnet* and the post-war papers are read by much the same public, but the mental age aimed at seems to have risen by a year or two years—an improvement probably corresponding to the improvement in elementary education since 1909.

The other thing that has emerged in the post-war boys' papers, though not to anything like the extent one would expect, is bully-worship and the cult of violence.

If one compares the *Gem* and *Magnet* with a genuinely modern paper, the thing that immediately strikes one is the absence of the leader-principle. There is no central dominating character; instead there are fifteen or twenty characters, all more or less on an equality, with whom readers of different types can identify. In the more modern papers this is not usually the case. Instead of identifying with a schoolboy of more or less his own age, the reader of the *Skipper*, *Hotspur*, etc is led to identify with a G-man, with a Foreign Legionary, with some variant of Tarzan, with an air ace, a master spy, an explorer, a pugilist—at any rate with some single all-powerful character who dominates everyone about him and whose usual method of solving any problem is a sock on the jaw. This character is intended as a superman, and as physical strength is the form of power that boys can best understand, he is usually a sort of human gorilla; in the Tarzan type of story he is sometimes actually a giant, eight or ten feet high. At the same time the scenes of violence in nearly all these stories are remarkably harmless and unconvincing. There is a great difference in tone between even the most bloodthirsty English paper and the threepenny Yank Mags, *Fight Stories*, *Action Stories*, etc (not strictly boys' papers, but largely read by boys). In the Yank Mags you get real blood-lust, really gory descriptions of the all-in, jump-on-his-testicles style of fighting, written in a jargon that has been perfected by people who brood endlessly on violence. A paper like *Fight Stories*, for instance, would have very little appeal except to sadists and masochists. You can see the comparative gentleness of the English civilisation by the amateurish way in which prize-fighting is always described in the boys' weeklies. There is no specialised vocabulary. Look at these four extracts, two English, two American:

When the gong sounded, both men were breathing heavily, and each had great red marks on his chest, Bill's chin was bleeding, and Ben had a cut over his right eye.

Into their corners they sank, but when the gong clanged again they were up swiftly, and they went like tigers at each other. (*Rover.*)

He walked in stolidly and smashed a clublike right to my face. Blood spattered and I went back on my heels, but surged in and ripped my right under his heart. Another right smashed full on Sven's already battered mouth, and, spitting out the fragments of a tooth, he crashed a flailing left to my body. (*Fight Stories.*)

It was amazing to watch the Black Panther at work. His muscles rippled and slid under his dark skin. There was all the power and grace of a giant cat in his swift and terrible onslaught.

He volleyed blows with a bewildering speed for so huge a fellow. In a moment Ben was simply blocking with his gloves as well as he could. Ben was really a past-master of defence. He had many fine victories behind him. But the Negro's rights and lefts crashed through openings that hardly any other fighter could have found. (*Wizard.*)

Haymakers which packed the bludgeoning weight of forest monarchs crashing down under the ax hurled into the bodies of the two heavies as they swapped punches. (*Fight Stories.*)

Notice how much more knowledgeable the American extracts sound. They are written for devotees of the prize-ring, the others are not. Also, it ought to be emphasised that on its level the moral code of the English boys' papers is a decent one. Crime and dishonesty are never held up to admiration, there is none of the cynicism and corruption of the American gangster story. The huge sale of the Yank Mags in England shows that there is a demand for that kind of thing, but very few English writers seem able to produce it. When hatred of Hitler became a major emotion in America, it was interesting to see how promptly "anti-Fascism" was adapted to pornographic purposes by the editors of the Yank Mags. One magazine which I have in front of me is given up to a long, complete story, "When Hell Came to America", in which the agents of a "blood-maddened European dictator" are trying to conquer the USA with death-rays and invisible aeroplanes. There is the frankest appeal to sadism, scenes in which the Nazis tie bombs to women's backs and fling them off heights to watch them blown to pieces in mid-air, others in which they tie naked girls together by their hair and prod them with knives to make them dance, etc etc. The editor comments solemnly on all this, and uses it as a plea for tightening up restrictions against immigrants. On another page of the same paper: "LIVES OF THE HOTCHA CHORUS GIRLS. Reveals all the intimate secrets and fascinating pastimes of the famous Broadway Hotcha girls. NOTHING IS OMITTED. Price 10c." "HOW TO LOVE. 10c." "FRENCH PHOTO RING, 25c." "NAUGHTY NUDIES TRANSFERS. From the outside of the glass you see a beautiful girl, innocently dressed. Turn it around and look through the glass and oh! what a difference! Set of 3 transfers 25c." etc etc etc. There is nothing at all like this in any English paper likely to be read by boys. But the process of Americanisation is going on all the same. The American ideal, the "he-man", the "tough guy", the gorilla who puts everything right by socking everybody else on the jaw, now figures in probably a majority of boys' papers. In one serial now running in the *Skipper* he is always portrayed, ominously enough, swinging a rubber truncheon.

The development of the *Wizard*, *Hotspur*, etc, as against the earlier boys' papers, boils down to this: better technique, more scientific interest, more bloodshed, more leader-worship. But, after all, it is the *lack* of development that is the really striking thing.

To begin with, there is no political development whatever. The world of the *Skipper* and the *Champion* is still the pre-1914 world of the *Magnet* and the *Gem*. The Wild West story, for instance, with its cattle-rustlers, lynch-law and other paraphernalia belonging to the 'eighties, is a curiously archaic thing. It is worth noticing that in papers of this type it is always taken for granted that adventures only happen at the ends of the earth, in tropical forests, in Arctic wastes, in African deserts, on Western prairies, in Chinese opium dens—everywhere, in fact, except the places where things really *do* happen. That is a belief dating from thirty or forty years ago, when the new continents were in process of being opened up. Nowadays, of course, if you really want adventure, the place to look for it is in Europe. But apart from the picturesque side of the Great War, contemporary history is carefully excluded. And except that Americans are now admired instead of being laughed at, foreigners are exactly the same figures of fun that they always were. If a Chinese character appears, he is still the sinister pigtailed opium-smuggler of Sax

Rohmer; no indication that things have been happening in China since 1912—no indication that a war is going on there, for instance. If a Spaniard appears, he is still a "dago" or "greaser" who rolls cigarettes and stabs people in the back; no indication that things have been happening in Spain. Hitler and the Nazis have not yet appeared, or are barely making their appearance. There will be plenty about them in a little while, but it will be from a strictly patriotic angle (Britain versus Germany), with the real meaning of the struggle kept out of sight as much as possible. As for the Russian Revolution, it is extremely difficult to find any reference to it in any of these papers. When Russia is mentioned at all it is usually in an information snippet (example: "There are 29,000 centenarians in the USSR"), and any reference to the Revolution is indirect and twenty years out of date. In one story in the *Rover*, for instance, somebody has a tame bear, and as it is a Russian bear, it is nicknamed Trotsky—obviously an echo of the 1917–23 period and not of recent controversies. The clock has stopped at 1910. Britannia rules the waves, and no one has heard of slumps, booms, unemployment, dictatorships, purges or concentration camps.

And in social outlook there is hardly any advance. The snobbishness is somewhat less open than in the *Gem* and *Magnet*—that is the most one can possibly say. To begin with, the school story, always partly dependent on snob-appeal, is by no means eliminated. Every number of a boys' paper includes at least one school story, these stories slightly outnumbering the Wild Westerns. The very elaborate fantasy-life of the *Gem* and *Magnet* is not imitated and there is more emphasis on extraneous adventure, but the social atmosphere (old grey stones) is much the same. When a new school is introduced at the beginning of a story we are often told in just about those words that "it was a very posh school". From time to time a story appears which is ostensibly directed *against* snobbery. The scholarship-boy (cf Tom Redwing in the *Magnet*) makes fairly frequent appearances, and what is essentially the same theme is sometimes presented in this form; there is great rivalry between two schools, one of which considers itself more "posh" than the other, and there are fights, practical jokes, football matches, etc always ending in the discomfiture of the snobs. If one glances very superficially at some of these stories it is possible to imagine that a democratic spirit has crept into the boys' weeklies, but when one looks more closely one sees that they merely reflect the bitter jealousies that exist within the white-collar class. Their real function is to allow the boy who goes to a cheap private school (*not* a Council school) to feel that his school is just as "posh" in the sight of God as Winchester or Eton. The sentiment of school loyalty ("We're better than the fellows down the road"), a thing almost unknown to the real working class, is still kept up. As these stories are written by many different hands, they do, of course, vary a good deal in tone. Some are reasonably free from snobbishness, in others money and pedigree are exploited even more shamelessly than in the *Gem* and *Magnet*. In one that I came across an actual *majority* of the boys mentioned were titled.

Where working-class characters appear, it is usually either as comics (jokes about tramps, convicts, etc) or as prize-fighters, acrobats, cowboys, professional footballers and Foreign Legionaries—in other words, as adventurers. There is no facing of the facts about working-class life, or, indeed, about *working* life of any description. Very occasionally one may come across a realistic description of, say, work in a coal mine, but in all probability it will only be there as the background of some lurid adventure. In any case the central character is not likely to be a coal miner. Nearly all the time the boy who reads these papers—in nine cases out of ten a boy who is going to spend his life working in a shop, in a factory or in some subordinate job in an office—is led to identify with people in positions of command, above all with people who are never troubled by shortage of money. The Lord Peter Wimsey figure, the seeming idiot who drawls and wears a monocle but is always to the fore in moments of danger, turns up over and over again. (This character is a great favourite in Secret Service stories.) And, as usual, the heroic characters all have to talk BBC; they may talk Scottish or Irish or American, but no one in a star part is ever permitted to drop an aitch. Here it is worth comparing the social atmosphere of the boys' weeklies with that of the women's weeklies, the *Oracle*, the *Family Star*, *Peg's Paper*, etc.

The women's papers are aimed at an older public and are read for the most part by girls who are working for a living. Consequently they are on the surface much more realistic. It is taken for granted, for example, that nearly everyone has to live in a big town and work at a more or less dull job. Sex, so far from being taboo, is *the* subject. The short, complete stories, the special feature of these papers, are generally of the "came the dawn" type: the heroine narrowly escapes losing her "boy" to a designing rival, or the "boy" loses his job and has to postpone marriage, but presently gets a better job. The changeling-fantasy (a girl brought up in a poor home is "really" the child of rich parents) is another favourite. Where sensationalism comes in, usually in the serials, it arises out of the more domestic type of crime, such as bigamy, forgery or sometimes murder; no Martians, death-rays or international anarchist gangs. These papers are at any rate aiming at credibility, and they have a link with real life in their correspondence columns, where genuine problems are being discussed. Ruby M. Ayres's column of advice in the *Oracle*, for instance, is extremely sensible and well written. And yet the world of the *Oracle* and *Peg's Paper* is a pure fantasy-world. It is the same fantasy all the time, pretending to be richer than you are. The chief impression that one carries away from almost every story in these papers is of frightful, overwhelming "refinement". Ostensibly the characters are working-class people, but their habits, the interiors of their houses, their clothes, their outlook and, above all, their speech are entirely middle class. They are all living at several pounds a week above their income. And needless to say, that is just the impression that is intended. The idea is to give the bored factory-girl or worn-out mother of five a dream-life in which she pictures herself—not actually as a duchess (that convention has gone out) but as, say, the wife of a bank-manager. Not only is a five-to-six-pound-a-week standard of life set up as the ideal, but it is tacitly assumed that that is how working-class people really *do* live. The major facts are simply not faced. It is admitted, for instance, that people sometimes lose their jobs; but then the dark clouds roll away and they get better jobs instead. No mention of unemployment as something permanent and inevitable, no mention of the dole, no mention of trade unionism. No suggestion anywhere that there can be anything wrong with the system *as a system*; there are only individual misfortunes, which are generally due to somebody's wickedness and can in any case be put right in the last chapter. Always the dark clouds roll away, the kind employer raises Alfred's wages, and there are jobs for everybody except the drunks. It is still the world of the *Wizard* and the *Gem*, except that there are orange-blossoms instead of machine-guns.

The outlook inculcated by all these papers is that of a rather exceptionally stupid member of the Navy League in the year 1910. Yes, it may be said, but what does it matter? And in any case, what else do you expect?

Of course no one in his senses would want to turn the so-called penny dreadful into a realistic novel or a Socialist tract. An adventure story must of its nature be more or less remote from real life. But, as I have tried to make clear, the unreality of the *Wizard* and the *Gem* is not so artless as it looks. These papers exist because of a specialised demand, because boys at certain ages find it necessary to read about Martians, death-rays, grizzly bears and gangsters. They get what they are looking for, but they get it wrapped up in the illusions which their future employers think suitable for them. To what extent people draw their ideas from fiction is disputable. Personally I believe that most people are influenced far more than they would care to admit by novels, serial stories, films and so forth, and that from this point of view the worst books are often the most important, because they are usually the ones that are read earliest in life. It is probable that many people who could consider themselves extremely sophisticated and "advanced" are actually carrying through life an imaginative background which they acquired in childhood from (for instance) Sapper and Ian Hay. If that is so, the boys' twopenny weeklies are of the deepest importance. Here is the stuff that is read somewhere between the ages of twelve and eighteen by a very large proportion, perhaps an actual majority, of English boys, including many who will never read anything else except newspapers; and along with it they are absorbing a set of beliefs which would be regarded as hopelessly out of date in the Central Office of the Conservative Party. All the better because it is done indirectly, there is being pumped into them the conviction that the major problems of our time do not exist, that there is nothing wrong with *laissez-faire* capitalism, that foreigners are unimportant comics and that the British Empire is a sort of charity-concern which will last for ever. Considering who owns these papers, it is difficult to believe that this is unintentional. Of the twelve papers I have been discussing (i.e. twelve including the *Thriller* and *Detective Weekly*) seven are the property of the Amalgamated Press, which is one of the biggest press-combines in the world and controls more than a hundred different papers. The *Gem* and *Magnet*, therefore, are closely linked up with the *Daily Telegraph* and the *Financial Times*. This in itself would be enough to rouse certain suspicions, even if it were not obvious that the stories in the boys' weeklies are politically vetted. So it appears that if you feel the need of a fantasy-life in which you travel to Mars and fight lions bare-handed (and what boy doesn't?) you can only have it by delivering yourself over, mentally, to people like Lord

Camrose. For there is no competition. Throughout the whole of this run of papers the differences are negligible, and on this level no others exist. This raises the question, why is there no such thing as a left-wing boys' paper?

At first glance such an idea merely makes one slightly sick. It is so horribly easy to imagine what a left-wing boys' paper would be like, if it existed. I remember in 1920 or 1921 some optimistic person handing round Communist tracts among a crowd of public-school boys. The tract I received was of the question-and-answer kind:

> *Q*. "Can a Boy Communist be a Boy Scout, Comrade?"
> *A*. "No, Comrade."
> *Q*. "Why, Comrade?"
> *A*. "Because, Comrade, a Boy Scout must salute the Union Jack, which is the symbol of tyranny and oppression," etc etc.

Now, suppose that at this moment somebody started a left-wing paper deliberately aimed at boys of twelve or fourteen. I do not suggest that the whole of its contents would be exactly like the tract I have quoted above, but does anyone doubt that they would be *something* like it? Inevitably such a paper would either consist of dreary uplift or it would be under Communist influence and given over to adulation of Soviet Russia; in either case no normal boy would ever look at it. Highbrow literature apart, the whole of the existing left-wing press, in so far as it is at all vigorously "left", is one long tract. The one Socialist paper in England which could live a week on its merits *as a paper* is the *Daily Herald*, and how much Socialism is there in the *Daily Herald*? At this moment, therefore, a paper with a "left" slant and at the same time likely to have an appeal to ordinary boys in their teens is something almost beyond hoping for.

But it does not follow that it is impossible. There is no clear reason why every adventure story should necessarily be mixed up with snobbishness and gutter patriotism. For, after all, the stories in the *Hotspur* and the *Modern Boy* are not Conservative tracts; they are merely adventure stories with a Conservative bias. It is fairly easy to imagine the process being reversed. It is possible, for instance, to imagine a paper as thrilling and lively as the *Hotspur*, but with subject-matter and "ideology" a little more up to date. It is even possible (though this raises other difficulties) to imagine a women's paper at the same literary level as the *Oracle*, dealing in approximately the same kind of story, but taking rather more account of the realities of working-class life. Such things have been done before, though not in England. In the last years of the Spanish monarchy there was a large output in Spain of left-wing novelettes, some of them evidently of Anarchist origin. Unfortunately at the time when they were appearing I did not see their social significance, and I lost the collection of them that I had, but no doubt copies would still be procurable. In get-up and style of story they were very similar to the English fourpenny novelette, except that their inspiration was "left". If, for instance, a story described police pursuing Anarchists through the mountains, it would be from the point of view of the Anarchists and not of the police. An example nearer to hand is the Soviet film *Chapaiev*, which has been shown a number of times in London. Technically, by the standards of the time when it was made, *Chapaiev* is a first-rate film, but mentally, in spite of the unfamiliar Russian background, it is not so very remote from Hollywood. The one thing that lifts it out of the ordinary is the remarkable performance by the actor who takes the part of the White officer (the fat one)—a performance which looks very like an inspired piece of gagging. Otherwise the atmosphere is familiar. All the usual paraphernalia is there—heroic fight against odds, escape at the last moment, shots of galloping horses, love interest, comic relief. The film is in fact a fairly ordinary one, except that its tendency is "left". In a Hollywood film of the Russian civil war the Whites would probably be angels and the Reds demons. In the Russian version the Reds are angels and the Whites demons. That also is a lie, but, taking the long view, it is a less pernicious lie than the other.

Here several difficult problems present themselves. Their general nature is obvious enough, and I do not want to discuss them. I am merely pointing to the fact that, in England, popular imaginative literature is a field that left-wing thought has never begun to enter. *All* fiction from the novels in the mushroom libraries downwards is censored in the interests of the ruling class. And boys' fiction above all, the blood-and-thunder stuff which nearly every boy devours at some time or other, is sodden in the worst illusions of 1910. The fact is only unimportant if one believes that what is read in childhood leaves no impression behind. Lord Camrose and his colleagues evidently believe nothing of the kind, and, after all, Lord Camrose ought to know.

Written 1939

Horizon, March 1940 (abridged); ITW; (slightly revised) CrE; DD; CE.

[Shortly after "Boys' Weeklies" appeared in *Horizon*, the editor, Cyril Connolly, was amazed to receive a letter from Frank Richards, very much alive, and asking for space to reply to "the charges" made against him. His reply reprinted here, appeared in *Horizon*, May 1940 and was much discussed and enjoyed in London literary circles at the time and by Orwell himself although, before seeing it, he expressed his apprehension about it to Geoffrey Gorer. See 165.]

Frank Richards Replies to George Orwell

The Editor has kindly given me space to reply to Mr Orwell, whose article on Boys' Weeklies appeared in *Horizon* No 3. Mr Orwell's article is a rather remarkable one to appear in a periodical of this kind. From the fact that *Horizon* contains a picture that does not resemble a picture, a poem that does not resemble poetry, and a story that does not resemble a story, I conclude that it must be a very high-browed paper indeed: and I was agreeably surprised, therefore, to find in it an article written in a lively and entertaining manner, and actually readable. I was still more interested as this article dealt chiefly with my work as an author for boys. Mr Orwell perpetrates so many inaccuracies, however, and flicks off his condemnations with so careless a hand, that I am glad of an opportunity to set him right on a few points. He reads into my very innocent fiction a fell scheme for drugging the minds of the younger proletariat into dull acquiescence in a system of which Mr Orwell does not approve: and of which, in consequence, he cannot imagine anyone else approving except from interested motives. Anyone who disagrees with Mr Orwell is necessarily either an antiquated ass or an exploiter on the make! His most serious charge against my series is that it smacks of the year 1910: a period which Mr Orwell appears to hold in peculiar horror. Probably I am older than Mr Orwell: and I can tell him that the world went very well then. It has not been improved by the Great War, the General Strike, the outbreak of sex-chatter, by make-up or lipstick, by the present discontents, or by Mr Orwell's thoughts upon the present discontents! But Mr Orwell not only reads a diehard dunderheaded Tory into a harmless author for boys: he accuses him of plagiarism, of snobbishness, of being out of date, even of cleanliness of mind, as if that were a sin also. I propose to take Mr Orwell's indictment charge by charge, rebutting the same one after another, excepting the last, to which I plead guilty. After which I expect to receive from Mr Orwell a telegram worded like that of the invader of Sind.

To begin with the plagiarism. "Probably," says Mr Orwell, "the *Magnet* owes something to Gunby Hadath, Desmond Coke, and the rest." Frank Richards had never read Desmond Coke till the nineteen-twenties: he had never read Gunby Hadath—whoever Gunby Hadath may be—at all. "Even the name of the chief comic among the Greyfriars masters, Mr Prout, is taken from *Stalky & Co.*," declares Mr Orwell. Now, it is true that there is a formmaster at Greyfriars named Prout, and there is a housemaster in *Stalky* named Prout. It is also true that the *Magnet* author is named Richards: and that there is a Richards in *Stalky & Co.* But the Fifth-form master at Greyfriars no more derives from the Stalky Prout, than the *Magnet* author from the *Stalky* Richards. *Stalky*'s Prout is a "gloomy ass", worried, dubious, easily worked on by others. The Greyfriars Prout is portly, self-satisfied, impervious to the opinions of others. No two characters could be more unlike. Mr Prout of Greyfriars is a very estimable gentleman: and characters in a story, after all, must have names. Every name in existence has been used over and over again in fiction.

The verb "to jape", says Mr Orwell, is also taken from *Stalky*. Mr Orwell is so very modern, that I cannot suspect him of having read anything so out of date as Chaucer. But if he will glance into that obsolete author, he will find "jape" therein, used in precisely the same sense. "Frabjous" also, it seems, is borrowed from *Stalky*! Has Mr Orwell never read *Alice*? "Frabjous", like "chortle" and "burble", derives from Lewis Carroll. Innumerable writers have borrowed "frabjous" and "chortle"—I believe Frank Richards was the first to borrow "burble", but I am not sure of this: such expressions, once in existence, become part of the language, and are common property.

"Sex," says Mr Orwell, "is completely taboo." Mr Noel Coward, in his autobiography, is equally amused at the absence of the sex-motif in the *Magnet* series. But what would Mr Orwell have? The *Magnet* is intended chiefly for readers up to sixteen; though I am proud to know that it has readers of sixty! It is read by girls as well as boys. Would it do these children good, or harm, to turn their thoughts to such matters? Sex, certainly, does enter uncomfortably into the experience of the adolescent. But surely the less he thinks about it, at an early age, the better. I am aware that, in these "modern" days, there are people who think that children should be told things of which in my own childhood no small person was ever allowed to hear. I disagree with this entirely. My own opinion is that such people generally suffer from disordered digestions, which cause their minds to take a nasty turn. They fancy that they are "realists", when they are only obscene. They go grubbing in the sewers for their realism, and refuse to believe in the grass and flowers above ground—which, nevertheless, are equally real! Moreover, this "motif" does not play so stupendous a part in real life, among healthy and wholesome people, as these "realists" imagine. If Mr Orwell supposes that the average Sixth-form boy cuddles a parlour-maid as often as he handles a cricket-bat, Mr Orwell is in error.

Drinking and smoking and betting, says Mr Orwell, are represented as "shady", but at the same time "irresistibly fascinating". If Mr Orwell will do me the honour of looking over a few numbers of the *Magnet*, he will find that such ways are invariably described as "dingy"—even the "bad hats" are a little ashamed of them: even Billy Bunter, though he will smoke a cigarette if he can get one for nothing, is described as being, though an ass, not ass enough to spend his money on such things. I submit that the adjective "dingy" is not equivalent to the adjective "fascinating".

Mr Orwell finds it difficult to believe that a series running for thirty years can possibly have been written by one and the same person. In the presence of such authority, I speak with diffidence: and can only say that, to the best of my knowledge and belief, I am only one person, and have never been two or three.

"Consequently," says Mr Orwell, cheerfully proceeding from erroneous premises to a still more erroneous conclusion, "they must be written in a style that is easily imitated." On this point, I may say that I could hardly count the number of authors who have striven to imitate Frank Richards, not one of whom has been successful. The style, whatever its merits or demerits, is my own, and—if I may say it with due modesty—inimitable. Nobody has ever written like it before, and nobody will ever write like it again. Many have tried; but as Dryden—an obsolete poet, Mr Orwell—has remarked:

> The builders were with want of genius curst,
> The second building was not like the first.

Mr Orwell mentions a number of other papers, which—egregiously—he classes with the *Magnet*. These papers, with the exception of the *Gem*, are not in the same class. They are not in the same street. They are hardly in the same universe. With the *Magnet*, it is not a case of *primus inter pares*: it is a case of Eclipse first and the rest nowhere. Mr Orwell in effect admits this. He tells us, quite correctly, that Billy Bunter is a "real creation": that he is a "first-rate character": that he is "one of the best-known in English fiction". He tells us that in the *Magnet* the "characters are so carefully graded, as to give every type of reader a character he can identify himself with". I suggest that an author who can do this is not easily imitated. It is not so easy as Mr Orwell supposes. It cannot be acquired: only the born story-teller can do it. Shakespeare could do it as no man ever did it before or since. Dickens could do it. Thackeray could not do it. Scott, with all his genius, could only give us historical suits of clothes with names attached. Can Bernard Shaw make a character live? Could Ibsen or Tchekov? To the highbrow, I know, a writer need only have a foreign name, to be a genius: and the more unpronounceable the name, the greater the genius. These duds—yes, Mr Orwell, Frank Richards really regards Shaw, Ibsen, and Tchekov, as duds—these duds would disdain to draw a schoolboy. Billy Bunter, let us admit, is not so dignified a character as an imbecile Russian, or a nerve-racked Norwegian. But, as a nineteenth-century writer, whom Mr Orwell would not deign to quote, remarked, "I would rather have a Dutch peasant by Teniers than his Majesty's head on a signpost."

Mr Orwell accuses Frank Richards of snobbishness: apparently because he makes an aristocratic character act as an aristocrat should. Now, although Mr Orwell may not suspect it, the word "aristocrat" has not wholly lost its original Greek meaning. It is an actual fact that, in this country at least, noblemen generally are better fellows than commoners. My own acquaintance with titled Nobs is strictly limited; but it is my experience, and I believe everybody's, that—excepting the peasant-on-the-land class, which is the salt of the earth—the higher you go up in the social scale the better you find the manners, and the more fixed the principles. The fact that old families almost invariably die out in the long run is proof of this: they cannot and will not do the things necessary for survival. All over the country, old estates are passing into new hands. Is this because Sir George up at the Hall is inferior to Mr Thompson from the City—or otherwise? Indeed, Mr Thompson himself is improved by being made a lord. Is it not a fact that, when a title is bestowed on some hard man of business, it has an ameliorating effect on him—

that he reacts unconsciously to his new state, and becomes rather less of a Gradgrind, rather more a man with a sense of his social responsibilities? Everyone must have observed this. The founder of a new family follows, at a distance, in the footsteps of the old families; and every day and in every way becomes better and better! It was said of old that the English nation dearly loves a lord. The English nation, in that as in other things, is wiser than its highbrowed instructors. Really, Mr Orwell, is it snobbish to give respect where respect is due: or should an author, because he doesn't happen to be a peer himself, inspire his readers with envy, hatred, malice, and all uncharitableness?

But Mr Orwell goes on to say that the working classes enter only as comics and semi-villains. This is sheer perversity on Mr Orwell's part. Such misrepresentation would not only be bad manners, but bad business. Every paper desiring a wide circulation must circulate, for the greater part, among the working classes, for the simple reason that they form nine-tenths of the population. A paper that is so fearfully aristocratic that it is supported only by marquises and men-servants must always go the way of the *Morning Post*. *Horizon*, I do not doubt, has a circle of readers with the loftiest brows; but I do doubt whether Sir John Simon will bother it very much for the sinews of war. Indeed, I have often wondered how so many young men with expansive foreheads and superior smiles contrive to live at all on bad prose and worse poetry. Directors, editors, and authors, must live: and they cannot live by insulting the majority of their public. If Frank Richards were the snob Mr Orwell believes him to be, he would still conceal that weakness very carefully when writing for the *Magnet*. But a man can believe that the "tenth possessor of a foolish face" has certain qualities lacking in the first possessor of a sly brain, without being a snob. I am very pleased to be an author, and I think I would rather be an author than a nobleman; but I am not fool enough to think that an author is of such national importance as a farmer or a farm labourer. Workmen can, and often do, get on quite well without authors; but no author could continue to exist without the workmen. They are not only the backbone of the nation: they *are* the nation: all other classes being merely trimmings. The best and noblest-minded man I ever knew was a simple wood-cutter. I would like Mr Orwell to indicate a single sentence in which Frank Richards refers disrespectfully to the people who keep him in comfort. There are three working-class boys in the Greyfriars Remove; Mr Orwell mentions all three by name: each one is represented as being liked and respected by the other boys; each in turn has been selected as the special hero of a series: and Mr Orwell must have used a very powerful microscope to detect anything comic or semi-villainous in them.

It is true that if I introduce a public-house loafer, I do not make him a baronet: and the billiard-marker does not wear an old school tie. But something, surely, is due to reality: especially as Mr Orwell is such a realist. If Mr Orwell has met public-house loafers who are baronets, or billiard-markers wearing the old school tie, I have never had a similar experience.

Of strikes, slumps, unemployment, etc, complains Mr Orwell, there is no mention. But are these really subjects for young people to meditate upon? It is true that we live in an insecure world: but why should not youth feel as secure as possible? It is true that burglars break into houses: but what parent in his senses would tell a child that a masked face may look in at the nursery window? A boy of fifteen or sixteen is on the threshold of life: and life is a tough proposition; but will he be better prepared for it by telling him how tough it may possibly be? I am sure that the reverse is the case. Gray —another obsolete poet, Mr Orwell!—tells us that sorrows never come too late, and happiness too swiftly flies. Let youth be happy, or as happy as possible. Happiness is the best preparation for misery, if misery must come. At least, the poor kid will have had something! He may, at twenty, be hunting for a job and not finding it—why should his fifteenth year be clouded by worrying about that in advance? He may, at thirty, get the sack—why tell him so at twelve? He may, at forty, be a wreck on Labour's scrap-heap—but how will it benefit him to know that at fourteen? Even if making miserable children would make happy adults, it would not be justifiable. But the truth is that the adult will be all the more miserable if he was miserable as a child. Every day of happiness, illusory or otherwise—and most happiness is illusory—is so much to the good. It will help to give the boy confidence and hope. Frank Richards tells him that there are some splendid fellows in a world that is, after all, a decent sort of place. He likes to think himself like one of these fellows, and is happy in his day-dreams. Mr Orwell would have him told that he is a shabby little blighter, his father an ill-used serf, his world a dirty, muddled, rotten sort of show. I don't think it would be fair play to take his twopence for telling him that!

Now about patriotism: an affronting word to Mr Orwell. I am

aware, of course, that the really "modern" highbrow is an "idiot who praises with enthusiastic tone, All centuries but this, and every country but his own". But is a country necessarily inferior because it is one's own? Why should not a fellow feel proud of things in which a just pride may be taken? I have lived in many countries, and talked in several languages: and found something to esteem in every country I have visited. But I have never seen any nation the equal of my own. Actually, such is my belief, Mr Orwell!

The basic political assumptions, Mr Orwell goes on, are two: that nothing ever changes, and that foreigners are funny. Well, the French have a proverb that the more a thing changes, the more it is just the same. Temporary mutations are mistaken for great changes—as they always were. Decency seems to have gone—but it will come in again, and there will be a new generation of men who do not talk and write muck, and women with clean faces. Progress, I believe, goes on: but it moves to slow time. No real change is perceptible in the course of a single lifetime. But even if changes succeeded one another with kaleidoscopic rapidity, the writer for young people should still endeavour to give his young readers a sense of stability and solid security, because it is good for them, and makes for happiness and peace of mind.

As for foreigners being funny, I must shock Mr Orwell by telling him that foreigners *are* funny. They lack the sense of humour which is the special gift to our own chosen nation: and people without a sense of humour are always unconsciously funny. Take Hitler, for example, with his swastika, his "good German sword", his fortifications named after characters from Wagner, his military coat that he will never take off till he marches home victorious: and the rest of his fripperies out of the property-box. In Germany they lap this up like milk, with the most awful seriousness; in England, the play-acting ass would be laughed out of existence. Take Mussolini—can anyone imagine a fat man in London talking the balderdash that Benito talks in Rome to wildly-cheering audiences, without evoking, not wild cheers, but inextinguishable laughter? But is Il Duce regarded as a mountebank in Italy? Very far from it. I submit to Mr Orwell that people who take their theatricals seriously *are* funny. The fact that Adolf Hitler is deadly dangerous does not make him less comic.

But what I dislike most is Mr Orwell telling me that I am out of date. Human nature, Mr Orwell, is dateless. A character that lives is always up to date. If, as Mr Orwell himself says, a boy in 1940 can identify himself with a boy in the *Magnet*, obviously that boy in the *Magnet* is a boy of 1940.

But it is quite startling to see what Mr Orwell regards as up to date. The one theme that is really new, quoth he, is the scientific one —death-rays, Martian invasions, invisible men, interplanetary rockets, and so on. Oh, my Hat! if Mr Orwell will permit that obsolete expression. This kind of thing was done, and done to death, when I was a small boy; long before the *Magnet* was born or thought of. Before I reached the age of unaided reading, a story was read to me by an elder brother, in which bold travellers hiked off to the moon, packed inside a big bullet discharged from a tremendous gun. The greatest of submarine stories—Jules Verne's *20,000 Leagues*—was published before I was born. The Martians invaded the earth, while I was still mewling and puking in the nurse's arms. In the nursery I knew the Invisible Man, though his invisibility was then due to a cloak of darkness. More than twenty years ago I wrote a death-ray story myself: but did not fancy that it was a new idea; even then it had an ancient and fish-like smell. Some of my earliest reading was of flying: there was a strenuous character in those days, who sailed the skies in what he called an aeronef: a direct descendant, I think, of Verne's *Clipper of the Clouds* of twenty years earlier: and Verne, I fancy, had read *Peter Wilkins* of seventy years earlier still; and I believe that the author of *Peter Wilkins* had not disdained to pick up a tip or two from Swift's writings in the eighteenth century. Did not Lucian tell them something about a trip to the moon in the second century? The oldest flying story I have read was written in Greek about three thousand years ago; but I don't suppose it was the earliest: I have no doubt that when they finish sorting over the Babylonian bricks they will find a flying story somewhere among the ruins, and very likely a death-ray and an invisible man keeping it company. If this stuff is new, Mr Orwell, what is old?

To conclude, Mr Orwell hopes that a boys' paper with a left-wing bias may not be impossible. I hope that it is, and will remain, impossible. Boys' minds ought not to be disturbed and worried by politics. Even if I were a Socialist, or a Communist, I should still consider it the duty of a boys' author to write without reference to such topics: because his business is to entertain his readers, make them as happy as possible, give them a feeling of cheerful security, turn their thoughts to healthy pursuits, and above all to keep them away from unhealthy introspection, which in early youth can do only harm. If there is a Tchekov among my readers, I fervently hope that the effect of the *Magnet* will be to turn him into a Bob Cherry!

Horizon, May 1940

164. Inside the Whale

I

When Henry Miller's novel, *Tropic of Cancer*, appeared in 1935, it was greeted with rather cautious praise, obviously conditioned in some cases by a fear of seeming to enjoy pornography. Among the people who praised it were T. S. Eliot, Herbert Read, Aldous Huxley, John dos Passos, Ezra Pound—on the whole, not the writers who are in fashion at this moment. And in fact the subject-matter of the book, and to a certain extent its mental atmosphere, belong to the 'twenties rather than to the 'thirties.

Tropic of Cancer is a novel in the first person, or autobiography in the form of a novel, whichever way you like to look at it. Miller himself insists that it is straight autobiography, but the tempo and method of telling the story are those of a novel. It is a story of the American Paris, but not along quite the usual lines, because the Americans who figure in it happen to be people without money. During the boom years, when dollars were plentiful and the exchange-value of the franc was low, Paris was invaded by such a swarm of artists, writers, students, dilettanti, sight-seers, debauchees and plain idlers as the world has probably never seen. In some quarters of the town the so-called artists must actually have outnumbered the working population—indeed, it has been reckoned that in the late 'twenties there were as many as 30,000 painters in Paris, most of them impostors. The populace had grown so hardened to artists that gruff-voiced lesbians in corduroy breeches and young men in Grecian or medieval costume could walk the streets without attracting a glance, and along the Seine banks by Notre Dame it was almost impossible to pick one's way between the sketching-stools. It was the age of dark horses and neglected genii; the phrase on everybody's lips was "Quand je serai lancé". As it turned out, nobody was "lancé", the slump descended like another Ice Age, the cosmopolitan mob of artists vanished, and the huge Montparnasse cafés which only ten years ago were filled till the small hours by hordes of shrieking poseurs have turned into darkened tombs in which there are not even any ghosts. It is this world—described in, among other novels, Wyndham Lewis's *Tarr*—that Miller is writing about, but he is dealing only with the under side of it, the lumpenproletarian fringe which has been able to survive the slump because it is composed partly of genuine artists and partly of genuine scoundrels. The neglected genii, the paranoiacs who are always "going to" write the novel that will knock Proust into a cocked hat, are there, but they are only genii in the rather rare moments when they are not scouting about for the next meal. For the most part it is a story of bug-ridden rooms in working-men's hotels, of fights, drinking bouts, cheap brothels, Russian refugees, cadging, swindling and temporary jobs. And the whole atmosphere of the poor quarters of Paris as a foreigner sees them—the cobbled alleys, the sour reek of refuse, the bistros with their greasy zinc counters and worn brick floors, the green waters of the Seine, the blue cloaks of the Republican Guard, the crumbling iron urinals, the peculiar sweetish smell of the Métro stations, the cigarettes that come to pieces, the pigeons in the Luxembourg Gardens—it is all there, or at any rate the feeling of it is there.

On the face of it no material could be less promising. When *Tropic of Cancer* was published the Italians were marching into Abyssinia and Hitler's concentration camps were already bulging. The intellectual foci of the world were Rome, Moscow and Berlin. It did not seem to be a moment at which a novel of outstanding value was likely to be written about American dead-beats cadging drinks in the Latin Quarter. Of course a novelist is not obliged to write directly about contemporary history, but a novelist who simply disregards the major public events of the moment is generally either a footler or a plain idiot. From a mere account of the subject-matter of *Tropic of Cancer* most people would probably assume it to be no more than a bit of naughty-naughty left over from the 'twenties. Actually, nearly everyone who read it saw at once that it was nothing of the kind, but a very remarkable book. How or why remarkable? That question is never easy to answer. It is better to begin by describing the impression that *Tropic of Cancer* has left on my own mind.

When I first opened *Tropic of Cancer* and saw that it was full of unprintable words, my immediate reaction was a refusal to be impressed. Most people's would be the same, I believe. Nevertheless, after a lapse of time the atmosphere of the book, besides innumerable details, seemed to linger in my memory in a peculiar way. A year later Miller's second book, *Black Spring*, was published. By this time *Tropic of Cancer* was much more vividly present in my mind than it had been when I first read it. My first feeling about *Black Spring* was that it showed a falling-off, and it is a fact that it has not the same unity as the other book. Yet after another year there were many passages in *Black Spring* that had also rooted themselves in my memory. Evidently these books are of the sort to leave a flavour behind them—books that "create a world of their own", as the saying goes. The books that do this are not necessarily good books, they may be good bad books like *Raffles* or the *Sherlock Holmes* stories, or perverse and morbid books like *Wuthering Heights* or *The House with the Green Shutters*. But now and again there appears a novel which opens up a new world not by revealing what is strange, but by revealing what is familiar. The truly remarkable thing about *Ulysses*, for instance, is the commonplaceness of its material. Of course there is much more in *Ulysses* than this, because Joyce is a kind of poet and also an elephantine pedant, but his real achievement has been to get the familiar on to paper. He dared—for it is a matter of *daring* just as much as of technique—to expose the imbecilities of the inner mind, and in doing so he discovered an America which was under everybody's nose. Here is a whole world of stuff which you have lived with since childhood, stuff which you supposed to be of its nature incommunicable, and somebody has managed to communicate it. The effect is to break down, at any rate momentarily, the solitude in which the human being lives. When you read certain passages in *Ulysses* you feel that Joyce's mind and your mind are one, that he knows all about you though he has never heard your name, that there exists some world outside time and space in which you and he are together. And though he does not resemble Joyce in other ways, there is a touch of this quality in Henry Miller. Not everywhere, because his work is very uneven, and sometimes, especially in *Black Spring*, tends to slide away into mere verbiage or into the squashy universe of the Surrealists. But read him for five pages, ten pages, and you feel the peculiar relief that comes not so much from understanding as from *being understood*. "He knows all about me," you feel; "he wrote this specially for me." It is as though you could hear a voice speaking to you, a friendly American voice, with no humbug in it, no moral purpose, merely an implicit assumption that we are all alike. For the moment you have got away from the lies and simplifications, the stylised, marionette-like quality of ordinary fiction, even quite good fiction, and are dealing with the recognisable experiences of human beings.

But what kind of experience? What kind of human beings? Miller is writing about the man in the street, and it is incidentally rather a pity that it should be a street full of brothels. That is the penalty of leaving your native land. It means transferring your roots into shallower soil. Exile is probably more damaging to a novelist than to a painter or even a poet, because its effect is to take him out of contact with working life and narrow down his range to the street, the café, the church, the brothel and the studio. On the whole, in Miller's books you are reading about people living the expatriate life, people drinking, talking, meditating and fornicating, not about people working, marrying and bringing up children; a pity, because he would have described the one set of activities as well as the other. In *Black Spring* there is a wonderful flashback of New York, the swarming Irish-infested New York of the O. Henry period, but the Paris scenes are the best, and, granted their utter worthlessness as social types, the drunks and dead-beats of the cafés are handled with a feeling for character and a mastery of technique that are unapproached in any at all recent novel. All of them are not only credible but completely familiar; you have the feeling that all their adventures have happened to yourself. Not that they are anything very startling in the way of adventures. Henry gets a job with a melancholy Indian student, gets another job at a dreadful French school during a cold snap when the lavatories are frozen solid, goes on drinking bouts in Le Havre with his friend Collins, the sea captain, goes to brothels where there are wonderful negresses, talks with his friend Van Norden, the novelist, who has got the great novel of the world in his head but can never bring himself to begin writing it. His friend Karl, on the verge of starvation, is picked up by a wealthy widow who wishes to marry him. There are interminable, Hamlet-like conversations in which Karl tries to decide which is worse, being hungry or sleeping with an old woman. In great detail he describes his visits to the widow, how he went to the hotel dressed in his best, how before going in he neglected to urinate, so that the whole evening was one long crescendo of torment, etc etc. And after all, none of it is true, the widow doesn't even exist—Karl has simply invented her in order to make himself seem important. The whole book is in this vein, more or less. Why is it that these monstrous trivialities are so engrossing? Simply because the whole atmosphere is deeply familiar, because you have all the while the feeling that these things are happening to *you.* And you have this feeling because somebody has chosen to drop the Geneva language of the ordinary novel and drag the *real-politik* of the inner mind into the open. In Miller's case it is not so much a question of exploring the mechanisms of the mind as of owning up to everyday facts and everyday emotions. For the truth is that many ordinary people, perhaps an actual majority, do speak and behave in just the way that is recorded here. The callous coarseness with which the characters in *Tropic of Cancer* talk is very rare in fiction, but it is extremely common in real life; again and again I have heard just such conversations from people who were not even aware that they were talking coarsely. It is worth noticing that *Tropic of Cancer* is not a young man's book. Miller was in his forties when it was published, and though since then he has produced three or four others, it is obvious that this first book had been lived with for years. It is one of those books that are slowly matured in poverty and obscurity, by people who know what they have got to do and therefore are able to wait. The prose is astonishing, and in parts of *Black Spring* it is even better. Unfortunately I cannot quote; unprintable words occur almost everywhere. But get hold of *Tropic of Cancer*, get hold of *Black Spring* and read especially the first hundred pages. They give you an idea of what can still be done, even at this late date, with English prose. In them, English is treated as a spoken language, but spoken *without fear*, i.e. without fear of rhetoric or of the unusual or poetical word. The adjective has come back, after its ten years' exile. It is a flowing, swelling prose, a prose with rhythms in it, something quite different from the flat, cautious statements and snack-bar dialects that are now in fashion.

When a book like *Tropic of Cancer* appears, it is only natural that the first thing people notice should be its obscenity. Given our current notions of literary decency, it is not at all easy to approach an unprintable book with detachment. Either one is shocked and disgusted, or one is morbidly thrilled, or one is determined above all else not to be impressed. The last is probably the commonest reaction, with the result that unprintable books often get less attention than they deserve. It is rather the fashion to say that nothing is easier than to write an obscene book, that people only do it in order to get themselves talked about and make money, etc etc. What makes it obvious that this is *not* the case is that books which are obscene in the police-court sense are distinctly uncommon. If there were easy money to be made out of dirty words, a lot more people would be making it. But, because "obscene" books do not appear very frequently, there is a tendency to lump them together, as a rule quite unjustifiably. *Tropic of Cancer* has been vaguely associated with two other books, *Ulysses* and *Voyage au Bout de la Nuit*, but in neither case is there much resemblance. What Miller has in common with Joyce is a willingness to mention the inane squalid facts of everyday life. Putting aside differences of technique, the funeral scene in *Ulysses*, for instance, would fit into *Tropic of Cancer*; the whole chapter is a sort of confession, an *exposé* of the frightful inner callousness of the human being. But there the resemblance ends. As a novel, *Tropic of Cancer* is far inferior to *Ulysses*. Joyce is an artist, in a sense in which Miller is not and probably would not wish to be, and in any case he is attempting much more. He is exploring different states of consciousness, dream, reverie (the "bronze-by-gold" chapter), drunkenness, etc, and dovetailing them all into a huge complex pattern, almost like a Victorian "plot". Miller is simply a hardboiled person talking about life, an ordinary American businessman with intellectual courage and a gift for words. It is perhaps significant that he *looks* exactly like everyone's idea of an American businessman. As for the comparison with *Voyage au Bout de la Nuit*, it is even further from the point. Both books use unprintable words, both are in some sense autobiographical, but that is all. *Voyage au Bout de la Nuit* is a book-with-a-purpose, and its purpose is to protest against the horror and meaninglessness of modern life—actually, indeed, of *life*. It is a cry of unbearable disgust, a voice from the cesspool. *Tropic of Cancer* is almost exactly the opposite. The thing has become so unusual as to seem almost anomalous, but it is the book of a man who is happy. So is *Black Spring*, though slightly less so, because tinged in places with nostalgia. With years of lumpenproletarian life behind him, hunger, vagabondage, dirt, failure, nights in the open, battles with immigration officers, endless struggles for a bit of cash, Miller finds that he is enjoying himself. Exactly the aspects of life that fill Céline with horror are the ones that appeal to him. So far from protesting, he is *accepting*. And the very word "acceptance" calls up his real affinity, another American, Walt Whitman.

But there is something rather curious in being Whitman in the nineteen-thirties. It is not certain that if Whitman himself were alive at this moment he would write anything in the least degree resembling

Leaves of Grass. For what he is saying, after all, is "I accept", and there is a radical difference between acceptance now and acceptance then. Whitman was writing in a time of unexampled prosperity, but more than that, he was writing in a country where freedom was something more than a word. The democracy, equality and comradeship that he is always talking about are not remote ideals, but something that existed in front of his eyes. In mid-nineteenth-century America men felt themselves free and equal, *were* free and equal, so far as that is possible outside a society of pure Communism. There was poverty and there were even class-distinctions, but except for the Negroes there was no permanently submerged class. Everyone had inside him, like a kind of core, the knowledge that he could earn a decent living, and earn it without boot-licking. When you read about Mark Twain's Mississippi raftsmen and pilots, or Bret Harte's Western gold miners, they seem more remote than the cannibals of the Stone Age. The reason is simply that they are free human beings. But it is the same even with the peaceful domesticated America of the Eastern states, the America of *Little Women*, *Helen's Babies* and "Riding Down from Bangor". Life has a buoyant, carefree quality that you can feel as you read, like a physical sensation in your belly. It is this that Whitman is celebrating, though actually he does it very badly, because he is one of those writers who tell you what you ought to feel instead of making you feel it. Luckily for his beliefs, perhaps, he died too early to see the deterioration in American life that came with the rise of large-scale industry and the exploiting of cheap immigrant labour.

Miller's outlook is deeply akin to that of Whitman, and nearly everyone who has read him has remarked on this. *Tropic of Cancer* ends with an especially Whitmanesque passage, in which, after the lecheries, the swindles, the fights, the drinking bouts and the imbecilities, he simply sits down and watches the Seine flowing past, in a sort of mystical acceptance of the thing-as-it-is. Only, what is he accepting? In the first place, not America, but the ancient bone-heap of Europe, where every grain of soil has passed through innumerable human bodies. Secondly, not an epoch of expansion and liberty, but an epoch of fear, tyranny and regimentation. To say "I accept" in an age like our own is to say that you accept concentration camps, rubber truncheons, Hitler, Stalin, bombs, aeroplanes, tinned food, machine-guns, putsches, purges, slogans, Bedaux belts, gas-masks, submarines, spies, *provocateurs*, press censorship, secret prisons, aspirins, Hollywood films and political murders. Not *only* those things, of course, but those things among others. And on the whole this is Henry Miller's attitude. Not quite always, because at moments he shows signs of a fairly ordinary kind of literary nostalgia. There is a long passage in the earlier part of *Black Spring*, in praise of the Middle Ages, which as prose must be one of the most remarkable pieces of writing in recent years, but which displays an attitude not very different from that of Chesterton. In *Max and the White Phagocytes* there is an attack on modern American civilisation (breakfast cereals, cellophane, etc) from the usual angle of the literary man who hates industrialism. But in general the attitude is "Let's swallow it whole". And hence the seeming preoccupation with indecency and with the dirty-handkerchief side of life. It is only seeming, for the truth is that life, ordinary everyday life, consists far more largely of horrors than writers of fiction usually care to admit. Whitman himself "accepted" a great deal that his contemporaries found unmentionable. For he is not only writing of the prairie, he also wanders through the city and notes the shattered skull of the suicide, the "grey sick faces of onanists", etc etc. But unquestionably our own age, at any rate in western Europe, is less healthy and less hopeful than the age in which Whitman was writing. Unlike Whitman, we live in a *shrinking* world. The "democratic vistas" have ended in barbed wire. There is less feeling of creation and growth, less and less emphasis on the cradle, endlessly rocking, more and more emphasis on the teapot, endlessly stewing. To accept civilisation *as it is* practically means accepting decay. It has ceased to be a strenuous attitude and become a passive attitude—even "decadent", if that word means anything.

But precisely because, in one sense, he is passive to experience, Miller is able to get nearer to the ordinary man than is possible to more purposive writers. For the ordinary man is also passive. Within a narrow circle (home life, and perhaps the trade union or local politics) he feels himself master of his fate, but against major events he is as helpless as against the elements. So far from endeavouring to influence the future, he simply lies down and lets things happen to him. During the past ten years literature has involved itself more and more deeply in politics, with the result that there is now less room in it for the ordinary man than at any time during the past two centuries. One can see the change in the prevailing literary attitude by comparing the books written about the Spanish civil war with those written about the war of 1914–18. The immediately striking thing about the Spanish war books, at any rate those written in English, is their shocking dullness and badness. But what is more significant is that almost all of them, right-wing or left-wing, are written from a political angle, by cocksure partisans telling you what to think, whereas the books about the Great War were written by common soldiers or junior officers who did not even pretend to understand what the whole thing was about. Books like *All Quiet on the Western Front*, *Le Feu*, *A Farewell to Arms*, *Death of a Hero*, *Good-Bye to All That*, *Memoirs of an Infantry Officer* and *A Subaltern on the Somme* were written not by propagandists but by *victims*. They are saying in effect, "What the hell is all this about? God knows. All we can do is to endure." And though he is not writing about war, nor, on the whole, about unhappiness, this is nearer to Miller's attitude than the omniscience which is now fashionable. The *Booster*, a short-lived periodical of which he was part-editor, used to describe itself in its advertisements as "non-political, non-educational, non-progressive, non-cooperative, non-ethical, non-literary, non-consistent, non-contemporary", and Miller's own work could be described in nearly the same terms. It is a voice from the crowd, from the underling, from the third-class carriage, from the ordinary, non-political, non-moral, passive man.

I have been using the phrase "ordinary man" rather loosely, and I have taken it for granted that the "ordinary man" exists, a thing now denied by some people. I do not mean that the people Miller is writing about constitute a majority, still less that he is writing about proletarians. No English or American novelist has as yet seriously attempted that. And again, the people in *Tropic of Cancer* fall short of being ordinary to the extent that they are idle, disreputable and more or less "artistic". As I have said already, this is a pity, but it is the necessary result of expatriation. Miller's "ordinary man" is neither the manual worker nor the suburban householder, but the derelict, the *déclassé*, the adventurer, the American intellectual without roots and without money. Still, the experiences even of this type overlap fairly widely with those of more normal people. Miller has been able to get the most out of his rather limited material because he has had the courage to identify with it. The ordinary man, the "average sensual man", has been given the power of speech, like Balaam's ass.

It will be seen that this is something out of date, or at any rate out of fashion. The average sensual man is out of fashion. The passive, non-political attitude is out of fashion. Preoccupation with sex and truthfulness about the inner life are out of fashion. American Paris is out of fashion. A book like *Tropic of Cancer*, published at such a time, must be either a tedious preciosity or something unusual, and I think a majority of the people who have read it would agree that it is not the first. It is worth trying to discover just what this escape from the current literary fashion means. But to do that one has got to see it against its background—that is, against the general development of English literature in the twenty years since the Great War.

II

When one says that a writer is fashionable one practically always means that he is admired by people under thirty. At the beginning of the period I am speaking of, the years during and immediately after the war, the writer who had the deepest hold upon the thinking young was almost certainly Housman. Among people who were adolescent in the years 1910–25, Housman had an influence which was enormous and is now not at all easy to understand. In 1920, when I was about seventeen, I probably knew the whole of *A Shropshire Lad* by heart. I wonder how much impression *A Shropshire Lad* makes at this moment on a boy of the same age and more or less the same cast of mind? No doubt he has heard of it and even glanced into it; it might strike him as rather cheaply clever—probably that would be about all. Yet these are the poems that I and my contemporaries used to recite to ourselves, over and over, in a kind of ecstasy, just as earlier generations had recited Meredith's "Love in a Valley", Swinburne's "Garden of Proserpine", etc etc.

> With rue my heart is laden
>   For golden friends I had,
> For many a rose-lipt maiden
>   And many a lightfoot lad.
>
> By brooks too broad for leaping
>   The lightfoot boys are laid;
> The rose-lipt girls are sleeping
>   In fields where roses fade.

It just tinkles. But it did not seem to tinkle in 1920. Why does the bubble always burst? To answer that question one has to take account of the *external* conditions that make certain writers popular at certain times. Housman's poems had not attracted much notice when they were first published. What was there in them that appealed so deeply to a single generation, the generation born round about 1900?

In the first place, Housman is a "country" poet. His poems are full of the charm of buried villages, the nostalgia of place-names, Clunton and Clunbury, Knighton, Ludlow, "on Wenlock Edge", "in summer time on Bredon", thatched roofs and the jingle of smithies, the wild jonquils in the pastures, the "blue, remembered hills". War poems apart, English verse of the 1910–25 period is mostly "country". The reason no doubt was that the *rentier*-professional class was ceasing once and for all to have any real relationship with the soil; but at any rate there prevailed then, far more than now, a kind of snobbism of belonging to the country and despising the town. England at that time was hardly more an agricultural country than it is now, but before the light industries began to spread themselves it was easier to think of it as one. Most middle-class boys grew up within sight of a farm, and naturally it was the picturesque side of farm life that appealed to them—the ploughing, harvesting, stack-thrashing and so forth. Unless he has to do it himself a boy is not likely to notice the horrible drudgery of hoeing turnips, milking cows with chapped teats at four o'clock in the morning, etc etc. Just before, just after and, for that matter, during the war was the great age of the "nature poet", the heyday of Richard Jefferies and W. H. Hudson. Rupert Brooke's "Grantchester", the star poem of 1913, is nothing but an enormous gush of "country" sentiment, a sort of accumulated vomit from a stomach stuffed with place-names. Considered as a poem "Grantchester" is something worse than worthless but as an illustration of what the thinking middle-class young of that period *felt* it is a valuable document.

Housman, however, did not enthuse over the rambler roses in the week-ending spirit of Brooke and the others. The "country" motif is there all the time, but mainly as a background. Most of the poems have a quasi-human subject, a kind of idealised rustic, in reality Strephon or Corydon brought up to date. This in itself had a deep appeal. Experience shows that over-civilised people enjoy reading about rustics (key-phrase, "close to the soil") because they imagine them to be more primitive and passionate than themselves. Hence the "dark earth" novels of Sheila Kaye-Smith etc. And at that time a middle-class boy, with his "country" bias, would identify with an agricultural worker as he would never have thought of doing with a town worker. Most boys had in their minds a vision of an idealised ploughman, gypsy, poacher, or gamekeeper, always pictured as a wild, free, roving blade, living a life of rabbit-snaring, cock-fighting, horses, beer and women. Masefield's *Everlasting Mercy*, another valuable period piece, immensely popular with boys round about the war years, gives you this vision in a very crude form. But Housman's Maurices and Terences could be taken seriously where Masefield's Saul Kane could not; on this side of him, Housman was Masefield with a dash of Theocritus. Moreover all his themes are adolescent —murder, suicide, unhappy love, early death. They deal with the simple, intelligible disasters that give you the feeling of being up against the "bedrock facts" of life:

The sun burns on the half-mown hill,
  By now the blood is dried;
And Maurice amongst the hay lies still
  And my knife is in his side.

And again:

They hang us now in Shrewsbury jail:
  The whistles blow forlorn,
And trains all night groan on the rail
  To men that die at morn.

It is all more or less in the same tune. Everything comes unstuck. "Dick lies long in the churchyard, and Ned lies long in jail." And notice also the exquisite self-pity—the "nobody loves me" feeling:

The diamond tears adorning
  Thy low mound on the lea,
Those are the tears of morning,
  That weeps, but not for thee.

Hard cheese, old chap! Such poems might have been written expressly for adolescents. And the unvarying sexual pessimism (the girl always dies or marries somebody else) seemed like wisdom to boys who were herded together in public schools and were half-inclined to think of women as something unattainable. Whether

Housman ever had the same appeal for girls I doubt. In his poems the women's point of view is not considered, she is merely the nymph, the siren, the treacherous half-human creature who leads you a little distance and then gives you the slip.

But Housman would not have appealed so deeply to the people who were young in 1920 if it had not been for another strain in him, and that was his blasphemous, antinomian, "cynical" strain. The fight that always occurs between the generations was exceptionally bitter at the end of the Great War; this was partly due to the war itself, and partly it was an indirect result of the Russian Revolution, but an intellectual struggle was in any case due at about that date. Owing probably to the ease and security of life in England, which even the war hardly disturbed, many people whose ideas were formed in the 'eighties or earlier had carried them quite unmodified into the nineteen-twenties. Meanwhile, so far as the younger generation was concerned, the official beliefs were dissolving like sand-castles. The slump in religious belief, for instance, was spectacular. For several years the old-young antagonism took on a quality of real hatred. What was left of the war generation had crept out of the massacre to find their elders still bellowing the slogans of 1914, and a slightly younger generation of boys were writhing under dirty-minded celibate schoolmasters. It was to these that Housman appealed, with his implied sexual revolt and his personal grievance against God. He was patriotic, it was true, but in a harmless old-fashioned way, to the tune of red coats and "God save the Queen" rather than steel helmets and "Hang the Kaiser". And he was satisfyingly anti-Christian—he stood for a kind of bitter, defiant paganism, a conviction that life is short and the gods are against you, which exactly fitted the prevailing mood of the young; and all in charming fragile verse that was composed almost entirely of words of one syllable.

It will be seen that I have discussed Housman as though he were merely a propagandist, an utterer of maxims and quotable "bits". Obviously he was more than that. There is no need to under-rate him now because he was over-rated a few years ago. Although one gets into trouble nowadays for saying so, there is a number of his poems ("Into my heart an air that kills", for instance, and "Is my team ploughing?") that are not likely to remain long out of favour. But at bottom it is always a writer's tendency, his "purpose", his "message", that makes him liked or disliked. The proof of this is the extreme difficulty of seeing any literary merit in a book that seriously damages your deepest beliefs. And no book is ever truly neutral. Some tendency or other is always discernible, in verse as much as in prose, even if it does no more than determine the form and the choice of imagery. But poets who attain wide popularity, like Housman, are as a rule definitely gnomic writers.

After the war, after Housman and the Nature poets, there appears a group of writers of completely different tendency—Joyce, Eliot, Pound, Lawrence, Wyndham Lewis, Aldous Huxley, Lytton Strachey. So far as the middle and late 'twenties go, these are "the movement", as surely as the Auden–Spender group have been "the movement" during the past few years. It is true that not all of the gifted writers of the period can be fitted into the pattern. E. M. Forster, for instance, though he wrote his best book in 1923 or thereabouts, was essentially pre-war, and Yeats does not seem in either of his phases to belong to the 'twenties. Others who were still living, Moore, Conrad, Bennett, Wells, Norman Douglas, had shot their bolt before the war ever happened. On the other hand, a writer who should be added to the group, though in the narrowly literary sense he hardly "belongs", is Somerset Maugham. Of course the dates do not fit exactly; most of these writers had already published books before the war, but they can be classified as post-war in the same sense that the younger men now writing are post-slump. Equally of course, you could read through most of the literary papers of the time without grasping that these people *are* "the movement". Even more then than at most times the big shots of literary journalism were busy pretending that the age-before-last had not come to an end. Squire ruled the *London Mercury*, Gibbs and Walpole were the gods of the lending libraries, there was a cult of cheeriness and manliness, beer and cricket, briar pipes and monogamy, and it was at all times possible to earn a few guineas by writing an article denouncing "highbrows". But all the same it was the despised highbrows who had captured the young. The wind was blowing from Europe, and long before 1930 it had blown the beer-and-cricket school naked, except for their knighthoods.

But the first thing one would notice about the group of writers I have named above is that they do not look like a group. Moreover several of them would strongly object to being coupled with several of the others. Lawrence and Eliot were in reality antipathetic, Huxley worshipped Lawrence but was repelled by Joyce, most of the others would have looked down on Huxley, Strachey and Maugham, and

Lewis attacked everyone in turn; indeed, his reputation as a writer rests largely on these attacks. And yet there is a certain temperamental similarity, evident enough now, though it would not have been so a dozen years ago. What it amounts to is *pessimism of outlook*. But it is necessary to make clear what is meant by pessimism.

If the keynote of the Georgian poets was "beauty of Nature", the keynote of the post-war writers would be "tragic sense of life". The spirit behind Housman's poems, for instance, is not tragic, merely querulous; it is hedonism disappointed. The same is true of Hardy, though one ought to make an exception of *The Dynasts*. But the Joyce-Eliot group come later in time, puritanism is not their main adversary, they are able from the start to "see through" most of the things that their predecessors had fought for. All of them are temperamentally hostile to the notion of "progress"; it is felt that progress not only doesn't happen, but *ought not* to happen. Given this general similarity, there are, of course, differences of approach between the writers I have named as well as very different degrees of talent. Eliot's pessimism is partly the Christian pessimism, which implies a certain indifference to human misery, partly a lament over the decadence of western civilisation ("We are the hollow men, we are the stuffed men" etc etc), a sort of twilight-of-the-gods feeling which finally leads him, in "Sweeney Agonistes" for instance, to achieve the difficult feat of making modern life out to be worse than it is. With Strachey it is merely a polite eighteenth-century scepticism mixed up with a taste for debunking. With Maugham it is a kind of stoical resignation, the stiff upper lip of the pukka sahib somewhere East of Suez, carrying on with his job without believing in it, like an Antonine Emperor. Lawrence at first sight does not seem to be a pessimistic writer, because, like Dickens, he is a "change-of-heart" man and constantly insisting that life here and now would be all right if only you looked at it a little differently. But what he is demanding is a movement away from our mechanised civilisation, which is not going to happen, and which he knows is not going to happen. Therefore his exasperation with the present turns once more into idealisation of the past, this time a safely mythical past, the Bronze Age. When Lawrence prefers the Etruscans (*his* Etruscans) to ourselves it is difficult not to agree with him, and yet, after all, it is a species of defeatism, because that is not the direction in which the world is moving. The kind of life that he is always pointing to, a life centring round the simple mysteries—sex, earth, fire, water, blood

—is merely a lost cause. All he has been able to produce, therefore, is a wish that things would happen in a way in which they are manifestly not going to happen. "A wave of generosity or a wave of death", he says, but it is obvious that there are no waves of generosity this side of the horizon. So he flees to Mexico, and then dies at forty-five, a few years before the wave of death gets going. It will be seen that once again I am speaking of these people as though they were not artists, as though they were merely propagandists putting a "message" across. And once again it is obvious that all of them are more than that. It would be absurd, for instance, to look on *Ulysses* as *merely* a show-up of the horror of modern life, the "dirty *Daily Mail* era", as Pound put it. Joyce actually is more of a "pure artist" than most writers. But *Ulysses* could not have been written by someone who was merely dabbling with word-patterns; it is the product of a special vision of life, the vision of a Catholic who has lost his faith. What Joyce is saying is "Here is life without God. Just look at it!" and his technical innovations, important though they are, are there primarily to serve this purpose.

But what is noticeable about all these writers is that what "purpose" they have is very much up in the air. There is no attention to the urgent problems of the moment, above all no politics in the narrower sense. Our eyes are directed to Rome, to Byzantium, to Montparnasse, to Mexico, to the Etruscans, to the subconscious, to the solar plexus—to everywhere except the places where things are actually happening. When one looks back at the 'twenties, nothing is queerer than the way in which every important event in Europe escaped the notice of the English intelligentsia. The Russian Revolution, for instance, all but vanishes from the English consciousness between the death of Lenin and the Ukraine famine—about ten years. Throughout those years Russia means Tolstoy, Dostoievski and exiled counts driving taxi-cabs. Italy means picture-galleries, ruins, churches and museums—but not Blackshirts. Germany means films, nudism and psychoanalysis—but not Hitler, of whom hardly anyone had heard till 1931. In "cultured" circles art-for-art's-saking extended practically to a worship of the meaningless. Literature was supposed to consist solely in the manipulation of words. To judge a book by its subject-matter was the unforgivable sin, and even to be aware of its subject-matter was looked on as a lapse of taste. About 1928, in one of the three genuinely funny jokes that *Punch* has produced since the Great War, an intolerable youth is pictured informing his aunt that he intends to "write". "And what are you going to write about, dear?" asks the aunt. "My dear aunt," says the youth crushingly, "one doesn't write *about* anything, one just *writes.*" The best writers of the 'twenties did not subscribe to this doctrine, their "purpose" is in most cases fairly overt, but it is usually a "purpose" along moral-religious-cultural lines. Also, when translatable into political terms, it is in no case "left". In one way or another the tendency of all the writers in this group is conservative. Lewis, for instance, spent years in frenzied witch-smellings after "Bolshevism", which he was able to detect in very unlikely places. Recently he has changed some of his views, perhaps influenced by Hitler's treatment of artists, but it is safe to bet that he will not go very far leftward. Pound seems to have plumped definitely for Fascism, at any rate the Italian variety. Eliot has remained aloof, but if forced at the pistol's point to choose between Fascism and some more democratic form of Socialism, would probably choose Fascism. Huxley starts off with the usual despair-of-life, then, under the influence of Lawrence's "dark abdomen", tries something called Life-Worship, and finally arrives at pacifism—a tenable position, and at this moment an honourable one, but probably in the long run involving rejection of Socialism. It is also noticeable that most of the writers in this group have a certain tenderness for the Catholic Church, though not usually of a kind that an orthodox Catholic would accept.

The mental connection between pessimism and a reactionary outlook is no doubt obvious enough. What is perhaps less obvious is just *why* the leading writers of the 'twenties were predominantly pessimistic. Why always the sense of decadence, the skulls and cactuses, the yearning after lost faith and impossible civilisations? Was it not, after all, *because* these people were writing in an exceptionally comfortable epoch? It is just in such times that "cosmic despair" can flourish. People with empty bellies never despair of the universe, nor even think about the universe, for that matter. The whole period 1910–30 was a prosperous one, and even the war years were physically tolerable if one happened to be a non-combatant in one of the Allied countries. As for the 'twenties, they were the golden age of the *rentier*-intellectual, a period of irresponsibility such as the world had never before seen. The war was over, the new totalitarian states had not arisen, moral and religious taboos of all descriptions had vanished, and the cash was rolling in. "Disillusionment" was all the fashion. Everyone with a safe £500 a year turned highbrow and began training himself in *taedium vitae*. It was an age of eagles and of crumpets, facile despairs, backyard Hamlets, cheap return tickets to the end of the night. In some of the minor characteristic novels of the period, books like *Told by an Idiot*, the despair-of-life reaches a Turkish-bath atmosphere of self-pity. And even the best writers of the time can be convicted of a too Olympian attitude, a too great readiness to wash their hands of the immediate practical problem. They see life very comprehensively, much more so than those who come immediately before or after them, but they see it through the wrong end of the telescope. Not that that invalidates their books, as books. The first test of any work of art is survival, and it is a fact that a great deal that was written in the period 1910–30 has survived and looks like continuing to survive. One has only to think of *Ulysses*, *Of Human Bondage*, most of Lawrence's early work, especially his short stories, and virtually the whole of Eliot's poems up to about 1930, to wonder what is now being written that will wear so well.

But quite suddenly, in the years 1930–5, something happens. The literary climate changes. A new group of writers, Auden and Spender and the rest of them, has made its appearance, and although technically these writers owe something to their predecessors, their "tendency" is entirely different. Suddenly we have got out of the twilight of the gods into a sort of Boy Scout atmosphere of bare knees and community singing. The typical literary man ceases to be a cultured expatriate with a leaning towards the Church, and becomes an eager-minded schoolboy with a leaning towards Communism. If the keynote of the writers of the 'twenties is "tragic sense of life", the keynote of the new writers is "serious purpose".

The differences between the two schools are discussed at some length in Mr Louis MacNeice's book *Modern Poetry*. This book is, of course, written entirely from the angle of the younger group and takes the superiority of their standards for granted. According to Mr MacNeice:

> The poets of *New Signatures*,[1] unlike Yeats and Eliot, are emotionally partisan. Yeats proposed to turn his back on desire and hatred; Eliot sat back and watched other people's emotions with ennui and an ironical self-pity. . . . The whole poetry, on the other hand, of Auden, Spender and Day-Lewis implies that they have desires and hatreds of their own and, further, that they think some things *ought* to be desired and others hated.

[1] Published in 1932. [Author's footnote.]

And again:

> The poets of *New Signatures* have swung back . . . to the Greek preference for information or statement. The first requirement is to have something to say, and after that you must say it as well as you can.

In other words, "purpose" has come back, the younger writers have "gone into politics". As I have pointed out already, Eliot & Co. are not really so non-partisan as Mr MacNeice seems to suggest. Still, it is broadly true that in the 'twenties the literary emphasis was more on technique and less on subject-matter than it is now.

The leading figures in this group are Auden, Spender, Day-Lewis, MacNeice, and there is a long string of writers of more or less the same tendency, Isherwood, John Lehmann, Arthur Calder-Marshall, Edward Upward, Alec Brown, Philip Henderson, and many others. As before, I am lumping them together simply according to tendency. Obviously there are very great variations in talent. But when one compares these writers with the Joyce-Eliot generation, the immediately striking thing is how much easier it is to form them into a group. Technically they are closer together, politically they are almost indistinguishable, and their criticisms of one another's work have always been (to put it mildly) good-natured. The outstanding writers of the 'twenties were of very varied origins, few of them had passed through the ordinary English educational mill (incidentally, the best of them, barring Lawrence, were not Englishmen), and most of them had had at some time to struggle against poverty, neglect, and even downright persecution. On the other hand, nearly all the younger writers fit easily into the public-school–university–Bloomsbury pattern. The few who are of proletarian origin are of the kind that is declassed early in life, first by means of scholarships and then by the bleaching-tub of London "culture". It is significant that several of the writers in this group have been not only boys but, subsequently, masters at public schools. Some years ago I described Auden as "a sort of gutless Kipling". As criticism this was quite unworthy, indeed it was merely a spiteful remark, but it is a fact that in Auden's work, especially his earlier work, an atmosphere of uplift—something rather like Kipling's "If" or Newbolt's "Play Up, Play Up, and Play the Game!"—never seems to be very far away. Take, for instance, a poem like "You're leaving now, and it's up to you boys."[1] It is pure scoutmaster, the exact note of the ten-minutes' straight talk on the dangers of self-abuse. No doubt there is an element of parody that he intends, but there is also a deeper resemblance that he does not intend. And of course the rather priggish note that is common to most of these writers is a symptom of release. By throwing "pure art" overboard they have freed themselves from the fear of being laughed at and vastly enlarged their scope. The prophetic side of Marxism, for example, is new material for poetry and has great possibilities:

> We are nothing.
> We have fallen
> Into the dark and shall be destroyed.
> Think though, that in this darkness
> We hold the secret hub of an idea
> Whose living sunlit wheel revolves in future years outside.
>
> (Spender, *Trial of a Judge*.)

But at the same time, by being Marxised literature has moved no nearer to the masses. Even allowing for the time-lag, Auden and Spender are somewhat farther from being popular writers than Joyce and Eliot, let alone Lawrence. As before, there are many contemporary writers who are outside the current, but there is not much doubt about what *is* the current. For the middle and late 'thirties, Auden, Spender & Co. *are* "the movement", just as Joyce, Eliot & Co. were for the 'twenties. And the movement is in the direction of some rather ill-defined thing called Communism. As early as 1934 or 1935 it was considered eccentric in literary circles not to be more or less "left", and in another year or two there had grown up a left-wing orthodoxy that made a certain set of opinions absolutely *de rigueur* on certain subjects. The idea had begun to gain ground (*vide* Edward Upward and others) that a writer must either be actively "left" or write badly. Between 1935 and 1939 the Communist Party had an almost irresistible fascination for any writer under forty. It became as normal to hear that so-and-so had "joined" as it had been a few years earlier, when Roman Catholicism was fashionable, to hear that so-and-so had "been received". For about three years, in fact, the central stream of English literature was more or less directly under Communist control. How was it possible for such a

[1] This is in fact the first line of Poem No. 10 in Cecil Day-Lewis's early volume of poetry *The Magnetic Mountain*.

thing to happen? And at the same time, what is meant by "Communism"? It is better to answer the second question first.

The Communist movement in western Europe began as a movement for the violent overthrow of capitalism, and degenerated within a few years into an instrument of Russian foreign policy. This was probably inevitable when the revolutionary ferment that followed the Great War had died down. So far as I know, the only comprehensive history of this subject in English is Franz Borkenau's book, *The Communist International.* What Borkenau's facts even more than his deductions make clear is that Communism could never have developed along its present lines if any real revolutionary feeling had existed in the industrialised countries. In England, for instance, it is obvious that no such feeling has existed for years past. The pathetic membership figures of all extremist parties show this clearly. It is only natural, therefore, that the English Communist movement should be controlled by people who are mentally subservient to Russia and have no real aim except to manipulate British foreign policy in the Russian interest. Of course such an aim cannot be openly admitted, and it is this fact that gives the Communist Party its very peculiar character. The more vocal kind of Communist is in effect a Russian publicity agent posing as an international Socialist. It is a pose that is easily kept up at normal times, but becomes difficult in moments of crisis, because of the fact that the USSR is no more scrupulous in its foreign policy than the rest of the Great Powers. Alliances, changes of front, etc which only make sense as part of the game of power politics have to be explained and justified in terms of international Socialism. Every time Stalin swaps partners, "Marxism" has to be hammered into a new shape. This entails sudden and violent changes of "line", purges, denunciations, systematic destruction of party literature, etc etc. Every Communist is in fact liable at any moment to have to alter his most fundamental convictions, or leave the party. The unquestionable dogma of Monday may become the damnable heresy of Tuesday, and so on. This has happened at least three times during the past ten years. It follows that in any western country a Communist Party is always unstable and usually very small. Its long-term membership really consists of an inner ring of intellectuals who have identified with the Russian bureaucracy, and a slightly larger body of working-class people who feel a loyalty towards Soviet Russia without necessarily understanding its policies. Otherwise there is only a shifting membership, one lot coming and another going with each change of "line".

In 1930 the English Communist Party was a tiny, barely legal organisation whose main activity was libelling the Labour Party. But by 1935 the face of Europe had changed, and left-wing politics changed with it. Hitler had risen to power and begun to re-arm, the Russian five-year plans had succeeded, Russia had reappeared as a great military power. As Hitler's three targets of attack were, to all appearances, Great Britain, France and the USSR, the three countries were forced into a sort of uneasy *rapprochement*. This meant that the English or French Communist was obliged to become a good patriot and imperialist—that is, to defend the very things he had been attacking for the past fifteen years. The Comintern slogans suddenly faded from red to pink. "World revolution" and "Social-Fascism" gave way to "Defence of democracy" and "Stop Hitler!" The years 1935–9 were the period of anti-Fascism and the Popular Front, the heyday of the Left Book Club, when red duchesses and "broad-minded" deans toured the battlefields of the Spanish war and Winston Churchill was the blue-eyed boy of the *Daily Worker*. Since then, of course, there has been yet another change of "line". But what is important for my purpose is that it was during the "anti-Fascist" phase that the younger English writers gravitated towards Communism.

The Fascism–democracy dogfight was no doubt an attraction in itself, but in any case their conversion was due at about that date. It was obvious that *laissez-faire* capitalism was finished and that there had got to be some kind of reconstruction; in the world of 1935 it was hardly possible to remain politically indifferent. But why did these young men turn towards anything so alien as Russian Communism? Why should *writers* be attracted by a form of Socialism that makes mental honesty impossible? The explanation really lies in something that had already made itself felt before the slump and before Hitler: middle-class unemployment.

Unemployment is not merely a matter of not having a job. Most people can *get* a job of sorts, even at the worst of times. The trouble was that by 1930 there was no activity, except perhaps scientific research, the arts and left-wing politics, that a thinking person could believe in. The debunking of western civilisation had reached its climax and "disillusionment" was immensely widespread. Who now could take it for granted to go through life in the ordinary middle-class way, as a soldier, a clergyman, a stockbroker, an Indian Civil Servant or what not? And how many of the values by which our grandfathers lived could now be taken seriously? Patriotism, religion, the Empire, the family, the sanctity of marriage, the Old School Tie, birth, breeding, honour, discipline—anyone of ordinary education could turn the whole lot of them inside out in three minutes. But what do you achieve, after all, by getting rid of such primal things as patriotism and religion? You have not necessarily got rid of the need for *something to believe in.* There had been a sort of false dawn a few years earlier when numbers of young intellectuals, including several quite gifted writers (Evelyn Waugh, Christopher Hollis and others), had fled into the Catholic Church. It is significant that these people went almost invariably to the Roman Church and not, for instance, to the C of E, the Greek Church or the Protestant sects. They went, that is, to the Church with a world-wide organisation, the one with a rigid discipline, the one with power and prestige behind it. Perhaps it is even worth noticing that the only latter-day convert of really first-rate gifts, Eliot, has embraced not Romanism but Anglo-Catholicism, the ecclesiastical equivalent of Trotskyism. But I do not think one need look farther than this for the reason why the young writers of the 'thirties flocked into or towards the Communist Party. It was simply something to believe in. Here was a church, an army, an orthodoxy, a discipline. Here was a Fatherland and—at any rate since 1935 or thereabouts—a Fuehrer. All the loyalties and superstitions that the intellect had seemingly banished could come rushing back under the thinnest of disguises. Patriotism, religion, empire, military glory—all in one word, Russia. Father, king, leader, hero, saviour—all in one word, Stalin. God—Stalin. The devil—Hitler. Heaven—Moscow. Hell—Berlin. All the gaps were filled up. So, after all, the "Communism" of the English intellectual is something explicable enough. It is the patriotism of the deracinated.

But there is one thing that undoubtedly contributed to the cult of Russia among the English intelligentsia during these years, and that is the softness and security of life in England itself. With all its injustices, England is still the land of habeas corpus, and the overwhelming majority of English people have no experience of violence or illegality. If you have grown up in that sort of atmosphere it is not at all easy to imagine what a despotic régime is like. Nearly all the dominant writers of the 'thirties belonged to the soft-boiled emancipated middle class and were too young to have effective memories of the Great War. To people of that kind such things as purges, secret police, summary executions, imprisonment without trial, etc etc are too remote to be terrifying. They can swallow totalitarianism *because* they have no experience of anything except liberalism. Look, for instance, at this extract from Mr Auden's poem "Spain" (incidentally this poem is one of the few decent things that have been written about the Spanish war):

> Tomorrow for the young, the poets exploding like bombs,
> The walks by the lake, the weeks of perfect communion;
> Tomorrow the bicycle races
> Through the suburbs on summer evenings. But today the struggle.
>
> Today the deliberate increase in the chances of death,
> The conscious acceptance of guilt in the necessary murder;
> Today the expending of powers
> On the flat ephemeral pamphlet and the boring meeting.

The second stanza is intended as a sort of thumbnail sketch of a day in the life of a "good party man". In the morning a couple of political murders, a ten-minutes' interlude to stifle "bourgeois" remorse, and then a hurried luncheon and a busy afternoon and evening chalking walls and distributing leaflets. All very edifying. But notice the phrase "necessary murder". It could only be written by a person to whom murder is at most a *word*. Personally I would not speak so lightly of murder. It so happens that I have seen the bodies of numbers of murdered men—I don't mean killed in battle, I mean murdered. Therefore I have some conception of what murder means —the terror, the hatred, the howling relatives, the post-mortems, the blood, the smells. To me, murder is something to be avoided. So it is to any ordinary person. The Hitlers and Stalins find murder necessary, but they don't advertise their callousness, and they don't speak of it as murder; it is "liquidation", "elimination" or some other soothing phrase. Mr Auden's brand of amoralism is only possible if you are the kind of person who is always somewhere else when the trigger is pulled. So much of left-wing thought is a kind of playing with fire by people who don't even know that fire is hot. The warmongering to which the English intelligentsia gave themselves up in the period 1935–9 was largely based on a sense of personal immunity. The attitude was very different in France, where the military service is hard to dodge and even literary men know the weight of a pack.

Towards the end of Mr Cyril Connolly's recent book, *Enemies of Promise*, there occurs an interesting and revealing passage. The first part of the book is, more or less, an evaluation of present-day literature. Mr Connolly belongs exactly to the generation of the writers of "the movement", and with not many reservations their values are his values. It is interesting to notice that among prose writers he admires chiefly those specialising in violence—the would-be tough American school, Hemingway, etc. The latter part of the book, however, is autobiographical and consists of an account, fascinatingly accurate, of life at a preparatory school and Eton in the years 1910–20. Mr Connolly ends by remarking:

> Were I to deduce anything from my feelings on leaving Eton, it might be called *The Theory of Permanent Adolescence*. It is the theory that the experiences undergone by boys at the great public schools are so intense as to dominate their lives and to arrest their development.

When you read the second sentence in this passage, your natural impulse is to look for the misprint. Presumably there is a "not" left out, or something. But no, not a bit of it! He means it! And what is more, he is merely speaking the truth, in an inverted fashion. "Cultured" middle-class life has reached a depth of softness at which a public-school education—five years in a lukewarm bath of snobbery—can actually be looked back upon as an eventful period. To nearly all the writers who have counted during the 'thirties, what more has ever happened than Mr Connolly records in *Enemies of Promise*? It is the same pattern all the time; public school, university, a few trips abroad, then London. Hunger, hardship, solitude, exile, war, prison, persecution, manual labour—hardly even words. No wonder that the huge tribe known as "the right left people" found it so easy to condone the purge-and-Ogpu side of the Russian régime and the horrors of the First Five Year Plan. They were so gloriously incapable of understanding what it all meant.

By 1937 the whole of the intelligentsia was mentally at war. Left-wing thought had narrowed down to "anti-Fascism", i.e. to a negative, and a torrent of hate-literature directed against Germany and the politicians supposedly friendly to Germany was pouring from the press. The thing that, to me, was truly frightening about the war in Spain was not such violence as I witnessed, nor even the party feuds behind the lines, but the immediate reappearance in left-wing circles of the mental atmosphere of the Great War. The very people who for twenty years had sniggered over their own superiority to war hysteria were the ones who rushed straight back into the mental slum of 1915. All the familiar war-time idiocies, spy-hunting, orthodoxy-sniffing (Sniff, sniff. Are you a good anti-Fascist?), the retailing of incredible atrocity stories, came back into vogue as though the intervening years had never happened. Before the end of the Spanish war, and even before Munich, some of the better of the left-wing writers were beginning to squirm. Neither Auden nor, on the whole, Spender wrote about the Spanish war in quite the vein that was expected of them. Since then there has been a change of feeling and much dismay and confusion, because the actual course of events has made nonsense of the left-wing orthodoxy of the last few years. But then it did not need very great acuteness to see that much of it was nonsense from the start. There is no certainty, therefore, that the next orthodoxy to emerge will be any better than the last.

On the whole the literary history of the 'thirties seems to justify the opinion that a writer does well to keep out of politics. For any writer who accepts or partially accepts the discipline of a political party is sooner or later faced with the alternative: toe the line, or shut up. It is, of course, possible to toe the line and go on writing—after a fashion. Any Marxist can demonstrate with the greatest of ease that "bourgeois" liberty of thought is an illusion. But when he has finished his demonstration there remains the psychological *fact* that without this "bourgeois" liberty the creative powers wither away. In the future a totalitarian literature may arise, but it will be quite different from anything we can now imagine. Literature as we know it is an individual thing, demanding mental honesty and a minimum of censorship. And this is even truer of prose than of verse. It is probably not a coincidence that the best writers of the 'thirties have been poets. The atmosphere of orthodoxy is always damaging to prose, and above all it is completely ruinous to the novel, the most anarchical of all forms of literature. How many Roman Catholics have been good novelists? Even the handful one could name have usually been bad Catholics. The novel is practically a Protestant form of art; it is a product of the free mind, of the autonomous individual. No decade in the past hundred and fifty years has been so barren of imaginative prose as the nineteen-thirties. There have been good poems, good sociological works, brilliant pamphlets, but practically no fiction of any value at all. From 1933 onwards the mental climate was increasingly against it. Anyone sensitive enough to be touched by the *zeitgeist* was also involved in politics. Not everyone, of course, was definitely *in* the political racket, but practically everyone was on its periphery and more or less mixed up in propaganda campaigns and squalid controversies. Communists and near-Communists had a disproportionately large influence in the literary reviews. It was a time of labels, slogans and evasions. At the worst moments you were expected to lock yourself up in a constipating little cage of lies; at the best a sort of voluntary censorship ("Ought I to say this? Is it pro-Fascist?") was at work in nearly everyone's mind. It is almost inconceivable that good novels should be written in such an atmosphere. Good novels are not written by orthodoxy-sniffers, nor by people who are conscience-stricken about their own unorthodoxy. Good novels are written by people who are *not frightened*. This brings me back to Henry Miller.

III

If this were a likely moment for the launching of "schools" of literature, Henry Miller might be the starting-point of a new "school". He does at any rate mark an unexpected swing of the pendulum. In his books one gets right away from the "political animal" and back to a viewpoint not only individualistic but completely passive—the viewpoint of a man who believes the world-process to be outside his control and who in any case hardly wishes to control it.

I first met Miller at the end of 1936, when I was passing through Paris on my way to Spain. What most intrigued me about him was to find that he felt no interest in the Spanish war whatever. He merely told me in forcible terms that to go to Spain at that moment was the act of an idiot. He could understand anyone going there from purely selfish motives, out of curiosity, for instance, but to mix oneself up in such things *from a sense of obligation* was sheer stupidity. In any case my ideas about combating Fascism, defending democracy, etc etc were all boloney. Our civilisation was destined to be swept away and replaced by something so different that we should scarcely regard it as human—a prospect that did not bother him, he said. And some such outlook is implicit throughout his work. Everywhere there is the sense of the approaching cataclysm, and almost everywhere the implied belief that it doesn't matter. The only political declaration which, so far as I know, he has ever made in print is a purely negative one. A year or so ago an American magazine, the *Marxist Quarterly*, sent out a questionnaire to various American writers asking them to define their attitude on the subject of war. Miller replied in terms of extreme pacifism, but a merely personal pacifism, an individual refusal to fight, with no apparent wish to convert others to the same opinion—practically, in fact, a declaration of irresponsibility.

However, there is more than one kind of irresponsibility. As a rule, writers who do not wish to identify themselves with the historical process of the moment either ignore it or fight against it. If they can ignore it, they are probably fools. If they can understand it well enough to want to fight against it, they probably have enough vision to realise that they cannot win. Look, for instance, at a poem like "The Scholar Gypsy", with its railing against the "strange disease of modern life" and its magnificent defeatist simile in the final stanza. It expresses one of the normal literary attitudes, perhaps actually the prevailing attitude during the last hundred years. And on the other hand there are the "progressives", the yea-sayers, the Shaw-Wells type, always leaping forward to embrace the ego-projections which they mistake for the future. On the whole the writers of the 'twenties took the first line and the writers of the 'thirties the second. And at any given moment, of course, there is a huge tribe of Barries and Deepings and Dells who simply don't notice what is happening. Where Miller's work is symptomatically important is in its avoidance of any of these attitudes. He is neither pushing the world-process forward nor trying to drag it back, but on the other hand he is by no means ignoring it. I should say that he believes in the impending ruin of western civilisation much more firmly than the majority of "revolutionary" writers; only he does not feel called upon to do anything about it. He is fiddling while Rome is burning, and, unlike the enormous majority of people who do this, fiddling with his face towards the flames.

In *Max and the White Phagocytes* there is one of those revealing passages in which a writer tells you a great deal about himself while talking about somebody else. The book includes a long essay on the diaries of Anais Nin, which I have never read, except for a few fragments, and which I believe have not been published. Miller claims that they are the only truly feminine writing that has ever appeared, whatever that may mean. But the interesting passage is one in which he compares Anais Nin—evidently a completely subjective, introverted writer—to Jonah in the whale's belly. In passing he refers to an essay that Aldous Huxley wrote some years ago about El Greco's picture "The Dream of Philip the Second". Huxley remarks that the people in El Greco's pictures always look as though they were in the bellies of whales, and professes to find something peculiarly horrible in the idea of being in a "visceral prison". Miller retorts that, on the contrary, there are many worse things than being swallowed by whales, and the passage makes it clear that he himself finds the idea rather attractive. Here he is touching upon what is probably a very widespread fantasy. It is perhaps worth noticing that everyone, at least every English-speaking person, invariably speaks of Jonah and the *whale.* Of course the creature that swallowed Jonah was a fish, and is so described in the Bible (Jonah 1 :17), but children naturally confuse it with a whale, and this fragment of baby-talk is habitually carried into later life—a sign, perhaps, of the hold that the Jonah myth has upon our imaginations. For the fact is that being inside a whale is a very comfortable, cosy, homelike thought. The historical Jonah, if he can be so called, was glad enough to escape, but in imagination, in day-dream, countless people have envied him. It is, of course, quite obvious why. The whale's belly is simply a womb big enough for an adult. There you are, in the dark, cushioned space that exactly fits you, with yards of blubber between yourself and reality, able to keep up an attitude of the completest indifference, no matter *what* happens. A storm that would sink all the battleships in the world would hardly reach you as an echo. Even the whale's own movements would probably be imperceptible to you. He might be wallowing among the surface waves or shooting down into the blackness of the middle seas (a mile deep, according to Herman Melville), but you would never notice the difference. Short of being dead, it is the final, unsurpassable stage of irresponsibility. And however it may be with Anais Nin, there is no question that Miller himself is inside the whale. All his best and most characteristic passages are written from the angle of Jonah, a willing Jonah. Not that he is especially introverted—quite the contrary. In his case the whale happens to be transparent. Only he feels no impulse to alter or control the process that he is undergoing. He has performed the essential Jonah act of allowing himself to be swallowed, remaining passive, *accepting*.

It will be seen what this amounts to. It is a species of quietism, implying either complete unbelief or else a degree of belief amounting to mysticism. The attitude is "Je m'en fous" or "Though He slay me, yet will I trust in Him", whichever way you like to look at it; for practical purposes both are identical, the moral in either case being "Sit on your bum". But in a time like ours, is this a defensible attitude? Notice that it is almost impossible to refrain from asking this question. At the moment of writing we are still in a period in which it is taken for granted that books ought always to be positive, serious and "constructive". A dozen years ago this idea would have been greeted with titters. ("My dear aunt, one doesn't write *about* anything, one just *writes.*") Then the pendulum swung away from the frivolous notion that art is merely technique, but it swung a very long distance, to the point of asserting that a book can only be "good" if it is founded on a "true" vision of life. Naturally the people who believe this also believe that they are in possession of the truth themselves. Catholic critics, for instance, tend to claim that books are only "good" when they are of Catholic tendency. Marxist critics make the same claim more boldly for Marxist books. For instance, Mr Edward Upward ("A Marxist Interpretation of Literature", in *The Mind in Chains*):

> Literary criticism which aims at being Marxist must . . . proclaim that no book written *at the present time* can be "good" unless it is written from a Marxist or near-Marxist viewpoint.

Various other writers have made similar or comparable statements. Mr Upward italicises "at the present time" because he realises that you cannot, for instance, dismiss *Hamlet* on the ground that Shakes-speare was not a Marxist. Nevertheless his interesting essay only glances very shortly at this difficulty. Much of the literature that comes to us out of the past is permeated by and in fact founded on beliefs (the belief in the immortality of the soul, for example) which now seem to us false and in some cases contemptibly silly. Yet it is "good" literature, if survival is any test. Mr Upward would no doubt answer that a belief which was appropriate several centuries ago might be inappropriate and therefore stultifying now. But this does not get one much farther, because it assumes that in any age there will be *one* body of belief which is the current approximation to truth, and that the best literature of the time will be more or less in harmony with it. Actually no such uniformity has ever existed. In seventeenth-century England, for instance, there was a religious and political cleavage which distinctly resembled the left–right antagonism of today. Looking back, most modern people would feel that the bourgeois–Puritan viewpoint was a better approximation to truth than the Catholic–feudal one. But it is certainly not the case that all or even a majority of the best writers of the time were Puritans. And more than this, there exist "good" writers whose world-view would in *any* age be recognised as false and silly. Edgar Allan Poe is an example. Poe's outlook is at best a wild romanticism and at worst is not far from being insane in the literal clinical sense. Why is it, then, that stories like "The Black Cat", "The Tell-tale Heart", "The Fall of the House of Usher" and so forth, which might very nearly have been written by a lunatic, do not convey a feeling of falsity? Because they are true within a certain framework, they keep the rules of their own peculiar world, like a Japanese picture. But it appears that to write successfully about such a world you have got to believe in it. One sees the difference immediately if one compares Poe's *Tales* with what is, in my opinion, an insincere attempt to work up a similar atmosphere, Julian Green's *Minuit.* The thing that immediately strikes one about *Minuit* is that there is no reason why any of the events in it should happen. Everything is completely arbitrary; there is no emotional sequence. But this is exactly what one does *not* feel with Poe's stories. Their maniacal logic, in its own setting, is quite convincing. When, for instance, the drunkard seizes the black cat and cuts its eye out with his penknife, one knows exactly *why* he did it, even to the point of feeling that one would have done the same oneself. It seems therefore that for a creative writer possession of the "truth" is less important than emotional sincerity. Even Mr Upward would not claim that a writer needs nothing beyond a Marxist training. He also needs talent. But talent, apparently, is a matter of being able to *care*, of really *believing* in your beliefs, whether they are true or false. The difference between, for instance, Céline and Evelyn Waugh is a difference of emotional intensity. It is the difference between genuine despair and a despair that is at least partly a pretence. And with this there goes another consideration which is perhaps less obvious: that there are occasions when an "untrue" belief is more likely to be sincerely held than a "true" one.

If one looks at the books of personal reminiscence written about the war of 1914–18, one notices that nearly all that have remained readable after a lapse of time are written from a passive, negative angle. They are the records of something completely meaningless, a nightmare happening in a void. That was not actually the truth about the war, but it was the truth about the individual reaction. The soldier advancing into a machine-gun barrage or standing waist-deep in a flooded trench knew only that here was an appalling experience in which he was all but helpless. He was likelier to make a good book out of his helplessness and his ignorance than out of a pretended power to see the whole thing in perspective. As for the books that were written during the war itself, the best of them were nearly all the work of people who simply turned their backs and tried not to notice that the war was happening. Mr E. M. Forster has described how in 1917 he read "Prufrock" and others of Eliot's early poems, and how it heartened him at such a time to get hold of poems that were "innocent of public-spiritedness":

> They sang of private disgust and diffidence, and of people who seemed genuine because they were unattractive or weak. . . . Here was a protest, and a feeble one, and the more congenial for being feeble. . . . He who could turn aside to complain of ladies and drawing-rooms preserved a tiny drop of our self-respect, he carried on the human heritage.

That is very well said. Mr MacNeice, in the book I have referred to already, quotes this passage and somewhat smugly adds:

> Ten years later less feeble protests were to be made by poets and the human heritage carried on rather differently. . . . The contemplation of a world of fragments becomes boring and Eliot's successors are more interested in tidying it up.

Similar remarks are scattered throughout Mr MacNeice's book. What he wishes us to believe is that Eliot's "successors" (meaning Mr MacNeice and his friends) have in some way "protested" more effectively than Eliot did by publishing "Prufrock" at the moment when the Allied armies were assaulting the Hindenburg Line. Just where these "protests" are to be found I do not know. But in the contrast between Mr Forster's comment and Mr MacNeice's lies all the difference between a man who knows what the 1914–18 war was like and a man who barely remembers it. The truth is that in 1917 there was nothing that a thinking and sensitive person could do, except to remain human, if possible. And a gesture of helplessness, even of frivolity, might be the best way of doing that. If I had been a soldier fighting in the Great War, I would sooner have got hold of "Prufrock" than *The First Hundred Thousand* or Horatio Bottomley's *Letters to the Boys in the Trenches*. I should have felt, like Mr Forster, that by simply standing aloof and keeping touch with pre-war emotions, Eliot was carrying on the human heritage. What a relief it would have been at such a time, to read about the hesitations of a middle-aged highbrow with a bald spot! So different from bayonet drill! After the bombs and the food queues and the recruiting posters, a human voice! What a relief!

But, after all, the war of 1914–18 was only a heightened moment in an almost continuous crisis. At this date it hardly even needs a war to bring home to us the disintegration of our society and the increasing helplessness of all decent people. It is for this reason that I think that the passive, non-cooperative attitude implied in Henry Miller's work is justified. Whether or not it is an expression of what people *ought* to feel, it probably comes somewhere near to expressing what they *do* feel. Once again it is the human voice among the bomb-explosions, a friendly American voice, "innocent of public-spiritedness". No sermons, merely the subjective truth. And along those lines, apparently, it is still possible for a good novel to be written. Not necessarily an edifying novel, but a novel worth reading and likely to be remembered after it is read.

While I have been writing this book[1] another European war has broken out. It will either last several years and tear western civilisation to pieces, or it will end inconclusively and prepare the way for yet another war which will do the job once and for all. But war is only "peace intensified". What is quite obviously happening, war or no war, is the break-up of *laissez-faire* capitalism and of the liberal-Christian culture. Until recently the full implications of this were not foreseen, because it was generally imagined that Socialism could preserve and even enlarge the atmosphere of liberalism. It is now beginning to be realised how false this idea was. Almost certainly we are moving into an age of totalitarian dictatorships—an age in which freedom of thought will be at first a deadly sin and later on a meaningless abstraction. The autonomous individual is going to be stamped out of existence. But this means that literature, in the form in which we know it, must suffer at least a temporary death. The literature of liberalism is coming to an end and the literature of totalitarianism has not yet appeared and is barely imaginable. As for the writer, he is sitting on a melting iceberg; he is merely an anachronism, a hangover from the bourgeois age, as surely doomed as the hippopotamus. Miller seems to me a man out of the common because he saw and proclaimed this fact a long while before most of his con-

[1] *Inside the Whale.*

temporaries—at a time, indeed, when many of them were actually burbling about a renaissance of literature. Wyndham Lewis had said years earlier that the major history of the English language was finished, but he was basing this on different and rather trivial reasons. But from now onwards the all-important fact for the creative writer is going to be that this is not a writer's world. That does not mean that he cannot help to bring the new society into being, but he can take no part in the process *as a writer*. For *as a writer* he is a liberal, and what is happening is the destruction of liberalism. It seems likely, therefore, that in the remaining years of free speech any novel worth reading will follow more or less along the lines that Miller has followed—I do not mean in technique or subject-matter, but in implied outlook. The passive attitude will come back, and it will be more consciously passive than before. Progress and reaction have both turned out to be swindles. Seemingly there is nothing left but quietism—robbing reality of its terrors by simply submitting to it. Get inside the whale—or rather, admit that you are inside the whale (for you *are*, of course). Give yourself over to the world-process, stop fighting against it or pretending that you control it; simply accept it, endure it, record it. That seems to be the formula that any sensitive novelist is now likely to adopt. A novel on more positive, "constructive" lines, and not emotionally spurious, is at present very difficult to imagine.

But do I mean by this that Miller is a "great author", a new hope for English prose? Nothing of the kind. Miller himself would be the last to claim or want any such thing. No doubt he will go on writing—anybody who has once started always goes on writing—and associated with him there is a number of writers of approximately the same tendency, Lawrence Durrell, Michael Fraenkel and others, almost amounting to a "school". But he himself seems to me essentially a man of one book. Sooner or later I should expect him to descend into unintelligibility, or into charlatanism; there are signs of both in his later work. His last book, *Tropic of Capricorn*, I have not even read. This was not because I did not want to read it, but because the police and customs authorities have so far managed to prevent me from getting hold of it. But it would surprise me if it came anywhere near *Tropic of Cancer* or the opening chapters of *Black Spring*. Like certain other autobiographical novelists, he had it in him to do just one thing perfectly, and he did it. Considering what the fiction of the nineteen-thirties has been like, that is something.

Miller's books are published by the Obelisk Press in Paris. What will happen to the Obelisk Press, now that war has broken out and Jack Kahane, the publisher, is dead, I do not know, but at any rate the books are still procurable. I earnestly counsel anyone who has not done so to read at least *Tropic of Cancer.* With a little ingenuity, or by paying a little over the published price, you can get hold of it, and even if parts of it disgust you, it will stick in your memory. It is also an "important" book, in a sense different from the sense in which that word is generally used. As a rule novels are spoken of as "important" when they are either a "terrible indictment" of something or other or when they introduce some technical innovation. Neither of these applies to *Tropic of Cancer*. Its importance is merely symptomatic. Here in my opinion is the only imaginative prose writer of the slightest value who has appeared among the English-speaking races for some years past. Even if that is objected to as an overstatement, it will probably be admitted that Miller is a writer out of the ordinary, worth more than a single glance; and, after all, he is a completely negative, unconstructive, amoral writer, a mere Jonah, a passive accepter of evil, a sort of Whitman among the corpses. Symptomatically, that is more significant than the mere fact that five thousand novels are published in England every year and four thousand nine hundred of them are tripe. It is a demonstration of the *impossibility* of any major literature until the world has shaken itself into its new shape.

ITW; *New Directions in Prose and Poetry*, 1940; SJ; EYE; CE.

165. Letter to Geoffrey Gorer

The Stores
Wallington
Nr Baldock, Herts.
3 April 1940

Dear Geoffrey,

I was very glad to get your letter & know you are at any rate fairly comfortable & congenially employed. All is very quiet on the Wallington front. Like nearly everyone else I have completely failed to get any kind of "war work". But I am trying very hard to join a Govt training centre & learn machine draughtsmanship, partly because I want a job, partly because I think it would interest me &

as I fancy we are all going to be conscripted in one form or another within about a year I'd rather do something more or less skilled, & partly because I think it might be well to come out of the war having learned a trade. However I don't know whether it will go through yet. Eileen is still working in a Govt department but if we can possibly afford it when our affairs are settled I want to get her out of it, as they are simply working her to death besides its making it impossible for us to be together. I dare say we *could* get by if I stuck simply to writing, but at present I am very anxious to slow off & not hurry on with my next book, as I have now published 8 in 8 years which is too much. You didn't I suppose see my last (*Inside the Whale*) which came out a few weeks back. There is one essay in it that might interest you, on boys' weekly papers, as it rather overlaps with your own researches. You remember perhaps my saying to you some years back that very popular fiction ought to be looked into & instancing Edgar Wallace. This essay was published first in a slightly abridged form in Cyril Connolly's monthly paper *Horizon*, & now the editor of the *Magnet*, which you no doubt remember from your boyhood, has asked for space in which to answer my "charges". I look forward to this with some uneasiness, as I've no doubt made many mistakes, but what he'll probably pick on is my suggestion that these papers try to inculcate snobbishness. I haven't a copy left to send you but you might be able to get it from the library. There is an essay on Dickens that might interest you too. I find this kind of semi-sociological literary criticism very interesting & I'd like to do a lot of other writers, but unfortunately there's no money in it. All Gollancz would give me in advance on the book was £20! With novels it's easier to be sure of a sale, but I've now got an idea for a really big novel, I mean big in bulk, & I want to lie fallow before doing it. Of course God knows what hope there is of making a living out of writing in the future or where we'll all be a few years hence. If the war really gets going one may get a chance of a scrap after all. Up to date I haven't felt greatly moved to join the army because even if one can get past the doctors they make all the older men into pioneers etc. It's ghastly how soon one becomes "older".

There is not much happening in England. As far as I can gather people are fed up with the war but not acutely so. Except for small sections such as Pacifists etc. people want to get it settled & I fancy they'd be willing to go on fighting for 10 years if they thought the sacrifices were falling equally on everybody, which alas isn't likely with the present Government in office. The Government seem to have done all their propaganda with the maximum of stupidity & there'll probably be hell to pay when people begin to grasp that fighting the war means a 12-hour day etc etc. The new paper *Horizon* is going very well, sells abt 6000 or 7000 already. Gollancz has grown a beard & fallen out with his Communist pals, partly over Finland etc, partly because of their general dishonesty which he's just become alive to. When I saw him recently, the first time in 3 years, he asked me whether it was really true that the GPU had been active in Spain during the civil war, & told me that when he tied up with the Communists in 1936 he had not known that they had ever had any other policy than the Popular Front one. It's frightful that people who are so ignorant should have so much influence. The food situation is quite OK, & I think what rationing there is (meat, sugar, butter) is actually unnecessary & done just to teach people a lesson. They've recently had to double the butter ration as they found the stocks going bad on them. I am busy getting our garden dug & am going to try & raise ½ ton of potatoes this year, as it wouldn't surprise me to see a food shortage next winter. If I thought I was going to be here all the time I'd breed a lot more hens & also go in for rabbits.

Eileen would send love if she was here.

Yours
Eric

166. Letter to Humphry House

The Stores
Wallington
Nr Baldock, Herts.
11 April 1940

Dear Mr House,[1]
Many thanks for your letter. I was glad to hear from you. With ref to the manifesto,[2] I haven't a copy of it by me, but as to the specific

[1] Humphry House (1908–55), English scholar, Fellow of Wadham College, Oxford. His works include an edition of the *Notebooks and Papers of Gerard Manley Hopkins*, *The Dickens World* and three essays in *Ideas and Beliefs of the Victorians*.

[2] Sir Richard Acland, Bt. (1906–), had become a Liberal MP in 1935. From 1936 he was active in the campaign for a Popular Front. At the outbreak

point you raise, about "the churches", I should say that it is a good rule of thumb never to mention religion if you can possibly avoid it. I don't know how many practising religious believers there are in England, but it couldn't conceivably be more than 10 million (probably more like 6 million), and even among those there is an active minority which will be offended by the suggestion that the churches don't put their professions into practice. In any case the churches no longer have any hold on the working class, except perhaps for the Catholic Irish labourers. On the other hand you can always appeal to common decency, which the vast majority of people believe in without the need to tie it up with any transcendental belief. As to the "white-man–coloured-man" business, I can't give an opinion.

As to the manifesto in general. If I had been drawing it up I would of course have put it quite differently. Whether that kind of thing can ever have a wide appeal, except when something has happened which brings the issue into the ordinary person's mind, I am not sure. The very fact that this manifesto of "common men" has to be drawn up by a baronet MP and handed out to fifty persons to sign on the dotted line, instead of coming spontaneously from the people themselves, carries its own suggestion. I was willing to give what little help I could, because I was in general agreement, i.e. I think it is vitally necessary to do something towards equalising incomes, abolishing class privilege and setting free the subject peoples. Not to put it on any wider ground, I don't believe the war can otherwise be won, if it goes to full lengths, and one simply can't see the present or any probable future government doing anything of the kind unless they are bullied into it. But had the manifesto been anything like Acland's book, *Unser Kampf*, I would have had nothing to do with it. The actual effect of a book like that, whatever the intention might be, is simply to spread defeatism. One has got to remember that most people see things in very simple terms and that the urgent question of the moment is "Do we fight Hitler or do we surrender?" Ninety-nine people of a hundred would conclude from reading *Unser Kampf* that we ought to surrender as quickly and ignominiously as possible.

---

of war he announced his conversion to Socialism, or, as he preferred to call it, "Common Ownership". In February 1940 he published *Unser Kampf* (one of the most successful of all Penguin Specials), asking its readers to write and give him their support. On 12 March 1940 about 150 of these correspondents assembled at a meeting convened by Acland in the House of Commons and agreed on the draft of *The Manifesto of the Common Man*, to which Orwell refers here.

Acland seems to me an almost complete ass, though of course well-meaning enough. All through the pre-war years, when it was just conceivably possible to avert war by reviving the international Socialist movement, he tied himself up with the warmongering Popular Front gang, and now that war has started, under the influence of the same people, he suddenly discovers that Hitler is no worse than we are and in fact rather better. He allows himself to become the tool of . . . like Pritt[1] and is apparently not capable of seeing that Nazi propaganda in this country has to pose as Russian propaganda. However, in the manifesto he steered clear of that kind of thing, so I was willing to associate myself with it, because I do agree about the absolute necessity of moving towards equality. But I would have worded the manifesto more strongly and emphasised both ends of the programme (defeat Hitler—equalise incomes) more plainly.

As to Dickens. You evidently know much more about him than I do. I have never really "studied" him, merely read and enjoyed him, and I dare say there are works of his I have never read. The point you took up, about Dickens not writing about work, was one I did not express very well. What I should have said was that when Dickens gives a detailed description of someone working, it is always someone seen from the outside and usually a burlesque (like Wemmick or Venus). I avoided following this up because it would have led me into a discussion of the burlesque in English novels which would have strayed too far afield. As to D's "discontent", I think I stick to it that some such quality is necessary, and I think the disappearance of it in the modern intelligentsia is a very sinister thing. Dickens, of course, had the most childish views on politics etc, but I think that because his *moral* sense was sound he would have been able to find his bearing in any political or economic milieu. So I think would most Victorians. The thing that frightens me about the modern intelligentsia is their inability to see that human society must be based on common decency, whatever the political and economic forms may be. To revert to Acland and his *Unser Kampf*, he is apparently incapable of seeing that there is something wrong with the present Russian régime. Private property has been abolished, therefore (so he argues) everything *must* be more or less all right. This seems to me

[1] D. N. Pritt (1887–), QC, Labour MP 1935–40. After his expulsion from the Labour Party for policy disagreements he became an Independent Socialist MP until 1950. Well known as a barrister and fervent supporter of left-wing causes and the Soviet Union.

to indicate the lack of a moral nose. Dickens, without the slightest understanding of Socialism etc, would have seen at a glance that there is something wrong with a régime that needs a pyramid of corpses every few years. It is as Nietzsche said about Christianity (I'm quoting from memory), if you are all right inside you don't have to be *told* that it is putrid. You can smell it—it stinks. All people who are morally sound have known since about 1931 that the Russian régime stinks. Part of the trouble, as I pointed out in my book,[1] is that the English intelligentsia have been so conditioned that they simply cannot imagine what a totalitarian government is like. They have also become infected with the inherently mechanistic Marxist notion that if you make the necessary technical advance the moral advance will follow of itself. I have never accepted this. I don't believe that capitalism, as against feudalism, improved the actual quality of human life, and I don't believe that Socialism *in itself* need work any real improvement either. Hitler is perhaps a large-scale demonstration of this. I believe that these economic advances merely provide the opportunity for a step forward which, as yet, hasn't happened. A year ago I was in the Atlas mountains, and looking at the Berber villagers there, it struck me that we were, perhaps, 1000 years ahead of these people, but no *better* than they, perhaps on balance rather worse. We are physically inferior to them, for instance, and manifestly less happy. All we have done is to advance to a point at which we *could* make a real improvement in human life, but we shan't do it without the recognition that common decency is necessary. My chief hope for the future is that the common people have never parted company with their moral code. I have never met a genuine working man who accepted Marxism, for instance. I have never had the slightest fear of a dictatorship of the proletariat, if it could happen, and certain things I saw in the Spanish war confirmed me in this. But I admit to having a perfect horror of a dictatorship of theorists, as in Russia and Germany.

I would like to meet some time. I am rather tied down here, as, apart from other things, I am trying to join a Government training centre and they may possibly call me up some time soon. Thank you for writing.

Yours sincerely
George Orwell

[1] *Inside the Whale.*

167. The Limit to Pessimism

Mr Malcolm Muggeridge's "message"[1]—for it is a message, though a negative one—has not altered since he wrote *Winter in Moscow*. It boils down to a simple disbelief in the power of human beings to construct a perfect or even a tolerable society here on earth. In essence, it is the Book of Ecclesiastes with the pious interpolations left out.

No doubt everyone is familiar with this line of thought. Vanity of vanities, all is vanity. The Kingdom of Earth is forever unattainable. Every attempt to establish liberty leads directly to tyranny. One tyrant takes over from another, the captain of industry from the robber baron, the Nazi gauleiter from the captain of industry, the sword gives way to the cheque book and the cheque book to the machine-gun, the Tower of Babel perpetually rises and falls. It is the Christian pessimism, but with this important difference, that in the Christian scheme of things the Kingdom of Heaven is there to restore the balance:

Jerusalem, my happy home,
Would God I were in thee!
Would God my woes were at an end,
Thy joys that I might see!

And after all, even your earthly "woes" don't matter so very greatly, provided that you really "believe". Life is short and even Purgatory does not last for ever, so you are bound to be in Jerusalem before long. Mr Muggeridge, needless to say, refuses this consolation. He gives no more evidence of believing in God than of trusting in Man. Nothing is open to him, therefore, except an indiscriminate walloping of all human activities whatever. But as a social historian this does not altogether invalidate him, because the age we live in invites something of the kind. It is an age in which every *positive* attitude has turned out a failure. Creeds, parties, programmes of every description have simply flopped, one after another. The only "ism" that has justified itself is pessimism. Therefore at this moment good books can be written from the angle of Thersites, though probably not very many.

I don't think Mr Muggeridge's history of the 'thirties is strictly truthful, but I think it is nearer to essential truth than any "constructive" outlook could have made it. He is looking only on the

[1] *The Thirties* by Malcolm Muggeridge.

black side, but it is doubtful whether there is any bright side to look on. What a decade! A riot of appalling folly that suddenly becomes a nightmare, a scenic railway ending in a torture-chamber. It starts off in the hangover of the "enlightened" post-war age, with Ramsay Macdonald soft-soaping into the microphone and the League of Nations flapping vague wings in the background, and it ends up with twenty thousand bombing planes darkening the sky and Himmler's masked executioner whacking women's heads off on a block borrowed from the Nuremberg museum. In between are the politics of the umbrella and the hand-grenade. The National Government coming in to "save the pound", Macdonald fading out like the Cheshire Cat, Baldwin winning an election on the disarmament ticket in order to rearm (and then failing to rearm), the June purge, the Russian purges, the glutinous humbug of the Abdication, the ideological mix-up of the Spanish war, Communists waving Union Jacks, Conservative MPs cheering the news that British ships have been bombed, the Pope blessing Franco, Anglican dignitaries beaming at the wrecked churches of Barcelona, Chamberlain stepping out of his Munich aeroplane with a misquotation from Shakespeare, Lord Rothermere acclaiming Hitler as "a great gentleman", the London air-raid sirens blowing a false alarm as the first bombs drop on Warsaw. Mr Muggeridge, who is not loved in "left" circles, is often labelled "reactionary" or even "Fascist", but I don't know of any left-wing writer who has flayed Macdonald, Baldwin and Chamberlain with equal ferocity. Mixed up with the buzz of conferences and the crash of guns are the day-to-day imbecilities of the gutter press. Astrology, trunk murders, the Oxford Groupers with their "sharing" and their praying-batteries, the Rector of Stiffkey (a great favourite with Mr Muggeridge: he makes several appearances) photographed with naked female acquaintances, starving in a barrel and finally devoured by lions, James Douglas and his dog Bunch, Godfrey Winn with his yet more emetic dog and his political reflections ("God and Mr Chamberlain—for I see no blasphemy in coupling these names"), spiritualism, the Modern Girl, nudism, dog racing, Shirley Temple, BO, halitosis, night starvation, should a doctor tell?

The book ends on a note of extreme defeatism. The peace that is not a peace slumps into a war that is not a war. The epic events that everyone had expected somehow don't happen, the all-pervading lethargy continues just as before. "Shape without form, shade without colour, paralysed force, gesture without motion." What Mr Muggeridge appears to be saying is that the English are powerless against their new adversaries because there is no longer anything that they believe in with sufficient firmness to make them willing for sacrifice. It is the struggle of people who have no faith against people who have faith in false gods. Is he right, I wonder? The truth is that it is impossible to discover what the English people are really feeling and thinking, about the war or about anything else. It has been impossible all through the critical years. I don't myself believe that he is right. But one cannot be sure until something of a quite unmistakable nature—some great disaster, probably—has brought home to the mass of the people what kind of world they are living in.

The final chapters are, to me, deeply moving, all the more because the despair and defeatism that they express is not altogether sincere. Beneath Mr Muggeridge's seeming acceptance of disaster there lies the unconfessed fact that he does after all believe in something—in England. He does not want to see England conquered by Germany, though if one judges merely by the earlier chapters one might well ask what difference it would make. I am told that some months back he left the Ministry of Information to join the army, a thing which none of the ex-warmongers of the Left has done, I believe. And I know very well what underlies these closing chapters. It is the emotion of the middle-class man, brought up in the military tradition, who finds in the moment of crisis that he is a patriot after all. It is all very well to be "advanced" and "enlightened", to snigger at Colonel Blimp and proclaim your emancipation from all traditional loyalties, but a time comes when the sand of the desert is sodden red and what have I done for thee, England, my England? As I was brought up in this tradition myself I can recognise it under strange disguises, and also sympathise with it, for even at its stupidest and most sentimental it is a comelier thing than the shallow self-righteousness of the left-wing intelligentsia.

New English Weekly, 25 April 1940

168. My Country Right or Left

Contrary to popular belief, the past was not more eventful than the present. If it seems so it is because when you look backward things that happened years apart are telescoped together, and because very few of your memories come to you genuinely virgin. It is largely because of the books, films and reminiscences that have come between that the war of 1914–18 is now supposed to have had some tremendous, epic quality that the present one lacks.

But if you were alive during that war, and if you disentangle your real memories from their later accretions, you find that it was not usually the big events that stirred you at the time. I don't believe that the Battle of the Marne, for instance, had for the general public the melodramatic quality that it was afterwards given. I do not even remember hearing the phrase "Battle of the Marne" till years later. It was merely that the Germans were 22 miles from Paris—and certainly that was terrifying enough, after the Belgian atrocity stories—and then for some reason they had turned back. I was eleven when the war started. If I honestly sort out my memories and disregard what I have learned since, I must admit that nothing in the whole war moved me so deeply as the loss of the *Titanic* had done a few years earlier. This comparatively petty disaster shocked the whole world, and the shock has not quite died away even yet. I remember the terrible, detailed accounts read out at the breakfast table (in those days it was a common habit to read the newspaper aloud), and I remember that in all the long list of horrors the one that most impressed me was that at the last the *Titanic* suddenly up-ended and sank bow foremost, so that the people clinging to the stern were lifted no less than three hundred feet into the air before they plunged into the abyss. It gave me a sinking sensation in the belly which I can still all but feel. Nothing in the war ever gave me quite that sensation.

Of the outbreak of war I have three vivid memories which, being petty and irrelevant, are uninfluenced by anything that has come later. One is of the cartoon of the "German Emperor" (I believe the hated name "Kaiser" was not popularised till a little later) that appeared in the last days of July. People were mildly shocked by this guying of royalty ("But he's such a handsome man, really!"), although we were on the edge of war. Another is of the time when the army commandeered all the horses in our little country town, and a cabman burst into tears in the market-place when his horse, which had worked for him for years, was taken away from him. And another is of a mob of young men at the railway station, scrambling for the evening papers that had just arrived on the London train. And I remember the pile of peagreen papers (some of them were still green in those days), the high collars, the tightish trousers and the bowler hats, far better than I can remember the names of the terrific battles that were already raging on the French frontier.

Of the middle years of the war, I remember chiefly the square shoulders, bulging calves and jingling spurs of the artillerymen, whose uniform I much preferred to that of the infantry. As for the final period, if you ask me to say truthfully what is my chief memory, I must answer simply—margarine. It is an instance of the horrible selfishness of children that by 1917 the war had almost ceased to affect us, except through our stomachs. In the school library a huge map of the Western Front was pinned on an easel, with a red silk thread running across on a zig-zag of drawing-pins. Occasionally the thread moved half an inch this way or that, each movement meaning a pyramid of corpses. I paid no attention. I was at school among boys who were above the average level of intelligence, and yet I do not remember that a single major event of the time appeared to us in its true significance. The Russian Revolution, for instance, made no impression, except on the few whose parents happened to have money invested in Russia. Among the very young the pacifist reaction had set in long before the war ended. To be as slack as you dared on OTC parades, and to take no interest in the war, was considered a mark of enlightenment. The young officers who had come back, hardened by their terrible experience and disgusted by the attitude of the younger generation to whom this experience meant just nothing, used to lecture us for our softness. Of course they could produce no argument that we were capable of understanding. They could only bark at you that war was "a good thing", it "made you tough", "kept you fit", etc etc. We merely sniggered at them. Ours was the one-eyed pacifism that is peculiar to sheltered countries with strong navies. For years after the war, to have any knowledge of or interest in military matters, even to know which end of a gun the bullet comes out of, was suspect in "enlightened" circles. 1914–18 was written off as a meaningless slaughter, and even the men who had been slaughtered were held to be in some way to blame. I have often laughed to think of that recruiting poster, "What did you do in the Great War, daddy?" (a child is asking this question of its shame-stricken father), and of all the men who must have been lured into the army by just that poster and afterwards despised by their children for not being Conscientious Objectors.

But the dead men had their revenge after all. As the war fell back into the past, my particular generation, those who had been "just too young", became conscious of the vastness of the experience they had missed. You felt yourself a little less than a man, because you had missed it. I spent the years 1922–7 mostly among men a little older than myself who had been through the war. They talked about it unceasingly, with horror, of course, but also with a steadily growing nostalgia. You can see this nostalgia perfectly clearly in the English war-books. Besides, the pacifist reaction was only a phase, and even the "just too young" had all been trained for war. Most of the English middle class are trained for war from the cradle onwards, not technically but morally. The earliest political slogan I can remember is "We want eight (eight dreadnoughts) and we won't wait". At seven years old I was a member of the Navy League and wore a sailor suit with "HMS *Invincible*" on my cap. Even before my public-school OTC I had been in a private-school cadet corps. On and off, I have been toting a rifle ever since I was ten, in preparation not only for war but for a particular kind of war, a war in which the guns rise to a frantic orgasm of sound, and at the appointed moment you clamber out of the trench, breaking your nails on the sandbags, and stumble across mud and wire into the machine-gun barrage. I am convinced that part of the reason for the fascination that the Spanish civil war had for people of about my age was that it was so like the Great War. At certain moments Franco was able to scrape together enough aeroplanes to raise the war to a modern level, and these were the turning-points. But for the rest it was a bad copy of 1914–18, a positional war of trenches, artillery, raids, snipers, mud, barbed wire, lice and stagnation. In early 1937 the bit of the Aragon front that I was on must have been very like a quiet sector in France in 1915. It was only the artillery that was lacking. Even on the rare occasions when all the guns in Huesca and outside it were firing simultaneously, there were only enough of them to make a fitful unimpressive noise like the ending of a thunderstorm. The shells from Franco's six-inch guns crashed loudly enough, but there were never more than a dozen of them at a time. I know that what I felt when I first heard artillery fired "in anger", as they say, was at least partly disappointment. It was so different from the tremendous, unbroken roar that my senses had been waiting for for twenty years.

I don't quite know in what year I first knew for certain that the present war was coming. After 1936, of course, the thing was obvious to anyone except an idiot. For several years the coming war was a nightmare to me, and at times I even made speeches and wrote pamphlets against it. But the night before the Russo-German pact was announced I dreamed that the war had started. It was one of those dreams which, whatever Freudian inner meaning they may have, do sometimes reveal to you the real state of your feelings. It taught me two things, first, that I should be simply relieved when the long-dreaded war started, secondly, that I was patriotic at heart, would not sabotage or act against my own side, would support the war, would fight in it if possible. I came downstairs to find the newspaper announcing Ribbentrop's flight to Moscow.[1] So war was coming, and the Government, even the Chamberlain Government, was assured of my loyalty. Needless to say this loyalty was and remains merely a gesture. As with almost everyone I know, the Government has flatly refused to employ me in any capacity whatever, even as a clerk or a private soldier. But that does not alter one's feelings. Besides, they will be forced to make use of us sooner or later.

If I had to defend my reasons for supporting the war, I believe I could do so. There is no real alternative between resisting Hitler and surrendering to him, and from a Socialist point of view I should say that it is better to resist; in any case I can see no argument for surrender that does not make nonsense of the Republican resistance in Spain, the Chinese resistance to Japan, etc etc. But I don't pretend that that is the emotional basis of my actions. What I knew in my dream that night was that the long drilling in patriotism which the middle classes go through had done its work, and that once England was in a serious jam it would be impossible for me to sabotage. But let no one mistake the meaning of this. Patriotism has nothing to do with conservatism. It is devotion to something that is changing but is felt to be mystically the same, like the devotion of the ex-White Bolshevik to Russia. To be loyal both to Chamberlain's England and to the England of tomorrow might seem an impossibility, if one did not know it to be an everyday phenomenon. Only revolution can save England, that has been obvious for years, but now the revolution has started, and it may proceed quite quickly if only we can keep Hitler out. Within two years, maybe a year, if only we can hang on, we shall see changes that will surprise the idiots who have no foresight. I dare say the London gutters will have to run with blood. All right, let them, if it is necessary. But when the red militias are billeted

[1] On 21 August 1939 Ribbentrop was invited to Moscow and on 23 August he and Molotov signed the Russo-German Pact.

in the Ritz I shall still feel that the England I was taught to love so long ago and for such different reasons is somehow persisting.

I grew up in an atmosphere tinged with militarism, and afterwards I spent five boring years within the sound of bugles. To this day it gives me a faint feeling of sacrilege not to stand to attention during "God save the King". That is childish, of course, but I would sooner have had that kind of upbringing than be like the left-wing intellectuals who are so "enlightened" that they cannot understand the most ordinary emotions. It is exactly the people whose hearts have *never* leapt at the sight of a Union Jack who will flinch from revolution when the moment comes. Let anyone compare the poem John Cornford wrote not long before he was killed ("Before the Storming of Huesca") with Sir Henry Newbolt's "There's a breathless hush in the Close tonight". Put aside the technical differences, which are merely a matter of period, and it will be seen that the emotional content of the two poems is almost exactly the same. The young Communist who died heroically in the International Brigade was public school to the core. He had changed his allegiance but not his emotions. What does that prove? Merely the possibility of building a Socialist on the bones of a Blimp, the power of one kind of loyalty to transmute itself into another, the spiritual need for patriotism and the military virtues, for which, however little the boiled rabbits of the Left may like them, no substitute has yet been found.

Folios of New Writing, Autumn 1940

Appendix I

BOOKS BY OR CONTAINING CONTRIBUTIONS BY GEORGE ORWELL

Down and Out in Paris and London, London, 1933; New York, 1933.
Burmese Days, New York, 1934; London, 1935.
A Clergyman's Daughter, London, 1935; New York, 1936.
Keep the Aspidistra Flying, London, 1936; New York, 1956.
The Road to Wigan Pier, London, 1937; New York, 1958.
Homage to Catalonia, London, 1938; New York, 1952.
Coming Up for Air, London, 1939; New York, 1950.
Inside the Whale, London, 1940.
The Lion and the Unicorn, London, 1941.
The Betrayal of the Left, by Victor Gollancz, George Orwell, John Strachey and others, London, 1941.
Victory or Vested Interest? by G. D. H. Cole, George Orwell and others, London, 1942.
Talking to India, edited with an introduction by George Orwell, London, 1943.
Animal Farm, London, 1945; New York, 1946.
Critical Essays, London, 1946; (American title) *Dickens, Dali and Others*, New York, 1946.
James Burnham and the Managerial Revolution, London 1946. (Pamphlet)
Love of Life and Other Stories, by Jack London. Introduction by George Orwell, London, 1946.
The English People, London, 1947.
British Pamphleteers, Vol. 1, edited by George Orwell and Reginald Reynolds. Introduction by George Orwell, London, 1948.
Nineteen Eighty-Four, London, 1949; New York, 1949.

POSTHUMOUS COLLECTIONS

Shooting an Elephant, London, 1950; New York, 1950.
Such, Such Were the Joys, New York, 1953.
England Your England, London, 1953.
The Orwell Reader, edited by Richard H. Rovere, New York, 1956.
Collected Essays, London, 1961.

Appendix II: Chronology

1903

Eric Arthur Blair was born on 25 June 1903 at Motihari, Bengal. His parents, Richard Walmesley Blair and Ida Mabel Blair, already had a daughter, Marjorie Frances, born at Gaya, Bengal, on 21 April 1898.

Richard Walmesley Blair, a sub-deputy agent in the Opium Department of the Indian Civil Service, was born in 1857 in Dorset. His father, the Reverend Thomas Richard Arthur Blair, vicar of Milborne St Andrew, had earlier served in the Indian Army and had lived at the Cape of Good Hope where he met his wife. He had been born in 1802 at Ensbury, Dorset, the grandson of Charles Blair and Lady Mary Blair, who had lived at Whatcombe in the same county.

Ida Mabel Blair was born in 1875 at Penge, Surrey, while her parents, Frank and Theresa Limouzin, were on leave. Her father, of French extraction, was a teak merchant in Moulmein, Burma, who later lost much of his money investing unsuccessfully in rice growing.

1907–11

In the summer of 1907 the Blairs came to England on leave, Richard Blair returning in the autumn to India, leaving his wife and children behind to settle at Nutshell, Western Road, Henley-on-Thames, where a second daughter, Avril Nora, was born on 6 April 1908. The Blair children attended a local Anglican convent school.

1911–13

In September Eric Blair was sent to St Cyprian's, a private preparatory school at Eastbourne on the Sussex coast, going home only for school holidays. Two of his contemporaries at St Cyprian's were Cecil Beaton and Cyril Connolly. Richard Blair retired from the Opium Department in January 1912 and not long after his permanent return to England the Blairs moved a few miles in the same county, Oxfordshire, to Roselawn, Shiplake.

1914–16

On 2 October 1914 Eric Blair made his first appearance in print when a local newspaper, the *Henley and South Oxfordshire Standard*, published his short patriotic poem, "Awake! Young Men of England". It also printed another, entitled "Kitchener", on 21 July 1916. Richard Blair joined the British army and was commissioned a second lieutenant in September 1917. In 1915 the Blair home was moved back to Henley-on-Thames, to 36 St Mark's Road. Eric Blair left St Cyprian's at Christmas 1916.

1917–21

He spent the Lent term of 1917 as a scholar at Wellington College and entered Eton as a King's Scholar in May the same year. While at Eton he wrote satirical verses and short stories for various of the College magazines, contributing to and being business manager of the handwritten magazine, the *Election Times*, and contributing to and helping to edit *College Days*, a printed magazine. (For an account of St Cyprian's and Eton while Blair was at both schools, see *Enemies of Promise* by Cyril Connolly.) He left Eton at Christmas 1921.

In autumn 1917 Ida Blair moved to London, to 23 Cromwell Crescent, Earl's Court, and took a job with the Ministry of Pensions. In spring 1918 she rented a flat, 23 Mall Chambers, Notting Hill Gate, not far from her sister, Nellie Limouzin, Eric Blair's favourite aunt, who lived in Portobello Road. In December 1919 Richard Blair was demobilised with the rank of lieutenant and in July 1920 Marjorie Blair married Humphrey Dakin, a doctor's son she had known since childhood in Henley-on-Thames. In 1922 Humphrey Dakin joined the National Savings Committee and eventually became Commissioner for the East Midlands.

In December 1921 the Blairs moved to 40 Stradbroke Road, Southwold, on the Suffolk coast, where Anglo-Indian friends were living.

1922–27

Eric Blair did not go to a university and exactly why he joined the Indian Imperial Police in Burma is not known. But with family approval he did so and arrived in Mandalay on 29 November 1922. He was trained in Mandalay and Maymyo as an assistant district superintendent and served successively at Myaungmya, Twante,

Syriam, Insein, Moulmein and, as headquarters assistant, at Katha. In August 1927 he went home on leave and in September while on holiday with his family in Cornwall he decided not to return to Burma and left the Indian Imperial Police on 1 January 1928. (For his account of his stay in Burma and his return to England, see Chapters 8 and 9 of *The Road to Wigan Pier*.)

In the autumn of 1927 Blair went to the East End of London on the first of the expeditions which were to occupy much of his time during the next five years in his quest to get to know the poor and the exploited.

Throughout the autumn and winter of 1927 he lived in a cheap room next door to the workshop of the poet, Ruth Pitter, in Portobello Road, Notting Hill.

1928–29

In spring 1928 he went to Paris and took a room at 6 Rue du Pot de Fer in the fifth arrondissement, a working-class district. Nellie Limouzin was living in Paris throughout the time he was there.

On 6 October 1928 "La Censure en Angleterre", Blair's first article as a professional writer, appeared in Henri Barbusse's paper, *Monde*, as did another, "John Galsworthy", on 23 March 1929. Four other articles, also in French translation, on unemployment in England, a day in the life of a tramp, the beggars of London, and on Burma, appeared between December 1928 and May 1929 in the paper, *Progrès Civique*. His first article to appear in England, "A Farthing Newspaper", was printed on 29 December 1928 in *G. K.'s Weekly*.

In February 1929 Blair fell ill with pneumonia and spent some weeks in the Hôpital Cochin.

By summer 1929 he had also written a "ballade", some articles entitled "Ayant Toujours Trait au Quartier Montparnasse", and several short stories, three of which were "The Sea God", "The Petition Crown" and "The Man in Kid Gloves". Their appearance in print has not been traced. He had also completed two novels which he did not succeed in getting published. None of the scripts of these writings has survived.

For about ten weeks in the late autumn of 1929 Blair worked as a dishwasher and kitchen porter in a luxury hotel and a restaurant in Paris. He returned to England at the end of the year.

1930–31

Until April 1932 Blair used his parents' home at 3 Queen Street, Southwold, as his base, spending the greater part of his time writing there, but going off from time to time in the south east of England to tramp and live with down and outs and stay for short periods in working-class districts of London. He also stayed for several weeks at a time with his sister, Marjorie Dakin, and her family in Leeds.

For several months after his return from Paris Blair tutored a backward boy in Walberswick, near Southwold. Then, for three school holidays in 1930 and 1931, he was tutor to three schoolboys while their father, C. R. Peters, was away from Southwold in the Indian Imperial Police.

Except for a review in the *New English Weekly* and two articles in the *New Statesman and Nation*, Blair placed all his occasional writing—documentary sketches, reviews and poems—with the *Adelphi* from March 1930 until August 1935.

By October 1930 he had completed a version of *Down and Out in Paris and London.*

Blair spent August 1931 in London, picked hops in Kent for the first half of September, lived in a cheap lodging house in Bermondsey for the rest of the month and took a room at 2 Windsor Street, Paddington for October and November.

By the late autumn of 1931 he had made a start on *Burmese Days.* He had also written two short stories for *Modern Youth*, a magazine which failed to appear, and sent two others, one of them entitled "An Idiot", to Leonard Moore, who in the spring of 1932 became his literary agent. These stories are not known to have been printed nor have their scripts survived.

1932

By March Jonathan Cape and Faber & Faber had turned down versions of *Down and Out in Paris and London.* In April Blair took up a teaching post at The Hawthorns, a small private school for boys, in Station Road, Hayes, Middlesex. In July he altered the longer version of *Down and Out in Paris and London* for Victor Gollancz who in August contracted to publish it. He spent the school summer holiday at Southwold writing *Burmese Days.*

1933

Down and Out in Paris and London, by George Orwell, was published on 9 January by Victor Gollancz and on 30 June in New York by

Harper and Brothers. Orwell changed schools and in September began teaching at Frays College, Uxbridge, Middlesex, a private school for boys and girls. By the beginning of December he had typed the final version of *Burmese Days*. Just before Christmas he went into Uxbridge Cottage Hospital seriously ill with pneumonia and, on recovery, gave up teaching.

1934

In mid-January Orwell went down to Southwold to live with his parents at 36 High Street and began writing *A Clergyman's Daughter*. Unable to find an English publisher for *Burmese Days* (Gollancz rejected it for fear of the offence it might give in Burma and India), Orwell made a few stylistic alterations to it for Harpers, who published it in New York on 25 October, and this remained the definitive text. By 3 October Orwell had finished *A Clergyman's Daughter* and in the middle of the month he left Southwold and took a room at 3 Warwick Mansions, Pond Street, Hampstead to become a part-time assistant in a nearby bookshop, Booklovers' Corner, 1 South End Road.

1935

By February Orwell had begun writing *Keep the Aspidistra Flying*. He was asked to make last-minute alterations in the proofs of *A Clergyman's Daughter*—once again for fear of libel—in February and on 11 March it was published by Victor Gollancz and on 17 August 1936 in New York by Harpers. In early March Orwell rented a room at 77 Parliament Hill, Hampstead, and in the same month met his future wife, Eileen O'Shaughnessy, who was reading for a psychology MA degree at University College London. On 24 June Victor Gollancz published *Burmese Days* with slight alterations. About the beginning of August Orwell rented a flat, 50 Lawford Road, Kentish Town.

In August he began reviewing novels for the *New English Weekly*. Edited by Philip Mairet, the *New English Weekly* paid its contributors at best nominal rates and often nothing at all but allowed them great freedom, and Orwell wrote reviews and articles regularly for it until April 1940.

1936

By the beginning of 1936 Orwell had finished *Keep the Aspidistra Flying*, but in February, because of a last minute scare over libel, he had to make drastic changes in it. It was published by Victor Gollancz on 20 April.

At the end of January he stopped working at Booklovers' Corner, gave up the flat in Lawford Road and, from 31 January until 30 March, he gathered material for a next book Victor Gollancz had commissioned him to write on the depressed areas in the north of England.

On 2 April Orwell moved to The Stores, Wallington, in Hertfordshire and in early May began writing *The Road to Wigan Pier*, from the material he had collected during his period in the North. Also this month he reviewed some novels for *Time and Tide* and continued to write for it until 1943.

On 9 June he married Eileen O'Shaughnessy. On 12 June he sent "Shooting an Elephant" to John Lehmann for *New Writing.*

On 18 July the Spanish civil war broke out. A few days before Christmas, having sent off the completed manuscript of *The Road to Wigan Pier* to Leonard Moore on 15 December, Orwell left for Spain. On 30 December at the Lenin Barracks in Barcelona he enlisted in the militia of the POUM (Workers' Party of Marxist Unification).

1937

In early January he went to the front line at Alcubierre. Towards the end of the month he transferred, as a corporal, to the Independent Labour Party contingent which had arrived from England to serve with the POUM militia on the Aragon front. In February Eileen Blair arrived in Barcelona and about 13 March she spent two days at the front near Monflorite with the ILP contingent.

On 8 March *The Road to Wigan Pier* was published by Victor Gollancz in a public edition and as a Left Book Club choice.

At the end of April Orwell went on leave to Barcelona and applied for his discharge papers, intending to join the International Brigade to get to Madrid, but the Communist attempt to suppress the revolutionary parties, including the POUM, in Barcelona in the first week in May made Orwell henceforward a bitter opponent of Stalinist Communism. On 10 May he returned, as a second lieutenant, to the ILP contingent and, ten days later, he was wounded in the throat by a Fascist sniper.

On 8 June, in a letter to Cyril Connolly, Orwell wrote, "I . . . at last really believe in Socialism, which I never did before."

He convalesced until 14 June and, while he was at the front collecting his discharge papers, the POUM was declared illegal by the Spanish Government on 16 June. From 20 to 22 June he was in Barcelona on the run from the Communist police and, with his wife, managed to get across the French border on 23 June.

By the first week of July Orwell was back at The Stores, Wallington and by the middle of the month he had started writing *Homage to Catalonia*. His concern to make known the facts about the struggle going on between the Spanish Republican parties led him into serious differences with the powerful sections of the English Left which supported or acquiesced in the domination of the Spanish Government by the Communists in the belief that any breach in the unity of the Left would lead to Franco's victory. Gollancz refused to publish *Homage to Catalonia* before Orwell had written a word of it and Kingsley Martin, editor of the *New Statesman and Nation*, rejected Orwell's review of Borkenau's *The Spanish Cockpit* for political reasons. He was able to express his political views in the *New English Weekly* and *Time and Tide*, for whom he resumed writing in July, and by contributing to *Controversy* and the *New Leader*. On 1 September Fredric Warburg contracted to publish *Homage to Catalonia* which Orwell completed by the middle of January 1938.

1938

In early March Orwell fell ill with a tubercular lesion in one lung and had to give up the idea of going to India to be a leader writer for the *Pioneer* (Lucknow) and collect material for a book. Later in the month he went into a sanatorium, Preston Hall, Aylesford, Kent. On 25 April *Homage to Catalonia* was published. In June Orwell became a member of the ILP. By July he had projected his next novel, but from the time he entered the sanatorium until he left it on 1 September he was not allowed to do any writing beyond an occasional review and had to turn down the offer to write a book, *Poverty in Practice*, he was interested in doing for Thomas Nelson & Sons, the publishers. The doctors had advised him to spend the winter in a warm climate and L. H. Myers, the novelist, anonymously gave Orwell, through Dorothy Plowman, £300 to enable him to do so. Orwell accepted it as a loan and on 2 September he and his wife set sail from Tilbury for Morocco. They arrived in Marrakech on 12 September and later in the month Orwell started *Coming Up for Air*.

1939

After finishing the first draft of *Coming Up for Air*, Orwell and his wife took a week's holiday at Taddert in the Atlas mountains. On their return to Marrakech on 27 January Orwell fell ill for three weeks. On 26 March Orwell sailed from Casablanca and arrived in London on 30 March, bringing with him the completed manuscript of *Coming Up for Air*.

After staying in Southwold, Orwell and his wife arrived home in Wallington on 11 April. When not writing, Orwell for the next twelve months spent most of his time working on the plot of land that went with The Stores, growing vegetables and flowers and rearing ducks, hens and goats. After staying nearly three weeks at 24 Crooms Hill, Greenwich, the home of Eileen Blair's brother, Laurence O'Shaughnessy, Orwell returned to Wallington on 24 May and began working on the essays for *Inside the Whale*. On 12 June Victor Gollancz published *Coming Up for Air*. On 24 June Orwell went to Southwold where four days later his father, aged 82, died of cancer. From 24 to 31 August Orwell stayed with L. H. Myers at his home at Ringwood, Hampshire.

With the outbreak of war on 3 September Orwell entered on a period of waste and frustration. Despite repeated efforts, he found himself unable to serve his country in any capacity (he was rejected by the army as medically unfit) and he made almost nothing from journalism. (He wrote five short reviews in the first four months of the war.) Eileen Blair went to live at 24 Crooms Hill, partly to be company for her sister-in-law, Gwen, whose husband, Laurence O'Shaughnessy, had gone into the Royal Army Medical Corps, but principally to take up a job in the Censorship Department in order to supplement Orwell's meagre earnings. Because of this she was able to go down to Wallington only at week-ends. Early in the war Orwell left the ILP. By mid-December he had finished *Inside the Whale*.

1940

Orwell spent a fortnight at Christmas and six weeks from 30 January 1940 at 24 Crooms Hill, part of the time being ill with 'flu. He made his first contribution, a book review entitled "The Lessons of War", to the February issue of *Horizon* and his first to *Tribune*, the Socialist weekly, a review of *The Memoirs of Sergeant Bourgogne*, appeared on

29 March. On 11 March *Inside the Whale* was published by Victor Gollancz. In April Orwell was projecting a long novel in three parts which he had had in his mind since the late autumn of 1938. It is doubtful whether he ever started writing it.

Ian Angus

INDEX

Compiled by Oliver Stallybrass

All numbers refer to pages, not items. Footnotes are indicated by "n" or "(n)" after the page-number: "n" refers *only* to the footnote, "(n)" to text *and* footnote. The *first* footnote on any individual person usually includes a brief biographical outline.

Subheadings are arranged in order of first page reference, except where chronological order (e.g. Orwell: *chronology*) or alphabetical order (e.g. Orwell: *writings:* individual titles) is clearly more appropriate.

George Orwell is abbreviated to GO throughout.

A la Belle de Nuit (Roberti), 72, 73, 78
Abdication, *see* Edward VIII
Acland, Sir Richard, 529n, 530–2; *The Manifesto of the Common Man*, 529–30(n); *Unser Kampf*, 530–2
Action, 202(n)
Action Stories, 461, 476
Adam, Karl: *The Spirit of Catholicism*, 79–81, 82(n), 85n
Adam, Nellie (*née* Limouzin), 133n, 544
Adelphi, The (and *New Adelphi*), 15n, 27n, 28n, 72n, 109, 152n, 163, 163n, 164n, 168, 168n, 169n, 173, 187, 194, 215, 218, 228; GO's contributions to, 19–21, 22–4, 25–7, 33–6, 36–43, 44–8, 95–7, 118, 123(n), 123–5, 134–5, 148–50, 233(n), 234n, 375–6, 394–8, 546
Adelphi Centre, 15n, 232–3(n)
Adventure, 461
Adventures of a Black Girl in Her Search for God, The (Shaw), 192
Adventures of Mr Verdant Green (Bede), 457(n)
Air Raid Precautions, 346; in French Morocco, 352
Alcott, Louisa M.: *Little Women*, 499
Aldine Boxing Novels, 461
Aldington, Richard: *Death of a Hero*, 232
Alexander Pope (Sitwell), 22–4, 285
All the Year Round, 442n
Almayer's Folly (Conrad), 227
Amalgamated Press, 461, 473–4, 482
America, *see* United States
Ami du Peuple, 12–15
Anarchism, 298, 344
Anarchists: and Spanish civil war, 269, 271, 272, 275, 277, 279, 284, 300, 316–18, 340, 412; GO regrets not having joined, 289; achievements of, 290–1
Anderson, Mrs, of Wallington, 352(n), 393(n)
Angel Pavement (Priestley), 25–7
Anglo-Catholicism: "ecclesiastical equivalent of Trotskyism", 515
Animals: GO's feeling for, 235–42, 388, 392
Anthropology: and literature, 222
Antisemitism: in Germany, 247–8; in Morocco, 390; absence in Dickens, 433
Arabs, 368–9
Aristophanes: play by GO in imitation of, 2
Armies, *see* British army; French army
Arnold, Matthew: "The Scholar Gypsy", 520
Art: "all art is propaganda", 448. *See also* Literature, *subheading* and politics
Aryan Path, 304
Asch, Scholem: *The Calf of Paper*, 247–8
Ashton, Helen: *Dr Serocold*, 166
Asquith, Margot: *Autobiography*, 167

Assignment in Utopia (Lyons), 332–4
Astor, Lady, 121(n)
Athenaeum, The, 28n
Atholl, Duchess of: *Searchlight on Spain*, 344–7
Auden, W. H., 313, 386, 506, 511–12(n), 518; GO retracts "gutless Kipling" criticism, 511; "Spain" quoted, 516
Authors Take Sides (Cunard), 312
Autobiography (Margot Asquith), 167
Ayres, Ruby M., 481

Baldwin, Stanley, 534
Bali and Angkor (Gorer), 222(n)
Balzac, Honoré de, 456; *Eugénie Grandet*, 54
Bankers: GO's fear of, 121
Barbusse, Henri, 545; *One Looks at Russia*, 257
Barcelona, *see* Spanish civil war
Barham, R. H., 452
Barnaby Rudge, *see* Dickens, C.
Barnes, E. W., Bishop of Birmingham, 121(n)
Barnsley, Yorkshire, 198–214
Barrie, J. M., 244, 520
Bartimeus, *pseud.*: *Naval Occasions*, 166–7
Barton, Andrew: *The People of Clopton*, 437
Bartz, Karl: *The Horrors of Cayenne*, 28(n)
Basily, N. de: *Russia under Soviet Rule*, 378–81
Bastard Death (Fraenkel), 219–20
Baths, public: at Barnsley, 204
Baudelaire (Starkie), 123n
Beachcomber, *pseud.*, 189 (n), 251
Beaton, Cecil, 543
Bechhofer-Roberts: *This Side Idolatry*, 414
Bede, Cuthbert, *pseud.*: *The Adventures of Mr Verdant Green*, 457(n)
Belief in God (Gore), 102
Belisha, Leslie Hore-, *see* Hore-Belisha
Bennett, Arnold, 506; and J. B. Priestley, 26; and Dickens, 428; *Riceyman Steps*, 25
Berbers, 382, 532
Besteiro, Julian, 411
Bible: quoted, 366
Bible Society, 50
Birkett, Norman, 333
Birmingham, 170
Black Spring, *see* Miller, H.
Blackshirts, *see* Fascists
Blair, family, 11n, 49n, 543
Blair, Avril Nora, GO's sister, 543
Blair, Eileen (*née* O'Shaughnessy), GO's first wife, 150n, 153(n), 154(n), 163, 263, 278–9, 282, 315, 330, 339, 347–8, 354, 364, 370, 381, 383, 393, 411, 547–50; marries GO, 222(n), 224; letter from GO, 264–6; works in Censorship Department, 410(n), 528
Blair, Eric Arthur, real name of George Orwell, *see* Orwell
Blair, Ida Mabel, GO's mother, 543–4; letter from GO, 347–8
Blair, Marjorie, GO's sister, later married to Humphrey Dakin, *see* Dakin
Blair, Richard Walmesley, GO's father, 347–8, 370, 543–4; death, 410(n), 550
Blake, Sexton, fictional character, 465, 473
Blake, William, 24; plagiarised by GO, 1; understanding of nature of capitalism, 427
Bleak House, *see* Dickens, C.
Blimp, Colonel, 276, 346, 403, 535, 540
Blum, Léon, 349
Blurbs, *see* Publishers
Book reviewers and reviewing, *see* Reviewers etc.
Booklovers' Corner, 142n, 148, 150, 154, 242–6
Bookshops and bookselling, 222, 242–6. *See also* Booklovers' Corner
Boothby, Guy: *Dr Nikola*, 101
Borkenau, Franz: *The Spanish Cockpit*, 276–8, 279, 281, 297, 299, 348; *The Communist International*, 348–51, 513
Bottomley, Horatio: *Letters to the Boys in the Trenches*, 524
Bourgeoisie: a Communist's hatred of, 191, 194; relative self-confidence of, 197, 326; Socialist, contempt for working class, 216; militarisation of, in England, 404. *See also* Class
Bourgogne, Sergeant: *Memoirs*, 550–1
Bouvard et Pécuchet (Flaubert), 456

Boy Scout movement, 465, 483, 510, 512
Boys' Friend Library, 461
Boy's Own Paper, 461
Boys' weeklies, 413, 461–93, 528
Bradley, Edward, *see* Bede, Cuthbert, *pseud.*
Brailsford, H. N., 301(n)
Brea, Juan, *see* Low, Mary
Breton, André, 377n
British army: "democracy" in, 401–5
British Broadcasting Corporation: broadcast by GO, 264
British Empire, *see* Imperialism
British Government: and Spanish civil war, 345, 347, 412; war preparations, 345–6; and Russia, 398; incompetent propaganda, 529
British Union of Fascists, *see* Fascists
Brock, Alan Clutton-, *see* Clutton-Brock
Brockway, Fenner: *Workers' Front*, 304–6
Brontë, Emily: *Wuthering Heights*, 456, 495
Brooke, Rupert, 503
Brown, Alec, 511; *The Fate of the Middle Classes*, 168(n), 215(n); *Daughters of Albion*, 258
Brown, Major F. Yeats-, *see* Yeats-Brown
Brown, George Douglas; *The House with the Green Shutters*, 495
Brown, William, 164(n)
Buddhism, 117
Burdett, Osbert: *The Two Carlyles*, 33–6
Burma, 4, 44–8, 113, 235–42, 306–7, 360, 403
Burmese Days, *see* Orwell, G.
Burns, Cecil Delisle, 136(n)
Burslem, Staffordshire, 171
Butler, Samuel (1835–1902), 119, 128, 151
Buttonshaw, in POUM militia with GO, 266(n)
Byrne, Donn: *Hangman's House*, 166
Byron and the Need of Fatality (du Bos), 95–7

Caballero, Francisco Largo, 268(n), 275, 412
Cage-Birds, 461
Cain, Paul: *Fast One*, 220
Caine, Hall, 138
Calder-Marshall, Arthur, 511
Calf of Paper, The (Asch), 247–8
Caliban Shrieks (Hilton), 148–50
Cambridge, 103
Camrose, Lord, 482–3, 484
Cape, Jonathan, Ltd, 141; rejects *Down and Out*, 77; rejects *Burmese Days*, 133n
Capital punishment, *see* Hanging
Capitalism, 337, 350, 532; and Socialist rehousing policy, 189; resemblance to Fascism, 284, 305; Blake's understanding of, 427; breaking up of, 525
Capone, Al, 334
Carlyle, Jane Welsh, 35–6
Carlyle, Thomas, 33–6, 117, 119
Carmen (Mérimée), 456
Carpenter, Edward, 216(n)
Carr, Mrs, of Southwold, 82
Casado, S.: *The Last Days of Madrid*, 411–12
Cashel Byron's Profession (Shaw), 220
Casual wards ("spikes"), 36–43, 150; Ide Hill, 57; West Malling, 59–60; Edmonton, 94
Catalonia Infelix (Peers), 291
Catholicism, *see* Roman Catholicism
Céline, L. F., 523; *Voyage au Bout de la Nuit*, 498
Censorship: predicted by GO, 337, 377–8, 386–7; Censorship Department: GO's wife works in, 410(n), 528
Cervantes: and Dickens, 435, 440
Challaye, Félicien, 300(n)
Chamberlain, Neville, 345–7, 356, 359, 386, 534, 539
Champion, The, 461, 475, 478
Charles Dickens (Gissing) 414, 444; (Jackson), 414(n)–15
Chatto & Windus Ltd, 78
Chesterton, G. K., 189, 234, 500; and Dickens, 414–15, 434, 458
Children's papers, *see* Boys' weeklies
Christianity, 28; divided ("long may they fight"), 50; and pessimism, 155; as an escape from "the awful thraldom of money", 226; Housman's opposition to, 505; Nietzsche on, 532. *See also* Anglo-Catholicism;

Christianity—(*contd.*)
Church Army; Church of England; Roman Catholicism
Christmas Carol, A, see Dickens, C.
Christy & Moore Ltd, *see* Moore, Leonard
Chums, 461
Church Army, 94
Church of England: "the poor, unoffending old" C of E, 81; "life in the poor old dog yet", 103
Church Times, 103, 121, 258
Churchill, Winston: fantasy concerning, 332–3; "posing as a democrat", 395; "blue-eyed boy of the *Daily Worker*", 514
Civil War in Spain, The (Jellinek), 340–3
Class consciousness and distinctions: experienced by GO as a tramp, 37, 59, 64; expressed by *Daily Worker* vendor calling GO "sir"; lurking tensions, 216; class-hatred as theme of *Le Rouge et le Noir*, 400; in Dickens, 434–41; in boys' weeklies, 466–7, 479–80; need to abolish distinctions, 530. *See also* Bourgeoisie; Working class
Classicism: in English literature, 22–4
Clé, La, 377n, 378
Clergyman's Daughter, A, see Orwell, G.
Clifford, Martin, *pseud. see* Richards, F.
"Clink", 86–94
Clutton-Brock, Alan, 163(n), 224
Coal miners: in Wigan, 163, 164, 174–6, 181–3; in Barnsley, 199, 200, 202, 204, 211; a woman miner, 205–6
Coal mines: slag-heaps, 176, 181, 212; accidents, 177, 205, 211; descended by GO, 184–7, 202, 206–8, 209–11; pithead baths, 205, 208, 211
Coal-stealing, 181–3
Coke, Desmond, 466, 486
College Days, 544
Collings, Dennis: 82(n), 102(n), 103, 117, 138, 222; letters from GO, 49(n)–51, 51(n)
Collings, Eleanor (*née* Jaques), 51n, 138; letters from GO, 81–3, 83, 85–6, 101–2, 102–4, 105–6, 107–8, 108–9, 117, 119–20, 122, 122–3
Collins, Norman, 168(n)
Collis, Maurice: *Trials in Burma*, 306–7
Colour prejudice: absence of in Morocco, 360; among working class, 369
Coming Up for Air, see Orwell, G.
Comintern, *see* Communism etc.
Common, Jack, 217, 218; letters from GO, 168(n)–9, 214–15, 215–17, 233–4, 288–90, 296, 303–4, 310–11, 314, 329–30, 338–9, 351–2, 352–4, 355–7, 367–71, 393–4; lives in GO's cottage, 338–9, 347, 351–2, 354–5, 370–1; *Seven Shifts*, 310(n), 314; *The Freedom of the Streets*, 329(n), 335–6
Common lodging houses, *see* Lodging houses
Communism and Communist Party: and literature, 256–9; compared or linked with Fascism, 259, 275, 334; and Spanish civil war, 269–75, 277–8, 285, 297, 300, 316–17n, 370; counter-revolutionary nature of, 270, 272, 273, 277, 281, 284, 285; propaganda methods and *volte-faces*, 273–5, 279, 285, 287, 300–1, 327, 333–4, 349, 365–6, 483, 513–14; likely role in war, 284; GO's declared hostility to, 313; appeal of to wealthy people, 344–7, 365; Comintern, 305, 348–51, 513; changing membership of parties, 349–50, 513–14; "pure Communism", 499; fascination for writers in 1930s, 510, 512–16; definition and summary, 513; as instrument of Russian foreign policy, 513; as surrogate for religion, 515. *See also* Communists; Russia; Socialism
Communism and Man (Sheed), 383–5
Communist International, The (Borkenau), 348–51, 513
Communists, British: a suspected one calls GO "sir", 104; spreading rumours about T. E. Lawrence, 153; in Wigan, 176; a case-history, 187–8; a bourgeois-hater, 190–1, 194; a meeting in Barnsley, 212; characteristics of ex-, 350; "waving Union Jacks", 395, 534; influence of in literary reviews, 519. *See also* Communism; *Daily Worker*; Intelligentsia, left-wing; Left, the

Connolly, Cyril, 409, 543; letters from GO, 162(n)–3, 268–9, 290, 309, 328–9, 343–4, 362–3; articles on Spanish civil war, 269; and *Horizon*, 411, 485, 528; *The Rock Pool*, 162(n), 225–7, 229(n); *Enemies of Promise*, 309(n), 362(n), 517
Conrad, Joseph, *pseud.*, 26, 33, 234, 506; *Almayer's Folly*, 227; *The Secret Agent*, 25
Conservative Party and MPs, 356, 359; and Spanish civil war, 534
Constant Nymph, The (Kennedy), 138, 252
Controversy, 357–8, 361. *See also Left; Left Forum*
Cooke, Rupert Croft-, *see* Croft-Cooke
Corelli, Marie: *Thelma*, 138
Cornford, John, 540
Coty, François, 13
Country of the Blind, The (Wells), 362–3
Course of English Classicism, The (Vines), 22–4
Coventry, 170
Cricket, 315(n), 344(n), 357
Cricket on the Hearth, The, *see* Dickens, C.
Crime and criminals, 69, 89–94; "Ginger", 54–5, 57–9, 62–3, 66–70; burglars' slang and methods, 71(n); "Charlie" and "Snouter", 90–1; coiners, 179; in Dickens, 434–5
Criterion, The, 151, 252–3
Croft-Cooke, Rupert, 411
Crozier, Brig.-Gen. F. P.: *The Men I Killed*, 282–3
Cunard, Nancy: *Authors Take Sides*, 312
Curle, Richard: *Who Goes Home?*, 161
Czechoslovakia: crisis of 1938, 351, 353, 355–6, 359, 377

Daily Express: and Spanish civil war, 281. *See also* Beachcomber
Daily Herald, 483; and Spanish civil war, 301
Daily Mail, 460
Daily Telegraph, 482
Daily Worker, 104, 265n, 514; and Spanish civil war, 269, 281, 365; calls GO pro-Fascist, 285, 289
Dakin, Humphrey, 164n, 193n, 197, 544
Dakin, Jane, 348
Dakin, Marjorie (*née* Blair), GO's sister, 164(n), 193(n), 196, 197, 348(n) 543–4
Dartmoor prison, 368
Daughters of Albion (Brown), 258
David Copperfield, *see* Dickens, C.
Day-Lewis, Cecil, 511–12(n)
Death of a Hero (Aldington), 232
De Basily, N., *see* Basily
Decency: fundamental, of an exhibitionist tramp, 96; of a Sheffield working-class family, 193; "ordinary decent people", 332; men only decent when powerless, 336; of Bertrand Russell's intellect, 376; of Clarence Streit's mind, 395; as Dickens's message, 417, 458, 459; "decent labouring poor", 435; value of appealing to, 530; need for, 531, 532
Deeping, Warwick, 244, 520
Defoe, Daniel, 460
Degnan, Tommy, 204–5, 213
Deiner, J. S. and May, 164(n), 187
Delafield, E. M., 166
Dell, Ethel M., 244, 520; *The Way of an Eagle*, 252
Democracy and democracies: relation of bourgeois variety to Fascism, 273–4, 284; in British army, 401–5; which nations qualify as?, 406–8; Socialist variety, *see* Socialism
Denmark: disinclination to visit, 283
Destitution, *see* Poverty
Detective Weekly, 475, 482
Dickens, Charles, 245, 413–60, 466, 475, 507, 531–2; and J. B. Priestley, 27; and his critics, 414–15, 434, 444, 448–9, 458; and Charles Reade, 416; and H. G. Wells, 428–9, 445, 456; and Thackeray, 430–1; and Cervantes, 435, 440; and Smollett, 440, 455; and Trollope, 442; and Bulwer Lytton, 448; and Tolstoy, 456; *Barnaby Rudge*, 419, 429, 436, 458; *Bleak House*, 25, 28(n), 418, 429–31, 438–9, 446, 450, 455; *A Christmas Carol*, 417–18, 422; *The Cricket on the Hearth*, 414; *David Copperfield*, 139, 415, 417–19, 424–7, 429, 434–9, 441, 443, 445, 449–50, 454–5, 457–9; *Dombey and Son*, 425–6, 430, 456; *Great Expectations*, 417, 424–6, 433,

Dickens, Charles—(*contd.*) 435–6, 438–9, 441, 442n, 444, 448, 450, 452–5; *Hard Times*, 414–15, 417–19, 430, 436–7, 442(n), 446, 448, 453–4, 457; *Little Dorrit*, 414–15, 418, 429–31, 435, 437, 439, 441–2, 444, 446, 457; *Martin Chuzzlewit*, 415–16, 433, 436, 439–42, 444–6, 448–50, 452, 454; *Nicholas Nickleby*, 417–18, 425–6, 430, 436, 441–3, 446–50, 452, 454–5, 457; *Oliver Twist*, 414–16, 426, 430, 433, 437, 442, 450; *Our Mutual Friend*, 140, 416, 418, 430–1, 433, 436, 438, 440, 442, 446, 449, 454; *Pickwick Papers*, 415–16, 429–30, 434, 436, 439, 442, 446, 448–53, 457; *A Tale of Two Cities*, 417, 419–23, 433, 437–8, 442(n), 450, 453, 458

Dictatorship, *see* Totalitarianism

Dockers: in Liverpool, 188

Doctor Faustus (Marlowe), 82

Dr Nikola (Boothby), 101

Dr Serocold (Ashton), 166

Dombey and Son, *see* Dickens, C.

Dos Passos, John, 493

"Doss houses", *see* Lodging houses

Dostoievski, Fyodor, 508

Douglas, Major C. H., 120n

Douglas, James, 534

Douglas, Norman, 226, 506

Down and Out in Paris and London, *see* Orwell, G.

Doyle, Arthur Conan: Sherlock Holmes books, 465, 495

Drinkwater, John, 386(n)

Du Bos, Charles: *Byron and the Need of Fatality*, 95–7

Duff, Charles: *James Joyce and the Plain Reader*, 117

Durrell, Lawrence, 526

Dynasts, The (Hardy), 128–9

Ede, Dr, 136

Edward VIII: "glutinous humbug" of abdication, 534

Edwards, Robert (Bob), 265(n), 266

Elections: predictions concerning, 337, 353, 356, 359, 361, 386

Election Times, 544

Elephant: shooting of, 235–42

Eliot, T. S., 493, 506, 507, 512, 515; letters from GO, 72(n), 73; opinion of *Down and Out*, 77; attitude of *Church Times* to, 121, 258; on the servant problem, 151; Sweeney poems, 230, 507; "Prufrock", 524

Encounter: letters of GO published in, 162–3, 217–18, 224–5, 268–9, 290, 311–12, 328–9, 362–3

Ends and Means (Huxley), 332(n)

Enemies of Promise (Connolly), 309(n), 362(n), 517

Enemy, The (ed. Lewis), 82

England, *passim*; mood of young after 1918, 505; nihilism around 1930, 514–15; sheltered recent history, 514–16; 1930s summarised, 534. *See also* British Government; *and specific topics*

English language: working-class speech reproduced, 86–7, 92–3; Lancashire dialect, 175; spoken and written, 314; Communist vocabulary of abuse (*see also* Trotskyism), 344; political jargon, 395. *See also* Slang

English literature: between the wars, 502–19. *See also* Classicism; Novels; *and individual writers*

Esquisse d'une Philosophie de la Dignité Humaine (Gille), 133n

Esther Waters (Moore), 166

Eton College, 11n, 343, 362–3, 517, 537–8, 544

Eugénie Grandet (Balzac), 54

Everlasting Mercy, The (Masefield), 504

Exchange and Mart, 461

Faber & Faber Ltd, 72(n), 73(n), 229; rejects *Down and Out*, 77

Fairchild Family, The (Sherwood), 101, 425(n)

Family Star, 480

Farlow, Denys King-, *see* King-Farlow

Farnol, Jeffery, 244

Farrar, Rev. H. W.: *St Winifred's*, 465

"Farthing Newspaper, A" 12–15

Fascism, 271, 275, 334, 337, 350; causes of, 259; Communist view of, 273–4; *News Chronicle* version of, 276; necessity of fighting, 280; only a development of capitalism, 284; two theories of how to combat, 366;

need for serious investigation of, 370. *See also* Germany; Italy; Spanish civil war
Fascists, British: violence in Barnsley, 169, 202–5. *See also Action*; Mosley, Sir O.
Fast One (Cain), 220
Fate of the Middle Classes, The (Brown), 168, 215(n)
Fiction, *see* Novels
Fielding, Henry: *Tom Jones*, 447
Fierz, Francis and Mabel, 49n, 77n
Fight Stories, 461, 476–7
Financial Times, 482
First Hundred Thousand, The (Hay), 524
First world war, 276, 280, 505, 523–5; GO's recollections of, 536–8
Firth, Ellis, 205(n), 211–12, 213
Flaubert, Gustave, 460; *Salammbô*, 370, 456; *Bouvard et Pécuchet*, 456
Flêche, La, 377
Fleming, Peter: *News from Tartary*, 286(n)
Folk-heroes, 459
Folios of New Writing: GO's contribution to, 535–40
Forbidden Journey (Maillart), 286(n)
"Fordification": GO's fear of, 121
Foreign Legion, 403, 467
Forster, E. M., 506; MacNeice's criticism of, 524; *A Passage to India*, 232, 506
Forster, John: *The Life of Charles Dickens*, 435
Fortnightly: GO's contribution to, 242–6
Fortress, The (Walpole), 101(n)
Fraenkel, Michael, 526: *Bastard Death*, 219–20
France and the French: pact with Russia, 272, 305; working class exploited by fear of Germany, 331; political apathy, 353–4, 382–3; in Morocco, 360–1, 369; dubiously democratic, 396; and Spainsh civil war, 412. *See also* French army; Paris
France, Anatole, 33
Franco, General, 270–1, 311, 312, 341n, 385, 411, 534, 538; British attitudes to, 344–7, 412
Frank Fairlegh (Smedley), 457(n)
Frankfort, Frank, 367(n)
Freedom and Organisation (Russell), 376
Freedom of the Streets (Common), 329(n), 335–6
French army, 403, 404. *See also* Foreign Legion
French Morocco, *see* Morocco
French Revolution, 420–3
Future, visions of the, *see* Orwell, G., *subheading* Predictions
Fyfe, Theodore, 103n, 108n, 109

G. K.'s Weekly: GO's contributions to: 12–15, 545
GPU, *see* Russia
Gallimard, publishers, 113
Galsworthy, John: *Glimpses and Reflections*, 307–8; *The Man of Property*, 252; *The Skin Game*, 198
Gangrel: GO's contribution to, 1–7
Garnett, Dr Richard: *The Twilight of the Gods*, 101
Garratt, G. T.: *Mussolini's Roman Empire*, 346
Garrett, George ("Matt Low"), 164(n), 187–8
Garstin, Crosbie: *The Owls' House*, 166
Garvin, J. L., 212(n), 270
Gaudy Night (Sayers), 161–2
Gem, The, 461–93 *passim*
General Election, *see* Elections
Germany, 337, 532; British attitudes to, 181, 198, 203, 331, 345, 356, 386, 508; French attitudes, 331; pact with Russia, 539(n). *See also* Fascism; Hitler, A.
Gibbs, Sir Philip, 506
Gibraltar: behaviour of troops in, 403
Gide, André: *Retour de l'URSS*, 433
Gille, Paul: *Esquisse d'une Philosophie de la Dignité Humaine*, 133n
Gipsies, *see* Gypsies
Girl's Own Paper, 246
Gissing, George: *Charles Dickens*, 414, 444
Glimpses and Reflections (Galsworthy), 307–8
Gollancz, Sir Victor, 266(n), 285, 303–4, 380, 394, 411, 529; letters from GO, 267, 409–10; and *Down and Out*, 84(n)–5, 104, 105, 107(n), 117; *and Burmese Days*, 130(n), 133(n), 141, 147–8, 150, 229; and *A Clergyman's*

Gollancz—(*contd.*)
Daughter, 142(n)–3, 147; and *Wigan Pier*, 163n, 165, 256, 263, 267; and *Homage to Catalonia*, 279, 285, 289; and *Coming Up for Air*, 309, 310, 394; and *Inside the Whale*, 413, 528. *See also* Collins, N.; Left Book Club
Gordon, Adam Lindsay, 308
Gordon Riots, 419–20
Gore, Bishop: *Belief in God*, 102
Gorer, Geoffrey, 154(n); letters from GO, 221–3, 280–2, 283–5, 381–3, 410–11, 527–9; reviews *Homage to Catalonia*, 315(n); *Bali and Angkor*, 222(n); *Himalayan Village*, 382(n)
Gould, Gerald, 252, 310
Gow, A. S. F., 224–5(n)
GPU, *see* Russia
Grady, Paddy, 174, 181, 204
Great Expectations, *see* Dickens, C.
Green, F. C.: *Stendhal*, 398–401
Green, Julian: *Minuit*, 248–9, 523
Green, Romney, 330(n)–2
Guns or butter, 331–2
Gupta, Sen, 307
Gypsies, 64–5

Habberton, John: *Helen's Babies*, 499
Hadath, Gunby, 466, 486
Haldane, J. B. S.: *Possible Worlds*, 101
Hamlet (Shakespeare), 20
Hanging: described, 44–8
Hangman's House (Byrne), 166
Hanley (Staffordshire), 171
Hanley, James: postcard from GO, 263(n)
Hannington, Wal, 176
Harcourt, Brace & Co., 316, 394
Hard Cash (Reade), 446–7
Hard Times, *see* Dickens, C.
Hardy, Thomas, 507; *The Dynasts*, 128–9
Harper Brothers, 113, 117, 133(n), 135. *See also* Saxton, E.
Harris, Frank, 119(n)
Hatchett, Mr, of Wallington, 352, 354, 355(n)
Haworth Parsonage, 197
Hay, Ian, 230, 482; *A Safety Match*, 232; *The First Hundred Thousand*, 524
Hayes, Middlesex: "one of the most godforsaken places I have ever struck", 81
Hearne, Lafcadio, "tiresome stuff", 138
Heinemann, William, Ltd: rejects *Burmese Days*, 133(n)
Helen's Babies (Habberton), 499
Hemingway, Ernest, 220, 517
Henderson, Alec, 354
Henderson, Sir Nevile: fantasy concerning, 353
Henderson, Philip, 511; *The Novel Today*, 256–9
Henley and South Oxfordshire Standard, 544
Heppenstall, Margaret, 278(n)
Heppenstall, Rayner: letters from GO, 152(n)–3, 153–4, 278–80
Herman Melville (Mumford), 19–21
Heroes of the Alcazar (Timmermans), 288
Hiddlestone, Reg, 367(n)
Higenbottam, Sam, 168, 169n
Hilton, Jack: *Caliban Shrieks*, 148–50
Himalayan Village (Gorer), 382(n)
Himmler, Heinrich, 534
Hind Let Loose, A (Montague), 232
Histoire de la Commune de 1871 (Lissagaray), 197
Hitler, Adolf, 247, 249, 270, 298, 305, 330, 353, 382, 389–90, 394, 397, 398, 479, 508, 514, 515, 532, 539; British views and attitudes, 403–4, 470–1, 494, 534
Hogg, Quintin, 363
Holdaway, N. A., 234(n), 280
Hollis, Christopher, 515
Homage to Catalonia, *see* Orwell, G.
Homosexuals and homosexuality: among tramps, 56–7; in London, 71
Hop-picking, 50, 57–8, 60–8
Hopkins, Gerard Manley, 23; "Felix Randal" helps GO on sentry-go, 311
Hore-Belisha, Leslie, 404
Horizon, 411, 529; GO's contributions to, 413, 460–84, 528, 550; Frank Richards's reply to GO, 485–93
Hornung, E. W.: Raffles books, 495
Horrors of Cayenne, The (Bartz), 28(n)
Hotspur, The, 461, 474–6, 478, 483
House, Humphry: letter from GO, 529(n)–32
House with the Green Shutters, The (Brown), 495
Household Words, 442n

Housman, A. E., 502–7; *A Shropshire Lad* memorised by GO at 17, 512
Hudson, W. H., 503
Hughes, Tom, 432; *Tom Brown's Schooldays*, 465
Hulbert, Jack, 138
Hunton, Doreen, later wife of Georges Kopp, *see* Kopp
Huxley, Aldous, 128, 226 456, 493, 506, 509; on being inside the whale, 520–1; *Ends and Means*, 332(n)
Huysmans, J. K.: *Sainte Lydwine de Schiedam*, 78

Ideas: compared with tunes, 137
ILP, *see* Independent Labour Party
Immortality: political implications of belief in, 383–4
Imperialism: and Kipling, 159–60; evils of, 235, 236, 337; effect of, in incident of shooting an elephant, 239–40; and "anti-Fascism", 345, 394; revolt of a subject people inevitable, 392–3; as a contradiction of democracy, 396–8; role of armies in, 402–3; incompatible with winning war, 530. *See also* Burma; India; Morocco
In Defence of Women (Mencken), 101
Independent Labour Party, 274, 279, 285n, 300, 300n, 301n, 367; GO's connection with, 269, 289, 302, 320; his reasons for joining, 336–7; GO leaves, 550
India: newspapers (*see also Pioneer*), 13; British rule "as bad as German Fascism", 284, 397; Civil Service's "exceptionally high traditions", 306
Inquisition, the, 137
Inside the Whale, *see* Orwell, G.
Insurance: GO seeks information on, 358–60
Intelligentsia, left-wing: "pansy", 329, 331–2, 357, 409–10, 516, 531–2; propensity to snigger, 518, 535, 537. *See also* Communists; Left, the; Socialists
Intelligentsia of Great Britain, The (Mirsky), 256, 258–9
International Brigade, *see* Spanish civil war
Intimate Diary of the Peace Conference (Riddell), 138
19*
Irujo, Manuel, 341
Isherwood, Christopher, 511
It Is Never Too Late to Mend (Reade), 434–5
Italy, 337; and Libya, 369; British attitudes, 508. *See also* Mussolini, B.

Jackson, T. A.: *Charles Dickens*, 414(n)–15
Jack the Giant-Killer, 459
Jacobs, W. W.: *Odd Craft*, 166
James, C. L. R.: *World Revolution*, 288
James Joyce and the Plain Reader (Duff), 117(n)
Jaques, Eleanor, later wife of Dennis Collings, *see* Collings
Jefferies, Richard, 503
Jellinek: letter from GO, 363–7; *The Civil War in Spain*, 340–3
Jerrold, Douglas: *Mrs Caudle's Curtain Lectures*, 457(n)
Jesuits: "sheer efficiency of", 340
Jews: customs of, 90, 356; Moroccan, 356, 388–9. *See also* Antisemitism
John Bull, 178(n), 180
Journey to Turkistan (Teichman), 286
Joyce, Alec Houghton: letter from GO, 302(n)–3
Joyce, James, 117, 506–8, 512; *Portrait of the Artist as a Young Man*, 129; *Ulysses*, 108, 121, 126–8, 139, 156, 230, 456, 495, 498, 510
Jungle, The (Sinclair), 232

Kahane, Jack, 162n, 527
Kaye, Len, 204, 212
Kaye-Smith, Sheila, 504
Keep the Aspidistra Flying, *see* Orwell, G.
Kennan, J., 174, 184, 185n
Kennedy, Margaret: *The Constant Nymph*, 138, 252
Kerensky, Alexander, 379
King-Farlow, Denys (formerly Nettleton), 162n, 309; letter from GO, 224(n)–5
Kingsley, Charles, 432
Kipling, Rudyard, 159–60, 475, 511; *Stalky and Co.*, 466, 486
Koestler, Arthur: *Spanish Testament*, 295–6
Kopp, Georges, 263n, 367, 370, 383
Krupskaya, Nadezhda: *Memories of Lenin*, 414

Kylsant, Lord, 94(n)

Labour Party, 356(n), 359, 361, 386, 395
Labour's Northern Voice, 164n, 173
Lady Chatterley's Lover (Lawrence), 409
Lancashire, 172–90
Landlords: ruthlessness of, 213
Large, E. C., 234(n)
Last Days of Madrid, The (Casado), 411–12
Lawrence, D. H., 245, 456, 506, 509–12; and the Bronze Age, 123, 507–8; *Lady Chatterley's Lover*, 409
Lawrence, T. E. 153
League of Nations, 534
Leech, John, 444
Leeds, Yorkshire, 193(n), 196–8
Left, the, in Britain, 386–7, 394–5; and jingoism, 346, 354, and war party, 356, 395; and imperialism, 369; *See also* Communists; Intelligentsia, left-wing; Socialists
Left, periodical, 358n. *See also Controversy; Left Forum*
Left Book Club, 256(n), 297(n)–8, 359, 411, 514
Left Forum, 358n; GO's contribution to, 401–5. *See also Controversy*; *Left*
Lehmann, John, 511; letter from GO, 221(n)
Leigh, Augusta: "vague and pliable to the point of idiocy", 95
Lenin, V. I., 381, 444; and Dickens, 414
"Lessons of War, The", 550
Letters to the Boys in the Trenches (Bottomley), 524
Leverhulme, Lord, 189
Lewis, Cecil Day-, *see* Day-Lewis
Lewis, D. B. Wyndham, 82(n), 101
Lewis, Sinclair: *Our Mr Wrenn*, 166
Lewis, Wyndham, 270, 506–7, 509, 526; *The Enemy*, 82, 101; *Snooty Baronet*, 101; *Tarr*, 494
Liberal Party, 361
Liberalism: liberal-Christian culture breaking up, 525
Liberals: in Spain, 270–1, 275
Libraries, 70
Licensed Victuallers Gazette: attack on *Down and Out*, 117
Life of Charles Dickens, The (Forster), 435
Life on the Mississippi (Twain), 101
"Limit to Pessimism, The", 533–5
Limouzin, Nellie, *see* Adam
Lissagaray, Prosper: *Histoire de la Commune de 1871*, 197
Listener, The: GO's contribution to, 306–7
Literature: and politics, 4, 5–6, 249, 256–9, 510–19; and anthropology, 222; proletarian, 314 "*impossibility* of any major literature" at present, 527. *See also* English literature; Novels; Reviewers etc.; War, *subheading* Literature
Little Dorrit, see Dickens, C.
Little Women (Alcott), 499
Lively Lady, The (Roberts), 160–1
Liverpool, 187–90
Llano, General Queipo de, *see* Queipo de Llano
Lloyd George, David, 345
Lodging houses, common, 97–100; regulations, 52; Westminster Bridge Road, 52; Southwark Bridge Road, 54; Tooley Street, 69–70; Manchester, 173
London: in fiction, 25–6; GO's interrest in low life of, 33; lodging houses, 52, 54, 69–70, 97–100; tramps in, 52–4; Dick's café, 52n; Saint Martin's Church, 53; Stewart's café, 53; Billingsgate, 69–70; Bermondsey public library, 70; homosexual vice in, 71; riots in, 103; GO's attitude to Bayswater, 137. *See also* Police; Saint Paul's
London County Council: and lodging house regulations, 52, 97–100
London Mercury, 506
Long Shadows (Sanderson), 161
Looe, Cornwall, 11n, 12
Low, Mary, and Juan Brea: *Red Spanish Notebook*, 287–8, 297
Low, Matt, *pseud., see* Garrett, G.
Lunn, Arnold: *Spanish Rehearsal*, 291
Lyons, Eugene: *Assignment in Utopia*, 332–4
Lytton, Bulwer: and *Great Expectations*, 448

Macartney, W. F. R.: *Walls Have Mouths*, 233

Macaulay, Lord: and Dickens, 417
Macaulay, Rose: *Told by an Idiot*, 510
Macbeth (Shakespeare), 106
MacDonald, Ramsay, 534
McDougall, Dr, of Wallington, 347
McGovern, John, 300(n)
Mackenzie, Compton: *Sinister Street* gets GO into trouble, 363
McNair, John, 264n, 265n, 318
MacNeice, Louis, ed.: *Modern Poetry*, 510–12, 524
Magistrates' courts, 91
Magnet, The, 461–93 *passim*, 528
Maillart, Ella K.: *Forbidden Journey*, 268(n)
Mairet, Philip, 547
Man of Property, The (Galsworthy), 252
Manchester, 172–4, 176
Manchester Guardian, 365; letter of GO to, 204; and Spanish civil war, 301, 341(n), 363–4
Manifesto of the Common Man, 529–530(n)
Manon Lescaut (Prévost), 456
Mapplewell, Yorkshire, 213
March, Juan, 340
Marlowe, Christopher: *Dr Faustus*, 82
Marrakech, 387–93. *See also* Morocco
Marryat, Captain, 452–3
Marshall, Arthur Calder-, *see* Calder-Marshall
Martin, Kingsley, 299(n), 310(n), 357(n)
Martin Chuzzlewit, *see* Dickens, C.
Martindale, Father C. C.: *The Roman Faith*, 79, 85(n)
Marx, GO's dog, 347(n)–8
Marx, Karl, 428
Marxism, *see* Communism
Marxist Quarterly, 519–20
Masefield, John: *The Everlasting Mercy*, 504
Matrimonial agency, in a weekly of 1851, 139–40
Matrimonial Times, 461
Maugham, W. Somerset, 33, 506; *Of Human Bondage*, 166, 510
Max and the White Phagocytes (Miller), 500, 520
Maxton, James, 285(n), 300(n)
Mayne, Ethel Colburn, 95, 97
Meade, Frank, and wife, 163(n), 165, 173–4, 218
Melville, Herman, 19–21, 521
Memoirs of Sergeant Bourgogne, The 550–1
Memories of Lenin (Krupskaya), 414
Men I Killed, The (Crozier), 282–3
Mencken, H. L.: *In Defence of Women*, 101
Meredith, George, 502; *Rhoda Fleming*, 437
Mérimée, Prosper: *Carmen*, 456
Mexico: and Spanish civil war, 272
Meynell, Godfrey, 224(n)
Mickey Mouse, 228, 231, 459
Middle class, *see* Bourgeoisie
Middlesmoor, Yorkshire, 197
Midlands: GO's travels in, 170–2
Midnight (Green), 248–9, 523
Miller, Henry, 220, 233, 493–502, 519–22, 525–7; letter from GO 227–9; and Walt Whitman, 498–500; on being inside the whale, 521; *Black Spring*, 227–9, 230–2, 495–8, 500, 526–7; *Max and the White Phagocytes*, 500, 520; *Tropic of Cancer*, 154–6, 219, 409, 493–5, 497–9, 501–2, 526; *Tropic of Capricorn*, 526
Milton, John, 2
Milton, Michael, *see* Wilton
Miners and mines, *see* Coal-miners etc.
Minuit (Green), 248–9, 523
Mirsky, Prince Dmitri: *The Intelligentsia of Great Britain*, 256, 258–9
Mitchell, Mairin: *Storm over Spain*, 290–1, 297
Modern Boy, 461, 475, 483
Modern Poetry (ed. MacNeice), 510–12, 524
Modern Youth, 50(n), 51(n), 546
Monde: GO's contributions to, 545
Money: "awful thraldom of", 226. *See also* Orwell, G., *subheading* Finances; Working class, *subheading* Income and expenditure
Montague, C. E.: *A Hind Let Loose*, 232
Moore, George, 506; *Esther Waters*, 166
Moore, Leonard, GO's agent, 107(n), 120, 279, 364; letters from GO, 77(n)–8, 84, 84–5, 104–5, 106–7,

Moore, Leonard—(*contd.*) 109–10, 115, 125, 129–30, 133, 134, 135–6, 141, 142–3, 147, 256
Morley, F. V.: *War Paint*, 160–1
Morocco, French: GO's impressions of, 352–4, 360–1, 362, 368–70, 382, 387–93
Mortimer, Raymond: letter from GO, 299(n)-302
Morton, J. B., *see* Beachcomber, *pseud.*
Mosley, Sir Oswald: speaks in Barnsley, 169(n), 202–4, 218
Mrs Caudle's Curtain Lectures (Jerrold), 457(n)
Muggeridge, Malcolm: *The Thirties*, 533–5; *Winter in Moscow*, 533
Mumford, Lewis: *Herman Melville*, 19–21
Munich crisis, *see* Czechoslovakia
Muriel, GO's goat, 370–1
Murry, John Middleton, 27–8(n), 29, 153, 154, 168–9(n), 280, 370(n)
Mussolini, Benito, 249, 270, 346, 370
Mussolini's Roman Empire (Garratt), 346
"My Country Right or Left", 535–40
My Man Jeeves (Wodehouse), 167
Myers, L. H.: anonymous loan to GO of £300, 367(n)
Mynors, Sir Roger, 11(n)

National Unemployed Workers' Movement, 164(n), 174, 176, 177, 181
Nationalism: vulgarity of English brand, 431–3; inculcated by boys' weeklies, 471–3. *See also* Patriotism
Naval Occasions (Bartimeus), 166–7
Nazism, *see* Fascism; Germany; Hitler, A.
Negrin, Juan, 411–12
Negroes: in French army, 392–3, 403
Nelson, Thomas, & Sons, 382n
Nettleton, Denys, later King-Farlow, *see* King-Farlow
New Adelphi, *see Adelphi*
New English Weekly, 120, 309, 362; GO's contributions to, 79–81, 82(n), 85n, 154–6, 159–60, 160–2, 163, 165–7, 219–20, 225–7, 228(n), 230–2, 233, 247–9, 249–55, 256–9, 269–76, 304–6, 329, 330–2, 332–4, 335–6, 344–6, 348–51, 378–81, 398–401, 533–5, 546
New Leader, 266, 301n, 310, 314, 361; and Spanish civil war, 269; GO's contributions to, 336–8, 340–3, 364(n)
New Signatures (ed. Roberts), 510(n)–11
New Statesman and Nation: 331, 346, 357(n), 358; GO's contributions to, 97–100, 103(n), 105(n), 108(n), 109, 282, 299n, 307–8, 395, 546; and Spanish civil war, 269(n); refusal to publish GO's views, 279, 281, 297, 299(n)–302; "under direct Communist influence", 365. *See also* Martin, K.
New Writing: GO's contributions to, 221(n), 235–42, 387–93
Newbolt, Sir Henry, 511, 540
News Chronicle, 331, 346, 405, 413; and Spanish civil war, 269, 281, 285; and Fascism, 276; "under direct Communist influence", 365
News from Tartary (Fleming), 286(n)
News of the World, 460
News Review, 413
Newsagents' shops, 460–1
Newspapers and periodicals: British, 15, 100–1, 255, 413; French, 12–15, 351; Indian, 13. *See also* Boys' weeklies; Camrose, Lord; Propaganda; Rothermere, Lord; Women's magazines; *and individual newspapers etc.*
Nicholas Nickleby, *see* Dickens, C.
Nicholls, Mr, of Wallington, 370
Nietzsche, Friedrich von: on war, 295; on Christianity, 532
Nin, Anais, 520–1
Nin, Andreas, 300, 341(n), 342
"*Not Counting Niggers*", 394–8
"Notes on the Spanish Militias", 316–28
Novel Today, The (Henderson), 256–9
Novels, 249–55, 256–9; sociological, 247; "a Protestant form of art", 518. *See also individual novels and novelists*
Nuffield, Lord, 333

Oak, Liston M., 269(n)
Obelisk Press, 162(n), 226–7, 409, 526–7
Obermeyer, Rosalind, 150n
Obscenity in literature, 497–8

Observer, The, 100–1, 161, 266(n); and POUM trial, 366
Odd Craft (Jacobs), 166
Of Human Bondage (Maugham), 166, 510
Officers' Training Corps, 404, 537–8
OGPU, *see* Russia
Oliver Twist, *see* Dickens, C.
One Looks at Russia (Barbusse), 257
Oracle, The, 461, 480, 481, 483
Orczy, Baroness: *The Scarlet Pimpernel*, 421
Orley Farm (Trollope), 442

Orwell, George (Eric Arthur Blair): *chronology of main non-literary events*: summarised by GO, 113–14, 302–3; by editors, 543–51; ancestry, 543. *1903–16*: early childhood, 1; at St Cyprian's school, 343, 362–3; impression made by loss of *Titanic*, 536; by outbreak of war, 536–7. *1917–21*: at Eton, 11n, 362; war memories, 537; an early adventure, 11–12. *1922–27*: service in Burma with Indian Imperial Police, effect on GO, 4; participates in a hanging, 44–8; shoots an elephant, 235–42; observes behaviour of soldiers, 403. *1928–29*: in Paris, 15, 113–14, 200. *1930*: at Southwold, 27. *1931*: in London, 33; lives as a tramp, 36–43, 52–70; at home of Mr and Mrs Fierz, 49, 50, 77; sees a ghost, 49–50; at 2 Windsor St, 51, 70, 72, 73; steals fruit etc, 56, 58–60, 63, 66, 68; picks hops, 60–8; succeeds in getting arrested but fails to get into prison, 86–94. *1932*: teaches at a day preparatory school at Hayes, Middlesex, 78, 81–2, 101, 104–5, 107, 110; finds himself going to church, 81–2, 100, 101, 103–4. *1933*: leaves school at Hayes, 120; teaches at similar school at Uxbridge, 120, 122, 123, 125, 129; has pneumonia and gives up teaching, 129(n). *1934*: at 36 High St, Southwold, 133; plans to move to London, 137, 140; moves to Pond St, Hampstead, 142; works in bookshop, 142(n), 148. *1935*: his regimen, 148, 150–1; moves to Parliament Hill, 150; buys chessmen and mends a fuse, 151; shares flat in Kentish Town with Rayner Heppenstall and Michael Sayers. 152. *1936*: commissioned to write about working-class conditions in north of England, 163n; passes through Midlands, 170–2; at Manchester, 172–4; lives with coal miners at Wigan, 163, 164, 174–87; goes down mines, 164, 184–7, 206–11; at Liverpool, 187–90; at Sheffield, 190–6; with married sister at Leeds, 196–8; with miners at Barnsley, 198–214; hears Mosley speak, 169, 202–4, 218; settles at Wallington, Hertfordshire, 164–5; opens a general shop, 214, 215–16, 217, 222, 224, 233; marries Eileen O'Shaughnessy, 222, 224; sees Spanish civil war as turning point in his life, 5; decides to fight, 256(n). *1937*: in action with POUM militia, 263, 316–28, 538; in hospital, 264–6, 268–9; in street fighting in Barcelona, 267; wounded in throat by a sniper, 268, 279–80, 281, 289, 329, 363, 366; escapes with wife into France, 279, 281, 289; back at Wallington, 278; libelled by *Daily Worker*, 285, 289. *1938*: offered appointment with Indian newspaper, 302–3; intends to accept, 304; prevented by illness, 309; in sanatorium with tubercular lesion, 310–15, 328–30, 338–9, 347–8; plans to winter abroad, 338–9, 343, 348; offers Jack Common use of cottage at Wallington, 338–9; accepts anonymous loan of £300 from L. H. Myers, 367(n); at Marrakech, French Morocco, 351–71; ill again, 360. *1939*: in Morocco, 377–8, 381–3, 385–7; more illnesses, 550, 393; returns to England, 385, 393; returns to Wallington, 393, 410; death of father, 410; rejected by army as medically unfit, 410. *1940*: still unable to get war work, 527, 539; tries to join a Government training centre, 532
—, *characteristics noted by himself* (*others may be suggested by entries under, e.g.* "Decency" *and other subjects of concern*): hatred of authority, 4; sense of failure, 4;

Orwell—(*contd.*)
patriotism, 535, 539–40; pessimism, 120–1, 140, 409 (*see also subheading* Predictions and forebodings); political concern, 5–7
—, *finances*: *1920*, 11–12; *1931*, 52, 55–6, 58, 60, 62, 66, 68–70, 86, 94; *1932*, 107, 108; *1934*, 133; *1935*, 148, 153, 154; *1936*, 165, 170–4, 190, 193, 214, 216, 222, 224, 233, 356; *1938*, 339, 351, 355–6, 367(n)–8; *1939*, 387; *1940*, 528
—, *miscellaneous observations*: on modern man, 154; on sluttish antinomianism, 226; on corrupt disposal of lucrative jobs, 271; on intellectual brutality, 313; on people with brown skins, 392; on smelly little orthodoxies, 460; on implications of "acceptance" 499
—, *predictions and forebodings*: civilisation doomed, 120; horrors of next decade, 121; over Spanish civil war, 275–6; over "fascisation" of Britain, 276, 284, 338, 356–7, 378, 386–7; over coming war, 280, 284, 286, 329, 338, 351, 358, 362, 377–8, 386, 538–9; over finishing up in a concentration camp, 330, 354, 360, 382; over censorship, 337, 377–8, 386–7; over the election that was never held, 337, 353, 359, 361, 386; over break-up of capitalism and liberal-Christian culture, 525; over red militias billeted in the Ritz, 539–40
—, *recreations and outdoor pursuits*: animal husbandry and poultry, 228, 233, 281, 339, 351, 354, 355, 356, 370–1, 529; chess, 151; cinema: "Jack Ahoy", with Jack Hulbert, 138; a crook film, 138; "Anna Karenina", with Garbo, 154; fishing, 83, 266; gardening 82, 119, 120, 122, 123, 214, 215, 217, 223, 265, 280, 281, 304, 338–9, 354, 369, 529; natural history 82, 83, 137–8, 170, 172, 190, 208, 212, 218, 310; swimming, 122, 123, 139; theatre: *Macbeth* at the Old Vic, 106; the Blackbirds at the Coliseum, 151; George Robey as Falstaff, 151; walking, 11–12, 54–60, 107, 108–9, 119–20, 170–2
—, *writing and writings* (*italic figures indicate texts*): books listed, 541; early development, 1–3; poems, 1, 2, *4–5*, 78, 81, *118*, 123n, *123–5*, *134–5*, 138, *142*, 233(n), 544; plays, 2, 103; motives, 3–7, 310–11; two unpublished novels and other early work, 78(n), 113(n), 545; first published work as professional writer, 545; preferences as a reviewer, 33; impossiblity of writing in a lodging house, 70; use of Bermondsey public library, 70; eagerness to translate from French, 72, 73, 78; decision to adopt a pseudonym, 85, 104; "George Orwell" and other suggestions, 106; writing habits, 148, 150–1, 217; an unidentified serial, 152, 153; interest in writing "semi-sociological literary criticism", 222, 528; in heavy demand, 289; inability to write short stories, 289; novel-writing inhibited by political situation, 330; an anti-war pamphlet, 357(n); projected Saga in three volumes, 368, 382, 410, 528, 551; projected book on poverty, 382; enjoyment of reviewing, 385. *Animal Farm*: attempt to fuse politics and art, 7. "Boys' Weeklies", 413, *460–84*, 528. *Burmese Days*, 3, 137(n); work on, 78(n), 100(n), 103(n), 104(n), 107(n), 110(n), 115(n) 117, 120, 123, 125, 546; with GO's agent, 120, 129; with Victor Gollancz, 129–30; rejected by Gollancz for fear of libel, Heinemann and Cape, 133n; accepted by Harper, 133n, 135; cuts and changes, 134, 141; published, 141; rejected draft material, *141–2*; reviewed in *Herald Tribune*, 143; reconsidered by Gollancz, 147–8; accepted, 150; admired by Geoffrey Gorer, 154n; fear of suppressal by India Office, 229; GO's favourite book (1936), 229. "Charles Dickens", *413–60*, 528. *A Clergyman's Daughter*, 151; projected, 129(n); work on, 136(n), 137(n); "that dreadful book", 136(n); "makes me spew", 138; "goes backwards with the most alarming speed", 139(n); sent to agent, 141; fear of libel, 141, 142–3; accepted by Gollancz, 147;

published, 150, 152; denigrated by GO, 229. "Clink", *86–94*, 103(n), 108(n). *Coming Up for Air*: projected, 304(n); announced by Gollancz, 309, 310; writing deferred, 329, 330, 344(n), 348; work on, 354, 367–8, 369, 377, 382; information sought on insurance offices, 358–60; completed, 394(n); published, 394. "Common Lodging Houses", *97–100*, 103(n). "Democracy in the British Army", *401–5*. *Down and Out in Paris and London* (originally *Days in London and Paris*), 29n, 43, 133n, 546; "not proud of it", 77–8; alterations, 84; *Lady Poverty* suggested as title, 85; in proof, 104(n), 105(n), 106; *Confessions of a Down and Out* suggested as title, 105; *Confessions of a Dishwasher* preferred by GO; advance copies, 109(n); Introduction to French edition, *113–14*; reply to attack in *The Times*, *115–16*, 117; attacked in *Licensed Victuallers Gazette*, 117; American rights sold, 117; copy obtained by Henry Miller, 228; most popular book in Dartmoor library, 368; Penguin edition, 368(n). "A Farthing Newspaper", *12–15*. "A Hanging", 33n, *44–8*. *Homage to Catalonia*, 6–7, 310, 311, 356, 364; projected, 267, 269; Gollancz refuses to publish, 279, 285; work on, 279(n), 280, 281, 285, 289; at press, 296; to be reviewed by Stephen Spender, 313; published, 316, 329; "boycotted", 330; liked by Cyril Connolly, 343; poor sales but good reviews, 368. "Hop-picking", 51(n), *52–71*. *Inside the Whale* (book and title essay), 409(n), 410(n), 413, *493–527*, 528. *Keep the Aspidistra Flying*, 218(n), 229; work on, 148(n), 152(n), 154(n), in proof, 163(n); fears of libel, 165(n), 168, 215(n); published, 219; admired by Anthony Powell, 223n. "The Lessons of War", 550. "The Limit to Pessimism", *533–5*. "Marrakech", *387–93*. "My Country Right or Left", *535–40*. "Not Counting Niggers", *394–8*. "Notes on the Spanish Militias", *316–28*. *The Road to Wigan Pier*, 268(n); commissioned by Gollancz, 163n; work on, 164, 168(n), 215(n), 217(n), 218(n), 222(n), 229, 233, 356; diary relating to, *170–214*; interests James Hanley, 263; published, 264; reviewed by Harry Pollitt, 265n; by Edward Shanks and Hugh Massingham, 266(n); introduction by Victor Gollancz, 267. "Shooting an Elephant", 221(n), *235–42*. "The Spike", 15n, 29(n), *36–43*. "Spilling the Spanish Beans", 276, *269–76*. "Why I joined the Independent Labour Party", *336–8*. "Why I Write", *1–7*

Osborne, Lewis: "Riding Down from Bangor", 499

O'Shaughnessy, Eileen, later GO's first wife, *see* Blair

O'Shaughnessy, Gwen, 263n, 550

O'Shaughnessy, Laurence, 263n, 309n, 352, 550

Othello (Shakespeare), 20

Oughton, Maurice, 153

Our Mr Wrenn (Lewis), 166

Our Mutual Friend, *see* Dickens, C.

Ovseenko, Antonov, 342

Owls' House, The (Garstin), 166

Oxford, Lady, *see* Asquith, M.

Oxford Group, 534

Pacifism and pacifists, 378, 528; GO's objections to, 280, 282–4; in relation to social problems, 331–2; GO's anti-war pamphlet, 357(n); "peculiar to sheltered countries with strong navies", 537. *See also* Peace Pledge Union; War

Paris, 113–14; newspapers, 12–15; Hôpital Cochin, 200, 545; and Henry Milller, 493–4

Parker, Buck, 266(n), 367(n)

Partido Obrero de Unificacion Marxista, *see* POUM

Passage to India, A (Forster), 232

Passos, John dos, *see* Dos Passos

Patriotism: GO settles for, 535, 539–40. *See also* Nationalism

Peace News: GO's contribution to, 383–5

Peace Pledge Union, 15n

Peers, E. Allison: *Catalonia Infelix*, 291
Peg's Paper, 149, 160, 162, 254, 461, 480, 481
Pendennis (Thackeray), 437, 459
Penguin Books, 165–7, 289, 368(n)
Penkridge, Staffordshire, 171
Penrose, Sir Roland, 387(n)
People of Clopton, The, (Barton), 437
People's Front, *see* Popular Front
Pessimism: and Christianity, 155; of Malcolm Muggeridge, 533–5
Peters, C. R., 546
Pickwick Papers, see Dickens, C.
Picture Post, 413
Poineer (Lucknow newspaper), 302–3, 549
Pitter, Ruth, 138(n)–9, 545
Pius XI, pope, 534
Plato and Aristotle (Thomson), 129
Plowman, Dorothy, 15n, 367n
Plowman, Max: letters from GO, 15(n), 27(n)–9, 33
Poe, Edgar Allan, 33, 249, 523
Poincaré, Raymond, 298
Police: GO arrested by, 86–7; Bethnal Green police station, 87–8; Old Street Police Court, 88–94; GO's imported books seized by, 409, 526
Politics: and literature, 4, 5–7, 249, 256–9, 510–14
Pollitt, Harry, 316–18: reviews *Road to Wigan Pier*, 265(n)
Pope, *see* Pius XI.
Pope, Alexander, 22–4
Popeye the Sailor, 459
Popular culture: "good-tempered antinomianism" of, 459. *See also* Boys' weeklies
Popular Front, 284, 304–6, 349, 377, 529n, 531; in Spain, 271; and "Rule Britannia", 305; agitation for a Popular Front government, 331; in Morocco, 514
Portrait of the Artist as a Young Man (Joyce), 129
Port Sunlight, 184
Possenti, Humbert: attacks *Down and Out* in *The Times*, 115(n)
Possible Worlds (Haldane), 101
POUM (Partido Obrero de Unificacion Marxista), 265n, 284, 317(n); GO in militia, 263(n), 265–6, 267, 269, 289, 317–28, 363–4, 367; persecution and suppressal, 274, 279, 340–2, 364–7; GO'S suppressed article on, 279, 281, 300–1, 365; review of a book defending, 287–8. *See also* Spanish civil war
Pound, Ezra, 493, 506, 508; and Fascism, 509
Poverty, 337; experience by GO, 4 and *passim*; among Irish immigrants, 53; in Morocco, 370, 382, 388–92; projected book on, 380(n); in India, 397, Dickens's horror of, 434. *See also* Lodging houses; Tramps; Unemployment; Working class
Powell, Anthony: letter from GO, 223(n)
Power (Russell), 375–6
Pozas, General, 328
Predictions, *see that subheading under* Orwell, G.
Preparatory (private) schools, 78, 81–2, 101, 104–5, 107, 110, 120, 122, 123, 125, 129, 141, 363. *See also* St Cyprian's
Press, the, *see* Newspapers etc.
Prévost, Abbé: *Manon Lescaut*, 456
Priestley, J. B., 117; *Angel Pavement*, 25–7
Pritt, D. N., 531(n)
Private schools, *see* Preparatory schools; Public schools
Progrès Civique: GO's contributions to, 545
"Progress": vision of, 121
Proletarian literature, 314
Propaganda, truth and lies, 376, 531; over Spanish civil war, 267, 269, 273–6, 277–8, 279, 281, 285, 297–8, 300–1, 318, 341, 365; over First world war, 276, 280; over Soviet Russia, 379–80; propaganda and art, *see* Politics, *subheading* and literature. *See also* Communist Party, *subheading* Propaganda etc.
Prophecies, *see* Orwell, G., *subheading* Predictions
Prostitutes and prostitution, 53–4, 287
Public (i.e. private) schools, 363; as reflected in boys' weeklies, 462–75. *See also* Eton
Publishers and publishing: blurbs, 310, 329–30. *See also names of individual firms*

Pulleyne, Collett Cresswell, 51(n), 83(n), 102(n), 103
Punch: unflattering references to, 155, 166, 256–7, 471, 508–9
Punishment, capital, *see* Hanging
Puritanism: Dickens and, 429; literature and, 523
Pygmalion (Shaw), 119

Quarterly Review, 361, 432
Queipo de Llano, General, 295

Raffles (Hornung), 495
Read, Sir Herbert, 493: letters from GO, 377–8, 385–7
Reade, Charles: and Dickens, 416; *Hard Cash*, 446–7; *It Is Never Too Late to Mend*, 434–5
Red Spanish Notebook (Low and Brea), 287–8, 297
Rees, Sir Richard, 28n, 72n, 77(n), 148, 152n, 169n, 215, 233, 290n, 354; letters from GO, 163–5, 217–18; and Spanish civil war, 280, 289, 311, 314(n)
Reforms, *see* Social reform
Religion: wisdom of not mentioning, 530. *See also* Buddhism; Christianity
Respectability, 140
Retour de l'URSS (Gide), 433
Reviewers and reviewing, 100–1, 223, 225, 250–5, 267, 289, 310, 385; mutual back-scratching, 309; in relation to advertising, 314, 330. *For GO's reviews, see titles*
Revolt, 385(n)–6
Revolutionaries: mostly potential Tories, 458
Reynolds News, 331
Rhoda Fleming (Meredith), 437
Rhondda, Lady 121(n)
Ribbentrop, Joachim von, 539(n)
Rice, Elmer: *A Voyage to Purilia*, 222
Riceyman Steps (Bennett), 25
Richards, Frank: sole author of *Gem* and *Magnet*, 461; replies to GO's article on boys' weeklies, 485–93, 528
Richards, Hilda, *pseud.*, 467n
Richards, Vernon, 385n
Riddell, Lord: *Intimate Diary of the Peace Conference*, 138
"Riding Down from Bangor" (Osborne), 499
Rivera, Diego, 377n
Road to Wigan Pier, The, *see* Orwell, G.
Roberti, Jacques: *A la Belle de Nuit*, 72, 73, 78
Roberts, C. E. Bechhofer-: *This Side Idolatry*, 414
Roberts, Kenneth: *The Lively Lady*, 160–1
Roberts, Michael, ed.: *New Signatures*, 510(n)–11
Robey, George, 151
Rock Pool, The (Connolly), 162(n), 225–7, 229(n)
Roman Catholicism and Roman Catholic Church, 189; unflattering references to, 50, 79–81, 81–2, 101, 137; and literature, 257–8, 522; in Spain, 271, 340; F. J. Sheed as apologist for, 383–5; leaning of writers towards in 1920s, 509, 512, 515
Roman Faith, The (Martindale), 79
Rotherham, Yorkshire, 194
Rothermere, Lord, 333, 345, 534
Roughing It (Twain), 138
Rover, The, 461, 477
Rowton Houses, 98
Runciman, The Hon. Steven: letter from GO, 11(n)–12
Ruskin, John, 455
Russell, Bertrand, 121, 387; *Freedom and Organisation*, 376; *Power*, 375–6
Russia: and Spanish civil war, 272–3, 412, 529; British attitudes and relations, 286, 398, 508, 513–15, 517; pact with France, 272, 305; rapid changes in, 305–6; as seen by Eugene Lyons, 332–4; the GPU, 334, 370, 383, 529; as seen by N. de Basily, 378–81; régime condemned by GO, 531–2; pact with Germany, 539(n). *See also* Communism; Stalin, J.
Russia under Soviet Rule (de Basily), 378–81
Russian Revolution: impact in England, 505, 508, 537

Sadism: in "Yank magazines", 478
Safety Match, A (Hay), 232
Saint Cyprian's school, 343, 362–3, 543–4

Saint Paul's Cathedral, 50–1
Saint Winifred's (Farrar), 465
Sainte Lydwine de Schiedam (Huysmans), 78
Saintsbury, George, 232
Salammbô (Flaubert), 370, 456
Salkeld, Brenda, 103; letters from GO, 100(n)–1, 119, 120–1, 125–9, 136–7, 137–9, 139–40, 147–8(n), 150–1
Salvation Army: attitude of tramps to, 39; hostels, 98
Salvemini, Gaetano: *Under the Axe of Fascism*, 379
Sanderson, Lady: *Long Shadows*, 161
Sapper, *pseud.*, 482
Saturday Review, 119
Saxton, Eugene, 133(n), 134
Sayers, Dorothy L.: *Gaudy Night*, 161–2
Sayers, Michael: 152n, 153, 154
Scarlet Pimpernel, The (Orczy), 421
Sceats, John: letters from GO, 357(n)–9, 360–1
Schoolgirl, The, 467n
Schoolgirl's Own Library, 461
Schools, *see* Eton; Preparatory schools; Public schools; Saint Cyprian's
Scotsmen: how to annoy, 223
Scrutiny, 253
Searchlight on Spain (Atholl), 344–7
Secker & Warburg Ltd, 303(n); known as "the Trotskyist publishers", 297; and *Homage to Catalonia*, 303, 315, 316; "Communists sabotaging their books", 314. *See also* Warburg, F. J.
Second world war: predicted by GO, 280, 284, 286, 329, 345–6, 351, 358, 362, 377–8, 538–9; Air Raid Precautions, 346(n); GO's intention to oppose, 377–8, 386–7; rumours and protests about conscription, 346, 395; effect of outbreak on GO, 410; prediction of its course, 525; public morale, 528–9; food supplies, 529; prescription for winning, 530; war aims, 531
Secrets, 461
Servant problem, as seen by T. S. Eliot, 151
Seven Shifts (Common), 310, 311
Sex: GO's views, 28; attitude and behaviour of tramps, 55, 56–7, 68; of "Charlie" and "Snouter", 93; taboo in boys' weeklies, 465; main theme of women's magazines, 480–1. *See also* Homosexuals; Obscenity; Prostitutes; Sadism
Shabby Genteel Story, A (Thackeray), 437
Shakespeare, William: "a mangy little book on", 82; "mortal moon" sonnet quoted, 356, 358; Falstaff, 435; misquoted by Chamberlain, 534; *Hamlet*, 20; *Macbeth*, 106; *Othello*, 20: *The Tempest* quoted ("bawling . . ."), 36; *Twelfth Night*, 439
Shaw, George Bernard: violently attacked by GO, 119; *The Adventures of a Black Girl in Her Search for God*, 192; *Cashel Byron's Profession*, 220; *Pygmalion*, 119
Sheed, F. J.: *Communism and Man*, 383–5
Sheffield, Yorkshire, 190–6
Sherwood, May M.: *The Fairchild Family*, 101, 425(n)
Shiel, M.P., 33
"Shooting an Elephant", 221(n), 235–42
Shropshire Lad, A (Housman): memorised by GO at 17, 502
Sinclair, Upton, 117; *The Jungle*, 232
Sinister Street (Mackenzie), 363
Sitwell, Edith, 285; *Alexander Pope*, 22–4, 285
Skin Game, The (Galsworthy), 198
Skipper, The, 461, 476, 478
Slang: words new to GO, 70–1; "gee", 88
Small House at Allington, The (Trollope), 437
Smedley, F. E.: *Frank Fairlegh*, 457(n)
Smith, C. A., 357–8n
Smith, Joseph, 334
Smollett, Tobias, 33, 119; compared with Dickens, 440, 455
Snooty Baronet (Lewis), 101
Social Credit, 120
Social reform: and war, 331–2
Socialism: democratic variety consistently advocated by GO, 5–6; "not easy to distinguish" from capitalism, 189; "I at last really believe in", 269; necessity of fighting for, 280; GO "of Socialist sympathies", 302; tactlessness of its propaganda, 305; and Independent

Labour Party, 337–8; F. J. Sheed's critique of, 383–5; incompatible with liberalism, 525; not enough, 532. *See also* Communism
Socialists, British: bourgeois contempt for working class, 216, 434; use of word "comrade", 233; attitude to Spanish political prisoners, 306; and jingoism, 346; contempt for sports, 444. *See also* Intelligentsia, left-wing; Left, the
Solidaridad Internacional Antifascista, 312(n)
Solidaridad Obrera, 366(n)
Sommerfield, John: *Volunteer in Spain*, 278
Southwold, Suffolk, 49n, 51(n), 77n, 82, 82n, 85–6, 100n, 102n, 122, 129, 148, 154, 347, 544; GO at, 27–9, 133–41, 393–4, 546–7
Soviet Union, *see* Russia
Spanish civil war, 263–302 *passim*, 311–29 *passim*, 340–7 *passim*, 363–7, 383, 411–12; profound influence on GO's political views, 5, 269, 289, 338, 377; GO's experiences in, 6–7, 263–9, 278–80, 281, 289, 316–28, 341, 363–4, 377, 538; fighting in Barcelona, 267, 269, 279, 285, 289, 300–1, 315, 341–2, 366; International Brigade, 267(n), 269, 278, 316, 540; distorted accounts of, in press etc., 267, 269, 273–6, 277–8, 279, 281, 285, 297–8, 318, 341, 365; GO's article in *New English Weekly*, 269–76; atrocities and atrocity stories, 269, 277, 290, 291, 295; Communist reign of terror, 207, 272, 274, 277, 279, 281, 298, 300–1; origins, 270–1, 340; Popular Front and, 271; divergent aims and dissension on Government side, 271–3, 275–6, 277–8, 279, 284–5, 287–8, 289, 412; military effects of this dissension, 323–5; foreign intervention and attitudes, 272–3, 412, 529, 534; deadlock prophesied by GO, 276; GO's review of books on, 276–8, 287–8, 290–1, 295–6, 340–3, 344–7, 411–13; political prisoners, 295, 300–1, 367, 370, 383; summary of political parties, 316–17n; militias, 317–28, 404; food supply, 321–2; conditions at front, 321–3; battle for Huesca, 323–5, 328; morale on Government side, 325–8; Auden on, 516; "a bad copy of 1914–18", 538. *See also* Anarchists; POUM
Spanish Cockpit, The (Borkenau), 276–8, 279, 281, 297, 299
Spanish Rehearsal (Lunn), 291
Spanish Testament (Koestler), 295–6
Spender, Stephen, 290, 301, 506, 511, 518; letters from GO, 311–12, 312–13; GO's change of attitude to, 313, 329; and *Horizon*, 411; *Trial of a Judge*, 312(n)–13, 329, 512
"Spikes", *see* Casual wards
"Spilling the Spanish Beans", 269–76
Spirit of Catholicism, The (Adam): 79–81, 82(n), 85n
Squire, Sir John, 100, 386(n), 506
Stafford, 171
Stalin, Joseph, 330, 379–81, 515; likeable?, 334
Stalky and Co. (Kipling), 466, 486
Starkie, Enid: *Baudelaire*, 123n
Statistics: misleading nature of, 379–80
Steer, G. L.: *The Tree of Gernika*, 295(n)
Stein, Gertrude, 101
Stendhal, 460; F. C. Green's book on, 398–401
Stiffkey, Rector of, 534
Storm over Spain (Mitchell), 290–1, 297
Strachey, John, 218, 234, 316
Strachey, Lytton, 506–7
Straus, Ralph, 253(n), 255
Streit, Clarence K.: *Union Now*, 395–8
Sunday Times, 100, 250, 266(n)
Surrealism, 495
Surtees, R. S., 444, 452–3
Sweeney Todd, 450
Swift, Jonathan, 33, 138, 460
Swinburne, Algernon Charles, 502
Syndicalists: in Spain, 275, 290

Tale of Two Cities, A, *see* Dickens, C.
Tarr (Lewis), 494
Teichman, Sir Eric: *Journey to Turkistan*, 286
Tempest, The (Shakespeare): quoted ("bawling . . ."), 36
Temple, Shirley, 534
Tennyson, Lord, 445
Thackeray, William Makepeace, 460, 466; and Dickens, 430–1, 452;

Thackeray—(*contd.*)
Pendennis, 437, 459; *A Shabby Genteel Story*, 437; *Vanity Fair*, 431–3
Thaelmann, Ernst, 181(n)
Thelma (Corelli), 138
Theosophy, 304
Thirties, The (Muggeridge), 533–5
This Side Idolatry (Bechhofer-Roberts), 414
Thomas, Hugh, 317n
Thompson, Mr: letter from GO, 268
Thompson, Francis, 23
Thomson, D. C., & Co., 461, 474
Thomson, David H.: letter from GO, 413(n)
Thomson, J. A. K.: *Plato and Aristotle*, 129
Thorez, Maurice, 298
Three Clerks, The (Trollope), 437
Thriller, The, 475, 482
Time and Tide, 121n, 280, 303, 309, 315(n); GO's contributions to, 221, 234–5, 276–8, 281, 286, 287–8, 290–1, 295–6, 297–8, 299n, 346–7, 411–12, 548
Times, The: letters from GO to, 115–16, 169(n), 209
Timmermans, R.: *Heroes of the Alcazar*, 288
Tit-Bits, 461
Titanic, the, 536
Told by an Idiot (Macaulay), 510
Tolstoy, Count Leo, 508; and Dickens, 456–7
Tom Brown's Schooldays (Hughes), 465
Tom Jones (Fielding), 447
Totalitarianism: consistently opposed by GO, 5–6; dictatorship of the proletariat, 336, 532; of theorists, 532; dependence on deception, 376; favoured by most modern intellectuals, 459; attraction for those who have not tasted it, 515–16. *See also* Communism; Fascism
Towards a Free Revolutionary Art, 377(n)
Trade unions: and Dickens, 419
Tramps and tramping, 36–43, 52–71, 149, 353; in London, 52–4; as hop-pickers, 60–8. *See also* Criminals, Gypsies; Lodging houses; Poverty
Travel: useless without involvement, 353
Tree of Gernika, The (Steer), 295(n)
Trials in Burma (Collis), 306–7
Tribune: GO's contributions to, 550–1
Triumph, The, 461
Trollope, Anthony, 128, 430; *Orley Farm*, 442; *The Small House at Allington*, 437; *The Three Clerks*, 437
Tropic of Cancer, *see* Miller, H.
Trotsky, Leon, 381
Trotskyism and Trotskyists, 287–8, 297, 344, 365; defended by GO, 6–7, 361; as Communist bogey-words, 274, 279, 285, 289, 298, 300–1, 332–4, 342–3, 349, 365
Trusts: GO's fear of, 121
Tunes: curious histories of, 136–7
Twain, Mark, 33; *Life on the Mississippi*, 101; *Roughing It*, 138
Twelfth Night (Shakespeare), 439
Twilight of the Gods, The (Garnett), 101
Two Carlyles, The (Burdett), 33–6

Ulysses, *see* Joyce, J.
Under the Axe of Fascism (Salvemini), 379
Undset, Sigrid, 234
Unemployment, 514–15. *See also* National Unemployed Workers' Movement; Poverty; Working class
Union Now (Streit), 395–8
United States: in 19th century, 21, 499; may "pass inspection" as a democracy, 396
Unser Kampf (Acland), 530–2
Upward, Edward, 511–12, 522–3
USSR, *see* Russia

Vacandard, E.: *L'Inquisition*, 137
Vanity Fair (Thackeray), 431–3
Verne, Jules, 475
Verstone, Brenda, 153
Vie Parisienne, 28, 82
Villon, François, 33
Vines, Sherard: *The Course of English Classicism*, 22–4
Violet's Paper, 160
Volunteer in Spain (Sommerfield), 278
Voyage au Bout de la Nuit (Céline), 498
Voyage to Purilia, A (Rice), 222

Walberswick cemetery: GO sees ghost in, 49–50

Wallace, Edgar, 222, 528
Wallington, Hertfordshire: GO's cottage at, 164–5, 214–18, 221–5, 227–9, 256, 278–82, 283–5, 288–90, 296, 299–304, 409–11, 413, 527–42, 548–50; Jack Common at cottage, 338–9, 347, 351–2, 354–5, 370–1, 393–4; inhabitants mentioned by name, 347, 352, 354, 355n, 370, 393(n)
Walls Have Mouths (Macartney), 233(n)
Walpole, Hugh, 506; and J. B. Priestley, 26, 117; *The Fortress*, 101(n)
War: circumstances in which it occurs, 283; effect on human mind, 291; Nietzsche on, 295; qualities of good soldiers, 326; "a racket", 331–2; war literature, 500–1, 523–5. *See also* First world war; Pacifism etc; Second world war; Spanish civil war
War Paint (F. V. Morley), 160–1
Warburg, F. J., 304, 309, 310, 315, 329, 368, 549. *See also* Secker & Warburg Ltd
Wastage: of food in workhouses, 41; among working class, 178–9
Watson, J. H., 314(n)
Waugh, Evelyn, 515, 523
Way of an Eagle, The (Dell), 252
Wellington College, 544
Wells, H. G., 506; his Utopiae, 155; and Stalin, 334; and Dickens, 428–9, 445, 456; father of "Scientifiction", 475; *The Country of the Blind*, 362–3
Western Short Stories, 461
Whitman, Walt, 230; and Henry Miller, 498–500
Who Goes Home? (Curle), 161
"Why I Joined the Independent Labour Party", 336–8
"Why I write", 1–7
Wigan, Lancashire, 163, 164, 174–87, 189; summarised, 190; Wigan Pier joke explained, 264
Wilkinson, Ellen, 298
Williams, Robert, 370(n)
Wilton, Michael (also known as Milton), 266(n)
Winn, Godfrey, 534
Winter in Moscow (Muggeridge), 533
Wizard, The, 461, 474–5, 477–8, 481–2
Wodehouse, P. G.: *My Man Jeeves*, 167
Wöller, Johann: *Zest for Life*, 234–5
Wolverhampton, Staffordshire, 171
Women: like Esther Summerson or the *Vie Parisienne* illustrations equally non-existent, 28; inferior status among working class, 174, 195; ignorance of politics etc, 174, 193; as coal miners, 205–6; status in Morocco, 391
Women's magazines, 461, 480–1. *See also Peg's Paper*
Wordsworth, William: quoted ("Getting . . ."), 217; by a labourer, 54
Workers' Front (Brockway), 304–6
Workers' Party of Marxist Unification, *see* POUM
Workhouses, 40–1, 57
Working class, 173–214 *passim*; bourgeois tendencies, 41, 173; a labourer who quotes Wordsworth, 54; speech reproduced, 86–7, 92–3; examples of income and expenditure, 173, 174, 175–6, 178, 180, 193–4, 195n, 199, 208, 211–12; dress and footwear, 173, 180–1, 190, 192, 199; food and drink, 173, 174, 178–9, 180, 183–4, 195n, 208, 212; a Wigan household, 174–6; another, 178, 183–4; privileged domestic position of men, 174, 195; women's ignorance of politics etc, 174, 193; deference to upper classes, 174; to authority, 196–7; housing, 175–6, 177, 188–9, 190, 192, 199–200, 201, 204, 213–14; smell, 178, 179; docility, 181, 229; North–South and local hatreds, 191, 215; a Sheffield household, 193–4, 195; comparison with bourgeoisie, 196–7; discussion groups, 197–8; a Barnsley household, 199–200; patience with "Socialist bourgeoisie", 216; their real enemies, 332; and colour prejudice, 360; in fiction, 415; in Dickens, 435–41; in boys' weeklies, 472; churches' lost hold on, 530; rejection of Marxism, 532
Working men's clubs, 200–1
World Revolution (James), 298
World wars, *see* First world war; Second world war
Wuthering Heights (E. Brontë), 456, 495

Yank magazines, 88, 220, 461, 476–8
Yeats, W. B., 506
Yeats-Brown, Major F., 288
Yorkshire, 190–214
Youth hostels: Clent, 170; Manchester, 172

Zest for Life (Wöller), 234–5
Zola (Emile), 33, 78, 247